3/01

African American
Authors, 1745–1945

AFRICAN AMERICAN AUTHORS, 1745–1945

A Bio-Bibliographical Critical Sourcebook

Edited by
EMMANUEL S. NELSON

Greenwood Press
Westport, Connecticut • London

Library of Congress Cataloging-in-Publication Data

African American authors, 1745–1945 : a bio-bibliographical critical
   sourcebook / edited by Emmanuel S. Nelson.
      p.   cm.
   Includes bibliographical references (p.   ) and index.
   ISBN 0–313–30910–8 (alk. paper)
   1. American literature—Afro-American authors—Bio-bibliography
Dictionaries.   2. American literature—Afro-American authors
Dictionaries.   3. Afro-American authors—Biography Dictionaries.
4. Afro-Americans in literature Dictionaries.   I. Nelson, Emmanuel
S. (Emmanuel Sampath), 1954–   .
   PS153.N5A32   2000
   810.9'896073—dc21
   [B]   99–32527

British Library Cataloguing in Publication Data is available.

Library of Congress Catalog Card Number: 99–32527
ISBN: 0–313–30910–8

First published in 2000

Greenwood Press, 88 Post Road West, Westport, CT 06881
An imprint of Greenwood Publishing Group, Inc.
www.greenwood.com

Printed in the United States of America

The paper used in this book complies with the
Permanent Paper Standard issued by the National
Information Standards Organization (Z39.48–1984).

10 9 8 7 6 5 4 3 2 1

FOR ANIL, WITH LOVE

CONTENTS

CONTENTS   ix

PREFACE

Three landmark events in African American literary history took place in 1983. That year Alice Walker's *The Color Purple* won the Pulitzer Prize; Gloria Naylor received the American Book Award for her first novel, *The Women of Brewster Place*; and Harriet Wilson's *Our Nig*, first published in 1859, was republished. These events contributed substantially to the dramatic resurgence of academic as well as popular interest in African American literature during the 1980s. While Walker's and Naylor's achievements strengthened interest in the contemporary literary scene, the accidental rediscovery of Wilson's forgotten work from the mid-nineteenth century by Henry Louis Gates, Jr., and its republication by Random House in 1983 sparked new scholarly curiosity about early African American writing. In fact, since 1983, the works of dozens of nineteenth- and early twentieth-century writers have been recovered and reprinted. There is now a significant revival of interest in the Harlem Renaissance of the 1920s. In the last decade alone, several major assessments of eighteenth- and nineteenth-century African American literature have been published. Recent collections, such as *The Norton Anthology of African American Literature* (1997) and *Call & Response: The Riverside Anthology of the African American Literary Tradition* (1998), offer nearly comprehensive overviews of African American writing unavailable even in the 1980s. This reference volume is designed as a vital contribution to this ongoing recuperative project: it is intended as a scholarly guide to the lives and works of 78 writers from the first 200 years of African American tradition in literature.

The African American tradition in creative expression probably began in 1619, when a ship carrying human cargo from West Africa arrived in Jamestown, Virginia. The hundreds of thousands of enslaved Africans who were subsequently transported across the Atlantic Ocean to the emerging United States of America forged an expressive culture that reflected their imaginative responses to their individual distress and collective nightmare. As a preindustrial people systematically denied access to literacy in the New World, they created imaginative texts that existed exclusively in oral forms. Blending their West African cultural memories and their harsh American experiences, they developed a unique Afro-New World idiom that found expression in their work songs, folktales, spirituals, sermons, and other verbal structures that were orally transmitted across generations. Those folk art forms provided the foundation for the written tradition that emerged in the eighteenth century.

The transition from orality to written text, arguably, occurred in 1746, when Lucy Terry—a young woman who, as an infant, was sold into slavery in Rhode Island—composed a ballad titled "Bars Fight." Though the poem was not actually published until 1855, it is generally believed to be the oldest literary work written by an African American. By the end of the eighteenth century, at least two African Americans had published considerably more substantial works: Phillis Wheatley's collection of poems in 1773 and Equiano's massive autobiography in 1789.

Slave narratives, a uniquely American art form, began to appear in large numbers during the first few decades of the nineteenth century. Often ghostwritten by white abolitionists, these works narrated the life stories of escaped slaves. A nodal point in the development of African American writing was the publication of the *Narrative of the Life of Frederick Douglass* in 1845. Written by himself, Douglass' work was not only a compelling autobiography but also a stunningly eloquent indictment of the institution of slavery as well as its political, religious, and cultural underpinnings. While protest continued to be a dominant concern of African American writers during the postbellum nineteenth century as well, some writers—such as Charlotte Forten Grimké, Charles W. Chesnutt, Pauline E. Hopkins, Paul Laurence Dunbar, Frances W. Harper, and others—began to engage a variety of themes in diverse genres.

A foundational event in African American intellectual history and a defining moment in American history in general was the Harlem Renaissance of the 1920s. An extraordinary cultural phenomenon, the Harlem Renaissance was the result of an almost accidental gathering of dozens of writers, sculptors, musicians, painters, dancers, photographers, and other artists in Harlem—a gathering made possible in part by the Great Migration that brought huge numbers of rural southern blacks to the urban centers of the industrial North. The renaissance was given definition and direction by the nurturing guidance of W.E.B. Du Bois and Alain Locke—both Harvard Ph.D.'s and formidable intellectuals of their generation. The artistic revival in Harlem reflected a new mood that began to animate centers of power within African American communities. The establishment of the National Association for the Advancement of Colored People (NAACP) in 1909 and the National Urban League in 1910 gave black Americans a renewed belief in the possibilities of structured resistance to various forms of individual and institutionalized oppression. The nationalist rhetoric of Marcus Garvey, whose organization was headquartered in Harlem, captured the imaginations of millions of African Americans and helped galvanize their political energies into a coherent grassroots movement. Jack Johnson's spectacular performances in the boxing ring and defiance of the white power structure outside the ring became a symbol of black excellence as well as an embodiment of the new spirit of resistance. The post–World War I economic boom, which enlarged the increasingly self-confident black middle class, helped sustain the renaissance at least until the collapse of the national economy in 1929. Newly established black-owned periodicals, such as *Crisis*, *Opportunity*, *The Messenger*, and *The Challenge*, provided venues for the publication of short works by aspiring young writers. These emerging artists gradually redefined the nature and function of black art, established new paradigms for literary expression, and laid the foundations for the brave new worlds that the post-renaissance writers such as Richard Wright would explore in the mid-twentieth century.

A central objective of this sourcebook is to provide a wide-ranging introduction to the first 200 years of this fascinating African American literary history. Among the writers included here are essayists, novelists, short story writers, poets, playwrights, and autobiographers. They are the defining figures in an extraordinary story: how a people who were victims of the most appalling crimes of slavery and statutory segregation and who were too long denied access to literacy and even rudimentary civil rights created one of the great literatures of the world. This volume celebrates their magnificent achievement.

All major artists from the eighteenth to the mid-twentieth centuries are included in this volume: the works of Phillis Wheatley, Frederick Douglass, W.E.B. Du Bois, Nella Larsen, Zora Neale Hurston, Richard Wright, and others receive careful attention. But I have also included numerous lesser-known authors— such as Elizabeth Laura Adams, Marita Bonner, Edythe Mae Gordon, Juanita Harrison, and Zara Wright—whose lives and accomplishments deserve wider recognition. Though my goal is not to define a canon, I am acutely conscious of the fact that a reference volume such as this is, indeed, likely to be implicated in canon formation.

My primary purpose, rather, is to offer reliable, thorough, and up-to-date biographical, critical, and bibliographic information on the writers included. Advanced scholars will find this volume a useful research tool; its user-friendly style, format, and level of complexity, however, should make it accessible to a wider audience that includes undergraduate students and even general readers. Each chapter begins with relevant biographical information on the writer, offers an interpretive commentary on his or her works, provides an overview of the critical reception accorded, and concludes with a bibliography that lists, separately, the primary works and the secondary sources. To facilitate cross-referencing, whenever a writer who is also the subject of a chapter in this volume is first mentioned, an asterisk appears next to his or her name.

I would like to take this opportunity to thank all the contributors to this volume; without their effort it would not exist. Let me also thank Dr. George Butler, associate editor at Greenwood Press, for his enthusiastic support of this as well as many other projects.

African American
Authors, 1745–1945

ELIZABETH LAURA ADAMS
(1909–?)

Joyce Russell-Robinson

BIOGRAPHY

Elizabeth Laura Adams' life could be viewed as a spiritual-religious odyssey that began in kindergarten and culminated with her selection of the Catholic Church as her means of worship and Christian expression. This odyssey is recorded in *Dark Symphony* (1942), Adams' narrative of conversion, which is less formulaic than some other autobiographies of this kind in that Adams includes numerous details of her childhood and family life. Although she had written and published poems, essays (more properly, spiritual musings), and a short, serialized autobiography prior to the appearance of *Dark Symphony*, this work distinguished her as the first African American to write a book on the subject of Catholic conversion.

Born on February 9, 1909, in Santa Barbara, California, Adams, after the death of her infant brother, became and remained the only child of Lula Holden Adams and Daniel Adams, a Los Angeles restaurant headwaiter who insisted that his wife devote her life to full-time homemaking and mothering. Prior to their marriage, Ms. Adams had been a teacher at the Los Angeles School of Art and Design. All indications are that the family lived in relative comfort, even when the mother and daughter, for health reasons, resumed residency in Santa Barbara, leaving the man of the family in Los Angeles to continue working at his restaurant job. During that separation from her father, fourteen-year-old Elizabeth attended a Good Friday service at the Santa Barbara Mission and was spiritually awakened. Soon after that event she announced to her father that she should convert to Catholicism. He staunchly forbade it.

As a younger child, Adams had regularly attended a Methodist church, which left very negative impressions upon her. Some of her worst memories were acts of humiliation by various adults who criticized her for not learning the Bible verses assigned by her Sunday school teachers. Also, she was frightened by church-shouting, a display of intense religious excitement punctuated by screams and holy dancing. The frenzy of the services caused Adams to fear the conversion experience that, according to church leaders, would one day occur in the young girl's life and that would cause her to shout just as the adults did. Adams found only one positive aspect of the Methodist service: music. Her parents nurtured that interest by purchasing a violin for their daughter and hiring a private instructor for her as well.

Upon the death of her father in 1924, Adams once again seriously considered conversion and discussed it with her mother. When she graduated from high school, she received a gift that forever changed her life: parental permission to convert. Adams entered a convert class, was baptized, and eventually was confirmed when she was approximately twenty years of age. Following her confirmation, she had planned to enter a convent, but those plans were dashed when her mother separated from her second husband, forcing Adams to provide financial support for her, which she continued to do until her mother's death in 1952.

Racism was very much a part of Adams' life. She nevertheless remained optimistic and hoped that the barrier of color would one day disappear: "Tenaciously I clung to the opinion that if I were a respectable law-abiding citizen, a devout Christian and not sensitive as to my color, that race prejudice could easily be shoved out of my pathway" (156).

Adams' optimism, however, did little to soften the hearts of the hardened racists (and sexists) whom she encountered. A priest, for example, refused to serve her Holy Communion because of her race, and a Catholic school—after agreeing to admit her—rescinded the offer, explaining, "As they had never accepted a Colored applicant they had decided that it was unwise to change their policy" (150). An editor of a newspaper once refused to offer Adams employment as a reporter, making it clear to her that her race was the only reason that she was denied the job. Further, the editor advised Adams to abandon the idea of a writing career altogether, to marry while she was young, and to have a family.

Rejecting the suggestions of the editor, Adams did, in fact, have a career as a writer; she supplemented her income, however, with secretarial and domestic work. She never married, restricting her personal ties to her mother and to Edythe Tierney, a white woman of the Catholic Church who, similar to Adams, possessed the dream of eliminating racial prejudice through church work.

The date and circumstances of Adams' death have not yet been determined. It is assumed, however, that she died in Santa Barbara, the city of her birth and the city where for most of her life she lived and worked.

MAJOR WORKS AND THEMES

As mentioned before, Adams had published poems, spiritual musings, and a short, serialized autobiography prior to the appearance of *Dark Symphony*, her most important work. Clearly, she possessed talent in various literary forms. Regardless of her chosen genre, however, Adams' works are unified by her Catholicism, along with her racial consciousness. But both of those themes may not always be visible in each work. In the spiritual musing "The Finding of a Soul" (1930), for example, Catholicism alone is Adams' focus. In the poem "The Summons" (1941) her racial consciousness is manifested (a Negro trombone player, a jet-black Negro, a Negro spiritual). "There Must Be a God . . . Somewhere," Adams' serialized autobiography, takes race as its starting point, a focus that is sustained throughout the work (although Catholicism is also discussed). In a brief headnote to this work she boldly asserts, "I am a young colored woman," a statement possibly intended to prepare her predominantly white Catholic audience for her memories of racism, recollections that to some readers might appear incredible.

In *Dark Symphony* Adams' attempt is to offer evenhanded treatment of race and religion and always to give a positive spin to her circumstances, no matter how horrible. But there are times when one gets the impression that she is less than satisfied with the outcome of her decision to convert. Adams, in short, appears frustrated and conflicted because God, Christianity, and the Catholic Church have done too little to eradicate the racist attitudes of those who relegate her and other African Americans to the ranks of inferiority. "How would God like it," she writes, "if someone called Him nigger?" (25).

Two voices compete to tell the story of Adams' life and conversion: the voice of the adult Adams and the voice of the little girl Adams. The little girl's voice frequently is stronger, the result being that the language and tone of *Dark Symphony* are rather childlike. These childlike qualities, however, are not sufficient grounds for a negative assessment of the book. Such characteristics serve to broaden the appeal of the work, making it suitable reading for adults and adolescents alike.

CRITICAL RECEPTION

During the 1940s Adams was lauded by some reviewers (mostly white) and criticized by others (mostly black). One of her harshest critics was Ellen Tarry, the author of *The Third Door: The Autobiography of an American Negro Woman* (1955). She criticized *Dark Symphony* on the basis of its rather cursory treatment of the Great Depression and on the basis of its inauthenticity—referring to Adams' rather saintly depiction of her parents. "One wonders if they were also human," wrote Tarry. Another African American critic (a man), Theophilus Lewis, suggested that *Dark Symphony*, quite simply, is rather dull reading. White reviewers, in contrast, overwhelmingly approved of the book, finding it to be quite interesting and devoid of malice.

Although Adams' name has long been familiar to scholars of African American literature, hardly any of them have conducted long studies on her. She is mentioned in Rebecca Chalmers Barton's *Witness for Freedom: Negro Americans* in *Autobiography* (1948) and in Jay David's *Growing up Black* (1968). Others who give Adams a glance include Geraldine O. Mathews in *Black American Writers, 1773–1949: A Bibliography and Union List* (1975), Russel A. Brignano in *Black Americans in Autobiography* (1984), and Joanne M. Braxton in *Black Women Writing Autobiography: A Tradition within a Tradition* (1989). Very useful information on Adams' life and works is provided by Mary Anthony Scally in *Negro Catholic Writers 1900–1943: A Bio-Bibliography*, published in 1945, just three years after the publication of *Dark Symphony*.

Carla Kaplan appears to be the first scholar to conduct an in-depth study of Adams and her writings. As the editor of *Dark Symphony and Other Works* (1996), Kaplan has given a new birth to Adams and her literary creations. Kaplan's introduction to this text is thorough and carefully researched. In her opinion, Adams is "double-voiced," meaning that "her story of acquiescent, obedient girlhood is laced with private, sometimes coded rebellion" (xviii). Double-voicedness, however, Kaplan suggests, is not restricted to Adams' two autobiographies, namely, "There Must Be a God . . . Somehwere" and *Dark Symphony*. For careful readers, the coded rebellion of which Kaplan speaks is detectable throughout Adams' writings, whether one is exploring her autobiographies, her poetry, or her spiritual musings.

BIBLIOGRAPHY

Works by Elizabeth Laura Adams

Autobiographies

"There Must Be a God . . . Somewhere." *Torch* (October 1940): 4–6; (November 1940): 19–20, 30; (December 1940): 9–10; (January 1941): 16–18; (February 1941): 10–11; (March 1941): 23–24, 29. (serialized)
Dark Symphony. New York: Sheed and Ward, 1942.

Poetry

"Until I Found You." *Westward* (July 1936): 30–31.
"Consecrated." *Westward* (October 1936): 29–32.
"Yes, I'm Colored." *Westward* (October 1938): 24–25.
"Our Colored Servants." *Torch* (September 1941): 16–17.
"The Summons." *Torch* (May 1941): 16, 32.
"The Country Doctor." *Torch* (May 1942): 31.
"Hypocrisy." *Torch* (June 1942): 24.
"The Last Supper." *Torch* (June 1943): 9–12.

Spiritual Musings

"The Finding of a Soul." *Sentinel of the Blessed Sacrament* (October 1930): 97–101.
"She Talks Like We Do." *Interracial Review* (October 1940): 153–54.

Reviews

"The Art of Living Joyfully." *Torch* (December 1942): 29.
"Children under Fire." *Torch* (November 1943): 29.

Studies of Elizabeth Laura Adams

Barton, Rebecca Chalmers. *Witness for Freedom: Negro Americans in Autobiography*. New York: Harper and Brothers, 1948. 123–34.

Braxton, Joanne M. *Black Women Writing Autobiography: A Tradition within a Tradition.* Philadelphia: Temple University Press, 1989. 140.

Brignano, Russel A. *Black Americans in Autobiography*. Chapel Hill, NC: Duke University Press, 1984. 3.

David, Jay. *Growing up Black*. New York: William Morrow, 1968. 60–70.

Dwyer, Joseph. Rev. of *Dark Symphony*. *Torch* (June 1942): 27.

Kaplan, Carla. Introduction: "I Wanna March." *Dark Symphony and Other Works* xvii–lvii. Ed. Henry Louis Gates Jr. and Jennifer Burton. *African American Women Writers, 1910–1940*. New York: G. K. Hall, 1996.

LaFarge, John. "One God for All." Rev. of *Dark Symphony*. *America: A Catholic Review of the Week* (May 30, 1942): 215.

Lewis, Theophilus. Rev. of *Dark Symphony*. *Interracial Review* (May 1942): 20–81.

Mathews, Geraldine O. *Black American Writers, 1773–1949: A Bibliography and Union List.* Boston: G. K. Hall, 1975.

Scally, Mary Anthony. *Negro Catholic Writers 1900–1943: A Bio-Bibliography*. Detroit: Walter Romig, 1945. 19–23.

Tarry, Ellen. Rev. of *Dark Symphony*. *Catholic World* (July 1942): 504–5.

OCTAVIA VICTORIA ROGERS ALBERT
(1853 – 1890 ?)

Geetha Ravi

BIOGRAPHY

Octavia Victoria Rogers Albert was one of the perceptive black women writers who realized early the relevance of the oral literature of the unlettered black folks that now forms the "usable past" in their vernacular tradition. She began writing at a time when writing was a male prerogative. Unmindful of criticisms, with missionary zeal she carefully recorded the voice of the former slaves; her work has won a special place and significance now, a century later, in the African American literary tradition.

Albert was born on December 12, 1853, of slave parentage in Oglethorpe, Macon County, Georgia. (Inexplicably, the prestigious *The Oxford Companion to African American Literature* mentions 1824 as her year of birth.) The Reconstruction-era easing of crippling laws denying education to blacks enabled Albert to gain entry into Georgia's Atlanta University, which she attended after the Civil War. After graduating she got involved in a variety of activities. She mastered the art of interviewing, and the historian John Blassingame considers her one of the few "well-trained" in interviewing in the country (qtd. in Foster, Introduction xxxii). Later she became a biographer of freed slaves, a researcher, and a leader of her community.

Octavia met Reverend A.E.P. Albert in 1873. He was a teacher in Monteguma, Georgia, where Octavia got her first teaching assignment. In the following year, on October 21, they were married, and this union gave her a respectable position as the wife of a doctor of divinity. Then the couple moved to Houma, Louisiana, where their house became a refuge for former slaves. Octavia's genial spirit was a source of solace to the wounded spirits of the ex-slaves. Albert not only gave them food but also educated them in the face of considerable white hostility.

She also nurtured them spiritually by reading the Bible to them. She taught them to read and write. Above all, she helped them to articulate their experiences as slaves. These benevolent gestures were not unusual to one of her status. As a well-educated minister's wife she was expected to be helpful to her husband's parishioners. She became special because she did more for history by recording their woes in her work *The House of Bondage; or Charlotte Brooks and Other Slaves.*

In 1877 her husband was ordained a minister in the Methodist Episcopal Church, and the following year she converted to his church, leaving her African Methodist Episcopal Church. Their only daughter, Laura T. F. Albert, was primarily responsible for serializing the stories in *The House of Bondage*, which she did after her mother's death. The stories were first published in the *South Western Christian Advocate* from January to December 1890, after Octavia's death. This periodical was run by the General Conference of the Episcopal Church, and thus her work received the approval of the church members. The paper enjoyed large circulation in New Orleans, and her work got the necessary publicity. The popularity the serial won gave father and daughter the confidence to get the whole published in book form, and it was dedicated to the author as a memorial.

MAJOR WORK AND THEMES

The slave narrative *The House of Bondage* is one of several texts that belong to "the tradition within a tradition" (black women's literary tradition as a part of black literary tradition), "a coded literary universe" created by black women writers between 1890 and 1910. These remained in obscurity, in the safe racks of research libraries or in "overpriced and poorly edited reprints" (Foster, Introduction xviii–xvi). Rightly enough, Henry Louis Gates Jr. opens his Foreword with an excerpt from the "prototypical black feminist" (xiii)—Anna Julia Cooper's *A Voice from the South* (1892), which identifies accurately the problem of black women's inability to make their voice heard. Cooper finds the cry of half of the "human family stifled" (xiv), and affirms that not even black men can adequately reproduce the voice of black women.

A note from the Schomburg Center by Howard Dodson mentions the renewed interest in the 1960s in black writing of the past, which led to the reprinting of these obscure texts of the nineteenth century by the combined efforts of the Schomburg Center for Research in Black Culture, the New York Public Library, Henry Louis Gates Jr., and the Oxford University Press.

In her elaborate Introduction to the text, Frances Smith Foster claims that the prime purpose of *The House of Bondage* is to purge the stereotypes like "Uncle Tom, Aunt Jemima or Kunta Kinte" (xxix) of the African American literary scene who appeal to popular fancy. Her work consists of the honest narrations of blacks like Aunt Charlotte and Uncle Cephas. Albert displays skill in disguising her artistry and enters "an intense competition to describe and design the material and moral fabric of an emerging society" (xxviii). She re-creates history, joining the train of realists whose desire for the ideal makes them protest against the sentimentalizing and romanticizing of the slave past. Foster points out how Albert ran the risk of unsexing herself by attempting to write in an age that resented a black woman's writing and that on political issues to an audience outside her immediate circle. The publication required "three separate testimonies" (xxxiii) in its prefatory note: that the writer had an "angelic spirit" and led a "pure" life and was a "devoted mother and wife" (vi), so that the readers did not dub her a "lunatic" to point an accusing finger at the white audience who "sinned by commission and omission" (xxxiii).

Foster considers this work a "carefully crafted venture" (xxxvi) displaying the impact of various genres. She brings out the similarities and differences in *The House of Bondage* and Harriet Beecher Stowe's *Uncle Tom's Cabin*. She finds Albert's work a clear contrast to work like Thomas Nelson Page's *Ole Virginia*. Foster does not lose sight of Albert's earnestness to influence public opinion and affect national policies, thus making her work something more than a sacred personal mission. In her concluding remarks Foster repeats that this book is "valuable to modern readers for both its content and its intent" (xlii).

The text opens in very direct and simple terms, spelling out the why of Albert's narrative. "Much has been written about the negro" (1), but "the half was never told" about the millions of slaves tortured for about 250 long years (2). Few had confronted the whites with the disturbing question, "[W]ho is responsible for the immoral condition of the illiterate race in the South?" and answered it with an unequivocal, "[T]heir masters" (1). Albert appears quite convinced that enough had not been said to the whites who had introduced Christianity to the slaves to lift their souls to God and had simultaneously perpetrated immorality, for to them blacks were "brutes" and that the Christian nation was obliged to face the sin—"the execrable villainy" (Foster, Introduction xi) of slavery they had nurtured.

The twin strands that run through this narrative are the sufferings of the slaves and their deep Christian faith. It unfolds the African American history from the days of chattel slavery up to "a touching incident" (156) of reunion that took place in New Orleans in 1884. Aunt Charlotte Brooks is the first ex-slave to "recite" (102) her heartrending accounts of woe. Every mother desires to raise her child; but she, a slave mother, gave birth to her master's son's children, but they all died because of lack of attention. When she was freed, she owned just the dress on her back. Nellie Johnson, her acquaintance, had to wear men's clothes and "deer-horns" (20) with bells on her head whenever punished. Nellie's newborn was given away by the white overseer soon after its birth on the roadside. A black child and mother were always separated unfeelingly as if they were dogs.

Similarly, the slave husbands and wives were separated. Aunt Charlotte remembers how Richard and Betty, the most faithful partners, were forcibly separated, and Richard was forced to take a new partner. Uncle Stephen Jordon was forced to marry a woman old enough to be his mother. Ella, Charlotte's mistress' house servant, used to be hit on the head with anything handy until blood oozed from her head. Dogs were set on those who tried to run away. When George spoke of freedom, he received 900 lashes and then was washed with salt water. Eventually, an eye was gouged out. On several occasions Aunt Charlotte returned home half dead and collapsed even without supper in her leaking shack only to find leeches further bleeding her to death.

On the auction blocks the slaves were bought and sold like hogs. They were switched on their legs to make them jump to see if they were supple enough. According to Aunt Lorendo, Hattie, a slave in her neighborhood, escaped into the woods and returned half naked after burying her dead child, to be beaten to death herself. Sallie Smith had to pick 150 pounds of cotton only to get whipped at night. Slave insurrections during Civil War turned Andersonville into a "bloody spot" (85). After emancipation ex-slaves were "let loose" with no support. In the South the Ku Klux Klan launched a reign of terror. These "white Camelias" and the "white Cohorts" (135) were the "hyenas" (136) who "bruised, stabbed" (111) the children returning from schools, for "an educated nigger is a dangerous thing" (111); they were "the fire-eaters" (139) who instituted fierce race riots and flooded New Orleans with the blood of the freed slaves.

In this sea of trouble the Holy Book served as "the sheet-anchor" (154) of their liberties, and Christ was "a Rock" (74) in a weary land. The name of Jesus was enough to calm their souls, for "God only wanted the heart" (13). Aunt Charlotte's soul feasted on Jesus when she had no bread. To her, "religion is good anywhere—at the plow-handle, at the hoe-handle, anywhere" (23). Black slave narrators adopted traditional Christian images with ease. Early instances of the use of the metaphor of "Mr. Christian" of the *Pilgrim's Progress*, which James Olney identifies in the slave narrative, are seen in Albert's narrative. "Mr. Christian" is a metaphor of "simple substitution" for religious persecutions of Aunt Charlotte. After reaching the Catholic belt of Louisiana, the Protestant Aunt Charlotte found Aunt Jane's prayer meetings the only alternative "to make peace with the Lord" (12). She desired to learn to read only to read the Bible. Lena, a member of their prayer meeting, remembered even while dying to say, "Glory be to God and the Lamb forever!" (28). The spirit of God so filled their souls with joy that Charlotte desired more problems, which would mean more prayers. Sallie Smith, hiding in the woods, had no religion, and she just blindly invoked "Daniel's God" (91) and simply repeated her mother's prayers from memory. Later she and her brother received good treatment, and Sallie felt happy that her prayers were answered. Catholicism is not treated favorably in the text. Catholic landlords made the slaves slog on Sabbath day and believed "God has made the black man to serve the white man" (70). This religion did not help those who practiced it, but the " 'Merican religion" (68) seemed to effect a miraculous change. Nancy, John's first wife, received religion and cried all the way home and said, "I am washed clean by the blood of Jesus" (66). The sable-hued and the white-skinned practiced the same religion; but the so-called brutes were filled with the love of God and humanity, whereas the whites practiced brutality. Charlotte felt sorry when her master met with an accident. Albert is not blind to the follies of the black; but their drunkenness, immorality, and belief in voodooism were caused by the curious institution of slavery, which kept them perennially poor and ignorant.

The blacks of this generation realized that religion and politics could not be divorced from each other. Uncle Cephas observes: "I never thought our salvation depended so much upon politics" (127). Religion alone gave them strength to survive and see the days of freedom. The blacks were sure that the "Yankees done the fighting" (55), because they did the praying, and God heard their prayers and led them out of the valley of misery. Freedom was the only thing they desired. Death in swamps was preferred to life in the stockade. But just in a matter of twenty-seven years there was a miraculous change in their community, and the blacks entered all avenues of civilized life. Uncle Cephas rose up in social status, and one of his sons became a physician, and the other a pastor. The educated blacks exploded the myth "O, he can't learn" (133). The myth of "he can't fight" (133) was exploded by the verdict that "the colored troops fought nobly" (132). Andrew Johnson's plan of Reconstruction might have excluded the blacks, but the "divine supervision" intervened to make many of their leaders eminent, like Oscar J. Dunn, the "first negro lieutenant governor" (142). Albert has immortalized General U. S. Grant, who sundered their fetters and who is enshrined in the memory of the blacks.

The black folk dialect has been employed by Albert, unself-consciously retaining its natural flavor without artificial mutilation of spelling and pronunciation. We hear the "La, me's" of Aunt Charlotte and illiterate Old Tim's "Me lover my Lord like my Lord lover me" (95), but it is observed by Albert herself that Uncle Cephas speaks "very properly for one that was a slave" (122). The entire work is a string of "call and response"—a technique that forms the very soul of the African American musical literary creation. Albert's call is responded to by various slaves; and the musical effect is heightened with the riffing of the refrain "nobody knows the trouble I have seen" (3), which rings through the narration with subtle alterations like, "None but Jesus knows what I have passed through" (27) and "nobody but God knows the trouble we poor black folks had to undergo" (102). Singing was not a ritual but the only escape for their troubled psyche; and music in its various forms such as hymns, gospels, work songs, and spirituals reverberates throughout. We hear Aunt Jane's "Guide me, O thou great Jehovah" (9), Richard's "I wish I was in heaven, hallelu" (26), the famous spiritual "My God Delivered Daniel" (31), and several other hymns. The text ends with the grand finale of the "touching incident" of Doctor Coleman Lee's "wonderful reunion" with his "long-separated" (160) mother. Albert has treasured these oral recitals to be transmitted to "our children's children" (130). The uniqueness of the text lies in the narration of the lives of others and not the author's. Her work is purely "mimetic," where the individuality of the writer is effaced, giving importance to the recital of facts of ordinary slaves.

CRITICAL RECEPTION

The only available exhaustive study on Albert's *House of Bondage* is Frances Smith Foster's essay *Written by Herself: Literary Production by African American Women, 1746–1892*. Foster places the work in its context of postbellum slave narrative, calling it a "text of confrontation and community" (162). Its intertextuality enables the text to be linked with the works of several black writers as well as those of the regionalist tradition then popular among the whites. Foster compares the experiences of Aunt Charlotte of *The House of Bondage* with those of Aunt Chloe of Frances Harper's *Sketches of Southern Life*. In recording the lives of the ordinary slaves and those blacks who rose to fame, Albert's work is close to Josephine Brown's *Biography of an American Bondman* (1856) and Frances Rollin's *Life and Public Service of Martin R. Delany* (1868).

Foster lists signifiers of authority used by Albert's publishers to receive sanction from the audience of her times; they would necessarily have questioned the propriety and the capability of black women to write and the validity and authenticity of the material that is slave history and race politics—an area that few would have been allowed to tread. Without these "signifiers" Albert's work could not have possibly been published without serious problems. Albert lived at a time when writing was an unwomanly act, and to write on political issues and of slavery, which everyone desired to forget, was no less than an "audacious act" (xxxii). Albert's education, which sets her above the former slaves and affords her social sanction, and her marital status as the wife of a minister, which gives her work a theological sanction, are discussed in the prefatory note. The narratives are actual oral presentations of former slaves and therefore are valid and authentic.

Albert's skillful manipulation of "the discourse of distrust" (164) is then elaborated: Despite proclamation of the lack of artifice in the text and strong avowals that the text is a simple record of slaves' experiences as "recited" by themselves, Stepto's theory of "discourse of distrust" helps to tear open this mask of "race ritual" (165) and to unravel the artistry in the storytelling mode adopted by Albert. Foster rightly compares the deceptively simple repetitions in the text with the African American innovative jazz musical techniques where behind the facade of repetitive lines or melody there are always subtle, yet startling, differences. The storytelling mode enables the author to make her work a readerly text and gives her a chance "to abort the contest of authorship and authority that writerly texts tend to produce" (170).

In her careful analysis of the text Foster finds Albert both "listener and teller" (167) of the slave's experiences. In spite of her slave past Albert does not sentimentalize but maintains a scholarly objectivity. This is seen in her distancing herself from her narration, introducing words like "this race" (167) and "them" (168). Her role is that of a medium, and through her we hear their stories; and being an educated listener, she interprets their experiences for the readers without compromising objectivity. Foster shows how Albert begins her narration with the recitals of ordinary slaves who picture the sordid conditions of the slave past and proceeds to introduce members from the black middle class, also ex-slaves, who help to interpret the present and suggest fruitful plans for the future. Foster perceives the ardent hope of Albert to "charm, subdue and bring forth tears" (150) in the readers just as the speech of Dr. Minor does.

Throughout, the narrator's interruptions provide the necessary links, and hers is the voice of a "concerned Christian" who is determined to prove to her white, Protestant, Christian brethren that the institution of slavery was a "sin against God and mankind" (169), and none could glorify the antebellum days as writers like Nelson Page have done. Foster is not sure if Albert ever had a chance to read Page's "Ole Virginia," but both Page and Albert wrote to remove misconceptions about the slave South, but they differed in their versions of truth. To Page the days of slavery were golden days when all was right with the world. But to Albert they were the days when brutality was in vogue, and both races should thank God slavery has been completely erased from the earth. Both are studies with metaphors like the "house of bondage" and "Ole Virginia," which refer to the South. Albert has not only challenged "the remythologizing of the plantation school" (162), which has romanticized the antebellum South, but also broken other equally popular myths of the "illiteracy, intellectual inferiority and lack of historical perspective" of the blacks. Foster concludes her study reiterating the fact that besides confronting her opponents, Albert has "defined her vision of the community" (176) that could be born in the United States. This she has achieved by using the "discourse of discontent" (164)—which is an African American literary tradition and has given a model that African American women writers could emulate.

BIBLIOGRAPHY

Work by Octavia Victoria Rogers Albert

Slave narrative

The House of Bondage: or Charlotte Brooks and Other Slaves. Ed. Frances Smith Foster. New York: Oxford University Press, 1988.

Studies of Octavia Victoria Rogers Albert

Foster, Frances Smith. Written by Herself: Literary Production by African American Women, 1746–1892. Bloomington: Indiana University Press, 1993.
———. "Introduction." In The House of Bondage: or Charlotte Brooks and Other Slaves. Ed. Frances Smith Foster, 1988. i–xlii.
The Oxford Companion to African American Literature. Ed. William L. Andrews, Frances Smith Foster, and Trudier Harris. New York: Oxford University Press, 1997. 10–11.

JAMES MADISON BELL
(1826–1902)

Robert L. Milde

BIOGRAPHY

James Madison Bell was born April 3, 1826, in Gallipolis, Ohio. At seventeen he moved to his brother-in-law's in Cincinnati to learn plastering, the trade that would support him most of his life. In winter he studied at the new "colored" high school associated with Oberlin College, working his trade the rest of the year; in later years as a traveling orator he would follow the same schedule. He married Louisiana Sanderlin in 1847 and, an impassioned abolitionist, chose to move his family to Chatham, Ontario, in 1854. He raised funds and recruits for John Brown from at least 1857 to the famous raid in 1859, and his home served as headquarters during Brown's planning and organizing trip to Canada in 1858. In the political aftermath of the raid, Bell "only escaped the fate of many of John Brown's men by the providence of God" (Arnett 7) and in 1860 moved without his wife and children to San Francisco, where he lived until 1866.

In San Francisco Bell began his career as a poet/orator. He was active in many organizations, from civil rights conventions, to the African Methodist Episcopal (AME) church, to the new San Francisco Literary Institute. Both his poems and his trade advertisements appeared in the *San Francisco Elevator* and *Pacific Appeal*; at least once he received mention as a "plasterer, brickmason, and poet" (Abajian 142). In 1862 he began giving public orations of long poems, which were sold in pamphlet form. These include "A Poem" on Emancipation (1862), "The Day and the War" (1864), a "Poem" on the death of Lincoln (1865), his "Valedictory on Leaving San Francisco" (1866), and "The Progress of Liberty" (1866) on the end of the war.

After relocating his family from Canada to Toledo, Ohio, Bell toured nationally with "Modern Moses" (1866). On tour in 1867, he met William Wells

Brown* in Washington. After "The Triumph of Liberty" (1870), Bell began a political career as a delegate to the state and national Republican conventions for Grant in 1872 and later writing a campaign poem for Harrison. In 1874 newspaper records suggest that his eldest son and his wife died at the same time or within a few days (Abajian 143). A memorial speech for his son is presumed to be by the same James Madison Bell. In 1901, at the insistence of his friend AME bishop Benjamin W. Arnett, Bell published *The Poetical Works of James Madison Bell*. "The Bard of the Maumee" died in 1902. Arnett's "Biographical Sketch" is the main source of all later biographies.

MAJOR WORKS AND THEMES

Bell thought of poetry as a public performance, designed to move a crowd into strong feelings on political and moral issues. His poems move almost exclusively in regular *aabb* or *abab* rhyme schemes with monotonous iambic tetrameter rhythms that were brought to life by a dramatic reading style. His major poems could be strung into a single narrative comment on the history of abolition, civil war, and their political aftermath. They record the logical, emotional, and political appeals of an ardent propagandist for abolition and civil rights.

His series of long political poems attempts an epic scope and makes a continuous, logical, moral argument for freedom in the United States and everywhere. Bell called himself the "Poet of Hope" for his faith in the ultimate progress of justice, freedom, truth, and a modern, equitable society. His first "Poem" celebrates abolition in the District of Columbia and the British West Indies, taking them as harbingers of the ultimate victory of freedom. His first Civil War oration, "The Day and the War," is dedicated to John Brown; it celebrates black Union soldiers (comparing them to the Light Brigade of Tennyson's poem) and recounts the history of the war to date. His "Poem" on Lincoln compares the late president nonironically to Moses, an attitude Bell would reverse to great effect in calling Johnson the "Modern Moses." "The Progress of Liberty" celebrates the end of the war, mourns Lincoln, evokes William Tell as a romantic hero, and earnestly prays for Johnson to fulfill promises to freed slaves. "The Triumph of Liberty," coming after "Modern Moses," is a return from satire to didactic oratory, recounting the political history of the years 1860–1870.

Bell reworks his earnest closing lines on Johnson from "Progress" in his satirical "Modern Moses, or 'My Policy' Man," which scathingly and entertainingly attacks Johnson on political and personal grounds. While Bell's other long poems are today nearly unreadable for their turgid, clichéd imagery and conventional emotional appeal, "Modern Moses" remains fresh and amusing. Here Bell abandons the rhetorical decorum and logical coherence of his other work to berate Johnson's policies, his inconsistent career, his manners, his drinking, his nose, and his ancestry.

All of Bell's political poems espouse a belief that the American Revolution left a legacy for blacks as well as whites; that black Americans had a public sphere and a duty as citizens; that the Constitution was not inherently pro-slavery; that moral consistency and justice exerted a compelling force on a nation's history. His logical arguments frequently turn on the theme of consistency. "The Dawn of Freedom" (1868) argues that to free slaves while denying them all civil rights is a moral contradiction, implicitly contrasting the incomplete American emancipation with the praiseworthy British West Indian emancipation. "Sons of Erin" exhorts Irish immigrants, in the name of consistency, not to help the oppression of blacks. "The Future of America, in the Unity of the Races" argues theologically against all prejudice, on the theme of consistency with God's creation of a diverse human family.

Some of Bell's nonpolitical poems explore nature and the wonders of creation, which include, for Bell, the marvels of human progress. "Creation Light" expresses nineteenth-century optimism regarding technology as part of God's work in the world. So does Bell's only "Sonnet," in which nature is "the daguerrotype of God" (220). Bell also praises motherhood, celebrates a wedding, gives moral advice to girls, describes a sea voyage, and retells the expulsion from Eden in various short poems.

CRITICAL RECEPTION

Bell has received short evaluations in anthologies of African American verse, first as a recent and valuable poet in the 1920s and 1930s, then as an interesting historical figure of minimal poetic worth in anthologies of the last three decades. Bell's works were praised in the nineteenth century for their uplifting sentiment, abundant heroic imagery, optimism, and moral and political commitment. Most of all, Bell's dramatic performances were admired. William Wells Brown says Bell combined "the highest excellence of the poet with the best style of the orator," a style "not easily described" but exemplifying the "negro's . . . great delight in rhetorical exercise, his inward enthusiasm, his seeming power to transport himself into the scene which he describes, or the emotion he has summoned" (504–5). Bell's friend and former pastor, Bishop Arnett, describes Bell's poetry as a "crystalline stream, which came bubbling, sparkling, leaping, rolling, tumbling and jumping down the mountain side" (10). Both men had seen Bell in performance and shared nineteenth-century rhetorical tastes.

In the early twentieth century, Bell figured into the earliest academic anthologies of African American verse as a champion of liberty and racial uplift. His stock quickly dropped, however, among modernist concerns for technical excellence and emotional honesty in poetry. Where Arnett describes Bell with "the trowel in one hand and his pen in the other" (11) writing "crystalline" poetry, current readers see Bell's imagery and sentimentality as more like opaque plaster.

Kerlin (1923), a rather patronizing white compiler of contemporary black poets, includes Bell in his history of important precursors. He finds "something of Byronic power in the roll of his verse" (33). White and Jackson (1924) find Bell important for his life's political work. Benjamin Brawley (1935) also notices

Byron's influence and calls Bell "an able speaker" who wrote "nothing . . . of high technical excellence" (279). J. Saunders Redding (1939), in his important history of African American poetry, gives the longest early critical treatment. Redding notes Bell's "imitations of Pope and Scott, Tennyson and Bryant" with sympathy for Bell's moral earnestness and sense of ceremony. He finds, however, "that [Bell] had neither the skill nor the power to sustain pieces of such length," which suffer from a "steady drop in emotional force and the frequent shifting of metrical form." He sees Bell as the last black poet able to celebrate optimistically the "liberty" of post–Civil War years (45–47).

From the 1930s through the 1960s, the literary profession ignored all nineteenth-century African American poets before Dunbar.* Robinson (1969) first revived some of them in his anthology. He comments astutely that "it is helpful to remember that Bell is best appreciated as something of an actor, his poems regarded as scripts" (82). He calls the ad hominem attack on Johnson in "Modern Moses" inappropriate, as it surely was on ethical grounds. Bell's departure from decorum, other critics say, makes "Modern Moses" the only enjoyable Bell poem for the post–New Critical reader. Joan R. Sherman, the main modern appreciator of Bell, finds "Modern Moses" to be Bell's "most inventive and readable work" (1992, 192) because of its "skillful combination of the rhymed couplet form, concrete topicality, and uninhibited personal (rather than corporate) emotion" (1989, 87). Redmond (1976) finds that "Modern Moses" "anticipates 'signifying' poets of the 1960s and '70s" (96). All critics agree with Blyden Jackson's (1989) assessment that Bell was morally and politically sincere and eloquent but "light as a passing breeze" in his poetic skills (256).

The most complete, authoritative, and fair evaluation of Bell's poetry to date is Sherman's in *Invisible Poets* (1974, 1989). Her biography is the first accurate and detailed account since Arnett's, and her critical evaluations account for both text and context. Bell's strongest moments, she finds, are when "amid the generalities references to specific events, persons, or places rouse momentary interest" (83); thus, "Modern Moses" with its specific personal expression is Bell's best work. In a 1992 anthology, Sherman agrees with Redding that Bell is a "transitional figure" between the "militant ardor" of abolitionism and the politic avoidance of controversy in turn-of-the-century black poets (7).

BIBLIOGRAPHY

Works by James Madison Bell

Memoriam, John Frye Bell. Died August 4, 1874: A Father's Tribute to the Memory of His Eldest Son. Northampton, MA, 1874. Held by the Library of Congress.

The Poetical Works of James Madison Bell. Lansing, MI: Wynkoop Hallenbeck Crawford, 1901; New York: AMS Press, 1973.

Studies of James Madison Bell

Abajian, James de T. *Blacks in Selected Newspapers, Censuses, and Other Sources*. Vol. 1. Boston: G. K. Hall, 1977.

Arnett, Benjamin W. "Biographical Sketch." In Bell, *Poetical Works*. 3–14.

Brawley, Benjamin. *Early Negro American Writers*. Chapel Hill: University of North Carolina Press, 1935.

Brown, William Wells. *The Rising Son: or, the Antecedents and Advancement of the Colored Race*. Boston: A. G. Brown, 1874; Miami: Mnemosyne, 1969.

Jackson, Blyden. *A History of Afro-American Literature*. Vol. 1. Baton Rouge: Louisiana State University Press, 1989.

Kerlin, Robert T. *Negro Poets and Their Poems*. Washington, DC: Associated, 1923, 1935.

Loggins, Vernon. *The Negro Author: His Development in America, 1900*. New York: Columbia University Press, 1931.

Redding, J. Saunders. *To Make a Poet Black*. Chapel Hill: University of North Carolina Press, 1939.

Redmond, Eugene B. *Drumvoices: The Mission of Afro-American Poetry*. Garden City, NY: Anchor Books, 1976.

Robinson, William H., Jr. *Early Black American Poets*. Dubuque, IA: W. C. Brown, 1969.

Sherman, Joan R., ed. *African-American Poetry of the Nineteenth Century*. Chicago: University of Illinois Press, 1992.

———. *Invisible Poets: Afro-Americans of the Nineteenth Century*. Chicago: University of Illinois Press, 1974, 1989.

White, Newman Ivey, and Walter Clinton Jackson. *An Anthology of Verse by American Negroes*. Durham, NC: Trinity College Press, 1924.

GWENDOLYN BENNETT
(1902–1981)

Gwendolyn S. Jones

BIOGRAPHY

Gwendolyn Bennett was a writer, artist, teacher, administrator, and community activist but is most remembered as a Harlem Renaissance poet. She was a multitalented literary artist whose creations included poetry, short stories, essays, scholarly articles, and critical reviews. In her career as a graphic artist, she was accomplished in easel work and batik work, illustrations (five appeared on the covers of the National Association for the Advancement of Colored People's [NAACP] *Crisis: A Record of the Darker Races* and the Urban League's *Opportunity, a Journal of Negro Life*), pen and ink, watercolor, and oil and held positions in art education and art administration. During her career, this versatile woman also worked with the Federal Writers Project in New York City and the Federal Arts Project, becoming the director of the Harlem Community Art Center; taught at Howard University, Tennessee State College, and the Jefferson School for Democracy; and was director at George Washington Carver School in Harlem.

Gwendolyn Bennett was born in Giddings, Texas, on July 8, 1902. When she was a toddler, her family moved to Nevada, where her parents taught on Indian reservations. While living in Washington, D.C., her parents separated when she was five or six years old. The courts awarded her mother custody, but her father kidnapped Bennett and frequently changed locations to avoid detection and finally settled in Brooklyn, New York.

Bennett received her secondary education in New York at Brooklyn's Girl's High School, where she was active in the literary and drama societies, being the first African American elected to both. As a high school student, she often designed art projects, won first prize in a poster contest, wrote the class graduation speech, and composed lyrics for the class song. She also began to write poetry. At Girl's High School, Bennett was influenced and mentored by her teachers in art and in literature.

Upon graduation from high school in 1921, Bennett enrolled in the Fine Arts Department at Teachers College, Columbia University, where she studied for two years. She transferred to Pratt Institute and studied art and drama there for two years. At Pratt Institute, she wrote the class play both years and had a lead role in the junior class play. After graduating in 1924, Bennett accepted a faculty position at Howard University in the Department of Fine Arts, where she taught design, watercolor, and crafts. When she arrived at Howard, Bennett was already an established artist: she had illustrated a cover for *Crisis*, was well known in the offices of *Crisis* and *Opportunity*, and had a poem, "To Usward," selected to commemorate the debut of younger writers at an affair sponsored by New York's Civic Club. While at Howard, she published articles about the Negro in the *Howard University Record*, and she submitted poems to *Crisis*, *Opportunity*, and other magazines.

Delta Sigma Theta sorority awarded Gwendolyn Bennett a $1,000 scholarship to study art in Paris for a year, beginning in June 1925. She studied at Academie Julian, Ecole de Pantheon, the Academie Colorassi, and the Sorbonne. Her studies included watercolor, oils, pen and ink, batik, and French literature. Her proficiency enabled her to mount hangings in batik. Returning to the United States, Bennett spent the summer of 1926 in Harlem, where she worked as assistant to the editor (Charles S. Johnson) of *Opportunity*, was a member of the editorial board of *Fire!!*, and studied art at the Charles C. Barnes Foundation in Merion, Pennsylvania.

Bennett returned to Howard University in the fall of 1926, continued to write "The Ebony Flute," a column for *Opportunity*, mounted exhibits, and submitted poems for publication. After her marriage to Alfred Jackson (who had been a medical student at Howard University) in the spring of 1927, Bennett resigned from her teaching position, returned to New York City, where she worked in a batik factory by passing as a Javanese woman, and continued to paint and to write. During the summer of 1927, she taught art education and English at Tennessee State College, then moved to Florida in the fall to join her husband. While living in Eustis, Florida, she stopped writing "The Ebony Flute" and stopped producing art and literature. In the early 1930s, at her insistence, Bennett and her husband moved to New York City; he completed the medical licensing examination and established a private practice. By that time, the Harlem Renaissance was ending. They lived well for a while, despite the Great Depression. Alfred Jackson died in the early 1930s.

After the renaissance, Gwendolyn Bennett worked with the Federal Arts Project and for the Consumers Union. She later moved to Kutztown, Pennsylvania, where she was an antique collector and dealer with her second husband. She died May 30, 1981, in Kutztown.

MAJOR WORKS AND THEMES

Gwendolyn Bennett's most productive years were from 1923 to 1928. She wrote in a number of genres but is most often identified as a poet. Her poems, numbering approximately twenty, were published in *Crisis, Opportunity*, and contemporary anthologies. Some of the poems express race consciousness, while others are private and introspective. "Heritage" presents a series of images describing her African heritage. It was published two years before Countee Cullen's* poem with the same title and a similar theme. "To Usward" was dedicated to Jessie Redmon Fauset* in honor of the publication of her novel, *There Is Confusion*. This poem captures unity through the metaphor of a ginger jar and celebrates youth and diversity. It extols the cultural riches of Africa and reflects folk culture. "Heritage" and "To Usward" invoke the merging of African and African American experiences.

"Hatred" won a second honorable mention in a 1926 *Opportunity* contest. The poem is personal and emotional. The object of the hate is ambiguous. Sounds and metaphors are similar to a painting's contradictory colors (Roses and Randolph). "To a Dark Girl" expresses pride in black beauty. "Lines Written at the Grave of Alexander Dumas" recognizes a black author and expresses unrequited love.

A significant body of work produced by Gwendolyn Bennett was her literary and arts column "The Ebony Flute," which appeared monthly from August 1926 to May 1928 in *Opportunity* and was widely read. It is an organized chronicle of news about writers, painters, sculptors, and musicians, whether they lived in New York City or elsewhere. She was well suited for this activity because she lived in, and had contacts in, New York and Washington, D.C., and she was talented in literature and in art. The articles, usually 1,200–1,500 words, celebrate the black artists and their works: Georgia Douglas Johnson's* literary salon at her home in Washington, D.C.; Helene Johnson* and her membership in the Saturday Evening Quill Club in Boston; Aaron Douglas's illustrations; and concerts by Eva Jessye's Dixie Jubilee Singers, for example. "The Ebony Flute" represents the bulk of Bennett's published work.

Bennett wrote two short stories: "Wedding Day," published in *Fire!!* in 1926, and "Tokens," published in Charles Johnson's *Ebony and Topaz: A Collectanea* in 1927. Both are about the black American expatriate living in Paris. The protagonist in "Wedding Day," Paul Watson, and the protagonist in "Tokens," Jenks Barnett, are bitter, alienated, and destroyed by unrequited love. Jazz music and musicians are featured in both. Details about weather, specific locations in the city, and local color reflect Bennett's familiarity with Paris.

Gwendolyn Bennett served on the editorial board of *Fire!!*, along with Langston Hughes,* Wallace Thurman,* Bruce Nugent,* Zora Neale Hurston,* and Aaron Douglas. This magazine was to provide an outlet for the younger writers and artists of the period; however, the November 1926 issue was the only one ever published. Budgetary problems and an actual fire prevented publication of subsequent issues.

In addition to writing poetry, fiction, and news columns, Bennett's journalism activities included literary reviews, scholarly articles, critiques, columns, and rewrites of technical reports. Following the Great Depression, Bennett spent much of her time in public service and in helping promote artists and their works.

CRITICAL RECEPTION

Many of the renaissance themes—the beauty of blackness, racial pride, and contradictory experiences—are reflected in Gwendolyn Bennett's poetry. Sandra Govan notes that Bennett's peers were complimentary of her work and that she was held in high regard. James Weldon Johnson described her poetry as lyrical. Sterling Brown observed that her poems were "race conscious" (74). Arna Bontemps, in *Harlem Renaissance Remembered*, describes her Romanticism as "the Romanticism of the best poetry of the Harlem Renaissance" (266). In "To a Dark Girl," for example, African and African American experiences by women meld. Countee Cullen felt that the poetry in *Caroling Dusk* would not be complete without selections by Bennett. That her poems are included in *Palms* is an indication of her artistry.

Although Alain Locke* selected "Song" for publication in *The New Negro*, Eugene Redmond thinks this piece is "not representative of her generally high craftsmanship; it is flawed by imbalance and an attempt to say too many things in one poem" (200). Bennett's "sharp, crisp and precise imagery employed in poems that appeared in magazines and other anthologies show her as a poet with many gifts and resources" (200).

Other recent critics reviewing Bennett's work are also complimentary. Gloria Hull, in *Sturdy Black Bridges*, writes that Gwendolyn Bennett's "poetry is rather good. She was, by occupation, an artist, and consequently in her work she envisions scenes, paints still lifes, and expresses herself well in color" (81). Ann Shockley declares that Bennett, who gained a reputation as a visual artist and a respected art teacher, was as talented a poet as she was an artist.

Govan notes that a shortcoming is the uneven quality of Bennett's work, perhaps the result of the division of her creative energy. She was so talented that she may have lacked sufficient concentration; perhaps she was not single-minded in purpose. Gwendolyn Bennett's best writing is evident when she combines renaissance themes with incidents growing out of her personal experiences.

BIBLIOGRAPHY

Works by Gwendolyn Bennett

Poetry

"Heritage." *Opportunity: A Journal of Negro Life* 1 (December 1923): 371.
"To Usward." *Crisis: A Record of the Darker Races* 28 (May 1924): 19 and *Opportunity* 2 (May 1924): 143–44.

"Wind." *Opportunity* 2 (November 1924): 335.

"Purgation." *Opportunity* 3 (February 1925): 56.

"On a Birthday." *Opportunity* 3 (September 1925): 276.

"Street Lamps in Early Spring." *Opportunity* 4 (May 1926): 152.

"Hatred." *Opportunity* 4 (June 1926): 190.

"Dirge." *Palms* 4 (October 1926): 22.

"Song." *Palms* 4 (October 1926): 21.

"Dear Things." *Palms* 4 (October 1926): 22.

"Advice." *Caroling Dusk: An Anthology of Verse by Negro Poets*. Ed. Countee Cullen. New York: Harper and Row, 1927. 156–57.

"Fantasy." *Caroling Dusk: An Anthology of Verse by Negro Poets*. Ed. Countee Cullen. New York: Harper and Row, 1927. 158.

"Lines Written at the Grave of Alexander Dumas." *Caroling Dusk: An Anthology of Verse by Negro Poets*. Ed. Countee Cullen. New York: Harper and Row, 1927. 159.

"Moon Tonight." *Anthology of Magazine Verse for 1927*. Ed. William S. Braithwaite. Boston: B. J. Brimmer, 1927. 32.

"Quatrains." *Caroling Dusk: An Anthology of Verse by Negro Poets*. Ed. Countee Cullen. New York: Harper and Row, 1927. 155.

"Secret." *Caroling Dusk: An Anthology of Verse by Negro Poets*. Ed. Countee Cullen. New York: Harper and Row, 1927. 155–56.

"Sonnet I." *Caroling Dusk: An Anthology of Verse by Negro Poets*. Ed. Countee Cullen. New York: Harper and Row, 1927. 160–61.

"Sonnet II." *Caroling Dusk: An Anthology of Verse by Negro Poets*. Ed. Countee Cullen. New York: Harper and Row, 1927. 161–62.

"To a Dark Girl." *Caroling Dusk: An Anthology of Verse by Negro Poets*. Ed. Countee Cullen. New York: Harper and Row, 1927. 157.

"Your Songs." *Caroling Dusk: An Anthology of Verse by Negro Poets*. Ed. Countee Cullen. New York: Harper and Row, 1927. 157–58.

"Nocturn." *The Book of American Negro Poetry*. Ed. James Weldon Johnson. New York: Harcourt, Brace, and World, rev. ed., 1931. 244.

Short Stories

"Wedding Day." *Fire!!* 1 (November 1926): 25–28; reprinted in *Voices from the Harlem Renaissance*. Ed. Nathan Huggins. New York: Oxford University Press, 1976. 191–97.

"Tokens." *Ebony and Topaz: A Collectanea*. Ed. Charles S. Johnson. New York: National Urban League, 1927; Freeport, NY: Books for Libraries Press, 1971. 149–50.

Nonfiction

"The Future of the Negro in Art." *Howard University Record* 19 (December 1924): 65–66.

"Negroes: Inherent Craftsmen." *Howard University Record* 19 (February 1925): 172.

"The Ebony Flute." *Opportunity* (a monthly column published August 1926–May 1928).

"The American Negro Paints." *Southern Workman* 57 (1928): 111–12.

"I Go to Camp." *Opportunity* 12 (August 1934): 241–43.

"Rounding the Century: Story of the Colored Orphan Asylum and Association for the Benefit of Colored Orphans in New York City." *Crisis* (June 1935): 180–81, 188.

Reviews

Sorrow in Sunlight, by Ronald Firbank. *Opportunity* (June 1926): 195–96.
The Grand Army Man of Rhode Island. *Opportunity* (September 1926): 295.
The Lonesome Road, by Paul Green. *Opportunity* (September 1926): 294.
My Spirituals, by Eva Jessye. *Opportunity* (November 1927): 338–39.
Banjo, by Claude Mckay. *Opportunity* (August 1929): 254–55.
Plum Bun, by Jessie Redmon Fauset. *Opportunity* (September 1929): 287.
Salah and His American, by Leland Hall. *Opportunity* (March 1934): 92.

Studies of Gwendolyn Bennett

Bontemps, Arna, ed. *Harlem Renaissance Remembered: Essays Edited with a Memoir*. New York: Dodd, Mead, 1972.
Brown, Sterling. *Negro Poetry and Drama*. Washington, DC: Associates in Negro Folk Education, 1937.
Cullen, Countee. *Caroling Dusk: An Anthology of Verse by Negro Poets*. New York: Harper and Row, 1927.
Daniel, Walter, and Sandra Y. Govan. "Gwendolyn Bennett." *Dictionary of Literary Biography*. Ed. Thadious M. Davis and Trudier Harris. Detroit: Gale, 1984. 3–10.
Govan, Sandra Y. "Portrait of an Artist Lost." Diss., University of Michigan, 1980.
———"Bennett, Gwendolyn." *The Oxford Companion to African American Literature*. Ed. William L. Andrews, Frances Smith Foster, and Trudier Harris. New York: Oxford University Press, 1997. 57.
Hull, Gloria, 1. "Black Women Poets from Wheatley to Walker." *Sturdy Black Bridges: Visions of Black Women in Literature*. Ed. Roseann P. Bell, Bettye J. Parker, and Beverly Guy-Sheftall. Garden City, NY: Anchor Books/Doubleday, 1979. 69–86.
———. *Color, Sex, and Poetry*. Bloomington: Indiana University Press, 1987.
Johnson, James Weldon. *The Book of American Negro Poetry*. New York: Harcourt, Brace, and World, 1922.
Lewis, David Levering. *When Harlem Was in Vogue*. New York: Knopf, 1981.
Locke, Alain, ed. *The New Negro: His Heritage and Literature*. 1925. New York: Arno Press, 1968.
Redmond, Eugene B. *Drumvoices: The Mission of Afro-American Poetry. A Critical History*. Garden City, NY: Anchor Books, 1976.
Roses, Lorraine Elena, and Ruth Elizabeth Randolph. *The Harlem Renaissance and Beyond Literary Biography of 100 Black Women Writers, 1900–1945*. Boston: G. K. Hall, 1990. 11–15.
———*Harlem's Glory: Black Women Writing 1900–1950*. Cambridge: Harvard University Press, 1997.
Shockley, Ann Allen. *Afro-American Women Writers 1746–33: An Anthology and Critical Guide*. New York: New American Library, 1989.
Stetson, Erlene, ed. *Black Sister: Poetry by Black American Women, 1746–1980*. Bloomington: Indiana University Press, 1981.
Wall, Cheryl A. *Women of the Harlem Renaissance*. Bloomington and Indianapolis: Indiana University Press, 1995.
Watson, Steven. *The Harlem Renaissance; Hub of African-American Culture, 1920–1930*. New York: Pantheon Books, 1995.

HENRY WALTON BIBB
(1815–1854)

Jesse G. Swan

BIOGRAPHY

Born on May 10, 1815, to Mildred Jackson, a slave on Willard Gatewood's Shelby County, Kentucky, plantation, Henry Bibb became an indefatigable critic of slavery and activist, especially on behalf of refugee slaves. Bibb's childhood and young adulthood were spent variously in Kentucky, Ohio, Michigan, Canada West, Louisiana, and the territory that was to become Oklahoma either as a slave, despite his father's being Kentucky state senator James Bibb, or refugee during his numerous periods of escape. Until it became impossible, Bibb continually returned to the South to rescue his wife and daughter, only to be betrayed and sold farther south into ever-crueler conditions, the worst being that of Baptist deacon Francis Whitfield, a Claiborn parish plantation owner. Of seven owners, this Christian, Bibb stresses, was "one of the basest hypocrites that I ever saw" (*Narrative* 118), and this slave owner forced the complete separation of Bibb from his wife, Malinda, and daughter, Frances. Further, this deacon slaveholder sold Malinda to another to serve as concubine. While this fact "was a death blow" to Bibb, he insisted that there be "no charge of guilt against her" (Malinda) given Malinda's inhuman environment (*Narrative* 162–63).

Upon giving Malinda up as "dead to me as a wife" (163) in the winter of 1845, Bibb devoted himself entirely to the antislavery cause in Michigan, Ohio, Pennsylvania, and New England. Having learned to read and write in a Louisville prison and having attended classes of the Reverend William C. Monroe in Detroit for only three weeks, being unable to afford more, Bibb created evocative and sardonic orations rivaled only by those of William Wells Brown* and Frederick Douglass.* As an activist in New York in May 1847, Bibb met free black abolitionist Mary Elizabeth Miles (c. 1820–1877) of Boston, and after a shy and then very rational courtship—having "mutually engaged ourselves" to marry in one year, the couple agreed to "this condition, viz: that if either party should see any reason to change their mind within that time, the contract [to marry] should not be considered binding" (*Narrative* 164)—they married in June 1848 (Ripley 2: 110). Between their marriage and their move to Canada in response to the Fugitive Slave Law of 1850, Bibb published, in New York and at his own expense, his *Narrative of the Life and Adventures of Henry Bibb, an American Slave Written by Himself* in October 1849. In Canada during the early 1850s, then, the noted couple were instrumental in starting the short-lived North American League and the longer-lived Refugees' Home Society, both designed to encourage black immigration to Canada and black separatism. Allied to these efforts, the couple started and edited *The Voice of the Fugitive*, a semimonthly newspaper directed to blacks who viewed themselves as temporary exiles. The paper also served as the print outlet for the Refugees' Home Society. In these endeavors, the Bibbs were severely criticized, ultimately being accused of defrauding benefactors and refugees alike by Mary Ann Shadd, famous educator and later lawyer known for her advocacy of temperance, abolition, integration, and education. Whatever the motive and substance of the accusations, the charges distressed the Bibbs. Henry died on August 1, 1854 (Ripley 2: 110), having seen his printing office burn to the ground the previous October 9, while Mary died in 1877 in Brooklyn, New York, after having married Isaac N. Cary and after having accumulated a considerable estate. As John W. Blassingame concludes, "Before his death at thirty-nine in the summer of 1854, Henry Bibb had made a permanent impression on his times" (44).

MAJOR WORKS AND THEMES

Bibb's major work is his *Narrative*, a work marked by reason, dignity, and modulating plainness and eloquence, even in its unflinching descriptions of mortifying physical and psychological tortures. A source for Harriet Beecher Stowe's *Uncle Tom's Cabin*, the narrative, introduced by Lucius C. Matlack, vocal Methodist Episcopal minister who lost his license to preach around 1845 for being an abolitionist, served to complement thematically, factually, and rhetorically the more famous *Narrative of the Life of Frederick Douglass, an American Slave, Written by Himself* of 1845.

The major themes are of the ways American slavery dehumanizes everyone, black and white, though southern white men are also represented at times as essentially inhuman. The worst effect of slavery on whites, the narrative insists, is turning white Christians into hypocrites. While Deacon Whitfield serves as the most extensive instrument for developing this theme, all the slave owners and the entire system are indicted for false, perverted piety, as is suggested by the explanation of Dan Lane, slave-hunter or "man stealer," regarding Bibb's incredible escape from him: Lane attributes Bibb's escape to Bibb's "goodness," which then makes Lane affirm that he "should never again have any thing to do with a praying negro" (100). All the white South, the narrative implies, entirely understands this sentiment, a sentiment that lies behind the common practice of flogging slaves who hold or attend prayer meetings (124). Such hypocrisy complements what is asserted to be an essential trait of southern white men, licentiousness. Having detailed several sexual abuses against Malinda and having done so to convey the torment both to Malinda and to him—having to be "eye witness to her insults, scourgings and abuses . . . to the insults and licentious passions of wicked slavedrivers and overseers . . . [to] the lash laid on by an un-merciful tyrant" was devastating to him (80)—Bibb makes clear in his concluding chapter that he has "long thought . . . that the strongest reason why southerners stick with such tenacity to their 'peculiar institution,' is because licentious white men could not carry out their wicked purposes among the defenceless colored population as they now do, without being exposed and punished by law" (169). Slavery dehumanizes whites—makes them Christian hypocrites—but slavery also derives from inhuman whites, people who steal everything from blacks, even, in the case of Bibb, to the point of having "almost entirely robbed me of my dark complexion" (83).

The dehumanizing consequences and inhuman origins of slavery, another re-lated theme suggests, force blacks to deceive and steal themselves, but because the system so perverts human relations, the deception and theft on the part of blacks are radically annulled or even made requisite. Indeed, in the penultimate chapter, Bibb provides an extensive argument for why he "had a just right to what [he] took" (166), mostly because he was unfree and said to be the property of the person he "stole" from, because he was not paid for his labor, and because he was not provided even a sustenance living. Similarly, Bibb explains that de-ception "is the most effective defense a slave can use" (95) in interacting with white slave owners and drivers. Deception and theft by slaves are actions of self-defense and self-preservation. All of this unnatural perverseness generated by the institution of slavery is further communicated throughout the narrative by par-alleling slave owners with vicious animals, such as wolves (126–27), in contrast to slaves as hunted victims, such as deer (97), or by depicting degenerate southern life enforcing work "under the flesh-devouring lash during life, without wages" in contrast to pastoral scenes of "free soil" with its "green trees and wild flowers of the forest; the ripening harvest fields waving with the gentle breezes of Heaven" (93).

Such themes of white degeneracy and requisite black resourcefulness and nim-bleness are allied to two of the narrative's other distinctive features: its signal descriptions and its rhetorical fluency. For detailed pictures of slave prisons and slave sales, Bibb's narrative is considered most reliable, and for use of devices such as the rhetorical question and energeia, as in "For while the slave is regarded as property, how can he steal from his master?" (166) and "With manacled limbs; with wounded spirit; with sympathising tears and with bleeding heart, I entreated Malinda to weep not for me, for it only added to my grief, which was ever greater than I could bear" (105), Bibb's narrative is exceptional.

Such rhetorical eloquence, coupled with his oratorical sardonicism, characterizes some of the writing of Bibb's other work, the newspaper *The Voice of the Fugitive*. Most notably, the paper ran Bibb's editorials and essays attacking southern whites and promoting black separatism and immigration to Canada. In one series of essays ironically entitled "To Our Old Masters," for instance, Bibb outlined the history of the "Anglo-Saxons" to show that southern whites were "the most inconsistent race of slaveholders that the world has yet produced" (Ripley 2: 122) and that their British "predecessors were once naked savages . . . and [now] the descendants of the Anglo-Saxons in England are ashamed of their monstrous offspring" (Ripley 2: 124) in the American South. As Roger W. Hite notes, Bibb and his newspaper were essential to a new "intellectual leadership dedicated to separatism and to rejection of militant assimilationist arguments of people like Frederick Douglass" (269).

CRITICAL RECEPTION

Other than by summary and though extremely limited, Bibb's narrative and newspaper have received some attention. John W. Blassingame counts the narrative among one of the "most informative of the autobiographies" by former slaves (374), and William L. Andrews shows how it creates an "implied reader" who is involved in "a decision about his own identity and his own position vis-a-vis the black and white categories of any socio-moral system of thought" (30). Robert B. Stepto, in addition to tracing some influence on Stowe ("Sharing the Thunder"), examines the front matter of Bibb's narrative and finds "[m]any race rituals enacted here," most significantly, the editor's conversation with other white Americans to prove that Bibb actually exists, an effort to make the invisible visible (*From behind the Veil* 8). Such prefatory material, though well meaning, "relegates [Bibb] to a posture of partial literacy" (*From behind the Veil* 10). Looking at Bibb's narrative, Maria Diedrich finds that Bibb uses white racist stereotypes of Indians rhetorically to shame white racists: Bibb's Indian master was by far his best master despite his barbarousness, most obvious in his apparent lack of intelligence and affinity for drunkenness. With *The Voice of the Fugitive*, Robin W. Winks notes that it was much quoted in the northern abolitionist press and realized more influence than its rival, *The Provincial Freeman*, edited by Bibb's nemesis, Mary Ann Shadd. Finally, Roger W. Hite offers an extended analysis of Bibb's rhetoric in his contributions to *The Voice* and concludes that "Bibb's rhetoric was both a success and a failure. It succeeded on a limited scale when directed toward satisfying the immediate needs of fugitive slaves. . . . When Bibb conceived of a more grandiose plan . . . he was ahead of his time" (281). Still, no one has pursued Gilbert Osofsky's recommendations for further investigation of especially Bibb's narrative (43), nor has anyone pursued the extent to which Bibb's wife, Mary, contributed to Henry's writing, a suggestion made by Ripley (2: 111). Much remains to be understood about Henry Bibb, sardonic black separatist.

BIBLIOGRAPHY

Works by Henry Walton Bibb

Narrative of the Life and Adventures of Henry Bibb, an American Slave Written by Himself. Intro. Lucius C. Matlack. New York: Henry Bibb, 1849. Reprinted in *Puttin' on Ole Massa.* Ed. Gilbert Osofsky. New York: Harper Torchbooks, 1969. 51–171.
The Voice of the Fugitive, founding editor and contributor. January 1, 1851–October 1854. Selections reprinted in Ripley.

Studies of Henry Walton Bibb

Andrews, William L. *To Tell a Free Story: The First Century of Afro-American Autobiography. 1760–1865.* Urbana: University of Illinois Press, 1986.
Blassingame, John W. *The Slave Community: Plantation Life in the Antebellum South.* Rev. ed. New York: Oxford University Press, 1979.
Davis, Charles T. "The Slave Narrative: First Major Art Form in an Emerging Black Tradition." In his *Black Is the Color of the Cosmos.* New York: Garland, 1982. 83–119.
Davis, Charles T., and Henry Louis Gates Jr., eds. *The Slave's Narrative.* New York: Oxford University Press, 1985.
Diedrich, Maria. "The Characterization of Native Americans in the Antebellum Slave Narrative." *CLA Journal* 31.4 (1988): 412–35.
Drew, Benjamin. *The Refugee: Narratives of Fugitive Slaves in Canada.* 1856. Reprinted, New York: Johnson Reprint, 1968.
Foster, Frances Smith. *Witnessing Slavery: The Development of Ante-Bellum Slave Narratives.* Westport, CT: Greenwood Press, 1979.
Fulcher, James. "Deception and Detection: Some Epistemological Themes of Ethnic Americans in the Nineteenth Century." *Markham Review* 8 (1979): 72–77.
Hill, Daniel. *The Freedom Seekers: Blacks in Early Canada.* Agincourt, Ontario: Book Society of Canada, 1981.
Hite, Roger W. "Voice of a Fugitive: Henry Bibb and Antebellum Black Separatism." *Journal of Black Studies* 4.3 (1974): 269–84.
Howe, S. G. *The Refugees from Slavery in Canada West: Report to the Freedman's Inquiry Commission.* 1864. New York: Arno Press and New York Times, 1969.
Jackson, Blyden. *A History of Afro-American Literature.* Vol. 1: *The Long Beginning, 1746–1895.* Baton Rouge: Louisiana State University Press, 1989. 141–42.
Koike, Sekio. "The Narrative of Henry Bibb." *Kyushu American Literature* 16 (1975): 21–33.
Landon, Fred. "Henry Bibb, a Colonizer." *Journal of Negro History* 5.4 (1920): 437–47.
Lowance, Mason L., Jr. "Bibb, Henry." *The Oxford Companion to African American Literature.* Ed. William L. Andrews, Frances Smith Foster, and Trudier Harris. New York: Oxford University Press, 1997. 58–59.
Matlack, Lucius C. *Narrative of the Anti-Slavery Experience of a Minister in the Methodist E. Church: Who Was Twice Rejected by the Philadelphia Annual Conference, and Finally Deprived of Licence [sic] to Preach for Being an Abolitionist.* Philadelphia: Martin and Boden, 1845.

Mullen, Harryette. "African Signs and Spirit Writing." *Callaloo* 19.3 (1996): 670–89.

Osofsky, Gilbert. "Introduction: Puttin' on Ole Massa: The Significance of Slave Narratives." *Puttin' on Ole Massa.* New York: Torchbooks, 1969. 9–44.

Ripley, C. Peter, et al., eds. *The Black Abolitionist Papers.* 5 vols. Chapel Hill: University of North Carolina Press, 1985.

Salzman, Jack, David Lionel Smith, and Cornel West, eds. *Encyclopedia of African-American Culture and History.* 5 vols. New York: Simon and Schuster Macmillan, 1996.

Silverman, Jason H. "Mary Ann Shadd and the Search for Equality." *Black Leaders of the Nineteenth Century.* Ed. Leon Litwack and August Meier. Urbana: University of Illinois Press, 1988. 87–100.

———. *The Unwelcome Guest: Canada's Response to American Fugitive Slaves 1800–1865.* Millwood, NY: National University Publications, 1985.

Starling, Marion Wilson. *The Slave Narrative: Its Place in American History.* Washington, DC: Howard University Press, 1988. 147–52.

Stepto, Robert B. *From behind the Veil: A Study of Afro-American Narrative.* Urbana: University of Illinois Press, 1979.

———. "Sharing the Thunder: The Literary Exchanges of Harriet Beecher Stowe, Henry Bibb, and Frederick Douglass." In Sundquist, 135–53.

Sundquist, Eric J., ed. *New Essays on Uncle Tom's Cabin.* Cambridge: Cambridge University Press, 1986.

Winks, Robin W. *The Blacks in Canada: A History.* 2nd ed. Montreal: McGill-Queen's University Press, 1997.

MARITA BONNER
(1898 – 1971)

Heather E. Spahr

BIOGRAPHY

Marita Odette Bonner was born on June 16, 1898, to Joseph Andrew and Mary Anne (Noel) Bonner. While most accounts of Bonner list her birth year as 1899, Lorraine Roses and Ruth Randolph note in "Marita Bonner: In Search of Other Mothers' Gardens" that it was actually 1898–a fact taken from records held by the City of Boston Registry of Records and Vital Statistics (165).

While attending Brookline High School, Bonner contributed regularly to *The Sagamore*, a student magazine. She excelled in her study of music and German and continued her pursuit of each during her attendance at Radcliffe College between 1918 and 1922. She won the song competitions on two occasions at Radcliffe, where she majored in English and comparative literature. As a black student, Bonner was not allowed to live in a campus dormitory, so she commuted from home. However, she participated in campus activities and founded the Radcliffe chapter of Delta Sigma Theta, a black sorority. She also earned one of sixteen coveted spots in Professor Copeland's writing class.

Bonner taught at Cambridge High School during the last part of her college career and continued to teach after graduation, first in Bluefield, West Virginia, and then in Washington, D.C. During her eight years in D.C., 1922–1930, Bonner attended the "S" Street Salon, a weekly writers' group at the home of Georgia Douglas Johnson,* where she shared her ideas with writers like May Miller, Langston Hughes,* Countee Cullen,* Alain Locke,* Jessie Fauset,* S. Randolph Edmonds, Willis Richardson, and Jean Toomer.*

After marrying William Almy Occomy in 1930, Bonner relocated to Chicago, where she would remain for the rest of her life. The couple raised three children,

William Almy Jr., Warwick Gale, and Marita Joyce, who would be instrumental in helping to recover Bonner's texts for publication in *Frye Street and Environs*.

Bonner stopped writing after 1941, concentrating instead on teaching mentally handicapped children until her death in 1971. Some critics link the end of her writing career with the beginning of her association with the Christian Science Church, to which she devoted much of her time and energy. Bonner died on December 6, 1971, as a result of injuries she suffered when her apartment caught fire.

MAJOR WORKS AND THEMES

Bonner published essays, plays, short stories, and serial fictional narratives (once under the pseudonym Joseph Maree Andrews) between 1922 and 1942 in the magazines *Crisis* and *Opportunity*. In 1925 she published her first, and what was to be her most influential, essay, "On Being Young—A Woman—and Colored." The essay, which appeared in *Crisis*, warns of the inevitable violence to come as a result of racial tension in America (Hine 148). It also explores the deplorable conditions that black Americans, particularly women, endured in Bonner's time. She separates the trials faced by blacks from those faced by women, foretelling the "double jeopardy" that Gloria Wade-Gayles would later describe as a common condition of black women writers (Roses and Randolph 170). Through her plays, short stories, and essays, Bonner discusses a wide variety of issues, including miscegenation, the tragic mulatto, generational conflicts, definitions of female respectability, the destructiveness of cities, racial revolution, infidelity, class bias, and interracial ties (Hine 148).

Bonner's participation in the "S" Street Salon inspired her to try her hand at playwriting. While her plays were never produced in her lifetime, they were read by artists of the Harlem Renaissance and influenced later writers, such as Alice Walker, Toni Morrison, Gloria Naylor, Toni Cade Bambara, and Gayl Jones (Roses and Randolph 166).

Bonner's plays contain strong messages: *The Pot Maker* speaks against infidelity, *The Purple Flower* warns of the danger of violent revolution to temper racism, and *Exit, an Illusion* discusses the complications of mixed ancestry. *The Pot Maker* is a morality play written in dialect. Like her other plays, stories, and even essays, Bonner uses a second-person narrator in *The Pot Maker* to direct the reader/ viewer's focus. Bonner meant for the plays to be read rather than performed, as is reflected in their subtitles: *The Pot Maker, (A Play to Be Read)* and *The Purple Flower, A Phantasy That Had Best Be Read* (Burton xxxviii). Bonner's final published play, *Exit, an Illusion*, combines her characteristic second-person narration with theatrical self-reflexivity to explore gender and race issues as well as the nature of theater (Burton xxxix).

When Bonner moved to Chicago with her husband in 1930, she took a three-year hiatus from writing. Bonner's stories from 1933 on reflect new subject matter

arising from the difficulties she saw in city life and its effects on the black population of Chicago, as well as a more complex writing style that would better
suit the telling of these new stories. During this time, Bonner concentrated exclusively on her fiction and won several literary contests in Crisis and Opportunity.
Her Chicago stories take place on the fictitious Frye Street of Chicago and deal
with themes that she would continue to develop in her later writing, such as
"class and color demarcations, poverty, and poor housing. Some of Bonner's
stories written in the early 1930s may have influenced Richard Wright,* who
knew Bonner and her work" (Hine 148).

One story from the Chicago period, "Hate Is Nothing" (1938), focuses on a
woman named Lee as she negotiates between her unsupportive husband and his
domineering mother, with whom they live. Lee's mother-in-law judges people's
worthiness by the lightness of their skin tone rather than by their actions. At
one point in the story, Lee takes a drive to escape her overbearing mother-in-
law and ends up in a poor colored settlement. She wishes she had driven in the
other direction and avoided the collection of tar paper and tin houses, but the
narrator argues against trying to escape ugliness, which must be "seen through—
and lived through—or fought through" (Frye Street and Environs 165). Bonner's
work as a whole faces the ugliness head-on.

Bonner wrote six stories between 1937 and 1941—"On the Altar," "High
Stepper," "One True Love," "Stones for Bread," "Reap It as You Sow It," and
"Light in Dark Places"—but they remained unpublished until sixteen years after
her death. According to Roses and Randolph, the stories constitute "a series of
dualities in black and white that emanate from a feminist perspective: black
female versus black male, black female versus white female, and black female
versus black female" (170). Bonner's exploration of prejudice and oppression
culminates in "Reap It as You Sow It," one of the last stories she wrote. The
story pits two women of the same race and class against one another, forcing their conflict to be moral, rather than racial or social, and therefore seems
to be exploring the deeper causes for conflicts than those arising from external
differences (179). Essentially, Bonner's stories show women searching for self-
realization. "Through marriage, children, education, religion, and sexual expression, they aspire to give birth to themselves, a dream that is elusive and perhaps
impossible because of the odds they face. . . . [Bonner] holds out the possibility
that women can find their own voices and achieve wholeness" (180).

CRITICAL RECEPTION

While few critical works have been written on Bonner's stories and plays,
interest has increased over the last couple of decades both in Bonner's work and
in that of other previously marginalized American writers. According to Darlene
Hine in Black Women in America, Bonner's major literary contribution is "her
characterization of the urban environment as a corrupting force. . . . Her characters belong to a lost world that cramps people in substandard housing, turns

middle-class African-Americans against recently immigrated, uneducated south-erners, and allows homeless and other poor people to die unattended" (149). The prevailing opinion among critics of Bonner's work is that it was ahead of its time in foretelling the violence to come in America as a result of racial tension. "Miscegenation emerges as another important theme in the drama of the period. . . . However, interracial marriage, as in *Exit, An Illusion* by Marita Bonner, offers no solution to the plight of blacks, and will not insure their integration in the white community" (French et al. 255).

The Purple Flower, Bonner's one-act play that won *Crisis'* 1928 playwriting contest, has been described as "non-realistic," "expressionistic," or "allegorical" (Kelly 309) and has been called "possibly the most provocative play" by an African American woman in the first part of the twentieth century, as well as "one of the most unusual plays ever written on the subject of black liberation" (309, citing Wilkerson and Hill). Elizabeth Brown-Guillory also notes Bonner's "preoccupation with the destructiveness of the rural south and the urban North in her writings" as a probable source of influence for Richard Wright and other Chicago Renaissance writers of the 1940s and 1950s (1).

In her introduction to *Frye Street and Environs*, Joyce Flynn discusses several aspects of Bonner's playwriting style, including second-person narration, which serves to involve the reader in the story, and allegory. While much of Bonner's work incorporates some allegorical elements, *The Purple Flower* is entirely an allegory of race relations (Kelly 310) and has been called Bonner's most "ambi-tious . . . effort to represent a black quest for 'Life-At-Its-Fullest' " (Gilbert and Gubar 1577).

Lorraine Roses and Ruth Randolph provide one of the most important studies of Bonner's life and works in their article entitled "Marita Bonner: In Search of Other Mothers' Gardens." They interviewed Bonner's three children for infor-mation on Bonner that goes beyond that listed in most biographical entries. Roses and Randolph also explore the six stories Bonner never published that she had copied into a notebook along with word counts and names—information that suggests the stories were written for publication in particular periodicals. The stories, which date from 1937 to 1941, were published for the first time in 1987 in *Frye Street and Environs: The Collected Works of Marita Bonner*. Katherine Kelly sums up the sentiments of other critics that the attention now being paid to Bonner and other women writers of the Harlem Renaissance is long overdue. The narrator of *The Purple Flower* ends the play with a question, "Is it time?" Now, like the Old Man, we answer, "Thank God! It's time then!"

BIBLIOGRAPHY

Works by Marita Bonner

Book

Frye Street and Environs: The Collected Works of Marita Bonner. Ed. Joyce Flynn and Joyce
    Occomy Stricklin. Boston: Beacon Press, 1987.

Short Stories

"The Hands—A Story." *Opportunity* 3 (August 1925): 235–37.
(As Joseph Maree Andrews). "One Boy's Story." *Crisis* 34 (November 1927): 297–99,
    326–30.
"Drab Rambles." *Crisis* 34 (December 1927): 335–36, 354.
"A Possible Triad on Black Notes." *Opportunity* 11 (1933): 205–7, 242–44, 269–71.
"Of Jimmy Harris." *Opportunity* 1 (August 1933): 242–44.
"Three Tales of the Living." *Opportunity* 11 (September 1933): 269–71.
"Tin Can." *Opportunity* 12 (July 1934): 202–5; 12 (August 1934): 236–40.
"A Sealed Pod." *Opportunity* 14 (March 1936): 88–91.
"Black Fronts." *Opportunity* 16 (July 1938): 210–14.
(As Joyce N. Reed.) "Hate Is Nothing." *Crisis* 45 (December 1938): 388–90, 394,
    403–4.
"The Makin's." *Opportunity* 17 (January 1939): 18–21.
"The Whipping." *Crisis* 46 (June 1939): 172–74.
"Hongry Fire." *Crisis* 46 (December 1939): 360–62, 367–77.
"Patch Quilt." *Crisis* 47 (March 1940): 71, 72, 92.
"On the Altar." *Frye Street and Environs: The Collected Works of Marita Bonner.* Ed. Joyce
    Flynn and Joyce Occomy Stricklin. Boston: Beacon Press, 1987. (Written 1937–
    1940.)
"High Stepper." *Frye Street.* (Written 1938–1940.)
"Stones for Bread." *Frye Street.* (Written 1940.)
"Reap It as You Sow It." *Frye Street.* (Written 1940–1941.)
"Light in Dark Places." *Frye Street.* (Written 1941.)
"One True Love." *Frye Street.* (Written 1941.)

Drama

The Pot Maker (A Play to Be Read). *Opportunity* 5 (February 1927): 43–46.
The Purple Flower. *Crisis* 35 (January 1928): 9–11.
Exit, an Illusion. *Crisis* 36 (1929): 355–57.

Essays

"On Being Young—A Woman—and Colored." *Crisis* 31 (December 1925): 225–26.
"The Prison-Bound." *Crisis* 32 (September 1926): 225–26.
"The Young Blood Hungers." *Crisis* 35 (May 1928): 151, 172.

Studies of Marita Bonner

Abramson, Doris E. "Angelina Weld Grimké, Mary T. Burrill, Georgia Douglas Johnson,
    and Marita O. Bonner: An Analysis of Their Plays." *SAGE* 2.1 (1985): 9–12.

Allen, Carol. *Black Women Intellectuals: Strategies of Nation, Family, and Neighborhood in the Works of Pauline Hopkins, Jessie Fauset, and Marita Bonner.* New York: Garland, 1998.

Brown-Guillory, Elizabeth, comp. and ed. *Wines in the Wilderness: Plays by African American Women from the Harlem Renaissance to the Present.* New York: Greenwood Press, 1990.

Burton, Jennifer, ed. *Zora Neale Hurston, Eulalie Spence, Marita Bonner, and Others: The Prize Plays and Other One-Acts Published in Periodicals.* New York: G. K. Hall, 1996.

Chick, Nancy. "Marita Bonner's Revolutionary Purple Flowers: Challenging the Symbol of White Womanhood." *The Langston Hughes Review* 13 (1994–1995): 21–32.

Fairbanks, Carol, and Eugene Engeldinger. *Black American Fiction: A Bibliography.* Metuchen, NJ: Scarecrow Press, 1978.

Flynn, Joyce. "Marita Bonner Occomy." In *Dictionary of Literary Biography: Afro-American Writers from the Harlem Renaissance to 1940.* Ed. Trudier Harris. Vol. 51. Detroit: Gale Research, 1987. 222–28.

French, William P., et al. *Afro-American Poetry and Drama, 1760–1975: A Guide to Information Sources.* Detroit: Gale Research, 1979.

Gates, Henry Louis, Jr. *Bearing Witness: Selections from African-American Autobiography in the Twentieth Century.* New York: Pantheon Books, 1991.

Gilbert, Sandra, and Susan Gubar, eds. *The Norton Anthology of Literature by Women: The Traditions in English.* 2d ed. New York: Norton, 1996.

Hatch, James V., and Ted Shine, eds. *Black Theater USA: Plays by African Americans 1847 to Today.* New York: Free Press, 1996.

Hine, Darlene C. "Bonner, Marita." *Black Women in America. An Historical Encyclopedia.* Vol. 1. Brooklyn, NY: Carlson, 1993, 148–49.

Isaacs, Diane. "Marita Bonner." *The Harlem Renaissance: A Dictionary for the Era.* Ed. Bruce Kellner. Westport, CT: Greenwood Press, 1984. 45.

Kelly, Katherine E., ed. *Modern Drama by Women 1880s–1930s: An International Anthology.* London: Routledge, 1996.

Roses, Lorraine E., and Ruth E. Randolph. "Marita Bonner: In Search of Other Mothers' Gardens." *Black American Literature Forum* 21, 1–2 (1987): 165–83.

Rush, Theresa Gunnels, Carol F. Myers, and Esther S. Arata. "Marita Bonner." In *Black American Writers Past and Present: A Biographical and Bibliographical Dictionary.* 2 vols. Metuchen, NJ: Scarecrow Press, 1975. 79.

Wade-Gayles, Gloria. *No Crystal Stair: Visions of Race and Sex in Black Women's Fiction.* New York: Pilgrim Press, 1984.

Wall, Cheryl A. "Poets and Versifiers, Singers and Signifiers: Women of the Harlem Renaissance." In *Women, the Arts, and the 1920s in Paris and New York.* Ed. Kenneth W. Wheeler and Virginia L. Lussier. New Brunswick, NJ: Transaction Books, 1982. 74–98.

———. *Women of the Harlem Renaissance.* Bloomington: Indiana University Press, 1995.

ARNA BONTEMPS
(1902–1973)

Jacqueline C. Jones

BIOGRAPHY

Arnaud (Arna) Wendell Bontemps was born on October 13, 1902, in Alexandria, Louisiana. His mother was a teacher, and his father worked as a brick mason and a carpenter. When he was three years old, his family moved to Los Angeles due to his father's treatment by racist whites. Soon after relocating to California, the family converted from Catholicism to the Seventh-Day Adventist faith. Arna, who was educated at church schools, would spend a large part of his life in Seventh-Day Adventist educational institutions. After his mother's death when he was eleven years old, Bontemps became more interested in reading and in African American history. The first book that Bontemps recalled reading was Booker T. Washington's* *The Story of My Life and Work*, a precursor to the more famous autobiography *Up from Slavery*.

In May 1922 Bontemps graduated from Pacific Union College in California, where he majored in English and minored in history. He then took a job in the Los Angeles post office, where Wallace Thurman* was also employed. During the summer of 1924 Bontemps learned that his poem "Hope" would be published in *Crisis*. Given the rise in literary activity, it is no surprise that Bontemps headed for Harlem in August 1924.

Bontemps found employment at Harlem Academy, a Seventh-Day Adventist school in Harlem, and also took graduate classes at Columbia University. He became friends with Countee Cullen,* who in late 1924 introduced him to his lifelong friend and correspondent, Langston Hughes.* As a core member of the literati, Bontemps enjoyed the camaraderie and support that the writers, painters, poets, and singers offered each other. Bontemps was the recipient of *Opportunity* magazine's Alexander Pushkin Poetry Prize in 1926 for "Golgotha Is a Mountain" and again in 1927. His short story "A Summer Tragedy" won *Opportunity*'s literary prize in 1932. He wrote reviews and poems for *Opportunity* during Countee Cullen's tenure as editor from 1926 to 1928. His first novel was rejected by publishers, leading Bontemps to conclude that "publishers were not ready or were in no mood for a first novel with autobiographical overtones about a sensitive black boy in a nostalgic setting" ("Awakening" 25).

Arna Bontemps married Alberta Johnson, a fellow Seventh-Day Adventist, on August 26, 1926. They had six children together (four daughters, Joan, Poppy, Constance, and Camille, and two sons, Paul and Arna Alexander). Alberta provided a stable home environment that made it possible for Bontemps to pursue his literary career. Yet having a growing family put financial pressure on Bontemps. With a family to support, the financial success of his literary efforts was more important to Bontemps than critical attention. His biographer, Kirkland Jones, attributes Bontemps' death to his busy work schedule. Bontemps wrote under conditions that were different from those of his fellow writers. Having a family dictated the need for steady employment, and Bontemps struggled to meet his responsibilities as a husband and father and fulfill his need to write. In his first autobiography, *The Big Sea*, Langston Hughes* describes how Bontemps' marriage set him apart from the other writers. "Arna Bontemps, poet and coming novelist, quiet and scholarly, looking like a young edition of Dr. Du Bois,* was the mysterious member of the Harlem literati, in that we knew that he had recently married, but none of us had ever seen his wife" (248). (Mrs. Bontemps' frequent pregnancies were the cause of her absence.) "But the labor of producing an average of two books and several shorter works each year, for nearly fifty years, not to mention his other duties and responsibilities, took its toll" (Jones, *Renaissance Man* 170).

Bontemps' friendship with Langston Hughes led to their collaboration on a series of important projects related to sustaining the literature and folklore of people of African descent. Their most famous project is *The Book of Negro Folklore*, a collection of folktales, songs, myths, and prose. Published in 1958, *The Book of Negro Folklore* is an extension of their earlier project, *The Poetry of the Negro*. The two men shared a deep and abiding friendship. They each agreed that they never had even one quarrel. The correspondence between the two men spanned from 1925 to Hughes' death in 1967. In 1980, 850 of their most important letters were published in book form by Dodd, Mead, Bontemps' longtime publisher. At his death Bontemps, a coexecutor of Hughes' estate, was working on a biography of Langston Hughes.

Bontemps taught at Oakwood Junior College (now Oakwood College) in Huntsville, Alabama, from 1931 to 1934. His return to the South took him back to African American folk culture in a variety of forms. He completed his historical novel, *Black Thunder*, in 1935, and it was published in 1936 to favorable reviews. Yet his tenure at Oakwood was not without its problems. Seen as strange because he read books, Bontemps was under more suspicion when his good friend Langston Hughes came to town for the nearby Scottsboro trial. The administration at Oakwood actually demanded that Bontemps burn his personal library. He did not comply. Finding the South and Oakwood College restrictive, Bontemps moved his family to Chicago in 1934. There he found employment as the principal of the Seventh-Day Adventist school Shiloh Academy. In 1938 he worked for the Federal Writers Project and gained a Rosenwald Fellowship. Bontemps graduated with a master's in library science from the University of Chicago in 1943. He was employed as chief librarian at Fisk University in Nashville, Tennessee, in 1942 and remained in that position until he resigned in 1965. He managed to perform his duties as head librarian, help to raise his family, and continue to produce literary works. The number of slave narratives in Fisk's archives led Bontemps to collect and publish them in *Great Slave Narratives*. Bontemps was the recipient of a 1954 Guggenheim Fellowship for creative writing. He also was a resident of both the Yaddo and MacDowell artist colonies. While at Fisk, Bontemps compiled an impressive archive of material relating to African Americans.

After leaving Fisk, Bontemps had appointments at the University of Illinois (Chicago Circle) and Yale University. He received honorary doctorates from Berea College and Morgan State University. He suffered a stroke during the winter of 1968 while on the faculty of the University of Illinois, Chicago Circle. Bontemps made a complete recovery from the stroke and resumed his lecturing and teaching. During the 1969–1970 academic year Bontemps taught at Yale University, which bestowed upon him the honorary title of curator of the James Weldon Johnson* Memorial Collection. Largely due to his wife's desire to return to their Nashville home, Bontemps left Yale after the 1970–1971 year. He continued to give lectures about African American literature throughout the country, despite being almost seventy years old. Fisk University wanted Bontemps back and offered him the position of writer in residence, which he accepted. Bontemps died on June 4, 1973, at the age of seventy-one in Nashville.

MAJOR WORKS AND THEMES

Bontemps' entire oeuvre is a celebration of the experiences of African Americans. Perhaps in response to the restrictions he suffered under the Seventh-Day Adventists, Bontemps' work focuses on freedom. Robert Bone found that Bontemps' work is marked by a distinct change after 1935, when his Harlem Renaissance themes turned to a more "revolutionary" tone (285). The term "revolutionary" certainly describes Bontemps' short story "A Summer Tragedy." Published in *Opportunity* in June 1933, the acclaimed story explores the unique way in which an old sharecropping couple liberate themselves from an economic system that oppresses them. By choosing their own form of death rather than a life of economic hell, the couple becomes powerful and remains dignified even in the face of their own demise.

Published in 1931, *God Sends Sunday*, Bontemps' first novel, explores colorism, masculinity, and blues ideology through the experiences of Little Augie, an African American jockey. This novel later served as the basis for Bontemps' and Countee Cullen's play *St. Louis Woman*. Bontemps incorporates the experiences of average African Americans in *God Sends Sunday*. Inspired by Bontemps' fun-loving and loud Uncle Buddy, Augie migrates from South to North and sings the blues as a form of self-expression (Jones, *Renaissance* 73).

Black Thunder: Gabriel's Revolt: Virginia 1800 is a work of fiction based on historical fact. It is generally considered to be Bontemps' most successful novel. "By manipulating the facts of the Gabriel Prosser revolt, he reveals the timeless problems man has in overpowering color and class oppression to achieve freedom and social equality" (Bell 104). The book did not sell well despite its good reviews. Bontemps expressed his thoughts about the book's initial reception in a new Introduction published in 1968. "But the theme of self-assertion by black men whose endurance was strained to the breaking point was not one that readers of fiction were prepared to contemplate at that time" ("Introduction" xv). The importance of *Black Thunder* lies largely in Bontemps' use of the genre of the historical novel.

Arna Bontemps' introductions to his anthologies are insightful commentaries on the African American literary tradition. In his introduction to *Great Slave Narratives* Bontemps argues that the slave narratives influence African American writers of the twentieth century such as Richard Wright* and James Baldwin. He finds that the themes of the slave narrative, bondage and freedom, are present in African American literature and that the debt of current writer to former slaves should not be forgotten (x). In "The Awakening: A Memoir," his Introduction to *The Harlem Renaissance Remembered*, Bontemps gives both an insider's account and a historical view of the Harlem Renaissance. Particularly interesting is his description of meeting Langston Hughes and being mistaken for Hughes by Countee Cullen's father.

Through books such as *100 Years of Negro Freedom* and his biographies of figures such as Frederick Douglass,* Bontemps educated children and adults about African American history. Bontemps' historical fiction and his books on the Harlem Renaissance and slave narratives, along with his children's books, make him an important figure in American literary history.

CRITICAL RECEPTION

Although not totally forgotten, Arna Bontemps has not received the type of attention from scholars that he so richly deserves. Five of his early poems and his masterful short story "A Summer Tragedy" appear in the *Norton Anthology of African American Literature*, but no selections from Bontemps appear in *Call and Response: The Riverside Anthology of the African American Literary Tradition*. Certainly, Bontemps' contribution to the study of the slave narrative is acknowledged as a significant step in African American literary history. Recently, more attention has been paid to his children's literature, so hopefully there will be a resurgence of interest in his work.

Bontemps' early poetry was well received, although he was not pleased with the reception of his early fiction. Du Bois did not like *God Sends Sunday* and compared it to Mckay's *Home to Harlem*. Poet Gwendolyn Bennett* praised Bontemps in her review of *God Sends Sunday* for the *New York Herald Tribune Books*. "One cannot read this book without realizing that Arna Bontemps has taken his place as one of the important writers of his race." *Black Thunder* received better reviews but did not sell well. *Black Thunder* gave Bontemps some of his best reviews and continues to attract attention from scholars. Richard Wright described *Black Thunder* as "the only novel dealing forthrightly with the historical and revolutionary traditions of Negro people." In a recent assessment of the novel, Eric Sundquist finds that "Bontempts's careful fluctuation between the worlds of slave and master makes historicism a means of recovering the 'subtext' of African America" (114). Arna Bontemps led a remarkably full life that was a testament to his commitment to a life of writing.

BIBLIOGRAPHY

Works by Arna Bontemps

Poetry

"Hope." *Crisis* 28 (August 1924): 176.
"Spring Music." *Crisis* 30 (June 1925): 93.
"Dirge." *Crisis* 32 (May 1926): 25.
"Golgotha Is a Mountain." *Opportunity* 32 (June 1926): 34.
"Holiday." *Crisis* 32 (July 1926): 121.
"Nocturne at Bethesda." *Crisis* 33 (December 1926): 66.
"Tree." *Crisis* 43 (April 1927): 48.
Personals. 1963. London: Paul Berman, 1973.
Hold Fast to Dreams: Poems Old and New. Chicago: Follett, 1969.

Short Stories

"A Summer Tragedy." *Opportunity* 11 (June 1933): 174–77, 190.
"Barrell Slaves." *New Challenge* 1 (March 1934): 16–24.
"Saturday Night: Alabama Town." *New Challenge* 1 (September 1934): 5–9.
The Old South: "A Summer Tragedy" and Other Stories of the Thirties. New York: Dodd, Mead, 1973.

Novels

God Sends Sunday. New York: Harcourt, Brace, 1931.
Black Thunder. New York: Macmillan, 1936.
Drums at Dusk. New York: Macmillan, 1939.

Drama

(With Countee Cullen). *St. Louis Woman.* (Unpublished)

Nonfiction

"Introduction." *Black Thunder*. 1936. Boston: Beacon Press, 1968.
"Sad-Faced Author." *The Horn Book Magazine* 15 (January–February 1939): 7–12.
"Special Collections of Negroana." *Library Quarterly* 14 (July 1944): 187–206.
(With Jack Conroy). *They Seek a City*. Garden City, NY: Doubleday, 1945. Later revised
  as *Anyplace but Here*. New York: Hill and Wang, 1966.
"Negro Poets, Then and Now." *Phylon* 11.4 (1950): 328–37.
The Story of George Washington Carver. New York: Grosset and Dunlap, 1954.
Chariot in the Sky: A Story of the Jubilee Singers. 1951. New York: Holt, Rinehart, and
  Winston, 1971.
Story of the Negro. New York: Knopf, 1958.
Frederick Douglass: Slave, Fighter, Freeman. New York: Knopf, 1959.
100 Years of Negro Freedom. 1961. Westport, CT: Greenwood Press, 1980.
Famous Negro Athletes. New York: Dodd, Mead, 1964.
"The *Lonesome Boy* Theme." *The Horn Book Magazine* 42 (December 1966): 672–80.
"The Negro Renaissance: Jean Toomer and the Harlem Writers of the 1920s." *Anger and
  Beyond*. Ed. Herbert Hill. New York: Harper and Row, 1966, 20–36.
Free at Last: The Life of Frederick Douglass. New York: Dodd, Mead, 1971.
"The Awakening: A Memoir." *The Harlem Renaissance Remembered*. New York: Dodd,
  Mead, 1972. 1–26.
Young Booker: Booker T. Washington's Early Days. New York: Dodd, Mead, 1972.
Five Black Lives. Middletown, CT: Wesleyan University Press, 1987.

Children's Literature

(With Langston Hughes). *Popo and Fifina: Children of Haiti*. New York: Macmillan, 1932.
You Can't Pet a Possum. New York: Morrow, 1934.
Sad Faced Boy. Boston: Houghton Mifflin, 1937.
(With Jack Conroy). *The Fast Sooner Hound*. Boston: Houghton Mifflin, 1942.
We Have Tomorrow. Boston: Houghton Mifflin, 1945.
(With Jack Conroy). *Slappy Hooper: The Wonderful Sign Painter*. Boston: Houghton Mif-
  flin, 1946.
The Story of the Negro. 1948. New York: Knopf, 1955.
(With Jack Conroy). *Sam Patch, the High, Wide and Handsome Jumper*. Boston: Houghton
  Mifflin, 1951.
Lonesome Boy. Boston: Houghton Mifflin, 1955.
Mr. Kelso's Lion. Philadelphia: Lippincott, 1970.

Anthologies

Golden Slippers: An Anthology of Negro Poetry for Young Readers. New York: Harper, 1941.
(With Langston Hughes). *The Poetry of the Negro, 1746–1949*. New York: Doubleday,
  1949.
(With Langston Hughes). *The Book of Negro Folklore*. New York: Dodd, Mead, 1958.

Editor

Father of the Blues: An Autobiography by W. C. Handy. New York: Macmillan, 1941.
American Negro Poetry. New York: Hill and Wang, 1963.

Great Slave Narratives. Boston: Beacon, 1969.
The Harlem Renaissance Remembered. New York: Dodd, Mead, 1972.

Studies of Arna Bontemps

Alexander, Roberta May. "The Fictional Portrayal of Popular Movements." Diss., University of California, Riverside, 1980.

Alvarez, Joseph A. "The Lonesome Boy Theme as Emblem for Arna Bontemps's Children's Literature." *African American Review* 32.1 (1998): 23–31.

Ashe, Betty Taylor. "A Study of the Fiction of Arna Wendell Bontemps." Diss., Howard University, 1978.

Bell, Bernard. *The Afro-American Novel and Its Tradition.* Amherst: University of Massachusetts Press, 1987.

Bennett, Gwendolyn. "A Poet's Novel." *New York Herald Tribune Books* (March 22, 1931): 16.

Bone, Robert. *Down Home: A History of Afro-American Short Fiction from Its Beginnings to the End of the Harlem Renaissance.* New York: G. P. Putnam's Sons, 1976.

Canaday, Nicholas. "Arna Bontemps: The Louisiana Heritage." *Callaloo* 4.2 (1981): 163–69.

Carlton-Alexander, Sandra. "Arna Bontemps: The Novelist Revisited." *CLA Journal* 34 (1991): 317–30.

Davis, Arthur P. *From the Dark Tower: Afro American Writers, 1900–1960.* Washington, DC: Howard University Press, 1974.

Davis, Mary Kemp. "Arna Bontemps' *Black Thunder*: The Creation of an Authoritative Text of 'Gabriel's Defeat.' " *Black American Literature Forum* 23.1 (1989): 17–36.

———. "From Death unto Life: The Rhetorical Function of Funeral Rites in Arna Bontemps' *Black Thunder.*" *Journal of Ritual Studies* 1.1 (1987): 85–101.

———. "The Historical Slave Revolt and the Literary Imagination." Diss., University of North Carolina, Chapel Hill, 1984.

Debnam, Gwendolyn Y. "The Imaginative Fiction of Arna Wendell Bontemps." M.A. thesis, Atlanta University, 1977.

Fleming, Robert E. *James Weldon Johnson and Arna Wendell Bontemps: A Reference Guide.* Boston: Hall, 1978.

Gaudet, Marcia. "Images of Old Age in Three Louisiana Short Stories." *Louisiana English Journal* 1.1 (1993): 62–64.

Grayson, Sandra M. "African Culture as Tradition: A Reading of 'Tales of the Congaree,' 'Middle Passage,' 'Benito Cereno,' and 'Black Thunder.' " Diss., University of California, Riverside, 1994.

Grigsby, John L. "Jesus, Judas, Job or 'Jes a Happy Ole Nigga'; Or, Will the Real 'Uncle Tom' Please Step Forward?" *Publications of the Mississippi Philological Association* (1986): 51–62.

Harris, Violet J. "From Little Black Sambo to Popo and Fifina: Arna Bontemps and the Creation of African-American Children's Literature." *The Lion-and-the-Unicorn:-A-Critical-Journal-of-Children's-Literature* 14.1 (1990): 108–27.

Hughes, Langston. *The Big Sea.* 1940. New York: Thunder's Mouth Press, 1986.

James, Charles L. "Alberta Bontemps: Reflections on Flyleaves." *The Langston Hughes Review* 13.1 (1994): 45–49.

Jones, Kirkland C. "Bontemps and the Old South." *African-American Review* 27.2 (1993): 179–85.

———. *Renaissance Man from Louisiana: A Biography of Arna Wendell Bontemps.* Westport, CT: Greenwood, 1992.

Leroy-Frazier, Jill. "Exploding the Southern Text: Reconsidering Southern Literature as a Critically Constructed Genre (Women Writers, Minority Writers)." Diss., University of Michigan, 1998.

Nichols, Charles, ed. *Arna Bontemps–Langston Hughes Letters.* New York: Paragon House, 1990.

Reagan, Daniel. "Voices of Silence: The Representation of Orality in Arna Bontemps' *Black Thunder.*" *Studies in American Fiction* 19.1 (1991): 71–83.

Reid, Margaret Ann. "A Rhetorical Analysis of Selected Black Protest Poetry of the Harlem Renaissance and of the Sixties." Diss., Indiana University of Pennsylvania, 1980.

Rummage, Ronald Glynne. "The Raceless Novel of the 1930s: African American Fiction by Arna Bontemps, George Henderson, Countee Cullen, Jessie Fauset, and Zora Neale Hurston." Diss., Middle Tennessee State University, 1994.

Sadler, Lynn V. "The Figure of the Black Insurrectionist in Stowe, Bouve, Bontemps, and Gaither: The Universality of the Need for Freedom." *MAWA Review* 2.1 (1986): 21–24.

———. "The West Indies as a Symbol of Freedom in Johnston's *Prisoners of Hope* and *The Slave Ship* and in Bontemps' *Black Thunder.*" *Jack London Newsletter* 15.1 (January–April 1982): 42–48.

Singh, Amritjit. *The Novels of the Harlem Renaissance.* University Park: Pennsylvania State University Press, 1976.

Stone, Albert E. *The Return of Nat Turner: History, Literature, and Cultural Politics in Sixties America.* Athens: University of Georgia Press, 1992.

Sundquist, Eric J. *The Hammers of Creation: Folk Culture in Modern African-American Fiction.* Athens: University of Georgia Press, 1992.

Weil, Dorothy. "Folklore Motifs in Arna Bontemps' *Black Thunder.*" *Southern Folklore Quarterly* 35 (1971): 1–14.

Wright, Richard. "A Tale of Folk Courage." *Partisan Review and Anvil* 3 (April 1936): 31.

WILLIAM STANLEY BRAITHWAITE
(1878–1962)

Kirk Nuss

BIOGRAPHY

In Boston, on December 6, 1878, William Stanley Braithwaite was born to Emma Braithwaite, an ex-slave whose conception was probably due to the rape of her mother by her slaveholder, and William Smith Braithwaite, a physician's assistant of mixed racial heritage who had begun, but did not complete, medical studies. Because he was a very delicate baby, neither parent possessed much hope for his survival. However, he did survive, and his father took control of his development. His father forbade his son to play with any other children and tutored his son at home because he felt that the other children and the public schools were not good enough. Further, his father chose to raise his son in the style of an upper-class British child. By controlling his light-skinned son's education and social life, his father might have been trying to keep him from interacting with other African Americans in thought or person—although Braithwaite himself never arrives at this conclusion. It was not until his father died when Braithwaite was seven years old that this reclusive lifestyle came to an end. For the next four years, he attended public school. Despite enjoying his schooling, Braithwaite quit in order to find a job that would allow him to help his mother support the family. He never returned to school as a student.

Despite his father's controlling nature, Braithwaite was profoundly affected by his father's death; it left him with the "indefinable taint of the mystery of death" ("House" 11). Braithwaite experienced, sometime in the early 1890s, what he called the second great mystery of his life. One day as he watched the rain fall upon the sea, he sensed a "cosmic force" ("House" 130) at work. He was drawn to the "mystical signal" of the sea, which symbolized "the womb that gave birth to life, the mother who bred our visions, which held in its obscure and mysterious depths the secrets of creation" (130). To him, this mystical event testified to the wonder of God's creation. For young Braithwaite, the sea began to take on the image of the eternal and the sea's edge the bourne where humans could transcend, at least temporarily, the physical world. These images of the sea along with the earlier taint of death would continue to influence Braithwaite's outlook on life and his poetry.

Braithwaite's life was full of these types of mystical experiences. After he had occupied several menial jobs, he landed a job with a publisher of textbooks, Ginn and Company. While typesetting, he first discovered the work of Keats. He described this introduction as "a day of annunciation" that revealed to him "a strange, new mystery of life and nature!"(*William Stanley Braithwaite* [WSB] *Reader* 173). Keats opened up a new world; in fact, Braithwaite goes so far as to say, "I worshipped him as god" (174). Inspired by Keats' influence, he read more poetry and went on to compose and publish three books of poetry: *Lyrics of Life and Love* (1904), *The House of Falling Leaves* (1908), and *Selected Poems* (1948). His poetry also appeared in many magazines and journals, including, but not limited to, *Century, Voice of the Negro, Crisis*, and *Atlantic Monthly*. In addition to poetry, he wrote a history book of World War I for children, *The Story of the Great War* (1919), and the literary biography *The Bewitched Parsonage: The Story of the Brontës* (1950). However, Braithwaite did not make his name by writing his own books but by editing and compiling books of poetry and writing criticism and book reviews in magazines and journals. He compiled and edited *The Book of Elizabethan Verse* (1906), *The Book of Georgian Verse* (1908), *The Book of Restoration Verse* (1909), *The Book of Modern British Verse* (1919), and the influential *Anthology of Magazine Verse* (1913–1929, 1958). He also wrote book reviews and criticism in several newspapers and magazines but most prominently for the *Boston Evening Transcript*. He edited and contributed to the *Poetry Journal* from 1912 to 1914 and the *Poetry Review* from 1916 to 1917 and was president of B. J. Brimmer, a publishing company, from 1922 until its demise in 1925. In 1918 he was awarded the Springarn Medal by the National Association for the Advancement of Colored People (NAACP) for his body of work. During all this output, Braithwaite married Emma Kelly in June 1903, and together they raised three daughters and four sons. Like many families, they were hurt by the Depression, leading Braithwaite to accept a professorship at Atlanta University in 1935, where he taught for ten years. After he retired from teaching, he continued to write and edit, but his output was minimal. He died on June 9, 1962, at the age of eighty-three.

MAJOR WORKS AND THEMES

On his twenty-first birthday, Braithwaite sat in his room and meditated on his future. In New York that previous year, he had had "a taste . . . of what difficulties and injustices were for one of color" (*WSB Reader* 177) when he unsuccessfully sought a job at bookstores and for newspapers. He had also heard Charles Chesnutt* referred to as "Page's darky" (180)—Chesnutt had been discovered by Walter Hines Page of *Atlantic Monthly*. Because of these types of racial obstacles, Braithwaite concluded that writings "confined to racial materials . . . would be appraised and judged by a different standard" (178). Thus, he chose to avoid writing racial material until he was first accepted by a universal standard. In all three books of his poetry, he makes no direct reference to race. He successfully concealed his race, leading James Weldon Johnson* to write that "for many years he [Braithwaite] had been a figure in the American literary world before it was known generally that he is a man of color" (99).

Instead of writing with a racial voice, Braithwaite chose a persona resembling the late Romantics, particularly Keats. Much of his poetry focuses on the moment when one is able to transcend an earthly existence and access the supernatural and eternal meaning behind it. For Braithwaite, our earthly experiences are "but footnotes to reality," and poetry is the attempt "to translate the language of the spirit—the invisible, immaterial character of another existence that is as real as our own" (qtd. in Redding, *To Make a Poet* 91). His poetry often utilizes the sea and the stars to represent the eternal and the sea's edge and the dreamscape to indicate the boundary where the temporal can access the eternal. While these experiences are beautiful, they also reveal the painfully ephemeral nature of human existence. Thus, in his poetry, Braithwaite unites the two mysteries that affected him as a child: the mystical sea and the taint of death.

In addition to his poetry, Braithwaite wrote some short fiction in magazines. In May 1902, Braithwaite published the short story "The Quality of Color" for the *Colored American Magazine*. While this tragic story of interracial love is not particularly well written, it is significant since it shows that, at least once, Braithwaite did take on racial issues in his own art. However, he did address racial issues more frequently in his criticism. For example, in *The Boston Globe* in 1906 he wrote against racial caricatures, in the June 1902 issue of the *Colored American Magazine* he criticized Thomas Dixon's *The Leopard's Spots*, and in his 1918 anthology he condemns Vachel Lindsay's depiction of the aborigine in the poem "The Congo." Thus, while his verse did not address race, his criticism and one short story did.

Braithwaite was known primarily for his work as an editor and compiler. His *Anthology of Magazine Verse* sought to collect the best magazine verse each year. Despite the fact that his own poetry was fairly traditional, he did not refrain from publishing a wide variety of poetry. In fact, while many critics were criticizing imagism, he published both H. D. and Amy Lowell. He also published many other noteworthy poets, including Robert Frost, Carl Sandburg, James Weldon Johnson, Wallace Stevens, and Edwin Arlington Robinson. His anthologies are sometimes credited with helping these poets receive recognition and helping poetry thrive in general.

CRITICAL RECEPTION

Braithwaite's poetry has received little recent attention but did receive some praise from his peers. As early as 1907, W. M. Pickens proclaimed that "Braithwaite has thus far made the highest bid" (119) to replace Paul Laurence Dunbar* as the top African American poet. In a similar vein, in 1968 John Daniels wrote that Braithwaite was "the leading poet of his race" (204) since Dunbar's death. James Weldon Johnson also applauded Braithwaite's poetry for its "delicate beauty" (99). While these same critics noted that Braithwaite avoided references to race in his poetry, they did not condemn his poetry because of it. However, later critics did condemn Braithwaite's raceless verse. In 1974 the French critic Jean Wagner claimed that Braithwaite's "work constitutes a disavowal of the race" (127); therefore, he did not deserve examination within the pages of *Black Poets of the United States*. In *Black Poetry in America*, Louis D. Rubin, Jr., suggests that the critic must determine whether or not Braithwaite's avoidance of race had a harmful effect on his poetry. Rubin concludes that in "suppressing his blackness, he suppressed his human uniqueness, producing a poetry of surface effects, deficient in importance both for society and self" (Jackson and Rubin 32). Like Wagner and Rubin, most later critics of Braithwaite dismiss both Braithwaite and his poetry.

Like his poetry, Braithwaite's *Anthology of Magazine Verse* provoked strong opinions. Some critics credit Braithwaite with discovering and mentoring many new poets who might not have gotten their chance if it was not for his anthology. W.E.B. Du Bois called Braithwaite "the most prominent critic of poetry in America," while William Dean Howells described him as "the most intelligent historian of contemporary poetry" (qtd. in *WSB Reader* 1). However, his anthologies also received backlash from the critics and even the poets he published in the anthologies. Conrad Aiken, his most notable opponent, claimed that "when I survey Mr. Braithwaite's page . . . I must confess that I am smitten with cold nausea. All these fireworks, this preening and attitudinizing, over so much sentimental and vulgar mediocrity" (Aiken, "Prizes" 96). While he admits there is an occasional worthwhile poem in the anthologies, in order to find it "one must wade through pages and pages of mawkishness, dulness [sic], artificiality, and utter emptiness" (Aiken, *Scepticisms* 50). While Aiken is the most brutal critic, poets such as Allen Tate, Genevieve Taggard, and Louis Untermeyer—all of whom were published in the anthologies—questioned the quality of the publication. Untermeyer, in 1927, called the anthology "Braithwaite's yearly blunder" and a "monument of mediocrity" (qtd. in Abbott 154).

Notably, Braithwaite never published an anthology of African American poetry, a point Wagner brings up. However, he did attempt to publish the *Anthology of Negro Authors: Prose and Verse* prior to 1906 but was turned down. Further, in 1934 he had plans to publish the *Omnibus of Negro Literature*, which he hoped would "stun the country into recognition and acceptance of the spiritual and cultural equality of the Race" (*WSB Reader* 284), and in the mid-1950s he pro-

posed a book of essays on African American novelists such as Richard Wright*
and Ralph Ellison. All of these projects failed to get published, and it is unclear
how hard Braithwaite worked to get them in print.

BIBLIOGRAPHY

Works by William Stanley Braithwaite

Short Story

"The Quality of Color." *Colored American Magazine* 5.1 (May 1902): 67–75.

Poetry

Lyrics of Life and Love. Boston: Herbert B. Turner, 1904.
The House of Falling Leaves. Boston: John W. Luce, 1908.
Selected Poems. New York: Coward-McCann, 1948.

Nonfiction Prose

The Story of the Great War. New York: Frederick A. Stokes, 1919.
"The House under Arcturus: An Autobiography." *Phylon* 2 (1st Quarter 1941): 9–26; 2
    (2nd Quarter 1941): 121–36; 2 (3rd Quarter 1941): 250–59; 3 (1st Quarter 1942):
    31–44; 3 (2nd Quarter 1942): 183–94.
The Bewitched Parsonage: The Story of the Brontës. New York: Coward-McCann, 1950.
The William Stanley Braithwaite Reader. Ed. Philip Butcher. Ann Arbor: University of
    Michigan Press, 1972.

Books Edited

The Book of Elizabethan Verse. Boston: Herbert B. Turner, 1906.
The Book of Georgian Verse. New York: Brentano's, 1908.
The Book of Restoration Verse. New York: Brentano's, 1909.
Anthology of Magazine Verse (1913–1929 and 1958) and Yearbook of American Poetry. [*Year-
    book* not included in 1913 and 1958.] Cambridge, MA: issued by WSB 1913–1914;
    New York: Gomme and Marshall, 1915–1916; Boston: Small, Maynard, 1917–
    1922; Boston: B. J. Brimmer, 1923–1927; New York: Harold Vinal, 1928; New
    York: George Scully, 1929; New York: Schulte, 1958.
The Poetic Year for 1916: A Critical Anthology. Boston: Small, Maynard, 1917.
The Golden Treasury of Magazine Verse. Boston: Small, Maynard, 1918.
The Book of Modern British Verse. Boston: Small, Maynard, 1919.
Victory! Celebrated by Thirty-Eight American Poets. Boston: Small, Maynard, 1919.
Anthology of Massachusetts Poets. Boston: Small, Maynard, 1922.
Our Lady's Choir: A Contemporary Anthology of Verse by Catholic Sisters. Boston: Bruce
    Humphries, 1931.

Studies of William Stanley Braithwaite

Abbott, Craig S. "Magazine Verse and Modernism: Braithwaite's Anthologies." *Journal of
    Modern Literature* 19.1 (Summer 1994): 151–59.

Aiken, Conrad. "Looking Pegasus in the Mouth." *Poetry Journal* 5.1 (February 1916): 20–28.

———. "Prizes and Anthologies." *Poetry Journal* 4.3 (November 1915): 95–100.

———. *Scepticisms: Notes on Contemporary Poetry*. New York: Alfred A. Knopf, 1919.

Bardolph, Richard. *The Negro Vanguard*. New York: Negro Universities Press, 1971.

Biram, Brenda M. "Paid Servant." *Negro Digest* 18 (April 1969): 92–93.

Bloom, Harold, ed. *Black American Prose Writers before the Harlem Renaissance*. New York: Chelsea House, 1994.

Brawley, Benjamin. *The Negro in Literature and Art in the United States*. New York: Duffield, 1930.

Butcher, Philip. "Introduction." In *The William Stanley Braithwaite Reader*. Ed. Philip Butcher. Ann Arbor: University of Michigan Press, 1972. 1–7.

———. "William Stanley Braithwaite and the College Language Association." *CLA Journal* 15.2 (December 1971): 117–25.

———. "William Stanley Braithwaite's Southern Exposure: Rescue and Revelation." *Southern Literary Journal* 3.2 (Spring 1971): 49–61.

Clairmonte, Glenn. "The Cup-Bearer: William Stanley Braithwaite of Boston." *CLA Journal* 17.1 (September 1973): 101–8.

———. "He Made Writers Famous." *Phylon* 30 (Summer 1969): 184–90.

Daniels, John. *In Freedom's Birthplace: A Study of the Boston Negroes*. New York: Negro Universities Press, 1968.

Frances Teresa, Sister. "Poet's Discovery." *Phylon* 5 (4th Quarter 1944): 375–78.

Jackson, Blyden, and Louis D. Rubin Jr. *Black Poetry in America*. Baton Rouge: Louisiana State University Press, 1974.

Johnson, James Weldon, ed. *The Book of American Negro Poetry*. New York: Harcourt, Brace, and World, 1958.

McKay, Claude. *A Long Way from Home*. New York: Arno Press, 1969.

Pickens, W. M. "Braithwaite." *The Voice of the Negro* 4.2 (March 1907): 119–21.

Redding, J. Saunders. *To Make a Poet Black*. Ithaca, NY: Cornell University Press, 1988.

———. "William Stanley Beaumont Braithwaite." In *Dictionary of American Negro Biography*. Ed. Rayford W. Logan and Michael R. Winston. New York: W. W. Norton, 1982. 58–60.

Robinson, William H. "William Stanley Braithwaite." In *Dictionary of Literary Biography: American Poets, 1890–1945*. Ed. Peter Quartermain. Vol. 54. Detroit: Gale Research, 1987. 3–12.

Rush, Theressa Gunnels, Carol Fairbanks Myers, and Esther Spring Arata, eds. *Black American Writers Past and Present*. Vol. 1. Metuchen, NJ: Scarecrow Press, 1975.

Wagner, Jean. *Black Poets of the United States: From Paul Laurence Dunbar to Langston Hughes*. Trans. Kenneth Douglas. Urbana: University of Illinois Press, 1974.

Williams, Kenny J. "An Invisible Partnership and Unlikely Relationship: William Stanley Braithwaite and Harriet Monroe." *Callaloo* 10.3 (Summer 1987): 548–50.

———. "William Stanley Braithwaite." In *Dictionary of Literary Biography: Afro-American Writers before the Harlem Renaissance*. Ed. Trudier Harris. Vol. 50. Detroit: Gale Research, 1986. 7–18.

CLAUDE BROWN
(1937-)

Robin Lucy

BIOGRAPHY

Claude Brown was born in Harlem on February 23, 1937, two years after his parents migrated from South Carolina. He had two sisters and a younger brother. His father was a railroad worker, and his mother was employed as a domestic.

By the time Brown started grade school he was, in the parlance of his day, a juvenile delinquent: playing hooky, fighting, stealing, and experimenting with alcohol, marijuana, and sex. At the age of ten, he was "adopted" by the Forty Thieves, part of a larger "bebopping" or criminal gang, the Buccaneers (*Manchild* 259). In 1948 he was sent to the Wiltwyck School for Boys. Its director, Ernest Papanek, became Brown's counselor and mentor after he was released two years later.

In Harlem, however, Brown resumed many of his previous activities and, while stealing laundry from neighborhood clotheslines, was shot in the stomach. He was sent to Warwick, an institution for young, if experienced, offenders. By the summer of 1953, Brown had returned to Warwick twice. During this period, Harlem was inundated by heroin.

When he returned to Harlem at the age of sixteen, Brown began selling marijuana and cocaine. A year later, he abandoned drug dealing and moved to Greenwich Village, where he supported himself at various jobs while going to high school at night. When he graduated in 1957, he once again moved back to Harlem. In 1959 he was awarded a scholarship by a church group and enrolled at Howard University in Washington, D.C. In the early 1960s Ernest Papanek encouraged Brown to write about Harlem. His article in the magazine *Dissent* attracted the attention of the Macmillan Publishing Company, which gave Brown an advance to write a book about his life. In 1965, the same year Brown received his B.A., Macmillan published his autobiography, *Manchild in the Promised Land*.

Brown went on to study at both Stanford and Rutgers Law Schools. In 1976 he published *The Children of Ham*. He has published articles in *Dissent, Esquire*, and other magazines.

MAJOR WORKS AND THEMES

In the Foreword to *Manchild in the Promised Land*, Brown writes that his own experience is, in fact, representative of "the first Northern urban generation of Negroes. . . . a misplaced generation" (7) struggling to survive and adapt in an unfamiliar and often hostile environment. His autobiography is also representative of what Albert E. Stone describes as black "personal history": interwoven narratives of individual and collective identity, history, and literature ("Patterns" 171). Brown represents the generation of blacks who came of age in America's cities after World War II—the first generation of the second Great Migration—as a group who found themselves in a dangerously liminal position: connected, through their parents, to life in the South but uncertain of their identity and of strategies for survival in the North, the "Promised Land" of the title. To Brown, the exodus of southern blacks to the North had "produced a generation of new niggers" (*Manchild* 287) in an urban New World: "There was nothing that was old. I really didn't have any familiar ground. . . . my generation was like the first Africans coming over on the boat" (288). Brown's autobiography delineates this movement across the historical threshold of black urban experience while it traces his personal journey from manchild to man.

Harlem has been virtually abandoned by the larger white world: "a slum ghetto . . . of a great city" (8). The fact that "nobody gave a fuck about some niggers and some Puerto Ricans" (190) is made especially clear to Brown when Harlem finds itself with few resources to cope with the heroin epidemic of the mid-1950s. While the theme of abandonment remains in the background of his autobiography, it is literally foregrounded in *The Children of Ham*. The young men and women whose lives the narrator documents live in a condemned Harlem tenement: "The air of abandonment is so pervasive . . . that every sign and sound of human life conforms to the motif. . . . humanity had abandoned the members of the group" (*Ham* 9). The "children of Ham" are, in fact, the children of Brown's generation, now two generations removed from life in the South. A measure of their personal and historical distance from this reality is the incisive and comprehensive nature of their critique of the quality of black life, as they have known it, in the urban North. In his autobiography, Brown registers an implicit critique in his acts of personal "rebellion" (*Manchild* 282).

Brown argues that his anger at the control and indifference of the white world provoked his youthful criminality. To a black Muslim friend's call for black "revolution," Brown replies, "I've had that revolution since I was six years old" (*Manchild* 328). Having abandoned it in favor of school and a steady job, he argues

that "[t]hat revolution was hopeless," particularly in light of the increasing number of heroin addicts in Harlem: these "revolutionaries" are only "cutting their
own throats" (329). Brown, in fact, reaches a crisis when he realizes that in order
for him to continue drug dealing—and living—in Harlem he must kill an addict
who has stolen from him and take his "place along with the bad niggers of the
community": those who are willing to kill and be killed (122). Instead, he gives
away his gun and moves to Greenwich Village, suddenly aware that his "positive
anger" (413) at the world is tainted by fear. As a result, for the first time in his
life he experiences freedom (193).

Brown's moment of recognition and his move to the Village are implicitly
linked to the literal worlds of possibility that the exercising of literacy opened
up for him while at Warwick: "I wanted to know things: and I wanted to do
things. It made me start thinking about what might happen if I . . . didn't go back
to Harlem" (Manchild 151). He is able to imagine a new life narrative for himself:
one that does not involve literal or figurative imprisonment, whether within an
institution or his own fears (Manchild 178). The link between the experience of
freedom and the power of the written word is an archetypal moment in African
American autobiography: from the slave narratives of Frederick Douglass* and
Harriet Jacobs* to Malcolm X's education in black history while in prison.

Brown's relationship to the white world remains, however, largely abstract.
His place within Harlem and, specifically, his relationship to the migrant generation of his parents are the central themes of his autobiography. While Brown
recognizes the disillusionment of the "colored pioneers" (8) who left the violence
and virtual slavery of the South only to be faced with the punitive realities of
the North, his sense of bitterness at their de facto abandonment of his generation—"they didn't know just what was to follow, so how could they tell me?"
(413)—is pervasive. Brown, in fact, is unable to see any positive or resistant
adaptations to the North on the part of his elders; instead, like many of Richard
Wright's* migrants, they exhibit the ostensible pathologies of a generation that
"didn't seem to be ready for urban life" (Manchild 279).

The "Harlem tradition," Brown writes, comes from the same southern "backwoods" his parents had fled (278): a "tradition" of "[l]iquor, religion, sex, and
violence. . . . a prayer that . . . somebody might hit the sweepstakes or get lucky"
(281). His mother is a member of a storefront church who preaches "that old
crazy shit that should have been left down there in the woods" (187–88). His
father is aligned with the other aspects of transplanted southern life: his "religion"
is liquor (27); he slit a man's throat for insulting his wife, has a similar scar on
his own neck, and beats his children; he regularly plays the numbers. The degree
to which this picture is a distortion can be measured, in part, by the fact that
Brown never mentions the working life of his parents. His home life drives him
into the streets as an avenue of escape: "I never thought of Harlem as being in
the house" (415; emphasis added). For Brown, life on the streets is a form of
rebellion against the "personal" world of his parents as well as the historical

dominance of white Americans: "when people start ruling people and they rule 'em wrong . . . they have to stop them. They've got to rebel" (282).

Brown's father is rendered figuratively impotent in the text. Unlike his son, he cannot manipulate language, and his conversations with Claude almost always end in violence "because it came easier to him than talking" (44). In addition, in a seminal scene in the book, his father's acquiescence to a white judge transforms him, in Brown's twelve-year-old eyes, from "a real bad nigger" to "just a head nodder" (94). Brown's relationship to his father reflects an angst about masculine identity that pervades much of his autobiography. Harlem's ethos of code-bound masculine violence, the enforcement of "a man's principles" (256), is disrupted by the rampant use of heroin. Many of Brown's peers use drugs to get away from the "bebopping" life of violence (147). Brown marks the shift in the masculine culture of Harlem between 1947, when he became a member of the Buccaneers, and that of a decade later as the difference between "The Knife" and "Drugs," respectively (253). Although he turns his back on violence, Brown's autobiography is pervaded by a conflicted nostalgia for "[y]oung Harlem, happy Harlem, Harlem before the plague" (215).

By the early 1960s, many of Brown's generation are dead or in jail. However, Brown is spared the effects of "the shit plague" of heroin (185) through the intervention of a then-drug-addicted friend, one of the few people in the book who subsequently kick their habit. *Manchild in the Promised Land* is Brown's narrative of survival. He concludes by declaring that the "plague wave" (406) has swept over Harlem, and, in its wake, the community will realize the collective dream "that all Harlem would be completely changed in about ten years" (408).

The Children of Ham depicts Harlem almost exactly ten years later and belies *Manchild*'s hopeful end. A blend of reportage and fiction, it documents a second, more virulent drug "plague" sweeping the community. According to one of the book's informants, its effects are "worse than slavery" (111). Harlem's "promise" has been reduced to a state of virtual bondage. The characters in the book, each of them the subject and the vernacular voice of a chapter that bears his or her name, acquire disturbing insights into the power relations that drive the drug epidemic: Harlem is compared to a vast prison or to the slave quarters of an urban neoplantation (160); the operations of the nation's drug economy employ as many Americans, "officially or unofficially," as General Motors (198–99). The critical literacy skills that Brown exercises in his autobiography are matched by this generation's ability to measure and claim the larger world through other media, particularly television: "We up here peepin' everything that the white folks're peepin'. . . . We peepin' what's happenin' out there with whitey and the bucks" (65).

The title, *The Children of Ham*, refers to the Genesis story (9, 20–27). When Ham spies on his drunken and naked father, Noah, Ham's son is cursed by Noah and made a slave to his brothers. Because some of Ham's descendants are black, the story has been used to justify the enslavement and oppression of people of

African origin. The title also invokes intergenerational conflict, the central theme of Brown's work. Harlem's "children of Ham" have been "cursed" and literally abandoned by their drug-addicted parents. These children, however, form a "family" (16) in which each member performs a role essential to the group's survival. Black women assume a central place as well as critical subject positions within this unit, in contrast to the dominant construction of women as mute objects in *Manchild*. The group's will to survive prompts the only adult figure in the book, other than the narrator himself, to declare that "for the first time . . . *in more than two generations*, there seems to be a relatively large group of kids who are going to make it" (171, emphasis added). Twice removed from life in the South, these "children" continue the struggle to survive in the urban North. However, the strategy of collective survival and resistance, signified by the fact that together the group's voices form a critical chorus, is in an uneasy balance with the highly individual American dreams of each character. The last sentence in the book is indicative of this attitude: "You know, you go on out there and go along with the game, too, but only for what you want—Numero Uno" (224). The narrator ends the book on an ambivalent note. He writes, "There is an epilogue to this book, but only time can write it."

CRITICAL RECEPTION

Published in the midst of the Civil Rights movement and in the wake of the nationwide urban riots of 1964, *Manchild in the Promised Land* was widely reviewed. In 1970 the black critic Albert Murray wrote a bitter response to what he perceived to be the position of many of these reviews, "that *Manchild* reveals what it is really like to be a Negro" (145). He argues that Brown ignores the complex, everyday existence of African Americans, particularly the functional interdependencies of black urban life. Brown's worldview and consequently his writing are "structured" by the ideology and language of the social sciences (145), disciplines that, Murray writes, are primarily concerned with "the fakelore of black pathology" (143).

Houston A. Baker Jr., acknowledges that *Manchild* can be read as the social history of an "epoch" in black urban life (54). However, he focuses on its literary elements, specifically, Brown's modification of the conventions of naturalistic writing. Baker points out that the Harlem environment is initially depicted as inimical. Harlem is, in fact, the colonial outpost of a white, downtown metropole. The South and the penal institutions to which Brown is sent for his "rebellion" against this colonial system are but versions of Harlem as colony; they function to equip him with "new," but always futile, strategies for survival. Brown's "exile" from Harlem, however, engenders a romantic nostalgia for its streets. This cycle of banishment and longing is broken only when he leaves Harlem for Greenwich Village. Nostalgia is transformed into a clinical realism that allows him to objectively see and describe the inimical aspects of the Harlem environment. For

Baker, this balance between nostalgia and objectivity revises "the ideological rigidities of naturalistic conventions" (58). When Brown returns to Harlem, he is able to both confront and survive its hostile elements and, for the first time, to tap into beneficial forces such as the church community that funds his education. To Baker, this fact signals Harlem's transformation from a place of danger to one that is, at least potentially, "tame and beneficent" (58): this is Brown's contribution to the record of an epoch in Harlem's history.

Albert E. Stone's article locates Manchild within a tradition of African American autobiographical writing. Stone argues that Brown's text is an example of a novelistic autobiography. Although permeated by history, its focus is on the personal: it "dramatize[s] by fictional techniques the truth of . . . recreated lives" ("Patterns" 171). Stone describes several signal characteristics of this autobiographical form, all of which Manchild incorporates: a title that invites the reader to generalize the author's experience; the use of the present tense and first-person narrative, which impart immediacy to the text; an opening scene, such as that of Brown's shooting, that compresses the work's major themes into one provocative and often violent image (182–83). Particularly significant to a critical reading of Manchild is the distinction Stone makes between the author and the "actor" or protagonist of an autobiography. Novelistic autobiographies tend to sacrifice the interplay between the older, more experienced author and the inexperienced, if not naive, actor who is in the process of becoming that person (183). This resonates with Baker's delineation of the tension between the nostalgic and realistic aspects of Manchild. In addition, it suggests a strategy for understanding, if not fully resolving, the conflicts and contradictions in Brown's delineation, as "actor" in the text, of aspects of his Harlem experience.

Roger Rosenblatt points out that Manchild incorporates elements of three distinct American literary traditions: folk humor, the success story, and the Gothic tale. Within a specifically African American tradition, he compares the comic talents of Brown's persona, Sonny, to those of Langston Hughes'* fictional creation Simple. Both employ humor as a method of critique, a didactic tool, and a source of visionary possibility for a better world.

The Children of Ham generated a much more limited critical response than Manchild. Arnold Rampersad's review, however, argues passionately for its importance, comparing its urgency and power to Stephen Crane's Maggie: A Girl of the Streets and The Diary of Anne Frank (26). Rampersad argues that as a narrative of return to a Harlem Brown had escaped, Children is permeated by a "survivor's guilt" raised to biblical proportions: "Harlem is in apocalypse and the story is revelation itself" (25). Noting the tension between the informants' often critical stance and their individual optimism, Rampersad argues that although they are "[a]ncient" by virtue of exposure to the harsh realities of the world, they "are as childlike as their most recent fantasy, illusion or dream" (25). The book's realism should put an end to the lingering elements of the early twentieth century's "myth of Harlem" (25).

BIBLIOGRAPHY

Works by Claude Brown

Manchild in the Promised Land. 1965. New York: Macmillan, 1971.
The Children of Ham. New York: Stein and Day, 1976.

Studies of Claude Brown

Baker, Houston A., Jr. "The Environment as Enemy in a Black Autobiography: *Manchild in the Promised Land.*" *Phylon* 32.1 (1971): 53–59.
Goldman, Robert M., and William D. Crano. "*Black Boy* and *Manchild in the Promised Land*: Content Analysis in the Study of Value Change over Time." *Journal of Black Studies* 7.2 (1976): 169–80.
Murray, Albert. *The Omni-Americans: New Perspectives on Black Experience and American Culture.* 1970. New York: Discus-Avon, 1971.
Rampersad, Arnold. Rev. of *The Children of Ham. The New Republic* 8 (May 1976): 25–26.
Rosenblatt, Roger. *Black Fiction.* Cambridge: Harvard University Press, 1974.
Stone, Albert E. "After *Black Boy* and *Dusk of Dawn*: Patterns in Recent Black Autobiography." *Phylon* 39.1 (1978): 18–34. Reprinted, with a postscript, in *African American Autobiography: A Collection of Critical Essays.* Ed. William L. Andrews. Englewood Cliffs, NJ: Prentice-Hall, 1993. 171–95.

STERLING A. BROWN
(1901–1989)

Leela Kapai

BIOGRAPHY

Sterling Allen Brown was born in Washington, D.C., on May 1, 1901. His father was Rev. Sterling Nelson Brown, a professor of religion at Howard University and minister of Lincoln Temple Congregational Church; his mother, Adelaide Allen Brown, was a valedictorian of her class at Fisk University. The senior Brown was born a slave in eastern Tennessee and put himself through Fisk and Oberlin by working as a manual laborer and later as a farmer. Sterling A. Brown grew up on the campus of Howard University, surrounded not only by intellectuals but also by those who had been close to the experience of slavery. He attended Dunbar High School, a bastion of excellence in the days of segregated educational institutions. Among his teachers were the writers Angelica Weld Grimke* and Jessie Redmon Fauset,* and of his classmates many grew up to have distinguished careers: Mercer Cook, an ambassador to Senegal; John Dewey, professor of education at the University of Chicago; Charles Drew, known for his research in blood plasma; Ralph Bunche, the U.S. representative to the United Nations and the winner of the Nobel Peace Prize in 1950; William Hastie, a federal judge; and W. Montague Cobb, a well-known anthropologist.

Brown graduated Phi Beta Kappa from Williams College, Massachusetts, in 1922. He won a scholarship to Harvard, where he received a master's degree in 1923 and embarked on a teaching career that took him south to Virginia Theological Seminary, then to Fisk University. His stay in the South was a turning point in his career, for it enriched his understanding of his people, their strength, their wit, and their tenacity that allowed them to survive indignities and unimaginable horrors. It was also at Virginia Seminary that he met his wife, Daisy Turnbull, who was his companion and his inspiration for over fifty years. Brown joined the faculty of Howard University in 1929 and remained there until his retirement.

Brown distinguished himself as a poet and a perceptive critic at an early age. In 1925 he won a prize in the *Opportunity* magazine contest for his essay on Roland Hayes, a renowned tenor. He published several reviews, poems, and sketches in *Opportunity* and contributed to several anthologies before his first book of poems, *Southern Road*, was published by Harcourt, Brace in 1932. The book received rave reviews and earned him a name among his contemporaries. From 1936 to 1939, he was an editor of *Negro Affairs* for the Federal Writers Project and also served on the staff of Gunnar Myrdal, who later published *An American Dilemma* (1944), a study of the American Negro. Brown's knowledge of black folklore, culture, and literature proved an invaluable source for the Carnegie-Myrdal study.

During his tenure at Howard University, Brown mentored many students who later became writers, poets, and activists. Despite a large number of publications in periodicals and anthologies, he did not get the acclaim that he richly deserved until the late 1960s, when the political activists of the black power movement and the aestheticians of the black arts movement brought his works to public attention. He had a tumultuous relationship with his colleagues and the administration at Howard University and underwent periods of depression. He retired in 1969 but at the insistence of students was asked to return in 1974. He finally won long-overdue recognition when Howard University awarded him an honorary doctorate in 1971. He taught classes, gave readings, and lectured extensively until 1978, when ill health forced him to give up his position. In 1980 he was honored to become the first poet laureate of Washington, D.C.

Brown's loneliness after his beloved wife's death in 1979 was mitigated, to some extent, by his erstwhile students and scholars who continued to visit him to share his knowledge and extensive collection of music, delightful recounting of his literary friends, and his memories of many colorful folks he had encountered during his life. He died of leukemia in Washington, D.C., on January 17, 1989.

MAJOR WORKS AND THEMES

Sterling Brown's poems clearly reflect the literary tendencies of the period. As he acknowledges in his speech "A Son's Return: 'Oh, Didn't He Ramble,' " George Dutton at Williams taught him critical realism, and Bliss Perry at Harvard exposed him to the richness of American poetry. He was influenced by the realists among American poets, chief among them Walt Whitman, Carl Sandburg, Edward Arlington Robinson, Edgar Lee Masters, A. E. Housman, and Robert Frost (*A Son's Return* 14–15). From the imagists, he learned the importance of sharp, concise pictures in words and creation of new rhythms (Gabbin 25–26). He was also influenced by Paul Laurence Dunbar,* Claude Mckay,* and other members of what he termed the New Negro Renaissance. One can hear in his poems the echoes of dialogues in dramatic situations of Robinson, Masters, and Frost; however, Brown's language, black vernacular, makes them distinctively his own.

Brown's first collection of poetry, *Southern Road*, published in 1932, reflected his experiences in the South and laid the groundwork for themes and techniques for his later poems. The poems in *Southern Road* are grouped under four headings: "Road So Rocky," "On Restless River," "Tin Roof Blues," and "Vestiges." In the words of Valerie Smith, the road is used as "the unifying motif of his book. . . . Among the forms that the road has taken are the creeks and the rivers, the railroad, the Underground Railroad, the gospel train, the way of survival, the slippery path to hell, the lonesome valley, the Big Road of Life" (49). When his publisher rejected *No Hiding Place* in 1937, he made no effort to bring out another collection of poems until *The Last Ride of Wild Bill and Eleven Narrative Poems* was published by Broadside Press in 1975. *The Collected Poems of Sterling A. Brown* (1980), edited by Michael Harper, has finally made most of Brown's poems conveniently available in one place. It brings together *Southern Road*, *The Last Ride of Wild Bill*, and *No Hiding Place* (published for the first time).

Sterling Brown's poems seem to answer James Weldon Johnson's* call for a new poetics. In the Preface to the first edition of *The Book of American Negro Poetry* (1921), Johnson had declared that the African American poet needed to do what J. M. Synge had done for the Irish and find an appropriate form "to express the racial spirit by symbols from within rather than by symbols from without, such as the mere mutilation of English spelling and pronunciation. He needs a form that is freer and larger than dialect but which will still hold the racial flavor; a form expressing the imagery, the idioms, the peculiar turns of thought, and the distinctive humor and pathos, too, of the Negro, but which will also be capable of voicing the deepest and highest emotions and aspirations, and allow of the widest range of subjects and the scope of treatment" (41–42).

Sterling Brown's poems present all that Johnson had asked for. He employs a variety of forms to express an equally wide range of emotions and situations in his poems. In keeping with his interest in the oral folk literature of his people, he writes work songs, spirituals, blues, and ballads and often an amalgamation of several forms. This synthesis, "cross-pollination," of diverse traditions is a distinguishing mark of his art (Gabbin 117). He is equally adept in more traditional forms as sonnets, lyrics, and literary ballads. However, what makes his work unique is his use of the folk material to present memorable portraits of people he came across.

Several themes are discernible in these poems. A common thread that runs through many of the poems is a desire to escape from the surrounding bleak conditions. Sometimes, a need to seek adventure governs this wanderlust. Thus, the speaker in "Long Gone" keeps roving, for it's not "nachal" for a railroad man to "stay long," even by his beloved's side. In "Maumee Ruth," the young wander off in search of better lives, leaving the old to die unmourned. Georgie Grimes leaves after stabbing his woman, muttering that he had no other recourse to redress the wrong done to him. "Bessie" laments the loss of innocence of the young girl who moves to the city to escape the grim squalor of her surroundings.

Another theme reiterated in *Southern Road* is the courage of the seemingly weak and helpless. Several poems depict memorable characters whose attitude toward life and its adversity makes them heroic figures even when they lack any worldly accomplishments. These men and women, mostly old, reflect a dignified and stoic approach to life's hardships. "Virginia Portrait" depicts an old woman who has lost many of her loved ones, has lived through "heavy years," yet continues to maintain "a courtly dignity of speech and carriage." Religion is the unfailing prop for most. "Sister Lou," a remarkable monologue, captures in homely imagery the pleasures that await in heaven for a dying woman who has toiled all her life. "Southern Road," a combination of work song and blues, depicts a member of a chain gang recalling the tragedies following his conviction. As he heaves and strikes the hammer, he warns his mate to be patient and slow, for there is no end to their toil in sight. "The Last Ride of Wild Bill," a ballad, sings of the hero who defies the Establishment and succeeds in frustrating the authorities for a long time. Perhaps, "Strong Men," the best-known poem of Brown, inspired by Carl Sandburg, sums up his tribute succinctly. "They," the men in power, "dragged," "chained," "scourged," "branded"—and the litany of cruelties swells—but his people kept on, singing songs of faith and sorrow and never breaking down. He ends on the note that the chain of strong men will remain unbroken.

Humor is a valuable means of coping with life's tragedies. Brown captures the whimsical nature of his characters—men and women—and sometimes with gentle irony makes us see the humor in their lives. Slim Greer's adventures attest to his skill. In the five poems about Slim Greer, Slim is depicted as the greatest "liar," a teller of tall tales, a trickster, and a folk hero. Nothing fazes him; he tries passing as white and almost succeeds; using hyperbolic statements, he shows the absurdities of the laws enforcing segregation and in the process makes the readers laugh with him.

Nevertheless, Brown makes it clear that his people are not all exemplary; some are dishonest, wayward, sometimes foolish, yet even these receive a loving portrayal. Mandy Jane comes back with a basket of goods stolen from her mistress; Luke Johnson, the speaker, never asks her but understands well, for he recalls how the grandfather of the lady at the big house had exploited Mandy Jane's grandfather; thus, no compensation—rightful or wrong—can ever suffice. Johnny in "Johnny Thomas" is a "consarned fool" who ends up lynched, but his odyssey through life shows the odds against his ever coming out a winner. In the ballad "Frankie and Johnny," Johnny's foolishness makes him forget the reality of sexual relationships in the South to allow himself to be seduced by Frankie, "a half-wit" white, a seduction that leads to his tragic end.

Romantic love and reminiscences of places visited also find a place in Brown's early poems. Grouped in "Vestiges" section of *Southern Road* are several sonnets addressed to his wife; "Challenge" and "Rain," among them, are especially charming. There are other lilting lyrics, "To a Certain Lady, in Her Garden," and reflections on fleeting life in "Thoughts of Death" and "Against That Day."

Brown's contributions to African American literature go beyond his poetic works. He distinguished himself by his criticism as well. As the editor of *Negro Affairs*, he coordinated the studies by and about blacks, notably the collection of ex-slave narratives. *The Negro in Virginia* (1940) became the prototype of similar studies to follow. As the literary editor of *Opportunity*, he wrote a monthly review of new books. He published critiques of plays, sketches, and his observations on the contemporary scene in many periodicals, now cataloged in the bibliography by O'Meally. His anthology, The *Negro Caravan* (1941), coedited with Ulysses Lee and Arthur P. Davis, remains a valuable resource. Among some of the most cited essays of Brown are "The American Race Problem as Reflected in American Literature," "Negro Character as Seen by White Authors," "The New Negro in Literature (1925–1955)," and "Negro Folk Expression: Spirituals, Seculars, Ballads and Work Songs." In these essays he analyzed the stereotypical portrayal of African Americans in literature with its unfair treatment of his people and suggested instead a realistic critical assessment of their rich heritage.

Originally published in various journals and anthologies or delivered as lectures, several of Brown's essays are now available in A *Son's Return: Selected Essays of Sterling A. Brown* (1996) and reveal his deep understanding of literary history and the place of African Americans in it. He attempted to end "the plantation tradition" by showing the real life of his people. While he celebrated their lives, he refused to see "Negro" literature as anything but a part of mainstream American literature. He perpetuated the black folk tradition but saw no reason to denounce the classical tradition in literature. Despite the fact that these essays were written mostly in the 1940s and 1950s, the critical insights in them are as relevant today as they were at that time.

CRITICAL RECEPTION

Brown's work appeared at the end of the Harlem Renaissance, a name that he never accepted. Alain Locke* hailed Sterling Brown as a "significant new Negro poet" in "a new era in Negro poetry" (3). Brown's capturing the voice of his speakers, his use of dialect, was not new in itself; it had been used by Charles Chesnutt,* Dunbar, and James Weldon Johnson before him. James Weldon Johnson had characterized most poetry in the dialect as being in the "minstrel traditions of Negro life, traditions that had but slight relation—often no relation at all—to actual Negro life, or . . . permeated with artificial sentiment" (4). However, introducing the first edition of *Southern Road*, Johnson conceded that Brown "has actually absorbed the spirit of his material, made it his own, and without diluting its primitive frankness and raciness, truly re-expressed it with artistry and magnificent power. In a word, he has taken this raw material and worked it into original and authentic poetry" (17).

Sterling Stuckey, in his Introduction to *The Collected Poems of Sterling Brown*, provides a panoramic view of the contemporary reviews of *Southern Road*. The *New York Times*, *The New Republic*, the *Saturday Review of Literature*, and critics—Louis Untermeyer and William Rose Benet among them—found Brown's accomplishments commendable. Especially appreciated were the absence of "maudlin sentimentality and outlandish humor" and the evidence of "genuine originality" (Stuckey 6).

Although Brown continued to steadily publish critical essays and reviews in the 1950s and 1960s, his reputation remained eclipsed until the 1970s, when the new generation of African American writers and critics once again recognized his unique contributions. The publication of his *Collected Poems* brought renewed literary appreciations from critics such as Stephen Henderson, John F. Callahan, Addison Gayle, Philip Levine, Henry Louis Gates Jr., and Robert G. O'Meally. They focused on the language and use of folk materials, especially Brown's twist on some of the original forms of blues and spirituals.

Joanne Gabbin's full-length study *Sterling A. Brown: Building the Black Aesthetic Tradition* (1985) remains an invaluable work, for she has incorporated interviews and recorded materials along with other sources available in the archives of the Institute of Arts and Sciences at Howard University in her detailed biography and perceptive critical analysis. Essays on Brown's art in his verse, specifically, the ballads and the blues, and on several well-known poems continue to appear periodically in journals. In October 1998, the Office of the U.S. Poet Laureate at the Library of Congress and *Callaloo*, which devoted the entire fall 1998 issue to Sterling Brown, held a three-day symposium in Washington, D.C., to celebrate his accomplishments. Undoubtedly, Brown's place in the literary annals as a poet, an authority on folk material, and a pioneer in criticism is assured forever.

BIBLIOGRAPHY

Works by Sterling A. Brown

Poetry

Southern Road. New York: Harcourt, Brace, 1932.
The Last Ride of Wild Bill and Eleven Narrative Poems. Detroit: Broadside Press, 1975.
The Collected Poems of Sterling A. Brown. Selected by Michael S. Harper. New York: Harper and Row, 1980. Reprinted, Chicago: TriQuarterly Books, 1989.

Criticism

"The Blues as Folk Poetry." In *Folk-Say*. Vol. 1. Ed. Benjamin A. Botkin. Norman: University of Oklahoma Press, 1930. 324–39.
Outline for the Study of the Poetry of American Negroes. New York: Harcourt, Brace, 1931. Supplement to James Weldon Johnson's anthology *The Book of American Poetry*.
"The Negro Character as Seen by White Authors." *Journal of Negro Education* 2 (April 1933): 179–203.

The Negro in American Fiction. Washington, DC: Associates in Negro Folk Education, 1938.

Negro Poetry and Drama. Washington, DC: Associates in Negro Folk Education, 1938.

"The American Race Problem as Reflected in American Literature." *Journal of Negro Education* 8 (July 1939): 275–90.

The Negro Caravan. Ed. Sterling A. Brown, Arthur P. Davis, and Ulysses Lee. New York: Dryden Press, 1941.

"The Negro in American Theater." In *Oxford Companion to the Theater.* Ed. Phyllis Harnoll. London: Oxford University Press, 1950. 672–79.

"A Century of Negro Portraiture in American Literature." *Massachusetts Review* 7 (Winter 1966): 73–96.

A Son's Return: Selected Essays of Sterling Brown. Ed. Mark A. Sanders. Boston: Northeastern University Press, 1996.

Studies of Sterling A. Brown

Gabbin, Joanne. *Sterling A. Brown: Building the Black Aesthetic Tradition.* Westport, CT: Greenwood Press, 1985.

Gates, Henry Louis, Jr. "Songs of a Racial Self: On Sterling A. Brown." In *Figures In Black: Words, Signs, and the Racial Self.* New York: Oxford University Press, 1987. 225–34.

Henderson, Stephen E. "The Heavy Blues of Sterling Brown: A Study of Craft and Tradition." *Black American Literature Forum* 14 (1980): 32–44.

Johnson, James Weldon. "Preface" to *The Book of American Negro Poetry.* New York: Harcourt, Brace, 1921. Revised, 1931; reprinted, 1983.

Locke, Alain. *The New Negro.* New York: A & C Boni, 1925.

O'Meally, Robert G. O. "An Annotated Bibliography of the Works of Sterling A. Brown."*The Collected Poems of Sterling Brown.* 255–67. Reprinted in *A Son's Return.* 293–304.

Rowell, Charles. "Sterling A. Brown and the Afro-American Folk Tradition." In *The Harlem Renaissance Re-Examined.* Ed. Victor A. Kramer. New York: AMS Press, 1987. 317–37.

Sanders, Mark A. "Foreword." *A Son's Return: Selected Essays of Sterling A. Brown.* Boston: Northeastern University Press, 1996. ix–xxii.

———. "Sterling A. Brown's Master Metaphor: *Southern Road* and the Sign of Black Modernity." *Callaloo* 21.4 (Fall 1998): 917–30.

Smith, Gary. "The Literary Ballads of Sterling Brown." *College Language Association Journal* 32.4 (June 1989): 393–409.

Smith, Valerie. "Sterling Brown." In *African American Writers.* New York: Charles Scribner, 1991. 45–57.

Stuckey, Sterling. "Introduction." *The Collected Poems of Sterling A. Brown.* Chicago: TriQuarterly Press, 1989. 3–15.

WILLIAM WELLS BROWN
(1814 – 1884)

Loretta G. Woodard

BIOGRAPHY

William Wells Brown was born sometime in 1814 on a plantation near Lexington, Kentucky, to a slave mother known as Elizabeth and a white, slaveholding father. His boyhood and teenage years were spent in St. Louis, Missouri, where he was often "hired out" and even sold by his various masters, working for several years in hotels and on steamboats. During this period, forced employment revealed to William slavery's full range of inhumanity, shaped the major beliefs of his mature years, convinced him that he must escape, and provided vivid materials for his abolitionist activities and major literary works.

In 1830 William began working in the printing office of Elijah P. Lovejoy, an antislavery editor and part-time owner of the newly founded *Saint Louis Times* who was later murdered by a pro-slavery mob for his liberal views. Though William acquired a rudimentary education under Lovejoy's direction, he remained functionally illiterate for some time. After six months with Lovejoy, William was hired out again as a steward on board the *Chester*. While it was docked at a small town on the Ohio River, William, at age nineteen, escaped to freedom in 1834. While a fugitive, he was befriended by Wells Brown, an Ohio Quaker whose name he adopted, and he was thereafter known as William Wells Brown. New Year's Day, the day of his freedom, marked the closing out of a year in which slavery was banned throughout the English empire. It was also a time when William Lloyd Garrison of Boston established the American Anti-Slavery Society, along with its abolitionist newspaper, *The Liberator*. Both Garrison's organization and newspaper were to play a key role in making Brown an internationally famous orator and author.

After seizing his freedom, Brown made his way to Cleveland and began a new life in the Great Lakes region, where he worked as a steward on Lake Erie steamboats and began educating himself. In 1834 he met and married Elizabeth Betsey Schooner, a free Negro. After two and a half years, the Brown family moved to Buffalo, New York, where he maintained a home for nine years and became an expert conductor on the Underground Railroad.

By the early 1840s Brown quickly emerged as a lecturer for the Western New York Anti-Slavery Society and a new writer of note. Moving to Boston in 1847, Brown wrote his first major work, *Narrative of William W. Brown, a Fugitive Slave*, which earned him international fame. A year later, *The Anti-Slavery Harp: A Collection of Songs for Anti-Slavery Meetings* was published.

Brown traveled to England in the summer of 1849 to attend the International Peace Congress in Paris and to encourage British support for the antislavery movement in the United States. While there, Brown delivered more than 1,000 antislavery lectures at several institutions and many antislavery, benevolent, and religious societies. In 1852 he helped to found and run a London newspaper, the *Anti-Slavery Advocate*, and published his epistolary travel book, *Three Years in Europe; or, Places I Have Seen and People I Have Met*, the first by a black man. Another first and Brown's greatest contribution, *Clotel; or, The President's Daughter: a Narrative of Slave Life in the United States*, was published in London in 1853. *Clotel* was revised and republished in America under different titles for a period of fourteen years. During his five years in England, Brown studied medicine with Dr. Young, a renowned British physician.

By the time Brown was forty years old, his English friends purchased his freedom for $300 on July 7, 1854, and he returned to Boston in the fall of 1854. Brown accepted a lecturer's position with Garrison's American Anti-Slavery Society and continued advocating for abolitionism until the end of the Civil War. His lecture featuring Toussaint L'Ouverture, the black Haitian revolutionary, was published as a pamphlet entitled *St. Domingo: Its Revolutions and Its Patriots* in 1855. Three years later, although never produced, he wrote the first play, *The Escape; or, A Leap for Freedom*, based on his experiences as a slave.

After the death of Betsey Schooner in 1851, Brown married twenty-five-year-old Annie Elizabeth Gray in 1860. After his marriage and the Civil War, Brown promoted temperance work and actively practiced medicine in Boston, which he had been practicing since his early work under Dr. Young and during his stay in England. Also in this period Brown's interest shifted from literature to sociohistorical writings.

Realizing the importance of blacks in American culture, Brown wrote some of his "most ambitious works." *The Black Man: His Antecedents, His Genius, and His Achievements* was published in 1862. This work was followed by *The Negro in the American Rebellion: His Heroism and His Fidelity* in 1867, and *The Rising Son; or, The Antecedents and Advancement of the Colored Race* in 1873. Brown's final and perhaps best work appeared in 1880 as *My Southern Home; or, The South and Its People*, his second autobiographical narrative, which recounts experiences and reassesses events and circumstances in Brown's life.

Generally regarded as one of the most remarkable men of the nineteenth century, Brown is remembered, nationally and internationally, as a committed writer and abolitionist lecturer who devoted his life and his work to the freedom and dignity of his people. Brown died in Chelsea, a suburb of Boston, of increasing ailments associated with a tumor of the bladder on November 6, 1884, and was buried in the Cambridge, Massachusetts, Cemetery.

MAJOR WORKS AND THEMES

Clotel; or, The President's Daughter (1853) is a propagandistic condemnation of slavery designed to advance the cause of abolition. Set in the South during the nineteenth century, this sentimental novel is interspersed with tales of the cruelty practiced by whites against slaves.

The complex plot and numerous subplots of *Clotel* revolve around a mulatto woman, Currer Bell, a quadroon, said to have been the mistress of Thomas Jefferson in her youth, and her two octoroon daughters, Clotel, age sixteen, and Althesa, age fourteen, who are sold as slaves after the death of their owner. As the separate careers of the three women are traced, the emphasis is on one of the daughters, Clotel, who ends up near Richmond and has a daughter named Mary. When the new owner's wife discovers his relationship with Clotel, she, like Mrs. Gaines in *The Escape*, demands that she be sold.

Mary is left behind, and Clotel is sold to yet another owner in Mississippi, where she is subjected to tremendous cruelty by the owner's wife and the other slaves. Together she and William, the slave who befriends her, manage to escape to Ohio, but he is unable to persuade her to continue on to freedom in Canada. She returns to Virginia, disguised as a man, to get her daughter, Mary, but her identity is disclosed, and she is arrested and sent to the "negro pens." Her persistence allows her to escape again, but when she realizes that she cannot escape the slave catchers, she plunges into the Potomac River. Significant is the fact that she commits suicide within sight of the White House, occupied by Thomas Jefferson, her alleged father.

By casting as his heroine of *Clotel* the slave daughter of Thomas Jefferson, author of the Declaration of Independence, Brown sought to depict the horror and irony of the "peculiar institution" of slavery, a system that would allow the daughter of a president to be sold into bondage. Brown used such a character and others in his works to document the sordid facts of slavery and used romantic, even melodramatic literary forms to portray the internal black perspective, as well as the typical experience of the black in white society. More significantly, in his development of the character Clotel, Brown does not rely totally upon the stereotypes and conventions of his time. Clotel's persistence and her bravery, like Melinda's in *The Escape*, make her an admirable character.

To portray convincingly the actual horrors and hypocrisies of the institution of slavery, Brown draws substantially upon his own personal experience as a slave in the descriptions of the slave traders, especially "Dick" Walker's slave-trading activities, and of slave auctions, coffles of slaves, slave pens, murder and on the slave narrative and antislavery novel traditions. Though the action literally whirls the reader from one incident to another, Brown's technique of bombarding the reader with a potpourri of material and forms works to create a melodramatic tension.

Though *The Escape* was never performed on stage, it grew in popularity from Brown's dramatic readings of it to friends and in various parts of the country. Like *Clotel*, *The Escape* (1858), a drama in five acts and seventeen scenes, is primarily an antislavery argument that centers on the crisis of two slaves, Glen and Melinda, who are in love with each other. The slave master, Dr. Gaines, a physician, politician, and a connoisseur of beautiful slave women, wants to exploit Melinda sexually. Mrs. Gaines, the jealous mistress, aware of her husband's passion for slave women, insists that her husband sell Melinda to Walker, a slave trader. However, instead of selling Melinda, as he leads his wife to believe, Dr. Gaines hides her in a cottage on Poplar Farm and again tries to coax her to become his mistress. When she does not encourage his advances, and when he learns that she has been secretly married to Glen for four weeks, Glen is imprisoned but eventually escapes, and both he and Melinda set out together for Canada.

Brown's play not only attacks slavery but further dramatizes three of his old and growing personal concerns throughout his works. The lustfulness of white men is evidenced in the play by their sexual exploitation of slave women who bear the mulatto children on the plantation. These children resemble their slave masters, a fact they cannot deny, since Brown often describes the light-skinned slave child as "a white slave" and since they are often mistaken by slave traders and other slave owners as the master's son or daughter.

The viciousness of white women is precipitated by the infidelity and perversity of their husbands, and this knowledge torments and deforms them into hard and cruel tyrants. By scolding and whipping the slaves, Mrs. Gaines releases considerable hostility. When she finds Melinda at the cottage, she first tries to compel Melinda to commit suicide by drinking poison, but Melinda refuses to drink it. Then Mrs. Gaines' fury and frustration explode as she attacks and attempts to murder her with a dagger.

Brown's own orientation to slavery taught him the meaning of powerlessness of the black man, as evidenced in his own autobiography. Consequently, it is a prevailing concern in all of his works. As slaves, black men could not react violently against their oppressors to defend slave women. Because they were whipped, sold, put in jail, or killed, they had to mask their true feelings by being submissive. Though Glen expresses his anger in the play, it is to no avail. The mere property of Dr. Gaines' brother-in-law, he is put in prison, where he is powerless to act to defend the honor of his slave wife and his own dignity as a black man until he successfully makes his "leap for freedom."

Most interesting about the play are its hyperbolic language, comedy, satire, and setting. Although the characters, themes, and plot are drawn from Brown's life and other abolitionist materials, what Brown does with these materials is unique and important for black literature.

CRITICAL RECEPTION

Brown's works have received serious scholarly attention. However, most of the critical responses have varied over time, and most of them have been about his well-known novel and play and are found in several excellent articles and chapters in books. Dismissing Brown "as a novelist of style," the general critical assessment of *Clotel* is on its "structural chaos." Arthur Davis voices this response when he notes that Brown "tried to cram too many things into one work: antislavery lectures and verse; enough situations to supply at least five novels; newspapers accounts, minstrel jokes and sketches; and every slavery anecdote he considered even remotely pertinent" (Introduction to *Clotel*).

Other scholars have approached Brown's work from a variety of directions. Robert Stepto surveys Brown's writing techniques and his process of "authentication." He argues, "Since *Clotel* is not fully formed as either a fiction or a slave narrative, it requires completion of some sort, and finds this when it is transformed into a fairly effective antislavery device through linkage with its prefatory authenticating text [Brown's personal narrative]" (29–30). Addison Gayle Jr., condemns Brown's creating unrealistic, almost white characters for a white audience, thereby calling the author an "unconscious propagator of assimilationism" (8–9). Other critics argue that as disorganized and melodramatic as *Clotel* seems to be, it still deserves more critical attention than simply as the first novel written by a black man.

Reviewers of Brown's play, *The Escape*, like those of his novel, tend to find weaknesses, but Brown himself states at the end of his Preface that he owed the public no apology for the defects in the drama, because "I was born in slavery, and never had a day's schooling in my life." Still, most critics cannot overlook how the play is "marred by didacticism and heroic sentimentality" and is "a hodge-podge with some humor and satire" (Redding, *They Came in Chains* 27–28).

In spite of the play's defects, it has received some positive reviews. Though leading Brown scholar W. Edward Farrison claims the play abounds in "artificial dialogue," he, nevertheless, sees it as "an authentic and vivid portrayal of slavery" (*William Wells Brown: Author and Reformer* 304). Doris M. Abramson, the first of the critics to treat *The Escape* as a serious work of art, defends Brown's play. She sees it as "a well-made play by standards of the period ... [which] ... has variety of characterization, careful exposition, a well-designed if obvious plot, ... spine-chilling scenes of seduction and revenge," and it is "an interesting document both from a social and a theatrical point of view" ("William Wells Brown" 375).

Given the fact that Brown's successes are considerable and of great importance to the history of African American culture, there is still a great need for more critical assessments on his lesser-known works.

BIBLIOGRAPHY

Works by William Wells Brown

Novel

Clotel; or, The President's Daughter: A Narrative of Slave Life in the United States. London: Partridge and Oakey, 1853.

Play

The Escape; or, a Leap for Freedom, a Drama in Five Acts. Boston: R. F. Walcutt, 1858.

Songs and Poems

The Anti-Slavery Harp: A Collection of Songs for Anti-Slavery Meetings. Boston: Bela Marsh, 1848.

Other Works

A Lecture Delivered before the Female Anti-Slavery Society of Salem, at Lyceum Hall, 14 November 1847. Boston: Anti-Slavery Society, 1847.
Narrative of William W. Brown, a Fugitive Slave, Written by Himself. Boston: Anti-Slavery Office, 1847.
Three Years in Europe; or, Places I have Seen and People I Have Met. London: Gilpin, 1852. Published as *The American Fugitive in Europe: Sketches of Places and People Abroad.* Boston: J. P. Jewett, 1855.
St. Domingo: Its Revolutions and Its Patriots. Boston: Bela Marsh, 1855.
Memoir of William Wells Brown, an American Bondsman. Written by Himself. Boston: Anti-Slavery Office, 1859.
The Anti-Southern Lecturer. London: Partridge & Oakey, 1862.
The Black Man: His Antecedents, His Genius, and His Achievements. Boston: R. F. Walcutt, 1862.
The Negro in the American Rebellion: His Heroism and His Fidelity. Boston: Lee and Shepard, 1867.
The Rising Sun; or, The Antecedents and Advancement of the Colored Race. Boston: A. G. Brown, 1873.
My Southern Home; or, The South and Its People. Boston: Brown, 1880.

Studies of William Wells Brown

Abramson, Doris M. *Negro Playwrights in the American Theatre, 1925–1959.* New York: Columbia University Press, 1969. 8–14, 18–19.
———. "William Wells Brown: America's First Negro Playwright." *Educational Theatre Journal* 20.3 (October 1968): 370–75.

Andrews, William L. *To Tell a Free Story: The First Century of Afro-American Autobiography, 1760–1865*. Urbana: University of Illinois Press, 1986.

Bardolph, Richard E. *The Negro Vanguard*. New York: Rinehart, 1959.

Bell, Bernard W. *The Afro-American Novel and Its Tradition*. Amherst: University of Massachusetts Press, 1987.

Bone, Robert A. *The Negro Novel in America*. New Haven, CT: Yale University Press, 1965.

Bontemps, Arna. "The Negro Contribution to American Letters." In *The American Negro Reference Book*. Ed. John P. Davis. Englewood Cliffs, NJ: Prentice-Hall, 1966. 850–78.

Brawley, Benjamin. "William Wells Brown." In *Early Negro American Writers: Selections with Biographical and Critical Introductions*. Freeport, NY: Books for Libraries Press, 1968. 168–74.

Brown, Josephine. *Biography of an American Bondsman, by His Daughter*. Boston: R. F. Walcutt, 1856.

Candela, Gregory L. "William Wells Brown." In *Dictionary of Literary Biography*. Vol. 50: *Afro-American Fiction Writers before 1955*. Ed. Thadious M. Davis and Trudier Harris. Detroit: Gale, 1986. 18–31.

Coleman, Edward M. "William Wells Brown as an Historian." *Journal of Negro History* 31 (1946): 47–49.

Davis, Arthur. "Introduction" to *Clotel; or, The President's Daughter*. New York: Collier-Macmillan, 1970.

Davis, John P., ed. *The American Negro Reference Book*. Englewood Cliffs, NJ: Prentice-Hall, 1966. 867–70.

Draper, James P., ed. "William Wells Brown." *Black Literature Criticism*. Vol. 1. Detroit: Gale, 1992. 292–306.

duCille, Ann. "The Coupling Convention: Novel Views of Love and Marriage." In *The Coupling Convention*. Ed. Ann duCille. New York: Oxford University Press, 1993. 17–29.

Emanuel, James A., and Theodore Gross. *Dark Symphony: Negro Literature in America*. New York: Free Press, 1968. 365–66.

Farrison, W. Edward. Brown's First Drama. *CLA Journal* 2 (1958): 104–10.

———. "A Flight across Ohio: The Escape of William Wells Brown from Slavery." *Ohio State Archeological and Historical Quarterly* 61 (1952): 272–82.

———. "One Ephemerer after Another." *CLA Journal* 13 (December 1969): 192–97.

———. "The Origin of Brown's Clotel." *Phylon* 15 (1954): 347–54.

———. "Phylon Profile, XVI: William Wells Brown." *Phylon* 9 (1948): 13–24.

———. "A Theologian's Missouri Compromise." *Journal of Negro History* 48 (1963): 33–43.

———. "William Wells Brown: America's First Negro Man of Letters." *Phylon* 9 (1948): 13–23.

———. *William Wells Brown: Author and Reformer*. Chicago: University of Chicago Press, 1969.

———. "William Wells Brown: Social Reformer." *Journal of Negro Education* 18 (1949): 29–39.

Foster, Frances S. "The Plot of Ante-Bellum Slave Narratives." *Witnessing Slavery: The Development of Ante-Bellum Slave Narratives*. Westport, CT: Greenwood Press, 1979. 87–91, 148–49.

Garrison, William Lloyd. Rev. of William Wells Brown's *Experience, or How to Give a Northern Man a Backbone*. *The Liberator* (August 1, 1856): 124.

Gayle, Addison, Jr. "Paradigms of the Early Past." In *The Way of the New World: The Black Novel in America*. New York: Anchor Press, 1975. 1–24.

Gloster, Hugh M. *Negro Voices in American Fiction*. Chapel Hill: University of North Carolina Press, 1948.

Heermance, Noel J. *William Wells Brown and Clotelle, a Portrait of the Artist in the First Negro Novel*. Hamden, CT: Archon, 1969.

Hill, Patricia L., ed. *Call and Response: The Riverside Anthology of the African American Literary Tradition*. Boston: Houghton Mifflin, 1998.

Hopkins, Pauline. "William Wells Brown." *Colored American Magazine* 2 (1901): 232–36.

Hughes, Carl Milton. *The Negro Novelist*. New York: Citadel, 1953.

Jackson, Blyden. *A History of Afro-American Literature*. Vol. 1: *The Long Beginning, 1746–1895*. Baton Rouge: Louisiana State University Press, 1989.

Kamme-Erkel, Sybille. *Happily Ever After? Marriage and Its Rejection in Afro-American Novels*. (Ph.D. diss., Philipps University, 1988.) Frankfurt am Main: Peter Lang, 1989.

Katz, William L., ed. *Five Slave Narratives: A Compendium*. New York: Arno, 1968. 1–110.

Loggins, Vernon. *The Negro Author: His Development in America to 1900*. New York: Columbia University Press, 1931.

Margolies, Edward. "Ante-Bellum Slave Narratives: Their Place in American Literature." *Studies in Black Literature* 4 (Autumn 1973): 1–8.

Meier, August. *Negro Thought in America, 1880–1915*. Ann Arbor: University of Michigan Press, 1963.

Moore, Alonzo D. "Memoir of the Author." In *The Rising Son; or, The Antecedents and Advancement of the Colored Race*, by William Wells Brown. 1874. Reprinted New York: Negro Universities Press, 1970. 9–35.

Nelson, John Herbert. "Negro Characters in American Literature." *Humanistic Studies of the University of Kansas* 4 (1932): 583–85.

Osofsky, Gilbert. *Puttin' on Ole Massa: The Slave Narratives of Henry Bibb, William W. Brown, and Solomon Northrup*. New York: Harper, 1969.

Pawley, Thomas D. "The First Black Playwrights." *Black World* (April 1972): 16–24.

Phillips, Porter Williams. *W. W. Brown, Host*. New York: Fleming H. Revel, 1941.

Redding, Saunders J. "Let Freedom Ring." In *To Make a Poet Black*. 1939. New York: Cornell University Press, 1988. 19–48.

———. *They Came in Chains*. Philadelphia: J. B. Lippincott, 1959.

Sekora, John. "William Wells Brown." In *Fifty Southern Writers before 1900: A Bibliographical Sourcebook*. Ed. Robert Bain and Joseph M. Flora. New York: Greenwood Press, 1987. 44–55.

Starke, Juanita C. "Archetypal Patterns." In *Black Portraiture in American Fiction*. New York: Basic Books, 1971. 90–92.

Stepto, Robert B. "I Rose and Found My Voice: Narration, Authentication, and Authorial Control in Four Slave Narratives." In *From behind the Veil: A Study of Afro-American Narrative*. Urbana: University of Illinois Press, 1979. 3–31.

Takaki, Ronald. "Violence in Fantasy: The Fiction of William Wells Brown." In *Violence in the Black Imagination*. New York: Oxford University Press, 1993. 215–30.

Tischler, Nancy M. *Black Masks: Negro Characters in Modern Southern Fiction*. University Park: Pennsylvania State University Press, 1969.

Trent, Toni. "Stratification among Blacks by Black Authors." *Negro History Bulletin* 34.8 (December 1971): 179–82.

Turner, Darwin T. *In a Minor Chord: Three Afro-American Writers and Their Search for Identity*. Carbondale: Southern Illinois University Press, 1971.

Woodson, Carter G. *The Mind of the Negro as Reflected in Letters Written during the Crisis, 1800–1860*. New York: Negro Universities Press, 1926. 213–16, 349–83.

Yellin, Jean Fagan. "William Wells Brown." In *The Intricate Knot: Black Figures in American Literature, 1776–1863*. New York: New York University Press, 1972. 154–81.

CHARLES WADDELL CHESNUTT
(1858 – 1932)

Tracie Church Guzzio

BIOGRAPHY

Charles Waddell Chesnutt was born in 1858 in Cleveland, Ohio. His parents were free African Americans who left Fayetteville, North Carolina, in 1856. The family returned to Fayetteville in 1866. Chesnutt's life in Fayetteville would later form the basis for many of his works' important issues (Fayetteville would become Patesville in his fiction). Here Chesnutt became aware of the "color line." Both of Chesnutt's parents were the illegitimate children of white fathers, and some of Chesnutt's relatives were light enough to "pass." Chesnutt was soon forced to confront issues of color and race that would inform most of his writing. He would give special concern in some work to "passing." Also, Chesnutt would see first-hand the problems facing the South during and following Reconstruction, and he would hear folktales and stories about the days of slavery from patrons in his father's store. All of these experiences would in some way later be reflected in his writing.

In 1871 Chesnutt's mother died, and soon after he was forced to drop out of school to help support the family. Chesnutt continued his studies at home. At the age of fifteen, he became a teacher, and two years later, a principal. In 1878 he married Susan Perry (and would later become a father to two daughters). His new marital responsibilities and the rise in racial tension in the South following the Compromise of 1877 convinced Chesnutt that it was time to leave North Carolina. He first moved to New York, where he became a journalist and a stenographer. A year later, he returned to his birthplace, Cleveland. In 1887 Chesnutt passed the Ohio bar, and "The Goophered Grapevine," the first of his "conjure" stories, appeared in *Atlantic Monthly*. The following year he opened his own court reporting business, but he continued to write. Entries in journals that he kept during the years he was a teacher indicate that Chesnutt had long desired to be a writer (Brodhead, *The Journals* 139). But Chesnutt knew this was a risky dream; he had a family to support, and the chances of his becoming a successful writer in post-Reconstruction America were slim.

Still, Chesnutt continued writing in his spare time. Several of his short stories were published in the late 1880s. He also worked on *Rena Walden*, a novella that was rejected several times. In the mid-1890s, Chesnutt was asked to submit a collection of his short stories, and even though the manuscript was initially rejected, editor Walter Hines Page suggested that a collection of "conjure stories" might be accepted for publication. Chesnutt promptly composed six new stories (Brodhead, *The Conjure* 16); four of these new stories and three older ones were published together in 1899 as *The Conjure Woman*. Later the same year, Houghton Mifflin published another collection of short stories, *The Wife of His Youth and Other Stories of the Color Line*. Chesnutt felt confident enough at last to pursue writing full-time and closed his business.

Chesnutt revised and retitled *Rena Walden*, and in 1900 Houghton Mifflin published it as the novel *The House behind the Cedars*. It did not bring the attention that the short stories had; nevertheless, Houghton Mifflin published Chesnutt's next novel, *The Marrow of Tradition*, in 1901. Based on the Wilmington, North Carolina, massacre of 1898, the novel elicited harsh criticism and controversy. Chesnutt began to feel that his career was not going to sustain his family. He returned to stenography work while he continued writing. In 1904 his last published story, "Baxter's Procrustes," appeared in *Atlantic Monthly*. The following year his last novel, *The Colonel's Dream*, was published. Even before its publication, Chesnutt was forced to give up his writing career and return to stenography full-time.

Chesnutt remained active in the arts and in social protest, arguing in 1915 against the showing of the film *The Birth of a Nation* in Cleveland. Chesnutt's enmity toward the film (and the novel it was based on, Thomas Dixon's *The Clansmen*) was obvious to those who knew the man and his work; the film presented the very visions of the South and the African American that Chesnutt had spent his literary career trying to dispute and rewrite. The protest was successful. Even though he never published works of fiction again, he continued to write. He was awarded the Spingarn Medal for literary service from the National Association for the Advancement of Colored People (NAACP) in 1928. When he died in 1932, he left six unpublished novels, including *Mandy Oxendine*, which finally saw publication in 1997.

MAJOR WORKS AND THEMES

In a journal entry dated May 29, 1880, Chesnutt writes that if he were to become a writer, the purpose of his work "would be not so much of the elevation of the colored people as the elevation of the white" (Brodhead, *The Journals* 139). It is generally accepted by scholars that this idea guided Chesnutt throughout his career.

This is certainly the case in his first published story collection, *The Conjure Woman*. The work (generally considered a short story cycle) seemed to its nineteenth-century readers to follow in the vein of popular southern plantation fiction written by Thomas Nelson Page and Joel Chandler Harris. The work, a frame narrative, comprises several tales told by Uncle Julius to his employer, John, and John's wife, Annie, both northerners living in the South. The work is most often compared to Harris' "Uncle Remus" stories. But to a critical reader, *The Conjure Woman* is not a mimetic piece of folklore; it is a work designed to "elevate" its white readers. It manipulates the conventions of plantation fiction in an attempt to criticize portraits that suggested that ex-slaves longed for the "good old days of slavery." Such portraits perpetuated the romantic myth of the Old South that the plantation "school" sought to fashion. Uncle Julius uses his stories, through indirection, to indict the system of slavery. The stories also allow Julius to present his own historiography of slavery, question the idea that white experience is more valid than that of the African American (through the frame narrative that balances Julius' stories with John's narration), and judge an economic system that "dehumanized him and which continues to emasculate him in his present relationship with his employer" (Dixon 190). As Craig Werner has pointed out, the work is a "folk deconstruction," an act of "signifying" (8). Such signifying and subversion Eric Sundquist calls "Chesnutt's cakewalk," a style that defines the majority of his expression (*To Wake* 279). John Edgar Wideman suggests that this characteristic of Chesnutt's work qualifies him as a "major innovator" in using literature to validate African American experience while celebrating African American oral cultural forms ("Charles Chesnutt and" 60). "Conjure" is transformation, as the stories and these critics suggest, but it is also used in its true sense as medicine. Julius often tells his stories to soothe the ailing Annie, and metaphorically, Chesnutt implies that sharing stories, thus promoting cultural understanding, can cure the disease of racism and begin to heal the wounds of slavery.

The Wife of His Youth and Other Stories of the Color Line focuses on the history of miscegenation, primarily on the stories of African Americans living on the "color line," many middle-class and living in Groveland (Cleveland). These were stories representative of Chesnutt's own life. Chesnutt displaced in these stories the popular stereotype of the tragic mulatto. The stories examine the effects of miscegenation on individuals and the caste and color system that dehumanizes them. The themes expressed in these stories are developed further in Chesnutt's novels where one of the central issues for mixed-race characters is their articulation of identity and their relationship to the past and future of America (Wonham 57). This is the case in the novel *The House behind the Cedars*, where the heroine, Rena Walden, decides to "pass" in order to achieve happiness and prosperity. The novel's examination of these issues revises the traditional tragic mulatta story into a criticism of the false promises of the American Dream.

Chesnutt's second novel, *The Marrow of Tradition*, continues to explore life on the color line in the context of the Wilmington massacre (here called Wellington). Here the metaphor of twins or doubles illustrates the interconnectedness of white and black Americans, their inherent "mulatto" culture, history, and identity (Knadler 440). It also explores the inevitability of violence in a society that systematically refuses to see these interrelationships. That refusal also suggests to Sundquist the novel's argument that the post-Reconstructionist era is a time of "second slavery" (also examined in Mark Twain's *Pudd'nhead Wilson*) (*To Wake* 453; Kawash 90). While many early critics suggested that Chesnutt posited Dr. Miller in the novel as the ideal American, recent scholars have argued that Chesnutt's ideal is Janet Miller (George and Pressman 298), who stands up to those who have destroyed her but shows them mercy and compassion in the spirit of humanity and healing.

Chesnutt's final novel, *The Colonel's Dream*, follows the course of Colonel French, whose dream of the Old South inspires him to rebuild his old home and community. The absolute failure of his dream and the community's inability to change illustrate Chesnutt's own "waning faith in the capacity of whites to advance the cause of democracy by dismantling the color bar" (Bell 64). It may have been this belief that convinced Chesnutt that he had failed in "elevating" the consciousness of white America, furthering his decision to give up his literary career.

CRITICAL RECEPTION

Early critics praised Chesnutt's work for his characterization, psychological insight, and attention to realistic details, and William Dean Howells mentioned him in the same breath as "Mr. James and Miss Jewett" (Render, *Charles* 141–42). Reaction to *The House behind the Cedars* was more mixed, however. Critics still praised his style and purpose, but some white reviewers sensed that the subject matter might be too sensitive for southern readers (Render, *Charles* 143). *The Marrow of Tradition* received even harsher reviews. The consensus was that this was an important, but disturbing and inflammatory, work (Sundquist, *The Marrow* xliii). Howells called the novel "bitter" (Farnsworth 39). Reaction to *The Colonel's Dream* was also mixed, and some have argued (Andrews, "Baxters"; Hemenway, "Baxter's") that Chesnutt's final short story, "Baxter's Procrustes," is a bitter response to those critics who failed to see the purpose behind his work and judge his ability by the color of his skin (Hemenway, "Baxter's" 183). Chesnutt's popularity waned in the 1920s (his books had already gone out of print). Later he received little critical notice, with some notable exceptions, one being J. Saunders Redding's assessment of him as an important "transitional figure" between the Civil War and the Harlem Renaissance (68). But it was not until the 1960s that Chesnutt began to seriously reappear on the literary scene. A few of his short stories were anthologized, and scholars inspired by the resurgent interest in African American literature reexamined Chesnutt's work, which Wideman noted had been seriously neglected by readers and critics ("Charles W. Chesnutt" 128). This omission soon changed. Important work done by Trudier Harris, William Andrews, Robert Hemenway, and other young critics reevaluated Chesnutt's position in the African American literary tradition. Sylvia

Lyons Render edited Chesnutt's previously uncollected stories, including "Baxter's Procrustes," in 1974. For the first time, critics examined the purpose and style of Chesnutt's conjure stories within an African American literary context. Literary historians today acknowledge Chesnutt's importance in "inaugurating" the African American short story, in showing that African American life was worthy material for literature (Andrews, *The Collected* xvi–xvii), in the development of modernism and the Harlem Renaissance (Baker 41–47), and in influencing the development of new forms such as the neoslave narrative. Most of the new scholarship centered on *The Conjure Woman*, but his novels also received renewed attention, much going to *The Marrow of Tradition*, which would be called, in a complete turnaround from early criticism, "one of the most significant historical novels in American Literature" (Sundquist, *The Marrow* vii). Chesnutt is now firmly in place as one of the important writers of American literature, a position that he desired and worked for during his lifetime but couldn't achieve until 100 years after his first book was published. Chesnutt's literary career is a testament to the difficulties that early African American novelists had breaking the color line that kept their voice restricted or silenced.

BIBLIOGRAPHY

Works by Charles Waddell Chesnutt

Novels

The House behind the Cedars. Boston: Houghton Mifflin, 1900.
The Marrow of Tradition. Boston: Houghton Mifflin, 1901.
The Colonel's Dream. New York: Doubleday Page, 1905.
Mandy Oxendine. Urbana: University of Illinois Press, 1997.

Short Story Collections

The Conjure Woman. Boston: Houghton Mifflin, 1899.
The Wife of His Youth and Other Stories of the Color Line. Boston: Houghton Mifflin, 1899.

Studies of Charles Waddell Chesnutt

Andrews, William L. " 'Baxter's Procrustes': Some More Light on the Biographical Connection." *Black American Literature Forum* 11 (1977): 75–78, 89.
———. "Chesnutt's Patesville: The Presence and Influence of the Past in *The House behind the Cedars*." *CLA Journal* 15 (1972): 284–94.
———, ed. and intro. *The Collected Stories of Charles W. Chesnutt*. New York: Penguin, 1992.
———. *The Literary Career of Charles W. Chesnutt*. Baton Rouge: Louisiana State University Press, 1980.
Baker, Houston. *Modernism and the Harlem Renaissance*. Chicago: University of Chicago Press, 1987.
Baldwin, Richard. "The Art of *The Conjure Woman*." *American Literature* 43 (1971): 383–98.

Bell, Bernard W. *The Afro-American Novel and Its Tradition*. Amherst: University of Massachusetts Press, 1987.

Bone, Robert. *Down Home: Origins of the Afro-American Short Story*. New York: Columbia University Press, 1975.

Brodhead, Richard, ed. and intro. *The Conjure Woman and Other Conjure Tales*. Durham: Duke University Press, 1993.

———. *The Journals of Charles W. Chesnutt*. Durham, NC: Duke University Press, 1993.

Chesnutt, Helen. *Charles Waddell Chesnutt: Pioneer of the Color Line*. Chapel Hill: University of North Carolina Press, 1952.

Delmar, P. Jay. "The Mask as Theme and Structure: Charles W. Chesnutt's 'The Sheriff's Children' and 'The Passing of Grandison.' " *American Literature* 51 (1979): 364–75.

Dixon, Melvin. "The Teller as Folk Trickster in Chesnutt's *The Conjure Woman*." *CLA Journal* 18 (1974): 186–97.

Duncan, Charles. *The Absent Man: The Narrative Craft of Charles Chesnutt*. Athens: Ohio University Press, 1998.

Elder, Arlene. *The 'Hindered Hand': Cultural Implications of Early African-American Fiction*. Wesport, CT: Greenwood, 1978.

Ellison, Curtis W., and E. W. Metcalf, Jr. *Charles W. Chesnutt: A Reference Guide*. Boston: G. K. Hall, 1977.

Farnsworth, Robert. "Charles Chesnutt and the Color Line." *Minor American Novelists*. Ed. Charles Hoyt. Carbondale: Southern Illinois University Press, 1971. 28–40.

Fienberg, Lorne. "Charles W. Chesnutt's *The Wife of His Youth*: The Unveiling of the Black Story-Teller." *American Transcendental Quarterly* 4 (1990): 219–37.

George, Marjorie, and Richard Pressman. "Confronting the Shadow: Psycho-Political Repression in Chesnutt's *The Marrow of Tradition*." *Phylon* 48 (1987): 287–98.

Hackenberry, Charles, ed. and introduction. *Mandy Oxendine*, by Charles W. Chesnutt. Urbana: University of Illinois Press, 1997.

Harris, Trudier. "Chesnutt's Frank Fowler: A Failure of Purpose?" *CLA Journal* 22 (1979): 215–28.

Hattenhaur, Darryl. "Racial and Textual Miscegenation in Chesnutt's *The House behind the Cedars*." *Mississippi Quarterly* 47 (1993–1994): 26–45.

Heermance, J. Noel. *Charles Waddell Chesnutt: America's First Great Black Novelist*. Hamden, CT: Archon, 1974.

Hemenway, Robert. " 'Baxter's Procrustes': Irony and Protest." *CLA Journal* 18 (1974): 172–85.

———. "The Functions of Folklore in Charles Chesnutt's *The Conjure Woman*." *Journal of the Folklore Institute* 13 (1976): 283–309.

———. "Gothic Sociology: Charles Chesnutt and the Gothic Mode." *Studies in the Literary Imagination* 7.1 (1974): 101–19.

Kawash, Samira. *Dislocating the Color Line: Identity, Hybridity, and Singularity in African-American Narrative*. Stanford, CA: Stanford University Press, 1997.

Keller, Frances Richardson. *An American Crusade: The Life of Charles Waddell Chesnutt*. Provo: Brigham Young University Press, 1978.

Knadler, Stephen P. "Untragic Mulatto: Charles Chesnutt and the Discourse of Whiteness." *American Literary History* 8 (1996): 426–48.

MacKethan, Lucinda. *The Dream of Arcady: Place and Time in Southern Literature*. Baton Rouge: Louisiana State University Press, 1980.

McElrath, Joseph R., Jr., and Robert C. Leitz III, eds. *"To Be an Author:" Letters of Charles W. Chesnutt, 1899–1905.* Princeton: Princeton University Press, 1997.

McGowan, Todd. "Acting without the Father: Charles Chesnutt's New Aristocrat." *American Literary Realism* 30.1 (1997): 59–74.

Molyneaux, Sandra. "Expanding the Collective Memory: Charles W. Chesnutt's Conjure Woman Tales." *Memory, Narrative, and Identity: New Essays in Ethnic American Literatures.* Ed. Amiritjit Singh et al. Boston: Northeastern University Press, 1994. 164–78.

Myers, Karen Magee. "Mythic Patterns in Charles Waddell Chesnutt's *The Conjure Woman* and Ovid's *Metamorphoses.*" *Black American Literature Forum* 13 (1979): 13–17.

Nowatzki, Robert. "Passing in a White Genre: Charles W. Chesnutt's Negation of the Plantation Tradition in *The Conjure Woman.*" *American Literary Realism* 27 (1995): 20–36.

Pettis, Joyce. "The Literary Imagination and the Historic Event: Chesnutt's Use of History in *The Marrow of Tradition.*" *South Atlantic Review* 55.4 (1990): 37–48.

Pickens, Ernestine Williams. *Charles W. Chesnutt and the Progressive Movement.* New York: Pace University Press, 1994.

Redding, J. Saunders. *To Make a Poet Black.* Chapel Hill: University of North Carolina Press, 1939.

Render, Sylvia Lyons. *Charles W. Chesnutt.* Boston: Twayne, 1980.

———, ed. and Intro. *The Short Fiction of Charles W. Chesnutt.* Washington, D.C.: Howard University Press, 1974.

Sollors, Werner. "The Goopher in Charles Chesnutt's Conjure Tales: Superstition, Ethnicity, and Modern Metamorphosis." *Letterature d'America* 6 (1986): 107–29.

Stepto, Robert B. " 'The Simple but Intensely Human Inner Life of Slavery': Storytelling and the Revision of History in Charles W. Chesnutt's 'Uncle Julius Stories.' " *History and Tradition in Afro-American Culture.* Ed. Gunter Lenz. Frankfurt: Campus Verlag, 1984. 29–55.

Sundquist, Eric, ed. and introduction. *The Marrow of Tradition.* New York: Penguin, 1993.

———. *To Wake the Nations: Race in the Making of American Literature.* Cambridge: Harvard University Press, 1993.

Werner, Craig Hansen. *Playing the Changes: From Afro-Modernism to the Jazz Impulse.* Urbana: University of Illinois Press, 1994.

White, Jeanette. "Baring Slavery's Darkest Secrets: Charles Chesnutt's Conjure Tales as Masks of Truth." *Southern Literary Journal* 27 (Fall 1997): 85–103.

Wideman, John Edgar. "Charles W. Chesnutt: *The Marrow of Tradition.*" *American Scholar* 42 (1973): 128–34.

———. "Charles Chesnutt and the WPA Narratives: The Oral and Literate Roots of Afro-American Literature." *The Slave's Narrative.* Ed. Charles T. Davis and Henry Louis Gates Jr. New York: Oxford University Press, 1985. 59–78.

Wonham, Henry B. *Charles W. Chesnutt: A Study of the Short Fiction.* New York: Twayne, 1998.

ANNA JULIA COOPER
(1858?–1964)

Vivian M. May

BIOGRAPHY

Anna Julia Cooper was born into slavery in Raleigh, North Carolina. Her mother, Hannah Stanley Haywood, was a slave, and her father, George Washington Haywood, was her mother's master. Living to the age of about 105, Cooper led a long life of activism as an author, educator, community activist, Pan-Africanist, and woman's rights advocate.

After learning to read and write from her mother, Cooper attended St. Augustine's Normal and Collegiate Institute from 1868 to 1877. Following the 1879 death of her husband, George Cooper, whom she had married in 1877, Cooper attended Oberlin College in Ohio, where she earned her B.A. in 1884 and M.A. in 1887. Later, while still teaching at the M Street High School in Washington, Cooper earned her Ph.D. in 1925 at the Sorbonne, University of Paris, the fourth African American woman to earn a Ph.D. Her thesis was entitled, "L'Attitude de la France a l'Egard de l'Esclavage Pendant la Revolution." Cooper also studied at the Guilde Internationale, Paris, from 1911 to 1913 and at Columbia University from 1914 to 1917; at this time, she published an updated version of a French text, *Le Pèlerinage de Charlemagne: Voyage à Jérusalem et à Constantinople*. Additionally, Cooper raised seven children—two foster and five adopted.

Spanning her entire life, Cooper's academic career included teaching at Oberlin, Wilberforce, and St. Augustine's; serving as principal at Washington's M Street (later, Dunbar) High School from 1902 to 1906 and as teacher from 1910 to 1930; chairing the Department of Languages, Lincoln University, Missouri, from 1906 to 1910; and founding and serving as president of Frelinghuysen University, Washington, D.C., from 1930 to 1941.

Best known for her 1892 book, *A Voice from the South*, Cooper's writing is but one element of a lifetime of activism. Her academic career can be considered activist because Cooper approached knowledge as a form of power to be used to benefit others and because she worked to dismantle stereotypes about the "inherent" intellectual deficiencies of African Americans. Personally, Cooper fought for the right to pursue "classical" (i.e., "masculine") studies at the baccalaureate level and beyond. Moreover, Cooper did not see herself as an isolated individual but as one element of a larger body politic. As Elizabeth Alexander argues, "Cooper articulates a philosophy that runs directly counter to the notion of the singular intellect or genius" (351).

Cooper's activism, especially regarding class issues, is somewhat embryonic in *Voice*, but her community work during the decades following this publication demonstrates the range of her commitment and outreach. Cooper saw herself as among the intellectual leaders of her time. In other words, her self-definition fits both W.E.B. Du Bois'* "Talented Tenth" as well as the "lifting as we climb" sense of collective responsibility in the Club movement. However, living her entire adult life as a single woman (except for two years of marriage), Cooper never benefited, as did many of her contemporaries, from the economic privileges of heterosexuality (Lemert and Bhan 19). Cooper was rich in cultural capital, but never economically wealthy.

Cooper's position as an intellectual leader is evidenced not only by her membership in the elite Negro Academy and her education at Oberlin, Columbia, and the Sorbonne but also by her participation in the 1890 American Conference of Educators, 1893 Congress of Representative Women, Second Hampton Negro Conference in 1894, 1896 Conference of the National Federation of Colored Women, and the 1900 Pan African Conference, where Cooper presented a paper, "The Negro Problem in America."

Cooper saw her intellectual position as integral to her membership in, and responsibility to, a diverse black community. Not only did she help found the first colored Young Women's Christian Association (YWCA) (the Phillis Wheatley* Y) and division of the Camp Fire Girls, but she also helped to establish and run a colored settlement house, which was entirely volunteer-run for its first three decades. It offered child care for working mothers, milk for babies, activity clubs for boys and girls, training for kindergarten teachers, and evening classes for adults in literacy, music, and art. The house also offered domestic service training under the ideal that black women could thereby demand higher wages.

In addition, as principal and teacher at Washington's M Street High School (razed in 1976), Cooper firmly advocated that black students be offered college preparatory courses in Greek, Latin, mathematics, and language arts. Like Du Bois, Cooper disagreed with Booker T. Washington's* philosophy of vocational education as exemplary for African Americans. In fact, there is some evidence that Washington's colleagues on the all-white school board were behind Cooper's de facto dismissal as principal of M Street High School amid false accusations that she was romantically involved with her foster child John Love (Lemert and Bhan 9–10).

Personally and professionally, Cooper advocated for a range of educational models. She did not disdain education that did not lead to Ivy League degrees (which many M Street/Dunbar students went on to gain). Cooper believed that all people should have access to reading, writing, and mathematics. She therefore helped to found Frelinghuysen University and later served as president, even allowing her home to be used for classrooms. The school had "satellite" locations around Washington, D.C., for easy access and offered courses at night when working people could attend.

MAJOR WORKS AND THEMES

Cooper is best known for her privately published 1892 collection of speeches and essays, *A Voice from the South by a Black Woman of the South*. Her later essays, pamphlets, booklets, memoirs, and doctoral dissertation build upon themes present in *A Voice* and demonstrate a lifelong commitment to analyzing what contemporary black feminist scholars name the politics of domination. Such theorists examine how intersecting racial, gender, class, and colonial dominations function in concert and are experienced simultaneously. Like Cooper, they argue that seemingly separate forms of oppression must be addressed holistically and simultaneously, not hierarchically and atomistically.

Cooper's multifaceted genre in *A Voice* is interesting in this context, combining third- and first-person narration, autobiography, cultural criticism, and literary and historical analysis. Frances Smith Foster explains that black women writing at the turn of the century redefined "the uses and possibilities of literature and of language in ways that served their own purposes" (22). Thus, Cooper questions scientific, historical, and cultural theories of her time that relegate African American women to the farthest margins of American society. Simultaneously, Cooper places her writing within those marginal spaces, creating an embodied analysis that is both individually marked and collectively significant— what Patricia Hill Collins, a century later, identifies as an Afrocentric feminist epistemology.

In *A Voice*, Cooper underscores how sexual, racial, class, and colonial oppressions are interconnected. She writes against dualistic and oppositional categories, revealing how "opposites" such as man/woman or black/white are relational and interdependent. Cooper explains how systems of oppression are institutionalized and mutually reinforcing, and she criticizes white feminists for not recognizing this and acting accordingly. She writes,

The cause of freedom is not the cause of a race or a sect, a party or a class,—it is the cause of human kind, the very birthright of humanity. . . . It is not the intelligent woman vs. the ignorant woman; nor the white woman vs. the black, the brown, and the red,—it is not even the cause of woman vs. man. . . . [Woman's] cause is linked with that of every agony that has been dumb—every wrong that needs a voice. (120–22)

Cooper also points to a key paradox of domination: simultaneous privilege and oppression. Whiteness mitigates white women's oppression just as maleness privileges black men in some contexts. Cooper sarcastically describes "Wimodaughsis (. . . a woman's culture club whose name is made up of the . . . four words wives, mothers, daughters, and sisters)." One day, "Pandora's box is opened . . . when a colored lady . . . applies for admission" because the white women had "not calculated that there were any wives, mothers, daughters, and sisters, except white ones." She ironically suggests, "*Whimodaughsis* would sound just as well, and then it need mean just *white mothers, daughters and sisters*" (80, 81).

Analogously, Cooper criticizes "race men," emphasizing the impossibility of elevating the race without elevating black women: African Americans "might as well expect to grow trees from leaves as hope to build up a civilization or a manhood without taking into consideration our women" (78). Just as she points to the futility of a "women's" movement that includes only some women, Cooper draws attention to the paradox underlying racial uplift that "lifts" only half of a people, for women are "at once both the lever and the fulcrum for uplifting the race" (45).

Cooper also points to class or "caste" as an important consideration in working toward social transformation. She asks, "Is not woman's cause broader, and deeper, and grander, than a blue stocking debate or an aristocratic pink tea?" (123). Cooper writes of tenements in which the urban poor are forced to live, the profitless and short lives of rural tenant farmers, and black women's limited access to adequate employment. Cooper queries, "[H]ow many have ever given a thought to the pinched and down-trodden colored women bending over wash-tubs and ironing boards—with children to feed and house rent to pay, wood to buy, soap and starch to furnish?" (254–55).

Cooper articulates a black feminist viewpoint rooted in her distinct experiences in American society. She writes, "The colored woman of to-day occupies, one may say, a unique position in this country . . . She is confronted by both a woman question and a race problem, and is as yet an unknown or unacknowledged factor in both" (134). Thus, lest it remain "unacknowledged," Cooper identifies a multifaceted black women's tradition that contests race and gender oppression. Cooper recognizes Frances Watkins Harper,* Sojourner Truth,* Amanda Smith, Charlotte Forten Grimké,* Hallie Quinn Brown, and Fannie Jackson Coppin, among many others. She argues that black women's voices and experiences should be heard and considered and reminds readers of an extant body of knowledge. Moreover, Cooper asserts that black women's marginality is key to the depth of their cultural analysis: "The colored woman, then, should not be ignored because her bark is resting in the silent waters of the sheltered cove. She is watching the movements of the contestants none the less and is all the better qualified, perhaps, to weigh and judge and advise because not herself in the excitement of the race" (138).

Rejecting dualistic hierarchies that tore apart political coalitions during abolition and Reconstruction, Cooper pointedly asks, "Why should woman become plaintiff in a suit versus the Indian, or the Negro or any other race or class who have been crushed under the iron heel of Anglo-Saxon power and selfishness?" (123). Radically, Cooper suggests that race, gender, and class are social constructs and not biological essences. She declares that "there is nothing irretrievably wrong in the shape of the black man's skull" (26) and that "race, color, sex, [and] condition" should be "realized to be the accidents, not the substance of life" (125).

Further rejecting determinist arguments for human hierarchies, Cooper suggests that social Darwinism, sexism, classism, racism, violence, and imperialism interconnect under overly prevalent "masculine" thought. She asks,

Whence came this apotheosis of greed and cruelty? Whence this sneaking admiration we all have for bullies and prize-fighters? Whence the self-congratulation of 'dominant' races . . . ? Whence the scorn of so-called weak or unwarlike races and individuals, and the very comfortable assurance that it is their manifest destiny to be wiped out as vermin before this advancing civilization? . . . The world of thought under the predominant man-influence, unmollified and unrestrained by its complementary force, would become like Daniel's fourth beast. (51, 53)

Cooper asserts that a balance of complementary masculine and feminine forces of power is necessary for a "progressive peace" (149).

Her concepts of masculine and feminine forces and spheres of thought are not biologically determined. There are masculine and feminine spheres of action, thought, and influence—not male and female spheres. Thought is not determined or constrained by one's "natural" body; men can (and should) think "feminine" thoughts, and women, "masculine" ones. Cooper calls for women to be self-reliant and independent and for men to be tender and sensitive (61–69).

Cooper's social philosophy substantiates her visionary status. Cooper writes, for example, that a social settlement creates "a 'level bridge' reaching sheer to the shores of complete emancipation" ("The Social Settlement"; Lemert and Bhan 223). At the close of the twentieth century, we continue to debate a level playing field in politics, education, economics, and culture. Thus, not only did Cooper anticipate Du Bois' assertion that race would be pivotal in the twentieth century—she also anticipated many ideas central to contemporary analysis and debate.

CRITICAL RECEPTION

Critical analyses of Cooper include literary, historical, sociological, and theoretical approaches. Hutchinson's and Gabel's analyses are primarily biographical and historical in nature. Hutchinson's is authoritative for countless details about Cooper's life, such as Cooper's cofounding the Colored Woman's League and her active participation in the National Negro Women's Club. James examines how Du Bois borrowed from Cooper, but often without credit: she scrutinizes his paternalism. Alexander and Foster attend to form, examining genre innovations as political strategies and creative sites of agency. Alexander identifies corporeality in Cooper's work that writes black female subjectivity into existence while refusing a mind/body split. Foster reads Cooper as a prophet who fought silencing through linguistic experimentation. Collins and hooks connect their black feminist theories to Cooper's, building from a frequently overlooked intellectual tradition, much as Cooper identifies numerous black women to whom she is indebted.

hooks also contributes to debates about whether Cooper adopts (white) essentialist notions of true womanhood—contending that she did use questionable notions of femininity. Washington asserts that Cooper problematically swallows Victorian ideals of domesticity and therefore demonstrates indifference for ordinary black women. Nonetheless, Washington praises Cooper's "forceful, well-argued . . . black feminist thought" ("Introduction" li). Baker-Fletcher identifies womanist vocality in A Voice, describing Part I as solo and Part II as chorus. Yet she also contends that Cooper unreflexively speaks "for" African Americans as an elite person.

du Cille contends Cooper's ideals lay beyond most black women's economic realities but views Cooper as conflicted, internalizing ideals of true womanhood and ethnocentrism while also fighting them. According to Tate, Cooper used the language of true womanhood as a rhetorical strategy to focus on black women as a group. Carby argues that Cooper critiqued true womanhood and was clearly antiessentialist in her radically connecting domestic and international colonialism by identifying the intersections of racism, sexism, and imperialism. Lemert and Bhan explore such ambiguities in critical approaches to Cooper's image and ideas, suggesting that Cooper's words be read in the context of her life's actions to understand such amibiguities in their appropriate intellectual and historical contexts.

BIBLIOGRAPHY

Works by Anna Julia Cooper

Manuscripts and Papers

Moorland-Springarn Research Center, Howard University.

Essays

A Voice from the South by a Black Woman of the South. 1892. New York: Oxford University Press, 1988.
"The Intellectual Progress of the Colored Women in the United States since the Emancipation Proclamation: A Response to Fannie Barrier Williams." 1893. In Lemert and Bhan 201–5.
"The Ethics of the Negro Question." [N.p. 1902]. In Lemert and Bhan 206–15.

"The Social Settlement: What It Is, and What It Does." Washington, DC: Murray Bros.
  Press, c. 1913. In Lemert and Bhan 216–23.
"Sketches from a Teacher's Notebook: Loss of Speech through Isolation." N.p., 1923? In
  Lemert and Bhan 224–29.
"The Humor of Teaching." *Crisis* (November 1930). In Lemert and Bhan 232–35.
"My Racial Philosophy." N.p., 1930. In Lemert and Bhan 236–37.
"The Negro's Dialect." N.p., 1930s? In Lemert and Bhan 238–47.
"On Education." N.p., 1930s? In Lemert and Bhan 248–58.
"Angry Saxons and Negro Education." *Crisis* (May 1938). In Lemert and Bhan 259–61.
"Hitler and the Negro." N.p., 1942? In Lemert and Bhan 262–65.

History

Ed. and Foreword. *Le Pèlerinage de Charlemagne: Voyage à Jérusalem et à Constantinople.*
  N.p., 1917.
"L'Attitude de la France a l'Egard de l'Esclavage Pendant la Revolution." Diss., University
  of Paris, 1925. Trans. Frances Richardson Keller as *Slavery and the French Revolu-
  tionists (1788–1805).* Lewiston, NY: Mellen Press, 1988.
"Equality of Races and the Democratic Movement." N.p., (1925) 1945. In Lemert and
  Bhan 291–98.
"Legislative Measures concerning Slavery in the United States." N.p., 1925? 1942? In
  Lemert and Bhan 299–304.

Memoirs and Reflections

The Third Step. N.p., 1945–1950? In Lemert and Bhan 320–30.
*Personal Recollections of the Grimke Family and the Life and Writings of Charlotte Forten
  Grimke.* N.p., 1951.

Studies of Anna Julia Cooper

Alexander, Elizabeth. " 'We Must Be about Our Father's Business'; Anna Julia Cooper
  and the In-Corporation of the Nineteenth-Century African-American Woman
  Intellectual." *Signs* 20.2 (Winter 1995): 336–56.
Baker-Fletcher, Karen. *A Singing Something: Womanist Reflections on Anna Julia Cooper.*
  New York: Crossroads, 1994.
Carby, Hazel V. *Reconstructing Womanhood: The Emergence of the Afro-American Woman
  Novelist.* New York: Oxford University Press, 1987.
Chateauvert, Melinda. "The Third Step: Anna Julia Cooper and Black Education in the
  District of Columbia, 1919–1960." *Sage,* Student Supplement (1988): 7–13.
Collins, Patricia Hill. *Black Feminist Thought: Knowledge, Consciousness, and the Politics of
  Empowerment.* London: Unwin Hyman, 1990.
duCille, Anne. *The Coupling Convention.* New York: Oxford University Press, 1993.
———. "The Occult of True Black Womanhood: Critical Demeanor and Black Feminist
  Studies." *Signs* 19.3 (1994): 591–629.
Foster, Frances Smith. "Testing and Testifying: The Word, the Other, and African Amer-
  ican Women Writers." In *Written by Herself: Literary Production by African Amer-
  ican Women. 1746–1892.* Bloomington: Indiana University Press, 1993. 1–22.

Gabel, Leona C. *From Slavery to the Sorbonne and Beyond: The Life and Writings of Anna J. Cooper*. Northampton, MA: Smith College History Department, 1982.

Giddings, Paula. *When and Where I Enter: The Impact of Black Women on Race and Sex in America*. New York: Bantam, 1984.

Harley, Sharon. "Anna J. Cooper: A Voice for Black Women." In *The Afro-American Woman: Struggles and Images*. Ed. Paula Giddings, Hazel Carby, Sharon Harley, and Rosalyn Terborg-Penn. Port Washington, NY: Kennikat Press, 1978. 87–96.

hooks, bell. *Ain't I a Woman: Black Women and Feminism*. Boston: South End Press, 1981.

Hutchinson, Louise Daniel. *Anna J. Cooper: A Voice from the South*. Washington, DC: Smithsonian Press, 1981.

James, Joy. "The Profeminist Politics of W.E.B. Du Bois with Respect to Anna Julia Cooper and Ida B. Wells Barnett." In *W.E.B. Du Bois on Race and Culture: Philosophy, Politics and Poetics*. Ed. Bernard W. Bell, et al. New York: Routledge, 1996. 141–60.

Lemert, Charles, and Esme Bhan, eds. *The Voice of Anna Julia Cooper*. New York: Rowman and Littlefield, 1998.

Tate, Claudia. *Domestic Allegories of Political Desire*. New York: Oxford University Press, 1992.

Washington, Mary Helen. "Anna Julia Cooper: The Black Feminist Voice of the 1890s." *Legacy: A Journal of American Women Writers* 4.2 (1987): 3–15.

———. "Introduction." In *A Voice from the South*, by Anna Julia Cooper. 1892. New York: Oxford University Press, 1988. xxvii–liv.

COUNTEE CULLEN
(1903 – 1946)

Gilbert N.M.O. Morris

BIOGRAPHY

Countee Cullen was born Countee Porter, May 30, 1903. By all accounts, no one is certain where he was born. Some say Louisville, Kentucky; others, Baltimore; others still, New York City. Cullen's origins are shrouded in this sort of mystery. The poet himself gave conflicting accounts of his birthplace. Gerald Early explicates, in his brilliant Introduction to an anthology of Cullen's poetry, on the complications of determining even the poet's height. While our knowledge of his parentage is more secure, it seems typical that he should have had two sets of parents as well. Moreover, since he was not adopted until 1918 at age fifteen—by Dr. and Mrs. Frederick A. Cullen—he was old enough to remember another life, particularly with his maternal grandmother, giving further credence to a dual origin. Perhaps, without becoming too Freudian, this elusivity of origins set Cullen against all forms of explicit categorization in his later life, which came to be a central issue in the way he regarded himself as a poet.

The Reverend Dr. Cullen imbued the young Countee with an indelible sense of Christian anxiety, which shows itself remarkably in poems such as "Yet Do I Marvel," "Simon the Cyrenian," and particularly "Shroud of Color." His relationship with his adoptive parents was apparently an intimate one. Particularly, he loved his mother's singing—again, perhaps an influence over the way he perceived poetry as muse-song, though that may have come from a familiarity with the classical Roman poets, from whom his ersatz paganism seems derived. The young Cullen was an excellent student who distinguished himself at every school he attended. Most famous among these schools was DeWitt Clinton, which was also attended by James Baldwin—who was taught by Cullen himself. As a man of prodigious accomplishments, Countee's academic success must have made the Reverend Cullen quite proud. He took the young man on numerous trips to Europe and the Middle East and within the United States, where they traveled as father and son, alone. Countee himself seemed reciprocally affectionate. He wrote a number of poems directly concerning his paternal love—"Lines for My Father, Dad" and "Fruit of the Flower."

Countee Cullen attended New York University (NYU) from 1922 to 1925 for his undergraduate studies at a time when it was still offering the "classical tripos" of languages, sciences, and philosophy. Here Cullen showed an experimental impulse associated in this century mostly with W. H. Auden. Shakespearean sonnets, Spencer's turn, quatrains, rime and terza rima—all seem to find their way into his expressive forms. It appears to have been this education that flowered in Cullen's imagination. Although he had shown a tendency away from the vocabulary of the hymnbook and the King James version (having redacted Alan Seeger's "I Have a Rendezvous with Death" into "I Have a Rendezvous with Life" in high school), he wrote nearly all the poems upon which his renown has been established as an undergraduate. His poems were the first (with exceptions for Paul Laurence Dunbar*) wholly sustained by an independent personality that was not merely reactionary but learned. As such, he was the first poet who was black whose work demonstrated metaphorical tensions between sensibilities, without actively selecting one of them. This may be seen plainly in the poem "Yet Do I Marvel," but it appears more simply in "Incident."

"Incident," short as it is, has a slight elegiac feel but without being enveloped in "baptismal jargon." The most subtle moments are extended in the use of the words "old" and "whit." At first one slips easily over the word "old" in the opening line. Yet, without it, one loses the first level of penetration in the poem. "Old Baltimore" projects the right economy of reflection. A child in an old city would obviously be fascinated: "Head-filled, heart-filled with glee." This is what one might call the "elevation," which sets up the reader for the decline. "Whit" is an old word, meaning "the least amount." For some reason, we trust the poet's learning on this score. But such is the texture of its resonance that its ambiguity makes it a catchall. If the reader supposes the "Baltimorean" to have been an adult, it only adds to the abusiveness of the incident itself. However, "whit" would mean that the Baltimorean was not much bigger than a "very small" Countee Cullen. The conditional phrase of the seventh line referring to the poet's smile reveals that the eight-year-old made a determination that it was safe to be friendly. This is the "elevation" extended to its maximum followed by the shocking decline that the Baltimorean poked his tongue at the poet and called him "Nigger." In the last stanza, Cullen shows that he is not vulgar. He does not leave us trapped in a reaction to an experience we cannot penetrate. Instead, we are left to ponder its effects. Therefore, if we have never had such an experience, we can replace some incident of our own that penetrated and overwhelmed our own sensibilities. This was the first time a black poet had shown this sort of detached mastery, and no American poet had shown it with such sweet musical efficiency.

The first and arguably the finest collection of Countee Cullen's poems appeared in 1925, titled *Color*. The complex, indefatigable poem "Shroud of Color" actually appeared in 1924 in H. L. Mencken's *American Mercury*. Along with "Incident," which we have examined, "Yet Do I Marvel" appears as well as the Wordsworthian "A Brown Girl Dead." The single most important poem of refined technique and penetration in this volume was "Heritage," of which we shall speak at length later.

Countee Cullen graduated from NYU Phi Beta Kappa, and, fortified by these credentials, he went on to Harvard University, where he read for the degree of master of arts in English and French, which he completed in 1927. By this time Countee Cullen was easily the best-known poet in America. He had won an impressive array of poetry prizes, including the John Reed Memorial Prize and the Amy Spingarn Award from *Crisis* magazine and a host of others. In the fall of 1926, Cullen began to write a column, "The Dark Tower," for *Opportunity* magazine, which was sponsored by the National Urban League, thus assuring him an influence beyond his poems. I agree with Gerald Early that it was Cullen's success that sprang forth as the essential energy of the Harlem Renaissance and not the publication of Jean Toomer's *Cane* (Early 19).

Countee Cullen's second volume, *Copper Sun*, appeared in 1927, which contained the much heralded poem "Threnody for a Brown Girl." In his powerful treatise on faith, Søren Kierkegaard wrote that true poetry is a "clash of emotions" but that modern poets thrash about in single series of emotions. Cullen is supremely guilty of this charge in the foregoing poem. Here we observe a gifted poet caught in a struggle for an original expression of his sensibilities in which he seems to have lost out to stock phrases and pastiche. Except for the economy of the opening stanza, which promises the austerity of "Heritage," the poem appears clumsy and mundane. The third line of the second stanza begins the ruin with its jarring musicality and the simile of the line following that is simply pedestrian. These adjectives do not get to the real problem facing Cullen or any poet, especially ones of genius, however. He clearly could not juxtapose a competing emotion to set in tension against his initial impulse. A simple read through the poem reveals that it does not evolve toward some resolution that places the reader in a position of "sensuous intensity" in which there is irresolution no matter which side of the poet's juxtaposition one takes. Without a force of opposition, the imagery in the poem seems impotent and possesses little or no metaphorical force, and the poem could, ostensibly, ramble on ad infinitum. In my view, the better poems in *Copper Sun* are "Lines to My Father," "From the Dark Tower," "Youth Sings of Rosebuds," "Ultimatum," and the brilliant "More than a Fool's Song," of which I speak later.

In 1927 came the release of *The Ballad of the Brown Girl: An Old Ballad Retold*, which demonstrated competence with the ballad form and dealt with miscegenation. It is not regarded as significant among Cullen's works. The year 1928 held high promise for the young literary star. He was at the height of his influence, if no longer of his powers. He received a Guggenheim Fellowship, which he undertook in Paris, thereby setting in train a passage to distance, escape, and acceptance for many black artists. On April 9, 1928, Cullen married Yolande Du Bois, the only offspring of W.E.B. Du Bois.* It was the society event of the year in Harlem and perhaps the "black community" nationwide. As typical of such unions, it fell into disrepair almost immediately and was ended by divorce in 1930. In 1929 Cullen published his penultimate volume of poems, *The Black Christ and Other Poems*. The poems in this volume are less well written than any other of the poet's works. The best of them are "For Helen Keller," "Song in Spite of Myself," "The Street Called Crooked," and, for its statement of the poet's intellectual state of mind, "To Certain Critics." Cullen was disappointed deeply that critics did not exalt the long poem in this volume, "The Black Christ." But again it is hopelessly unmusical, without the clever twists of "Heritage" and very much overwrought by mundane imagery. The poet seemed to be suffering in the way T. S. Eliot suffered in his "Choruses from the Rock," speaking didactically to his audience, not caring to distance himself from an interest in the poem's resolution, which in this case happens to be its beginning, middle, and end.

The final collection of poems by Countee Cullen, *The Medea and Some Poems*, included a translation of the Greek tragedy by that name, but only the poem "Magnets" from this collection strikes me as worthwhile. To last beyond his twenties, a poet must increase his learning and the means by which he transfers imagery. His audience, well schooled in his forms and methods, are accustomed to look for the same old signs, and, finding them with ease, they grow disinterested and soon think their poet predictable. Cullen seemed at this stage of life unable to develop a coherent philosophical perspective out of which he could weave poems that drew the reader inward before the inevitable encounter with old familiar signs.

In 1932 he published a novel, *One Way to Heaven*, which constitutes an attempt at satire but is wholly without skillful ridicule or ironical turn. It should be of interest to us that a poet with Cullen's gifts failed in this regard, and we may note that for all his "paganism," he shows in his novel no fully satirical representations of Christianity or black life. No people can claim to have arrived at a replenishing maturity regarding their historical position, where they cannot demonstrate by succinct parody an artistic detachment from their circumstances. Certainly, we have nothing in the entire Harlem Renaissance approaching irony in respect of these most ironically placed people in the world, black Americans— a phenomenon more explicit in Cullen's time. Countee Cullen kept employment for the rest of his life as a teacher at Frederick Douglass Junior High School in New York City. The poet ended his writing career with two children's books, *The Lost Zoo* and *My Lives and How I Lost Them*. In 1945 he was working on a musical with Arna Bontemps*. He died on January 9, 1946, of complications from high blood pressure.

MAJOR WORKS AND THEMES

Every poet has what may be called a "logic of sensibility" in which his or her imagery is given. Wordsworth's poetry dealt primarily with innocence juxtaposed against an encroaching world that had begun to regulate the "sensuous sublime" to either primitivity or naïveté. T. S. Eliot's works concerned the impossibility and impotence, and yet necessity, of belief. At the core of Countee Cullen's poetic sensibility is a paradox that he could not set into relief, the geometry of which he seemed unable to align and that he mistook for irony. When poets are young, they may perceive the world a certain way and, without knowing it, may have promulgated some new vision. As they grow older, either they work out the logic of their sensibility or they are condemned to attempted repetitions of past successes. In the poem "More than a Fool's Song," Cullen struck upon, rather than worked out, his vision; more specifically, he seemed to have stumbled across, rather than knowingly promulgated, his ontological concept of existence. In the second stanza of that poem he poetized the paradoxical relations of human knowledge, or rather the assumptions thereof, and the wisdom of insight and experience.

I find those "Heraclitean" lines to be some of Cullen's finest phrases and the most philosophically penetrating of all of his lines. In addition the poet manages there an adroit economy of musicality in which no sound seems forced or trite, and this while ushering the reader into the paradoxical philosophical worldview of the pre-Socratics. "More than a Fool's Song" addresses the human limitation of perspective and the indecipherability of God. The word "Perhaps," as used in the poem's last line, whenever well employed in poetry, is a beautiful modifier of feeling, and in the foregoing poem it is used with skill to great effect. That is, Cullen does not press his conclusion; he is not desperate for agreement. He maintains throughout the very judicious equilibrium that is the poem's subject, merely "suggesting" against those who would evangelize that they "know" who is or is not "hurtling down" into hell. There are those who will overlook such a poem as this, thinking of it as a respite from the poet's "racial theme." Cullen must have in some way believed this as well, since he never enlarged upon the philosophical principles he struck upon there. However, if we are unable to see the relevance of this poem for race, then we may not wonder any longer at the condition not only of our poetry today but of the lack of penetration of our sensibilities—in which is withheld a more profound existential conception of ourselves.

Fundamentally, that entire poem addresses the question of "certainty." Cullen seeks to undermine the comfort we gain from our preoccupation with moral and religious certitude, a preoccupation that has consumed the Western world since Plato that has shaped our quotidian psychology, and that lies at the root of so many of our wars and is the chief instigator in conceptions of difference that may not have led to slavery but is at the heart of racial prejudice and the attitudes of superiority from which it is derived. I am not saying that Cullen literally set out to make these points. Rather, the case I am making is that whether he did so or not, they are implicit in the poem we are now considering. If he had specifically addressed the poem's underlying logic, he would not have had to depend on his pseudopaganism, which grew so tiresome, when philosophical doubt offered a much more sincere, historical, and extended mechanism through which he could have expressed his concept of life.

If we turn our attention to the poem "Yet Do I Marvel," I think we find an early more racial expression of the paradoxical mode in which Cullen was writing. Critics often say that this poem concerns "race and spirituality." Not so; not so simply, in any case. One also suggested that the poem was "Blakean" in its sensibility. Not so again. This is Percy Bysshe Shelley's influence, most nearly seen in the "Asia Replies" section of *Prometheus Unbound*. Cullen's poem itself concerns a mode of existence, later expressed in "More than a Fool's Song." The most crucial lines in the poem ask about the capricious nature of Sisyphus' suffering. That is, Cullen does not want us to merely sympathize with Sisyphus; rather, he refers to him in the manner done by Albert Camus in his *Myth of Sisyphus*. The reference is purely existential. The question is, in paraphrase, Are we condemned by mere chance to toil ceaselessly? This is what we might call an "eternal question" or, as Eliot put it in *Prufrock*, an "overwhelming question." As such, answering this sort of interrogative answers not for blacks alone but something for all humankind. It is this universalization or detachment or distance through philosophical doubt that Cullen seemed unable to sustain after the mid-1920s, despite his genius. In addition, the "spirituality" mentioned by some critics is not within the four walls of the poem. Rather, it is part of the result of the poet's skill in leaving the reader exiled to his or her own limitations before the "inscrutability" of God and existence. I would stand therefore upon the statement that Countee Cullen's "Yet Do I Marvel" is perhaps the finest sonnet ever written in America.

CRITICAL RECEPTION

In Carl Van Vechten's review of Cullen's poetry for *Vanity Fair* in June 1925, he wrote that "his only Negro forebear . . . is the poet Pushkin, whose verses dwelt on Russian history and folklore, although he was the great-grandson of a slave" (62). Two of Countee Cullen's long poems not only reveal his application of various philosophical perspectives as a self-critical mechanism but also his intimacy with, and separation from, "being black" in similar sense to Pushkin. In "Shroud of Color" and "Heritage" Cullen sets the question of race as an ironist with a skill not seen again until Ralph Ellison's *Invisible Man*—a work that is as infinitely existential as it is racial. The first poem is less mature but more robust in its demands upon the reader. It is the poem of a young mind in command of its voice and the experience it modulates. Again, not the nineteenth-century Romantics but Dante and the Bible (even Donne and Milton) seem to have been the principal influences in these two frames of Cullen's work. Keats wrote sweetly, but he was incapable of the philosophical freight that purloined Cullen's poetic sense. Shelley had something of that quality but lost it by emphasizing thought over experience, and Byron's "mock heroism" could offer Cullen little. Pushkin, though not an influence, at least in *Eugene Onegin*, outlined the tragedy of living with dual identities, while belonging to a single culture—which is somewhat comparable to Cullen's most profound artistic ambitions.

In addition, Cullen in "Shroud of Color" seemed to manage the oppositional turnstiles of intimacy and distance, which were central to Pushkin's mastery. There Cullen exhibited a patience that he failed to show in "Black Christ" or that is not found in the whole corpus of Langston Hughes,* for instance; there he held his resolution in the poem until the very end, allowing the reader to enter the poem's sensibility without having to "argue the way in." That is, he began by claiming intimacy and empathy with the suffering darker brother. Instead of offering encouragement, Cullen placed himself in the position of the weak and broken-spirited, writing of how he lacked the strength to sacrifice. This may have said as much about what he sacrificed as an artist as much as it speaks about the suffering man. He set himself so low in the poem that probably any reader encountering the poet would have to pity his despair. (This move we have earlier called the "exaltation," which establishes a juxtaposition of tensions in poetry.)

It is exactly these insights that lay behind J. Saunders Redding's analysis of Cullen's artistic contribution in *To Make a Poet Black*. "Countee Cullen is decidedly a gentle poet . . . whose vision of life is interestingly distorted by too much of the vicarious" (109). The poet's principal tool is language. Because of the "enigmas of arrival" of the Negro in America, Cullen not only had to fashion selfhood in a language adopted but had to show the experience from the most interior vantage point of the dominant culture itself. As such, from the "racial" vantage point (though that should include whites), he seemed concerned with color, and from the standpoint of blacks, he seemed to deal with color only "vicariously." Therefore, racial color in the poems of Countee Cullen seems to show the poet seeking an "interobjective correlative" between both worlds—one black, the other white—and his own poetic musings. This phenomenon can be seen in the name and in the relief sought in the first of two rhyming couplets in "Shroud of Color," in which Cullen extends the moment of prophetic realization through a familiar, powerful, and well-placed lamentation concerning the omen of the "sacrificial lamb"—as appeared, for example, for Abraham in his moment of relief. Like Dante's vision in the *Purgatorio*, the poet, by epiphany, sees a moral vision of the ebb and flow of germ and birth; he notes the fragility of the survival of lower living beings, fortified only by their "determination" to survive. The entire vision culminates in the fall of man, which unnerves the poet. That is, he is now so enamored of his suffering condition that he is unable to assimilate the lesson of the vision. (This exactly is the import of his warning to black people.) In the poetic vision, another lesson is offered, and its accompanying song lights the poet's imagination. Immediately, he apprehends the resolution that in the "harmony" of creation, all things—including the suffering of blacks and seeming superiority of whites—will come to an end. By these lights, this poem concerns fundamentally Christian redemption in exchange for unearned suffering. Essentially, the poet is saying to us as well that if we think our suffering is great, consider how Christ suffered for us—not yet the Christ of Calvary, but in the beginning. As I indicated, the poet demonstrates that the fall of man is emblematic of the fall of all who raise themselves up in superiority—to wit, whites over blacks. It is noteworthy that the poet does this without oversanctifying blacks, thus allowing them to remain existential and subject to the human weakness the poem condemns. Therefore, while the theme is not original, its method of presentation is unique in the manner that it distributes the vision to the reader, seeming to indicate that neither blacks nor whites but only the poetic vision is pure. That is, only in the artistic vision is there an unadulterated vantage point in which all may be seen as they are.

In apprehending the preceding points, we should have some further insight into Cullen's tenuous hold on his paganism and the strength of his Christian tendencies, which, in the poem we are discussing, insofar as suffering is concerned, run counter to his defiant resolution in "From the Dark Tower" that the Negro now suffering was not made to weep eternally.

If "Heritage" is the opposite side of the same coin with "Shroud of Color," the former side is itself split in two. Heritage is the "schizophrenia" into which one falls, when the lessons from the moral vision in "Shroud of Color" lose their effect. Perhaps the most effective way to read this poem is to juxtapose the opening chorus, which ends with a question of the meaning of Africa to the poet himself, against the line, "So I lie . . ." The chorus carries a stock description of Africa with an exotic, pseudoanthropological profile. The poet presents this as his immediate perception of Africa. But then he lets the reader in on the ruse: "So I lie," he says, then tells us about his true impressions of Africa through its haunting effects over his mind, body, and spirit, in spite of his lack of actual familiarity with the continent. The technique of the poem is, in this respect, quite skillful.

Referring to Cullen's technical mastery, Alan R. Shucard in his *Countee Cullen* was right to say, "'Heritage' is an attempt to determine what Africa means to the speaker: finally, he realizes that it is his essential soul that must be suppressed in a civilization that is inimical to it" (22). Therefore, the technique is in part the theme, that is, this poetry is a search for identity. In "Heritage," there is a marvelous measurement of tonality, and again, as with "Yet Do I Marvel," the music is perhaps as refined as Cullen has produced. In addition, there are several brilliant enjambments, an art lost to "free verse" in the latter half of the twentieth century. Returning to the phrase "So I lie," I disagree with Gerald Early that it concerns lying in toto (Early 59). When the poet says, "What is Africa to me?" he is asking, rhetorically, What do I know or care about Africa? After all, we may imagine his saying, I am not even African. Immediately, he follows this with the juxtaposing phrase, "So I lie." With that the poet explains the nature of the aforementioned "hauntings," and so the "lying" here is more like, So I go along to get along or So I pretend not to have any real interest in Africa. It is almost as if he is asking, What will you have me do? After all, those people serve heathen Gods, and the poet saw himself as belonging to "traditional" Christianity. Although in the poem Cullen admits that he is now Western and Christian, he also admits that as a "Christian" he feels the double identity I spoke of earlier, in part, because of an enormous sense of cultural loss. This is not unlike T. S. Eliot's comment that though he found something more profound in Hinduism, for reasons of convenience, he stuck with Christianity. Cullen is saying that despite his pretense that Africa is little more that a menu of exotica to him, still he cannot forgo his Christian heritage. However, he then turns to Christ and reveals that he sometimes wished that Christ was black. As such, the poem treats the converse, obverse, and contrapositive impulses of historical dislocation and religious commitment through a deliberately anemic conception of historical imagination.

Finally, Countee Cullen in "Yet Do I Marvel," "Shroud of Color," and "Heritage" most nearly embodies the philosophical perspective that extends his poetic force into the present. In struggling between his race and his art, he was not consistent in maintaining such a vision. Implicit in such an outlook is a self-critical mode that many blacks found tantamount to betrayal. Cullen added to this with his insistence on being seen as a poet who happened to be black rather than a black poet. In this he was opposed, among others, by none other than Langston Hughes,* who was, in my view, Cullen's most severe critic. The tension between them was the poetic vision versus a political one and Hughes' insistence on the latter.

BIBLIOGRAPHY

Works by Countee Cullen

Color. New York: Harper and Brothers, 1925.
The Ballad of the Brown Girl: An Old Ballad Retold. New York: Harper and Brothers 1927.
Caroling Dusk. New York: Harper and Brothers, 1927.
Copper Sun. New York: Harper and Brothers, 1927.
The Black Christ and Other Poems. New York: Harper and Brothers, 1929.
One Way to Heaven. New York: Harper and Brothers, 1932.
The Medea and Some Poems. New York: Harper and Brothers, 1935.
The Lost Zoo. New York: Harper and Brothers, 1940.
My Lives and How I Lost Them. New York: Harper and Brothers, 1942.
On These I Stand. New York: Harper and Brothers, 1947. (posthumously).

Studies of Countee Cullen

Baker, Houston, Jr. "The Poetry of Countee Cullen." In Major Modern Black American Writers. Ed. Harold Bloom. New York: Chelsea House, 1995. 29–30.
Bronz, Stephen H. Roots of Negro Consciousness in the 1920s: Three Harlem Renaissance Authors. New York: Libra, 1964.
Collier, Eugenia. "I Do Not Marvell, Countee Cullen." College Language Association Journal 11 (1967): 73–87.

Daniel, Walter C. "Countee Cullen as Literary Critic." *College Language Association Journal* 14 (1971): 281–90.

Early, Gerald. *My Soul's High Song: The Collected Writings of Countee Cullen, Voice of the Harlem Renaissance*. New York: Anchor Books, 1991.

Ferguson, Blanche E. *Countee Cullen and the Negro Renaissance*. New York: Dodd, Mead, 1966.

Hughes, Langston. "The Negro Artist and the Racial Mountain." *Nation* 122 (June 23, 1926): 692–94.

Perry, Margaret. *A Bio-Bibliography of Countee Cullen*. Westport, CT: Greenwood, 1971.

Redding, Saunders J. *To Make a Poet Black*. College Park, MD: McGrath, 1968.

Reimonenq, Alden. "Countee Cullen and Uranian 'Soul Windows.' " In *Critical Essays: Gay and Lesbian Writers of Color*. Ed. Emmanuel S. Nelson. New York: Haworth, 1993. 143–65.

Shackleford, Dean D. "The Poetry of Countee Cullen." In *Masterpieces of African American Literature*. Ed. Frank N. Magill. New York: HarperCollins, 1992. 382–86.

Shucard, Alan. *Countee Cullen*. Boston: Twayne, 1984.

Turner, Darwin T. *In a Minor Chord: Afro-American Writers and Their Search for Identity*. Carbondale: Southern Illinois University Press, 1971.

Tuttleton, James W. "Countee Cullen at 'The Heights.' " In *The Harlem Renaissance: Revaluations*. Ed. Amritjit Singh et al. New York: Garland, 1989. 101–37.

Vechten, Carl Van. Rev. of *Color*. *Vanity Fair* (June 1925): 62.

LUCY A. DELANEY
(c. 1828–19??)

Verner D. Mitchell

BIOGRAPHY

In her 1891 autobiography, a sketch of her life in slavery and in freedom, Delaney writes that she was born Lucy Ann Berry in St. Louis, Missouri. Her only sibling, a sister, Nancy, escaped to Toronto in the early 1840s. In February 1844, with the help of her mother, Delaney won her own freedom. The following year she married Frederick Turner and moved to Quincy, Illinois. Unfortunately, a few months later Turner was killed in a steamboat explosion. His young widow then returned home to St. Louis, where in 1849 she married again: "I became the wife of Zachariah Delaney, of Cincinnati, with whom I have had a happy married life, continuing forty-two years" (58), an obviously pleased Delaney wrote in 1891. Two of their children died in childhood, and the other two in their early twenties; thus, Delaney and her husband left no heirs.

Delaney's only extant photograph, which she placed on the inside cover of her autobiography, reveals a striking resemblance to Mahalia Jackson, the renowned gospel singer. She signed the picture, "Yours truly, Lucy A. Delaney."

MAJOR WORK AND THEMES

A sixty-four-page autobiography, *From the Darkness Cometh the Light; or, Struggles for Freedom*, is Delaney's single literary work. She employs many of the standard slave narrative conventions and themes, but, unlike the more famous narratives of Frederick Douglass,* Harriet Jacobs,* and Booker T. Washington,* Delaney's does not have an authenticating preface written by someone other than the author. The primary function of such prefaces—generally written by a white person—was to verify the truthfulness of the author's story. Hence in choosing to author her own Preface, Delaney signals that she needs no inter-mediaries, that she is fully capable of authenticating her own story.

Nonetheless, her Preface does contain signs of self-deprecation, a common feature in slave narratives. For example, she asks that if the narrative is deficient in unity or coherence, "be charitable and attribute it to lack of knowledge and experience in literary acquirements" (viii). She concludes, "I leave you to the perusal of my little tale" (viii). Delaney's work, however, is far from "a little tale." Instead, this modest description is merely the first instance of the narrative's fruitful use of "masks" as a trope.

As a little girl, Delaney has little understanding of slavery. Accordingly, she is unable to read or to decipher her mother's "masks": "As I carelessly played away the hours, mother's smiles would fade away . . . ah! only too soon when I learned the secret of her ever-changing face" (13). Later, she reiterates: "Oh! The impenetrable mask of these poor black creatures! How much joy, of sorrow, of misery and anguish have they hidden from their tormentors?" (18). Delaney, then, is initially a young, naïve reader. But after being initiated into the horrors of slavery, she of necessity becomes a more sophisticated reader who sees beyond her mother's and other enslaved people's exterior masks. Delaney as author therefore provides a model or theory of reading for her narrative. Put differently, her "little tale" requires a complex reading that looks beyond the literal words/masks.

Central to the narrative is the description of Delaney's "pathway" from slavery to freedom. "My pathway," she underscores, "was thorny enough, and though there may be no roses without thorns, I had thorns in plenty with no roses" (19). When Delaney was twelve, her mother—Polly Berry—escaped to Chicago and thus to "freedom." But fearing that her erstwhile "owner" would wreak his ven-geance on young Lucy, Berry soon returned to St. Louis, this time determined to sue for her freedom. With the help of an able lawyer, she proved that she was born free but subsequently kidnapped in Illinois, carried across the Mississippi River, and sold into slavery in St. Louis. Emboldened by the jury's verdict that "she was a free woman" (24), Berry next endeavored to secure Lucy's freedom.

"On the morning of the 8th of September, 1842," reports Delaney, "my mother sued Mr. D. D. Mitchell for the possession of her child, Lucy Ann Berry" (33). Afterward, Lucy suffered many hardships, including "seventeen long and dreary months" in jail (34) while her case was being adjudicated. "My only crime," she explains, "was seeking for that freedom which was my birthright!" (35). Finally, with the court's belated ruling that—born to a freeborn mother, Lucy is therefore free—comes the autobiography's overarching theme: the heroic struggle of the enslaved mother to achieve freedom for both herself and her progeny.

From the Darkness Cometh the Light is, above all, the triumphant story of a daughter and mother. Inspired by her mother's example, Delaney, in turn, seeks to inspire courage, self-confidence, and probity in her narrative's readers. She stresses this very point in the book's final chapter, concluding that surely blacks can succeed "as well as the whites, if given the same chance" (64).

CRITICAL RECEPTION

Although Delaney's writing has received little critical attention, what it has received is decidedly favorable. In his "Introduction" to the 1988 reprint of Delaney's autobiography, the historian and literary critic William L. Andrews notes that Delaney ably builds upon, and extends, the black female literary tradition. Not only does she reiterate many of the themes of her literary predecessors, but she "extends her story beyond her family's reunion in freedom to record, in brief, the success she has made in the quarter-century since the end of the Civil War" (xxx). For Lindon Barrett, Delaney reveals that "to write African American autobiography is not only to write 'from behind the veil' but also to write in the public, yet confining 'constitutional' space of American custom and law" (123).

BIBLIOGRAPHY

Work by Lucy A. Delaney

From the Darkness Cometh the Light; or, Struggles for Freedom. St. Louis: J. T. Smith, 1891. Reprinted, *Six Women's Slave Narratives.* Ed. William L. Andrews. New York: Oxford University Press, 1988.

Studies of Lucy A. Delaney

Andrews, William L. "Introduction." In *Six Women's Slave Narratives.* New York: Oxford University Press, 1988. xxix–xli.
Barrett, Lindon. "Self-Knowledge, Law, and African American Autobiography: Lucy A. Delaney's *From the Darkness Cometh the Light.*" In *The Culture of Autobiography: Constructions of Self-Representation.* Ed. Robert Folkenflik. Stanford, CA: Stanford University Press, 1993. 104–24.

MARTIN ROBINSON DELANY
(1812–1885)

Adenike Marie Davidson

BIOGRAPHY

Martin Robinson Delany was born in Charles Town, West Virginia, on May 6, 1812, to Samuel Delany, an enslaved man, and Pati Peace Delany, a free African American woman. Both sets of his grandparents were African natives brought to the United States and enslaved. Growing up, Delany was told tales of the homeland; his paternal grandfather was a Mandingo prince, and the other a Golah village chieftain. The Delanys fled to Chambersburg, Pennsylvania, in 1822 when white neighbors discovered their literary abilities and threatened Pati with imprisonment. At nineteen, Delany left home and settled in Pittsburgh; he briefly studied under a white doctor and became a physician's assistant. When black suffrage was rescinded in Pennsylvania in 1838, Delany traveled alone to Texas, then independent, in hopes of its being a place of political potential for free African Americans—a possible emigration site—but was disappointed. Delany lived in Pittsburgh until 1856 and quickly became a leader in the African American community, helped to organize literacy, temperance, and moral reform societies, and cofounded the Theban Literary Society.

In 1843 Delany married Catherine Richards, the granddaughter of Benjamin Richards, a butcher, and the wealthiest African American in Pittsburgh. The Delanys had seven surviving children, whom they named after prominent and important blacks: Toussaint L'Ouverture, Charles Lenox Redmond, Alexander Dumas, Saint Cyprian, Faustin Soulouque, Ramses Placido, and Ethiopia Halle Delany (his only daughter). In the same year of the marriage, Delany began a publishing career with *The Mystery*, the first African American newspaper west of the Allegheny Mountains. It folded in 1847 due to lack of financial support. Delany then joined Frederick Douglass* as coeditor of *The North Star*. Delany resigned after a year and a half due to political differences and the paper's inability to support both men. He decided to resume his medical studies.

His applications to Pennsylvania and New York medical schools were rejected, but in November 1850, he was admitted to Harvard College, along with two other African American men planning to practice medicine in Liberia. By the end of the term, white students had petitioned for the removal of the men. Delany and his colleagues were allowed to finish the term but were barred from further study at Harvard. He returned to Pittsburgh and continued to practice medicine throughout his life. Delany's dismissal from Harvard, the passing of the Fugitive Slave Law in 1850, and his being denied a patent because he was not recognized as a citizen, sparked his consideration of leaving the United States and the serious planning of a mass black emigration. In 1854 he organized a National Emigration Convention and argued for leaving the States as the only solution for African American progress.

He briefly moved his family to Chatham, Canada, in 1856 yet maintained ties to the antislavery movement in the United States. In 1858 Delany acted as intermediary between John Brown and the Canadian black community, organizing a secret convention and recruiting black men to fight. Yet Delany was in Africa when Brown's raid took place.

In 1859 Delany traveled through the Niger Valley with Robert Campbell in search of a territory to which African Americans could emigrate and build a black nation. Delany and Campbell signed a treaty in Abbeokuta, which is now Nigeria, to establish a self-governing colony. The treaty was later voided.

Delany recommitted himself to the United States after Lincoln issued the Emancipation Proclamation in 1863. He became an official recruiter for the Union's African American military units and was commissioned as a major in the army, the first African American field officer of high rank. After the war, Delany became a subassistant commissioner in the Freedmen's Bureau, assigned to Hilton Head Island. In 1873 he was appointed customs inspector in Charleston, South Carolina, and in 1874 he was appointed trial justice in Charlestown's Third Ward. By 1874, disenchanted with Reconstruction, he ran unsuccessfully for lieutenant governor, and two years later he supported the Democrats. By 1878 Delany turned once again toward emigration and supported the Liberian Exodus Joint Stock Exchange Company to carry emigrants to Liberia. Yet he himself never left and died on January 24, 1885.

MAJOR WORKS AND THEMES

Delany is considered the most prominent advocate of cultural black nationalism in the nineteenth century. His works explore black self-reliance, emigration, elevation, and the hypocrisy of Christianity. His first book, *The Condition, Elevation, Emigration, and Destiny of the Colored People of the United States: Politically Considered* (1852), is the first full-length formulation of black nationalism, describing in detail how African Americans are alienated in their birthland by the condescension and animosity of whites. Delany reports on the achievements of black men and women, despite the political pressure to keep African Americans in positions of servility, critiques abolitionists for not consistently fighting for integration, and recommends emigration as a solution to the race problem, calling African Americans a nation within a nation: "That there have in all ages, in almost every nation, existed a nation within a nation—a people who although forming a part and parcel of the population, yet were from force of circumstances, known by the peculiar position they occupied, forming in fact, by the deprivation of political equality with others, no part, and if any, but a restricted part of the body politic of such nations, is also true" (12). In this text, Delany also calls for a new perception of religion and Christianity, seeing southern Christianity as a tool used by slaveholders to pacify enslaved African Americans: "The colored races are highly susceptible of religion; it is a constitute principle of their nature, and an excellent trait in their character. But unfortunately for them, they carry it too far" (37).

The Origin and Objects of Ancient Freemasonry; Its Introduction into the United States, and Legitimacy among Colored Men (1853) is a defense of black Freemasonry. Delany outlines America's attempts at preventing black men from organizing and connects Freemasonry to the biblical Moses, an Ethiopian, and thereby to Africans: "To Africa is the world indebted for its knowledge of the mysteries of ancient freemasonry. . . . thus to deny to black men the privilege of Masonry, is to deny to a child the lineage of its own parentage. From whence sprung Masonry but from Ethiopia, Egypt, and Assyria—all settled and peopled by the children of Ham?" (37). In responding to white American men's attempts to prevent African American men from forming Masonry lodges, Delany argues for Masonry as an African fraternity and therefore more legitimate for African Americans than for white Americans.

"Political Destiny of the Colored Race of the American Continent" examines "the great issue [facing the world, which] will be a question of black and white, and every individual will be called upon for his identity with one or the other" (335). Delany attempted to convince African Americans that emigration was the only solution in the face of such blatant racism and forced inferior status. To stay in the States meant acknowledgment and compliance with second-class status, for "no person can be free who themselves do not constitute an essential part of the *ruling element* of the country in which they live" (329).

Blake; or, The Huts of America, Delany's only attempt at a novel, first appeared incomplete in *The Anglo-African Magazine* between January and July 1859. A more complete version of the novel appeared serially in *The Weekly Anglo-African* from November 26, 1861, until late May 1862. Because of the editor's claim of eighty chapters in a promotion for the text, it is believed that the complete novel contains six uncovered chapters, possibly appearing in the first four issues in May 1862, but they have not yet been found. Divided into two major parts, *Blake* is the story of Henry Blake, an enslaved Cuban living in the South whose wife, Maggie, is sold away by their owner, Colonel Franks. Part One traces his adventures as a fugitive slave while he searches for his wife, transports his son and extended family to Canada, and organizes fellow slaves in the Deep South for a mass rebellion: " 'I have laid a scheme, and matured a plan for a general insurrection of the slaves in every state, and the successful overthrow of slavery!' " (39). Blake also redefines Christianity into a liberation theology, convincing the masses that " '[y]ou must make your religion subserve your interests, as your oppressors do theirs!' " (41). Part Two takes the reader to Cuba, reunites the married couple, gives a brief description of the Middle Passage with Blake working on a slave ship and organizing a mutiny, and shows Blake making concrete plans for an international insurrection: " 'Whatever liberty is worth to the whites, it is worth to the blacks; therefore, whatever it cost the whites to obtain it, the blacks would be willing and ready to pay, if they desire it' " (192). Blake is teamed with a poet, Placido, who speaks emotionally to the masses, and a militant slave, Gondolier, who incites physical violence. The novel as we have it ends on the eve of a possible revolution: " 'Woe be unto those devils of whites, I say!' " (313).

Principia of Ethnology: The Origin of Races and Color, with an Archeological Compendium of Ethiopian and Egyptian Civilization, from Years of Careful Examination and Enquiry (1879), his last full-length text, interprets the origins of the three races (Caucasian, Asian, and Negroid) and connects them to Noah's three sons Ham, Shem, and Japheth. He spends most of the text, naturally, tracing the lineage of Ham through Egypt and Ethiopia. He concludes with a discussion of the Egyptians' forming a trinity Godhead as in Christianity. Delany may have written more, but his papers, which were stored at Wilberforce University, were lost in a fire in April 1865.

CRITICAL RECEPTION

Delany's work on *The Mystery* did not attract significant attention outside Pittsburgh, but his work as a lecturer and his commitment to racial uplift and the African American community made him well known in abolitionist circles. After becoming coeditor of the *North Star* with Douglass, his lecturing activities were reported regularly in that paper, making him a recognized name nationally. *Condition* was given mixed reviews by a few important abolitionist newspapers and ignored by *North Star* and other African American periodicals. Most abolitionists were troubled by Delany's blatant call for emigration and the hopeless tone of possible success in the States.

Aside from brief notices about the appearance of the novel, critical response to *Blake* was virtually nonexistent, partly because of its publication in serial form. Although Delany as an author failed to receive much notice during his lifetime, his position as an activist in the African American emigrationist movement and in political affairs earned him considerable attention, the subject of a biography during his lifetime.

Along with an increased interest in African American literature and culture came renewed attention in Delany and his writings, although most critics thought his novel was weak and poorly written. In the 1950s, as historians examined the nineteenth century as important in developing a tradition of black nationalism, critical attention was given to Delany's political prose and his commitment to emigration and separatism. This interest increased in the 1960s, along with efforts to establish Delany as the original theorist of black nationalism in the United States. Delany seemed to have been given his due respect and attention with the proclaiming of him as nationalism's "founding father." Perhaps even more important, Delany's major works were reprinted: *Condition* in 1968 and *Official Report* twice in the following year. Delany's fiction also received more attention. *Blake* was compared favorably to other antebellum African American novels, such as William Wells Brown's* *Clotel*, because of its positive affirmation of black identity. *Blake* is also included in the African American literary tradition as the third novel published by an African American. In the early 1970s interest in Delany reached an all-time high with four books solely or significantly about Delany published between 1970 and 1975. Miller discovered and republished most of the text of *Blake* as it had appeared in *Weekly Anglo-African*, presenting it as an important novel of black pride that suggested political revolution. Published incomplete, Miller suggests that "the very inconclusiveness of the novel as it now exists—the rebellion—is perhaps more relevant today than any ending Delany could possibly have conceived" (xxv). Delany continues to be given more critical attention, all of his major texts have been reprinted and are available, and he seems to have secured a place within African American literature and the tradition of black nationalism.

BIBLIOGRAPHY

Works By Martin Robinson Delany

Fiction

Blake; or, The Huts of America. 1970. Ed. Floyd Miller. Boston: Beacon Press, 1989.

Nonfiction

Elegy on the Life and Character of the Rev. Fayette Davis. Pittsburgh: Benjamin Franklin Peterson, 1847.
The Condition, Elevation, Emigration, and Destiny of the Colored People of the United States: Politically Considered. 1852. New York: Arno Press, 1968. Baltimore: Black Classic Press, 1993.
The Origin and Objects of Ancient Freemasonry; Its Introduction into the United States, and Legitimacy among Colored Men. Pittsburgh: W. S. Haven, 1853; Xenia, OH: Aldine, 1904.
"Comets." *The Anglo-African Magazine* (February 1859): 59–60.
"The Attraction of Planets." *The Anglo-African Magazine* (January 1859): 17–20.
Official Report of the Niger Valley Exploring Party. New York: T. Hamilton, 1861. Ann

Arbor: University of Michigan Press, 1968. Philadelphia: Rhetorical Publications, 1968.

"Political Destiny of the Colored Race on the American Continent." In *Life and Public Services of Martin R. Delany.* Ed. Frank A. Rollin. Boston: Lee and Shephard, 1868. 327–67.

A Series of Four Tracts on National Policy: To the Students of Wilberforce University, being Adapted to the Capacity of the Newly Enfranchised Citizens, First Series. Charleston, SC: Republican Book and Job Office, 1870.

Principia of Ethnology: The Origin of Races and Color, with an Archeological Compendium of Ethiopian and Egyptian Civilization, from Years of Careful Examination and Enquiry. 1879. Baltimore: Black Classic Press, 1990.

Studies of Martin Robinson Delany

Adeleke, Tunde. "Martin Robinson Delany: The Economic and Cultural Contexts of Imperialism." In *UnAfrican Americans: Nineteenth-Century Black Nationalists and the Civilizing Mission.* Lexington: University Press of Kentucky, 1998. 43–69.

Austin, Allan D. "The Significance of Martin R. Delany's *Blake; or, The Huts of America.*" Ph.D. diss., University of Massachusetts, 1975.

Bell, Howard H. "Introduction." In *Search for a Place: Black Separatism and Africa, 1860,* by M. R. Delany and Robert Campbell. Ann Arbor: University of Michigan Press, 1969.

Bienvenu, Germain J. "The People of Delany's *Blake.*" *CLA Journal* 36.4 (June 1993): 406–29.

Blackett, Richard. "In Search of International Support for African Colonization: Martin Robinson Delany's Visit to England, 1860." *Canadian Journal of History* 10 (December 1975): 307–24.

Cobb, William. "Martin Robinson Delany." *National Medical Association Journal* 44 (May 1952): 232–38.

Crane, Gregg D. "The Lexicon of Rights, Power, and Community in *Blake*: Martin Delany's Dissent from *Dred Scott.*" *American Literature* 68.3 (September 1996): 527–53.

Du Bois, W. E. B. "A Forum of Fact and Opinion." *Pittsburgh Courier,* July 25, 1936.

Ellison, Curtis W., and E. W. Metcalf Jr. *William Wells Brown and Martin R. Delany: A Reference Guide.* Boston: G. K. Hall, 1978.

Ernest, John. "The White Gap and the Approaching Storm: Martin R. Delany's *Blake.*" In *Resistance and Reformation in Nineteenth-Century African-American Literature: Brown, Wilson, Jacobs, Delany, Douglass and Harper.* Jackson: University Press of Mississippi, 1995.

Fauset, Jessie. "Rank Imposes Obligations." *Crisis* 33 (November 1926): 9–12.

Fleming, Robert E. "Black, White, and Mulatto in Martin R. Delaney's [*sic*] *Blake.*" *Negro History Bulletin* 36 (February 1973): 37–39.

"Great Men in Negro History: Union Army Doctor Was Advocate of Education." *Sepia* 8 (February 1960): 61.

Griffith, Cyril E. *The African Dream: Martin R. Delany and the Emergence of Pan African Thought.* University Park: Pennsylvania State University Press, 1975.

Hite, Roger W. "Stand Still and See the Salvation: The Rhetorical Design of Martin Delany's *Blake.*" *Journal of Black Studies* 5 (December 1974): 192–202.

Holly, James T. "In Memorium." *A.M.E. Church Review* 3 (October 1886): 117–25.

Kahn, Robert M. "The Political Ideology of Martin Delany." *Journal of Black Studies* 14 (1984): 415–40.

Levine, Robert S. *Martin Delany, Frederick Douglass, and the Politics of Representative Identity.* Chapel Hill: University of North Carolina Press, 1997.

Magdol, Edward. "Martin R. Delany Counsels Freedmen, July 23, 1865." *Journal of Negro History* 56 (October 1971): 303–9.

Malveaux, Julianne. "Revolutionary Themes in Martin Delany's *Blake.*" *Black Scholar* 4 (July–August 1973): 52–56.

Marx, Jo Ann. "Myth and Meaning in Martin Delany's *Blake; or, The Huts of America.*" *CLA Journal* 38. 2 (December 1994): 183–92.

Miller, Floyd J. "The Father of Black Nationalism: Another Contender." *Civil War History* 17 (December 1971): 310–19.

———. "Introduction." In *Blake; or, The Huts of America.* Boston: Beacon Press, 1970. xi–xxix.

———. "Search for a Black Nationality: Martin R. Delany and the Emigrationist Alternative." Ph.D. diss., University of Minnesota, 1970.

Painter, Nell. "Martin R. Delany: Elitism and Black Nationalism." In *Black Leaders of the Nineteenth Century.* Ed. Leon Litwack and August Meier. Chicago: University of Illinois Press, 1988. 149–71.

Reid-Pharr, Robert. "Violent Ambiguity: Martin Delany, Bourgeois Sadomasochism, and the Production of a Black National Masculinity." In *Representing Black Men.* Ed. Marcellous Blount and George P. Cunningham. New York: Routledge, 1996. 73–94.

Rollin, Frank A. *Life and Public Services of Martin R. Delany.* Boston: Lee and Shephard, 1868.

Sanja, Mike. "*The Mystery* of Martin Delany." *Carnegie Magazine* (July/August 1990): 36–40.

Sterling, Dorothy. *The Making of an Afro-American: Martin Robinson Delany, 1812–1885.* Garden City, NY: Doubleday, 1971.

Ullman, Victor. *Martin R. Delany: The Beginnings of Black Nationalism.* Boston: Beacon Press, 1971.

Wallace, Maurice. " 'Are We Men?': Prince Hall, Martin Delany, and the Masculine Ideal in Black Freemasonry, 1775–1865." *American Literary History* 9.3 (Fall 1997): 396–424.

Whitlow, Roger. "The Revolutionary Black Novels of Martin R. Delany and Sutton Griggs." *MELUS* 5.3 (1978): 26–36.

Zeugner, John F. "A Note on Martin Delany's *Blake* and Black Militancy." *Phylon* 32 (March 1971): 98–105.

FREDERICK DOUGLASS
(1818–1895)

Harish Chander

BIOGRAPHY

Frederick Douglass, the father of the American Civil Rights movement, was born into slavery at a farm in Tuckahoe, Maryland, in February 1818. His mother was Harriet Bailey, a slave of Captain Aaron Anthony, and his father was a white person who never acknowledged paternity but was whispered to be Captain Anthony himself. The exact date of his birth is not known, but since his mother once called him her "valentine," Douglass celebrated his birthday on Valentine's Day. Captain Anthony, who had a farm and slaves of his own, worked as the chief manager of the vast plantation estate of Colonel Edward Lloyd V, who served at different times as U.S. senator and Maryland governor.

Douglass was taken away from his mother as soon as he was weaned because she had been hired out to work on a distant farm. Douglass was taken to live with his grandparents, who lived in a log cabin on the banks of Tuckahoe Creek. Manumitted in 1797, Grandpa Bailey was a freeman who worked as a sawyer, but Grandma Bailey was Captain Anthony's slave. Douglass' relatively carefree childhood with his grandparents ended abruptly when, one day in 1824, Grandma Bailey took him to Captain Anthony's plantation house, twelve miles away. It was a long distance to walk for a child of six, so Grandma Bailey alternately made him walk and carried him on her shoulders. Upon arrival, she told Frederick to play with the other children there and then quietly left. That was the last time Frederick saw his grandmother.

At Captain Anthony's plantation house, Frederick Douglass gradually learned the grim realities of slave life. Because of his young age, he was assigned light household duties, such as cleaning the yard, keeping the chickens out of the garden, and running errands for Captain Anthony's daughter Lucretia, who had married Thomas Auld, the captain of Colonel Lloyd's sloop. Lucretia often re-warded him with a piece of real bread and butter when he sang for her. Douglass was chosen to be the companion of twelve-year-old Daniel Lloyd, who took him along when he went hunting, as well as protected him from harm. Though he was spared physical abuse, he witnessed the abuse suffered by other slaves. One night, awakening to screams, he peered out to see Captain Anthony mercilessly whipping his Aunt Hester on her bare back. On another occasion, Frederick saw his badly beaten cousin Betsey begging Captain Anthony in vain for protection from a drunken overseer.

Frederick Douglass' mother could see him only rarely and briefly, as she worked from sunrise on at a farm miles from the plantation house. His mother passed away when Douglass was just seven. Captain Anthony died shortly thereafter. In *Life and Times of Frederick Douglass* (1881), Douglass expresses his sorrow over his mother's absence from his life: "To me it has ever been a grief that I knew my mother so little, and have so few of her words treasured in my remembrance" (36).

In 1826 Frederick Douglass was sent to Baltimore to care for the two-year-old son of Sophia and Hugh Auld. Douglass spent the next seven years in Baltimore, except for a brief return to Talbot County in October 1827 during the settlement of Captain Anthony's estate. Upon Captain Anthony's death in 1826, his estate, which included his slaves, was divided among his heirs. Douglass was given to Thomas Auld, who at once sent him back to Baltimore to his brother Hugh Auld's home.

The Baltimore setting proved to be relatively congenial. Douglass worked as a house servant and then as a laborer in Auld's shipyard. Sophia Auld, who had never before had a slave, treated him kindly. She began to teach him to read, but when she told her husband how good a student Douglass was, Thomas Auld, in Douglass' presence, forbade her to give him any further instruction. He said that "learning" would spoil even the best slave in the world, making him or her unfit to be a slave. In *Narrative of the Life of Frederick Douglass, an American Slave*, Douglass says that Hugh Auld's objections to the education of slaves helped him understand the secret of the master's power, thereby revealing the "pathway from slavery to freedom" (78). Sophia followed Hugh's order and desisted, but Douglass found other means of receiving instruction. When sent on errands, he would carry extra bread, which he would exchange for reading lessons from poor white children.

In 1829, at the age of eleven, Douglass started working at the shipyard as a general assistant. His duties included beating and spinning oakum, stoking fires under pitch boilers, turning grindstones, and running errands. He learned to write by copying out letters written on lumber by carpenters to indicate their positions in the vessel. At night, he practiced writing by copying out words written by Sophia and Hugh Auld's son in the blank spaces left in their son's used copy-books. Douglass describes in his *Narrative* that "after a long, tedious effort for years, I finally succeeded in learning how to write" (87).

In 1831, at the age of thirteen, two important events deeply influenced Douglass. First, after experiencing a revelation, he accepted Jesus Christ as his Redeemer and Savior. He joined the Bethel African Methodist Episcopal Church in Baltimore and studied the Bible with Charles Lawson, a free black drayman. Later in life, however, Douglass became disillusioned with a religious establishment that not only tolerated but supported slavery. Second, 1831 was the year he bought a secondhand copy of *The Columbian Orator*, a collection of essays on liberty, for fifty cents he had earned by blacking boots. In one essay, a recaptured slave ably defends himself against his master's charge of ingratitude, convincing his master that it is wrong to hold a person in bondage. The speeches of Richard Brinsley Sheridan, Lord Chatham, and William Pitt, which Douglass read again and again, increased his knowledge and added to his vocabulary, enabling him to give "tongue" to his thoughts. Douglass observes in *Life and Times of Frederick Douglass* (1881) regarding Sheridan's speeches on Catholic emancipation in England that "from the speeches of Sheridan I got a bold and powerful denunciation of oppression and a most brilliant vindication of the rights of man" (85).

In 1833 Sophia and Hugh Auld, dissatisfied with the work of a crippled slave, Douglass' cousin Henny, sent her back to her master, Thomas Auld. This led to a quarrel between the two brothers, leading Thomas Auld to demand that Douglass be returned to him as well. In March Douglass was sent to Caroline County, where Thomas Auld then lived with his second wife, Rowena. As Douglass describes in his *Narrative*, he found both Thomas and Rowena Auld to be "equally mean and cruel" (95). Douglass faced hunger, as well as whippings from Thomas Auld. As Douglass describes in *My Bondage and My Freedom*, Auld found biblical sanction for his cruelty. Finding Douglass stubborn, Auld hired Douglass out as a field hand to the notorious Edward Covey "to be broken" (203). Covey proved to be a merciless tyrant, repeatedly beating Douglass until he felt broken in body and spirit. However, one day in August 1834, Covey pushed Douglass too far. Working at the wheat threshing machine in the oppressive heat, Douglass collapsed. After Douglass failed to get up, Covey bashed him on his head with a hickory board, leaving him bleeding. Douglass then trekked through seven miles to Auld's home to report Covey's assault, but Auld remained indifferent and sent him back to Covey. Upon Douglass' return, Covey tried to tie him up with a rope, but Douglass resisted. After a lengthy fight, Covey retreated. This fight set Douglass on the road to freedom. To quote his *Narrative*: "My long-crushed spirit rose . . . and I now resolved that, however long I might remain a slave in form, the day had passed forever when I could be a slave in fact" (113). In the five subsequent months he worked for Covey, he did not receive another beating.

In January 1835 Douglass was hired out to William Freeland, who gave him enough to eat and did not overwork him. Douglass secretly ran a Sabbath school where he taught his fellow slaves how to read. In the *Narrative*, Douglass calls Freeland "the best master I ever had, *till I became my own master*" (121). During this time, he launched a plan to escape with five fellow slaves to the free state of Pennsylvania. However, the plan was betrayed, and Douglass, the leader of the plot, was thrown into jail. After a week, Thomas Auld secured Douglass' release, at which time he sent Douglas back to his brother Hugh Auld in Baltimore. From 1836 to 1838, Douglass again worked in the shipyards, first as an apprentice and then as a caulker, a job he was allowed to hold only because his wages went to a white man. On one occasion, four white workers attacked Douglass with stones and spikes, viciously beating him. Douglass could not seek legal redress because Maryland law did not permit a black person to offer evidence against a white person.

On September 3, 1838, Douglass escaped slavery. Dressed in a sailor's suit and carrying a seaman's protection paper, which he had borrowed from a retired sailor, he boarded a train to New York City. There, he found the home of David Ruggles, a key figure in the Underground Railroad. From Ruggles' home, Douglass wrote to his fiancée, Anna Murray, a free black woman whom he had met in Baltimore and who had helped arrange his escape, about his safe arrival. After she joined him a few days later, they were married. At Ruggles' suggestion, the couple moved to New Bedford, Massachusetts. In order to hide his identity, Douglass changed his name, adopting the surname of the Scottish hero of Sir Walter Scott's *Lady of the Lake*. In Bedford, Massachusetts, Douglass found work as a general laborer after failing to find better-paid work as a caulker because of discrimination. Anna Douglass helped support the family by taking in washing and doing domestic work.

Douglass' career as an abolitionist began in 1841 at a Massachusetts Anti-Slavery Society convention. Asked at the convention to tell of his experiences as a slave, Douglass delivered such a stirring and eloquent account of his life as a slave that he was offered a job as a lecturer for the society, a position that he accepted and held for four years. At the society, he helped defeat a new Rhode Island constitution that would have extended the franchise to unpropertied white men while denying the same right to blacks. Despite being heckled and beaten for being a black abolitionist, Douglass was a key figure in the famous "One Hundred Conventions," during which he lectured on the evils of slavery.

To counter skeptics who doubted that anyone so articulate could have been a slave, Douglass published a narrative of his life as a slave in 1845. *Narrative of the Life of Frederick Douglass, an American Slave* proved an instant success, but its bold recital of the facts of his life put Douglass in jeopardy. Seeking to avoid recapture by his former owner, Douglass set sail for the U.K. and Ireland, where he spent two years lecturing against slavery. His oratory won widespread support for the abolitionist cause in the U.K., and two Quakers, Ellen and Anna Richardson, raised money to purchase his emancipation in December 1846 for 150 pounds sterling.

Douglass returned to the United States in 1847 with an international reputation as a figure who symbolized the latent potentialities of the black people held in bondage. His English friends sent him off with a purse containing $2,175 to start a newspaper. Douglass moved to Rochester, New York, where he launched *The North Star* despite the opposition of the white abolitionist William

Lloyd Garrison, who feared competition for his own paper, *Liberator*, which had two-thirds of its circulation in the black community. Douglass' paper sought "to attack slavery in all of its forms and aspects" and to "promote the moral and intellectual improvement of the colored people." With the assistance of Julia Griffiths, Douglass ran the paper successfully, himself writing most of the editorials and articles, and renamed it in 1851 as *Frederick Douglass's Paper* when it merged with the Liberty Party Paper. In 1858 Douglass also launched *Douglass's Monthly*, especially for British readers. It was in *Frederick Douglass's Paper* that Douglass in March 1853 first published his novella titled *The Heroic Slave*. Based on a historical slave uprising aboard the slave ship *Creole*, *The Heroic Slave* is considered the first work of prose fiction in African American literature. He continued publishing *Frederick Douglass's Paper* until 1860 and *Douglass's Monthly* until 1863, the year of the Emancipation Proclamation. During this time, Douglass' printing shop in Rochester served as a station on the Underground Railroad, helping over 400 slaves escape to Canada.

Douglass came to repudiate some central positions of Garrison's abolitionism. He rejected Garrison's "No Union with Slaveholders" doctrine, which argued for the dissolution of the Union. Arguing that slavery was incompatible with the noble goals set forth in the Constitution, he read that document as an antislavery charter, not the pro-slavery document Garrison saw. Douglass believed in political action, along with moral suasion, to attack the institution of slavery. Douglass' differences with Garrison led him to write his second autobiography, setting forth his positions, *My Bondage and My Freedom*, published in 1855. Douglass also opposed the 1859 raid on Harpers Ferry led by John Brown, the militant white abolitionist. Brown met with Douglass to enlist him in a plot to seize the federal armory at Harpers Ferry, but Douglass rejected the plan as doomed to failure. After Douglass learned of Brown's capture, he fled to England via Canada, fearing that he would be implicated as an accomplice. After five months abroad, he returned home in May 1860 after learning of the death of his youngest child, Annie.

Douglass' belief in human rights led him to take an active role in the woman's rights movement. At the inaugural meeting of the Women's Rights Movement at Seneca Falls, New York on July 19, 1848, he seconded Elizabeth Cady Stanton's suffrage resolution with the impassioned plea that "[t]he power to choose rulers and make laws is the right by which all others could be secured." His paper *The North Star* carried the masthead "Right is of no sex—Truth is of no Color." He cautioned white feminists not to advance their cause without regard to slave women.

Douglass saw the outbreak of the Civil War as the final means of abolishing slavery. In his editorial "How to End the War" in the May 1861 issue of the *Douglass's Monthly*, Douglass proposed that President Lincoln, for whom he had campaigned in the election, should declare the emancipation of slaves as the primary war objective and permit slaves and free blacks to enlist for the Union. While the cautious president was not initially inclined to accept either proposal, Douglass' views gradually gained support among the radical Republicans in Congress. Congress banned slavery in the District of Columbia in April 1862 and in the federal territories in June. Finally, in September 1862, Lincoln announced that, on January 1, 1863, he would issue a proclamation freeing all slaves in states in rebellion. The Emancipation Proclamation also permitted blacks to enter the U.S. military, and Douglass set about to recruit two regiments, the 54th and 55th Massachusetts colored regiments, with his own sons Charles and Lewis among the first to be recruited. In August 1863 Lincoln invited him for a private conference at which Douglass sought equal pay, equal promotion, and equal protection for black soldiers. After President Lincoln's assassination, Mrs. Lincoln sent Douglass President Lincoln's walking stick as a token of her husband's regard for Douglass.

After the war, Douglass led a black delegation in 1866 to discuss race relations with President Andrew Johnson. Johnson rejected their request for black suffrage on the grounds that such a step would increase racial tension and that it was the province of the states, not the federal government, to regulate suffrage. Douglass campaigned vigorously for the enactment of the civil rights amendments to the Constitution.

In the 1870s and 1880s Douglass' distinction as a national leader won him a number of political appointments. In 1871 President Ulysses Grant appointed him secretary of the commission on the annexation of Santo Domingo. In 1872 the Equal Rights Party nominated Douglass for the vice presidency on a ticket headed by Victoria Woodhull. Douglass nevertheless continued his efforts to support Grant's reelection. In 1872 a mysterious fire destroyed his Rochester home and newspaper files, and Douglass moved to Washington, D.C. In 1877 Douglass was appointed District of Columbia marshal by President Rutherford Hayes, and in 1881, recorder of deeds of the District of Columbia by President James Garfield. In 1878 Douglass bought "Cedar Hill," a fifteen-acre estate with a twenty-room Victorian house commanding a view of the Capitol, which ironically once belonged to General Robert E. Lee. In 1889 Douglass was appointed consul general to Haiti by President Benjamin Harrison.

His first wife, Anna, died in 1882. Two years later, Douglass married Helen Pitts, a white woman, who had been his secretary in the office of record of deeds. He was criticized by some whites and blacks for his interracial marriage, but he dismissed his critics with the remark that his first wife "was the color of my mother, and the second, the color of my father." Recent research suggests that Douglass had a long affair with the German journalist Otillie Assing. He twice updated his autobiography *Life and Times of Frederick Douglass*, first in 1881 and then in 1892. He died of cardiac arrest on February 20, 1895, having spent the day attending a meeting of the National Convention of Women.

MAJOR WORKS AND THEMES

The major theme of Frederick Douglass' life and work was his struggle against slavery and injustice. Through his autobiographies, speeches, and newspaper articles, he fought against slavery and racism and all forms of oppression and exploitation. In the 1881 edition of *Life and Times of Frederick Douglass*, Douglass sets forth the purpose of his writings: "My part has been to tell the story of the slave. The story of the master never wanted for narrators" (486–87).

In *Narrative of the Life of Frederick Douglass, an American Slave*, published in 1845, Douglass seeks to "do something toward throwing light on the American slave system, and hastening the glad day of deliverance to the millions of my brethren in bonds" (159). Relying on "the power of truth, love, and justice" (159), he believes that by exposing slavery, he will help end it. The book reveals how slavery degrades both the slaveholder and the slave. For example, Douglass describes how the "lamblike" Sophia Auld, when instructed by her husband that she must treat Douglass like a slave and not a fellow human being, is left with a "ston[y]" heart (82). Douglass' narrative also shows how slavery destroys the family, beginning with his own example as someone who never knew his father and barely knew his mother. Asserting one's manhood by resolutely resisting a tyrant provides another major theme of Douglass' *Narrative*. Douglass' fight with Covey, the climactic episode of the *Narrative*, represents the moment when Douglass feels that he has regained his manhood: he prefaces his description of this fight by saying, "You have seen how a man was made a slave; you shall see how a slave was made a man" (107). The *Narrative* condemns slaveholding Christians who profess faith yet practice the fiercest cruelty. Master Thomas Auld, for example, "would whip [Aunt Hester] to make her scream, and whip her to make her hush" (51), while the Reverend Rigby Hopkins "always managed to have one or more of his slaves to whip every Monday morning" (118). The book also explodes the myth that slaves are content with their lot as slaves and that they, for example, sing when they are happy; rather, slave songs give voice to grief: "[T]hey breathed the prayer and complaint of souls boiling over with the bitterest anguish" (57). He points out that if slaves do not criticize their masters, it is for fear of retaliation, especially the fear that they will be separated from their family (62).

Douglass' *The Heroic Slave* is a historical novella that retells the true story of Madison Washington, who led a mutiny on the slave ship *Creole*. After the ship reached a British island, the British refused to return the 130 slaves onboard to slavery in the United States, though the British eventually paid an indemnity of $110,000 to their American slaveholders. The novella exposes the infernal character of slavery in the antebellum South, showing, for example, the heartrending spectacle of slaves being taken to market: "Humanity converted into merchandise. . . . All sizes, ages, and sexes, mothers, fathers, daughters, brothers, sisters, all huddled together, on their way to market to be sold and separated from each other *forever*" (152). To Douglass, Madison Washington is no less an American hero than his namesake George Washington. Though two people, including the captain of the ship, fell during the mutiny, Douglass' hero defends his actions: "You call me a *black murderer*. I am not a murderer. God is my witness that LIBERTY, not *malice*, is the motive" (161).

In *My Bondage and My Freedom*, published in 1855, Douglass again seeks to reveal the "true nature, character, and tendency of the slave system" and to plead the cause of "my afflicted people" (vii). Appearing ten years after the *Narrative* and after his break with Garrison (who had written the Preface to the *Narrative*), *My Bondage* offers more details about his experiences as a slave and also his work as an abolitionist, this time with an Introduction by a black abolitionist and physician, Dr. James M'Cune Smith. In the book, Douglass rejects the Garrisonian abolitionist advice to stick to "the facts" and leave the "philosophy" to others: "It did not entirely satisfy me to *narrate* wrongs; I felt like *denouncing* them" (361–62). *My Bondage* tells some of the same stories told in the *Narrative*, but with additional and often more horrifying details, as in, for example, the description of Captain Anthony's whipping of Aunt Esther: "Each blow vigorously laid on, brought screams as well as blood" (87). Douglass points out that a slave is not bound by social morality: "Make a man a slave, and you rob him of moral responsibility" (191). Thus, Douglass feels no qualms of conscience in stealing from Master Thomas or other slaveholders. Douglass returns to his theme of the toll that slavery has on the family, noting that "[m]y poor mother . . . had many children, but NO FAMILY!" (48). Douglass also describes the racism he experiences as a freeman. He is sometimes stoned or insulted with racist slurs at lectures; he must often sit in segregated train cars and is denied entrance to hotels and restaurants. He recounts a humorous incident when he and a white abolitionist colleague are to stay at someone's house during their lecture circuit, but there is only one spare bed. Sensing the host's dilemma, Douglass addresses his colleague: "Friend White, having got entirely rid of my prejudice against color, I think as a proof of it, I must allow you to sleep with me tonight" (401–2).

In 1881 Douglass published his life story for the third time as *Life and Times of Frederick Douglass, Written by Himself*. Nearly twice as long as *My Bondage* (which had itself been four times as long as the *Narrative*), *Life and Times* updates his autobiography to the year 1881. *Life and Times* offers only slight changes in the account of his years as a slave provided in *My Bondage*, except for the addition of the story of his escape from slavery. It adds a number of chapters describing his role in the Civil War and in the post–Civil War era, exposing particularly the problems facing blacks in the post-Reconstruction era. Through his autobiographies, Douglass provides a black perspective that is not available in most works written by his contemporaries. However, the fact that Douglass tends to document rather than dramatize the conflicts, issues, and events by including numerous excerpts from his speeches and other writings makes his *Life and Times* (1881, 1892) much less interesting autobiography than the *Narrative* or *My Bondage*.

Frederick Douglass was one of the great American orators. His oratorical style was influenced by the African American oral tradition, black and white revivalist preachers, and his thoroughgoing study of Caleb Bingham's *The Columbian Orator*, which compiled examples of effective speeches. Gifted with a deep, rolling, sonorous voice and a commanding figure, Douglass was the envy of platform speakers of his day.

Brief excerpts from three speeches offer a glimpse of Douglass' rhetorical skills. In "What to the Slave Is the Fourth of July?" (1852), delivered before the Rochester Antislavery Sewing Society, Douglass answers the speech title's question in a number of accusatory phrases:

To him, your celebration is a sham; your boasted liberty, an unholy license; your national greatness, swelling vanity; . . . your denunciations of tyrants, brass fronted impudence; and your shouts of liberty and equality hollow mockery . . . a thin veil to cover up crimes which would disgrace a nation of savages. (119)

The reader can visualize Douglass' listeners squirming in collective guilt. In "The Color Line in America" (1883), Douglass bemoans the fact that "[t]he color line meets [the colored person] everywhere, and in a measure shuts him out from all respectable and profitable trades and callings." He offers specific examples of the injustice done to black people and exhorts blacks to challenge the nefarious codes that subjugate them: "Who would be free, themselves must strike the blow" (586). In "The Lessons of the Hour" (1894), delivered in the Metropolitan A.M.E. Church in Washington, D.C., Douglass tackles the "Negro Problem" postulated by the racist southern whites. He argues that those who accuse blacks of violence take a charge against an individual black man and make it a charge against the whole black race, so every black man becomes an object of suspicion. He turns the tables on the accusers by pointing out how black people have "become the sport of mob violence and murder" (341).

CRITICAL RECEPTION

Much of the critical analysis of Douglass' work focuses on his *Narrative*, which has received the highest critical acclaim among his three autobiographies. On its publication in 1845, the *Narrative* was generally received favorably by critics. Margaret Fuller, reviewing the book for the *New York Tribune* (June 10, 1845), offers high praise: "Considered merely as narrative, we have never read one more simple, true, coherent and warm with genuine feeling" (2). Ephraim Peabody, however, in his July 1849 *Christian Examiner* article, finds Douglass prone to using "extravagance and passionate and rhetorical flourishes," indicating that he might be "thinking more of his speech than of the end for which he professes to make it," which makes Douglass' commitment to the antislavery cause suspect (26). The public received the book enthusiastically, making it a best-seller. In 1969 the *Narrative* was included in Hennig Cohen's *Landmarks of American Writing*, signifying its acceptance into the American canon. In *Landmarks*, Benjamin Quarles calls the *Narrative* "a landmark in the literary crusade against slavery" and "one of the most influential pieces of reform propaganda in American literature" (101). He points out that the *Narrative* owes its popularity to its "strong storyline," its believability, its "simple and direct prose," its power to evoke sympathy, and its "sharply etched portraits" (104–7).

Writing in 1973, Houston Baker Jr. in *Long Black Song* sees the *Narrative* as a sophisticated literary autobiography and finds the chief features of Douglass' style to include irony, deft characterizations, clever use of animal imagery, and antithesis (58–78). Albert E. Stone, in a 1973 article in the *CLA Journal*, points out that the *Narrative* shows "the man revealed in the act of discovering and recreating his own identity in the face of slavery's denial of individuality and creativity" (65–66). In a 1978 essay, Henry Louis Gates Jr. points out that Douglass' narrative strategy employs "binary oppositions": "by opposing two seemingly unrelated elements, such as the sheep, cattle, or horses on the plantation, and the specimen of life known as slave, Douglass's language is made to signify the presence and absence of some quality—in this case, humanity" (86).

Recent works have applied modern critical theories to the *Narrative*. Ann Kibbey in "Language in Slavery" (1983) deconstructs the *Narrative*: "The silence of the slave was not the silence of ignorance, much less of ineptitude, but the silence of a human being whose enslavement had forced on him an extraordinary knowledge of language use" (151). Valerie Smith in *Self-Discovery and Authority in Afro-American Narrative* (1987) says that "Douglass' *Narrative* celebrates both explicitly and symbolically a slave's capacity to achieve humanity in a system that conspires to reduce him to nothing" and suggests that "the plot of the narrative offers a profound endorsement of the fundamental American plot, the myth of the self-made man" (26–27). Fred Lee Hord in *Reconstructing Memory: Black Literary Criticism* (1991) argues that "Douglass' *Narrative* is a study of the 'power of truth' triumphing over 'irresponsible power' " and that the " 'power of truth' was necessary to the slaves to demystify their predicament and to resist the dehumanization of an alien identity and ethos" (45). Ann Kibbey and Michele Stepto (1991) offer the Marxist perspective that alienation from the self and language is caused by the marketplace, and, thus, Douglass' awareness of the market's operation makes him "potentially free" (179). Deborah E. McDowell (1991) contends that the *Narrative* makes aggressive "manhood" identical with selfhood and points to Douglass' "complex and troubling relationship to slave women" (202–3).

Douglass' other works received much less critical attention than his *Narrative*. Richard Yarborough (1990), writing of *The Heroic Slave*, contends that Douglass makes Madison Washington into a "heroic exemplar who would both win white converts to the antislavery struggle and firmly establish the reality of black manhood" (179). Douglass' second autobiography, *My Bondage*, is described by Eric J. Sundquist as revealing that Douglass has thrown off the yoke of the "white father-figure," replacing him with "a self-fathered figure combining black and white ideals" (124). Wilson J. Moses (1990) criticizes *Life and Times* as a "literary act of self-presentation . . . skillfully engineered to produce desired effects on certain sets of white liberals" and contends that in this book "Douglass became a stereotype, limited by the constraints of the myths . . . the myth of rags to riches and the myth of the heroic slave . . . to which he so successfully contributed" (68–69). Jenny Franchot (1990) attacks Douglass for failing to give full due to the contributions of women to his struggle and reducing the description of the role of women to no more than a part of one chapter of his final autobiography, despite his prominence as a strong proponent of woman's rights (149).

BIBLIOGRAPHY

Works by Frederick Douglass

Narrative of the Life of Frederick Douglass, an American Slave, Written by Himself. Boston, 1845. Ed. Houston A. Baker Jr. New York: Penguin, 1986.

Oration Delivered in Corinthian Hall, Rochester, July 5th, 1852 (originally titled "What to the Slave Is the Fourth of July?"). Rochester, NY, 1852. In *The Oxford Frederick Douglass Reader*. New York: Oxford University Press, 1996.

The Heroic Slave. In *Autographs for Freedom*. Ed. Julia Griffiths. Boston, 1853. In *The Oxford Frederick Douglass Reader*. Ed. William L. Andrews. New York: Oxford University Press, 1996.

My Bondage and My Freedom. Intro. Dr. James M'Cune Smith. New York, 1855. Reprinted with the original intro., and a new intro. by Philip S. Foner. New York: Dover, 1969.

Life and Times of Frederick Douglass, Written by Himself. Intro. George L. Ruffin. New York, 1881. Facsimile. New York: Carol, 1995.

"My Escape from Slavery." *The Century Magazine* (November 1881): 125–31.

Life and Times of Frederick Douglass, Written by Himself. A new intro. by Rayford W. Logan. New York, 1881. New York: Collier Books, 1962.

"The Color Line in America." In *Three Addresses on the Relations between the White and Colored People of the United States*. Washington, DC, 1886. Reprinted, *The Annals of America*. Vol. 10: 1866–1883. Chicago: Encyclopedia Britannica, 1976.

The Lessons of the Hour. Baltimore, 1894. In *The Oxford Frederick Douglass Reader*. Ed. William L. Andrews. New York: Oxford University Press, 1996.

The Life and Writings of Frederick Douglass. Ed. Philip S. Foner. 5 vols. New Haven, CT: Yale University Press, 1950–1975.

The Frederick Douglass Papers. Ed. John W. Blassinghame. New Haven, CT: Yale University Press, 1979.

Journals Owned and Edited by Frederick Douglass

North Star (Rochester, NY), 1847–1851.

Frederick Douglass's Paper (Rochester, NY), 1851–1860.

Douglass's Monthly (Rochester, NY), 1859–1863; issues before January 1859 were supplements to *Frederick Douglass's Paper*.

New National Era (Washington, DC), 1870–1874.

Studies of Frederick Douglass

Baker, Jr., Houston A. *Long Black Song*. Charlottesville: University Press of Virginia, 1973. 58–78.

Cohen, Hennig, ed. *Landmarks of American Writing*. New York: Basic Books, 1969.

Dorsey, Peter A. "Becoming the Other: The Mimesis of Metaphor in Douglass's *My Bondage and My Freedom*. PMLA 111 (May 1996): 435–50.

Franchot, Jenny. "The Punishment of Esther: Frederick Douglass and the Construction of the Feminine." In *Frederick Douglass: New Literary and Historical Essays*. Ed. Eric J. Sundquist. Cambridge: Cambridge University Press, 1990. 141–65.

Fuller, Margaret. Rev. of *Narrative of the Life of Frederick Douglass, an American Slave*. *New York Tribune*, June 10, 1845: 2.

Gates, Henry Louis. "Binary Oppositions in Chapter One of *Narrative of the Life of Frederick Douglass, an American Slave, Written by Himself*." In *Afro-American Literature*. Ed. Dexter Fisher and Robert B. Stepto. New York: MLA, 1978. 212–32. In *Critical Essays on Frederick Douglass*. Ed. William L. Andrews. Boston: G. K. Hall, 1991. 79–93.

Hord, Fred Lee. *Reconstructing Memory: Black Literary Criticism*. Chicago: Third World Press, 1991.

Kibbey, Ann. "Language in Slavery." *Prospects: The Annual of American Cultural Studies* 8 (1983). In *Frederick Douglass's Narrative of the Life of Frederick Douglass*. Ed. Harold Bloom. New York: Chelsea House, 1988. 131–52.

Kibbey Ann, and Michele Stepto. "The Antilanguage of Slavery: Frederick Douglass's 1845 *Narrative*. In *Critical Essays on Frederick Douglass*. Ed. William L. Andrews. Boston: G. K. Hall, 1991. 166–91.

McDowell, Deborah E. "In the First Place: Making Frederick Douglass and the Afro-American Narrative Tradition." In *Critical Essays on Frederick Douglass*. Ed. William L. Andrews. Boston: G. K. Hall, 1991. 192–214.

Moses, Wilson J. "Writing Freely?: Frederick Douglass and the Constraints of Racialized Writing." *Frederick Douglass: New Literary and Historical Essays*. Ed. Eric J. Sundquist. Cambridge: Cambridge University Press, 1990. 66–83.

Peabody, Ephraim. Rev. of Douglass' *Narrative*. In "Narratives of Fugitive Slaves." *Christian Examiner* 47 (July 1849): 61–93. In *Critical Essays on Frederick Douglass*. Ed. William L. Andrews. Boston: G. K. Hall, 1991. 24–27.

Smith, Valerie. *Self-Discovery and Authority in Afro-American Literature*. Cambridge: Harvard University Press, 1987.

Stone, Albert E. "Identity and Art in Frederick Douglass's *Narrative*." *CLA Journal* 17 (1973): 192–213. In *Critical Essays on Frederick Douglass*. Ed. William L. Andrews. Boston: G. K. Hall, 1991. 62–78.

Sundquist, Eric J. "Frederick Douglass: Literacy and Paternalism." *Raritan* 2 (Fall 1986): 108–24. In *Critical Essays on Frederick Douglass*. Ed. William L. Andrews, Boston: G. K. Hall, 1991. 120–132.

Yarborough, Richard. "Race, Violence, and Manhood: The Masculine Ideal in Frederick Douglass's 'The Heroic Slave.' " In *Frederick Douglass: New Literary and Historical Essays*. Ed. Eric J. Sundquist. Cambridge: Cambridge University Press, 1990. 166–88.

Biographies and Histories

Blassinghame, John W. *The Slave Community: Plantation Life in the Antebellum South*. New York: Oxford University Press, 1972.

Buckmaster, Henrietta. *Let My People Go: The Story of the Underground Railroad and the Growth of the Abolition Movement*. Boston: Beacon, 1969.

Chesnutt, Charles W. *Frederick Douglass*. Boston: Small, Maynard, 1899.

Chiasson, Lloyd E., and Philip B. Damatteis. "Frederick Douglass." In *Dictionary of Literary Biography*. Vol. 79: *American Magazine Journalists, 1850–1900*. Detroit: Gale, 1989. 139–42.

Filler, Louis. *The Crusade against Slavery, 1830–1860*. New York: Harper, 1960.

Foner, Philip S. *Frederick Douglass*. New York: Citadel, 1964.

"Frederick Douglass." *Civil War Journal*. Narr. Danny Glover. Dir. Craig Haffner. Arts & Entertainment Network. April 6, 1993.

Frederick Douglass: When the Lion Wrote History. PBS Video. Narr. Alfree Woodard. Turner Home Entertainment. November 1994.

Gregory, James M. *Frederick Douglass, the Orator*. Intro. W. S. Scarborough. Chicago: Afro-Am Press, 1969.

Hively, Russell K. "Frederick Douglass." In *Dictionary of Literary Biography*. Vol. 50: *Afro-American Writers before the Harlem Renaissance*. Detroit: Gale, 1986. 80–91.

Holland, Frederic May. *Frederick Douglass: The Colored Orator*. Rev. ed. New York: Haskell House, 1969.

Huggins, Nathan Irvin. *Slave and Citizen: The Life of Frederick Douglass*. Boston: Little, Brown, 1980.

Lester, Julius. *To Be a Slave*. Illus. Tom Feelings. New York: Dell, 1968.

McFeeley, William S. *Frederick Douglass*. New York: W. W. Norton, 1991.

Miller, Douglass T. *Frederick Douglass and the Fight for Freedom*. New York: Facts on File, 1998.

Murphy, Sharon M. "Frederick Douglass." *Dictionary of Literary Biography*. Vol. 43: *American Newspaper Journalists, 1690–1872*. Detroit: Gale, 1985. 160–68.

Preston, Dickson J. *Young Frederick Douglass: The Maryland Years*. Baltimore: Johns Hopkins University Press, 1980.

Quarles, Benjamin. *Black Abolitionists*. London: Oxford University Press, 1969.

———. *Frederick Douglass*. Washington, DC: Associated, 1948. With revised Intro. by James M. Mcpherson. New York: Da Capo Press, 1997.

Unger, Irwin, and David Reimers. *The Slavery Experience in the United States*. New York: Holt, 1970.

Washington, Booker T. *Frederick Douglass*. Philadelphia: George W. Jacobs, 1907; New York: Greenwood, 1969.

Weinstein, Allen, Frank Otto Gatell, and David Sarasohn, eds. *American Negro Slavery: A Modern Reader*. 3d ed. New York: Oxford University Press, 1979.

W.E.B. DU BOIS
(1868–1963)

David L. Dudley

BIOGRAPHY

The impressively long, productive, and committed life of William Edward Burg-hardt Du Bois began on February 23, 1868, in Great Barrington, Massachusetts. The son of Alfred Du Bois and Mary Silvina Burghardt, Du Bois was born into a family struggling to scratch a living on the fringes of society in a predominantly white, small New England town. Before Du Bois was two, his father deserted the family, worsening its financial plight. But despite desperate circumstances at home, Du Bois succeeded in school, where his intellectual gifts were recognized and encouraged.

Perhaps the central realization of W.E.B. Du Bois' life came in his adolescence, on a day his classmates were exchanging visiting cards. A white girl refused Du Bois' card because he was an African American. At that moment, Du Bois understood that his individuality counted for little in the face of racial prejudice. As he recalls in *The Souls of Black Folk*, "it dawned upon me with a certain suddenness that I was different from the others; or like, maybe, in heart and life and longing, but shut from their world by a vast veil" (364). Du Bois spent the rest of his life fighting the injustice of American racism that saw color more strongly than ability, education, or character.

Du Bois graduated from Fisk University in 1888; that autumn he entered Harvard, earning the master's degree in 1891. After studies at the University of Berlin between 1892 and 1894, Du Bois completed his doctoral degree through Harvard, receiving the Ph.D. in 1895—the first African American to do so. In 1896 Du Bois accepted an offer from the University of Pennsylvania to write a sociological study of the black population of Philadelphia. That same year he married Nina Gomer, who would become the mother of his two children, Burghardt, who died of diphtheria in 1899, and a daughter, Nina Yolande. Du Bois also published his doctoral dissertation in 1896; this work, *The Suppression of the African Slave Trade to the United States of America, 1638–1870*, became the first volume of the Harvard Historical Monograph Series. More than a century later, it is still considered the standard work in its field.

Du Bois' research for the University of Pennsylvania ultimately resulted in the publication of *The Philadelphia Negro* in 1899. With this work, designed to demonstrate the impact of environmental forces on black life, Du Bois virtually created the discipline of urban sociology. After being refused a job at the University of Pennsylvania because of his race, Du Bois accepted a position at Atlanta University in 1897. Under his direction, the school sponsored yearly conferences between 1897 and 1914 and published sixteen Atlanta University Studies, covering numerous aspects of the sociology of African Americans.

During his Atlanta University years, W.E.B. Du Bois became embroiled in one of the great controversies of his life. As leader of a group he called the "Talented Tenth"—well-educated black intellectuals who he believed were best qualified to lead African Americans—Du Bois challenged the accommodationist philosophy of Booker T. Washington,* founder of Tuskegee Institute and the most powerful black man in the nation. Washington urged African Americans to accept temporary segregation while improving their condition economically; eventually, Washington believed, whites would recognize the worth of productive black citizens and come to grant them full social equality. The notorious lynching of Sam Hose in Atlanta helped jolt Du Bois out of his life of scholarly study and convinced him that Washington's advice to blacks to wait for equality was fatally flawed. That day of equality would never come; in the meantime, African Americans were being lynched. Du Bois challenged Washington in the essay "Of Mr. Booker T. Washington and Others," published in *The Souls of Black Folk* (1903). The ensuing conflict moved Du Bois in 1905 to help organize the Niagara Movement, an organization of black Americans dedicated to combating Washington and fighting for civil rights. In 1910 the Niagara Movement gave way to the National Association for the Advancement of Colored People (NAACP), with Du Bois a founding member. That same year Du Bois resigned his position at Atlanta University and moved to New York, where he became editor of *Crisis*, the official newspaper of the NAACP. In this position, Du Bois found the wide audience he had missed as a university professor. Du Bois saw *Crisis* expand to reach nearly 100,000 subscribers by 1918; his columns made him the most influential African American in the nation following the death of Booker T. Washington in 1915.

During his years with the NAACP, Du Bois was involved in another controversy, this time with Marcus Garvey,* founder of the Universal Negro Improvement Association. Initially a supporter of Garvey, Du Bois came to be critical of the Jamaican leader's advocacy of black Americans' mass emigration to Africa, as well as of Garvey's flashy style. Yet Du Bois shared Garvey's interest in Africa; between 1919 and 1927, Du Bois took the lead in four conferences on Pan-

Africanism. Du Bois had a lifelong interest in Africa and sought to promote African unity and worldwide appreciation for the continent's history and culture.

Du Bois remained with the NAACP until 1934, despite a long struggle with its other leaders over control of *Crisis* and the philosophy of the organization. Du Bois believed that the NAACP was neglecting the needs of the masses of black Americans while focusing too much on the black middle class. Long an advocate of integration, Du Bois was also coming to see the value of African Americans' working exclusively among themselves to form separatist economic and social structures. As early as 1905, he had had an interest in socialism, which grew in the years after his resignation from the NAACP.

In 1934 W.E.B. Du Bois returned to Atlanta University to chair the Department of Sociology. In six years, he wrote three books, including *Black Reconstruction* and *Dusk of Dawn*, an autobiography. In the latter work, subtitled *An Essay toward an Autobiography of a Race Concept*, Du Bois connects his individual life and destiny with that of the dark-skinned peoples of the world. He sees his own life as a representative example of the struggle facing people of color in the twentieth century.

Du Bois left Atlanta in 1944 and returned to the NAACP as director of special research, a position he held until 1948. That same year he became the honorary vice chairman of the Council on African Affairs, an organization labeled subversive by the office of the attorney general. In 1950 Du Bois' wife, Nina, died, and Du Bois was named chairman of the Peace Information Center. Ten months later he found himself indicted by the federal government for his association with an organization deemed an "agent of a foreign principal." At this time, Du Bois married Shirley Graham. Although acquitted of the charges against him in November 1951, Du Bois was embittered by the experience and by the failure of the NAACP to rally African Americans to his cause. After his passport was restored in 1958, Du Bois traveled extensively, particularly in the communist nations of Eastern Europe and Asia. He applied for membership in the American Communist Party in 1961, the year in which he left America permanently and expatriated himself to Ghana, where he was received with honor. W.E.B. Du Bois, who had been born during the presidency of Andrew Johnson, died in Accra, Ghana, on August 27, 1963, during the presidency of Lyndon Johnson. Appropriately, Du Bois died while the famous March on Washington was under way. He had lived long enough to see African Americans begin to receive the rights for which he had worked so long; ironically, it was by his own choice that he was buried outside the nation of his birth, doubting that African Americans would ever receive the full privileges of equal citizens.

MAJOR WORKS AND THEMES

W.E.B. Du Bois' career as a scholar and writer covered more than two-thirds of a century. During that time he produced twenty-three books and hundreds of articles, essays, editorials, and reviews. The sheer volume of his writing makes it necessary to limit discussion here to those few works generally regarded as his most important. But because, as Adolph L. Reed Jr. asserts, Du Bois held "certain core assumptions and values that he maintained over the course of his lengthy intellectual career" (72), a look at even a small number of his books will reveal the major themes of his total literary production.

The Suppression of the African Slave Trade (1896) established Du Bois as a historian. In it, he marshals facts revealing why the slave trade was started and continued so long, even after its legal abolishment. His tone is usually dispassionate, but critics agree that Du Bois reveals a partisan position, despite his training in the tenets of scientific objectivity. Jack B. Moore notes that in The Suppression of the African Slave Trade, Du Bois begins his lifelong "literary and personal task of rehabilitating the history of black people in Africa and America, of establishing a usable past for them in their constant, daily struggle to achieve a decent future" (27). Keith Byerman asserts that in this text, Du Bois first "defines his lifelong thesis: the need for a moral order in an immoral nation" (38).

At the end of The Suppression of the African Slave Trade, Du Bois advises America to study its history and profit from its mistakes. He asserts that his study raises an important question, "How far in a State can a recognized moral wrong safely be compromised?" (198). Had America abandoned the slave trade early on, Du Bois argues, it might have avoided the disaster of the Civil War. He closes his work with this moral: "[W]e may conclude that it behooves nations as well as men to do things at the very moment when they ought to be done" (198). Shamoon Zamir believes that this ending reveals Du Bois' belief at the time that moral argument has the power to change people's minds and move them toward right action (95). Du Bois would later abandon such an optimistic view; as Zamir notes, "Neither the appeal to a will to action nor the moralism of the critical judgments in Du Bois's social scientific works can offer an adequate account of social process or the individual experience of history or of the process of referral between self and world" (95). Although Du Bois would come to accept this truth, his next major work, The Philadelphia Negro, shows him still believing that the findings of objective social science could profitably serve social reform.

The Philadelphia Negro virtually invented the field of urban sociology. David Levering Lewis, author of the standard biography of Du Bois, remarks that the work is "remarkable as an example of the new empiricism that was fundamentally transforming the social sciences at the beginning of the twentieth century" (201). Influenced by Darwin and Spencer, most sociologists then believed heredity to be the strongest determinant in an individual's destiny. This made it all too easy to blame the poor and disadvantaged for their plight. The subject of The Philadelphia Negro is the city's Seventh Ward, an area plagued by poverty, crime, and disintegrating social structures. Under the guise of exhaustive objective investigation—Du Bois and his associates conducted literally thousands of interviews—Du Bois sets out to show that environment, not heredity, is responsible for the blighted lives of Philadelphia's poorest black citizens. This does not prevent Du

Bois from moralizing: he offers suggestions for changes that African Americans can undertake themselves in order to improve their own condition. Yet their problems would be helped most when the white world changed its thinking about them. At this time, notes Keith Byerman, Du Bois still thought that "prejudice is a matter of ignorance and unenlightened self-interest" (59). Du Bois believed he could help eliminate such prejudice: " 'The world was thinking wrong about race, because it did not know.' He would teach it to think right" (Lewis 189).

The Philadelphia Negro combines elements of the emerging field of objective sociology with older beliefs in the power of reason and persuasion to work social change. Byerman rightly notes that the work rests on "reformist objectives" but acts as if it is "disinterested science" (50). Jack Moore praises the work for humanizing the misery suggested by its numerous charts, graphs, and statistics. He further notes that Du Bois' optimism for a better future for African Americans is not supported by the facts Du Bois has collected (43). Moralizing and reason would not prove strong enough to effect the changes needed to help African Americans. When he wrote *The Philadelphia Negro*, Du Bois was not yet a radical. His study of power would make him one (Moore 50).

Many regard *The Souls of Black Folk* (1903) as Du Bois' greatest work; it is certainly his best known. Proclaiming it "epochal," David Levering Lewis claims that it "redefined the terms of a three-hundred-year interaction between black and white people and influenced the cultural and political psychology of peoples of African descent throughout the Western hemisphere, as well as on the continent of Africa" (277). The book also established Du Bois as a race leader and the leading opponent of Booker T. Washington. It advances ideas that are among Du Bois' great themes: African Americans are a people with a valuable history and culture of their own and have made cultural contributions to the world as great as those of the white Europeans. Perhaps even more important, in what Jack B. Moore calls "one of the most famous paragraphs in American literary history" (69), Du Bois identifies the "double consciousness" operating within the African American: "One ever feels his twoness,—an American, a Negro; two souls, two thoughts, two unreconciled strivings; two warring ideals in one dark body, whose dogged strength alone keeps it from being torn asunder" (364–65). As Lewis emphasizes, Du Bois not only identifies this twoness but celebrates it, crediting African Americans with a kind of "second sight" that enables them to see themselves "through the revelation of the other world" (*Souls* 364). Furthermore, this double consciousness will not destroy African Americans but strengthen them to triumph and show other immigrant peoples that the white European paradigm is not the only acceptable model for American identity (Lewis 283).

The Souls of Black Folk is a collection of essays on various subjects concerning African Americans, held together by an eloquent narrative voice that both presents detailed facts and observations about African American life in a white-dominated society and then makes comments and observations that are, in turn, nostalgic, ironic, celebratory, and critical. The first and third essays are the best known; in "Of Our Spiritual Strivings," Du Bois recalls his first experience of rejection for being an African American. He then proceeds to meditate on the African American's "double consciousness" and what it means to live behind the veil of color. The third essay, "Of Mr. Booker T. Washington and Others," caused the greatest stir when *Souls* was first published. In it, Du Bois challenges the policies and philosophies of Washington, who was advising his race to forgo— temporarily—political power, civil rights, and higher education for their young people while concentrating instead on "industrial education, the accumulation of wealth, and the conciliation of the South" (398–99). These policies were failing, without the vote, African Americans lacked the political power to defend their rights. No amount of material wealth could compensate for the sense of "civic inferiority" fostered by segregationist laws. Du Bois positions himself with the opponents of Washington, whom he calls, in the essay "Of the Training of Black Men," the "Talented Tenth." These individuals demand immediately that the nation grant African Americans "1. The right to vote. 2. Civic equality. 3. The education of youth according to ability" (*Souls* 400). In this essay, Du Bois lays claim to race leadership, a position he would finally assume after the death of Washington in 1915. The twelve years between the publication of *Souls* and Washington's demise were characterized by the struggle between two conflicting positions: the accommodationist, gradualist philosophy of Washington and the increasingly urgent demands of Du Bois and the Talented Tenth for immediate equality for African Americans. "Of Mr. Booker T. Washington and Others" is the opening volley in this war.

Other essays in *The Souls of Black Folk* are characteristic of Du Bois in thought, style, and method. The narrative voice often rises to heights of eloquence that have caused some to find the book's greatest value to be its artistic use of language. Du Bois the revisionist historian speaks in "Of the Dawn of Freedom," in which he defends the Freedmen's Bureau, created by the federal government after the Civil War to help former slaves in the South. Refuting the popular view that the bureau had been a failure, Du Bois demonstrates its successes, especially in bringing educational opportunities to illiterate ex-slaves. Two companion essays, "Of the Black Belt" and "Of the Quest of the Golden Fleece," show Du Bois as the sharp-eyed observer of people, landscapes, and social structures. In both essays, Du Bois takes the reader to the South and to its most oppressed people, poor black farmers and workers victimized by the greed of an emerging capitalist economy. The observations of Du Bois the social scientist are made to serve the musings of Du Bois the philosopher and prophet; here the two tendencies within him—to research and write according to the tenets of scientific objectivity and to exhort and persuade—find seamless fusion.

W.E.B. Du Bois, a man seemingly destined by virtue of his training and personality for a quiet life of academic writing and teaching, finds instead, in *The Souls of Black Folk*, the path he would henceforth pursue. Du Bois was born to put his enormous intellect, prodigious energy, and superb training at the service of African Americans' quest for freedom and acceptance. As Jack B. Moore notes,

"[I]n writing about black souls and his own, Du Bois transformed himself into a race leader who with both passion and scholarship revealed with shrewdness, honesty, and artistic sophistication a level of black existence that had never been shown before" (64). This would continue to be Du Bois' life work for the next sixty years.

In 1935, in the depths of the Great Depression, Du Bois published *Black Reconstruction*, which some consider his greatest work; he himself believed it to be his magnum opus. In this work, Du Bois, well into his sixties, grapples with a subject whose breadth and importance offered a challenge to which his wisdom, insight, and scholarly ability were more than equal. Covering the years 1850–1880, *Black Reconstruction* presents a history of the period through the Marxist focus on the importance of economics and class struggle as determinants of historical outcomes. But perhaps more importantly, Du Bois continues his lifelong work of correcting the racist propaganda that had taken over the field of American history, particularly in its treatment of African Americans.

In the closing chapter of *Black Reconstruction*, Du Bois summarizes the lies and distortions current in the history textbooks of his day. By and large, those books depicted African Americans during Reconstruction as ignorant, incapable of handling the political power placed into their hands by northern radicals, pawns of northern whites, and responsible for the corruption and economic collapse in southern states after the Civil War. Du Bois' task, as always, is to sweep away these lies and present a true history. Despite his own attraction to Marxism, it is not enough, he writes, to offer a simple, mechanistic version of events, to claim that economics was the only force operating in the history of the times and that individuals bore no personal responsibility for what was done:

Yet in this sweeping mechanistic interpretation, there is no room for the real plot of the story, for the clear mistake and guilt of rebuilding a new slavery of the working class in the midst of a fateful experiment in democracy; for the triumph of sheer moral courage and sacrifice in the abolition crusade; and for the hurt and struggle of degraded black millions in their fight for freedom and their attempt to enter democracy. (715)

Du Bois' task is clear: he will tell the story of the true hero of the time, the black folk, their wisdom, restraint, and what Jack B. Moore summarizes as their "charitability and tenacity in their struggle for right in an often unresponsive or hostile land" (128). To accomplish this task, Du Bois plays the role of prophet whose challenge to America to examine and learn from its past is based upon his exacting recovery of truth. If the nation will not see and accept this truth and make changes to correct its errors, then America had better acknowledge its true motives:

If, on the other hand, we are going to use history for our pleasure and amusement, for inflating our national ego, and giving us a false but pleasurable sense of accomplishment, then we must give up the idea of history either as a science or as an art using the results of science, and admit frankly that we are using a version of historic fact to influence and educate the new generation along the way we wish. (714)

W.E.B. Du Bois devoted his life to telling the truth about the African American, often to a world that did not want to hear or believe that truth. In so doing, Du Bois, more than any other black leader of the twentieth century, returned to African Americans their own history. Furthermore, he linked his personal destiny to that of millions of others forced to live "behind the veil." Du Bois lived long enough to see the beginning of the end of centuries of abuse and degradation: he admitted his surprise at hearing of the *Brown v. Board of Education* decision in 1954, which put a legal end to public school segregation. He supported the work of Dr. Martin Luther King Jr. Although he left the United States in 1961 and joined the Communist Party—Du Bois knew the value of dramatic gestures—he still followed with interest the preparations for the famous 1963 March on Washington, during which he died. How fitting that Du Bois passed on just as others were taking up, as strongly as he had, the work to which he had devoted so much passion, so much energy, so much of the deep power of his own soul, for so many years.

CRITICAL RECEPTION

W.E.B. Du Bois' writings met with mixed reviews during his lifetime, primarily because some critics disliked what he had to say and were offended by his uncompromising way of saying it. Today, while admitting that Du Bois was not equally successful in every literary undertaking (e.g., he was not a gifted novelist but wrote several novels anyway), critics celebrate his enormous contribution to American letters.

In *Black Literature in America*, Houston Baker summarizes the reasons that Du Bois' works were not as well received as they should have been. Commenting on *The Souls of Black Folk*, which he calls a "prophetic" work, Baker says simply that white America was not ready to accept Du Bois' contention that the great problem of the twentieth century was the color line (6–7). Harold Cruse and Carolyn Gipson, writing in *The New York Review of Books*, agree that Du Bois did not receive the recognition he deserved but acknowledge the magnitude of his achievement. According to Cruse and Gipson, Du Bois did more for African Americans than "redefine . . . their role in Western history" (22). As if that achievement were not enough by itself, they assert that Du Bois' even greater gift to black Americans was "the right of intellectual independence" and that Du Bois' truest legacy was his own "intellectual audacity" (22).

As a historian and writer, Du Bois was a man of many firsts. As Herbert Aptheker notes, in his *The Complete Published Works of W.E.B. Du Bois*, Du Bois pioneered study of the slave trade. He provided new insights into the true accomplishments of the Freedmen's Bureau after the Civil War. He showed the important contribution of African Americans to the abolitionist movement, countered the stereotypes that blacks were docile and contented slaves, and transformed the popular vision of the role of African Americans in the Civil War and Reconstruction. Furthermore, Du Bois was the first to write a history of Africans and did groundbreaking work in the fields of the study of southern agriculture and northern city life. In short, to him we owe credit for his "pioneering efforts in historiography" (271). Critics today are able to look back over his career and recognize these achievements.

Those who faulted Du Bois as a writer during his lifetime most often blamed what they believed to be his negativity, claiming to find excessive negativity, even hatred in his work. Some critics were bothered by his insistence on identifying himself personally with the wrongs suffered by his own people; others chided him for his insistence that the wrongs of the century could be reduced to the one problem of the wrongs against people of color. But whether they liked his work or not, one thing the critics over the years agreed upon: the writings of W.E.B. Du Bois were *passionate*. That is the adjective that turns up most often when critics evaluate the tone of his writing.

W.E.B. Du Bois and his work are today the subjects of numerous, excellent scholarly works. One must single out David Levering Lewis' superb biography, *W.E.B. Du Bois: Biography of a Race, 1868–1919*. The first volume of a projected two-volume work, it won the 1994 Pulitzer Prize in biography as well as many other awards. Other important works include Jack B. Moore's *W.E.B. Du Bois*, a useful, succinct introduction to the man's life and work, and more specialized books such as Keith Byerman's *Seizing the Word: History, Art, and Self in the Works of W.E.B. Du Bois*. It is gratifying to see that Du Bois, who may well have done more for African Americans than any other writer, is at last receiving the scholarly attention that he and his work so well deserve.

BIBLIOGRAPHY

Works by W.E.B. Du Bois

History, Sociology, Politics, and Philosophy

The Suppression of the African Slave Trade to the United States of America 1638–1870. 1896. In *W.E.B. Du Bois: Writings*. Ed. Nathan Huggins. New York: Viking/Library of America, 1986.

The Philadelphia Negro: A Social Study. 1899. Millwood, NY: Kraus-Thomson, 1973.

The Souls of Black Folk: Essays and Sketches. 1903. In *W.E.B. Du Bois: Writings*. Ed. Nathan Huggins. New York: Viking/Library of America, 1986.

John Brown. 1909. Millwood, NY: Kraus-Thomson, 1973.

The Negro. 1915. Millwood, NY: Kraus-Thomson, 1975.

The Gift of Black Folk: Negroes in the Making of America. 1924. Millwood, NY: Kraus-Thomson, 1975.

Africa, Its Geography, People, and Products. Africa—Its Place in Modern History. (2 vols. in one book). 1930. Ed. Herbert Aptheker. Millwood, NY: Kraus-Thomson, 1977.

Black Reconstruction in America. 1935. New York: Russell and Russell, 1966.
Black Folk Then and Now: An Essay in the History and Sociology of the Negro Race. 1939. Millwood, NY: Kraus-Thomson, 1975.
The World and Africa. 1965. Reprinted, Millwood, NY: Kraus-Thomson. 1968.

Autobiography

Darkwater: Voices from Within the Veil. 1921. Millwood, NY: Kraus-Thomson, 1969.
Dusk of Dawn: An Essay toward an Autobiography of a Race Concept. In *W.E.B. Du Bois: Writings.* 1940. Ed. Nathan Huggins. New York: Viking/Library of America, 1986.
The Autobiography of W.E.B. Du Bois. 1962. Millwood, NY: Kraus-Thomson, 1976.

Fiction

The Quest of the Silver Fleece: A Novel. 1911. Boston: Northeastern University Press, 1989.
Dark Princess: A Romance. 1928. Millwood, NY: Kraus-Thomson, 1975.
The Black Flame: A Trilogy. (*The Ordeal of Mansart,* 1957; *Mansart Builds a School,* 1959; *Worlds of Color,* 1961). Millwood, NY: Kraus-Thomson, 1976.

Collections

Against Racism: Unpublished Essays, Papers, Addresses 1887–1961. Ed. Herbert Aptheker. Amherst: University of Massachusetts Press, 1988.
The Complete Published Works of W.E.B. Du Bois. Ed. Herbert Aptheker. Millwood, NY: Kraus-Thomson, 1973–1986.
The Correspondence of W.E.B. Du Bois. 3 vols. Ed. Herbert Aptheker. Amherst: University of Massachusetts Press, 1997.
Newspaper Columns 1883–1944, 1945–61. Ed. Herbert Aptheker. Millwood, NY: Kraus International, 1986.
The Oxford W.E.B. Du Bois Reader. Ed. Eric J. Sundquist. New York: Oxford University Press, 1996.
W.E.B. Du Bois: A Reader. Ed. David Levering Lewis. New York: Henry Holt, 1995.
W.E.B. Du Bois on Race and Culture: Philosophy, Politics, and Poetics. Ed. Bernard Bell, Emily Grosholz, and James B. Stewart. New York: Routledge, 1996.
W.E.B. Du Bois Speaks: Speeches and Addresses, 1890–1919, 1920–63. 2 vols. Ed. Philip Foner. New York: Pathfinder Press, 1988.
Writings: The Suppression of the African Slave Trade: The Souls of Black Folk: Dusk of Dawn; Essays; Articles from the Crisis. Ed. Nathan I. Huggins. New York: Viking/Library of America, 1986.

Studies of W.E.B. Du Bois

Baker, Houston. *Black Literature in America.* New York: McGraw-Hill, 1971.
Broderick, Francis. *W.E.B. Du Bois: Negro Leader in Time of Crisis.* Stanford, CA: Stanford University Press, 1959.
Byerman, Keith. *Seizing the Word: History, Art, and Self in the Works of W.E.B. Du Bois.* Athens: University of Georgia Press, 1994.
Cruse, Harold, and Carolyn Gipson. "W.E.B. Du Bois and Black History." *New York Review of Books.* 19 (November 30, 1972): 22–26.

DeMarco, Joseph. *The Social Thought of W.E.B. Du Bois*. Lanham, MD: University Press of America, 1983.

Du Bois, Shirley Graham. *His Day Is Marching On: A Memoir of W.E.B. Du Bois*. Philadelphia: Lippincott, 1971.

Horne, Gerald. *Black and Red: W.E.B. Du Bois and the Afro-American Response to the Cold War, 1944–1963*. Albany: State University of New York Press, 1986.

Lewis, David Levering. *W.E.B. Du Bois: Biography of a Race 1868–1919*. New York: Henry Holt, 1993.

Logan, Rayford. *W.E.B. Du Bois: A Profile*. New York: Hill and Wang, 1971.

Manning, Marable. *W.E.B. Du Bois: Black Radical Democrat*. Boston: Twayne, 1986.

McDonnell, Robert W., and Paul G. Partington. *W.E.B. Du Bois: A Bibliography of Writings about Him*. Whittier, CA: Paul G. Partington, 1989.

Moore, Jack B. *W.E.B. Du Bois*. Twayne's U.S. Authors Series. Boston: Twayne, 1981.

Pobi-Asamani, Kwadwo. *W.E.B. Du Bois: His Contribution to Pan-Africanism*. San Bernardino, CA: Borgo Press, 1994.

Rampersad, Arnold. *The Art and Imagination of W.E.B. Du Bois*. New York: Schocken Books, 1990.

Reed, Adolph L., Jr. *W.E.B. Du Bois and American Political Thought: Fabianism and the Color Line*. New York: Oxford University Press, 1997.

Rudwick, Elliott. *W.E.B. Du Bois: Propagandist of the Negro Protest*. New York: Atheneum, 1968.

The W.E.B. Du Bois Virtual University. January 12, 1999. ⟨http://members.tripod.com/~DuBois/bibl.html⟩

Zamir, Shamoon. *Dark Voices: W.E.B. Du Bois and American Thought*. Chicago: University of Chicago Press, 1995.

PAUL LAURENCE DUNBAR
(1872–1906)

Pierre-Damien Mvuyekure

BIOGRAPHY

Paul Laurence Dunbar was born in Dayton, Ohio, where he graduated from high school with honors, wrote a school song, and worked as an elevator operator in Callahan Buildings, where, despite constant interruptions by passengers, he wrote many of his best poems. Working in Callahan Buildings became instrumental in Paul Laurence Dunbar's literary career. According to Addison Gayle, in *Oak and Ivy: A Biography of Paul Laurence Dunbar*, not only was Dunbar called an "elevator boy and a poet," a nickname he first received from his mother, but for "the rest of his life and long after his death" he "would be known by these two terms." But Gayle posits that Dunbar wrote poetry long before he operated an elevator insofar as "he began rhyming words at the age of six" (ix–x).

If it was in Callahan Buildings that Dunbar was caught off-guard writing a poem by a Mrs. Conover, who later introduced his work to Charles Thatcher, it was in Toledo that Dunbar would receive a great impetus to his career as a poet, for there he met all the men who would help him take his literary career to another level. Attorney Charles Thatcher, for example, played a momentous role in exposing Dunbar's poetry at West End Club, where Dunbar was frequently invited to read his poems. Dr. H. A. Tobey, another respected citizen of Toledo, helped Dunbar's career financially, including sending him a check that allowed him to participate at the Western Association of Writers meeting in 1895. More importantly, Tobey and Thatcher sponsored Dunbar's second collection of poems, *Majors and Minors*. Under Tobey's insistence Dunbar left a copy of *Majors and Minors* at the hotel where the playwright James A. Herne was staying, a copy that would later land in the hands of the powerful critic William Dean Howells.

Not only did William Dean Howells read *Majors and Minors*, but he wrote about Dunbar in *Harpers*, a gesture that was to put Dunbar on a literary pedestal. Howells praised Dunbar as a poet who had done what no other "English speaking Negro" had done until then, especially in putting black dialect in verse and rhyme. Thus, when "the oracle [Howells] spoke, his tone was forceful and ma-jestic. It was due to this oracle that Paul Laurence Dunbar went to bed one night and awoke to find himself famous" (Gayle 50). When Howells introduced Dun-bar's *Lyrics of Lowly Life*, however, he said something that forever pigeonholed Dunbar and haunted his entire career: that the dialect distinguished Dunbar, not the poems written in standard English. Yet, anyone who reads Dunbar would concur with Howells that it is in poems, stories, and novels written in black vernacular that Dunbar is at his best insofar as therein are successfully woven the concept of blackness and the black American experience.

MAJOR WORKS AND THEMES

Because of the voluminous nature of Dunbar's work—collections of poems, novels, and collections of short stories—and its versatility, it is rather difficult to identify one major theme as the thread running through his major works. Even from one collection of poems, themes can range from romanticism/ sentimentalism, to singing as the only way to express pain, to endurance and pride of black people despite slavery, to courtship and marriage, to the eating of possum. As far as Dunbar's poetics is concerned, critics have repeatedly and cogently pointed out how experimental in verse, rhyme, and tone Dunbar's po-etry is.

Before even W.E.B. Du Bois* invented the term "double consciousness"—the fact for black Americans that they are both black and American—Dunbar's work was permeated by double consciousness insofar as he consciously wrote in two different languages: standard English and the black English of the plantations known as black dialect. Noteworthy is how the titles of his poetry collections evoke this idea of double consciousness: *Oak and Ivy* (1892), *Majors and Minors* (1896), *Lyrics of Love and Laughter* (1903), *Poems of Cabin and Field* (1899), *Lyrics of Sunshine and Shadows* (1905). In his famous Introduction to *Lyrics of Lowly Life*, a collection of poems that combine poems from *Oak and Ivy* and *Majors and Minors*, William Dean Howells noted that "the poems in literary English," though "very good, and even more than very good," should not be regarded as "distinc-tively" Dunbar's "contribution to the body of American poetry" because any other good poet could have written those poems. For Howells, Dunbar had to be judged and distinguished by the "dialect pieces" insofar as therein are revealed not only "the range of the race" but also "a finely ironical perception of the Negro's limitations, with tenderness for them" (xviii–xx).

On the other hand, Addison Gayle has posited not only that Dunbar's "serious poems" are those written in standard English but that Dunbar himself did not like his dialect poems, which he saw as "humorous ditties written to entertain white audiences" (29–30). While Howells may have exaggerated his characterization of Dunbar's poetry, because not any poet writing in English would successfully do the experimentation in meter and rhyme that Dunbar was able to do, Gayle was probably misled by *Majors and Minors*, Dunbar's second collection, which combined *Oak and Ivy* with new poems, in which "Majors" refers to poems written in standard English and "Minors" to dialect poems. As a matter of fact, the poems in dialect in the second section of the collection are referred to as "Humor and Dialect."

The 100-plus poems in *Lyrics of Lowly Life* treat varied themes such as the essence of songs, love, nature, eulogies, and praises to black heroes. "Ere Sleep Comes Down to Soothe the Weary Blues," the opening poem, is a blueslike poem in which the hardships of the day produce "weary eyes" whose only hope is sleep. The hardships and toil of the day also permeate "The Poet and His Song," a poem that addresses the issue of being a black and a poet in America. In four stanzas, the poet laments that though no one listens to, or praises, him, he sings to live, laugh, and love. Furthermore, he sings both to express the pain produced by days of hard labor, wet brow, hot sun drying up his garden and to make things well again. Nowhere is this idea of singing to quell pain more eloquently expressed than in "A Banjo Song," a poem written in dialect. Despite the pains, troubles, and toils of the day, the poet looks forward to the evening, when he takes his banjo from the wall and plays music. This music cheers up all the family in the evening, as it provides joy and solace to the tired slaves. What is more, the banjo music becomes spiritual and celestial insofar as the musicians and dancers can hear their music reach heaven and the angels sing it.

There are also poems that celebrate black heroes and encourage the black race to remain hopeful. While in "Ante-Bellum Sermon" the preacher preaches about the coming of Moses to defeat Pharaoh but asks his congregation not to brag about it, in "Ode to Ethiopia" the poet exhorts his people to be proud "in mind and soul" as the children of Ethiopia. The poet's pride in the progress his race has made is also expressed in "Frederick Douglass," in which Ethiopia laments the death of Frederick Douglass* and glorifies his perennial teachings whereby he encouraged his race to be always hopeful. Racial pride is further explored in "The Colored Soldiers," a laudatory poem that honors and glorifies the "sons of Ham" who bravely responded to Uncle Sam's call to fight in the Civil War. Throughout the poem the poet recounts how at the beginning of the war blacks were scorned and not allowed to fight, but when the North was on the verge of losing the war, black soldiers were called upon to fight for freedom. Furthermore, the poet insists that freedom was not given to blacks on a platter, because they had to win it by shedding their blood in the southern fields.

Like *Lyrics of Lowly Life*, *Lyrics of the Hearthside* is characterized by double-voicedness of language, standard English and dialect; in this collection, too, Dunbar experiments with rhyme and rhythm in both standard English and dialect poems. Themes of love, romance, life, the right to die, faith, inspiration, and plantation life permeate the 109 poems. Noteworthy is the fact that some poems in this collection show to what extent Dunbar has exerted a great influence on contemporary African American writers, including Maya Angelou, whose *I Know Why the Caged Bird Sings* takes its title from Dunbar's poem "Sympathy." In "Sympathy," the poet examines the quest for freedom through the image of a caged bird beating and bruising its wings trying to get free. Finally, the poet understands that the caged bird's song is not an expression of joy but a heartfelt prayer sent to heaven. In "Mare Rubrum," the speaker plants his feet in "Life's Red Sea" in order to duplicate the parting of the water by Moses to save the children of Israel from the Pharaoh's soldiers, but when nothing happens, the speaker wonders if God is still sitting in his "ancient seat."

In "Harriet Beecher Stowe," a classic Italian sonnet, Dunbar lauds Harriet Beecher Stowe as a fearless lady who, by writing *Uncle Tom's Cabin*, sounded the alarm for the need for justice and freedom. In the poem the poet echoes what Abraham Lincoln may have told Harriet Beecher Stowe about her having caused the Civil War; he also credits her for having given freedom to the black race. In "Chrismus on the Plantation," however, the poet examines the meaning of emancipation and suggests that several blacks did not know what to do with their freedom, away from their former masters. Indeed, the poem dramatizes how after the emancipation blacks became unhappy when their master informed them that he was selling his homestead because he could not afford to pay them. One of the blacks delivered a speech in which he told his master that leaving him would mean that they had forgotten his kindness. Furthermore, he argued that if freedom and emancipation meant forgetting the kindness done to a person, black or white, then Lincoln can take them back. It is only when he proposed they work on the old plantation together in order to survive that everybody cheered and was merrily ready for Christmas. It is worth noting that in dialect poems like "Chrismus on the Plantation" Dunbar, under the mask of humor, genuinely explores black experiences on the plantation.

Black experiences on the plantation, including racial injustices, are more extensively explored in Dunbar's four novels and four collections of short stories. In 1898 Dunbar published *The Uncalled*, a novel in which Dunbar explored injustice and hypocrisy through the main character, a white boy whose ministry the community refuses to recognize. In 1900 and 1901 Dunbar respectively published his second and third novels, *The Love of Landry* and *The Fanatics*, both sentimental melodrama stories. Though these three novels have been overlooked by critics, either because Dunbar uses white characters as main characters or because critics have been more interested in Dunbar's poetry, *The Sport of the Gods*, Dunbar's fourth novel, has received some critical attention. In the novel Dunbar examines racial injustice and prejudice against blacks through a southern black family during late in the Reconstruction period. But it is in the short stories that Dunbar brilliantly portrays the experiences of black families in the South; all the four collections of stories, *In Old Plantation Days*, *Heart of Happy Hollow*, *Folks from Dixie*, and *The Strength of Gideon, and Other Stories*, portray black life on plantations in Virginia and Kentucky and in several southern and northern towns. In their Introduction to the stories in *The Paul Laurence Dunbar Reader*,

Jay Martin and Gossie H. Hudson have rightly pointed out how the world of Dunbar's fiction is "larger than any of his contemporaries" and how Dunbar surpassed "all the writers of his time" insofar as "he did not write of the same region over and over again" (64).

CRITICAL RECEPTION

In his famous Introduction to the *Lyrics of Lowly Life* William Dean Howells hailed Dunbar as "the only man of pure African blood and of American civilization to feel the negro aesthetically and express it lyrically" (xvi). Howells further concluded that Dunbar had made "the strongest claim for the negro in English literature that the negro has yet made" and that he had produced "a work of art" to enjoy (xx). Since Howells' favorable reviews, albeit exaggerated, Dunbar's work has enjoyed critical acclaim. Nevertheless, Darwin T. Turner has noted that the reputation of Dunbar as a poet rests on three false myths: that all Dunbar's poetry is written "in the dialect of the southern Negro"; that "Howells' well intended but misguided praise" for Dunbar's "ability to caricature southern Negroes" prevented critics from fully recognizing "Dunbar's talents as a poet in standard English"; and that Dunbar was "a black Robert Burns, instinctively singing about nature" (ii–viii). These myths, however, have not prevented critics from continuing to assess Dunbar's contribution to American letters, as attested by recent critical essays by Valerie J. Wheat in *Afro-Hispanic Review* (1996), Lawrence R. Rogers in *American Literary Realism* (1992), Casey Inge in *Callaloo* (1997), and John Keeling in *Southern Literary Review* (1993).

On the other hand, it is clear that there is a strong need for book-length critical studies of Dunbar's voluminous work. Also, except for *The Sport of the Gods*, Dunbar's fiction has been shamefully neglected. If critics had paid attention to Dunbar's short stories, for example, they would have discovered that Dunbar was a very gifted storyteller and that the black dialect, the racial consciousness, and the portrayal of black life are better and more fully appraised in the short stories than in the poems.

BIBLIOGRAPHY

Works by Paul Laurence Dunbar

Poems

Oak and Ivy. New York: Dodd, Mead, 1892.
Lyrics of Lowly Life. New York: Dodd, Mead, 1896; New York: Arno Press, 1969.
Majors and Minors. 1896. Miami: Mnemosyne, 1969.
Lyrics of the Hearthside. New York: Dodd, Mead, 1899; New York: AMS Press, 1972.
Poems of Cabin and Field. New York: Dodd, Mead, 1899.
I Greet the Dawn: Poems. New York: Dodd, Mead, 1903; New York: Atheneum, 1978.
Lyrics of Love and Laughter. New York: Dodd, Mead, 1903.

Lyrics of Sunshine and Shadow. New York: Dodd, Mead, 1905.
Joggin' Erlong. New York: Dodd, Mead, 1906; Miami: Mnemosyne, 1969.
The Complete Poems of Paul Laurence Dunbar. New York: Dodd, Mead, 1976.

Fiction

The Uncalled. New York: Dodd, Mead, 1898; College Park, MD: McGrath, 1969.
The Love of Landry. New York: Dodd, Mead, 1900; Miami: Mnemosyne, 1969.
The Fanatics. New York: Dodd, Mead, 1901; Upper Saddle River, NJ: Literature House, 1970.
The Sport of the Gods. 1902. New York: Arno Press, 1969.
In Old Plantation Days. New York: Dodd, Mead, 1903; New York: Negro Universities Press, 1969.
The Heart of Happy Hollow. New York: Dodd, Mead, 1904; Miami: Mnemosyne, 1969.
Folks from Dixie. New York: Dodd, Mead, 1922; Miami: Mnemosyne, 1969.
The Best Stories of Paul Laurence Dunbar. Ed. Benjamin Brawley. New York: Dodd, Mead, 1938.
Little Brown Baby. New York: Dodd, Mead, 1940.
The Strength of Gideon, and Other Stories. Miami: Mnemosyne, 1969.
The Paul Laurence Dunbar Reader: A Selection of the Best of Paul Laurence Dunbar's Poetry and Prose. Ed. Jay Martin and Gossie H. Hudson. New York: Dodd, Mead, 1975.

Studies of Paul Laurence Dunbar

Allen, Caffilene. "The Caged Bird Sings: The Ellison-Dunbar Connection." *CLA Journal* 40.2 (1996): 178–90.
Baker, Houston A., Jr. "The 'Limitless' Freedom of Myth: Paul Laurence Dunbar's *The Sport of the Gods* and the Criticism of Afro-American Literature." In *American Self: Myth, Ideology, and Popular Culture.* Ed. Sam B. Girgus. Albuquerque: University of New Mexico Press, 1981. 124–43.
Blount, Marcellus. "Caged Birds: Race and Gender in the Sonnet." *PMLA* 107.3 (1992): 582–93.
Brawley, Benjamin Griffith. *Paul Laurence Dunbar, Poet of His People.* Chapel Hill: University of North Carolina Press, 1936.
Cook, Will Marion. *In Dahomey. Vocal Score.* Ed. Thomas Riis. Madison, WI: A-R Editions, 1996.
Cunningham, Virginia. *Paul Laurence Dunbar and His Song.* New York: Dodd, Mead, 1947.
Engel, Bernard F. "Paul Laurence Dunbar's Civil War Verse." *Midwestern Miscellany* 11 (1983): 15–18.
Gayle, Addison, Jr. *Oak and Ivy: A Biography of Paul Laurence Dunbar.* Garden City, NY: Doubleday, 1971.
Howells, William Dean. "Introduction." In *Lyrics of Lowly Life.* New York: Dodd, Mead, 1904.
Inge, Casey. "Family Functions: Disciplinary Discourses and (De) Constructions of the 'Family' in *The Sport of the Gods.*" *Callaloo* 20.1 (1997): 226–42.
Jones, Gayl. "Breaking Out of the Conventions of Dialect: Dunbar and Hurston." *Presence Africaine: Revue Culturelle Du Monde Noir* 144 (1987): 32–46.

Keeling, John. "Paul Dunbar and the Mask of Dialect." *Southern Literary Review* 25.2 (1993): 24–38.

Kinnamon, Keneth. "Three Black Writers and the Anthologized Canon." *American Literary Realism* 23.3 (1991): 42–51.

Kunkel, Glenn E. "*The Sport of the Gods.*" *Masterpieces of African-American Literature.* Ed. Frank N. Magill. New York: HarperCollins, 1992. 522–30.

Martin, Jay, ed. *A Singer in the Dawn: Reinterpretations of Paul Laurence Dunbar.* New York: Dodd, Mead, 1975.

McGraw, Patricia Washington. "The Duality of Dialect and Dialogue in Dunbar." *Publications of the Arkansas Philological Association* 15.1 (1989): 53–66.

McKissack, Pat. *Paul Laurence Dunbar: A Poet to Remember.* Chicago: Children's Press, 1984.

Metcalf, E. W., Jr. *Paul Laurence Dunbar: A Bibliography.* Metuchen, NJ: Scarecrow Press, 1975.

Okeke, Ezigbo Emeka. "Paul Laurence Dunbar: Straightening the Record." *CLA Journal* 24.4 (1981): 481–96.

Revell, Peter. *Paul Laurence Dunbar.* Ed. Sylvia E. Bowman. Boston: Twayne, 1979.

Rogers, Lawrence R. "Paul Laurence Dunbar's *The Sport of the Gods*: The Doubly Conscious World of Plantation Fiction, Migration, and Ascent." *American Literary Realism* 24.3 (1992): 42–57.

Story, Ralph. "Paul Laurence Dunbar: Master Player in a Fixed Game." *CLA Journal* 27.1 (1983): 30–55.

Turner, Darwin T. "Preface". In *Lyrics of Lowly Life*, New York: Arno Press, 1969. i–viii.

Wheat, Valerie J. "Nineteenth Century Black Dialect Poetry and Racial Pride: Candelario Obeso's Cantos Populares de mi Teirra and Paul Laurence Dunbar's *Lyrics of Lowly Life.*" *Afro-Hispanic Review* 15.2 (1996): 26–36.

Williams, Roosevelt J. "The Poetry of Paul Laurence Dunbar." In *Masterpieces of African-American Literature.* Ed. Frank N. Magill. New York: HarperCollins, 1992. 394–98.

ALICE MOORE DUNBAR-NELSON
(1875–1935)

Lori Leathers Single

BIOGRAPHY

Alice Ruth Moore was born July 19, 1875, in New Orleans, the city that was to provide the setting for her first local-color stories, a genre to which she would return throughout her lifetime. The versatility that characterizes her career as a writer was evident from an early age. While she was still in her teens, she began contributing poems, essays, sketches, and short stories to black magazines like the New York *Age*, the Boston *Woman's Era*, and the *Colored American Magazine*. She also wrote the "Woman's Column" for the *Journal of the Lodge*, a fraternal organization newspaper. By the time she published *Violets and Other Tales* (1895), her first book at age twenty, Alice Ruth Moore was already well known as a " 'brilliant and versatile writer' " and as a respected member of Creole society (qtd. in Hull, *Color* 36). In 1892 she began teaching, one of the many vocations she would turn to when her writing failed to sustain her financially. Her multi-faceted career included work as a stenographer, typist, educator, parole officer, editor, journalist, racial and feminist activist, and public speaker. In 1896 she moved north, first to Medford, Massachusetts, and then to New York, where her teaching and mission work would provide her with material for what she called her "tenement stories."

On March 6, 1898, she married Paul Laurence Dunbar,* the first black American poet to support himself solely by his writing. Although the marriage was brief and tumultuous, it is arguably the single most important event in the history of her literary career. They were touted in Washington society as the dark-skinned version of Robert and Elizabeth Browning. Soon after their marriage, Paul Reynolds, Dunbar's agent, began marketing Dunbar-Nelson's short fiction to major magazines. In 1899 Dunbar's publisher Dodd, Mead, published her *The*

Goodness of St. Rocque, a collection of Creole stories, as a companion volume to Dunbar's *Poems of Cabin and Field*. In 1900 *the Smart Set* published *The Author's Evening at Home*, one of only two of her dramas ever published in her life. However, more significant than her brief role as Dunbar's wife was her twenty-nine-year role as Dunbar's widow. As Gloria Hull explains, this role was "her insurance against obscurity and a concrete means of livelihood" (*Color* 43). Even at her death, she was remembered by the *Philadelphia Afro-American* as the wife of the famous poet (Hull, *Color* 43). Significantly, she chose to keep the Dunbar name even after her second and third marriages.

In 1902 Alice Dunbar left Paul Dunbar and moved to Wilmington, Delaware, where she would be associated with Howard High School as a teacher and administrator for nearly twenty years. During this period she furthered her own education, taking courses at Cornell University, Columbia University, and the University of Pennsylvania. A part of her master's thesis from Cornell was published in *Modern Language Notes* in April 1909. Following a series of close personal relationships, on April 20, 1916, she married Robert J. Nelson, with whom she had worked in 1913 while editing *Masterpieces of Negro Eloquence* (1914). From the beginning, their life together was characterized by political activism. In response to the national debate over black participation in World War I, Dunbar-Nelson penned *Mine Eyes Have Seen* (1918), a propaganda drama in favor of black support notwithstanding their oppression at home. For two years, the Nelsons published the *Wilmington Advocate* (1920–1922), a liberal black newspaper. Also in 1920 Dunbar-Nelson published *The Dunbar Speaker and Entertainer*, a second anthology honoring the African American oral tradition. As an older member of the Harlem Renaissance, she contributed her conservative poetic voice and more radical journalistic voice. Between 1917 and 1931, her poems were published in *The Crisis, Opportunity*, Countee Cullen's* *Caroling Dusk*, James Weldon Johnson's* *The Book of American Negro Poetry*, and Charles S. Johnson's *Ebony and Topaz*, while her syndicated newspaper columns appeared in the *Pittsburgh Courier* (1926) and the *Washington Eagle* (1926–1930). However, her most lasting historical contribution may prove to be the diary that she kept in 1921 and between 1926 and 1931. It is one of only two book-length journals by a nineteenth-century black woman known to exist, and it illuminates aspects of this important era that only a black female participant could reveal. Her final literary effort, *This Lofty Oak*, a novel based on the life of Edwina B. Kruse, a friend and onetime principal of Howard High School, remains unpublished. Alice Dunbar-Nelson died at age sixty of heart trouble.

MAJOR WORKS AND THEMES

Violets and Other Tales, a collection of sketches, essays, poetry, short stories, and a review, is indicative of the diversity of her talent and the range of Dunbar-Nelson's interests. In it she introduces characteristic themes of love, gender, and

Creole life. Her first and only published collections, *Violets* and *The Goodness of St. Rocque and Other Stories*, established her as a competent poet given to romantic themes and conventional forms and as a talented local-colorist whose Creole stories and sketches rivaled those of Washington Cable and Grace King.

Like many late nineteenth-century black women writers, Dunbar-Nelson chose to eschew racial characters and subjects in her early fiction. Rather than pander to the literary establishment's taste for racial types, she presents Creole characters in all their diversity. The Creole stories in *The Goodness of St. Rocque* offer the best example of this multiplicity. In the ironically titled "Tony's Wife," a German woman lives with an abusive and drunken Italian man who refuses to marry her even on his deathbed. In "Mr. Baptiste," an old creole man is killed in a labor dispute between Irish and black stevedores. Although some of these stories hint at racial identity, like Miss Sophie's dusty eyes ("The Ball Dress") and Sister Josepha's brown hands ("The Little Mother"), overall racial issues are ignored in favor of issues of love, gender and "quiet heroism" (Whitlow 115). Although "Miss Sophie" and "Titee" from *St. Rocque* are frequently cited as representative of this later category, I recently discovered two Creole stories "Edouard" and "Esteve, the Soldier Boy," which also explore the theme of personal courage. Significantly, although Edouard is a wrongfully accused protagonist of ambiguous racial identity, the "very brown" Esteve is identified with Maman Louis, a free woman, and with a battalion of free men of color. However, only later would Nelson-Dunbar use her own personal experience as a fair-skinned person of color to write knowingly about the color line, passing, and interracial prejudice, as she does in her stories "The Pearl in the Oyster" and "Stones of the Village," in her essay "Brass Ankles Speaks," and in her play *Gone White*. Unfortunately, these and much of her more mature work were not published in her lifetime.

One such group of twelve stories was projected for a volume entitled *Women and Men*. Two of these, "Elisabeth" and "Ellen Fenton," treat the role of women in a modern society. Another projected volume, *The Annals of 'Steenth Street*, was to contain tales of New York's East Side's Irish ghetto youth. Of these "tenement stories," only "The Ball Dress" and "The Revenge of James Brown" were published. Interestingly, in the three of her unpublished stories that draw on her relationship with Paul Dunbar, the protagonists are white and wealthy. Two other unpublished pieces, "His Great Career" and "Summer Session," are detective stories.

Although Dunbar-Nelson is best known for her poetry and short fiction, her nonfiction prose consumed a considerable amount of her creative energy and represents a large portion of her work. As a renowned newspaper columnist, she "shines as literary critic, political analyst, social commentator, race theorist, humorist, and stage and film critic" (Hull, "Introduction" liii). These columns, along with her speeches, her diary, and her essays, provide an important context from which to view her more canonical work.

CRITICAL RECEPTION

The contemporary reception of *Violets* was favorable. Most reviewers were impressed by Dunbar-Nelson's versatile talent and saw promise in her work. They praised her poetry for its lyricism and sentiment and her stories for their characterization and pathos touched with humor. A few reviewers felt that *Violets* was a significant contribution to what was then called "race literature." The reception of *Goodness* was complicated by her marriage to Dunbar. One reviewer suggested that her husband was the only reason the book was published. Although she identified herself as a writer of short fiction, only her poetry received any serious critical attention in her lifetime. Until recently, her literary reputation was based on her poetic contributions to the Harlem Renaissance.

Since the 1980s, Dunbar-Nelson's fiction has begun to receive more critical attention. Scholars have been particularly interested in *Goodness* from a regionalist perspective. Central to this scholarly debate have been the absence of racial representation in the Creole stories and what this might mean in terms of Dunbar-Nelson's attitude toward race. Where Gloria Hull sees ambivalence, Violet Bryan sees camouflage, and Elizabeth Ammons sees carnivalization. Others have found these stories interesting for their treatment of gender issues. Most recently, Alisa Johnson has provided us with a historicized reading of "Ellen Fenton" as an innovative combination of a romantic plot with the feminine quest.

In her 1895 address to the First Congress of Colored Women of the United States, Victoria Earle Matthews defined "race literature" as all black-authored texts, not just those dealing with racial subjects and not just those written in canonical genres (Tate 83). In keeping with this, Dunbar-Nelson viewed all of her writing as " 'producing literature' " (Hull, "Introduction" xx) and was aware of her role in the formation of a new black literary tradition. In this context, there is clearly much more of Dunbar-Nelson's work that deserves serious consideration.

BIBLIOGRAPHY

Works by Alice Moore Dunbar-Nelson

Short Stories/Poetry/Nonfiction

Violets and Other Tales. Boston: Monthly Review Press, 1895.[†]

Short Stories

The Goodness of St. Rocque and Other Stories. New York: Dodd, 1899; reprinted, College Park, MD: McGarth, 1969.[†]

[†]Reprinted, *The Works of Alice Dunbar-Nelson.* Ed. Gloria T. Hull. 3 vols. New York: Oxford University Press, 1988.

"The Little Mother." *Brooklyn Standard Union*, March 19, 1900, 8.

"Edouard." *The Southern Workman* 29 (June 1900): 358–64.

"Esteve, the Soldier Boy." *The Southern Workman* 29 (November 1900): 631–37.

"The Ball Dress." *Leslie's Weekly*, December 2, 1901, 552.[†]

"The Pearl in the Oyster." *The Southern Workman* 29 (August 1902): 444–52.[†]

"Science in Frenchtown—A Short Story." *The Saturday Evening Mail*, December 7, 1912, 8–9, 26, 27.

"Hope Deferred." *The Crisis* 8 (September 1914): 238–42.[†]

"The Revenge of James Brown." *African Methodist Episcopal Church Review* 1929.[†]

Poetry

"Rainy Day." *Elmira (NY) Advertiser*, September 18, 1898, n.p.[†]

"A Song of Love." *Munsey's Magazine* (July 1902): 603.[†]

"Summit and Vale." *Lippincott's Magazine* 60 (December 1902): 715.[†]

"Violets." *The Crisis* 18 (August 1917): 198; reprinted as "Sonnet" in *The Books of American Negro Poetry*. Ed. James Weldon Johnson. New York: Harcourt, 1922. 164.[†]

"The Lights at Carney's Point." *The Dunbar Speaker and Entertainer*. Ed. Alice Dunbar-Nelson. Naperville, IL: Nichols, 1920. 132.[†]

"I Sit and Sew." *The Dunbar Speaker and Entertainer*. Ed. Alice Dunbar-Nelson. Naperville, IL: Nichols, 1920. 145.[†]

"To the Negro Farmers of the United States." *The Dunbar Speaker and Entertainer*. Ed. Alice Dunbar-Nelson. Naperville, IL: Nichols, 1920. 240.[†]

"To Madame Curie." *Philadelphia Public Ledger*, August 21, 1921, n.p.[†]

"Communion," "Music," and "Of Old St. Augustine." *Opportunity* 3 (July 1925): 216.[†]

"April Is on the Way." *Ebony and Topaz: A Collectanea*. Ed. Charles S. Johnson. 1927. Reprinted, Freeport, NY: Books for Libraries Press, 1971. 52.[†]

"Snow in October." *Caroling Dusk*. Ed. Countee Cullen. New York: Harper, 1927. 71.[†]

"Forest Fire." *Harlem: A Forum of Negro Life* 1 (November 1928): 22.[†]

"Cano—I Sing." *The American Interracial Peace Committee Bulletin* (October 1929), n.p.[†]

"The Proletariat Speaks." *The Crisis* 36 (1929): 378.[†]

"Little Roads." *Dunbar News*, March 11, 1931, n.p.[†]

"Harlem John Henry Views the Aimada." *The Crisis* 39 (January 1932): 458, 473.[†]

"Delta Sigma Theta, National Hymn." *The Official Ritual of Delta Sigma Theta Grand Chapter*. Washington, DC: Delta Sigma Theta Sorority, 1950. 192.

Drama

The Author's Evening at Home. *The Smart Set* (September 1900): 105–6.[†]

Mine Eyes Have Seen. *The Crisis* 15 (1918): 271–75.[†]

Essays/Articles

"The Black Farmers after Their Conference at Tuskegee." *Boston Evening Transcript*, March 18, 1899, n.p.

"Some of the Work of the National Association of Colored Women." *The Long Island Review* 7, 9 (November 1899): 338–39.

"Is It Time for the Negro Colleges in the South to Be Put into the Hands of Negro Teachers?" *Twentieth Century Negro Literature*. Ed. D. W. Culp. Toronto: Nichols, 1902; reprinted, New York: Arno Press and the New York Times, 1969. 139–41.

"Training of Teachers of English." *Education* 29 (October 1908): 97–103.

"The Compensations of a Teacher of English." *Educational Review* of Columbia University. (Cited by Hull, *Color* 61).

"Wordsworth's Use of Milton's Description of Pandemonium." *Modern Language Notes* 24 (April 1909): 124–25.

"What Has the Church to Offer the Men of Today?" *The A.M.E. Church Review* 30 (July 1913): 5–13.

"A Life of Social Service as Exemplified in David Livingstone." *Masterpieces of Negro Eloquence*. Ed. Alice Dunbar. Harrisburg, PA: Douglas, 1914. 425–44.

"The Poet and His Song." *Paul Laurence Dunbar: Poet Laureate of the Negro Race*. Special issue of *The A.M.E. Church Review* 21 (October 1914): 5–19. Reprinted, *Alice Moore Dunbar-Nelson/ The Dunbar Speaker and Entertainer/ The Poet and His Song*. New York: G. K. Hall, 1996. 321–38.

"The Single Standard." *The A.M.E. Church Review* 30 (January 1914): 189–92.

"People of Color in Louisiana." Part I. *Journal of Negro History* 1 (October 1916): 361–76.

"People of Color in Louisiana." Part II. *Journal of Negro History* 2 (January 1917): 51–78.

"Negro Women in War Work." *Scott's Official History of the American Negro in the World War*. Ed. Emmett J. Scott. n.p., 1919. 347–97.

"The Boys of Howard High." *The Dunbar Speaker and Entertainer*. Ed. Alice Dunbar-Nelson. Naperville, IL: Nichols, 1920. 226–28.

"Hysteria: The Old Time Mass Meeting Is Dead." *The Competitor* 1 (February 1920): 32–33.

"Lincoln and Douglas." *The Dunbar Speaker and Entertainer*. Ed. Alice Dunbar-Nelson. Naperville, IL: Nichols, 1920. 197–203.

"Negro Literature for Negro Pupils." *The Southern Workman* 51 (February 1922): 59–63.

"These 'Colored' United States; No. 16—Delaware: A Jewel of Inconsistencies." Part I. *The Messenger* 6 (August 1924): 244–46.

"These 'Colored' United States; No. 16—Delaware: A Jewel of Inconsistencies." Part II. *The Messenger* 6 (September 1924): 276–79.

"Politics in Delaware." *Opportunity* 2 (November 1924): 339–40.[†]

"Women's Most Serious Problem." *The Messenger* 9 (March 1927): 73, 86.[†]

"Textbooks in Public Schools: A Job for Negro Women." *The Messenger* 9 (May 1927): 149, 169.

"The Problem of Personal Service." *The Messenger* 9 (June 1927): 184.[†]

"Facing Life Squarely." *The Messenger* 9 (July 1927): 219.[†]

"The Negro Looks at an Outworn Tradition." *The Southern Workman* 57 (May 1928): 195–200.

"The Ultimate Insult." *Washington Eagle*, October 26, 1928, n.p. (Cited by Hull, *Color* 89).

"Women in Politics with an Emphasis on Negro Participation." *The Journal of the College Alumnae Club of Washington* (April 1932): n.p. (Cited by Williams, "Works by" 325).

"The Big Quarterly in Wilmington." *Wilmington* (DE) *Journal Every Evening*, August 27, 1932, 8–9.[†]

"Try the Golden Rule Next." *New York Amsterdam News*, June 1, 1935, n.p. (Cited by Hull, *Color* 103).

"Little Excursions Week by Week." Associated Negro Press. *Paul L. Dunbar Papers*. Ed.

Sara S. Fuller, microfilmed by Robert B. Jones. Reel 6, frame 1863, 64, 65, 66. Columbus Archives and Manuscript Division: Ohio Historical Society, 1972. 9 reels.

"The Mardi Gras and Denver's Festival Contrasted." Coauthor Paul L. Dunbar. n.p. *Paul L. Dunbar Papers*. Ed. Sara S. Fuller, microfilmed by Robert B. Jones. Reel 6, frame 0969. Columbus Archives and Manuscript Division: Ohio Historical Society, 1972. 9 reels.

Newspaper Columns

"From a Woman's Point of View." *Pittsburgh Courier*, January 2, 1926–February 20, 1926, n.p.

"Une Femme Dit." *Pittsburgh Courier*, February 20, 1926–September 18, 1926, n.p.

"As in a Looking Glass." *Washington Eagle*, 1926–1930, n.p.

"So It Seems to Alice Dunbar-Nelson." *Pittsburgh Courier*, January 1930–May 1930, n.p. (Selections from these columns are reprinted in *Works*.)

Anthologies Edited

Masterpieces of Negro Eloquence: The Best Speeches Delivered by the Negro from the Days of Slavery to the Present Time. Ed. Alice Dunbar-Nelson. Harrisburg, PA: Douglas, 1914.

The Dunbar Speaker and Entertainer: Containing the Best Prose and Poetic Selections by and about the Negro Race. Ed. Alice Dunbar-Nelson. Naperville, IL: Nichols, 1920.

Diary

Give Us Each Day: The Diary of Alice Dunbar-Nelson. Ed. Gloria T. Hull. New York: Norton, 1984.

Studies of Alice Moore Dunbar-Nelson

Ammons, Elizabeth. "The Limits of Freedom: The Fiction of Alice Dunbar-Nelson, Kate Chopin, and Pauline Hopkins." In *Conflicting Stories: American Women Writers at the Turn into the Twentieth Century*. New York: Oxford University Press, 1991. 59–85.

Bryan, Violet Harrington. "Creating and Re-creating the Myth of New Orleans: Grace King and Alice Dunbar-Nelson." POMPA 10 (1987): 185–96.

———. "Race and Gender in the Early Works of Alice Dunbar-Nelson." In *Louisiana Women Writers: New Essays and a Comprehensive Bibliography*. Ed. Dorothy H. Brown and Barbara C. Ewell. Baton Rouge: Louisiana State University Press, 1992. 120–38.

Hull, Gloria T. "Alice Dunbar-Nelson (1875–1935)." In *Color, Sex, and Poetry: Three Women Writers of the Harlem Renaissance*. Bloomington: Indiana University Press, 1987. 33–104.

———. "Alice Dunbar-Nelson: A Regional Approach." In *Teaching Women's Literature from a Regional Perspective*. Ed. Leonore Hoffmann and Deborah Rosenfelt. New York: MLA, 1982. 64–68.

———. *Color, Sex, and Poetry: Three Women Writers of the Harlem Renaissance*. Bloomington: Indiana University Press, 1987.

———. "Dunbar-Nelson, Alice Ruth Moore (1875–1935)." In *Black Women in America: An Historical Encyclopedia*. Vol. 1. Ed. Darlene Clark Hine. Brooklyn, NY: Carlson, 1993. 359–63.

"Introduction." In *The Works of Alice Dunbar-Nelson*. Vol. 1. Ed. Gloria Hull. New York: Oxford University Press, 1988. 3 vols.

Johnson, Alisa. "Writing within the Script: Alice Dunbar-Nelson's 'Ellen Fenton.' " *Studies in American Fiction* 19 (1991): 165–74.

Metcalf, E. W., ed. *The Letters of Paul and Alice Dunbar: A Private History*. 2 vols. Berkeley: University of California Press, 1973.

Tate, Claudia. *Domestic Allegories of Political Desire: The Black Heroine's Text at the Turn of the Century*. New York: Oxford University Press, 1992.

Whitlow, Roger. "Alice Dunbar-Nelson: New Orleans Writer." In *Regionalism and the Female Imagination: A Collection of Essays* Ed. Emily Toth. New York: Human Sciences Press, 1985. 109–25.

Williams, Ora R., ed. *An Alice Dunbar-Nelson Reader*. Washington, DC: University Press of America, 1978.

———. "Works by and about Alice Ruth (Moore) Dunbar-Nelson: A Bibliography." *CLA* 19 (1976): 322–26.

OLAUDAH EQUIANO
(1745–1797)

Gilbert N.M.O. Morris

BIOGRAPHY

Olaudah Equiano was born in what is considered by anthropologists to be the "cradle of civilization," near the lake region of southeast Nigeria, above Cameroon and Benin. In 1755 he was, by his own account, kidnapped and sold to English slave merchants. He was sent for resale to Barbados, with its treacherous reputation for the treatment of slaves, then onto Virginia, where he was purchased by an English captain—Michael Henry Pascal of the Royal Navy—who gave him the name of a revolutionary who became king of Sweden, Gustavus Vassa. Equiano undertook service aboard ship, sailing between the European metropolitan centers, the Caribbean, and the American colonies, and remained employed for the next decade in various forms of maritime commerce and naval warfare. By these means Equiano avoided the harsh realities of North American or Caribbean slavery—both of which he later came to denounce.

While aboard ship, Equiano developed a friendship with two white sailors, Richard Baker and Daniel Queen. They taught him to read and write, and Queen in particular introduced him to Methodism, the then-burgeoning Christian denomination. This was a significant event since the Methodists saw a close relationship between spiritual and social-intellectual development. That is, while they shared the Hebraic codes and evangelical inclinations of their fellow Protestants, they seemed less puritanical and more inclined toward free will and personal development—a key reference point for Equiano.

Equiano undertook further supplementary employments, when at the urging of a Thomas Farmer, his master was convinced to allow the young slave to purchase his freedom. On July 10, 1766, Olaudah Equiano purchased his freedom and was manumitted at Montserrat. A freeman, he returned to service on board ships, and in the years that followed he undertook voyages throughout the Mediterranean, the Middle East, and even the Arctics. When he finally settled in England, Equiano participated in a plan to "repatriate" blacks to the Sierra Leone Territories, which became an unmitigated failure. (In later years, though, that territory, along with Liberia, came to be populated by similar means.)

In 1792 Equiano married Susanna Cullen, an Englishwoman, and became father to two daughters. In the late 1780s, when the great debate for the abolition of slavery grew impatient, many noble citizens had already made their voices heard. Lord Mansfield had made his contribution with his landmark judgment in the Somerset case—exactly one day before the American Declaration of Independence; Granville Sharpe led many public discussions through pamphleteering; William Wilberforce led eloquently in Parliament; Turner, the fine English painter, painted his hauntingly beautiful *Slave Ship*, which terrorized even an indifferent Ruskin; and in the spirit of this time, Equiano decided to write a two-volume autobiography to tell of his life and to indict slavery. It created a sensation in that year of sensations, 1789—the year of the French Revolution.

MAJOR WORK AND THEMES

The Interesting Narrative of the Life of Olaudah Equiano, or Gustavus Vassa, the African, Written by Himself is the first book by a former black slave of which we have an account. It is not, however, the only work of Equiano's. As is customary in the music industry to release a single song as precursor to the release of an album, or as academics or novelists market their work by the expertly placed chapter to stimulate the public's interest, so, too, did Equiano whet the public's appetite for the forthcoming *Narrative*. Perhaps in agreement with the rule that conflict creates drama, he set himself publicly against the leading pro-slavery forces of the times. Particularly in book reviews and letters to newspapers, he attacked his prospective enemies and gave foretaste of the *Narrative*'s content. One of the main opponents at that time was the notorious "Civis"—a pseudonym of someone who not only defended slavery but ironically, through his grudging admission of Equiano's competence, assured the latter's place in the public's mind. Altogether, these means brought considerable notice to the former slave. The work was published by subscription. That is, confirmed purchases were solicited from potential subscribers, and by these methods, the cost of production and printing would have been met—leaving residual royalties to the author.

Subscription offers another form of kudos that, when it is revealed, must boost the esteem of an author. Among the list of over 300 subscribers to Equiano's first edition were approximately forty-seven noble, ranking members of the landed aristocracy and the royal household. This alone ensured that the *Narrative* would dominate conversation in all the great houses in England in general and London in particular. Upon this probability are raised the ironic specters analyzed by Edward Said in his *Culture and Imperialism*. There he raises an indictment against the novelist Jane Austen for a too-ready exaltation of English upper-class life, without the merest reference to the brutal plantations in the Caribbean through which such a life is afforded. In like manner, nearly all the gentrified subscribers to Equiano's *Narrative* attained their wealth and status in association, directly or otherwise, with the very ignobility of slavery, which the *Narrative* was written to address.

Moreover, in the title of the *Narrative*, the phrase, "Written by Himself" should apprise the reader of another curiosity particular to the foregoing class of subscribers. It ought to have been a superfluous gesture for Equiano to add this rider to his title page. However, there was, at the time, a vitriolic public debate concerning the intellectual capacity of blacks. Forty-five years earlier, this debate had entered the "mainstream" through the commentary of the Scottish Enlightenment philosopher David Hume (1711–1776). In his *Essays Moral and Political*, Hume implored that blacks were not capable of reason and that where there appeared to be a man who was black and a "man of parts" or learning, it was more likely that he had simply learned a few phrases well, not unlike a parrot. Immanuel Kant (1724–1804) followed Hume's reasoning with a stunning conclusion in his *Essays on the Sublime and the Beautiful*, which I render in paraphrase: This man was black from head to toe, a clear proof that he was stupid (110–11). In America Thomas Jefferson in his *Notes on Virginia* is often weary of blacks who are presented to him as having demonstrated independent acts of reasoning (*Works of Jefferson*, vol. 6, 309–20). Even when Benjamin Banneker—a surveyor and mathematician, whom Diderot recommends to the French Academy—is presented, Jefferson accuses his benefactors of "puffing" or promoting him. The first black writers, therefore, along with the necessity of producing their stories, had to prove their mental capacity to have written such stories. We know that Phillis Wheatley* had to have her authorship authenticated by seventeen gentlemen of Boston. Part of the difficulty was that Jefferson was right, in some degree, that the abolitionists constantly "ghosted" the writings of slaves to enforce a perception of competence concerning their intellectual capacities. Equiano, therefore, in placing his rider, "Written by Himself," sought to discharge any suspicion of "ghosting." In so doing he was also unleashing that independence that he found so tightly packed in the primitive power of the pen.

Many commentators on the *Narrative* have compared it to *The Confessions* of St. Augustine (A.D. 354–430). As formula, this may have some truth. However, there is a danger of categorizing the works of former slaves and interpreting them within the near limits of preestablished literary forms, rendering them more acceptable. Care must also be taken not to appear to be defending any form of writing, no matter its "quality," as competent in order to increase the store of black writers as proof of black people's humanity. As such, the writer, reader, and critic of slave works are often at risk, when raising comparisons, of failing to understand the "turnstiles of dislocation" in such works. I prefer to think of them differently. They are entirely new forms, the likes of which Western readers had not anticipated in their literary histories. The extent to which Equiano or other slave writers follow the methods of some writer from the dominant culture ought to leave us with an even greater sense of the difficulty of their projects—a difficulty about which I speak later. For these writers, too, close a following of Western literary forms would be an abnegation of oneself; too radical a departure would alienate potential readers, many of whom were readers with such hopes. In my view, what Equiano faced was infinitely more complex than what moved St. Augustine, and that complexity must be admitted as part of the form. Every aspect of slave writers' existence turns upon a dual track even before their representation of themselves is made. Once their opportunity to express themselves has been fulfilled, psychologically, they must know that any lapse in reason draws them again to the threshold of inhumanity—even where they are defended against it and even where that "defense" is taken to have succeeded.

At length, the *Narrative* tells of Equiano's homeland by means of litany. His descriptions are romanticized and bear striking resemblance to the literary portraiture of eighteenth-century travel books. When he talks of his hope for freedom, he adopts the florid style of John Lyly or Richard Hooker. He is at his best when he addresses the paradoxical fear and awe he feels encountering the Western world. He is, as well, quite poignant in his moral condemnation of the contradictory impulses of the Euro-American Christian world. His unembellished, if too understated, terrors of his remembered bondage are disturbing, but they are too smoothly written, to evenhandedly expressed to shock. Two things ring through the entire work, however: (1) Equiano is a confirmed Anglophile who identifies English culture and civilization with humanity, refinement, and prosperity and (2) he is constantly aware of the effect wrought upon his fellow Africans by the rapacious progression of Western economic and technological dominance.

CRITICAL RECEPTION

The Narrative of Olaudah Equiano has become an important and troubling piece of literature on the question of identity for Americans. It is important because it contains an implicit "phenomenology of dislocation," the particulars of which American scholars have failed to apprehend fully. The psychology of American history would be released from its binary formation through the study of Equiano's Christianity, his concepts of progress, and his apparent lack of revolutionary impulse. Yet, this is exactly the reason Equiano is dangerous for American racial politics, because his *Narrative* may be applied to sustain political arguments on both sides of the historical characterization of slavery, either as a benign institution or a great moral tragedy. His father, according to his own account, owned "many slaves" (46), and he managed a slave plantation for his former master (205). As such, he does not conform to the profile of the revolutionary hero, consistently committed to freedom.

The reception of the *Narrative* is open to a myriad of complexities. First, Equiano's book comes near the end of a substantial line of narrative accounts, beginning about 1770 and exploding in 1772, after the infamous Somerset case

mentioned before, in which Lord Mansfield held that English law did not recognize title to persons as property. Second, the success of the sale by subscription
was fueled more by the public's fascination with a Negro who writes than by
what is written. As such, the evaluation of the Negro's literacy was the principal
import of the initial critical reception. Mary Wollstonecraft, the renowned
woman's rights activist of the eighteenth century, in *The Analytical Review* (May
1789), seems to have been one of the few to put the *Narrative* into both cultural
and literary perspective: "How they are shaded down, from the fresh colour of
northern rustics, to the sable hue seen on African sands, is not our task to inquire,
nor do we intend to draw a parallel between the abilities of a negro and European
mechanic." Yet, even the sympathetic reviewer seemed unable to resist the comparison, which was held not to be their "task" and which Equiano himself hoped
would be judged in his favor. Wollstonecraft wrote further: "[W]e shall only
observe, that if these volumes do not exhibit extraordinary intellectual powers,
sufficient to wipe off the stigma, yet the activity and ingenuity, which conspicuously appear in the character of Gustavus, place him on a par with the general
mass of men, who fill the subordinate stations in a more civilized society than
that which he was thrown into at his birth" (18).

The foregoing draws on the history of the reception of Equiano's *Narrative* at
its time of publication. With the abolition of slavery in Britain and the saturation
of the reading public by narrative accounts, Equiano's book fell into obscurity.
In America during the heyday of the Civil Rights movement, black faculty demanded a curriculum highlighting black intellectual achievements, which gave
rise not only to the "rediscovery" but to the Americanization of Olaudah Equiano. That "Americanization" was and is nothing less than pleading the case for
black humanity in the very Hegelian terms through which blacks were excluded
in the first instance and showing Equiano as the forerunner in an African American canon—thereby implying that canonicity is a category by which a probative
humanity could (and should) be demonstrated. Further, Equiano's own aristocratic background was overlooked by these critics, since acknowledgment may
mean that he could not stand forth as symbolic and actual proof of Western
literariness and assimilation, which were at the heart of their politics.

In consideration of these themes, what calls for notice is the temper of Equiano's explanation. I refer to the seeming dissonance between the world he occupied and the mythology of justice to which he constantly appealed. I accept
that in each case there appeared to be persons undertaking his cause, speaking
for him. Yet, it is exactly that arbitrariness that is antithetical to all known
principles of justice and that ought to have given him assurances of the absence
of the justice he pursued so confoundingly. For instance, at Kingston, Jamaica,
Equiano is cheated of his wages after an employment by Captain Baker. Peti-
tioning the captain, he was threatened with violence. He recalled a similar instance of a breach of contract, in which another Negro was refused payment for
professional services (218). Yet, he showed no significant declension in his association of the West with forms of freedom, constantly closed to his fellow

Negroes and himself. In an earlier episode, that aforementioned "freedom" and its imputed auxiliary to Christianity came under direct threat when Equiano found himself bound, "unlawfully," aboard ship by a certain Captain Hughes. Equiano pleaded his case as a fellow Christian. This brought a volley of "imprecations" and remonstrative curses from Captain Hughes, who, now angered, ordered Equiano to be bound in preparation to be sold (212).

We cannot hope to apprehend the entire ground of Equiano's thinking at the quick of his condition, and I am uncertain whether that is at all the instructive issue. At best, we may assess the psychological resources available to one so situated as a lesson in the theologies of law and justice in the face of oppression and importantly the technologies of victimhood, against which the oppressed individual, in the scope of even a purchased freedom, must act still to attain it. The report of the Truth and Reconciliation Commission in South Africa, which implicates the apartheid government and the African National Congress, turns intimately upon this question of the victim's response, which in its resistance to imperialism throughout the twentieth century operated in as closed and confounding a space as Equiano's. Beyond that, there is a compelling reason to challenge the apparently obsequious impulses of Equiano himself: his request to the bishop of London to become missionary to the Africans (221). That Equiano should seek, of his own volition, to identify with a Christianity and its "civilizing project," which was so far unable to offer him safety against bondage or sureties of contract, betrays either an attraction of the Western civilization complex, a weakness of spirit in the man, or a profound insight into something universal— beyond the anthropology of particular cultures, which we have yet to examine properly, much less understand.

A distinction of degrees shows itself when juxtaposing the narratives of Jupiter Hammon* and Frederick Douglass* with that of Equiano. Douglass wins his freedom through violence and by appropriating his autonomy through his escape from slavery. Hammon does not exercise himself in violence but attains a cosmic belief in universal justice—in which an inevitable day of reckoning lurks upon the horizon, when the enslaver will account for his iniquities. Equiano engages in no violence and essentially writes of himself as victim and as one who has not been accorded the rights of one who holds a legal stake in the property of his person. He goes further than either Douglass or Hammon—recommending the West to itself, ignoring the absence of his own longed-for sense of belonging and the protocols of hospitality by which both are guaranteed.

It is astonishing, then, that Houston Baker and other American literary critics exalt Equiano's "independence" while condemning Frederick Douglass—whose response to bondage is more meaningful to us—for his collapse from revolutionary language (38). For in addition to his slave-supported native aristocracy, Equiano exalted English culture, apparently without any sense of loss. In fact, his description of Africa (a term itself nothing more than an imperialistic sign of amalgamation and indifference to cultural particularity) is little more than an Englishman's performance of cultural misappropriation. Joseph Fichtelberg, at least, twice gets to the root of the question that Equiano's life and *Narrative* impose upon blacks, Western capitalism, and its Christian sensibility: "[I]n purchasing his freedom, one might ask, has Equiano somehow distanced himself from the motives that produced enslavement, or has he simply found new footing on old ground? Is it possible to disown one's governing discourse?" (460). How shall we answer such a question without reassessing all of Western civilization? What would we have avoided in an attempt to answer? Fichtelberg points at what used to lie at stake: "The alienated forms of commodity dominating the Narrative have now returned to colonize mother Africa, turning the communal culture in which money was negligible into a mass consumer, an arena for expanding capitalism" (475).

Finally, Equiano's language does not offer a "counterword" in which a new freedom may be expressed. Perhaps that would have been too much to ask, but his is the mantra of an assimilation that either accepts or ignores the absence of reciprocal stores of identity. That is, every idea or ideal he offers his new culture is already derived from the culture itself. In other words, Equiano could see the possible humanity of his race only under the tutelage and even moral leadership of their former oppressors. This means that so far as it concerns equality, the former slave, in theory, will be forever shrouded in an incumbency in which the very culture and economic systems that destroyed his sense of wholeness will be in a position to offer him, arbitrarily, new identities formed through the unchanged perspectives that led to his oppression in the first instance. As such, we have our most profound lesson in the *Narrative* when we consider freedom conditioned by purchase and language attuned to a necessity that determined freedom's price.

BIBLIOGRAPHY

Work by Olaudah Equiano

The Interesting Narrative of the Life of Olaudah Equiano, or Gustavus Vassa, the African, Written by Himself. 1789. Ed. and Intro. Vincent Carretta. New York: Penguin, 1995.

Works about Olaudah Equiano

Baker Jr., Houston A. *Black Literature in America.* New York: McGraw-Hill, 1971.

Chinosole. "Tryin' to Get Over: Narrative Posture in Equiano's Autobiography." In *The Art of the Slave Narrative: Original Essays in Criticism and Theory.* Ed. John Sekora and Darwin Turner. MaComb: Eastern Illinois University Press, 1982. 45–54.

Costanzo, Angelo. *Surprising Narrative: Olaudah Equiano and the Beginnings of Black Autobiography.* Westport, CT: Greenwood Press, 1987.

Curtin, Philip D. *Africa Remembered: Narratives by West Africans from the Era of the Slave Trade.* Madison: University of Wisconsin Press, 1967.

Fichtelberg, Joseph. "Word between Worlds: The Economy of Equiano's Narrative." *American Literary History Journal* 5.3 (Fall 1993): 459–80.

Starkey, Marion L. *Striving to Make It My Home: The Story of an American from Africa.* New York: W. W. Norton, 1964.

Walvin, James. *An African's Life: The Life and Times of Olaudah Equiano 1745–1797.* London: Cassell, 1999.

Wollstonecraft, Mary. "African Slavery." *The Analytical Review* 2 (May 1789): 18.

JESSIE REDMON FAUSET
(1882–1961)

Emmanuel S. Nelson

BIOGRAPHY

Jessie Redmon Fauset is a frequently misunderstood writer in the African American literary tradition. Often perceived as a child of privilege, she has been dismissed by many of her critics as an apologist for the values of the urban black elite. In reality, however, Fauset was not born to wealth and unearned privilege, and her ideological orientation was far from reactionary. She was born on April 27, 1882, in rural Camden County in southeastern New Jersey. Her father, Redmon Fauset, was a minister in the African Methodist Episcopal Church. While her father's occupation ensured social respectability within the black community, the family for the most part was impecunious. Her mother, Anna Seamon Fauset, died young. So did five of Jessie's six siblings.

A firm believer in the value of education, Redmon Fauset encouraged his academically talented daughter to excel in her classes. She graduated from the prestigious Philadelphia High School for Girls in 1901. However, because she was black, she was denied a place at Bryn Mawr and several other colleges in the Philadelphia area. Cornell University, with its own history of racially exclusionary practices, gave her admission but not on-campus housing. A liberal white family in Ithaca offered her off-campus accommodations. The only black student on campus for four years, Fauset graduated from Cornell in 1905 with distinction. Indeed, it is quite probable that she was the first African American female to receive a degree from Cornell University.

Upon graduation Fauset taught for a summer at Fisk University in Nashville. Though she had endured subtle and overt forms of racist mistreatment in Philadelphia and in Ithaca, the few months she spent in the South gave her a firsthand knowledge of the raw brutality of statutory segregation maintained through force and custom. In the fall of 1905 Fauset moved to Washington, D.C., where she taught in predominantly black high schools for twelve years before moving to Harlem in 1919.

By then Fauset had published a few poems, short stories, and essays in *The Crisis*, the official journal of the recently established National Association for the Advancement of Colored People (NAACP). In 1919 she became the journal's literary editor and thus became a pivotal figure in the Harlem Renaissance, which had already begun to emerge. In her rather influential editorial position at *The Crisis*, she provided a forum for the publication of some of the early works of Langston Hughes,* Countee Cullen,* Nella Larsen,* and other aspiring young writers. In 1924 she published her first novel, *There Is Confusion*.

In 1925 Fauset traveled to Europe and studied for six months at the Sorbonne in Paris. Soon after she returned to the United States, she began to teach at DeWitt Clinton High School in New York until her retirement in 1944. During those years she published three more novels. She returned to the classroom in the fall of 1949—this time as a visiting professor—at Hampton Institute, Virginia, but only for a semester.

In 1929, at age forty-seven, Fauset married Herbert Harris, an insurance agent. After she was widowed in 1958, she relocated to Philadelphia to live with her stepbrother, Earl Huff Fauset, a distinguished anthropologist. Jessie Fauset died on April 30, 1961.

MAJOR WORKS AND THEMES

There Is Confusion, Fauset's first major work of fiction, was intended by the author as a deliberate challenge to T. S. Stibling's novel *Birthright*, published in 1922. Offended by the patronizing representation of mixed-race characters in that white-authored text, Fauset decided to write *There Is Confusion* in an attempt to present mulatto characters with greater realism and authenticity. The main plot of the novel centers around the troubled romantic relationship between Joanna Marshall and Peter Bye. Light-skinned, self-assured, ambitious, and decidedly middle-class in their views and aspirations, both Marshall and Bye dream of successful careers and comfortable lives. But both grow increasingly disillusioned as they encounter endless obstacles in a racist society. At the end of the novel, Joanna abandons her goals of career and autonomy and decides to marry Bye and become a traditional housewife. The fact that she sacrifices her personal goals for the apparent security of marriage has prompted many critics to conclude that Fauset, despite her willingness to raise intriguing questions about gender relations, ultimately endorses tradition over progressive change. Such a reading, however, fails to acknowledge the complexity of Fauset's political vision. Rather than validate conventional social arrangements, the novel offers a compelling commentary on the high personal price black women are made to pay for their color and gender in a culture that is insidiously racist as well as patriarchal. Fauset's intent is to undermine, not endorse, tradition and convention.

Though Fauset may have succeeded in her challenge to T. S. Stribling by addressing the dilemmas of mulatto characters with insight and empathy, the novel itself, on aesthetic grounds, does not entirely succeed. Its didactic tone is too strident; the main plot often veers into sentimentality and melodrama; the innumerable subplots and characters cause confusion; and at times Fauset's prose is far from engaging. These weaknesses, in varying degrees, characterize her other three novels as well.

The marriage plot, which is central to *There Is Confusion*, resurfaces in *Plum Bun*, Fauset's second and arguably her best novel. The plot once again provides her with an opportunity to examine racial and sexual politics. The protagonist, Angela Murray, is a young and artistic African American woman whose light complexion and European features enable her to pass for white. In order to access the social and economic privileges that whiteness confers, Angela does, indeed, pass for white. As the novel progresses, however, she begins to understand the enormous emotional cost of her racial masquerade and ultimately acknowledges, publicly, her cultural origins. This emancipatory journey toward healing and authentic selfhood, however, appears to take place only in racial terms. As a woman, Angela Murray remains remarkably conventional; she views marriage as "the only, the most desirable and natural end" (274). As in *There Is Confusion*, Fauset's resolution of the marriage plot makes her vulnerable to charges that she merely affirms the conventional cultural script that designates marriage as the defining metaphor in a woman's life. Yet it is just as easy to read the novel as an indictment of that very cultural script. Fauset's emphasis here, as in her first novel, is on the absence of significant and enabling choices in women's lives— especially in the lives of black women during the early decades of the twentieth century.

Fauset's last two novels—*The Chinaberry Tree* and *Comedy: American Style*— are largely disappointing works. In these narratives Fauset attempts to deal with provocative themes but retreats from exploring them fully and perceptively. In *The Chinaberry Tree*, for example, she presents a love relationship between a rich, white male (Colonel Holloway) and his black maid (Aunt Sal). But Fauset fails to examine the psychological complexities inherent in such a relationship and merely frames it in the stale conventions of nineteenth-century sentimental fiction. Such superficiality marks her final novel, *Comedy: American Style*, as well. Again, Fauset chooses to thematize a potentially explosive subject: racial self-hatred. The protagonist, Olivia Cary, hates her own blackness and despises other blacks, including her own dark-skinned son. However, to understand such an extreme form of internalized racism, one has to grasp the psychology of victimized individuals; to understand Olivia Cary, readers should be allowed to sense the depth of her racial injury. Fauset, regrettably, fails to provide the necessary psychological insights.

In addition to the four novels, Fauset published several short stories, poems, and formal essays. Almost all of those short works appeared in *The Crisis*, a journal over which she had editorial control. Some of the stories, such as "The Sleeper

Wakes," anticipate the themes she develops more elaborately in her novels. But almost all of her poems reveal an amateurish quality. Her formal essays, perhaps, constitute her best work: many of them reflect her analytical mind and sophisticated political insights.

CRITICAL RECEPTION

The novels of Jessie Fauset have received substantial critical attention. Carolyn Wedin Sylvander's *Jessie Redmon Fauset*, the only book-length study devoted exclusively to Fauset's work, contains meticulously researched biographical details as well as valuable close reading of each of Fauset's four novels. Jacquelyn Y. McLendon, Cheryl A. Wall, and Ann duCille devote substantial portions of their books to lively discussion of Fauset's life and work. Many critical surveys of African American writing, such as Barbara Christian's *Black Women Novelists* and Robert Bone's *The Negro Novel in America*, offer at least brief commentaries on Fauset.

The critical reception Fauset's works have elicited, however, is mixed. Many critics adopt a derisive tone in their discussions. David Littlejohn, for example, characterizes her novels as "vapidly genteel lace curtain romances" that conform to "the stuffy, tiny-minded circulating-library norm" (50–51). Robert Bone is even more blunt: he calls Fauset's novels "uniformly sophomoric, trivial, and dull" (97). Barbara Christian, usually a sympathetic reader of black women's narratives, declares that Fauset's "characters lack critical insight and complexity" and that "her plots seldom rise beyond the level of melodrama" (43). She concludes that Fauset's novels are "bad fairytales" (43). Even critics who sometimes admire Fauset's works feel compelled to identify her artistic shortcomings. Cheryl A. Wall correctly points out that Fauset has a "tin ear for black vernacular" (79), that her poems are easily "forgettable" (58), and that her tendency toward repetition can test "many readers' capacity to endure" (80).

However, it should be pointed out that recent feminist rereadings of Fauset's work point to its intrinsic worth. Sylvander, while acknowledging Fauset's artistic weaknesses, nevertheless contends that her work is "worth reading for the ideas and themes Fauset articulates" (*Dictionary of Literary Biography* 80). Those ideas and themes, as Cheryl A. Wall points out, "illuminate the ways in which race, gender, and class construct and constrain identity" (38). Fauset's political beliefs, often viewed as reactionary, receive careful attention in Jacqueline Y. McLendon's book. McLendon convincingly argues that Fauset, far from being a social conservative, was, in fact, remarkably progressive, even subversive, in her interrogation of the prevailing views on race, gender, and class.

BIBLIOGRAPHY

Works by Jessie Redmon Fauset

Novels

There Is Confusion. New York: Boni and Liveright, 1924.
Plum Bun. New York: Stokes, 1929.
The Chinaberry Tree. New York: Stokes, 1931.
Comedy: American Style. New York: Stokes, 1933.

Short Stories

"Emmy." *The Crisis* 5 (December 1912): 79–87; 5 (January 1913): 134–42.
"My House and a Glimpse of My Life Therein." *The Crisis* 8 (July 1914): 143–45.
" 'There Was One Time': A Story of Spring." *The Crisis* 13 (April 1917): 272–77; 14
    (May 1917): 11–15.
"Mary Elizabeth." *The Crisis* 19 (December 1919): 51–56.
"The Sleeper Wakes." *The Crisis* 20 (August 1920): 168–73; 20 (September 1920): 226–
    29; 20 (October 1920): 267–74.
"When Christmas Comes." *The Crisis* 25 (December 1922): 61–63.
"Double Trouble." *The Crisis* 26 (August 1923): 155–59; 26 (September 1923): 205–9.

Poems

"Rondeau." *The Crisis* 3 (April 1912): 252.
"The Return." *The Crisis* 17 (January 1919): 118.
"Oriflamme." *The Crisis* 19 (January 1920): 128.
"La Vie C'est La Vie." *The Crisis* 24 (July 1922): 124.
"Dilworth Road Revisited." *The Crisis* 24 (August 1922): 167.
"Song for the Lost Comrade." *The Crisis* 25 (November 1922): 22.
"Recontre." *The Crisis* 27 (January 1924): 122.
"Here's April." *The Crisis* 27 (April 1924): 277.
"Rain Fugue." *The Crisis* 28 (August 1924): 155.
"Stars in Alabama." *The Crisis* 35 (January 1928): 14.
" 'Courage!' He Said." *The Crisis* 36 (November 1929): 378.

Essays

"New Literature on the Negro." *The Crisis* 20 (June 1920): 78–83.
"Impressions of the Second Pan-African Congress." *The Crisis* 22 (November 1921): 12–
    18.
"What Europe Thought of the Pan-African Congress." *The Crisis* 22 (December 1921):
    60–69.
"The Enigma of the Sorbonne." *The Crisis* 29 (March 1925): 216–19.
"Dark Algiers the White." *The Crisis* 30 (April 1925): 16–20.

Studies of Jessie Redmon Fauset

Ammons, Elizabeth. "New Literary History: Edith Wharton and Jessie Redmon Fauset."
    College Literature 14.3 (Fall 1987): 207–18.

Bone, Robert. *The Negro Novel in America.* New Haven, CT: Yale University Press, 1965.

Chandler, Karen M. "Nella Larsen's Fatal Polarities: Melodrama and Its Limits in *Quicksand.*" *College Language Association Journal* 42.1 (September 1998): 24–47.

Christian, Barbara. *Black Women Novelists.* Westport, CT: Greenwood Press, 1980.

Conda, Mary. "Passing in the Fiction of Jessie Redmon Fauset and Nella Larsen." *Yearbook of English Studies* 24 (1994): 84–104.

duCille, Ann. *The Coupling Convention: Sex, Text, and Tradition in Black Women's Fiction.* New York: Oxford University Press, 1993.

Lewis, Vashti Crutcher. "Mulatto Hegemony in the Novels of Jessie Redmon Fauset." *College Language Association Journal* 35.4 (June 1992): 375–80.

Littlejohn, David. *Black on White: A Critical Survey of Writing by American Negroes.* New York: Viking, 1966.

Lupton, Mary Jane. "Bad Blood in Jersey: Jessie Fauset's *The Chinaberry Tree.*" *College Language Association Journal* 27.4 (June 1984): 383–92.

McCoy, Beth. " 'Is This Really What You Wanted Me to Be?': The Daughter's Disintegration in Jessie Redmon Fauset's *There Is Confusion.*" *Modern Fiction Studies* 40.1 (Spring 1994): 101–17.

McDowell, Deborah. "The Neglected Dimension of Jessie Redmon Fauset." In *Conjuring: Black Women, Fiction, and Literary Tradition.* Ed. Marjorie Pryse and Hortense J. Spillers. Bloomington: Indiana University Press, 1985. 86–103.

McLendon, Jacquelyn Y. *The Politics of Color in the Fiction of Jessie Fauset and Nella Larsen.* Charlottesville: University of Virginia Press, 1995.

Rueschmann, Eva. "Sister Bonds: Intersections of Family and Race in Jessie Redmon Fauset's *Plum Bun* and Dorothy West's *The Living Is Easy.*" In *The Significance of Sibling Relationships in Literature.* Ed. JoAnna Stephens Mink and Janet Doubler Ward. Bowling Green, OH: Popular Press, 1992, 120–31.

Singh, Amritjit. *The Novels of the Harlem Renaissance.* University Park: Pennsylvania State University Press, 1976.

Sylvander, Carolyn Wedin. *Jessie Redmon Fauset.* Troy, NY: Whitson, 1981.

———. "Jessie Redmon Fauset." In *Dictionary of Literary Biography.* Ed. Trudier Harris and Thadious Harris. Detroit: Gale Research, 1987. 76–85.

Wall, Cheryl A. *Women of the Harlem Renaissance.* Bloomington: Indiana University Press, 1995.

RUDOLPH FISHER
(1897–1934)

Harish Chander

BIOGRAPHY

Rudolph John Chauncey Fisher was born to Rev. John Wesley Fisher and Glendora Williamson Fisher on May 9, 1897, the youngest of three children. At the time of his birth, the Fisher family was living in Providence, Rhode Island, where Rev. Fisher was the pastor of a Baptist church. However, Mrs. Fisher wanted the baby to be delivered at her parents' home in Memphis, Tennessee, but on the way she experienced labor pains in Washington, D.C., so it was in a Washington hospital that Rudolph Fisher was born. Fisher grew up in Providence, except for two years in New York from 1903 to 1905, where his father had a pastorate during that period. At high school, he showed interest in both literature and science and was a member of the debating team. He graduated with high honors from Classical High School in 1915 and entered Brown University on a scholarship. At Brown, Fisher maintained his interest in both literature and science by double majoring in English and biology. He excelled in public speaking as well, winning first prize at an intercollegiate public speaking contest at Harvard University in his junior year. He was elected to three honor societies: Phi Beta Kappa, Delta Sigma Rho, and Sigma Xi. At his commencement in 1919, Fisher gave an oration titled "The Emancipation of Science," making the case for the compatibility of science and religion. Fisher stayed for another year at Brown to do his master's in biology and was admitted to Howard Medical School, Washington, D.C. He shone at his medical studies, graduating with highest honors in 1924. In his senior year at Howard, he met Jane Ryder, an intelligent, sprightly Washington, D.C., schoolteacher, whom he married on September 22, 1924. He then served as an intern at Washington's Freedman's Hospital for one year.

During his senior year in medical school, Rudolph Fisher began writing short stories, and in the spring of 1924 he completed his first story, "The City of Refuge," which was published in the *Atlantic Monthly* in February 1925. Before the end of 1925, Fisher had three more stories—"South Lingers On," "Ringtail," and "High Yaller"—published in *Survey Graphic*, the *Atlantic Monthly*, and *The Crisis*, respectively. "High Yaller" won the Amy Spingarn prize for fiction in 1926. He also arranged spirituals, many of them for the singer and actor Paul Robeson, and played piano in concerts, Robeson singing.

From September 1925 to October 1927, Dr. Fisher worked as a fellow of the National Research Council at Columbia University Medical School in New York. Within the next two years, he wrote two research papers on the influence of ultraviolet rays on viruses. The Fishers had a son, Hugh, in 1926, Rudolph affectionately nicknaming him the "New Negro."

Rudolph Fisher had divided loyalties between writing and medical practice, devoting time to both. In 1927 he became superintendent of the International Hospital in Harlem and set up his private practice as a radiologist, with an X-ray laboratory of his own, in New York. The year 1927 also saw the publication of many new short stories, such as "The Promised Land," "The Backslider," "Blades of Steel," and "Fire by Night." The next year, Fisher published his first novel, *The Walls of Jericho*, which was followed by a number of short stories, such as "Common Meter," "Guardian of the Law," and "Miss Cynthie." Fisher's second novel, *The Conjure Man Dies*, was published in 1932. Fisher adapted this novel for theatrical production but sadly did not live to see it performed. Rudolph Fisher died of intestinal cancer on December 26, 1934, at the young age of thirty-seven.

MAJOR WORKS AND THEMES

Rudolph Fisher is one of the important literary artists of the Harlem Renaissance, which began with the ending of World War I and flowered during the 1920s and early 1930s. This period of a decade and a half witnessed a resurgence of literary impetus and an unprecedented burst of creative activity among the African American artists who came together in Harlem, the "Culture Capital" of black America. It was a period of intense self-scrutiny and self-definition on the part of African American artists, who began to assert their own individual and racial souls, "shaking off the psychology of imitation and implied inferiority," to use Alain Locke's* phrase in his essay "Negro Youth Speaks" (4). Locke in "Negro Youth Speaks" points out that for the Harlem Renaissance artists, "[r]ace . . . is but an idiom of experience, a sort of added enriching adventure and discipline, giving subtler tones to life, making it more beautiful and interesting, even if more poignantly so" (48). Locke says that these artists "take their material objectively with detached artistic vision" (50). Fisher exemplifies this approach, conveying an unsentimental, dispassionate picture of reality, a sort of clinical realism. Fisher's chief forte lies in his depiction of the black urban scene, presented with the penetrating eye of a radiologist.

In his short stories, Fisher describes black urban life with its strengths and weaknesses. Eschewing propaganda, he depicts the problems of the Harlemites, including their interracial and intraracial conflicts, and also the charms of Harlem life. Fisher excels in his depiction of Harlem scenes—the cabaret, the barbershop, the café, the dance casino, and the Sunday promenade on Seventh Avenue. Of the sixteen stories he published, we consider here four representative ones.

"The City of Refuge" (1925) dramatizes the initial euphoria and subsequent disillusionment of a southern black migrant to Harlem. King Solomon Gillis, ecstatic to see black people everywhere, envisions Harlem not only as "the city of refuge" but as the place where "black was white" and where black people "had privileges, protected by law" (4) unlike his native South. However, Gillis proves easy prey to the machinations of a drug dealer and is nabbed by the police on charges of drug dealing. Fisher's handling of the local color is masterly, skillfully evoking the sights and sounds of Harlem. He presents the tableau of African American men "standing idly on the curb," "women, bundle-laden, trudging reluctantly homeward," and "children rattle-trapping about the sidewalks" (3). He faithfully renders the various English dialects spoken by Harlemites. Fisher also demonstrates a deft use of the ironic mode. "The City of Refuge" turns out to be the city of doom for King Solomon Gillis, and Mouse Uggams, his so-called friend, turns out to be his worst enemy.

Intraracial prejudice is the theme of "Ringtail" and intraracial prejudice and interracial enmity are the major themes of "High Yaller." "Ringtail" brings out the conflict between native Harlem blacks and Harlem's West Indian blacks. Subjected to a barrage of insulting epithets such as "ringtail monkey-chaser" by native blacks, the West Indian elevator operator Cyril Sebastian Best avenges himself by killing Punch Anderson, a native black who is his rival for Hilda Vogel's love. In "High Yaller," the light-skinned protagonist, Evelyn Brown, is first accused of having "yellow fever" (82) by her darker-skinned peers, as she favors fair-skinned individuals as friends. Later on, when she wholeheartedly aligns herself with the black community by dating the dark-skinned Jay Martin, whites look at her with contempt: "What a cheap drab she must be to tag around with a nigger!" (92). However, when her dark-skinned mother dies, Evelyn decides to pass for white.

"Miss Cynthie" (1933) is perhaps the most successful of Fisher's short stories. Rich in local color, it deals with the themes of reconciliation between generations, southern traditional values, and northern black values. The seventy-year-old Miss Cynthie, who is initially disappointed that her grandson has not chosen to become a doctor or a dentist or at least an undertaker, comes to take pride in his success as a singer-entertainer because he goes about it honestly, remembering her grandmother's advice: "Son, do like a church steeple—aim high and go straight" (78). As Miss Cynthie sees the audience sinlessly grinning, "enjoying the guileless antics" of her grandson, Dave Tappan, she whispers: "Bless my soul! They didn't mean nothin'. . . . they jes' didn' see no harm in it" (77). The local color is exemplified in the carnival-like atmosphere of Seventh Avenue: "Sidewalks teeming with leisurely strollers, at once strangely dark and bright. Boys in white trousers, berets, and green shirts, with slickened black heads and proud swagger. Bareheaded girls in crisp organdie dresses, purple, canary, gay scarlet" (72).

Rudolph Fisher wrote his first novel, *The Walls of Jericho* (1928), in response to a challenge that a short novel could not blend the extremes of Harlem society into a single coherent story. Fisher successfully meets the challenge, dexterously representing a cross-section of Harlem society. The novel has two plots—one concerning the love story of Joshua "Shine" Jones, a furniture mover, and Linda Young, a maid, and the other involving black attorney Fred Merrit's move into a house in an exclusive white neighborhood. The two plots merge when the men hired to move Fred Merrit into the new home are Joshua Jones, Bubber Brown, and Jinx Jenkins. The antics of the latter duo provide comic relief. Also, Linda Young works as the maid for Fred Merrit's new neighbor, Miss Agatha Cramp.

The Walls of Jericho attacks race and class prejudice as well as egomania and self-illusion and also brings out the need for racial unity for good causes. Black prejudice toward whites is evident from Fred Merrit's bold statement: "I hate fays [white people]. Always has. Always will. Chief joy in life is making them uncomfortable" (37). He believes that the only reason that a white man gives special attention to a colored woman "socially" is that he has sexual designs on her (106). When Tod Bruce, the rector of the St. Augustine Church, mentions that there is a white point of view, Meritt says that "we aren't supposed to see that" (42). The white prejudice against black people is explicit in Miss Agatha Cramp's remark to Fred Merrit that blacks are "primitive" people, "primeval" and "unspoiled by civilization" (108). While she enjoys talking with Fred Merrit at the General Improvement Association (GIA) officers' meeting and invites him to another meeting to discuss how to uplift the black race, her attitude changes the moment she comes to know that he is black. As reported by Linda, Miss Cramp confides in her friend Irene that " 'it's one thing to help them and quite another to live beside them as equals' " (173).

The novel also brings out the class prejudice among blacks in Harlem. While the men are unloading the truck, they begin to discuss what course to adopt if whites should try to evict Fred Merrit. They agree that they should not risk their lives for the lawyer because he is a "dickty" (upper-class black intelligentsia), and Shine (Joshua Jones) says to himself, "If this bird wasn't a dickty he'd be o.k. But they [*sic*] never was a dickty worth a damn" (51). Class enmity helps explain why the middle-class Henry Patmore burns down the upper-class Merrit's home in the white neighborhood.

Fisher uses the title metaphor of the walls of Jericho to explain the self-illusion with which people wrap themselves, such that they do not really know themselves. Just as the biblical Joshua had to battle to shatter the walls of Jericho, Fisher's Joshua Jones has to shatter the wall of self-illusion to know himself. As Tod Bruce, the author's spokesman, observes: "A man may . . . boast that he is evil and merciless and hard when all this is but a crust, shielding and hiding a spirit that is kindly, compassionate and gentle" (186). Joshua has so far wrongly believed that he is "hard and it's soft to fall for a girl" (258). It is only when he realizes that "[t]he guy that's really hard is the guy that's hard enough to be soft" (264), that the walls of Jericho come tumbling down for him.

Lastly, the novel brings out the need for black racial unity and interracial cooperation to fight racism. To create a black "business class" (282), Merrit proposes to buy a one-truck moving business to be run by Joshua Jones, with both dividing up the profits equally and with an option to buy from Jones in due course. Jones gratefully accepts the offer. While the GIA Costume Ball brings together blacks from all classes as well as interested whites to raise money for the advancement of colored people, the motivations of the participants are different. Some whites come to "enjoy themselves," some to "raise up the darker brother," and others to observe the behavior of black people (73). As for "Dicktie" women, the narrator reports that they come to show off their costumes and jewelry (73).

Fisher's second novel, *The Conjure Man Dies* (1932), is acknowledged to be the first mystery novel written by an African American with African American characters. The conjure man Frimbo, a psychic, is supposedly murdered with a stuffed handkerchief down his throat, and the physician John Archer is called by Jinx Jenkins and Bubber Brown, the comic characters taken from *The Walls of Jericho*, to examine Frimbo's body. The black detective Perry Dart is sent by the New York Police Department to investigate. Detective Dart and Dr. Archer combine their efforts to solve the murder mystery. They find a dental bridge, a turban, and a thigh bone at the crime scene, as well as bottles containing male sex glands in the psychic's laboratory. The circumstantial evidence suggests as murder suspects Jinx Jenkins, who was in the room to seek the conjure man's advice about the detective business; Doty Hicks, the drug addict and pusher; Spider Webbs, the number-runner working for the policy king Si Barandon; and Easely Jones, the railroad porter. Also present on the scene at the time of the crime were Mrs. Martha Crouch, the attractive wife of Frimbo's landlord, and Mrs. Aramintha Snead, who had come to consult Frimbo to cure her husband's drinking problem. As Archer and Dart explore the possible motivations of these suspects, Rudolph Fisher uses flashbacks and monologues to create suspense. Like other detective novels, the story takes surprising turns, including when Frimbo appears alive and well, and it turns out that the corpse is that of his assistant.

Frimbo emerges as a fascinating character in the story. Frimbo reveals that he is an African king who has given up his kingship to learn the lessons of Western civilization and has studied philosophy and psychology at Harvard. He has powers of "mental telepathy" (225) and claims that he "can study a person's face and tell his past, present, and future" (226). He adds that he believes in an "applied determinism" (226) and explains how he helps others: "I am a catalyst. I accelerate or retard a reaction without entering into it . . . so that the coincidences are different from what they would otherwise be. A husband reaches home twenty minutes too soon. A traveler misses his train—and escapes death in a wreck" (228).

CRITICAL RECEPTION

Rudolph Fisher's short stories have been favorably received. Scholars uniformly praise Fisher for his faithful presentation of Harlem life. Sterling Brown commends Fisher for his realism but adds, "At times his plots are too neat, with something of O'Henry's trickery" (136). Emmanuel and Gross (1968) point out that, in addition to providing local color, Fisher "humanizes the corrupt as well as innocent figures in his stories" (111). According to Oliver Henry, Fisher was primarily a writer of short stories rather than novels, and his evaluation as a writer "should be based primarily upon his short stories rather than on his novels" (150). Arthur P. Davis calls Fisher a "comic realist" who "laughed at the foibles of all classes of Harlemites" and adds that this laughter comes from "knowledge and a fondness" for the people of Harlem (98). Leonard J. Deutsch extols Fisher's short stories for their pictures of morals and manners of Harlem in the 1920s and for their presentation of "Harlem idioms and dialects, the old-time preacher's sermons; the West Indian speech pattern; the people of Harlem bantering in Harlemese" (170). Margaret Perry writes that Fisher felt impelled to capture the world of Harlem in the art form of the short story and asserts, "Full of wit, irony, humor, and some acerbity, Fisher has enriched the world of literature in a medium Frank O'Connor has called our 'national art form' " (254).

As compared to his short stories, Fisher's novels have received less critical attention. W.E.B. Du Bois* criticizes Fisher for his portraiture of his two characters, Jinx and Bubber, who are "only moderately funny, a little smutty, and certainly not humanly convincing," and advises him to write about the middle class to which he belongs: "Why does Mr. Fisher fear to use his genius to paint his own kind, as he has painted Shine and Linda?" (374). B. A. Botkin says about *The Walls of Jericho*: "Here are the suave aplomb and the easy assurance of one at home in his subject" (346). Sterling Brown admires *The Walls of Jericho* for its "jaunty realism, masterly irony and satiric genius" (135). Hugh M. Gloster contends that "[t]his novel reveals the first Negro author skilled in comic realism and able to use irony and satire not only upon whites but also upon various classes of his own people" (17). William H. Robinson writes, "*The Walls of Jericho* is an especially comprehensive display of the themes that are common in American Negro literature and Fisher's own brilliantly satirical treatment of such themes" (vi–vii). David Levering Lewis says, "*The Walls of Jericho* was a social novel with a perfect ending: working-class integrity survives; the best elements of the upper and lower classes ally to oppose an internal foe, symbolized by organized gambling; and lessons in demolishing the walls of class and race are taught" (230).

With regard to *The Conjure Man Dies*, Arthur Davis offers praise for its clever plot and striking characters such as Frimbo, Jinx, and Bubber. He commends Dr. Archer as "a good authentic detective story type" who has "the human quality that will bear the strain of repetition, and we sincerely hope that Dr. Fisher will carry him on" (320) (which Fisher indeed does in short stories). According to

Sterling Brown, "The novel is above the average in its popular field" (136). The anonymous *Time* reviewer ("Rev.") writes, revealing the blatant prejudice of the day, that "Negroes are suitable for mystery stories because they are hard to see in the dark and white folks not knowing much about them, believe them primitively prone to violence" (39). Stanley Elkin finds the influence of mystery writer Dashiell Hammett in Fisher's second novel: "Fisher's extremely complex plotting and his occasionally too-pedantic writing of descriptive and expository passages is in the classical mode, but the characters, their broad range of background, and the handling of dialogue are wholly of Hammett's realistic school" (v).

BIBLIOGRAPHY

Works by Rudolph Fisher

Short Stories

"The City of Refuge." *Atlantic Monthly* (February 1925): 178–87.
"The South Lingers On." *Survey Graphic* (March 1925): 644–47.
"Ringtail." *Atlantic Monthly* (May 1925): 652–60.
"High Yaller." *The Crisis* (October 1925): 281–86; (November 1925): 33–38.
"The Promised Land." *Atlantic Monthly* (January 1927): 37–45.
"The Backslider." *McClure's* (August 1927): 16–17, 101–4.
"Blades of Steel." *Atlantic Monthly* (August 1927): 183–192.
"Fire by Night." *McClure's* (December 1927): 64–67, 98–102.
"Common Meter." *Baltimore Afro-American* (February 1930). Reprinted, *The City of Refuge: The Collected Stories of Rudolph Fisher*. Ed. John McCluskey Jr. Columbia: University of Missouri Press, 1987. 145–57.
"Dust." *Opportunity* (February 1931): 46–47.
"Ezkiel." *Junior Red Cross News* (March 1932): 151–53.
"Ezkiel Learns." *Junior Red Cross News* (February 1933): 123–25.
"Guardian of the Law." *Opportunity* (March 1933): 82–85, 90.
"Miss Cynthie." *Story* (June 1933): 3–15.
"John Archer's Nose." *Metropolitan Magazine* (January 1935): 10–82.
The City of Refuge: The Collected Stories of Rudolph Fisher. Ed. John McCluskey Jr. Columbia: University of Missouri Press, 1987.

Unpublished Stories

Held at John Hay Library at Brown University
"Across the Airshaft"
"The Lindy Hop"
"The Lost Love Blues" (three versions)
"The Man Who Passed"
Held by Mrs. Jane Ryder Fisher
"One Month's Wages"
"A Perfect Understanding"
"Skeeter"

Novels

The Walls of Jericho. New York: Knopf, 1928. Reprinted, with a new Preface by William H. Robinson. New York: Arno, 1969.
The Conjure Man Dies: A Mystery Tale of Dark Harlem. New York: Covici-Friede, 1932. Intro. Stanley Elkin. New York: Arno, 1971.

Essays

(With Earl B. McKinley and Margaret Holden). "Action of Ultraviolet Light upon Bacteriophage and Filterable Viruses." *Proceedings of the Society of Experimental Biology and Medicine* 23 (1926): 408–12.
"The Caucasian Storms Harlem." *American Mercury* 11 (1927): 393–98.
(With Earl McKinley). "The Resistance of Different Concentrations of a Bacteriophage of Ultraviolet Rays." *Journal of Infectious Diseases* 40 (1927): 399–403.

Reviews

"A Black Machiavelli." Rev. of *Mamba's Daughters*, by DuBoise Heywood. *BookLeague Monthly* (May 1929): 201.
Rev. of *The White Girl*, by Vera Caspary. *Opportunity* 78 (1929): 255–56.
"A Novel That Makes Faces." Rev. of *Black No More*, by George Schuyler. *New York Herald Tribune*, February 1, 1931, 5.
"Where Negroes Are People." Rev. of *The Chinaberry Tree*, by Jessie Fauset. *New York Herald Tribune*, January 17, 1932, 6.
"Harlem Manor." Rev. of *Infants of the Spring*, by Wallace Thurman. *New York Herald Tribune*, February 21, 1932, 16.
"Revealing a Beauty That Is Black." Rev. of *One Way to Heaven*, by Countee Cullen. *New York Herald Tribune*, February 28, 1932, 3.
"White, High Yellow, Black." Rev. of *Gingertown*, by Claude Mckay. *New York Herald Tribune*, March 27, 1932, 3.

Studies of Rudolph Fisher

Botkin, B. A. "The Lighter Touch in Harlem." Rev. of *The Walls of Jericho*. *Opportunity* (November 1928): 346.
Brawley, Benjamin. *Negro Genius: A New Appraisal of the Achievement of the American Negro in Literature and the Fine Arts*. Washington, DC: Dodd, Mead, 1937. 231–32.
Brown, Sterling. *The Negro in American Fiction*. Associates in Negro Folk Education, 1937. Reissued, Port Washington, NY: Kennikat, 1968.
Davis, Arthur P. "Harlem Mysterious." Rev. of *The Conjure Man Dies*. *Opportunity* 10 (1932): 320.
Deutsch, Leonard J. "The Streets of Harlem: The Short Stories of Rudolph Fisher." *Phylon* 40.2 (June 1979): 159–71.
Du Bois, W.E.B. "The Browsing Reader." Rev. of *The Walls of Jericho*. *The Crisis* 35 (1928): 374.
Emanuel, James A., and Theodore L. Gross, eds. *Dark Symphony: Negro Literature in America*. New York: Free Press, 1968.

Gloster, Hugh M. "Rudolph Fisher." In *Negro Voices in American Fiction*. New York: Russell and Russell, 1965. 174–77.

Henry, Oliver Louis. "Rudolph Fisher: An Evaluation." *The Crisis* 78 (June 1971): 149–54.

Lewis, David Levering. *When Harlem Was in Vogue*. New York: Knopf, 1981. New Preface by the author. New York: Penguin, 1997.

Locke, Alain, ed. "Negro Youth Speaks." In *The New Negro*. New York: Albert and Charles Boni, 1925. Ed. with a new Preface by Robert Hayden, New York: Atheneum, 1969.

Perry, Margaret. "A Fisher of Black Life: Short Stories by Rudolph Fisher." In *The Harlem Renaissance Re-examined*. Ed. Victor A. Kramer. New York: AMS Press, 1987. 253–63.

"Rev. of *The Conjure Man Dies*." *Time Magazine* (August 1, 1932): 39.

"Rudolph Fisher." In *From the Dark Tower: Afro-American Writers, 1900 to 1960*. Washington, DC: Howard University Press, 1974. 98–103.

Singh, Amritjit. *The Novels of the Harlem Renaissance*. University Park: Pennsylvania State University Press, 1976.

Singh, Amritjit, William S. Shriver, and Stanley Brodwin, eds. *The Harlem Renaissance: Revaluations*. New York: Garland, 1989.

SARAH LEE BROWN FLEMING
(1876–1963)

Jacquelyn Y. McLendon

BIOGRAPHY

Wife, mother, teacher, activist, and writer, Sarah Lee Brown Fleming worked devotedly for human rights and racial uplift. Despite her considerable achievements, however, not much has been written about her, and the information that is available provides only a sketchy picture of her life. Born on January 10, 1876, in Charleston, South Carolina, she grew up in Brooklyn, New York. A few scholars list her date of birth as 1875, but the 1876 date is listed on her death certificate and corresponds with Ann Allen Shockley's statement in *Afro-American Women Writers, 1746–1933* that Fleming died five days before her eighty-seventh birthday. Little is known of her girlhood, except that she sometimes went without even the bare necessities and had parents who did not encourage her ambition. Her father, believing she would never attain her goal of becoming a teacher, advised her to get work as a domestic instead, but, overcoming obstacles of poverty and racism, she went on to become the first black teacher in the Brooklyn school system.

More is known of Fleming after she married Richard Stedman Fleming on November 5, 1902. They had two children, Dorothy and Harold, born in 1903 and 1906, respectively. When they moved to New Haven, Connecticut, Richard Fleming became the first black dentist to practice in that state. Sarah Fleming organized the New Haven Women's Civic League (1929), founded the Phillis Wheatley* Home for Girls (1936), "a refuge for young colored girls who came to the city as strangers," and became the first black woman to be elected Connecticut "Mother of the Year" (1952). She was cited before Congress in 1955 for her many community contributions, and that same year she also received the Sojourner Truth Scroll, an annual award sponsored by the National Association of Negro Business and Professional Women's Club. Interestingly, it is her husband who is included in at least two volumes of *Who's Who in Colored America* and not Fleming, but her accomplishments have been cited in articles appearing in the *New Haven Register* (1955) and in *Jet* magazine (1964).

MAJOR WORKS AND THEMES

Fleming has been most recognized for her civic work rather than her art. Yet, she had a great love of the arts and wrote songs, skits, and musicals, none of which have ever been published. Her first publication appears to have been a novel, *Hope's Highway*, in 1918, followed two years later by a poetry collection, *Clouds and Sunshine*. She also contributed two brief biographies to a volume entitled *Homespun Heroines and Other Women of Distinction* (1926), extolling the virtues of Eliza A. Gardner and Josephine St. Pierre Ruffin, two black women, much like herself, who devoted their lives to the social, economic, and political struggles of minorities and women.

Fleming's writings, both fiction and nonfiction, are informed by her belief in racial uplift. She participated fully in the uplift activities that were a preoccupation of the black women's club movement of her day, writing in a letter to Mary Church Terrell* that through the efforts of intellectuals such as Terrell herself, "much of the burden of the race would be lifted immeasurably." A predominant theme of *Hope's Highway* is unmistakably that the "Negro problem," as it were, is "a matter of condition plus color" (48–49). The other major themes put forth in the book are the necessity of integration and, more important, the need for educated blacks to lead the race. Inspired by William H. Ferris' *The African Abroad* (1913), *Hope's Highway* is dedicated to great black men such as Frederick Douglass,* Booker T. Washington,* and W.E.B. Du Bois,* all of whom are recognizable in the black protagonist, Thomas Brinley. Ferris' book may also have inspired the name of one of *Hope's Highway*'s black heroes, Enoch Vance. Vance, as Ferris says of his grandfather Enoch Jefferson on the dedication page of *Africans Abroad*, was a "faithful guardian of all interests intrusted to his care."

Hope's Highway, a historical romance, takes place during slavery in idyllic Santa Maria, a fictional southern plantation settlement. It traces briefly the life and work of Enoch Vance, who builds a school for blacks using property left to him by his former kind master. With the era of Reconstruction comes the rise of a group of powerful antiblack politicians who destroy Vance's school and with it all of his hopes for the race. Vance dies of a broken heart, and the focus turns to young Tom Brinley, alias Frank Hope, who is destined to carry on Vance's work. Eventually, Tom and a young white woman, Grace Ennery, who finances his Oxford education, successfully integrate Santa Maria, restoring peace and happiness.

Although the plot is melodramatic, and the outcome hardly surprising, *Hope's Highway* exhibits several unconventional narrative choices. First, a white woman, Grace Ennery, stands at the center of the novel in place of a mulatto, the conventional heroine of early black fiction. Indeed, there are no phenotypically white or racially indeterminate characters and no miscegenation themes, a fact that ensures the improbability of a "blood theory," the notion that blood "tells" and a donnée of early mulatto fiction, to explain the attitudes and attributes of the characters. Second, to protest a politics of white supremacy, Fleming has a black character and a white character share the status of hero, again challenging traditional novels in which black characters are usually peripheral to white elite subjects, most often in the roles of whites' servants. Finally, well before the end of the novel, Grace marries and has a child, but she continues her work as activist and artist, much like Fleming herself. Fleming chooses not to use the customary marriage ending as a narrative solution to women's problems, asserting instead a woman's right to a career even if married.

Issues of religion, class, race, and gender are all addressed in the book. Fleming's feminist views are manifested in the explicit protestation of violence against women, in the affirmation of women's right to vote, and in a reinterpretation of black domesticity. That is, black women domestics are given cultural authority to address significant social and political issues. The race problem is resolved through the efforts of both heroic, educated blacks and aristocratic whites. These whites, because of their religion, education, and breeding, are able to overcome prejudice and work with blacks who have not sunk to the level of the "idle class of Negroes" (31). Even with her integrationist ideology, Fleming did not miss an opportunity to condemn racism and the violence that often accompanied it. Like many other black writers of her day, she wrote about lynching, although it was not directly germane to her plot; she also addressed the issue of blacks in the military through Tom's enlistment in the French army and his rapid rise to the rank of a commander who leads a successful charge against the enemy, the point being that absent the oppression of racism, blacks can reach great heights. Both these issues were especially pressing at the time of her book's publication.

Fleming's poetry volume also expresses her political views and may be more important for its content than for the author's poetic skill. Dedicated to her children, *Clouds and Sunshine* is divided into three parts, the first of which contains poems on general topics of love, friendship, trust, patriotism, and religion, embodying in some fashion sentiments of sadness and happiness, as the title indicates. The second and third sections, subtitled "Dialect Poems" and "Race Poems," respectively, deal with racial themes. With few exceptions, her poetry adheres to predictable rhyme patterns and conventional structures. One notable exception is "Pictures," consisting of six nonrhyming stanzas that unfold like a series of snapshots captioned "Slavery," "War," "Freedom," "Lynching," "Discrimination," and "Future." It ends with the same optimistic, integrationist view as her novel that by forming "one united band" blacks and whites together can bring about freedom (51).

The only other unrhymed poem is "The Black Man's Plea," which seems to be addressed to whites, urging them to be tolerant of a race that still "totters from Slav'ry's blow." Implicit in this and other poems is Fleming's acceptance of the view of her people's inferiority, even though she places the blame on slavery's having wounded the heart where "nobler" man lives (36). Several of her poems perpetuate negative black stereotypes, suggesting that Fleming might herself have had difficulty identifying with poor, uneducated black women at the same time that she strove to help them. In a poem entitled "Radiant Woman," for example, the black mother's beauty is attributable to an inner Christian glow that out-shines her outer physical homeliness. The speaker entreats others to look beyond the woman's physical appearance to see the "Divinity" within (40–41). "Radiant Woman" is included in "Race Poems," the last section of the book, in which lofty language, except for three dialect poems, and lofty subjects help to portray the "deeper life" of black people (35). Fleming moves back and forth between slavery's lasting physical and mental damage, as in "The Black Man's Plea," and emancipation's aftermath of hope for black people, as in "Emancipation Cele-bration," all of these themes converging in "Pictures." The last two poems, "Night Song" and "Put Away That Ukelele and Bring Out the Old Banjo," are indeed curiously placed in light of their content; they do not fit into the category of "Race Poems" as neatly as do the others in the section. However, even with the eclecticism of the collection, it is abundantly clear that Fleming saw her duty as similar to that of the poet in "An Exhortation": to depict the story of a "burdened race of men" with "glory" (47).

CRITICAL RECEPTION

Hope's Highway and *Clouds and Sunshine* were reprinted in the 1970s and not again until 1995, as part of the African-American Women Writers 1910–1940 series, published by G. K. Hall. As Shockley notes, "the New Haven papers never informed their readers of [Fleming's] literary works during her life or afterward" (358). Thus, they have largely remained unknown, mentioned in only a few critical works such as Hugh Gloster's *Negro Voices in American Fiction* (1948) and Carl Milton Hughes' *The Negro Novelist* (1953). Gloster recounts the plot of *Hope's Highway*, discusses several characters, speculates about Fleming's narrative intent, and finally concludes that it "has the usual overstatements of novels of its kind" (97–98). Hughes states that the book "piously resolved the race problem in religion" (36), which is only a cursory reading of a complex theme. Both Hughes and Gloster call attention to Fleming's desire to glorify black leaders, and Hughes categorizes the novel as literature that lends itself to protest and reform. Fleming is one of 100 black women writers profiled in Lorraine E. Roses and Ruth E. Randolph's *Harlem Renaissance and Beyond* (1990). Not meant to serve as in-depth studies of these women, the book attempts only to resurrect them from obscurity. Thus, Roses and Randolph briefly summarize Fleming's novel, stating that its "sweeping style is . . . engaging and romantic," that "the plot is at times refreshingly unpredictable" (115), and that it is "extremely sen-sitive to all aspects of the racial conflict between whites and blacks in this coun-try" (116). They also state that Fleming "was a versatile writer who explored many forms of written expression." Overall, Shockley's book includes the most extensive biographical information, derived primarily from correspondence and interviews with Fleming's daughter. Jacquelyn Y. McLendon's Introduction to the 1995 reprint is the most in-depth analysis of both the novel and poetry to date.

All of her writing demonstrates that Sarah Lee Brown Fleming remained steadfast in her optimism and determination, the same qualities that had enabled her to realize her fondest dreams of becoming a teacher, of helping her race, and of becoming an artist.

BIBLIOGRAPHY

Works by Sarah Lee Brown Fleming

Fiction

Hope's Highway. 1918. New York: G. K. Hall, 1995.

Poetry

Clouds and Sunshine. 1920. New York: G. K. Hall, 1995.

Nonfiction

"Eliza A. Gardner" and "Josephine St. Pierre Ruffin." In *Homespun Heroines and Other Women of Distinction*. 1926. Ed. Hallie Q. Brown. New York: Oxford University Press, 1988. 117–18, 151–53.

Studies of Sarah Lee Brown Fleming

Gloster, Hugh. *Negro Voices in American Fiction*. Chapel Hill: University of North Carolina Press, 1948.

Hughes, Carl Milton. *The Negro Novelist, 1940–1950*. New York: Citadel Press, 1953.

McLendon, Jacquelyn Y. "Introduction." In *Hope's Highway* and *Clouds and Sunshine*. New York: G. K. Hall, 1995.

Roses, Lorraine E., and Ruth E. Randolph. *Harlem Renaissance and Beyond: Literary Biographies of 100 Black Women Writers, 1900–1945*. Boston: G. K. Hall, 1990. 115–17.

Shockley, Ann Allen. *Afro-American Women Writers, 1746–1933: An Anthology and Critical Guide*. Boston: G. K. Hall, 1988. 356–62.

MARCUS MOSIAH GARVEY JR.
(1887–1940)

Peggy Stevenson Ratliff and Roosevelt Ratliff Jr.

BIOGRAPHY

Marcus Mosiah Garvey Jr., was hailed as a redeemer, a "black Moses." Although he did not realize all of his goals, his movement still represents a liberation from the psychological bondage of racial inferiority. Garvey is responsible for forming the Universal Negro Improvement Association (UNIA), a critical link in black America's centuries-long struggle for freedom, equality, and justice. He is responsible for the largest organized national mass movement in black history and is the progenitor of the modern "black is beautiful" ideal. He was one of the strongest advocates of the back-to-Africa movement (UNIA Paper Projects 4).

He was born on August 7, 1887, in St. Ann's Bay, Jamaica. He was the eleventh and last child born to Malcus ("Marcus") Mosiah Garvey, a mason, and Sarah Jane Richards, a domestic servant and produce grower. His family was poor, unmixed blacks. His father was a strict disciplinarian, and his mother was a kind and humble churchgoer. Out of the eleven children, Marcus and his sister Indiana were the only two siblings to live to adulthood.

He attended Standard 6, Church of England High School in Jamaica. At fourteen, he left school to work as an apprentice to his godfather, Mr. Burrowes, a painter. Subsequently, he joined the Protonationalist National Club, which championed Jamaican self-rule. He was not satisfied with his lack of a formal education and always yearned to be a learned man like W.E.B. Du Bois.* As an apprentice at the country painting business, he was able to learn all facets of a trade. Garvey was always interested in books, and Burrowes' large library assisted Garvey in developing this interest.

When Garvey was sixteen, he made a series of moves that changed the direction of his life. He left his rural apprenticeship to take a job with his uncle as a printer in the city of Kingston. In Kingston, Garvey added to his knowledge of the newspaper business. Here, he also was impressed with the power of oratory. He was especially struck by the skills of preachers and other speakers he heard at barbershop forums and debates in local parks (Levine 107).

At the age of twenty, he was a master printer and foreman of the P. A. Benjamin Company. In 1907 the printer's union went on strike, and Garvey was the only foreman on the side of the union. He was named their leader. After the strike ended, most of the workers got their jobs back, but Garvey was blacklisted. This caused Garvey to distrust the role unions played in helping black workers.

In 1910 Garvey was employed by the government and created the *Watchman*. This was the first in a series of attempts before starting the UNIA movement. He quit his job and moved to Costa Rica in search of better opportunities. His uncle helped him to find a job as a timekeeper at the United Fruit Company's banana plantation. Disappointed by how black field-workers were treated, he went to Limon to protest to the British consul but was met with indifference. Garvey traveled to Central America: Panama, Equador, Nicaragua, Colombia, and Venezuela. In all of these places, he found the status of blacks as inferior. He met Duse Mohammed Ali, a Pan-Negro journalist and businessman and publisher of the influential *African Times and Orient Review*, in 1912.

Garvey returned to his birthplace, Jamaica, and established the Universal Negro Improvement Association (UNIA). In four years he was in Harlem opening American chapters of UNIA. In America he advocated black independence by speaking, opening black businesses, creating the Black Star Shipping Line, spreading the UNIA around the world, and encouraging African Americans' emigration to Africa. He had thousands of followers. Garvey was extravagant in creating titles and costumes for leaders of his movement.

Garvey's movement was not without problems. His business was hampered with problems, and there was harsh criticism of him. Some even insinuated he associated with the Ku Klux Klan in order to help to send blacks back to Africa. Garvey's problems continued, and in 1922 he was incarcerated for six months because of mail fraud, and the Black Star Shipping Line also failed.

He was married twice. From 1919 to 1922 he was married to Amy Ashwood, cofounder of the UNIA in Jamaica, a journalist, feminist, and playwright. He also married Amy Jacques, his legal assistant in Jamaica, before migrating to the United States, where she was his business manager and personal secretary from 1922 to 1940. To this union two children were born, Marcus Garvey Jr. and Julius Winston Garvey; both were born in Jamaica but are now residents of the United States (UCLA 2).

Garvey died June 10, 1940, in London, England, and was buried in Marcus Garvey Memorial National Heroes' Park in Kingston, Jamaica.

MAJOR WORKS AND THEMES

One cannot discuss Marcus Garvey's speeches and writings without talking about his life. Therefore, throughout this section, segments of his life are integrated within the themes and analysis of his speeches and essays.

Garvey was not a fiction writer. However, he wrote several essays and speeches. His addresses on the race problem and black nationalism caused many to refer to him as another Moses. He selected twelve disciples to help him to announce and reach his goals of establishing brotherhood among blacks universally and to advocate and promote love and pride. He wanted to assist in establishing scholarships and, above all, a strong Negro nation. To get his message out, he founded a weekly newspaper, *The Negro World*.

Garvey also established the Black Star Line and factories to build ships in order to carry out his programs. He wanted to bring the raw materials of Africa and of the West Indies to America to be manufactured and then send the materials by ship back to those countries. These ships would also be used to carry and settle blacks of the New World in Africa.

In all of Garvey's writing and speeches his major themes deal with establishing universal confraternity among the race, promoting the spirit of race pride and love, reclaiming the fallen of the race, administering and assisting the needy, assisting with educating the illiterate tribes of Africa, strengthening the independent African states; establishing commissaries or agencies in the principal countries of the world for protection of all blacks, irrespective of their nationality; promoting a conscientious Christian worship among the native tribes of Africa; establishing universities, colleges, and secondary schools for the further education of the boys and girls of the race; and conducting a worldwide commercial and industrial exchange.

His aims and goals were closely linked to his religious mission; his schools and economic organizations were often vehicles for the development of the colonies. His international outlook and demand for change emerged out of the Pan-African ideas and activities with which he came in contact while in London (Williams 1).

In his essay written in 1913 on the "West Indies," however, he articulated a set of goals that were sharply different from the ones he had declared at the start of UNIA (*The Philosophy*, Vol. I, 42–51). He stressed the production of wealth by black labor, the inhumane treatment of slaves, and their heroic revolts. He wrote the following: "With the characteristic fortitude of the African, the Blacks shouldered their burdens [after slavery] and set themselves to work, receiving scanty remuneration for their services. By their industry and thrift, they have been able to provide themselves with small holdings which they are improving, greatly to their credit" (Stein 31). He had criticized the society that hired "intellectually inferior" young whites to civil service positions that blacks deserved.

A year after his return to his homeland, he denied his intention to belabor the race question. He stated that his concern was the development of his people and country. The black people in Jamaica, as a society, needed a great deal of help. "To the cultured mind, the bulk of our people are in darkness and are really unfit for good Religion society" (Stein 31). He further stated that the achievements of a couple would always be limited by the condition of many. Therefore, the UNIA goal was to go among the uncultured and help them to lift their standards so that they could better be appreciated by the cultured classes. Garvey was fighting an uphill battle because the majority of black Jamaicans were also indifferent to his efforts to change their traditional values.

In Jamaica he was unable to implement his plans and objectives, such as obtaining government land to build a school. Therefore, Garvey departed for the United States in 1916, where he was introduced to black leaders such as W.E.B. Du Bois and others. Most were not impressed with his philosophy. He admired Booker T. Washington* and wrote to him to build a school similar to Tuskegee Institute. Washington invited him to visit Tuskegee but did not make any pledges to help him.

Garvey now saw black business enterprises as replacing black education as the critical civilizing agent for the race. He was impressed by the active part played by black men and women in the commercial and the industrial life of the nation. He predicted greater achievements in the future: "The acme of American Negro enterprise is not yet reached. You have still a far way to go. You want more stores, more banks, and bigger enterprises. And under the American tutelage West Indians could dress as well as the Blacks in the North of the United States . . . [and] live in good homes . . . with furniture on the installment plan" (Clarke and Garvey 81–91).

Garvey continued to celebrate the blacks of the United States and stated that black business was the result of new ideological forces at work. However, Pan-Africanism did not lead to progress. His selection of institutions was critical and always involved a certain degree of expediency. But the idea of the Jamaican school paled before the new economic opportunities, especially those opportunities established in the United States by World War I.

Many of Garvey's conclusions were that black leaders had no programs, that they were merely opportunists. He said, "Too much of the leadership was concentrated in the hands of Mulattoes and those part-white Blacks could not be trusted" (*Afro American Encyclopedia* 1037). He also was disturbed that the black leadership depended on the mercy of liberal whites.

The Negro World, Garvey's newspaper, was published in English, French, and Spanish and had a circulation at one time of over 200,000. In this paper he wrote of blacks' contribution to history and his interpretation of history. He also praised the greatness of the classical African civilization at a period when whites were savages and barbarians.

Garvey was a success in New York, and he and his followers had their first international convention of the UNIA in New York City in August 1920. Over twenty-five countries were represented, and over 25,000 blacks were present in the audience.

Garvey was a very flamboyant dresser, sartorially similar to a British monarch, and at these conventions he dressed in raiment that outdid even kings, and so did his followers. He spoke out against British imperialism, yet he imitated its forms.

Garvey also was unable to throw off the impact of British folderol and glitter of his colonial childhood. He referred to himself as president and named his followers Royal African Guards, established dukes such as duke of Nile and of Uganda and knights commander and other titles. A supreme showman, Garvey's behavior resembled that of Barnum and attracted the attention of not only un- educated blacks but many educated and cultured whites who would have ignored him otherwise.

Garvey's successful speeches stirred his adversaries to greater activity, thereby increasing the devotion of his followers. Admirers and sycophants swarmed around him. He was hailed as the greatest man who ever lived and as another Moses and messiah. Some even compared him to God. The two great Gs in the world, said one of his followers, were God and Garvey. Like Napoleon, Mussolini, Hitler, and other dictators, Garvey started believing his followers' praise and became a braggadocio. Many of his speeches and writings caused his admirers to want to attack whites anywhere.

Overall, Garvey believed sincerely that the best way to right the wrongs of blacks was to retort by adopting the modus operandi of the racial imperialists he was in opposition to. In brief, for everything white that they had, he would have something black. For instance, he promised a Black House in Washington. He declared that his movement was fascistic. Garvey stated, "We were the first Fas- cists. We had disciplined men, women, and children in training for the liberation in Africa." The Black masses saw that in this extreme nationalism lay their only hope and readily supported it. "Mussolini," he said, "copied fascism from me, but the Negro reactionaries sabotaged it" (Rogers 420).

Opposition to Garvey increased, and his supporters became fanatical. Fighting occurred within the organization, some by blacks better educated than he was who did not see him as an intellectual and others who were also envious. Still others were willing to do anything for him. Some denounced him as medieval, autocratic, and antimulatto. Even a number of his once-supportive followers eventually attacked him in print and created counterorganizations.

Much of the opposition to Garvey was due to the fact that this once-obscure immigrant from Jamaica was collecting millions of dollars and was more successful than many college-trained leaders who had to rely on the help of white philan- thropists. He was the first black man to appeal to the black masses too far down to be noticed by other leaders. He won their admiration by informing them not only that they were as good as upper-class blacks but that a black skin was just as good as a white one, and even better. He told them that because of their skin color they would never be successful in America and that their only remedy was to get out and go back to Africa. They believed and agreed with him completely.

Some of the opposition he encountered was motivated by sheer jealousy, but a great deal of it was honest and logical. His "Back to Africa" program was diverting attention from the fight for racial justice in America. He discouraged blacks from joining white trade unions and even the Negro organizations fighting for rights here at home. He also rejected the church. Garvey's movement was political, not social; he declared that anything white cannot be beneficial to the black man. "We cannot fill Christian churches that show pictures of God and Jesus as Caucasians. We cannot look at the Bibles which are filled with pictures of a white God, a white savior and all white heavenly host" (*Afro American Encyclopedia* 1038).

Incredible as it may sound, he endorsed the Ku Klux Klan, the greatest foe of the black American and of democracy. In Atlanta, Georgia, he called on the leader of the Klan and pledged him his support. He stated that he and the Klan had in common that the Klan was fighting to make America a white man's country, and he was working to make Africa a black man's country (*Afro American Encyclopedia* 403). Garvey was working with the Ku Klux Klan and the fanatical racist clubs of that period. They gave him their open support; Garvey then announced, "We do not want all the Blacks to settle in Africa; some are no good here, and naturally, will be no good there" (1038).

He wanted to begin his movement in Liberia and wanted the whites to get out of Africa "because we are coming four hundred million strong" (*Afro American Encyclopedia* 1039).

His endorsement of the Klan was incendiary for his opponents. Eight of them signed a petition to the Department of Justice, citing cases of violence committed by members of his organization, all of which they alleged had been initiated by Garvey himself.

Garvey was convicted of using the U.S. mail to commit fraud and was sentenced to prison in 1925. After two years, he was pardoned by President Coolidge and deported to Jamaica.

Blacks in Harlem had looked out of the windows of their crowded slum apartments and saw him as the Hebrews saw Moses. He was bringing them a dream and promising to lead them to the promised land.

Garvey's speech at his trial was undoubtedly the finest speech of his career. Justice, not sympathy, was his refrain. "I want no mercy, only justice," he stated, and one felt that he meant every word. "I have served my people, my race and my God; I have wronged not even a child of my own race or any other. I would not betray my struggling race. If I do, I deserve to be thrown into the nethermost depths of Hell. If I have committed any offense in truth, and it is a violation of the law, I say it's your duty to find me guilty, and let me have the full extent of the law, I ask no mercy. I ask no sympathy. I ask but justice based on the testimony given in this court" (*World's Great Men of Color* 425).

There can be no question of his ability. However, he had the potentialities of a Mussolini or Hitler. His cause was just, but his methods were twisted, perverse, and archaic. Undoubtedly, Garvey wanted to help the downtrodden blacks, but like every other dictator, he believed the end justified the means. Similar to all other false messiahs, he was a poet and romancer and knew how to soothe the suffering of his followers with hopes of utopia.

CRITICAL RECEPTION

The charismatic, flamboyant, and enigmatic Marcus Garvey, rising to the highest echelon of African American leadership in the 1920s, attracted widespread criticism. Although the philosophy he espoused and the separatist movement he championed were much more evident in his speeches than in his writing, the fundamental ideology of black nationalism is to be found in his book *Philosophy and Opinions of Marcus Garvey*, published in 1967. Garvey was outspoken and staunch in his belief. Garvey stated that "the white man of America will not to any organized extent, assimilate the Black, because in doing so, he feels he will be committing racial suicide" (21). "A race without authority and power, is a race without respect" (2).

Borrowing ideas from Edwin P. McCabe of Oklahoma, the first to popularize a "back to Africa" movement, Garvey founded the Universal Black Improvement Association (UNIA) and the Black Star Line to attract and mobilize African Americans in pursuit of black economic and political self-determination. To accomplish this goal, Garvey vigorously promoted the mass exodus of African Americans and blacks from other countries to relocate to Africa. Through the establishment of businesses, shops, grocery stores, industrial plants, and shipping lines, he envisioned a free and industrially strong black race in Africa.

The contrasting philosophy of W.E.B. Du Bois, a rival intellectual leader, writer, and spokesman, included the advocacy of the assimilation of African Americans into mainstream society; it was a philosophy that clashed with the separatist, capitalist, black self-determination philosophy of Garvey. According to Du Bois, the only way for African Americans to find success was for them to become the intellectual equals of whites. If African Americans could prove themselves worthy, they could find a place in America (Laidlaw 3). E. Franklin Frazier maintained, however, that this appeal to the masses by Du Bois was "too intellectual" (147). Du Bois himself described Garvey as a sincere, hardworking idealist, but he added that Garvey was a stubborn, domineering leader of the masses; he had worthy industrial and commercial schemes, but he was an inexperienced businessman. His dreams of black industry and commerce and the ultimate freedom of Africa were feasible; but his methods were bombastic, wasteful, illogical, ineffective, and almost illegal (Du Bois, "Back to Africa" 129).

Analogous to the age-old question of whether President Lincoln in 1863 emancipated slaves in the rebellious South for political expediency or for humanitarian reasons, the enigma of Marcus Garvey's efforts—were they sincere or merely for his own self-aggrandizement?—remains. Sean Wilentz states that "with its mystical separatism and its notion of black economic self-deliverance, Garveyism had little value to offer its followers beyond cathartic theatrics" (17). Levine states that despite the rhetoric, Garvey exalted blackness as a virtue rather than a curse or a crime (26). Garvey preached freedom, justice, and economic self-determination, but "his actual performance was grotesquely nil," according to Lovett (179). If the ill-fated and unwise political decision by Garvey to elicit

Ku Klux Klan's support, followed by the dissension it created within the UNIA organizations, did not totally cripple the movement, the conviction and incarceration of Garvey for defrauding his followers of their investments did lead to the UNIA's downfall. The UNIA and the Black Star Line lost some $800,000 and left numerous critics to question Garvey's integrity. However, several critics do credit Garvey with instilling hope and pride in African American history. Following the end of World War I and the return of African American soldiers to their communities, where they faced segregation, discrimination, brutality, and lynching, Garveyism appeared more attractive to the masses than it would have otherwise under different conditions.

Not only did he promise the disfranchised and second-class citizens a paradise on earth, but he helped enhance African American self-esteem. Frazier writes that "he invented honors and social distinctions and converted every social invention to his use in his effort to make his followers feel important" (147).

In his assessment of Garveyism, Laidlaw argues that the movement may have had its flaws, and it may have been more about glitz than substance, but it still had a profound effect on the mind of the average black person. Garvey boosted self-confidence and mastered a sense of race pride in those who could find nothing but despair in their lives (8). To Garvey's American followers, the idea of an African homeland was always more potent than any actual desire to abandon the United States. "The Back-to-Africa part was not important; pride was" (Levine 27). The significance of Garveyism, according to Judith Stein, involved more than a charismatic leader asserting ideas of black worth and power and mandating racial unity. The rudiments of black nationalism are continuous from the late nineteenth century to the present (275). Garvey, more so than any of his contemporaries, helped galvanize the political energies of the African American masses. He remains one of the most colorful and controversial figures in American political history.

BIBLIOGRAPHY

Works by Marcus Mosiah Garvey Jr.

Philosophy and Opinions of Marcus Garvey. London: Frank Cass, 1967.
The Philosophy and Opinions of Marcus Garvey or Africa for the African. Ed. Amy Jacques and Tony Martin. 2 vols. Dover, MA: Majority Press, 1986.

Studies of Marcus Mosiah Garvey Jr.

Afro American Encyclopedia. Vol. 4. North Miami, Florida: Education Book Publishers, Inc., 1974.
Burns, W. Haywood. Voices of Black Protest in America. New York: Oxford University Press, 1963.
Chambers, Bradford. Chronicles of Black Protest: A Background Book for Young People Documenting the History of Black Power. New York: Parents Magazine Press, 1968.

Clarke, John H., and Amy Jacques Garvey, eds. *Marcus Garvey and the Vision of Africa*. New York: Random House, 1974.

Cronan, David E. *Black Moses*. Madison: University of Wisconsin Press, 1955.

Du Bois, W.E.B. et al. *African American Political Thought–1890–1930*. Ed. Cary D. Wintz. New York: M. E. Sharpe, 1996.

———. "Back to Africa." *The Century Magazine* (February 1923): 539–40.

———. "Behold the Land." In *Documentary History of the Civil Rights Movement*. Ed. Peter B. Levy. New York: Greenwood Press, 1992. 14–18.

———. *The Souls of Black Folk*. Ed. David W. Blight. Boston: Bedford Books, 1997.

———. *The Souls of Black Folk. The Struggle for Racial Equality: A Documentary Record*. Ed. Henry Steele Commager. 1967. Gloucester, MA: Peter Smith, 1972.

———. *The Souls of Black Folk and the Black Problem. The Black in 20th Century America*. Ed. John Hope Franklin and Isadore Starr. New York: Vintage Books, 1967.

Fax, Elton C. *Garvey: The Story of a Pioneer Black Nationalist*. New York: Dodd, Mead, 1972.

Franklin, John Hope, and August Meier, eds. *Black Leaders of the Twentieth Century*. Chicago: University of Illinois Press, 1982.

Frazier, E. Franklin. "Garvey: A Mass Leader." *The Nation* (August 18, 1926): 147–48.

"Garvey, Marcus." Editorial. *Black World* (September 11, 1920). http://www.isop.ucla.edu/mgpp/sample03.htm (14 February 1998.)

"Gunning for the Black Moses." *The Literary Digest* (August 19, 1992): 43–45.

Laidlaw, Mark. "Televangelist of the Masses: The Effect of Marcus Garvey and His Philosophy on the Black Movement of the Nineteen Twenties." http://www.msu.edu/course/mc . . . 20s/Garvey-Dubois/doylep.htm (1995).

Levine, Lawrence W. "Marcus Garvey's Moment." *New Republic* (October 29, 1984): 26–31.

Lewis, Rupert, and Patrick Bryan, eds. *Garvey: His Work and Impact*. Mona, Jamaica: Institute of Social and Economic Research, 1988.

Marable, Manning. *W.E.B. Du Bois, Black Radical Democrat*. Boston: Twayne, 1986.

McKissack, Patricia, and Fredrick McKissack. *W.E.B. Du Bois*. New York: Franklin Watts, 1990.

Moon, Henry Lee. *The Emerging Thought of W.E.B. Du Bois*. New York: Simon and Schuster, 1972.

Parrish, Michael E. *Anxious Decades: America in Prosperity and Depression, 1920–1941*. New York: W. W. Norton, 1992.

Pickens, William. "Africa for the Africans—The Garvey Movement." *The Nation* (December 28, 1921): 750–51.

Rogers, J. A. "Marcus Garvey." In *World's Great Men of Color*. New York: Macmillan, 1972.

Salzman, Jack, David Smith, and Cornel West, eds. *Encyclopedia of African American Culture and History*. New York: Simon and Schuster and Macmillan, 1996.

Stein, Judith. *The World of Marcus Garvey: Race and Class in Modern Society*. Baton Rouge: Louisiana State University Press, 1986.

UCLA. "Marcus Garvey and UNIA Papers Project." http://www.ikim@isop.ucla.edu. (1995).

Wilentz, Sean. "Backward March." *The New Republic* (November 6, 1995): 16–18.

EDYTHE MAE GORDON
(c. 1898–?)

Russell Jay Nurick

BIOGRAPHY

Edythe Mae Chapman was born sometime between the years 1896 and 1900 in Washington, D.C. It is difficult to determine the exact year of her birth. Though there are three existing documents that note her birth date, on each of these documents the date is different: one Boston University document states that she was born on June 4, 1898; another shows her birth date as June 4, 1900; and a census record from 1900 recognizes her life beginning in June 1896. Coinciding with the ambiguity of Edythe's birth, many of the events in her life are still a mystery. However, a few significant facts about her life have been recovered.

Edythe began her formal education in a Washington, D.C., public school. During the years 1912 to 1916, she attended the District of Columbia's distinguished M Street School in preparation for secondary school. At that time, the school was recognized for its distinguished faculty, which included the poet and novelist Jessie Redmon Fauset.*

During her last year at the M Street School, Edythe married Eugene Gordon. After graduating from Howard University in 1917, Eugene became a writer for the *Boston Post*. He was also editor of the *Quill*, a small literary magazine. This periodical is the only existing source of Edythe's creative fiction. In 1928 the first issue of this magazine was published, and in this issue Edythe published her first short story: "Subversion." The O. Henry Memorial Award Prize Committee listed this piece of fiction as one of the distinguished short stories of 1928 and did so during a time when white publishing companies rarely acknowledged the talent of African American authors. Edythe published another short story in each of the following two years. The *Quill* also published thirteen of her poems.

While Eugene Gordon was writing for the *Boston Post*, Edythe pursued her bachelor of science degree at Boston University. In the year 1934, eight years after enrolling in the university, Edythe finally received a B.S. in religious education and social services. A year later, she received her master's degree from the School of Social Services, at a time when it was exceptionally rare for an African American woman to earn a postgraduate degree.

Though Edythe was a scholar, it appears that her relationship with her husband, rather than most of the material she studied in school, acted as the source for the majority of issues about which she wrote. Eugene was a member of the Communist Party and a Marxist who was in favor of achieving racial and gender equality. Edythe's master's thesis is written in hopes of achieving such equalities. In 1932 the Boston directory shows separate addresses for Eugene and Edythe. They remained separated until 1942, when she filed for divorce. After 1942 no information is available as to how Edythe lived the remaining years of her life. The time and circumstances of her death remain unknown.

MAJOR WORKS AND THEMES

There is a consistent theme throughout Gordon's short stories; her poetry contains a slight variation in theme from her short stories, and the central idea to her master's thesis is quite different from her creative writing altogether.

In Gordon's first short story, "Subversion," the main character, John Marley, borrows money and a fur coat from his longtime friend, Charlie Delany. Emasculated by poor health and poverty, Marley convinces himself that he can purchase more than material objects with the money Delany loans him. Marley comes to believe that when his wife sees a man in a fancy fur coat who is bearing gifts, she will be capable of rekindling the passion she has lost toward him. Much to Marley's disappointment, he discovers that his wife has already fallen in love with the person to whom the fur coat and money truly belong: Delany. After discovering his wife's infidelity, in the most startling scene in any of Gordon's stories, Marley becomes aware that the boy who he thought was his child is actually Delany's. The child becomes a painful symbol of his wife's gross betrayal.

In her next short story, "If Wishes Were Horses," Gordon improves on her writing style, while exploring a theme similar to that of her first story. Here Edythe employs the technique of foreshadowing: a soothsayer informs Fred Pomeroy that he will be responsible for the fulfillment of his wife's desires, without indicating how this will be accomplished. Ironically, his death provides Rachel with insurance money that enables her to realize her dream of traveling. Rachel's dissatisfaction with her husband, though kept internal, is the cause of her husband's death. Once again, Gordon uses a clever device, the fortune-teller, for uncovering the theme of betrayal in her story. In addition, Gordon makes this story powerful by making Rachel's dissatisfaction with her husband literally destroy him.

Gordon's talent as a short story writer culminates with her third and final short story, "Hostess." For the first time, Gordon creates a woman who is primarily responsible for her own destruction. The story's central character, Mazie, leaves her husband, Jack, for the capriciously stimulating Saxophone Bill. Though Mazie's husband satisfies her financial desires, she wants "someone like a red-hot sheik from Harlem" (*Selected Works of Edythe Mae Gordon* 4). When Mazie's money runs out, so does Saxophone Bill. She returns to her husband, only to discover not only that he has married an old friend of hers but that the old friend is the very woman who advised Mazie against becoming further involved with Saxophone Bill. The repercussions of Mazie's descent into adultery provoke her suicide: a systematic self-destruction. In all three of these stories, at least one person is betrayed, and money is perpetually associated with these betrayals. Thus, it appears that Gordon is communicating her belief in the possibility of betrayal in relationships, as well as her anticapitalistic attitude.

Unlike her tragic short stories, Edythe's poetry offers a positive view of love. In "Elysium," the speaker fondly reminisces of an old love; yet, she realizes that the fertility of such a love is possible only in "the land of dreams" (94). Edythe views death as an event that should make living all the more precious in "Buried Deep." "One Summer's Day" personifies love as a beautiful, but temporary, companion. "Young Love" is a poem about becoming enraptured by the love of another. It is about the desire to find a faithful lover and hold onto him forever. "April Night" is filled with powerful imagery that compares human nature to the natural world. It presents spring as the season of fecundity and desire, but seasons inevitably change, just as human beings do. This poem, as do all the others, contains the theme of ephemeral beauty.

Edythe's master's thesis, "The Status of the Negro Women," provides a powerful history of the origin of American slavery. Its purpose is to unveil the hardships African American women underwent between the American colonial era and the Emancipation Proclamation. Though Gordon carefully explains the inhumane treatment that most male and female slaves underwent, she is specifically concerned with the double hardship of the female slave, who was oppressed because of her race as well as her gender. By doing so, Gordon reveals not only a highly developed racial consciousness but also an emerging feminist awareness.

CRITICAL RECEPTION

There have been no articles written about Edythe Mae Gordon yet.

Edythe's master's thesis is a powerfully informative document, yet it tends to stray from its thesis statement. She claims to be concerned only with the Negro woman, yet the majority of her thesis discusses the conditions of all slaves. Perhaps she found it impossible to isolate the woman because such background information (e.g., what happened to their sons and husbands) is absolutely necessary in telling their story. The most inspiring part of this document is the section where Edythe highlights the special achievements of a few African American women. In this section, she includes stories of several great women such as Sojourner Truth* and Harriet Tubman.

Though Gordon wrote during the Harlem Renaissance, besides her master's thesis, only one of her stories specifically alludes to this time period and her African American descent: "Hostess." By having Mazie leave her husband for Saxophone Bill, Gordon reveals the magnetic power of a new art form—jazz—that captivated many African Americans during the 1920s.

Edythe's literary talent is best exemplified in her poetry. At its best, her visual imagery is as vivid as a pastel drawing, and her sensual imagery is powerful and highly imaginative.

BIBLIOGRAPHY

Work by Edythe Mae Gordon

Selected Works of Edythe Mae Gordon. Ed. Henry Louis Gates Jr. and Jennifer Burton. New York: G. K. Hall, 1996.

SUTTON E. GRIGGS
(1872–1933)

Roy Kay

BIOGRAPHY

Sutton E. Griggs was born in Chatfield, Texas, on June 19, 1872. The son of a Baptist preacher, the Reverend Allen R. Griggs, Sutton was both a college (Bishop College in Marshall, Texas) and seminary (Richmond Theological Seminary in Richmond, Virginia) graduate. He was ordained in 1893 and became the pastor of a Baptist church in Berkeley, Virginia. In 1899 Griggs published *Imperium in Imperio*, thereby beginning a literary career that lasted almost thirty years. Maintaining his position as a pastor, Griggs published five novels, an autobiography, and a number of books and pamphlets on the Negro race and the race problem in America. Grigg' work can be seen as an early articulation of what came to be known as "the New Negro" movement.

Griggs' career as a Baptist minister and writer changed with his move to Nashville, Tennessee. He became the pastor of the First Baptist Church in East Nashville, in addition to founding and operating Orion Publishing Company. For ten years Griggs published his fiction and nonfiction through Orion. During that time Griggs' fiction was financially unsuccessful, and Orion was forced to close before Griggs moved to Memphis in 1920. Subsequent works by Griggs, all nonfiction, were published by his second publishing venture, the Public Welfare League. This organization, dedicated to racial uplift, was located in Memphis.

In 1920 Griggs became the pastor of Tabernacle Baptist Church in Memphis. The Public Welfare League also suffered financial hardships and had to close. Griggs' career as a writer ended in 1927. In 1928 Griggs recorded a half dozen sermons with little commercial success (Tracy 159–66). Soon after his failures in Memphis, Griggs moved back to Texas and took over his father's church. On

January 3, 1933, the Reverend Sutton E. Griggs died. A bibliophile throughout his adult life, at the time of his death Griggs owned over 2,000 books.

MAJOR WORKS AND THEMES

The writings of the Reverend Sutton E. Griggs are held together by the idea of race. They can be characterized as race writings, and Griggs himself can be called a race man in the same vein as Alexander Crummell (1819–1898), Edward Blyden (1832–1912), W.E.B. Du Bois* (1868–1963), and Marcus Garvey* (1887–1940). In line with much of the racial logic of his day, Griggs presented two complementary concepts of race. First, race is a biological given. People are born into races, such as the Anglo-Saxon race and the Negro race, and racial differences are part of God's order. Phenotype in Griggs' writings is very important and in his novel constitutes an outward sign of one's inward character. For this reason Griggs' narrators take great care to describe characters' color, features, and hair texture.

Second, race is a spiritual given more substantial than the materiality of race. The spiritual dimension of race is mystical and romantic, but more importantly it is teleological. According to the German philosopher and theologian Johann Gottfried Herder, all nations have a destiny to fulfill that is both unique to them and simultaneously a contribution to the global destiny of the human race (*Outlines of a Philosophy of the History of Man* [1784–1791]). For Griggs Negroes cannot achieve their destiny because they are fettered by immaturity and hindered by racial injustice and its effects. Solving the arrested development of the Negro and thus putting the race on the right track constitute the subject and goals of Griggs' writings.

One way to put the race on the path to its destiny is to foster and promote racial consciousness and unity. The development of racial consciousness and unity, on both a national and international level, was a theme throughout nineteenth-century African American letters. Much of this discussion was based on interpretations of one biblical verse, Psalm 68:31 ("Prince shall come forth out of Egypt; Ethiopia shall soon stretch forth her hands to God")—the so-called Ethiopian Prophecy (also known as Ethiopianism) and its imperative that Negroes, armed with Christianity and a Western education, convert and civilize their racial brethren globally. Griggs as a Baptist pastor and well-read man was very familiar with the hermeneutical tradition of Psalms 68:31 in African American religious and political thought. All of Griggs' fictions are extended interpretations of the verse and the destiny of the Negro, especially his 1905 novel, *The Hindered Hand.*

In keeping with the nationalist and racialistic logic of Ethiopianism, *Overshadowed* dramatizes the problem of Negroes' immaturity and hence their inability to achieve their destiny. The cause of this immaturity is twofold. First, Negroes are only two generations out of savagery (*Overshadowed* 5). Second, because

Negroes, due to their historical and geographical context, are forced to mature alongside the Anglo-Saxon race, "the most cultured, aggressive and virile type of all times" (*Overshadowed* 5), the Negroes' growth has been hindered and reduced to a weak imitation of Anglo-Saxon civilization. In other words, the Negro is overshadowed by the Anglo-Saxon race. Despite the bleakness of the present, the future is guaranteed in the novel by the marriage of Astral Herdon and Erma Wysong and the birth of their son, Astral Herdon Jr. In messianic, melodramatic, and romantic language, the narrator concludes the novel with the following:

Under the influences which this child of destiny shall generate, the Negro shall emerge from his centuries of gloom, with a hope-emblazoned brow, a heart freighted with courage, and a chisel in his hand to carve, whether you will or not, his name in the hall of fame. (219)

In *Unfettered* Griggs articulates a plan of racial uplift and regeneration that will free the Negro from the shadow of the Anglo-Saxon race and its civilization. In the tradition of Ethiopianism, the hero, Dorlan Warthell (a man of pure African blood), takes on the race problem not only to free the Negro race but also to win the hand of Morlene Dalton. Written as another volume in the continuing saga of the Negro in the postbellum South, Dorlan sets forth a plan for Negro autonomy. Alluded to in the plot of *Unfettered*, "Dorlan's Plan" constitutes a sequel to the novel itself. This plan, organized around biblical phrases and nineteenth-century themes, argues for the Negro's common humanity but racial and hence spiritual difference.

Like Edward Blyden, Marcus Garvey, and the writers of the plantation tradition such as Thomas Dixon, Griggs did not write favorably of race mixing or of characters who were racially mixed. Even though mulattos/mulattas are called Negroes in Griggs' novels, their status is ambiguous and hence possibly dangerous to the race. There are two types of antagonists in Griggs' work, racist white people or groups and mulattos/mulattas. In *Imperium in Imperio* the mulatto Bernard Belgrave, driven to madness by unrequited love due to his status as a mulatto and the very nature of his turbulent blood, executes the true Negro and American patriot Belton Piedmont (a man of pure Negro blood) and forms a separate Negro government (the Imperium in Imperio) to break away from the United States. In *The Hindered Hand*, the pimp Leroy Crutcher is a mulatto and in a conflict reminiscent of that between Belton and Bernard, Esnal Ellwood (a pure Negro) and Earl Bluefield (a mulatto) struggle against racism, with the latter becoming insane, violent, and a pariah of biblical proportions, "Earl the Ishmaelite" (251). The former, however, in true Griggsian fashion, is heroic and, true to his race, states in unambiguous terms the primacy and importance of racial purity and its relationship to fulfilling the destiny of the race, the redemption of Africa (198).

As a modern writer and thinker Griggs believed not only that literature was an expression of the racial soul but that it constituted a sign of racial maturity. In a 1916 pamphlet, *Life's Demands; or, According to the Law*, Griggs wrote,

"Observe that all the races of mankind that have achieved greatness have developed a literature" (qtd. in Elder 69). These sentiments were echoed earlier in "Dorlan's Plan." Griggs' form of racial mysticism and romanticism recalls Herder's theory of the spiritual relationship among the nation, national language, and national literature. Griggs' commitment to writing fiction is his attempt to both educate and bind the race. In Griggs' novels the subject of the story (the Negro race) is more important than the medium of the story. Written in serial style, Griggs' plots are melodramatic, romantic, committed to both representing and protesting America's racial predicament and the suffering of the Negro. Characters are like cardboard figures, one-dimensional in these dramas in which class, region, and gender dynamics are collapsed under the category of race. In Griggs' fictional world everyone represents an ideological position. Names indicate a character's role in the plot, and disguises and pseudonyms (well-worn tropes of popular American fiction) function as plot devices to either build or relieve tension. Because of the overtly political goal of Griggs' fiction, language is purely referential in that it transparently speaks the world. All jokes, tropes, and figures function as either signs of ignorance (in the forms of dialect and malapropisms) or mere ornamentation.

CRITICAL RECEPTION

Hugh Gloster's 1943 essay in *Phylon*, "Sutton E. Griggs: Novelist of the New Negro," is the first extended critical engagement with Griggs' fiction. Gloster reads Griggs' novels, along with the works of other Negro writers such as Charles Waddell Chesnutt* and Pauline Elizabeth Hopkins,* as responses to the plantation tradition of Thomas Nelson Page and Thomas Dixon. In Gloster's estimation Griggs' fictions, despite their artistic weaknesses, "were probably more popular among the rank and file of Negroes than the fiction of Chesnutt and Dunbar" (337), a claim that has been echoed by other scholars of Griggs. Moreover, Gloster is also responsible for another often repeated characterization of Griggs' novels as political and revolutionary (345).

Despite the critical attention Griggs' works have received from numerous scholars since their reprinting in the late 1960s and early 1970s, the work of Arlene Elder and Wilson Jeremiah Moses is required reading for any student of Sutton Griggs. Elder's chapter on Sutton Griggs in her book entitled *The "Hindered Hand": Cultural Implications of Early African-American Fiction* is an extended and well-written *explication de texte* of Griggs' novels and also a primary source on his life. Complementary to Elder's work is Moses' situation of Griggs' novels within American history and modernity in general. Moses, a historian, was one of the first scholars to analyze and define "literary black nationalism" in African American literature, and the novels and poetics of Griggs were his texts. In 1979 Moses argued that Griggs' work demands to be studied "because Griggs was perhaps the first black writer consciously to attempt to create a distinctly Afro-American philosophy of literature and a body of writing to go with it" ("Literary"

204). Moses has continued his analysis of Griggs and has extended his critique to other black literary nationalists such as Pauline Hopkins* and W.E.B. Du Bois.*

BIBLIOGRAPHY

Works by Sutton E. Griggs

Novels

Imperium in Imperio. Cincinnati: Editor, 1899.
Overshadowed: A Novel. Nashville, TN: Orion, 1901.
Unfettered: A Novel. Nashville, TN: Orion, 1902.
The Hindered Hand: or, The Reign of the Repressionist. Nashville, TN: Orion, 1905.
Pointing the Way. Nashville, TN: Orion, 1908.

Autobiography

The Story of My Struggles. Memphis: National Public Welfare League, 1914.

Pamphlets and Other Writings

The One Great Question . . . Nashville, TN: Orion, 1907.
Needs of the South. Nashville, TN: Orion, 1909.
Wisdom's Call. Nashville, TN: Orion, 1911.
How to Rise. Memphis, TN: National Public Welfare League, 1915.
Life's Demands; or, According to the Law. Memphis, TN: National Public Welfare League, 1916.
The Reconstruction of a Race. Memphis, TN: National Public Welfare League, 1917.
Light on Racial Issues. Memphis, TN: National Public Welfare League, 1921.
Guide to Racial Greatness: or, The Science of Collective Efficiency. Memphis, TN: National Public Welfare League, 1923.
The Negro's Next Step. Memphis, TN: National Public Welfare League, 1923.
The Negro's Next Step. Memphis, TN: National Public Welfare League, 1923.
Kingdom Builders' Manual: Companion Book to Guide to Racial Greatness. Memphis, TN: National Public Welfare League, 1924.
Paths of Progress; or, Co-operation between the Races. Memphis, TN: National Public Welfare League, 1925.
The Winning Policy. Memphis, TN: National Public Welfare League, 1927.

Studies of Sutton E. Griggs

Bell, Bernard W. *The Afro-American Novel and Its Tradition.* Amherst: University of Massachusetts Press, 1987.
Bloom, Harold, ed. *Black American Prose Writers: Before the Harlem Renaissance.* New York: Chelsea House, 1994.
Bone, Robert A. *The Negro Novel in America.* New Haven, CT: Yale University Press, 1965.

Brown, Sterling. *Negro Poetry and Drama* and *The Negro in American Fiction*. New York: Atheneum, 1978.

Elder, Arlene A. "Sutton Griggs: The Dilemma of the Black Bourgeoisie." In *The "Hindered Hand": Cultural Implications of Early African-American Fiction*. Westport, CT: Greenwood Press, 1978.

Fleming, Robert E. "Sutton E. Griggs: Militant Black Novelist." *Phylon* 34.1 (March 1973): 73–77.

Fuller, Thomas O. *History of the Negro Baptists of Tennessee*. Memphis, TN: Hopkins Print, 1936.

Gloster, Hugh M. *Negro Voices in American Fiction*. New York: Russell and Russell, 1965.

———. "Sutton E. Griggs: Novelist of the New Negro." *Phylon* 4.4 (1943): 335–345.

Moses, Wilson Jeremiah. *Afrotopia: The Roots of African American Popular History*. Cambridge: Cambridge University Press, 1998.

———. *The Golden Age of Black Nationalism, 1850–1925*. New York: Oxford University Press, 1978.

———. "Literary Garveyism: The Novels of Reverend Sutton E. Griggs." *Phylon* 40.3 (Fall 1979): 203–16.

———. *The Wings of Ethiopia: Studies in African-American Life and Letters*. Ames: Iowa State University Press, 1990.

Payne, James Robert. "Griggs and Corrothers: Historical Reality and Black Fiction." *Explorations in Ethnic Studies* 6.1 (January 1983): 1–15.

Taylor-Thompson, Betty E. "Sutton Elbert Griggs." In *Dictionary of Literary Biography*. Vol. 50: *Afro-American Writers before the Harlem Renaissance*. Ed. Trudier Harris and Thadious M. Davis. Detroit: Gale, 1984. 140–48.

Tracy, Steven C. "Saving the Day: The Recordings of the Reverend Sutton E. Griggs." *Phylon* 47.2 (June 1986): 159–66.

ANGELINA WELD GRIMKÉ
(1880–1958)

Ymitri Jayasundera

BIOGRAPHY

Angelina Weld Grimké's family history includes a heritage of miscegenation. She was named after her great-aunt Angelina Grimké Weld, who, with her sister Sarah Grimké, left the family plantation, Caneacre in South Carolina, as a young woman to escape owning slaves. They settled in Hyde Park, Massachusetts, and became well-known abolitionists and advocates of woman's rights. After the Civil War, they discovered and acknowledged their brother Henry's two sons, Archibald and Francis, born to his slave Nancy Weston. The two sisters supported Archibald through Harvard Law School. He married Sarah Stanley, a white woman, whose father, a prominent Boston preacher, opposed the marriage. Soon after Grimké's birth, her mother was probably confined to a mental institution and definitely lived away from her in Detroit with her parents. Grimké never saw her, but they corresponded until her death in 1898. She was emotionally very close and dependent on her stern, exacting, but loving, father, sending him her work for his approval. She repressed her lesbian sexual desires to please him, but there are references to lesbian love affairs in her poetry and unpublished papers. Her closeted lesbianism probably contributed to her personal unhappiness that lasted throughout her life.

Grimké grew up in a liberal and cultured atmosphere, encouraged to write poetry by her family and meeting prominent people such as Frederick Douglass.* She was educated in Boston in private schools, frequently the only black child in her class, and received her college degree from Boston Normal School of Gymnastics (now part of Wellesley College) in 1902. She became a gym teacher first at Armstrong Manual Training School in Washington, D.C., but in 1907 transferred to M Street High School, later the famous Dunbar High School, where she taught English until 1926. After a disastrous love affair, she resolved, "I shall never know what it means to be a mother, for I shall never marry" (qtd. in Hull 124), and she did not marry. Shortly after her father's death in 1930, she moved to Brooklyn, living there until her death. Although she is included in the Harlem Renaissance movement, Grimké did not associate with the Harlem literati, and her main body of work was composed between 1900 and 1920, antedating the movement.

Grimké's literary reputation rests on her play *Rachel*, performed in 1916 and published in 1920, and a few of her published poems, frequently anthologized, such as in Alain Locke's* *The New Negro* (1925) and Countee Cullen's* *Caroling Dusk* (1927). Major portions of her oeuvre—many unpublished poems, *Rachel*, seven short stories (four never published), and selections from her diaries and sketches—were published in 1991 as part of the Schomburg Library of Nineteenth-Century Black Women Writers series by Oxford University Press, thus making her work accessible to readers and scholars. Her unpublished work and papers, archived at Howard University's Moorland Spingarn Research Center in Washington, D.C., include another 200 unpublished poems, several unfinished short stories, and an unfinished play titled *Mara*, in which an entire African American family is lynched after the father kills his daughter's white rapist.

MAJOR WORKS AND THEMES

Mara parallels *Rachel* and many of the short stories by focusing on women's reactions to the lynching of their men and seeming to advocate a type of self-genocide of African Americans. The title character in *Rachel*, previously anticipating motherhood, vows never to have children to prevent their being potentially lynched when she discovers that her father and brother were lynched. In "The Closing Door," Grimké develops this further when the mother suffocates her baby after learning that her brother was lynched. Grimké targeted her work to white women to educate them to the consequences of racism by appealing to motherhood, publishing two short stories in *Birth Control Review* with a white readership. Surrogate daughters form very loving relationships with surrogate mothers, such as in "The Closing Door" and "Jettisoned," the only story written in black English and focusing on the repercussions of passing that cause the daughter to pretend not to know her mother. The stories probably rework biographically Grimké's lifelong lack of, and wish for, the love and support of a mother.

Birth Control Review rejected "Blackness," an earlier version of "Goldie," in which the unnamed black narrator escapes after killing the man responsible for lynching his former love and her husband, slashing her womb, and trampling to death her unborn baby. Because the narrator escapes, it was probably deemed unpalatable to their white audience, but publication of "The Closing Door" makes self-genocide of African Americans appear as a viable form of birth control. It was Grimké's choice to publish the story in the journal. In an undated letter to the *Atlantic Monthly*, she cites the actual incident as her impetus for writing "Blackness," which suffers from too much framework and an insufficiently developed core story. But in "Goldie," published in *Birth Control Review*, the black narrator is lynched after he kills the white perpetrator. It is a much stronger story, successfully incorporating the stream-of-consciousness technique. "Black Is, As Black Does," part of Grimké's juvenalia, is a moralistic story on the theme of lynching. In a dream, the white narrator observes an African American man, recently lynched, entering heaven and his white murderer condemned to hell.

In two short stories Grimké uses white characters to focus on the lack of communication in a marriage and another relationship. In "The Drudge," she deals with domestic violence and how women endure it with stoicism and despair. In "The Laughing Hand," an artist breaks up with his fiancée because his lower face is mutilated by cancer, and he has lost the power of speech. Grimké creates a paradox with language seemingly castrated but with the handwriting substituting for speech. The title is literal as well as metaphorical. The inability of language to articulate the humiliation and pain of racism is also a major theme in *Rachel* and other stories. In the only article completely devoted to Grimké's fiction, David Hirsch discusses Grimké's strategies of embodying the silencing of African Americans that is caused by lynching. Lucy, the young narrator in "The Closing Door," and the two narrators in "Blackness" try to break this silence.

Unlike in her play and short stories, the subjects of motherhood, racial concerns, and lynching are minor themes in Grimké's poetry. She wrote elegies of her family and friends, love and nature lyrics, sonnets, and philosophical poems on the human condition; some of the themes include grief, death, and lost love and its accompanying despair. Most of her poetry is conservative—polished, formal, lyrical, and sentimental—but in her later poetry, she begins experimenting with form that looks forward to the Harlem Renaissance. Large portions of the poetry obliquely record lesbian love through the use of a male persona.

CRITICAL RECEPTION

Although frequently mentioned in passing in overview articles on Harlem Renaissance women playwrights or poets, Grimké's work, especially her short stories, has been mostly ignored by scholars, who have dismissed *Rachel* as a propaganda play of social protest and criticized it for its sentimentality, exposition, and awkwardness. But current scholarship is now beginning to reclaim Grimké, with feminist critics arguing, for example, that the play, while "us[ing] the sentimental language of dominant gender ideology which idealized motherhood, . . . does not support or concede to that ideology" (Stephens 334). Other scholars, now delving into the play's issues, themes, and structure, such as William Storm, argue for a psychoanalytic reading of the play focusing on Rachel's battle in the "arena of religious doubt and faith" (463), and Elizabeth Brown-Guillory focused her article on the conflicts and tensions between mothers and daughters. The major study of Grimké is in Gloria Hull's *Color, Sex, and Poetry*, which includes a chapter on her. Using a biographical approach, Hull discusses how the major themes in the play and stories relate to the poetry, as well as analyzes the poetry in depth. Before Grimké's *Selected Works* (1991), the short stories had been inaccessible to readers, and David Hirsch acknowledges this in his article on the stories.

The thread of sentimentality running through the stories and *Rachel* may be somewhat jarring to the modern reader unused to a nineteenth-century sensibility, but Grimké also takes an unflinching look at the consequences of racism as it affected African American women in their daily lives, thereby reclaiming the lives of this ignored and silenced group. As a result, Grimké is an important forerunner to the Harlem Renaissance movement, and she has the distinction of being the first twentieth-century black female playwright whose play was produced and acted by African Americans.

BIBLIOGRAPHY

Works by Angelina Weld Grimké

Collected Work

Selected Works of Angelina Weld Grimké. Ed. Carolivia Herron. The Schomburg Library of Nineteenth-Century Black Women Writers series. New York: Oxford University Press, 1991.

Short Stories

"Black Is, As Black Does: A Dream." *Colored American Magazine* 1 (August 1900): 160–63. Reprinted in *Short Fiction by Black Women 1900–1920*. Ed. Elizabeth Ammons. The Schomburg Library of Nineteenth Century Black Women Writers series. New York: Oxford University Press, 1991. 27–31.
"The Closing Door." *Birth Control Review* (September and October 1919): 10–14.
"Goldie." *Birth Control Review* (November–December 1920): 7–11.

Drama

Rachel. Boston: Cornhill, 1920; reprinted, College Park, MD: McGrath, 1969. Reprinted in *Black Theater, U.S.A.: Forty-Five Plays by Black Americans 1847–1974*. Ed. James V. Hatch and Ted Shine. New York: Free Press, 1974. 137–72.

Poetry

Black Writers of America: A Comprehensive Anthology. Ed. Richard Barksdale and Keneth Kinnamon. New York: Macmillan, 1972. 626–27.
Black Sister: Poetry by Black American Women, 1746–1980. Ed. Erlene Stetson. Bloomington: Indiana University Press, 1981. 60–63.
The Norton Anthology of African American Literature. Ed. Henry Louis Gates Jr. and Nellie Y. McKay. New York: Norton, 1997. 943–45.

Studies of Angelina Weld Grimké

Abramson, Doris E. "Angelina Weld Grimké, Mary T. Burrel, Georgia Douglas Johnson, and Marita O. Bonner: An Analysis of Their Plays." *Sage* 2.1 (1985): 9–13.

Brown-Guillory, Elizabeth. "Disrupted Motherlines: Mothers and Daughters in a Gendered, Sexualized, and Racialized World." In *Women of Color: Mother–Daughter Relationships in 20th-Century Literature*. Ed. Elizabeth Brown-Guillory. Austin: University of Texas Press, 1996. 188–207.

———. *Their Place on the Stage: Black Women Playwrights in America*. Westport, CT: Greenwood Press, 1988.

Hirsch, David A. Hedrich. "Speaking Silences in Angelina Weld Grimké's 'The Closing Door' and 'Blackness.'" *African American Review* 28.3 (1992): 459–74.

Hull, Gloria T. *Color, Sex, and Poetry: Three Women Writers of the Harlem Renaissance*. Bloomington: Indiana University Press, 1987.

Keyssar, Helene. "Rites and Responsibilities: The Drama of Black American Women." In *Feminine Focus: The New Women Playwrights*. Ed. Enoch Brater. New York: Oxford University Press, 1989. 226–40.

Miller, Jean Marie. "Angelina Weld Grimké: Playwright and Poet." *CLA Journal* 21 (1978): 513–24.

Schroeder, Patricia R. "Remembering the Disremembered: Feminist Realists of the Harlem Renaissance." In *Realism and the American Dramatic Tradition*. Ed. William W. Demastes. Tuscaloosa: University of Alabama Press, 1996: 91–106.

Stephens, Judith L. "Anti-Lynch Plays by African American Women: Race, Gender, and Social Protest in American Drama." *African American Review* 28.2 (1992): 329–39.

Storm, William. "Reactions of a 'Highly-Strung Girl': Psychology and Dramatic Representation in Angelina W. Grimké's *Rachel*." *African American Review* 27.3 (1993): 461–71.

Young, Patricia. "Shackled: Angelina Weld Grimké." *Women and Language* 15.2 (1992): 25–31.

CHARLOTTE LOTTIE FORTEN GRIMKÉ
(1837–1914)

Karen M. Davis

BIOGRAPHY

Charlotte Lottie Forten was born August 17, 1837, into a prominent Philadelphia family of free blacks with a long history of social responsibility. Charlotte's early education, provided primarily by private tutors, was greatly enhanced by her family, activists in their own right, as well as by the influential professional and social circles they moved in, which included abolitionists William Lloyd Garrison, William Wells Brown,* and numerous others.

In 1853, when Charlotte was sixteen, she enrolled in the integrated Higginson Grammar School of Salem, Massachusetts. During that first year away from home, boarding in the home of black abolitionists Charles and Amy Remond, she began her journal. She was an excellent student, and during her initial years in Salem she commenced a course of self-improvement in which she taught herself several foreign languages and read over the course of a year more than 100 contemporary and classical works by authors such as Lydia Maria Child, Elizabeth Barrett Browning, Shakespeare, and Milton. Her poem "A Parting Hymn" was read at her official graduation from Higginson in 1856. That year she attended Salem Normal School in preparation for a teaching career.

At the recommendation of administrators at Salem Normal she was hired at Epes Grammar School, where she successfully taught for approximately two years, periodically returning to Philadelphia to recuperate from respiratory illnesses and headaches that would challenge her for the rest of her life. The majority of Forten's poems, including "Wind among the Poplars" (1859) and "A Slave Girl's Prayer" (1860), were published in the *National Anti-Slavery Standard* and Garrison's *The Liberator* between 1858 and 1860.

Forten, ever conscious of her duty to her race, manifested her activism in 1862, when she pursued and was eventually offered a position with Philadelphia's Port Royal Relief Association, which sought to educate former slaves on South Carolina's Sea Islands. By this time in her young life, Forten had crossed several color barriers. She had been the only black student of 200 at Higginson, the first black person to instruct the white student population at Epes, and the first black teacher hired to work with the emancipated slaves. Abolitionist poet John Greenleaf Whittier, a friend and supporter of Charlotte's, published excerpts of her journal she had sent him that chronicled "Life on the Sea Islands" in the May and June 1864 issues of *Atlantic Monthly*. After her departure from St. Helena Island in 1864, she spent the next twelve years quietly, writing and studying. During that time, she supported herself through her literary efforts of writing children's stories and translating novels from French and German. She was employed in a variety of positions, from secretary of the Freedmen's Relief Association in Boston to clerk at the U.S. Treasury Department (Sumler-Edmond 506).

In 1878 Forten married Presbyterian minister Francis James Grimké, a man thirteen years her junior. He was the son of Nancy Weston and slaveholder Henry Grimké and nephew of feminist abolitionists Sarah and Angelina Grimké.* Their only child, Theodora Cornelia, was born in January 1880, dying months later that same year. Charlotte's poetry of her later years, most unpublished and appearing undated in her journals, reflects the introspection and experience of a mature woman. Her journal entries came few and far between as Forten experienced declining health. She spent the last thirteen months of her life bedridden, attended to by her husband. Charlotte Forten Grimké died in Washington, D.C., on July 23, 1914.

MAJOR WORKS AND THEMES

Although not intended for publication, the work for which Charlotte Grimké is most recognized is her five-volume journal, privately published after her death by Anna Julia Cooper in 1951. A version of her journal was edited by Dr. Ray Billington and published by Dryden Press in 1953. Grimké's journal is an artifact that covers a multitude of themes from public matters of political and historical import to private recollections of family and social relations as well as personal reflections.

Grimké was born a fourth-generation free black. Her family was quite active in the women's, temperance, and antislavery movements. As a result, she was exposed from a young age not only to the rhetoric of the aforementioned movements but to the activists themselves. She developed relationships with, for example, *Liberator* editor William Lloyd Garrison and attended lectures by Henry Ward Beecher, recording her impressions of the individuals and their philosophies in her journal. Given that the country of her birth insisted on oppressing a segment of its population based on its skin color alone, Grimké was critical of the hypocrisy of "a government which proudly boasts of being the freeest [sic] in the world" (June 2, 1854, Journal 1). The years she spent educating former slaves at St. Helena Island with the Port Royal Relief Association provided her with an opportunity to document the eagerness of her students "to enjoy both the rights and responsibilities of citizenship" (Sumler-Edmond 506). However, Grimké scholar Brenda Stevenson notices that "it seems Charlotte had difficulty considering these blacks her peers because of their cultural differences, personal histories, and lack of intellectual sophistication" (44). During her stay on the Sea Islands, she also recorded the experiences of the officers and African American soldiers of the First South Carolina Volunteers and the Fifty-Fourth Massachusetts Regiment.

Grimké's notations of a private nature document interactions with family, as well as with intimate friends and associates. Kinship ties were important. Numerous entries reflect her familiar relationships with women who had antislavery sympathies to one degree or another. She was close to her grandmother Charlotte, after whom she was named, as well as her aunt Margaretta Forten and Harriet Forten Purvis, with whom she lived at various times in her young life. She often mentions her "dear friend Miss Shepard," principal of Higginson Grammar School and personal mentor. Her entries indicate as well a fondness for Amy Remond, in whose home she stayed while achieving her education in Salem, Massachusetts, and whose death in 1856 saddened her.

The Journal of Charlotte L. Forten naturally touches on the inner workings of the author, who, though an excellent student, is very self-critical and lonely. She writes: "Have been under-going a thorough self-examination. The result is a mingled feeling of sorrow, shame and self-contempt. Have realized more deeply and bitterly than ever in my life my own ignorance and folly. Have had many advantages of late years; and it is entirely owing to my own want of energy, perseverance and application, that I have not improved them. It grieves me deeply to think of this. I have read an immense quantity, and it has all amounted to nothing,—because I have been too indolent and foolish to take the trouble of reflecting" (June 15, 1858, Journal 3). Longing to know more of her mother, who died when Charlotte was three, she writes: "Looked over some very old letters written by my dear, lost mother—years ago. As I read the words penned by that dear hand, a strange feeling of tenderness, of sadness, of *loneliness* came over me, and I could not refrain from tears. Dear, dear mother whom I have scarcely known, yet so warmly love;—who art now an angel in heaven,—my heart years for thee!" (July 16, 1857, Journal 2). Such sentiment expressed in several entries would influence her poem "The Angel's Visit" (1863). After her father's remarriage and subsequent move to Canada with his second wife and their two children, we see: "I too, have known but little of a father's love. It is hard for me to bear. To thee, alone, my journal, can I say with tears how *very* hard it is. I *have* a loving heart, though some may doubt it, and I long for a parent's love—for the love of my only parent; but it seems denied me;—I know not why" (August 21, 1857, Journal 2).

Accorded lesser import than her journal are her limited number of published poems, which reflect a variety of topics, including love, and admiration for prominent individuals of the day. Several of her poems are dedicated to persons whom she interacted with directly and indirectly, such as Wordsworth and U.S. senator Charles Sumner. Two poems, "A Parting Hymn" (1855) and "Poem for Normal School Graduation" (1856), allude to her commitment to using her education to labor for the betterment of others (of her race). Her essays, letters, poems, and journal spoke of what concerned her and reflect her personal journey.

CRITICAL RECEPTION

Although Anna Julia Cooper privately published Charlotte Forten's journals in 1951, the version of Forten's journals edited by Billington and published in 1953 brought attention to Forten. He concluded that her "conflicts—between modesty and talent, ambition and apparent lack of realization, affection and shyness—all stemmed from her constant awareness that she was a Negro" (9). Billington admits to focusing on the excerpts of Forten's journal that were of political and historical importance, eliminating those aspects that detail much of her daily life. Nevertheless, his version of Forten's journal was to be commended, considering not much had been known prior to its publication of free elite black women's lives.

Scholarship since Billington's effort has enlarged our perspective on Forten Grimké. In 1983 Gloria Oden pointed out that Billington's misidentification and omission of her "family members, . . . those with whom she lived in the Salem household, . . . (and) the small society which made up her social ambience" had created a distortion not only of Grimké's life but of the lives of free blacks she associated with as well (120). It is significant to know that family and friends were important in the lives of free blacks, as their activities were controlled by law (121).

Brenda Stevenson, editor of the 1988 edition of the journals, viewed Grimké's work not only as a window through which the reader may glimpse slices of antebellum American life but also as text testifying to "one woman's struggles and accomplishments" (3). African American scholar/poet Joanne Braxton initially became interested in Grimké after reading Billington's edition of the journal. Later reading Anna Julia Cooper's typed manuscripts of Forten's private document facilitated Braxton's recognizing Grimké as a woman/poet in "search of a public voice." Braxton observes "Forten's use of the diary as a tool for the development of her political and artistic consciousness and as a means of self-evaluation; for Forten, the diaries also represent a retreat from potentially shattering encounters with racism and a vehicle for the development of a black and female poetic identity, a place of restoration and self-healing" (256). We see that Grimké's journal is both historical and personal, public as well as private.

With regard to her poetry and essays, "Forten is considered a minor creator of sentimental verse and a competent if not exceptional essayist. Her highest praise came from contemporaries who knew and admired her as a person and were therefore influenced by her sincerity as much as by her admittedly meager talents" (Draper 808).

BIBLIOGRAPHY

Works by Charlotte Lottie Forten Grimké

Journals

The Journal of Charlotte L. Forten: A Free Negro in the Slave Era. Ed. Ray A. Billington. New York: Dryden Press, 1953.
The Journals of Charlotte Forten Grimké. Ed. Brenda Stevenson. New York: Oxford University Press, 1988.

Essays

"Glimpses of New England." National Anti-Slavery Standard, June 18, 1858. 2.
"Life on the Sea Islands." Parts 1 and 2. The Atlantic Monthly (May/June 1864). 14–15; 28–30.

Letters

Letter to the editor. The Liberator, December 19, 1862.
"New Year's Day on the Islands of South Carolina, 1863." The Liberator, January 23, 1863.

Poetry

"To W.L.G. on Reading His 'Chosen Queen.' " The Liberator, March 1855.
"Poem for Normal School Graduation." The Liberator, August 24, 1856.
"Flowers." The Christian Recorder, May 20, 1858.
"The Two Voices." National Anti-Slavery Standard, January 15, 1859.
"The Wind among the Poplars." The Liberator, May 27, 1859.
"In the Country." National Anti-Slavery Standard, 1860.
"A Slave Girl's Prayer." National Anti-Slavery Standard, January 14, 1860.
"The Angel's Visit." The Black Man, His Antecedents, His Genius, and His Achievements. Ed. William Wells Brown. New York: Thomas Hamilton, 1863.
"Charles Sumner." Life and Writings of the Grimké Family. Vol. 2. Ed. Anna J. Cooper. 1951.
"The Gathering of the Grand Army." Life and Writings of the Grimké Family. Vol. 2. Ed. Anna J. Cooper. n.p. 1951.
"Wordsworth." Life and Writings of the Grimké Family. Vol. 2. Ed. Anna J. Cooper. n.p. 1951.

Translation

Erckmann, Emilie, and Alexander Chartrian. Madame Therese, or the Volunteers of '92. New York: Scribners, 1868.

Studies of Charlotte Lottie Forten Grimké

Billington, Ray A. "Introduction." In The Journal of Charlotte Forten: A Free Negro in the Slave Era. Ed. Ray A. Billington. London: Collier Books, 1961. 7–27.

Braxton, Joanne M. "Charlotte Forten Grimké and the Search for a Public Voice." In *The Private Self: Theory and Practice of Women's Autobiographical Writings*. Ed. Shari Benstock. Chapel Hill: University of North Carolina Press, 1988. 254–71.

Brown, William Wells. "Charlotte L. Forten." In *The Black Man, His Antecedents, His Genius, and His Achievements*. New York: Thomas Hamilton, 1863. 190–99.

"Charlotte L. Forten." *Black Literature Criticism: Excerpts from Criticism of the Most Significant Works of Black Authors over the Past 200 Years*. Ed. James P. Draper. Vol. 2. Detroit: Gale Research, 1992. 807–23.

Cooper, Anna Julia. *Life and Writings of the Grimké Family*. 2 vols. Privately printed, 1951.

Koch, Lisa M. "Bodies as Stage Props: Enacting Hysteria in the Diaries of Charlotte Forten Grimké and Alice James." *Legacy* 15 (1998): 59–64.

Lapansky, Emma Jones. "Feminism, Freedom, and Community: Charlotte Forten and Women Activists in Nineteenth-Century Philadelphia." *The Pennsylvania Magazine of History and Biography* 113 (1989): 3–19.

Loewenberg, Bert James, and Ruth Bogin, eds. *Black Women in Nineteenth-Century American Life: Their Words, Their Thoughts, Their Feelings*. University Park: Pennsylvania State University Press, 1976. 283–95.

Oden, Gloria. "*The Journal of Charlotte L. Forten*: The Salem-Philadelphia Years (1854–1862) Reexamined." *Essex Institute Historical Collections* 119 (1983): 119–36.

Peterson, Carla. *Doers of the Word: African American Women Writers and Speakers in the North (1830–1880)*. New York: Oxford University Press, 1995.

Sherman, Joan R. "Charlotte L. Forten Grimké." *Invisible Poets: Afro-Americans of the Nineteenth Century*. Ed. Joan R. Sherman. Urbana: University of Illinois Press, 1974. 88–96.

Stevenson, Brenda. "Introduction." In *The Journals of Charlotte Forten Grimké*. Ed. Brenda Stevenson. New York: Oxford University Press, 1988. 3–55.

Sumler-Edmond, Janice. "Charlotte L. Forten Grimké." In *Black Women in America: An Historical Encyclopedia*. Ed. Darlene Clark Hine. Vol. 1. Brooklyn: Carlson, 1993. 505–7.

Vaught, Bonny. "Trying to Make Things Real." In *Between Women: Biographers, Novelists, Critics, Teachers, and Artists Write about Their Work on Women*. Ed. Carol Ascher, Louise De Salvo, and Sara Ruddick. Boston: Beacon, 1984. 55–69.

BRITON HAMMON
(late 1720s–?)

Harish Chander

BIOGRAPHY

Briton Hammon is acknowledged to be the first African American to publish a literary work in the North American colonies. His short autobiographical work, *A Narrative of the Uncommon Sufferings and Surprizing Deliverance of Briton Hammon, a Negro Man*, published in 1760, recounts his experiences of a journey to Jamaica, a shipwreck followed by capture by Native Americans and then Spaniards, and his subsequent escape and return to his master in Boston. Hammon's *Narrative* is regarded as the first American slave narrative and the first African American writing of religious prose.

The few biographical bits of information known about Briton Hammon are those culled from his narrative. Hammon, a slave of General Winslow, received permission from Master Winslow in December 1747 to take a brief voyage to Jamaica for logwood. He reached there safely, but on the return journey, his ship was wrecked off the coast of Florida, and he was overpowered by hostile Native Americans and taken prisoner. After seven years in captivity, he was rescued by the Spaniards, only to be imprisoned by them in Havana, Cuba, when he refused to serve on Spanish ships. Freed from Spanish captivity by the British navy, he then served on a British warship. Upon being wounded in battle, he was hospitalized at Greenwich in London. On recuperation, he worked as a cook on merchant ships and was happily reunited with his master, who happened to be a passenger on a Boston-bound ship on which Hammon was working.

This narrative tells the story of his tribulations—his sufferings in captivity by the Native Americans and then by the Spaniards and his providential escape. Hammon's account is rather unusual because, unlike other slave narratives of the eighteenth century, it makes no mention of his life as a slave under his master,

General Winslow, gives no clue how long he had been General Winslow's slave, and offers no account of the duties assigned to him as Winslow's slave. Nor does he give any hint as to his antecedents, family, and siblings. The probable reasons for withholding information on these essential particulars about Hammon and his family from the readers—for the omission of "a great many Things" (14)—are (1) the narrative was likely set down by an anonymous white amanuensis and (2) as a spiritual autobiography, the narrative is limited in its scope to offer thanks to God for preserving his life and delivering him from captivity and to invite others to "[m]agnify the Lord with me" (14).

MAJOR WORK AND THEMES

Like other writers of slave narratives, Briton Hammon insists that he is telling the truth and nothing but the truth, to the best of his knowledge and recollection. At the opening of the *Narrative*, Hammon appeals to the reader, "I shall only relate Matters of Fact as they occur to my Mind" (3), and he concludes in the same vein: "I think I have not deviated from Truth, in any particular of this my Narrative" (14). However, there are some striking differences between Hammon's *Narrative* and other classic slave narratives, such as Frederick Douglass'* *Narrative of the Life of Frederick Douglass, an American Slave, Written by Himself* (1845). Whereas Douglass in his narrative focuses on the degrading conditions of slavery and seeks deliverance from slavery, Hammon finds only Indian and Spanish captivity degrading and demeaning and does not find any fault with his condition of slavery under General Winslow, as he gladly returns to his master, thereby helping perpetuate the myth of the happy and contented slave. Hammon reports that he is so overjoyed to see his master that he "could not speak to him for some Time" (13), and the master is "exceeding glad to see me, telling me that I was like one arose from the Dead" (13). This kind of description of a master–servant relationship is perhaps unparalleled in slavery literature. Nor does Hammon fear any kind of reprisal or punishment from his master for his almost thirteen years of absence. As John C. Miller points out: "Slavery conferred power virtually unchecked by law; and whether that power was used for good or for ill, benevolently or cruelly, was left almost wholly to the slaveowner himself" (149–50). One cannot but infer either that Hammon's master belongs to the category of benevolent masters or that the manuscript is not honest in this respect.

Hammon offers angry words to describe his first captors, the Native Americans who kill all of the crew and passengers on the ship except for Hammon himself. Referring to them as "Savages" and "Devils" (6), Hammon says that they "led me to their Hutts [sic]" and told him in broken English that they intended to "roast me alive" (7). However, they do not carry out their threat, nor do they mistreat him or torture him, giving Hammon the same food that they themselves eat.

The Spaniards, by contrast, throw Hammon into "a close dungeon" where he is "confin'd Four Years and seven months" (8) and from which he is later transferred to confinement in a castle in Havana. His period of confinement is broken for seven months, during which time he is assigned with others the job of carrying the bishop around in his sedan chair.

Hammon's narrative being a spiritual autobiography, Hammon praises God's miraculous power for saving his life from "barbarous and inhuman Savages" (6). He praises the Providence of God for coming to his help in his difficult times and changing the minds of the Native Americans, so they spared his life and "were better to me then [sic] my fears" (7). Again, Hammon thanks "Kind Providence" for rescuing him from Spanish captivity (8).

CRITICAL RECEPTION

Hammon's *Narrative* has elicited some critical attention by virtue of its being the first slave narrative. Richard Van Der Beets observes that Hammon's *Narrative* employs the framework of an Indian captivity tale and shows "the salutary effects of the captivity, especially in the context of redemptive suffering; the captivity as test, trial, or punishment by God; and finally and most demonstrably, the captivity as evidence of divine Providence and of God's wisdom" (xiii). Frances Smith Foster points out that "Hammon, like other mid-eighteenth-century narrators in the British colonies, had an obvious political bias and used his narrative to promote England and colonies as countries of more noble men than those of France or Spain" (40). Blyden Jackson avers that the narrative reveals that Hammon, "like many . . . of his Christian contemporaries, . . . quite firmly believed that God's eye is on the sparrow, so that nothing, great or small, happens in this universe save by the direct intervention of God's will" (47). Mason I. Lowance says that, in Hammon's narrative, "deliverance from one group only meant enslavement by another; his 'liberation' comes when he is reunited with his 'old master' " (310).

BIBLIOGRAPHY

Work by Briton Hammon

Hammon, Briton. *A Narrative of the Uncommon Sufferings and Surprizing Deliverance of Briton Hammon, a Negro Man*. Boston: Green and Russell, 1760. Millwood, NY: Kraus Reprints, 1972.

Studies of Briton Hammon

Beets, Van Der, ed. *Held Captive by Indians: Selected Narratives, 1643–1836*. Knoxville: University of Tennessee Press, 1973.
Foster, Frances Smith. *Witnessing Slavery: The Development of Ante-Bellum Slave Narratives*. Westport, CT: Greenwood, 1979; 2d ed., Madison: University of Wisconsin Press, 1994.

Jackson, Blyden. *A History of Afro-American Literature*. Vol. 1: *The Long Beginning, 1746–1895*. Baton Rouge: Louisiana State University Press, 1989.
Lowance, Mason I., Jr. "The Slave Narrative in American Literature." In *African American Writers: Profiles of Their Lives and Works from the 1700s to the Present*. Ed. Valerie Smith, Lea Baechler, and A. Walton Litz. New York: Collier Books, 1993.
Miller, John C. *The First Frontier: Life in Colonial America*. New York: Dell, 1966.

JUPITER HAMMON
(1711–1806?)

Lonnell E. Johnson

BIOGRAPHY

Jupiter Hammon achieved a place in African American literature with the publishing of "An Evening Thought (Salvation by Christ, with Penetential [sic] Cries," a broadside printed on Christmas Day, 1760, the first literary work published by an African American. Other works include "An Address to Miss Phillis Wheatly* [sic]" (1778); two prose pieces "Essay on the Ten Virgins" (1779), a copy of which is yet to surface; "An Address to the Negroes in the State of New-York" (1787); "A Winter Piece," which includes "A Poem for Children with Thoughts in Death" (1782); and "An Evening's Improvement," which includes "A Dialogue Entitled, The Kind Master and the Dutiful Servant" (1783).

Little is known regarding Hammon's life. Born on the estate of the wealthy Henry Lloyd of Oyster Bay, Long Island, Hammon lived under a mild form of servitude in colonial New York, where he is believed to have been "a missionary and the lay preacher" (Schomburg 14). Described as "the gentleman slave" (Schomburg (14), Hammon comments on his particular status in his "Address to the Negroes . . . of New-York": "I suppose I have had more advantages and privileges than most of you who are slaves, have ever known, and I believe more than many white people have enjoyed" (Ransom 106). Evidence suggests that Hammon may have been tutored on the Lloyd estate or through the Society for the Propagation of the Gospel, a missionary outreach effort concerned with education of slaves in the Long Island area. He undoubtedly also had access to the Lloyd family library, all factors in Hammon's development as a poet.

MAJOR WORKS AND THEMES

All of Hammon's works center on the religious. His poetry is described as "sincere and enthusiastic, and . . . primarily religious: Hammon's poetry reflects his great intellectual and emotional involvement with religion to the point where it approaches intoxication" (Ransom 12).

Regarding more secular concerns, such as enslavement, Hammon is more moderate in his attitude. His response in "A Winter Piece," however, indicates that while he does not desire freedom for himself, he believes that the young enslaved should be set free.

Because he assimilates the predominant religious views of colonial New England, Hammon has been viewed as too conciliatory in his attitude toward enslavement. While he does not always speak out against slavery, he does speak for equality and unity of both the enslaved and master, notably, in "A Dialogue Entitled," The Kind Master and the Dutiful Servant."

Another factor influencing Hammon's work may well have been the Great Awakening or New Light movement, which ushered in a series of religious revivals, sweeping America around the mid-1800s, touching whites and blacks alike. A profoundly personal spiritual experience may have been the inspiration for Hammon's "An Evening Thought," which opens with the declaration: "Salvation comes by Jesus Christ alone" (Ransom 45).

The word "Salvation" subsequently appears in every stanza, as the poet hammers away with the term twenty-three times throughout the work. Written in alternate iambic tetrameter and iambic trimeter lines with *abab* rhyme scheme, the format of Hammon's first and subsequent poems is similar to the hymn stanza, revealing the influence of the popular hymns of Watts and Wesley, to whom Hammon was undoubtedly exposed.

CRITICAL RECEPTION

In-depth study of Hammon's poetry is sparse. *Jupiter Hammon: American Negro Poet* was produced by Oscar Wegelin in 1915. A notable source of Hammon's poetry is the 1970 edition of *America's First Negro Poet: The Complete Works of Jupiter Hammon of Long Island*, edited by Ransom with a biographical sketch of Hammon by Wegelin and critical analysis of his works by Loggins. Critical treatment of Hammon's poetry by Loggins is also found in *The Negro Author in America* (1939). Robinson offers a good critical introduction and selection of Hammon's poetry in *Early Black Poets* (1969). More recent discussions of Hammon's works include O'Neale's extensive biographical and critical study *Jupiter Hammon and the Beginnings of African-American Literature* (1993).

Hammon's contribution to African American literature goes beyond his being the first person of African extraction to publish poetry in America. He is a significant figure whose method of composing must have been similar to that of those who fashioned spirituals from their souls, yet his poetry is original. As Ransom comments:

It would seem likely that he was strongly affected by the renaissance of religious fervor which swept Long Island in the middle 18th century, for he expresses the deep evangelical feelings of the time. Yet the medium and form of expression, while owing much to the poetic forms of hymn writers, is his own, with stirring similarities to Negro spiritual and other religious folk poetry. (12)

Hammon's poetry has been described as rough-hewn and rugged, rhythmically heavy with at times awkward, forced rhymes. Nevertheless, the poetry does mark a transition leading from the artless beauty of the spirituals to the more formal verse poets following Hammon. Wagner speaks of "An Evening Thought" as "a halfway stage between the guileless art of the unknown composers of spirituals and the already much wordier manner of the popular preacher" (17).

Although Hammon's verse lacks the refinement, decorum, and fluency of his contemporary Phillis Wheatley,* admirable qualities are noteworthy in his works. Loggins states that Hammon's verse was composed to be heard with "that peculiar sense of sound, the distinguishing characteristics of Negro folk poetry" (12). Robinson classifies Hammon as an oratorical poet whose works are best suited for oral renderings" (xv). Porter sees Hammon's verse as "seldom matched by such occasional expressions as hymns, spiritual songs or didactic verse, however impassioned, on the subjects of freedom, slavery, or worldly bliss" (3). Though not often viewed as significant beyond having been the first black poet to publish, Hammon's contribution is noteworthy.

BIBLIOGRAPHY

Works by Jupiter Hammon

"Essay on the Ten Virgins." Hartford: Hudson and Goodwin, 1779.
"A Winter Piece: Being a Serious Exhortation, with a Call to the Unconverted: And a Short Contemplation on the Death of Jesus Christ." Hartford: Hudson and Goodwin(?); 1782.
"An Evening's Improvement: Shewing the Necessity of Beholding the Lamb of God, to Which Is Added, a Dialogue Entitled, The Kind Master and the Dutiful Servant." Hartford: Hudson and Goodwin(?), c. 1783.
"An Address to the Negroes in the State of New-York." New York: Carroll and Patterson, 1787.

Studies of Jupiter Hammon

Herron, Carolivia. "Early African American Poetry." In The Columbia History of American Poetry. Ed. Jay Parini and Brett Millier. New York: Columbia University Press, 1993. 16–32.
Johnson, Lonnell E. "Dilemma of the Dutiful Servant: The Poetry of Jupiter Hammon." In Language and Literature in the African American Imagination. Ed. Carol Aisha. Blackshire-Belay. Westport, CT: Greenwood, 1992. 105–17.
"Jupiter Hammon." Nineteenth Century Literature Criticism. Vol. 5. Detroit: Gale, 1984, 260–66.

Klinkowitz, Jerome. "Early Writers: Jupiter Hammon, Phillis Wheatley, and Benjamin Banneker." In *Black American Writers: Bibliographic Essays*. Vol. 1: *The Beginnings through the Harlem Renaissance and Langston Hughes*. Ed. M. Thomas Inge, Maurice Duke, and Jackson R. Bryer. New York: St. Martin's, 1978. 1–20.

Lee, A. Robert. "Selves Subscribed: Early Afro-America and the Signifying of Phillis Wheatley, Jupiter Hammon, Olaudah Equiano, and David Walker." In *Making America/Making American Literature*. Ed. A. Robert Lee and W. M. Verhoeven. Amsterdam: Rodopi, 1996. 275–95.

Loggins, Vernon. *The Negro Author in America*. New York: Columbia University Press, 1939.

O'Neale, Sondra A. "Jupiter Hammon." In *Dictionary of Literary Biography*. Vol. 50: *Afro-American Writers before the Harlem Renaissance*. Ed. Thadious M. Davis and Trudier Harris. Detroit: Gale, 1984. 156–63.

———. *Jupiter Hammon and the Beginnings of African-American Literature*. Metuchen, NJ: Scarecrow, 1993.

Palmer, R. Roderick. "Jupiter Hammon's Poetic Exhortations." *College Language Association Journal* 18 (1974): 22–28.

Peters, Erskine. "Jupiter Hammon: His Engagement with Interpretation." *Journal of Ethnic Studies* 8.4 (Winter 1981): 1–12.

———. "Jupiter Hammon: His Involvement with His 'Unconverted' Brethren." *Minority Voices: An Interdisciplinary Journal of Literature and the Arts* 4.1 (Spring 1980): 1–10.

Porter, Dorothy B., ed. *Early New Writing*. Boston: Beacon, 1971.

Ransom, Stanley A., Jr. *America's First Negro Poet: The Complete Works of Jupiter Hammon of Long Island*. Port Washington, NY: Kennikat, 1970.

Richards, Philip M. "Nationalist Themes in the Preaching of Jupiter Hammon." *Early American Literature* 25.2 (1990): 122–38.

Robinson, William H. *Early Black Poets*. Dubuque, IA: W. C. Brown, 1969. *Early Negro Writing*. Boston: Beacon, 1971.

Schomburg, Arthur A. "Jupiter Hammon, before the New York African Society." *Amsterdam News*, January 22, 1930, 14.

Versions, Charles A. "Jupiter Hammon, Early Long Island Poet." *Gnaws County Historical Journal* (Winter 1997): 1–17.

Wagner, Jean. *Black Poets of the United States*. Urbana: University of Illinois Press, 1973.

Wegelin, Oscar. *Jupiter Hammon, American Negro Poet: Selections from His Writings and a Bibliography*. Freeport, NY: Books for Libraries, 1915.

Whitlow, Roger. *Black American Literature: A Critical History*. Chicago: Nelson Hall, 1973.

FRANCES ELLEN WATKINS HARPER
(1825–1911)

Terry Novak

BIOGRAPHY

Frances Ellen Watkins Harper was born on September 24, 1825, in Baltimore to free parents, who died before Harper's third birthday. Harper's uncle, the Reverend William Watkins, became her guardian. Rev. Watkins was a staunch abolitionist who ran the William Watkins Academy for Colored Youth. Harper was formally educated at her uncle's school; she received a much deeper education regarding racial pride and the importance of the abolition movement from her close relationship with her uncle. After completing her education, Harper worked at a variety of jobs, including teaching. In 1853, after a law was passed in Harper's home state of Maryland declaring that free blacks entering the state could be sold as slaves, Harper decided to devote herself exclusively to abolition work. She began lecturing on the antislavery circuit in 1854 and continued to do so for most of her life. In addition, Harper was a committed supporter of the Underground Railroad.

Harper married Fenton Harper in 1860 and retired from public life for four years, until she was widowed. Widowhood freed her to resume her lecturing career. For a while she was accompanied on the lecture circuit by her daughter, who apparently died at a very young age. Along with her lecturing career, Harper became an extremely prolific writer. Her collection of poetry, *Poems on Miscellaneous Subjects*, was first published in 1854 and went through several editions. In 1859 her short story "The Two Offers" was published in the *Weekly Anglo-African*. With this story, Harper is credited with being the first African American author to publish a short story. Harper published several other short stories, along with scores of poems, letters, and essays, in various periodicals throughout her lifetime. She also published three serialized novellas in the *Christian Recorder*:

Minnie's Sacrifice in 1869, *Sowing and Reaping* from 1876 to 1877, and *Trial and Triumph* from 1888 to 1889. Additional books that were published during Harper's lifetime are the poetry collection *Moses, a Story of the Nile*, first published in 1869; *Poems*, first published in 1871; *Sketches of Southern Life*, first published in 1872; the novel *Iola Leroy*, first published in 1892; *The Martyr of Alabama and Other Poems*, published c. 1894; *Atlanta Offering Poems*, first published in 1895; and *Idylls of the Bible*, published in 1901.

In addition to her lecturing and writing, Harper was a social activist on quite equal footing with any white, middle-class woman of her time. She was a member of the American Women's Suffrage Association, the Women's Christian Temperance Union, the American Equal Rights Association, the National Council of Negro Women, the American Association for the Education of Colored Youth, the Universal Peace Union, and the John Brown Memorial Association of Women. She served leadership roles in many of these organizations and fully asserted her right to belong to such social change–minded organizations, without apology. Her deep commitment to the ideals of the various organizations repeatedly finds voice in her writings. Harper died on February 20, 1911.

MAJOR WORKS AND THEMES

Readers of Frances Ellen Watkins Harper cannot help but be impressed by the author's prolific output as well as by her steadfast following of a certain social agenda in her writing. Much of her poetry, such as the long narrative "Moses: A Story of the Nile" and the lyric "The Slave Mother," deals with Harper's abhorrence of slavery and the consequences of such a social institution. Harper goes beyond the norm with the issue of slavery in her poetry, however. She works hard to portray the slave in her poetry as a real person and succeeds in evoking strong emotions against slavery in her readers. Harper does not confine herself to the issue of slavery in her poetry, though. In many of her poems, Harper extols the mother–child relationship. In others she speaks of woman's role in society—oftentimes the role she describes is one of strength, courage, and great possibility. Many of Harper's poems deal with one of her favorite social themes—temperance. Poems such as "The Drunkard's Child" and "The Fatal Pledge" paint horrid pictures of the ills of alcohol. The importance of religious faith is a theme that can also be found with regularity in Harper's poetry. While much of Harper's poetry contains sentimental messages, most of the poems are crafted with great care. Harper pays attention to poetic structure in her work and experiments with various poetic forms, resulting in an interesting body of work.

Many of the themes found in Harper's poetry can also be found in her essays and speeches, although the essays and speeches deal more heavily with race issues. What the reader notices most in Harper's essays and speeches is her high degree of intelligence and education. She exudes confidence and strength in her writings about racial and other social concerns, and she makes perfect sense to the reader. One can imagine how powerful she must have sounded as an orator.

Despite her massive work with the poetry and essay forms, Harper can be seen most clearly as a fine crafter of fiction. Again, her fiction deals with the same issues as does her nonfiction, but with her fiction Harper seems to take more care and seems to be more comfortable. Harper's first work of fiction, the short story "The Two Offers," is significant in many ways. The story, first published in the *Weekly Anglo-African* in 1859, is considered the first published short story of any African American writer. It is also a story that markedly avoids the issue of race. The characters in the story are never assigned a race, nor is such an important factor in the larger themes of the story: temperance and a woman's right to choose against marriage. Both themes appear again in Harper's work, but it is interesting that she uses both in her first work of fiction. Certainly, the temperance issue was one with which her female readers would easily sympathize; the idea that a nineteenth-century woman would readily prefer spinsterhood over the possibility of a bad marriage was not a theme, however, that most of her readers would have found necessarily comforting. From the beginning of her fiction career, Harper exhibited the need to stand by her convictions in all areas of importance to her.

Harper continues to fulfill this need in her longer works of fiction. In the novella *Minnie's Sacrifice* (1869), Harper takes on the theme of racial identity with the characters Minnie and Louis. Both characters are biracial; both appear to be white; both are raised white. Not until they reach young adulthood do the characters discover their true heritage. Armed with this knowledge, the two join forces with the Negro race of their mothers—and with each other—first to fight against slavery and then to wholeheartedly help with the Reconstruction efforts of the South. It is especially with the Reconstruction work of Minnie and Louis that Harper brings forth her own agenda; the importance of education and political involvement to the newly freed race. Harper unabashedly concludes her novella with an editorial message:

The lesson of Minnie's sacrifice is this, that it is braver to suffer with one's own branch of the human race,—to feel, that the weaker and the more despised they are, the closer we will cling to them, for the sake of helping them, than to attempt to creep out of all identity with them in their feebleness, for the sake of mere personal advantages, and to do this at the expense of self-respect, and a true manhood, and a truly dignified womanhood, that with whatever gifts we possess, whether they be genius, culture, wealth or social position, we can best serve the interests of our race by a generous and loving diffusion, than by a narrow and selfish isolation which, after all, is only one type of the barbarous and antisocial state. (91–92)

Harper takes her didacticism to a much higher level in her second novella, *Sowing and Reaping* (1876–1877), and she returns to her theme of temperance. As in "The Two Offers," there is no discussion of race in *Sowing and Reaping*. The story revolves mainly around the characters of Belle Gordon, Jeanette Roland, and Charles Romaine, but a variety of other characters are included in the tale. Harper quite unabashedly takes a strong stand for temperance in this novel, to the point of having one character break off her marriage engagement with another because he accepts a glass of wine at a party. Indeed, in the sentimental fashion of nineteenth-century literature, the young man in question does end up ruining his life with alcohol.

In her third novella, *Trial and Triumph* (1888–1889), stylistically Harper changes course a bit. There is a strong element of romance in this story that is not included in Harper's prior work. Surrounding this romantic tale, though, are many instances of moral and social messages. Often these messages severely detract from the basic story line. There are plenty of warning messages to women concerning proper behavior, but there is also a respect given by the author to the main character, Annette, for her high-spiritedness and native intelligence that is somewhat reminiscent of the messages given in "The Two Offers." Harper's fondness for certain phrases becomes painfully obvious in this novella also.

Harper's only full-length novel, *Iola Leroy* (1892), brings together many of her previous themes. Harper presents the story of the biracial Iola, who, like Minnie in *Minnie's Sacrifice*, appears white, is raised white, and believes she is white until young adulthood. Unlike Minnie, though, Iola is sold as a slave and finds herself in the position of defending her virtue. As the country is in the midst of the Civil War, Iola has the good fortune of being rescued by the Union army. Iola serves as an army nurse and attracts a great deal of attention. Harper gives the reader romantic tension when a white doctor falls in love with Iola and, upon discovering her racial heritage, attempts to persuade her to marry him anyway and pass for white. Like Minnie, Iola is adamant about remaining true to the race of her mother. Iola does indeed cling to the Negro race and, after the war, works diligently for the Reconstruction effort. Though Iola does marry in the end, she remains the independent woman she proves herself to be when she states, "I have a theory that every woman ought to know how to earn her own living. I believe that a great amount of sin and misery springs from the weakness and inefficiency of women" (154). Harper also continues with her themes of temperance and education in this novel. In addition, she devotes much of the book to the intellectual discussions of Iola and her circle of friends, illustrating with certainty the lively existence of educated nineteenth-century African American professionals. Harper also illustrates the importance of the post–Civil War search for family members, especially through religious organizations. Harper's deep personal belief in the Christian faith is heavily evident in this novel.

In all of her work, Frances Ellen Watkins Harper commits her most pressing social concerns to the security of paper. There is no doubt that she steadfastly believed in working to "uplift the race," that she desperately abhorred the effects of alcohol, that she harbored a wondrous faith in God, and that she truly believed that women could—and should—effect meaningful changes in society.

CRITICAL RECEPTION

Frances Ellen Watkins Harper enjoyed public appreciation of her work since it was first published. In recent years, however, greater critical attention has been given to her work, and much of her work has been rediscovered and/or reprinted. Most critics note that Harper was certainly a product of her times and that her writings fit well into the realms of nineteenth-century American women's writing in general. Many also note the vast importance of her Reconstruction agenda. Frances Smith Foster notes this especially in regard to Harper's essays, lectures, and poems. Foster also points out that Harper blends her Reconstruction themes with her themes of woman's role in society. Speaking of Harper's narrative poem "Moses: A Story of the Nile," Foster writes, "Frances Harper creates an allegorical piece from Judeo-Christian mythology that reinterprets the roles of women and women's stories but does so in a distinctively African-American manner" (*Written* 138).

Harper's fiction in particular has enjoyed a resurgence in recent years. The three novellas serialized in the *Christian Recorder* during her lifetime—*Minnie's Sacrifice, Sowing and Reaping,* and *Trial and Triumph*—were recently resurrected from obscurity by Frances Smith Foster and reprinted in a single volume. Foster points out that in *Minnie's Sacrifice* Harper once again deals with the Moses story; she also makes an interesting correlation between the novel and modern-day political thought: "Harper's readers today may recognize that the author gives Minnie and Louis attitudes that combine those now commonly associated with Martin Luther King, Jr., and Malcolm X" (*Minnie's* xxix).

While other critics have begun discussing these three newly reprinted novellas, most critical attention has been paid to Harper's *Iola Leroy*. Not all of this attention has been positive. Many have argued that Harper used the ideas of William Wells Brown's* *Clotel*, published some forty years before her own novel, as the basis of *Iola Leroy*. Just as many others have chosen, however, to view Harper's work as a completely separate entity. Elizabeth Young calls *Iola Leroy* a war novel and says that it "gains specificity as a black woman's perspective on the war, one rooted in maternal and familial dimensions of black experience" (295). Young also points to *Iola Leroy* as the "first novel to address black participation in the war" (298). In addition, Young notes the importance of mothers to Harper's work. This same theme has been discussed by Foster and by Maggie Sale.

Critical attention has also been given to *Iola Leroy*'s message of the importance of education to the newly freed African American community. John Ernest writes, "Like other nineteenth-century African-American writers, Harper equates literacy and freedom, but her conception of literacy as presented in *Iola Leroy* involves not only the awareness that her own rhetorical skills will be used as a gauge of her (and her race's) inherent ability, but also the awareness that the dominant culture's conception of literacy offers only a dubious freedom at best" (196). In light of discussions on both the sentimental nature of Harper's fiction and the effectiveness of African American literature at large, Ernest's words take on particular significance. William L. Andrews is one critic who looks to *Iola Leroy* as an example of nineteenth-century sentimental writing both in style and in theme. Both Hazel Carby and Deborah E. McDowell have written extensively on Harper's aim of significantly aiding her race through the writing of *Iola Leroy*.

Discussion has also begun on comparisons of all of Harper's works of fiction.

Debra Rosenthal compares "The Two Offers" and *Sowing and Reaping* in regard to their lack of character race identity as well as to their shared temperance themes: "Because Harper is race-conscious and progressive in her other writings, her emptying this temperance fiction of racial markers serves specific purposes and aligns her thinking with some of the most radical assimilation discourse of her day. . . . Harper implicitly advocates an assimilationist agenda by absorbing one discourse into another" (156).

There is promise of much more discussion on Harper's canon at large, especially in light of the recent republication of her work. Certainly, Harper's themes of various social issues, the uplifting of the African American race in particular, will continue to be part of the discussion. With a more complete canon, however, more comparative criticism can assuredly be anticipated.

BIBLIOGRAPHY

Works by Frances Ellen Watkins Harper

Novels

Iola Leroy, or Shadows Uplifted. 1892. In *The African-American Novel in the Age of Reaction.* Ed. William L. Andrews. New York: Penguin Books, 1992.
Minnie's Sacrifice, Sowing and Reaping, Trial and Triumph: Three Rediscovered Novels by Frances E. W. Harper. Ed. Frances Smith Foster. Boston: Beacon Press, 1994.

Collected Short Stories, Essays, Speeches, Letters, and Poetry

A Brighter Day Coming: A Frances Ellen Watkins Harper Reader. Ed. Frances Smith Foster. New York: Feminist Press, 1990.

Poetry

Complete Poems of Frances E. W. Harper. Ed. Maryemma Graham. New York: Oxford University Press, 1988.

Studies of Frances Ellen Watkins Harper

Andrews, William L. "Introduction." In *The African-American Novel in the Age of Reaction.* Ed. William L. Andrews. New York: Penguin Press, 1992.
Boyd, Melba Joyce. *Discarded Legacy: Politics and Poetics in the Life of Frances E. W. Harper, 1825–1911.* Detroit: Wayne State University Press, 1994.
Carby, Hazel. *Reconstructing Womanhood: The Emergence of the Afro-American Woman Novelist.* New York: Oxford University Press, 1987.
Ernest, John. *Resistance and Reformation in Nineteenth-Century African-American Literature: Brown, Wilson, Jacobs, Delany, Douglass, and Harper.* Jackson: University of Mississippi Press, 1995.
Foster, Frances Smith. "Introduction." In *A Brighter Day Coming: A Frances Ellen Watkins Harper Reader.* Ed. Frances Smith Foster. New York: Feminist Press, 1990.
————. Introduction. *Minnie's Sacrifice, Sowing and Reaping, Trial and Triumph: Three*

Rediscovered Novels by Frances E. W. Harper. Ed. Frances Smith Foster. Boston: Beacon Press, 1994.

———. *Written by Herself: Literary Production by African-American Women, 1746–1892*. Bloomington: Indiana University Press, 1993.

McDowell, Deborah E. " 'The Changing Same': Generational Connections and Black Women Novelists." *New Literary History: A Journal of Theory and Interpretation* 18 (1987): 281–302.

Rosenthal, Debra J. "Deracialized Discourse: Temperance and Racial Ambiguity in Harper's 'The Two Offers' and *Sowing and Reaping*." In *The Serpent and The Cup: Temperance in American Literature*. Ed. David S. Reynolds and Debra J. Rosenthal. Amherst: University of Massachusetts Press, 1997. 153–64.

Sale, Maggie. "Critiques from Within: Antebellum Projects of Resistance." *American Literature* 64.2 (1992): 696–718.

Young, Elizabeth. "Warring Fictions: *Iola Leroy* and the Color of Gender." In *Subjects and Citizens: Nation, Race, and Gender from Oroonoko to Anita Hill*. Ed. Michael Moon and Cathy N. Davidson. Durham, NC: Duke University Press, 1995. 293–317.

JUANITA HARRISON
(1891–?)

Debra J. Rosenthal

BIOGRAPHY

Juanita Harrison was born in Mississippi, presumably in 1891, for she states that she began her travels around the world in 1927, when she was thirty-six years old. We can place her birthday as December 28, for she writes on that date in 1927, "Every Dec. 28 the calendar say I am another year old but 1927 found me the same age I was 15 years ago and I expect to be that same age at least 10 years more anyway" (18). Little is known about Harrison's life other than what her employer's daughter, Mildred Morris, writes in the Preface to Harrison's only publication, the autobiographical travelogue, *My Great, Wide, Beautiful World* (1936). Morris states that Harrison attended school for only a few months before she turned ten. Her life after that consisted of "an endless round of cooking, washing and ironing in an overburdened household" (ix), typical for black girls in the Deep South. Although a picture of Harrison appears along with Katherine Woods' review for the *New York Times*, it is quite blurry, and the only description we have of her comes from Morris: "Her slight form, fresh olive complexion, long hair braided about her head, made her appear younger than her years" (xi).

In her Preface, Morris writes that Harrison saw pictures of "templed cities in foreign lands" and longed to travel. Harrison began traveling at age sixteen, working along the way to support herself. She visited Canada and Cuba, always taking classes at a Young Women's Christian Association (YWCA) or at a night school, and learned Spanish and French. At one point she had saved $800, but she lost it all when a bank failed.

At one point Harrison worked in Los Angeles as a domestic for George W. Dickson and his wife, Myra K. Dickson, to whom she dedicates her book. Mr. Dickson invested Harrison's salary in mortgages and thus assisted her in saving enough money until it generated $200 a year in interest. With those funds, Harrison began working her way around the world from 1927 until 1936.

In France she worked as a maid for Mrs. Felix Morris, who first gave her the idea of writing down her adventures for publication. Her daughter, Mildred, a writer, helped Harrison compile and arrange her writings into a book.

MAJOR WORK AND THEMES

Harrison's only work, My Great, Wide, Beautiful World, appeared in 1936, though selections were published in the Atlantic Monthly in 1935. The book is an account of Harrison's round-the-world travels to twenty-two countries from 1927 to 1936, written as journal entries. Since Harrison's diary format concentrates on the here and now, she presents herself, as Barton argues, as a woman "who is not concerned about all the whys and wherefores of her past life but who only wants to convey her immediate joys to her readers" (89). Whenever she ran out of money, she either placed or answered an ad in a newspaper and worked as a domestic until she had enough saved to continue her adventures. Her book is remarkable for its freshness, vivid details, immediacy, and quirky and idiosyncratic grammar. Since Harrison had little formal education, she spells phonetically and has little sense of punctuation. Her friend Mildred Morris evidently believed Harrison's words should be published "just as I have written them misteakes and all. I said that if the misteakes are left out there'll be only blank" (243).

From her account, the reader can tell that Harrison enjoys life to the fullest. She details fruit and vegetable markets, foods, and eating experiences. Most journal entries include her meals for the day. For example, in Seville in 1930 she writes, "We had a good lunch of beans tomatoes and meat potatoes olives wine and oranges" (207). She embraces daily life heartily, writing on board a ship to Madras, "I am the first woman on deck each morning I enjoy seeing the Sun come up out of the Sea" (159).

Although her lack of grammatical skills may make her writing seem unsophisticated, her prose soars when she is inspired. In Cairo she records, "I went to a native sweet shop and finished up on sweets. I spent the afternoon with my Library Friend Mohomed Laki Hassan. It was like something pleasant and yet not sweet. It was like mint—our after noon on the Bank of the Nile River" (85). In Darjeeling she writes, "the Moon is bright and the houses on the many mountains are like pearl just below my cottage are a floor of white Clouds. the darkness of the tall fir trees and tea plants on the mountain sides beside the snow white clouds far below are to wonderful" (140).

For a woman who undoubtedly came from a racist, prejudiced society, Harrison's work is remarkably free of the question of race. She easily melds into any society and seems to be accepted by all. In Heliopolis she states that "At Aleppo they thought I was Chinese. Here they think I am Aribian" (65). Harrison wisely discovers the secret of the veil: "By making myself so native like with my vail I have visited many of their [Egyptians'] feasts" (81), and in India she smiles that "In my red shawl and black vail on my head no one would think I had seen Broadway" (112).

In every country she visits, Harrison quickly and easily makes friends, especially with local men. Harrison has a great sense of humor, and many of her lighter adventures occur with her male admirers. For example, in Barcelona she met a German man. "I was to meet the German at 9, but I layd down to rest and went to sleep woke up at 11 so that was the ending of the German" (188).

Harrison's recorded adventures end in 1936 in Hawaii. She writes, "This is the most wonderful part of the World and now that I have about finnish my travellers I feel very happy to have choosed this lovely part of the World" (314). In an Epilogue, the world-wise traveler buys a tent with the money she received from the *Atlantic Monthly* and lives on the beach. She chose Hawaii because "I want alway to be where wealth health youth beauty and gayness are altho I need very little for myself I just want to be in the midst of it" (318). Always buoyant and cheerful, Harrison serves as a model of curiosity and achievement: "I have reversed the saying of Troubles are like Babies the more you nurse them the bigger They grow so I have nursed the joys" (318). We do not know whether Harrison remained in Hawaii, whether she lived there during the bombing of Pearl Harbor, or when and where she died.

CRITICAL RECEPTION

My Great, Wide, Beautiful World was extremely well received and reviewed in prominent places, such as *Time*, the *New York Times*, and the *New Republic*. All reviewers were duly impressed by Harrison's shrewdness, spontaneity, and joy of life. Her faulty spelling and grammar only endeared her to readers. In fact, the reviewer for *Time* believes that readers "will admire not only Juanita's freedom from economic shackles but her impressionistic spelling, sometimes better than right" (83).

Despite such glowing reviews, Harrison's book has been long forgotten and long out of print. G. K. Hall republished it in 1996 in the thirty-volume series African-American Women Writers, 1910–1940.

Adele Logan Alexander, in her Introduction to the G. K. Hall reprint of *My Great, Wide, Beautiful World*, questions the "motivations of publishing houses that choose to present the public with unedited works by unknown authors" and suggests that perhaps Macmillan originally published the manuscript because white readers enjoyed the portrayal of blacks as humorous burlesques, a "clownish Aunt Jemima or latter-day Uncle Remus, whose narrative was readily acceptable to white America as part of a traditional and popular black dialect genre" (xvii). The favorable reception of Harrison's untutored language thus may cast her as a "dark primitive." Yet the *New York Times* reviewer protests such a view, for when she calls *My Great, Wide, Beautiful World* "inspiring," she means that "to say that the book is inspiring is not to indulge in sentimentality or condescension. It is an inspiration to see any human being having such a wide-eyed good time, any traveler throwing herself so completely into the experiences and rewards of traveling" (4).

Now that *My Great, Wide, Beautiful World* has been republished and appears in the same series as works by such prominent writers as Jessie Redmon Fauset,* Zora Neale Hurston,* and Alice Dunbar-Nelson,* perhaps it will receive the attention it deserves.

BIBLIOGRAPHY

Work by Juanita Harrison

My Great, Wide, Beautiful World. New York: Macmillan, 1936.

Studies of Juanita Harrison

Alexander, Adele Logan. "Introduction." In *My Great, Wide, Beautiful World.* New York: G. K. Hall, 1996, xv–xxviii.

Barton, Rebecca Chalmers. *Witnesses for Freedom: Negro Americans in Autobiography.* New York: Harper and Brothers, 1948.

Rev. of *My Great, Wide, Beautiful World. Booklist* 32 (June 1936): 288.

Rev. of *My Great, Wide, Beautiful World. Books* 17 (May 1936): 19.

Rev. of *My Great, Wide, Beautiful World. Christian Century* 53 (June 10, 1936): 843.

Rev. of *My Great, Wide, Beautiful World. Cleveland Open Shelf* (July 1936): 16.

Rev. of *My Great, Wide, Beautiful World. New Republic* 87 (June 3, 1936): 111.

Rev. of *My Great, Wide, Beautiful World. Saturday Review of Literature* 14 (June 20, 1936): 11.

Rev. of *My Great, Wide, Beautiful World. Springfield Republican,* May 17, 1936, 7.

Rev. of *My Great, Wide, Beautiful World. Time* 27 (May 18, 1936): 83.

Rev. of *My Great, Wide, Beautiful World. Wisconsin Library Bulletin* 32 (July 1936): 85.

Rev. of *My Great, Wide, Beautiful World. Yale Review* 25 (Summer 1936): 839.

Woods, Katherine. "Juanita Harrison Has Known Twenty-Two Countries." Rev. of *My Great, Wide, Beautiful World. New York Times,* May 17, 1936, 4.

GEORGE WYLIE HENDERSON
(1904–1965)

Peter G. Christensen

BIOGRAPHY

There is no biography of Henderson, and material on his life is hard to come by. George Wylie Henderson was born June 14, 1904, in Warrior Stand, Alabama, a very small town in Macon County. His father, pastor of the Butler's AME Zion Church in Tuskegee, was an 1899 graduate of the Tuskegee Institute, as David G. Nicholls shows (forthcoming book, Chapter 5). Elected class orator in his senior year, Henderson, Nicholls notes, had twice placed second in the school's annual Trinity Church Boston Oratorical Prize contest. He discussed "Booker T. Washington,* the Apostle of Industrial Education" in 1921 and "Muscle Shoals in the South" in 1922. He learned printing at the nearby Tuskegee Institute 1918–1922 and later went to New York City to use his skills. The self-reliance and economic autonomy ideals of the institute seem to have impressed Henderson greatly.

After several months in New York, Henderson was able to find a job as a linotype operator in the printing offices of the *New York Daily News*. Blyden Jackson recalls having gone to Henderson's place for a gathering of Harlem Renaissance luminaries in the fall of 1931 (xii). Henderson lived at the Dunbar Apartments with his first wife and son from that marriage. Although it is difficult to track down all of his short stories from this period, he published at least nine very short stories in the *New York Daily News* between January 1932 and June 1933. It seems as if after that date he stopped publishing for the *News* and moved to *Redbook*. At least one story appeared in this magazine before the publication of his first novel, *Ollie Miss*, in 1935. At least four more stories appeared in *Redbook* from 1936 to 1939. Around the year 1941 he met his second wife, who had a daughter of about eleven years old, now Roslyn Kirkland Allen, from a previous marriage. In 1946 he published his second, less successful novel, *Jule*, a sequel to *Ollie Miss*. Reviews seem to have driven him away from publishing further work. Except for a story in *Redbook* in 1947, his published works end here. Nicholls notes that he was working on an unfinished novel in the 1950s, *Baby Lou and the Angel Bud*, which was to have been the third part of a series of novels about Jule's family. He was proud of being a skilled worker and union member and worked up until his retirement age. He continued to reside in New York City until his death in 1965.

To some extent Henderson is an autobiographical novelist. *Ollie Miss* takes place in Macon County (Jackson 16), which young Jule, illegitimate son of Ollie Miss and the older Jule, leaves for Harlem at the end of the first half of the sequel. In the latter part of *Jule* the protagonist eventually joins a printer's union. No specific dates are given in Henderson's novels, and they are hard to pin down to specific years. Jule is eight at the beginning of *Jule* and about seventeen when he flees to New York after a white man, who is in love with the same black woman as he, tries to kill him. The rest of the novel takes place in Harlem over the course of about a year (summer to summer), at which time Jule is called back to Alabama because his mother has died, and he gets ready to take his girlfriend, teenaged Bertha Mae, back to New York. Henderson, born in 1904, left for New York about 1922, and these dates could well correspond to those in the novels. At the end of *Ollie Miss*, which covers less than a year, Ollie Miss is pregnant with young Jule.

If the novels are autobiographical in their dates, then perhaps it took Henderson a decade before he began to get his stories published. The Harlem in *Jule* does not seem to have yet experienced the Depression. It is a place of hope for the blacks who come there. The closest one gets to a designation of time comes in the last Harlem chapter when Jule goes with a friend to see some films. Henderson writes, "They watched William S. Hart and Theda Bara, Flora Finch and Rudolph Valentino, flickering on the screen. Silent pictures. Old pictures. Nickelodeon stuff" (223). Since Valentino's career is just beginning in 1922, perhaps Henderson is telescoping time here. Henderson died, fairly unknown, in 1965, not having portrayed his life after 1922 in print.

The Harlem settings and characters of the *Redbook* stories, such as Jake Simmons in "Redcap" and "Mister Simmons—Good Lord!," indicate that from 1933 to 1939 Henderson was publishing material that was to be channeled into *Jule*. Jake Simmons, who offers Jule one of his Harlem rooms to live in, has already "made it" in the novel. In this earlier story we find out more about his past, learning that, before he was thirty, he was a redcap at Grand Central Station. Whether Henderson finished the novel during World War II or whether it was complete in 1939, and he could not get it published until after World War II is hard to say. The Library of Alabama Classics Series reprinted *Ollie Miss* in 1988 and *Jule* in 1989, and both of these books are still in print in paperback.

MAJOR WORKS AND THEMES

The most striking quality of both *Ollie Miss* and *Jule* is the refusal of the narrator to enter into the thoughts of the characters. In each case, stories of 276 and 234 pages, respectively, are told over a short period of time by a narrator familiar with both an Alabama hamlet and 135th Street in Harlem who concentrates on the speech of the characters and their surroundings rather than on their inner lives. In *Ollie Miss* almost all the characters are blacks, but in *Jule* there are some key white figures.

Ollie Miss is told in a straightforward fashion with one flashback on the protagonists' love for Jule. Ollie Miss arrives from nowhere to take up a job as a hand on the farm of the friendly Uncle Alex and Aunt Caroline. This couple was better off than most of the other black citizens of the impoverished area. She is at eighteen a hard worker who does not want any men to show her special favors or court her. She goes back to her boyfriend's home to see if he, Jule, is still living with her rival Della. She discovers that Della has also been dumped by him and moved on. Ollie sympathizes with Della and stays with the lonely woman a while. On her return home, Ollie finds Jule at a camp meeting, and they spend the night together. He leaves, but she follows. When his new lover slashes her with a knife, she finds that she is expecting his child. She shows no hostility to the woman who almost killed her, and she rejects Jule's offer to stay with her.

Ollie is seen by most critics as a role model for independent black women who don't desire to marry their indecisive male lovers and who consider even their female rivals as sisters. She is without a shred of self-pity and doesn't have time to think about oppression by whites. More significant than the heroine's courage, so much praised by the critics, is the style of characterization. Ollie is opaque, and she comes almost without a past. Her future is an open book. The novel is not so much an example of realism as an attempt to present a heroine who is existentially free. She is undetermined psychologically and sociologically. She prefigures the type of heroes desired by Jean-Paul Sartre, who are not the puppets of their creators. One would suspect that Henderson disliked the view of blacks as victims and found not so much a credible heroine as a style that "just says no" to victimization.

In *Jule* the same narrative strategy is at work, even when the author approaches material more associated with the protest novel. (The novel has an opening that implies, contrary to *Ollie Miss*, that Jule had left Ollie.) Jule has to flee the South because a white man, who has taken Jule's girlfriend as his mistress, wants to kill him. When he arrives in Harlem, the problems he runs into concern his sexual affairs with Annie (a rather vulgar friend of Maisie and Jake Simmons, with whom Jule lives) and Lou Davis (a dishonest social climber of lighter skin, who has been educated at an eastern college). When Old Douglas tries to keep the printers' union closed to Jule because of his race, it does not take much time for Jule to overcome this obstacle and get Old Douglas to give him a union card.

When Ollie suddenly dies of unknown causes, Jule returns home, and, without many tears for his beloved mother or any premeditation that we can see, he decides to take his old girlfriend back to Harlem with him. Jule accepts whatever comes and is full of sayings, such as "Coke would be nice" (166). Except for being betrayed by his girlfriends, events that call forth his ire but from which he bounces back immediately, almost anything is "nice" for Jule. This style of characterization has turned off the critics since the novel appeared.

Again, what is at stake for Henderson is not characterization or protest but the creation of personalities with no psychological baggage and no longings for the future. One has to understand Henderson's two heroes as examples of the tendency toward the "abstract idealist" hero, the opposite of the "disillusioned romantic" in Georg Lukács' 1920 *Theory of the Novel*. For them, the world is always broader than their desires. Life is a series of hurdles to be overcome, and there is no time for regrets and contemplation of sad events. Unless we consider the two novels as attempts to achieve the same type of character with an open future, then we will misinterpret them. We will think that the second novel is a failing off from the first in terms of realism, when neither is aimed at being realistic. Even the time schemes are so vague that outside events cannot impinge on the freedom of the characters. Ollie Mae recovers from her horrible knife wound. Jule, in his lack of depth, is like a fairy-tale hero. He wins the kingdom (a decent job) and the princess (his old back-home girlfriend). As novels written during the depression-ridden, socialist-oriented American 1930s, these are odd protest novels. They protest against protest in order to set up moral examples to their readers. Victims become bitter, so one should not become bitter like the quarrelsome old Nan in *Ollie Miss*.

CRITICAL RECEPTION

Articles on *Ollie Miss* have generally praised the novel for its picture of its heroine. In the first scholarly journal article specifically devoted to Henderson, Patricia Kane and Doris Y. Wilkinson compare *Ollie Miss* to Iris in Chester Himes' *Cotton Comes to Harlem* (1965), concluding that they are "vivid pictures of two black women surviving in male-dominated worlds" (101). However, as the "central character in a realistic novel, Ollie assumes an authenticity more significant than Iris" (108). Lonnell Johnson has also written a comparative essay, matching up Ollie Miss with Janie Mae Crawford in Zora Neale Hurston's* *Their Eyes Were Watching God* (1937). Both characters exhibit defiance, independence, and rebellion (46), but Ollie is "far less fully developed than Janie Mae" (45). For Blyden Jackson, Ollie Miss is the "child of nature easily distinguishable from persons possessed, in the eyes of society, of a host of acquired sophistications" (xii). Jackson states that the "work that she does makes clear her close and instinctual relationship to an earth like that of Hesiod's *Works and Days* and with forms of labor rooted in elemental aspects of human culture" (xii–xiii).

Emmanuel S. Nelson says that *Jule* "lacks the intensity and power of Henderson's first novel but it has a more complicated plot and makes a bold social statement" (97). He considers it a novel of initiation from adolescence to young adulthood. In this novel Henderson "effectively handles social and racial protest, concerns so conspicuously absent in his first work" (100). Yet he finds that the novel is disappointing because it lacks realistic complexity and divides whites into simple "good" and "bad" characters. J. Lee Greene also prefers *Ollie Miss* and finds *Jule* a stereotypical southern black migration novel in an artistically flat style.

Unfortunately, a flood in the basement of the Harlem home of Henderson's stepdaughter, Roslyn Kirkland Allen, caused the destruction of many of the author's papers. David G. Nicholls' devoted efforts have attempted to restore Henderson's reputation. He wrote a chapter on him in his 1995 dissertation at the University of Chicago, contributed a working paper to the University of Michigan on Henderson in 1997, and published a primary and secondary bibliography on him in *Bulletin of Bibliography* in 1997, to which this article is highly indebted. Nicholls is currently publishing his revised dissertation (with a chapter on Henderson), compiling an edition of Henderson's collected stories, while Ms. Allen is working on archiving Henderson's surviving papers. There are files on Henderson in the Schomburg Center and at Tuskegee University.

BIBLIOGRAPHY

Works by George Wylie Henderson

Novels

Ollie Miss: A Novel. Blocks by Lowell Leroy Balcolm. New York: Frederick A. Stokes; London: Martin Secker, 1935.
Jule: A Novel. New York: Creative Age Press; London: W. H. Allen, 1946.

Short Stories

"Sinner Man's Wedding." *New York Daily News*, January 14, 1932, 29.
"Whistlin' Slim." *New York Daily News*, April 11, 1932, 29.
"Dance of Death." *New York Daily News*, June 13, 1932, 27.
"Thy Name Is Woman." *New York Daily News*, July 15, 1932, 29.
"Without Tears." *New York Daily News*, July 25, 1932, 25.
"Midnight in Harlem." *New York Daily News*, August 8, 1932, 25.
"Day of Judgment." *New York Daily News*, August 29, 1932, 25.
"Man in the Moon." *New York Daily News*, September 15, 1932, 31.
"A Brownskin's Revenge." *New York Daily News*, June 12, 1933, 25.
"Redcap." *Redbook* 62.6 (April 1934): 42–43.
"Harlem Calling." *Redbook* 62.6 (April 1934): 42–43, 100–103.
"Mister Simmons—Good Lord!" *Redbook* 63.2 (June 1934): 58–59, 72.
"Waitress." *Redbook* 66.3 (January 1936): 48–49, 98.
"Time for a Dance." *Redbook* 68.4 (February 1937): 42–43, 109–19.
"Home Style: An Episode." *Redbook* 72.4 (February 1939): 58–59, 112.

"Red Devil over Harlem." *Redbook* 73.24 (August 1939): 54–56.
"Only Mary and Me." *Redbook* 89.6 (October 1947): 40–41.

Studies of George Wylie Henderson

Baker, Howard. "Some Notes on New Fiction." Rev. of *Ollie Miss. Southern Review* 1 (1935): 178–91.
Cook, Fannie. "Somebody." Rev. of *Jule. New York Herald Tribune Weekly Book Review* (October 20, 1946): 22.
Creekmore, Hubert. "The Evolution of Jule." Rev. of *Jule. New York Times*, October 13, 1946, 22.
Dozier, Lois. "Mississippi Migrant." Rev. of *Jule. Phylon* 6.4 (1946): 400–401.
Gannett, Lewis. "Books and Things." Rev. of *Ollie Miss. New York Herald Tribune*, February 23, 1935, 9.
Greene, J. Lee. "Introduction." In *Jule*. Tuscaloosa: University of Alabama Press, 1989. vi–xix.
Greene, Lee. "Black Novelists and Novels, 1930–1950." In *The History of Southern Literature*. Ed. Louis D. Rubin. Baton Rouge: Louisiana State University Press, 1985. 383–98.
Gruening, Martha. "A Cabin, a Garden." Rev. of *Ollie Miss. The New Republic* 82 (April 17, 1935): 292.
Hart, Elizabeth. "Within the All-Negro World." Rev. of *Ollie Miss. New York Herald Tribune Books* (February 24, 1935): 4.
Holmes, J. Welfred. "Two Stories of Color." Rev. of *Jule. Opportunity* 25.1 (January–March 1947): 38–39.
Hughes, Langston. *The Big Sea: An Autobiography*. New York: Knopf, 1940.
Jackson, Blyden. "Introduction." In *Ollie Miss*. Tuscaloosa: University of Alabama Press, 1988. vi–xix.
Johnson, Charles Spurgeon. *Shadow of the Plantation*. Chicago: University of Chicago Press, 1934.
Johnson, Lonnell E. "The Defiant Black Heroine: Ollie Miss and Janie Mae—Two Portraits from the 30's." *The Zora Neale Hurston Forum* 4.2 (Spring 1990): 41–46.
Kane, Patricia, and Doris Y. Wilkinson. "Survival Strategies: Black Women in *Ollie Miss* and *Cotton Comes to Harlem*." *Critique: Studies in Modern Fiction* 16.1 (1974): 101–9.
Miller, Merle. "Lonely Boy." Rev. of *Jule. Saturday Review of Literature* 29 (October 12, 1946): 56.
Nelson, Emmanuel S. "George Wylie Henderson." In *Dictionary of Literary Biography*. Vol. 51: *Afro-American Writers from the Harlem Renaissance to 1940*. Ed. Trudier Harris and Thadious M. Davis. Detroit: Gale, 1987. 96–100.
Nicholls, David G. "Conjuring the Folk: Modernity and Narrative in African America, 1914–1945." Diss., University of Chicago, 1995: 124–62.
———. "George Wylie Henderson: A Primary and Secondary Bibliography." *Bulletin of Bibliography* 54.4 (1997): 335–38.
———. "Rural Modernity, Migration, and the Gender of Autonomy: Narrative and History: The Novels of George Wylie Henderson." In *Center for Afroamerican and African Studies Working Papers* 32. Ann Arbor: University of Michigan, 1997. [To

be the basis of Chapter 5 of the author's forthcoming revised, published dissertation]

———. *The Novels of George Wylie Henderson.* Forthcoming.

Perry, Edward G. "Our Bookshelf." Rev. of *Ollie Miss. Opportunity* 13.4 (April 1935): 123.

Quennell, Peter. "New Novels." Rev. of *Ollie Miss. New Statesman and Nation* 9 (June 1, 1935): 829–30.

Turner, Darwin. "The Negro Novelist and the South." *The Southern Humanities Review* 1.1 (Spring 1967): 21–29.

Walton, Edith H. "An Excellent Novel of Negro Life." Rev. of *Ollie Miss. New York Times Book Review* (February 24, 1935): 7.

Wilkins, Roy. Rev. of *Ollie Miss. The Crisis* 42.4 (April 1935): 121.

PAULINE ELIZABETH HOPKINS
(1859–1930)

Adenike Marie Davidson

BIOGRAPHY

Pauline Elizabeth Hopkins was born in Portland, Maine, in 1859 to Northup and Sarah Allen Hopkins. Her stepfather, William A. Hopkins, was a Civil War veteran. Her mother was a descendant of the well-known New England family that included Nathaniel Paul and Thomas Paul, who founded Baptist churches in Boston. Hopkins herself was the great-grandniece of the poet James Whitfield. The family relocated to Boston when Hopkins was an infant, and there she was educated in public schools and graduated from Girls High School.

Her literary talents were developed from an early age. When she was only fifteen, she entered an essay titled "The Evils of Intemperance and Their Remedy" in a writing contest sponsored by Boston's Congregational Publishing Society, supported by William Wells Brown.* Her essay won a prize of ten dollars in gold.

At the age of twenty she completed her first play, *Slaves' Escape: or, the Underground Railroad*. In 1880 the play was produced at Boston's Oakland Garden by the Hopkins Colored Troubadours; the cast included her mother, stepfather, and Hopkins, who was referred to as "Boston's Colored Soprano." The play was later published as *Peculiar Sam; or, The Underground Railroad*. She performed with the Colored Troubadours for twelve years, during which time she wrote at least one other play, *One Scene from the Drama of Early Days*, based on the biblical story of Daniel in the lion's den.

Hopkins left the stage and studied stenography as a means of earning a living while pursuing a writing career. In 1895 she passed the civil service examination and was appointed stenographer in the Bureau of Statistics for the Census.

In 1900 she published her first novel, *Contending Forces: A Romance Illustrative*

of Negro Life North and South and began a career as editor of, and frequent contributor to, the newly founded *Colored American Magazine*. Her first contribution
was a short story, "The Mystery within Us," published in the magazine's first
issue. She served as editor until September 1904, when she was relieved of her
position at the magazine's change in ownership. During her time as editor, she
published three novels in serial form, seven short stories, and numerous biographical and political sketches, sometimes under the pseudonym Sarah A. Allen.

After leaving *Colored American*, Hopkins became a regular contributor to the
Voice of the Negro and began a series of articles entitled "The Dark Races of the
Twentieth Century." In 1905 she founded her own publishing company and
published *A Primer of Facts Pertaining to the Early Greatness of the African Race*.
Hopkins' literary career virtually ceased after her contributions to *Voice*. In 1916
Hopkins pursued another publishing venture with the launching of the *New Era*
magazine, similar in format to the *Colored American*; unfortunately, the magazine
folded after two issues.

She returned to stenographic work, taking a position at Massachusetts Institute
of Technology. Living in virtual obscurity after 1916, she died on August 13,
1930, from burn injuries on her entire body when her dress caught fire in a tragic
home accident. She was buried in the Hopkins family plot in Chelsea, Massachusetts.

MAJOR WORKS AND THEMES

Contending Forces, Hopkins' first novel, is set in Bermuda and North Carolina
in the 1790s and shows the corrupting influence of the slave system. The first
part of the novel tells the tale of Charles Montforth, who leaves Bermuda for
North Carolina with his wife, children, and slaves to avoid compliance with a
British law ordering him to free his slaves. In the States, he meets up with Anson
Pollack, who has Montforth murdered, spreads a rumor that Mrs. Montforth is
black, causing her to commit suicide, and has the Montforth children remanded
into slavery. One son, Charles, Jr., is purchased and taken to England; the other,
Jesse, escapes to New Hampshire, where he eventually marries an African American woman. The second part of the novel traces Jesse's family, now the Smiths
100 years later, and the characters of Will Smith and his sister, Dora, and their
efforts to fulfill their goals in marriage and career. Will, a black civil rights leader,
falls in love with Sappho Clark, a mulatta. Sappho leaves Will rather than expose
his career to her background; at the age of fifteen she was abducted by a white
uncle, placed in a brothel, and birthed a son in secret. His dedication overcomes
her hesitation, and they are eventually married. Dora is engaged to John Langley,
an ambitious black lawyer, yet unscrupulous, being a direct descendant of Anson
Pollack. When she is betrayed by Langley—he discovers Sappho's secret and
attempts to blackmail her into submitting to him—Dora rejects him and turns
to Arthur Lewis, the president of a technical college for blacks in the South.
Lewis, unlike Langley, is dedicated to the betterment of the race, and he and

Dora are eventually married. The novel ends with a family reunion of the Smiths and the British strand of the Montforth family.

This novel introduces the reader to several of Hopkins' more favorite themes: miscegenation, racial uplift, mystery-hidden histories, and the issue of vulnerable black womanhood in the face of white male lust. One theme explored over and over again in her fiction is the unmasking of black characters passing for white. Such explorations suggest Hopkins' insistence that racial barriers are irrational. Often in her fiction, she explores the black community's search for social order within the aftereffects of slavery. The restoration of order usually entails the breaking down of the color line; Hopkins presents racial division as something that often separates members of the same family. Hopkins also continually stresses the political consciousness of African American women.

In the Preface to the novel, Hopkins explains, "Fiction is of great value to any people as a preserver of manners and customs—religious, political and social. . . . *No one will do this for us; we must ourselves develop the men and women who will faithfully portray the inmost thoughts and feelings of the Negro with all the fire and romance of which lie dormant in our history*" (13–14). Hopkins used her fiction and her position as editor of *Colored American* to promote the uplift of her race. She presented African American readers with moral guidance and instruction through exemplary African American characters who would be acknowledged by the white reader as human beings and embodiments of white bourgeois values, manners, and tastes.

The serialized novels, all of which are now included in *The Magazine Novels of Pauline Hopkins*, are situated within a white, rather than a black, social order and emphasize suspense, adventure, complex plotting, multiple and false identities, and the use of disguise. *Hagar's Daughter: A Story of Southern Caste Prejudice* (serialized March 1901–March 1902) is a generational novel. The characters are mostly white. In each generation, a beautiful, "white," and wealthy woman discovers herself to be black, forcing her to cope with racism and rejection. For each, blackness is a secret and a means of her victimization. The white world is represented as white villains of greed who have the power to oppress.

Winona: A Tale of Negro Life in the South and Southeast (serialized May 1901–March 1902) is a historical romance, her only long piece of fiction set entirely before the Civil War. The story features Winona and her brother, Judah, children of a white man who has become an Indian chief, and his quadroon wife. The siblings are captured by slave catchers and cast into bondage early in the text. The remainder of the novel focuses on their efforts to escape. They are befriended and helped by an Englishman, Maxwell. The three of them meet with John Brown and join the plans to fight for a free Kansas but then are transported to Canada. In the end, Maxwell and Winona marry and relocate to England; Judah follows and becomes a soldier for the queen. The novel calls for organized political resistance against contemporary persecution.

Of One Blood: or, the Hidden Self (serialized November 1902–November 1903) explores Hopkins' belief that blacks should revere their African origins. It also voices a Pan-African vision, unifying and celebrating black people all over the world. The story focuses on the career of Reuel Briggs, a Harvard medical student (believed to be white by fellow students) who is fascinated with trance states. At the beginning of the tale, Reuel has a dream in which he sees a beautiful woman; shortly afterward, he sees his vision in person—Dianthe, a soprano with the Fisk Jubilee singers. The two meet again in the hospital when Dianthe appears dead, but Reuel recognizes her state as suspended animation and revives her; the two marry, but because she suffers from amnesia, he doesn't disclose her racial identity to her or anyone else. Aubrey Livingston, Reuel's "friend," knowing of the racial identities of both Reuel and Dianthe, arranges for Reuel to take a position on an African expedition and plots to have him killed in the wilderness. Although he is engaged to Molly Vance, he seeks to seduce Dianthe and make her his mistress. Reuel escapes death and discovers a great underground African civilization. His lily-shaped birthmark proves him to be a descendant of the royal line. Although married to Dianthe, a union that was never consummated, he is married to the queen, Candace. Through psychic abilities, he learns of Dianthe's torment and Aubrey's plot, and returns to America, but too late to rescue her from death. He learns that Dianthe and Aubrey also possess the birthmark; they are all "of one blood" separated in slavery. Aubrey is taken prisoner and forced to commit suicide for his evil deeds. Reuel returns to Africa as ruler.

In *Primer of Facts*, her last full-length publication, Hopkins focused on recovering for the community the record of plundered African civilizations. In the last line of the text, Hopkins directs her attention to Africans in the United States, exhorting, "NEVER GIVE UP THE BALLOT."

CRITICAL RECEPTION

Hopkins was virtually forgotten until Shockley rediscovered her work in 1972. Since then her reputation has gradually reemerged. Her works have been reprinted, along with many others, as numerous forgotten nineteenth-century feminist and black nationalist texts are being recovered and given new consideration. Her dedication to racial uplift and her examination of Africa and historical African American figures earned her a place in the Pan-African literary tradition. Her use of strong African American female characters dedicated to the betterment of the community allows readers to see her as a precursor to well-known feminist authors such as Zora Neale Hurston* and Alice Walker. Her use of the supernatural as realistic shows her to be a forerunner to Toni Morrison. Hopkins' works had never been given the attention it merits until recently. Probably because of the size of its press, Hopkins' first novel was released with little fanfare and received no comment from the white mainstream literary community. The remainder of her work was published in African American magazines with small circulations; this no doubt contributed to her relative anonymity. If nothing else, the late acknowledgment of Hopkins' large body of work "should remind us of how difficult it was for black writers to reject widely accepted concepts of race and culture that were frequently employed to denigrate blacks and to justify racial oppression" (Yarborough xli).

BIBLIOGRAPHY

Works by Pauline Elizabeth Hopkins

Plays

Peculiar Sam; or, The Underground Railroad. N.d.
One Scene from the Drama of Early Days. N.d.

Fiction

Contending Forces. Boston: Colored Cooperative, 1900.
"The Mystery within Us." *Colored American Magazine* (May 1900).
"Talma Gordon." *Colored American Magazine* (October 1900).
"George Washington: A Christmas Story." *Colored American Magazine* (December 1900).
"Bro'r Abr'm Jimson's Wedding: A Christmas Story." 1901. In *Invented Lives: Narratives of Black Women, 1860–1960.* Ed. Mary Helen Washington. New York: Doubleday, 1987. 130–46.
"A Dash for Liberty." *Colored American Magazine* (August 1901).
"The Test of Manhood, a Christmas Story." *Colored American Magazine* (December 1902).
"As the Lord Lives, He Is One of Our Mother's Children," 1903. In *Revolutionary Tales: African American Women's Short Stories, from the First Story to the Present.* Ed. Bill Mullen. New York: Dell, 1995. 52–62.
"Topsy Templeton." *New Era* (1916).
The Magazine Novels of Pauline Hopkins. New York: Oxford University Press, 1988.

Nonfiction

"Famous Women of the Negro Race, Seven Educators." *Colored American Magazine* (September 1900): 125–30.
"The First Pan-African Conference of the World." *Colored American Magazine* (September 1900): 223–31.
"William Wells Brown." *Colored American Magazine* (January 1901).
"Famous Men of the Negro Race." *Colored American Magazine* (February 1901–September 1902).
"Club Life Among Colored Women." *Colored American Magazine* (August 1902): 273–77.
"Heroes and Heroines in Black." *Colored American Magazine* (January 1903): 206–11.
"Last Phases of the Race Problem in America." *Colored American Magazine* (February 1903): 244–51.
"Venus and Apollo Modeled from Ethiopians." *Colored American Magazine* (May/June 1903).
A Primer of Facts Pertaining to the Early Greatness of the African Race and the Possibility of Restoration by Its Descendants. Cambridge, MA: P. E. Hopkins, 1905.

Studies of Pauline Elizabeth Hopkins

Ammons, Elizabeth. "Afterword: Winona, Bahktin, and Hopkins in the Twenty-first Century." In *The Unruly Voice: Rediscovering Pauline Elizabeth Hopkins*. Ed. John Cullen Gruesser. Urbana: University of Illinois Press, 1996. 158–81.

————. "The Limits of Freedom: The Fiction of Alice Dunbar-Nelson, Kate Chopin, and Pauline Hopkins." In *Conflicting Stories: American Women Writers at the Turn into the Twentieth Century*. New York: Oxford University Press, 1991. 59–85.

Berg, Allison. "Reconstructing Motherhood: Pauline Hopkins' *Contending Forces*." *Studies in American Fiction* 24.2 (Autumn 1996): 131–50.

Brooks, Gwendolyn. "Afterword." In *Contending Forces: A Romance Illustrative of Negro Life North and South*, 1900. Carbondale: Southern Illinois University Press, 1978.

Brooks, Kristina. "Mammies, Bucks, and Wenches: Minstrelsy, Racial Pornography, and Racial Politics in Pauline Hopkins's *Hagar's Daughter*." In *The Unruly Voice: Rediscovering Pauline Elizabeth Hopkins*. Ed. John Cullen Gruesser. Urbana: University of Illinois Press, 1996. 119–57.

Brown, Lois Lamphere. " 'To Allow No Tragic End': Defensive Postures in Pauline Hopkins's *Contending Forces*." In *The Unruly Voice: Rediscovering Pauline Elizabeth Hopkins*. Ed. John Cullen Gruesser. Urbana: University of Illinois Press, 1996. 50–70.

Campbell, Jane. "Female Paradigms in Frances Harper's Iola Leroy and Pauline Hopkins's *Contending Forces*." In *Mythic Black Fiction: The Transformation of History*. Knoxville: University of Tennessee Press, 1986. 18–41.

————. "Pauline Elizabeth Hopkins." In *Afro-American Writers before the Harlem Renaissance: Dictionary of Literary Biography*. Vol. 50. Ed. Trudier Harris and Thadious M. Davis. Detroit: Bruccoli Clark, 1986. 182–89.

Carby, Hazel. " 'All the Fire and Romance': The Magazine Fiction of Pauline Hopkins." In *Reconstructing Womanhood: The Emergence of the Afro-American Woman Novelist*. New York: Oxford University Press, 1987. 145–62.

————. "Introduction." In *The Magazine Novels of Pauline Hopkins*. New York: Oxford University Press, 1988. xxiv–1.

————. " 'Of What Use Is Fiction?': Pauline Elizabeth Hopkins." In *Reconstructing Womanhood: The Emergence of the Afro-American Woman Novelist*. New York: Oxford University Press, 1987. 121–44.

————. " 'On the Threshold of Woman's Era': Lynching, Empire, and Sexuality in Black Feminist Theory." In *"Race," Writing, and Difference*. Ed. Henry Louis Gates Jr. Chicago: University of Chicago Press, 1986. 301–16.

Doreski, C. K. "Inherited Rhetoric and Authentic History: Pauline Hopkins at the Colored American Magazine." In *The Unruly Voice: Rediscovering Pauline Elizabeth Hopkins*. Ed. John Cullen Gruesser. Urbana: University of Illinois Press, 1996. 71–97.

Gable-Hover, Janet. "Pauline Elizabeth Hopkins." In *Nineteenth Century American Women Writers: A Bio-Bibliographical Critical Sourcebook*. Ed. Denise Knight. Westport, CT: Greenwood, 1997. 236–40.

Gaines, Kevin. "Black Americans' Racial Uplift Ideology as 'Civilizing Mission': Pauline E. Hopkins on Race and Imperialism." In *Cultures of United States Imperialism*. Ed.

Amy E. Kaplan and Donald E. Pease. Durham, NC: Duke University Press, 1993. 433–55.

Gillman, Susan. "Pauline Hopkins and the Occult: African American Revisions of Nineteenth-Century Sciences." *American Literary History* 8.1 (Spring 1996): 57–82.

Gruesser, John. "Pauline Hopkins's Of One Blood: Creating an Afrocentric Fantasy for a Black Middle Class Audience." In *Modes of the Fantastic: Selected Essays from the Twelfth International Conference on the Fantastic in the Arts.* Ed. Robert A. Latham. Westport, CT: Greenwood, 1995.

———. "Taking Liberties: Pauline Hopkins's Recasting of the Creole Rebellion." In *The Unruly Voice: Rediscovering Pauline Elizabeth Hopkins.* Ed. John Cullen Gruesser. Urbana: University of Illinois Press, 1996. 98–118.

Kassanoff, Jennie A. " 'Fate Has Linked Us Together': Blood, Gender, and the Politics of the Representation in Pauline Hopkins's Of One Blood." In *The Unruly Voice: Rediscovering Pauline Elizabeth Hopkins.* Ed. John Cullen Gruesser. Urbana: University of Illinois Press, 1996. 158–81.

Lamping, Marilyn. "Pauline Elizabeth Hopkins." In *American Women Writers: A Critical Reference Guide from Colonial Times to Present.* Ed. Lina Mainiero. Vol. 2. New York: Frederick Unger, 1980. 325–27.

Marcus, Lisa. " 'Of One Blood': Reimagining American Genealogy in Pauline Hopkins's *Contending Forces.*" In *Speaking the Other Self: American Women Writers.* Ed. Jeanne Reesman. Athens: University of Georgia Press, 1997. 117–43.

McCann, Sean. " 'Bonds of Brotherhood': Pauline Hopkins and the Work of Melodrama." *ELH* 64.3 (Fall 1997): 789–822.

McCullough, Kate. "Slavery, Sexuality, and Genre: Pauline Hopkins and the Representation of Female Desire." In *The Unruly Voice: Rediscovering Pauline Elizabeth Hopkins.* Ed. John Cullen Gruesser. Urbana: University of Illinois Press, 1996. 21–49.

McKay, Nellie Y. "Introduction." In *The Unruly Voice: Rediscovering Pauline Elizabeth Hopkins.* Ed. John Cullen Gruesser. Urbana: University of Illinois Press, 1996.

Otten, Thomas J. "Pauline Hopkins and the Hidden Self of Race." *ELH* 59.1 (Spring 1992): 227–56.

Pamplin, Claire. " 'Race' and Identity in Pauline Hopkins's *Hagar's Daughter.*" In *Redefining the Political Novel: American Women Writers, 1797–1901.* Ed. Sharon M. Harris. Knoxville: University of Tennessee Press, 1995. 169–83.

"Pauline E. Hopkins." *Colored American Magazine* 2 (January 1901): 218–19.

Peterson, Carla L. "Unsettled Frontiers: Race, History, and Romance in Pauline Hopkins's 'Contending Forces.' " In *Famous Last Words: Changes in Gender and Narrative Closure.* Ed. Alison Booth. Charlottesville: University of Virginia Press, 1993.

Porter, Dorothy B. "Pauline Elizabeth Hopkins." In *Dictionary of American Negro Biography.* Ed. Rayford W. Logan and Michael R. Winston. New York: W. W. Norton, 1982. 325–26.

Sawaya, Francesca. "Emplotting National History: Regionalism and Pauline Hopkins's *Contending Forces.*" In *Breaking Boundaries: New Perspectives on Regional Writing.* Ed. Sherrie A. Inness. Iowa City: University of Iowa Press, 1997. 72–87.

Schrager, Cynthia D. "Pauline Hopkins and William James: The New Psychology and the Politics of Race." In *Female Subjects in Black and White: Race, Psychoanalysis,*

Feminism. Ed. Elizabeth Abel. Berkeley: University of California Press, 1997. 307–29.

Shockley, Ann Allen. "Pauline Elizabeth Hopkins: A Biographical Excursion into Obscurity." *Phylon* 33 (1972): 22–26.

Somerville, Siobhan. "Passing through the Closet in Pauline E. Hopkins's *Contending Forces*." *American Literature* 69.1 (March 1997): 139–66.

Tate, Claudia. "Pauline Hopkins: Our Literary Foremother." In *Conjuring: Black Women, Fiction, and Literary Tradition*. Ed. Marjorie Pryse and Hortense J. Spillers. Bloomington: Indiana University Press, 1985. 53–66.

Yarborough, Richard. "Introduction." In *Contending Forces: A Romance Illustrative of Negro Life North and South*. New York: Oxford University Press, 1988.

GEORGE MOSES HORTON
(1797–1883?)

Lonnell E. Johnson

BIOGRAPHY

George Moses Horton, the first southern black to publish poetry, was born in 1797. Writing about slavery from the point of view of the slave, Horton is "the first clear black outcry in poetic form against slavery" (Richmond 82).

Into the world of plantation slavery, Horton was born the property of William Horton of Northampton County, North Carolina. His master moved to a new farm about ten miles southwest of Chapel Hill in Chatham County. In 1814 George was given to James Horton, who also had a farm in Chatham. The young slave carried produce to nearby Chapel Hill to sell. His contact with students at the University of North Carolina providentially changed the course of Horton's life.

While working at the Horton farm, the slave had taught himself to read and rhyme from listening to hymns heard at revival meetings and from hearing the Bible. When it was discovered that the young slave could recite original verse, Horton became a center of attraction for the young college students. Horton is distinguished as the first black "professional poet," in that he anonymously wrote occasional love poetry for the sweethearts of the male students at twenty-five or fifty cents per poem.

Eventually, Horton came to the attention of Caroline Lee Hentz, wife of a professor at the university. Through contact with Mrs. Hentz, Horton learned to write, as she encouraged his poetic efforts by acting as his mentor. She was also helpful in getting two of his poems, "Liberty and Slavery" and "Slavery" published in her hometown newspaper.

Horton's preoccupation for most of his life was the acquisition of his freedom. Horton's first published collection *The Hope of Liberty* (1829) was sold with the intention that profits would be used to purchase his freedom. Unfortunately, the scheme was not successful, nor were the attempts of Mrs. Hentz and several prominent white patrons and supporters.

The Hope of Liberty underwent two subsequent editions under the title Poems by a Slave (1837), published in Philadelphia, and a compilation with a memoir of Phillis Wheatley* along with a selection of her poetry published in Boston with the full title Memoir and Poems of Phillis Wheatley, a Native African and Slave: Also Poems by a Slave (1838).

Following the publishing of Horton's first collection, Mrs. Hentz departed from Chapel Hill, and his attempts to purchase his freedom continued to be thwarted. These events devastated the poet, as he turned to drinking as consolation in his seemingly unchangeable state of bondage.

Sixteen years after the publication of The Hope of Liberty, Horton published a second volume, Poetical Works of George M. Horton, the Colored Bard of North-Carolina to Which Is Prefixed the Life of the Author Written by Himself (1845).

Despite all efforts to the contrary, the poet remained in bondage until 1865, when he attached himself to the approaching Ninth Calvary from Michigan. The sixty-eight-year-old Horton traveled from Raleigh to meet the approaching Union troops and soon caught the attention of Captain William H. S. Banks of Michigan, a twenty-eight-year-old officer, with whom the poet collaborated on his third volume of verse, Naked Genius (1865).

In addition to the three extant works by Horton, indications are that the poet also produced a manuscript entitled The Museum, but a copy is yet to surface as a published work.

When Horton's last book, Naked Genius, was not as successful as anticipated, he ventured to Philadelphia. For whatever reasons, Horton did not thrive there but seems to have eked out a meager existence. The poet died in obscurity, either in Philadelphia or North Carolina or some place in between. Neither the time nor the place of his death is known.

MAJOR WORKS AND THEMES

To comprehend Horton's contribution to African American literature, one must examine his poetry, which mirrors the soul of a man who lived most of his life in slavery with the burning hope of someday being free. Although Horton covers a variety of subjects, some of the poet's strongest works deal explicitly with slavery. The basis for The Hope of Liberty is to raise funds to purchase the freedom of the poet that he might go to live in Liberia (although Horton never publicly acknowledged such a desire outside the introductory note in the book). The twenty-two poems are outstanding not only because of their underlying inspiration but because their author could read but not write at the time of publication. The poems were recited by the author and recorded by some un-known scribe. Freedom was an elusive state the poet longed to enjoy, yet it seemed just beyond his grasp. Horton's protest was not only against his personal status as a slave; he also expressed a concern for the plight of all slaves.

Horton's self-absorption with his state of bondage is evident in his use of flight imagery, particularly in his earlier poetry, beginning with "Praise of Creation," the opening poem of *The Hope of Liberty*. John Cobbs comments, "It is Horton's preoccupation with and development of the motif of flight that provides *Hope of Liberty* with a cohesive quality. . . . Freedom from slavery for Horton is freedom to soar, to ascend" (446–47).

For the romantic poet who yearns to escape, the ultimate escape is death, a subject Horton discusses in several poems. In his earlier poems Horton voices the belief that his state of bondage may be unending, as in "On Liberty and Slavery," "Dear Liberty," and "The Slave's Complaint." In "Death of a Favorite" he offers the oxymoronic description: "Death is a joyful doom" (*Naked Genius* 13).

In Horton's second collection, *Poetical Works*, the underlying impetus is not slavery; in fact, slavery is mentioned only in "Division of an Estate" and "Farewell to Frances." Although Horton still had the longing to purchase his freedom, he has been thoroughly disillusioned and disappointed by his failure with *The Hope of Liberty*.

In the Introduction to *Poetical Works* Horton expresses the motivation for its publication. According to Richmond, Horton's primary objective in publishing his literary work was to help "remove doubt of cavilists with regard to African genius" (127). His second volume has a wide range of topics: love, nature, religion, and praise of noted contemporaries—Andrew Jackson and Henry Clay. Poems reflect Horton's warm sense of humor, such as "The Fate of an Innocent Dog," "The Woodman and the Money Hunter," and "Trouble with the Itch and Rubbing with Sulphur." Horton also reveals his personal problems with money and alcohol in the forty-five poems.

Published in 1865, Horton's third work, *Naked Genius*, contains 132 poems, two of which are from *The Hope of Liberty* and forty-two from *Poetical Works*, with the remaining being previously unpublished works. As with the previous volumes Horton's poetry covers a wide range of subjects, including tributes to contemporaries Grant, Sherman, and Jefferson Davis and three poems on Lincoln's death. Loggins describes this work as "much more extensive, and at the same time a much more intimate volume" (113).

Like Jupiter Hammon* and Phillis Wheatley, Horton is strongly influenced by the Bible. Horton, however, differs in that he uses logic based on the Bible to reason with Christian slaveholders who attempt to justify slavery on the basis of the Scriptures. O'Neale discusses Horton's "use of Christian allusion to get his message above the heads of pro-slavery advocates who may not have known Scripture well enough to accept the indictment, and into the hearts of those who did" (19).

Overall, Horton, as a product of a later age, has a wider range of poetic possibilities than Hammon or Wheatley, displaying a versatility that may be simply a reflection of the tenor of his times. Brawley classifies Horton as "essentially a romantic poet" and points out the possible influence of William Cullen Bryant (386).

The most striking difference in the portrait of Horton is the distinct personality he projects through his works. Sherman offers this evaluation of Horton as compared to Wheatley:

He is more original, more inventive, his range is far broader in form, language and theme. Most important, a distinct human personality emerges from his verse, complex and contradictory and fudged at times, but an authentic personality that is self-assertive in its hopes and commentary on the human condition, that possesses irony and wit, that is, on occasion, bold enough to break convention. He has a sense of identity that, from available evidence, Wheatley did not and perhaps could not possess. (*Invisible Poets* 182–83)

CRITICAL RECEPTION

The earliest critical commentary on Horton's poetry is Collier Cobb's "American Man of Letters: George Moses Horton" (1909). His commentary dismisses Horton's antislavery poetry with the remark, "George never really cared for more liberty than he had, but was fond of playing to the grandstand"(qtd. in Richmond 178). A similar perspective is noted in *The Black Poet* (1967), comprehensive biography of Horton by Professor Richard Walser in discussing the period following *The Hope of Liberty* and Horton's failed efforts at manumission. Vernon Loggins also discusses Horton's poetry in *The Negro Author*. Stephen B. Weeks in a biographical essay in *The Southern Workman* comments on *The Hope of Liberty* as a reflection "upon the conditions of slaves in North Carolina at the date of its publication" (qtd. in Richmond 179).

Other noteworthy discussions of Horton's poetry include J. Saunders Redding's *To Make a Poet Black* (1939) and Merle Richmond's *Bid the Vassal Soar: Interpretive Essays on the Life and Poetry of Phillis Wheatley and George Moses Horton* (1974). Joan Sherman has edited and provided the Introduction to a critical discussion in *The Black Bard of North Carolina: George Moses Horton and His Poetry* (1997). Entries on Horton are found in the *Dictionary of Literary Biography* (Carroll) and the *Oxford Companion to African American Literature* (Sherman).

BIBLIOGRAPHY

Works by George Moses Horton

The Hope of Liberty. Raleigh, NC: J. Gales and Son, 1829.
The Poetical Works of George M. Horton, the Colored Bard of North-Carolina. Hillsboro, NC: D. Heartt, 1845.
Naked Genius. Raleigh, NC: William B. Smith, 1865.

Studies of George Moses Horton

Brawley, Benjamin. "Three Negro Poets: Horton, Mrs. Harper, and Whitman." *Journal of Negro History* 2 (October 1917): 384–92.

Carroll, William. "George Moses Horton." In *Dictionary of Literary Biography*. Vol. 50: *Afro-American Writers before the Harlem Renaissance*. Ed. Thadious M. Davis and Trudier Harris. Detroit: Gale, 1984. 190–201.

Cobb, Collier. "An American Man of Letters: George Moses Horton, the Negro Poet." *North Carolina Review* 3 (October 1909): 3–5.

Cobbs, John L. "George Moses Horton's *Hope of Liberty*: Thematic Unity in Early American Black Poetry." *College Language Association Journal* 24.4 (June 1981): 441–50.

Farrison, W. Edward. "George Moses Horton: Poet for Freedom." *College Language Association Journal* 14 (March 1971): 227–41.

Jackson, Blyden. "George Moses Horton: North Carolinian." *North Carolina Historical Review* 53 (1976): 140–47.

Loggins, Vernon. *The Negro Author in America*. New York: Columbia University Press, 1931.

O'Neale, Sondra. "Roots of Our Literary Culture: George Moses Horton and Biblical Protest." *Obsidian* 7.2–3 (Summer/Winter 1981): 18–28.

Redding, J. Saunders. *To Make a Poet Black*. Chapel Hill: University of North Carolina Press, 1939.

Richmond, Merle. *Bid the Vassal Soar: Interpretive Essays on the Life and Poetry of Phillis Wheatley and George Moses Horton*. Washington, D.C.: Howard University Press, 1974.

Sherman, Joan R., ed. *The Black Bard of North Carolina: George Moses Horton and His Poetry*. Chapel Hill: University of North Carolina Press, 1997.

———. "Horton, George Moses." In *Oxford Companion to African American Literature*. Ed. William L. Andrews, Frances Smith Foster, and Trudier Harris. New York: Oxford University Press, 1997. 367–68.

———. *Invisible Poets of the Nineteenth Century*. Urbana: University of Illinois Press, 1974.

Walser, Richard. *The Black Poet; being the Remarkable Story of George Moses Horton*. New York: Philosophical Library, 1966.

Weeks, Stephen B. "George Moses Horton: Slave Poet." *The Southern Workman* (October 1914): 571–77.

Whitlow, Roger. *Black American Literature: A Critical History*. Chicago: Nelson Hall, 1973.

JAMES H. W. HOWARD
(1856–?)

Ronald A. Tyson

BIOGRAPHY

There is little biographical information available on James H. W. Howard. According to I. Garland Penn, he was born in 1856 in Hamilton, Pennsylvania, and educated in Buffalo, New York. An artist's drawing opposite the title page of *Bond and Free* (1886), his only known novel to be published in book form, depicts Howard as a man of African descent. The Preface, signed by "the author," and numerous narrative intrusions throughout the novel are intended to inform readers that Howard is of African descent.

The title page of *Bond and Free* identifies Howard as "Late Editor of the State Journal." The *State Journal*, an African American newspaper, was published in Harrisburg, Pennsylvania between 1883 and 1886 as a continuation of the *Home Journal*, which was published from 1881 to 1883; Penn cites Howard as editor of both publications. He was publisher and editor of *Howard's Negro American Magazine*, a monthly effort that published under various titles in Harrisburg from 1889 to 1901. Blyden Jackson notes that *Howard's Negro American Magazine* serialized another novel by Howard, *The Color Struggles*, from 1889 to 1890, but he doubts that it was ever published in book form; the Library of Congress has no records suggesting that *The Color Struggles* was published in book form.

MAJOR WORK AND THEMES

Bond and Free is the romantic tale of the successful escape to Canada of an enslaved family, Purcey and William McCullar and their young son.

The Preface states, "The incidents related are true, while the adventures of the fugitives . . . are actual facts related by persons well known to me, some of them closely related, and for whose veracity I can safely vouch." This act of literary "authentication" places Howard's novel among the nineteenth-century texts published by African American and European American authors in which personal experiences (either enslavement or association with individuals who had been enslaved), published slave narratives, and newspaper and magazine accounts related to the "peculiar institution" formed the "true" foundations for works of fiction. Harriet Beecher Stowe's *Uncle Tom's Cabin*, Frederick Douglass'* *The Heroic Slave*, and William Wells Brown's* *Clotel; or The President's Daughter*—among other novels—are the predecessors of Howard's effort in this genre, which has modern incarnations in Sherley Anne Williams' *Dessa Rose*, Toni Morrison's *Beloved*, and David Bradley's *The Chaneysville Incident*.

Among other sources, Howard's novel draws from William Craft's *Running a Thousand Miles for Freedom; or, The Escape of William and Ellen Craft from Slavery* (London: William Tweedie, 1860) in its representation of Purcey's escape. Purcey, the daughter of a plantation owner and an enslaved woman, uses subterfuge to travel by public conveyances from Virginia to New York, where she is met by "conductors" of the Underground Railroad and ferried across Lake Erie into Canada. William's escape parallels several recorded incidents of slave rebellions, most notably, the 1829 revolt among the men and women in a coffle of slaves being driven into the Deep South that David Walker* cites in his "Appeal" and that partly inspired *Dessa Rose*.

More than a critique of slavery and—by way of its efforts to refute the pseudoscientific underpinnings of "race" theory—a critique of the post-Reconstruction racial status quo, *Bond and Free* is a refutation of antebellum proslavery fiction and the emerging "plantation" fiction of the 1880s, as well as a response to the sympathetic, but flawed, representations of African Americans in the work of European American novelists such as Stowe, Richard Hildreth, Lydia Maria Child, George Washington Cable, Mark Twain, and Rebecca Harding Davis. Perhaps most notable in this regard is the novel's representation of Purcey's mother, Elva. Howard uses the recorded experiences of Harriet Tubman and Sojourner Truth,* among other African American women, to give Elva—who is beaten to death by a sadistic overseer but keeps her lips sealed regarding Purcey's escape—the noble characteristics assigned to Tom in Stowe's novel.

Considering the nineteenth-century characterizations of African American women as lascivious, nonmaternal, and unfeminine, Howard's representations of Purcey, Elva, and other African American women are significant. Mother and daughter are metonymic representations of the "bond and free" women who resisted the objectifying forces of their day. Elva, as "subject," encourages and facilitates Purcey's escape, as well as the escapes of two of her other children. Purcey masterminds her own escape and—when faced with capture—defends herself and her young son with deadly force. In addition to these literary heroines, there is Judah, who escapes from the slave coffle with William, urges him on when his resolve falters, and takes her fate into her own hands by confronting the slave trader who is driving the coffle to ensure that he cannot pursue the escapees. When viewed as three parts of a whole, the characterizations of Elva, Purcey, and Judah serve to subvert the conventions of nineteenth-century literature that linked "femininity" with helplessness.

The central theme of *Bond and Free* is the gentility that enslaved men and women were able to maintain, despite the corrupting effects of their enslavement. As is noted by Dickson D. Bruce Jr., the application of Victorian ideals of proper attitudes and behaviors to depictions of African American men and women in the late nineteenth century "served not only as a standard for the positive portrayal of black heroism and black aspirations but also as a way of denouncing white oppression" (29). This narrative strategy juxtaposes idealized representations of African American men and women as quintessential Victorian "ladies" and "gentlemen" with those of the corruption and depravity of those European Americans who, through their active support of, or accommodation to, the slave system, are everything but model citizens.

The courtship of William and Purcey, for instance, is in keeping with nineteenth-century literary norms for proper conduct for a man and a woman. This representation gives enslaved men and women the same Christian virtues that were assigned to "moral" white men and women in Victorian fiction and counters the literary and historical discourses that represented enslaved men and women—and their free sisters and brothers—as incapable of refined expressions of love and devotion. Purcey's fight to keep herself "pure" prior to her marriage to William and to retain her virtue despite numerous attempts by profligate white men to compromise her honor casts her from the same mold from which such white literary heroines as Pamela Andrews emerged. Moreover, William's odyssey as he travels through the United States en route to freedom and his travels from town to town in Canada in search of his wife and son represent him as an ideal husband and father.

CRITICAL RECEPTION

Bond and Free has received minimal critical attention. Recent scholarship has generated new interest in the fiction produced by African American women in the late Victorian era, and there is a growing body of critical analyses of these texts. The work of Howard and other lesser-known African American male writers from this period has not received similar consideration. The historicism and the materialist base of contemporary African American feminist criticism provide appropriate analytic tools, and the renewed academic interest in nineteenth-century African American arts and letters presents the probability that this oversight will be remedied.

Prior to the 1969 reprint of *Bond and Free* by Mnemosyne (Miami), the only edition of the novel available was the 1886 printing. In December of that year, a review appeared in *The Conservator*, an African American newspaper published in Chicago. Almost three decades later, in an article entitled "Some Books by Negro Authors," published in *The Freeman*, an African American newspaper published in Indianapolis, Charles Alexander lists *Bond and Free* among other novels authored by African Americans in the late nineteenth and early twentieth centuries that he says present "interesting views" but doubts will be remembered "after this present generation has passed away."

Recent criticism of *Bond and Free* has been divided with regard to the representations in the novel. Arlene A. Elder notes the struggles that late nineteenth-century African American writers had with the racial zeitgeist and writes that several aspects of *Bond and Free* do "nothing to calm the widespread fear of miscegenation fanned by pro-slavery writers" (18). She is troubled by the narrator's assertion that one of the things that made Purcey attractive to William had to do with the "open secret which existed in the accursed days of slavery, and which exists among the race today. That secret is, that a real black man is generally extremely partial to very light women" (17). Elder also cites the narrative's attribution of Elva's "remarkable" intelligence to the "admixture of Indian and Anglo-Saxon blood in her veins" and the narrator's observation that "making such an admission as this strengthens a theory which was quite prevalent in the days of slavery . . . that a Negro is incapable of any deep thought" (Howard 40) to argue that "Howard's conclusion about this racial theory of intelligence remains ambiguous" (Elder 18).

Elder notes that many of the satiric elements in late nineteenth-century African American fiction, such as Howard's use of cattle in *Bond and Free* as a metaphor to represent the commodified status of enslaved women and men, are significant departures from the ways in which satire generally was employed in the work of European American novelists. She argues that while "popular fiction refrained, for the most part, from any sardonic view of American life," and satire in these texts "was generally directed against the foibles and egoism found in individuals, rather than against those same qualities in the social structure," African American novelists continued the slave narratives' "condemnation of an entire political and religious system" through satire (46).

Blyden Jackson does not perceive any "protest" in the novel and argues that it is not much more than "escapist reminiscence" (391), with little relevance to the realities of African Americans at the time of its publication. Referring to *Bond and Free*'s representation of Canada as a haven for escaped slaves, Jackson says that "Canada symbolizes nothing, no call to present or future action" (391).

Bernard W. Bell places *Bond and Free* in the antiplantation tradition. He interprets Howard's affirmation of the truth of the incidents related in the novel and the statement in the novel's Preface—"In commenting upon the cruelties of slavery, I have endeavored to suppress all rancorous feeling which would naturally arise in the bosom of one so closely identified with the race" [Howard 3]— as a "literary adaptation of the pseudo-apology introduced into black oratory by Frederick Douglass" (Bell 56–57).

Although he characterizes *Bond and Free* as "little more than an abolitionist novel published after the Civil War," Dickson D. Bruce Jr. writes favorably of its contrasts between the gentility of its major black characters and venality of its significant white characters. According to Bruce, Howard's use of "motifs connected with the ideals of gentility . . . provided an important background of feelings and ideals to underlie his more specific charges of racial injustice" (30). This background, Bruce writes, "tied his protest in with significant concerns in American culture as a whole as well as with dominant aspirations among middle-class black Americans" (30).

In Bruce's view, the use of genteel motifs by Howard and other nineteenth-century African American authors "also allowed them to approach American history and society with a touch of irony," because "White America . . . in its quest to keep blacks in an inferior position, had made itself inferior to black America" (30). He cites representations in *Bond and Free* to argue that Howard sought to highlight the point that white claims that blacks are incapable of "independent virtue and thus must be controlled" are belied by the fact that "[t]he system of control they created . . . so brutalized the white men that they lost the very virtues they claimed to defend" (30–31).

BIBLIOGRAPHY

Works by James H. W. Howard

Novels

Bond and Free: A True Tale of Slave Times. 1886. Miami: Mnemosyne, 1969.
The Color Struggles. Serialized in *Howard's Negro American Magazine* (1889–1890).

Studies of James H. W. Howard

Alexander, Charles. "Some Books by Negro Authors." *The Freeman: An Illustrated Colored Newspaper*, December 27, 1913, 2.
Bell, Bernard W. *The Afro-American Novel and Its Tradition*. Amherst: University of Massachusetts Press, 1987.
Bruce, Dickson D., Jr. *Black American Writing from the Nadir: The Evolution of a Tradition 1877–1915*. Baton Rouge: Louisiana State University Press, 1989.
Elder, Arlene A. *The Hindered Hand: Cultural Implications of Early African-American Fiction*. Westport, CT. Greenwood, 1978.
Jackson, Blyden. *A History of Afro-American Literature*. Vol. 1: *The Long Beginning, 1746–1895*. Baton Rouge: Louisiana State University Press, 1989.
Penn, I. Garland. *The Afro-American Press and Its Editors*. New York: Arno-New York Times, 1969.

LANGSTON HUGHES
(1902–1967)

Emmanuel S. Nelson

BIOGRAPHY

Langston Hughes was born on February 1, 1902, in Joplin, Missouri; he died in his sleep at a New York City hospital on May 22, 1967. During those sixty-five years he led one of the most eventful literary lives of the twentieth century. An exceptionally prolific writer, he was a poet, short story writer, librettist, playwright, novelist, autobiographer, translator, anthologist, essayist, and critic; he published dozens of books and hundreds of essays and reviews. Often called the "Dean of Black Letters," he remains one of the most influential and innovative writers of the twentieth century.

Hughes' early life was an unstable and troubled one. His father, James Nathaniel Hughes, left the family when Langston was an infant; a lawyer by training, James Hughes settled permanently in Mexico. Young Langston was largely raised by his mother and maternal grandmother. His mother moved from place to place, often in search of suitable employment, until she settled down in Cleveland, Ohio, for a few years. In 1920 Hughes graduated from Cleveland's Central High School, where he was a popular and impressive student.

In the fall of 1921 Hughes—after spending several unhappy months in Mexico with his father—entered Columbia University in New York City. He left after a year there, became a merchant seaman, and traveled to Europe and Africa. When he returned to the United States in 1924, he spent a year with his mother, who was living in Washington, D.C., at that time. Supporting himself by doing a variety of menial jobs, Hughes began to write seriously and was successful in publishing a number of poems in African American periodicals, such as *Crisis* and *Opportunity*. By the time he enrolled at Lincoln University in Pennsylvania in 1926, he was already the author of a published volume of poetry, *The Weary*

Blues. An elderly white woman, Charlotte Mason, became his benefactor in 1927; she offered moral and material support but insisted that he should emphasize in his creative work what she considered the "primitive" elements in African American culture. The professional relationship between the two ended on a bitter note in 1929—the year Hughes graduated from Lincoln University.

By the 1930s Hughes had become a reasonably established writer, and he began to publish prodigiously. He traveled all over the world. Like many American intellectuals of the time, Hughes was drawn to leftist political beliefs, which began to inform his art as well as his public speeches. His articulate criticism of racism and other maladies that he found endemic in capitalist societies began to generate controversy; eventually, in the early 1950s, his politics landed him in front of Senator Joseph McCarthy and the infamous House Committee on Un-American Activities. However, though the careers of many American artists were destroyed by McCarthy's anticommunist hysteria, Hughes' career remained largely undamaged.

While Hughes' prolificity was uncompromised by the controversy, he began to lose his preeminent position in the American literary scene by the mid-1950s. The dramatic emergence of other African American writers, such as Ralph Ellison and James Baldwin, meant that Hughes had to share the spotlight. The militant black voices of the 1960s made Hughes sound rather old-fashioned and not entirely in tune with the mood of black America. Yet he remained, until his death, one of the most respected African American writers of his generation, with a large and loyal audience both at home and abroad. The impressive body of work that he left behind has assured him a central place in the African American literary tradition.

Although there is consensus regarding Hughes' significance as an artist, the subject of his sexuality continues to remain a contested territory. There is overwhelming circumstantial and anecdotal evidence that Hughes, who never married or forged any significant relationship with women, was primarily homosexual in his orientation. Faith Berry, a superior biographer of Hughes, concludes that he was gay. Gregory Woods, in his encyclopedic *A History of Gay Literature*, finds in Hughes' poetry plenty of subtle evidence that points to Hughes' homosexual leanings. Isaac Julien's film *Looking for Langston* is based on the premise that Hughes, like many other writers of the Harlem Renaissance, was gay. In Claude Summers' *Gay and Lesbian Literary Heritage*, Hughes is counted as a gay writer. In fact, many African American gay activists have appropriated Hughes as a gay icon.

However, there is considerable resistance to such appropriation, and the opposition comes largely from the executors of Hughes' estate. They are determined to safeguard Hughes' privacy. Some opposition comes also from African American scholars who are uncomfortable with the subject of Hughes' sexuality. Arnold Rampersad, for example, concludes in his two-volume biography of Hughes that the legendary artist was not gay. His refusal to read the evidence dispassionately has elicited charges of homophobia. Charles I. Nero's article on Rampersad's biography is a brilliant analysis of Rampersad's determination to heterosexualize Hughes.

Other scholars who share Rampersad's views on the subject resort to curious strategies. R. Baxter Miller, for example, states in his biocritical essay that Hughes once "dated a seventeen-year-old black woman" who inspired him to write the poem "When She Wears Red." Miller goes on to add that this was "the first of many poems in which Hughes would celebrate the beauty of black women" ("Langston Hughes" 116). These comments seem carefully crafted and deliberately planted to counter the widespread perception that Hughes was gay. But Miller's tactic is unconvincing: he appears unaware that friendships between gay men and straight women are commonplace and that male heterosexuality is not a prerequisite to thematize female beauty. Catherine Daniels Hurst employs a tactic similar to Miller's: in her article on Hughes, she casually mentions that early in 1924, while living in Paris, Hughes fell in love "with a wealthy Nigerian girl" and that they even "planned to elope" to Italy and get married (317). Even if this information is correct, it does not prove conclusively that Hughes was straight: it was not uncommon for young gay men during those times to attempt relationships with women in a desperate effort at "normalcy." The fact that Hughes did not marry that Nigerian woman—or any other woman, for that matter—might be more significant than the appearance that he was in love with her. Indeed, Hughes' isolated connections with young women during his youth prove nothing; his life has to be viewed in its entirety before any conclusions can be drawn.

As scholars and students of Langston Hughes' work become increasingly more comfortable with examining his art in the context of his sexuality, substantial reassessments of his life and work are inevitable.

MAJOR WORKS AND THEMES

Perhaps the best way to understand Langston Hughes—the man and his art—is to begin with his two substantial autobiographies: *The Big Sea* and *I Wonder As I Wander*. The *Big Sea*, published in 1940, chronicles the first twenty-seven years of his life. Hughes speaks extensively about his impoverished childhood; his troubled relationship with his father; his university years both at Columbia and at Lincoln; his travels to Mexico, Europe, and Africa; and finally the Harlem Renaissance—an artistic movement that he himself helped energize. But *The Big Sea* is more than a mere recollection of his youthful years and picaresque adventures. At least in part, *The Big Sea* is a *Künstlerroman*: it offers a fascinating portrait of the artist as a young man. Here Hughes maps the evolution of his artistic consciousness. The second autobiography, *I Wonder As I Wander*, published in 1956, charts Hughes' life in the 1930s. Here again Hughes is on the road. He travels through the South, speaking at churches and on college campuses. He visits the Caribbean. Then he travels to Europe, Central Asia, China, Japan, and Hawaii before arriving in California. Later he travels to Spain as a journalist to report on the Spanish civil war. Full of fascinating anecdotes, the book is a testimony to Hughes' irrepressible curiosity about other peoples and cultures and his ability to interpret and record his experiences in an engaging and unpretentious style.

These two autobiographies are particularly useful in the context of the debate over Hughes' sexuality. The two texts cover the first forty years of his life. In both books he very briefly mentions women he met, both in the United States and abroad, who fell in love with him. There is no need to suspect that these occasional moments are necessarily fabrications: Hughes was a strikingly good-looking young man; his appearance, as well as his intellect, no doubt made him appealing to many women. But what is intriguing is the fact that none of these women seem to interest him for any significant period of time. They surface briefly in his narratives and then vanish; they leave no lasting imprints. He recalls none of them frequently or with desire and longing.

The sexual silences that characterize both autobiographies can indeed be read as textual markers of Hughes' unconventional sexuality. A very public man with a large circle of friends, Hughes paradoxically remained an intensely private—and lonely—man throughout his life. When read carefully, the two autobiographies reveal Hughes' weary solitude. While we as readers accompany him on his cross-continental sojourns, we learn very little about his inner life. He remains an enigma. His resolute sexual silences, one may argue, are part of Hughes' carefully orchestrated rhetorical strategy. In other words, in both narratives Hughes plays an elaborate rhetorical game: he stages a simultaneous drama of revelation and concealment. His refusal to acknowledge intimate emotional ties and his fleeting references to women are a coded way of speaking the unspeakable. Through the obfuscatory strategies of artful silences and careful distortions, he reveals what he conceals. This game he plays, however, is not unique; in fact, it is a pervasive feature of gay autobiographies until recent times. There are other clues as well. Hughes' fascination with the all-male environment of merchant ships on which he spent extended periods of time—despite poor pay and dreadful working conditions—raises interesting questions. His obsessive travels to exotic locations, another stock characteristic of gay male autobiographies, again link Hughes' books to the autobiographical tradition in gay male writing.

In addition to being an autobiographer, Hughes was the author of over a dozen plays, and he was one of the first African American playwrights to have his work staged on Broadway. Though none of his dramatic works gained the status of a modern classic—like Lorraine Hansberry's enduring A Raisin in the Sun, for example—Hughes' contribution to the American theater was not inconsequential. He helped found all-black theater companies in New York City as well as in Cleveland. Some of his works, despite mixed reviews, were commercial successes. Moreover, his plays helped counter the stereotypical portrayals of black characters that were the norm in the overwhelmingly white-oriented American theater during the first half of the twentieth century.

Hughes' dramatic works deal with a variety of themes. Emperor of Haiti, for example, reflects his interest in the history of the African diaspora: it focuses on the extraordinary life of Jean Jacques Dessalines, a Haitian slave who became an emperor. *Tambourines to Glory*, a play about two women who start a church to earn a living, testifies to Hughes' lifelong skepticism toward institutionalized religion. His left-wing views find expression in *Blood on the Fields*. The play offers a sharp commentary on how racial divisions and animosities among poor white and black laborers render all of them vulnerable to exploitation by wealthy white employers. In *Mother and Child*, Hughes explores one of his frequent themes: sexual connections across racial boundaries that often lead to tragedy in a violently racist culture.

This subject of cross-racial love is central to *Mulatto*, one of Hughes' best-known plays. The plot pivots on the relationships among three major characters: Cora, a black woman; Colonel Norwood, a white man involved in a sexual relationship with Cora; and Bert, their son. Norwood's rejection of his biracial son allows Hughes to expose the "blood" connections between many white and black southerners as well as the pathological hypocrisy of those whites who refuse to acknowledge the kinship. Its violence and melodrama notwithstanding, *Mulatto* remains one of the most compelling dramatic works by Hughes.

Equally memorable are *Don't You Want to Be Free?* and *Scottsboro Limited*. The first work maps African American history from slavery to the first few decades of the twentieth century. Many historical figures, such as Nat Turner, Harriet Tubman, and Sojourner Truth,* make their appearance. The content of the play reveals Hughes' deep interest in the recuperation and reenactment of enabling moments in African American history. More overtly confrontational is Hughes' *Scottsboro Limited*. An experimental drama that blends theatrical elements with agitprop poetry, it examines one of the most obscene moments in American legal history: the trial of nine young black men falsely accused of raping two white female prostitutes—a trial that provoked international outrage in 1931.

Though Hughes' dramatic works continue to elicit some scholarly interest, there is little popular interest in them. Few of his plays are now produced commercially. His fiction, however, has had a more lasting impact. Some of his short stories continue to be widely anthologized; his novel *Not without Laughter* is taught not infrequently on American campuses. Some of Hughes' best stories appear in his 1934 collection *The Ways of White Folks*. Often his stories tend to be very short. Hughes is less concerned about developing an elaborate plot and more interested in capturing a particular moment that reveals a larger truth. The tone is often informal, even folksy: many of his fictional narratives retain an "oral" quality. James A. Emanuel identifies in Hughes' fiction about "forty-odd distinct themes." He points out that Hughes' "main theme is racial prejudice; his much less intense thematic purposes are to present usually delinquent fathers, affection-seeking women, interracial love, the faddish misconception of Negroes by whites, religion and morality, the life of the artist, and jealousy" (148). Indeed, the subject of race is at the center of many of Hughes' stories. "Home," a particularly powerful piece, is about an African American musician who returns to his home in the American heartland after a successful career in Europe. He is lynched by a savage white mob for tipping his hat to a white woman, his former music teacher. Here Hughes, like Richard Wright,* William Faulkner, James Baldwin, and other American writers, sees a profound connection between racist hysteria and white male sexual paranoia. "Passing," a poignant tale told in epistolary form, is about racial passing. A young African American male who passes for white writes a painfully apologetic letter to his mother explaining why he ignored her on the street: acknowledging his mother could unravel his racial masquerade.

"Blues I'm Playing" is a story with autobiographical echoes. It examines the relationship between a young black female pianist and an elderly white woman who positions herself as her benefactor—a relationship that is strikingly similar to Hughes' own three-year friendship with Charlotte Osgood. The relationship fails when the benefactor places unreasonable demands on the pianist's creativity. The story is about cultural appropriation, but it is also an insightful commentary on how disparity in power can corrupt human relationships. Disparate power relationships are the subject of "Good Job Gone" and "Red-Headed Baby." Both stories are about sex between black women and white men. There is little love here, but there is plenty of pathology. In "Father and Son," a story that has received considerable critical attention, Hughes returns to the theme of interracial sexual connections. It is the story of a middle-aged white man who refuses to claim his biracial son. This theme of the tragic mulatto surfaces often in Hughes' work, but without the sentimentality with which it is sometimes handled by African American authors. Hughes, rather than exploit his biracial characters for pathos, presents them as telling embodiments of the secret connections between blacks and whites and as insistent personifications of the unacknowledged kinships that result from such furtive sexual alliances.

Beginning in 1942, Hughes began to write a regular column in the African American newspaper *Chicago Defender*. Within months his journalistic pieces began to read more like short narratives about a fictional character named Jesse B. Simple. Eventually, they began to take on all the qualities of full-fledged short stories. Called Simple stories, these narratives center around Jesse B. Simple, a working-class African American male who comments on a variety of personal and social issues with humor and an abundance of common sense. The columns became so popular that Hughes eventually published them as volumes of short stories. Eventually, *Simply Heavenly*—a play based on the Simple stories—was produced on Broadway.

Hughes published his novel *Not without Laughter* in 1930. The setting is Kansas. The plot focuses on six characters: an elderly black woman (Aunt Hager); her three adult daughters (Anjee, Harriet, Tempy); Anjee's husband (Jimboy); and the young son of Anjee and Jimboy (Sandy). The characters, on the surface, appear simple, but Hughes reveals their complex inner lives. He focuses on a variety of sharp conflicts: between blacks and whites, between older and younger blacks, between traditional faith and emerging secularism; between the desire for social respectability and the need for personal authenticity. The lives that Hughes portrays are difficult ones, but there is plenty of music, dancing, and joy. As the title declares, the lives of his characters may often be painful, but they are "not without laughter."

Many of the themes that Hughes deals with in his fiction surface in his poetry as well. Like his stories, his poems are deceptively simple; close readings, however, reveal considerable narrative and technical sophistication. Perhaps his greatest achievement as a poet is his seamless integration of certain Anglo-American poetic conventions and African American folk traditions. His poetry certainly shows the influence of Walt Whitman, Carl Sandburg, Amy Lowell, and other American poets he deeply admired. Yet his work also shows his indebtedness to black poets, such as Paul Laurence Dunbar,* James Weldon Johnson,* and Jean Toomer,* among others. However, Hughes' poetic voice is a distinct and singularly graceful one. He was the first American writer to integrate successfully into his poetry a variety of African American folk elements: the blue notes and the jazz idiom; the diction of folk speech and the wisdom of folkways; the simple eloquence of the spiritual and the grand cadences of the gospel music. In his first collection of poetry, *The Weary Blues*, Hughes demonstrates his sleek mastery of the blues as well as the ballad. *Ask Your Mama* contains some of his best jazz poems, although Hughes' poetry in general from the 1920s through the 1960s reflects the crucial changes in jazz music itself—from ragtime to bebop. *The Panther and the Lash*, one of his last books, shows his increasing preference for free verse, but even here the techniques of jazz—such as riffs, breaks, use of scat words, and synthesis—inevitably surface. A folk poet who celebrates the ordinary people, Hughes manages to find in the lives of plain folks an occasion for high art.

CRITICAL RECEPTION

An invaluable source for readers curious about the reception that Hughes' works have received from his contemporaries is Tish Dace's monumental *Langston Hughes: The Contemporary Reviews*. This volume includes not only reviews by eminent scholars in major periodicals but also reviews by anonymous critics in obscure newspapers. Dace's own superb introductory essay offers a judicious assessment of how Hughes' contemporaries responded to his work. In addition to helping us understand Hughes' place in American letters, Dace's volume offers valuable insights into the complex politics of literary reception.

Another indispensable tool for scholars interested in critical material on Hughes is *The Langston Hughes Review*. The official publication of the Langston Hughes Society, this periodical has served as a venue for some of the liveliest articles on Hughes since 1982.

In addition to these sources, there are over a dozen books, two dozen doctoral dissertations, and even more journal articles on Hughes' life and work. There are two fine biographies of Hughes: one by Faith Berry and the other, more recent, by Arnold Rampersad. Donna Akiba Sullivan Harper's *Not So Simple* is a comprehensive critical introduction to Hughes' Simple stories.

The reception granted Hughes' work, in general, is quite favorable. Although the books he published during the 1920s and 1930s received hostile responses from some black reviewers who were offended and embarrassed by Hughes' unapologetic celebration of working-class black life, more recent assessments of Hughes' work tend to be mostly laudatory.

Though Hughes' dramatic works have not elicited much critical attention, his autobiographies have generated a good deal of interest. Because Hughes effectively captures the tenor of his times in his autobiographical narratives, they have substantial historiographic value as well. His fiction continues to draw scholarly interest, but it is his poetry that has assured him a lasting place in the history of American literature. He is likely to be remembered largely for being, in the words of R. Baxter Miller, "one of Black America's greatest lyricists" ("Some Mark to Make" 154).

BIBLIOGRAPHY

Selected Works by Langston Hughes

Poetry

The Weary Blues. New York: Knopf, 1926.
Fine Clothes to the Jew. New York: Knopf, 1927.
The Dream Keeper and Other Poems. New York: Knopf, 1932.
Shakespeare in Harlem. New York: Knopf, 1942.
Fields of Wonder. New York: Knopf, 1947.
Montage of a Dream Deferred. New York: Holt, 1951.
Ask Your Mama. New York: Knopf, 1961.
The Panther and the Lash. New York: Knopf, 1967.

Drama

Five Plays by Langston Hughes: Tambourines to Glory, Soul Gone Home, Little Harm, Mulatto, Simply Heavenly. Ed. Webster Smalley. Bloomington: Indiana University Press, 1963.
(Other plays by Hughes are available only in manuscript form at the Beinecke Library at Yale.)

Fiction

Not without Laughter. New York: Knopf, 1930.
The Ways of White Folks. New York: Knopf, 1934.
Simple Speaks His Mind. New York: Simon and Schuster, 1950.
Simple Takes a Wife. New York: Simon and Schuster, 1954.
Simple Stakes a Claim. New York: Rinehart, 1957.
The Best of Simple. New York: Hill and Wang, 1961.

Autobiographies

The Big Sea. New York: Knopf, 1940.
I Wonder As I Wander. New York: Rinehart, 1956.

Selected Studies of Langston Hughes

Barksdale, Richard. *Langston Hughes: The Poet and His Critics*. Chicago: American Library Association, 1977.

Berry, Faith. *Langston Hughes: Before and Beyond Harlem*. Westport, CT: Lawrence Hill, 1983.

Bloom, Harold, ed. *Modern Critical Views: Langston Hughes*. New York: Chelsea House, 1989.

Bordon, Anne. "Heroic 'Hussies' and 'Brilliant Queers': Genderracial Resistance in the Works of Langston Hughes." *African American Review* 28.3 (1994): 333–42.

Dace, Tish. *Langston Hughes: The Contemporary Reviews*. New York: Cambridge University Press, 1997.

Emanuel, James. "The Short Fiction of Langston Hughes." In O'Daniel, 145–56.

Gates, Henry Louis, Jr., and K. Anthony Appiah. *Langston Hughes: Critical Perspectives Past and Present*. New York: Amistad, 1993.

Harper, Donna Akiba Sullivan. *Not So Simple*. Columbia: University of Missouri Press, 1995.

Hudson, Theodore R. "Technical Aspects of the Poetry of Langston Hughes." *Black World* (September 1973): 24–45.

Hurst, Catherine Daniels. "Langston Hughes." In *Dictionary of Literary Biography*. Vol. 7, Part I. Detroit: Gale Research, 1981.

Looking for Langston. Writ.-Dir. Isaac Julien. London: Sankofa Film and Video. 1989.

McLaren, Joseph. *Langston Hughes: Folk Dramatist in the Protest Tradition, 1921–1943*. Westport, CT: Greenwood Press, 1997.

Mikolyzk, Thomas. *Langston Hughes: A Bio-Bibliography*. Westport, CT: Greenwood Press, 1990.

Miller, R. Baxter. *The Art and Imagination of Langston Hughes*. Lexington: University Press of Kentucky, 1989.

———. " 'For a Moment I Wondered': Theory and Symbolic Form in the Autobiographies of Langston Hughes." *The Langston Hughes Review* 3.2 (Fall 1984): 1–6.

———. "Langston Hughes." In *Dictionary of Literary Biography*. Vol. 51. Detroit: Gale Research, 1987.

———. " 'Some Mark to Make': The Lyrical Imagination of Langston Hughes." In Mullen, 154–66.

Mullen, Edward J. *Critical Essays on Langston Hughes*. Boston: G. K. Hall, 1986.

Nero, Charles I. "Re/membering Langston: Homophobic Textuality and Arnold Rampersad's *The Life of Langston Hughes*." In *Queer Representations*. Ed. Martin Duberman. New York: New York University Press, 1997. 188–96.

O'Daniel, Therman. *Langston Hughes, Black Genius: A Critical Evaluation*. New York: Morrow, 1971.

Ostrum, Hans. *Langston Hughes: A Study of the Short Fiction*. New York: Twayne, 1993.

Rampersad, Arnold. *The Life of Langston Hughes*. Vol. 1. New York: Oxford University Press, 1986.

————. *The Life of Langston Hughes*. Vol. 2. New York: Oxford University Press, 1988.
Steven, Tracy. *Langston Hughes and the Blues*. Chicago: University of Illinois Press, 1988.
Summers, Claude J., ed. *The Gay and Lesbian Literary Heritage*. New York: Henry Holt, 1995.
Woods, Gregory. *A History of Gay Literature*. New Haven: Yale University Press, 1998.

ZORA NEALE HURSTON
(1891–1960)

Laurie Champion and Bruce A. Glasrud

BIOGRAPHY

Born on January 7, 1891, in Macon County, Alabama, the fifth child of Rev. John Hurston and Lucy Potts Hurston, Zora Neale Hurston was a more prolific writer than any of her African American women predecessors. In 1894 she moved to Eatonville, Florida, the African American community near Orlando that provides the setting for much of her work. After her mother's death in 1904, Hurston attended boarding school in Jacksonville and later moved to various cities, where she performed menial jobs. She graduated from Morgan Academy high school in Baltimore, enrolled at Howard University in Washington, D.C., and matriculated at Barnard College (1925) in New York City, where she studied anthropology under the guidance of anthropologists Franz Boas and Gladys Reichard.

In 1925 Hurston moved to New York City and became one of the most prominent women writers of the Harlem Renaissance. During the 1920s and 1930s she published short stories and essays in African American magazines such as *Opportunity* and *Journal of Negro History*. She coedited the literary magazine *Fire!*, in which her short story "Sweat" appeared, and she collaborated with Langston Hughes* to write the play *Mule Bone*.

Interested in African American folklore, in 1927 (the same year she married her first husband, Herbert Sheen) Hurston returned to the South to conduct fieldwork that consisted of gathering folktales, listening to sermons and songs, and visiting hoodoo doctors to learn their practices. Like many writers of the Harlem Renaissance, Hurston's research partially was funded by a white patron, and the relationship between Hurston and her patron was controversial and problematic. In 1932 their relationship ended, and with her new artistic independence, Hurston turned to theater, writing plays that were performed in New

York, Chicago, and Florida. A Guggenheim Fellowship allowed Hurston in 1936 to research West Indies obeah practices for her collection of African folklore, *Tell My Horse* (1938). In 1934 her first novel, *Jonah's Gourd Vine*, based loosely on her parents' lives, was published, followed by *Their Eyes Were Watching God* (1937) and *Moses, Man of the Mountain* (1939). Hurston received the prestigious Anisfield-Wolf Book Award for her autobiography *Dust Tracks on a Road* in 1942; she appeared on the cover of *Saturday Evening Post* in 1943. Five years later (1948), when her last novel, *Seraph on the Suwanee* appeared, Hurston was indicted for allegedly committing immoral acts with a ten-year-old boy. Although the charges were eventually proven groundless, the incident devastated Hurston and caused her to withdraw from public attention.

Although she never wrote another novel, during the 1950s Hurston published essays in magazines such as *Saturday Evening Post*, *American Legion Magazine*, and *Negro Digest*. In these later essays, Hurston frequently supported conservative views that culminated in her infamous 1954 letter to the *Orlando Sentinel* that condemned the Supreme Court's *Brown* decision that outlawed segregated public schools. She argued that the decision would harm the all-black schools of the South as well as the study of black culture. Hurston became increasingly reclusive for the rest of her life.

With neither meaningful employment nor money to support herself, Hurston's last ten years were spent in obscurity and in poverty. On January 28, 1960, she died in a welfare home in Fort Pierce, Florida, where she is buried in a segregated cemetery. Hurston's grave was unmarked until 1973, when Alice Walker marked the site with a tombstone embellished with the epitaph "A Genius of the South."

MAJOR WORKS AND THEMES

A significant twentieth-century author, Zora Neale Hurston wrote in several genres, including novel, autobiography, folklore, drama, short story, and essay. Both in her depiction of the folk customs of rural African Americans and in her portrayals of various struggles for personal and cultural identity, Hurston celebrates African American culture. While extolling African American culture, she frequently focuses on African American women and reveals their strength, their courage, and their ability to triumph in spite of sometimes devastating situations.

One of Hurston's significant contributions to African American literature is her authentic depiction of rural African Americans. She produced the first collection of African American folklore, *Mules and Men*, which consists of humorous and serious essay-like presentations of conversations, sermons, and jokes that reflect the social customs, religious and spiritual beliefs, and local folklore of the residents of rural Florida and Louisiana. Her award-winning autobiography, *Dust Tracks on a Road*, also reveals extensive African American folklore. Here, Hurston describes the history, culture, and residents of Eatonville, Florida, both indirectly and directly: when she recalls that throughout her childhood she listened to her elders tell stories, their tales provide a subtext wherein folk customs and traditions are revealed indirectly; when she recounts incidents in which she participated, customs and traditions are revealed directly.

Presented against the background of both African American folklore and Christian myth, *Moses, Man of the Mountain* is set in Egypt during the time of Hebrew captivity. An obvious retelling of the biblical story of Moses and the Israelites, the novel also demonstrates the plight of African Americans in the white-dominated United States. Told with tongue-in-cheek humor, the novel portrays folklore and folkways of the Hebrews, while showing how they have been enslaved. One of the strengths of *Moses, Man of the Mountain* is the humor that appears when the subtext that represents the African American slave experience is juxtaposed against the text that concerns Hebrews. Not only is the humor presented on a deeper level because Hurston allows the Hebrew experience to symbolize that of African American slaves, but the analogy created between the text and the subtext also provides a study of slave emancipation from a black viewpoint.

Hurston also presents African American folk customs throughout her short stories, many of which are set in Eatonville. "Eatonville Anthology," originally appearing in three installments in the magazine *Messenger*, consists of fourteen vignettes, each describing a specific character or incident. Many of these characters and incidents become the central subjects of other short stories or novels set in Eatonville. The tales are packed with descriptions of local customs, religious beliefs, folktales, and jokes. Among the portraits of characters in "Eatonville Anthology" are a pleading woman, a compulsive liar, a loner, and a silent woman.

Whereas "Eatonville Anthology" presents sketches of the Eatonville community, "Uncle Monday" and "Black Death" reveal hoodoo practices as an Eatonville custom. The title of "Uncle Monday" refers to a conjure doctor who has mysteriously arisen from water and come to a small village. Among his mystical powers, Uncle Monday can shed and regrow bodily limbs; he also possesses a singing stone, the greatest charm in the world. Hurston's narrator provides many folk customs and beliefs, such as a recipe for retrieving a singing stone from a serpent. In both "Uncle Monday" and "Black Death" women seek conjure doctors to punish men who have jilted their daughters. In "Black Death," the conjure doctor Old Man Morgan casts a spell on Beau Diddeley for refusing to marry Docia. In a scene packed with symbolism, puns, irony, and poetic justice, Beau dies of a heart attack while wooing another woman. Mysteriously, a powder burn appears over his heart.

Whether in novel, autobiography, or short story, Hurston depicts rural African Americans without condescending to the working-class population. She celebrates the social life and religious expression of rural African American communities and shows their hoodoo beliefs, their proverbs, and their children's games. In her characterizations of rural African Americans, Hurston creates strong portrayals of women who defy stereotypes. These women search for a sense of individuality that does not depend on men for definitions. They also overcome obstacles and find success.

Hurston's characterization of women from a feminist perspective is most apparent in the novel *Their Eyes Were Watching God*, her most critically acclaimed work. The novel presents Janie Crawford's quests for romantic love and for both personal and cultural identity. Janie develops from a woman who is denied a sense of self to one who experiences emotional and economic independence and a sense of shared community when she claims her African American heritage. When Janie leaves Logan, she marries Joe Starks and moves to Eatonville, only to realize that her need for economic security compels her to remain his wife, even though he abuses her. Long after Joe dies, Janie becomes romantically involved with the much younger Tea Cake, leaves the financial security of her store and home, and goes to southern Florida to aid migrant farm laborers. After Tea Cake's death, she returns to the security of her home to tell her story and share her experience of having fulfilled her quest for romantic love.

In *Their Eyes Were Watching God*, Hurston weaves Janie's quest for personal fulfillment with her search for identity as an African American. Janie eventually connects with the migrant farmworkers with her ability to tell stories and experiences a spiritual kinship. This sense of belonging to a community provides her with both cultural and self-identity. When she returns to Eatonville after Tea Cake dies, she has the strength and courage to tell her story to Pheoby. Because Pheoby will repeat Janie's story to others, Janie has shared with the entire community the knowledge she has gained about her heritage.

Whereas most of Hurston's work focuses exclusively on African Americans, her last novel, *Seraph on the Suwanee*, concerns the white protagonists Arvay Henson and Jim Meserve. The couple moves from Sawley to Citrabelle, where Jim becomes a successful citrus grower. When Jim leaves Arvay, she returns to Sawley, where she acknowledges her past, discovers self-identity, and comes to appreciate her heritage. After achieving self-respect and dignity and developing spiritual insights, she travels to the coast to find Jim and attempt to save their marriage. Although white, Arvay experiences personal growth in ways similar to Hurston's African American women.

Hurston also reveals strong, independent women in her short stories. For example, "Mother Catherine" depicts a spiritual leader who gives advice to people and who bears both black and white children. Among other mystical powers, Mother Catherine is able to heal the sick. In her depiction of Mother Catherine, Hurston disrupts stereotypes by characterizing an African American woman in a role traditionally attributed to white men. Similarly, Delia, the protagonist of "Sweat," is married to Sykes, who both mentally and physically torments her. Delia develops from a meek victim to one who verbally assaults her victimizer. At the end of the story, after Sykes puts a rattlesnake in the house so it will bite Delia, she does not warn him that it instead may bite him. When the snake bites Sykes, Delia knows that he will die before she has time to drive him to the distant hospital. Instead of feeling pity for her tormenter, Delia is relieved that poetic justice has occurred.

As her works demonstrate, Hurston successfully blends folklore with fiction to celebrate African American culture and heritage. As writer, anthropologist, and folklorist, Hurston is one of the most significant contributors to the appreciation of African American culture. During her lifetime, Hurston was criticized by her cohorts because she did not write in the protest tradition that exposes blatantly the ills of racism. She died a forgotten artist, homeless and penniless; however, fortunately, she is now recognized for her achievements that affirm African American identity.

CRITICAL RECEPTION

As reflected in Richard Wright's* criticism that *Their Eyes Were Watching God* failed to expose situations relevant to the political struggles of African Americans, Hurston's work was not always favorably received. Like many women writers of the first half of the twentieth century, Hurston became a forgotten writer until the 1970s, when the feminist movement prompted the rediscovery of women writers who had been critically neglected. During the 1970s, writers such as Alice Walker and Toni Cade Bambara acknowledged Hurston's influence, Hurston's out-of-print works reappeared, and her hitherto unpublished work was published for the first time. For a superb bibliographical essay that provides an extensive overview of the history of Hurston scholarship, see Daryl Dance's "Zora Neale Hurston."

Recent scholars examine Hurston's work chiefly from cultural and feminist perspectives. Many critics focus on ways Hurston blends anthropological knowledge with literary skills, what is now considered one of Hurston's most important contributions to African American literature. Klaus Benesch's "Oral Narrative and Literary Text: Afro-American Folklore in *Their Eyes Were Watching God*," Ellease Southerland's "The Influence of Voodoo on the Fiction of Zora Neale Hurston," Rachel Stein's "Remembering the Sacred Tree: Black Women, Nature, and Voodoo in Zora Neale Hurston's *Tell My Horse* and *Their Eyes Were Watching God*," and Howard J. Faulkner's "*Mules and Men*: Fiction as Folklore" address various ways Hurston uses folklore to celebrate African American culture.

From feminist perspectives, scholars examine Hurston's women characters and look at the social issues in Hurston's works that concern women. Alice Walker's "In Search of Zora Neale Hurston" notes that Hurston represents African American women who seek a political voice in the areas of race and gender. " 'This Infinity of Conscious Pain': Zora Neale Hurston and the Black Female Literary Tradition," by Lorraine Bethel, points out that throughout her works Hurston disrupts stereotypes of African American women portrayed by white males. Mary O'Connor, in "Zora Neale Hurston and Talking between Cultures," credits Hurston with establishing for women an African American literary tradition wherein talking is a tool used to blend race and gender. Similarly, Missy Dehn Kubitschek's " 'Tuh de Horizon and Back': The Female Quest in *Their Eyes Were Watching God*" suggests that Hurston's characterization of strong and courageous black women inspired future black women writers to depict nonstereotypical black women characters. Mary Helen Washington's " 'I Love the Way Janie Crawford Left Her Husbands': Zora Neale Hurston's Emergent Female Hero" sees Janie as a leader in her community and as a developing hero.

Similarly, Gay Wilentz, in "Defeating the False God: Janie's Self-Determination in Zora Neale Hurston's *Their Eyes Were Watching God*," suggests that Janie is one of the earliest African American women characters to develop cultural and personal identity. Cheryl Wall's "*Mules and Men* and Women: Zora Neale Hurston's Strategies of Narration and Visions of Female Empowerment" views Hurston as anthropologist and suggests ways Hurston's women are empowered. Many scholars examine Hurston as a female autobiographer: James Krasner, "The Life of Women: Zora Neale Hurston and Female Autobiography"; Elizabeth Fox-Genovese, "My Statue, My Self: Autobiographical Writings of Afro-American Women"; Francois Lionnet, "Autoethnography: The An-Archic Style of *Dust Tracks on a Road*"; and Nellie Y. McKay, "Race, Gender, and Cultural Context in Zora Neale Hurston's *Dust Tracks on a Road*."

Hurston's contribution to literary movements such as the Harlem Renaissance and the Southern Renaissance are other areas discussed by scholars. Among studies that examine her contribution to the Harlem Renaissance are Mary V. Dearborn's "Black Women Authors and the Harlem Renaissance," John Lowe's "Hurston, Humor, and the Harlem Renaissance," and Ralph D. Story's "Gender and Ambition: Zora Neale Hurston in the Harlem Renaissance." Jan Cooper, in "Zora Neale Hurston Was Always a Southerner Too," points out that although she should be included in discussions of the Southern Renaissance, Hurston is omitted because of racial bias. Geneva Cobb-Moore's "Zora Neale Hurston as Local Colorist" establishes Hurston as regionalist and local colorist who delineates a distinctive group of people.

Several book-length treatments of Hurston's works deserve mention. Although published in the 1970s, Robert E. Hemenway's *Zora Neale Hurston: A Literary Biography* remains the most insightful study. Another skillful biography is Lillie P. Howard, *Zora Neale Hurston*. A valuable book on Hurston's humor is John Lowe, *Jump at the Sun: Zora Neale Hurston's Cosmic Comedy*. Neither Deborah G. Plant, *Every Tub Must Sit on Its Own Bottom: The Philosophy and Politics of Zora Neale Hurston*, nor Karla Holloway, *The Character of the Word: The Texts of Zora Neale Hurston*, can be ignored. Henry Louis Gates Jr. and K. A. Appiah's *Zora Neale Hurston: Critical Perspectives Past and Present* is the most comprehensive collection of critical essays.

Thanks to the insights of these and other scholars, Hurston is finally gaining long overdue recognition for her achievements as author, folklorist, and anthropologist. As these critics remind us, Hurston's works provide accurate portrayals of rural African American life as well as demonstrating the many strengths of women who struggled to overcome obstacles they encountered while living in a society dominated by white males.

BIBLIOGRAPHY

Works by Zora Neale Hurston

Jonah's Gourd Vine. Philadelphia: Lippincott, 1934. (novel)

Mules and Men. London: Kegan, 1936. (folklore)

Their Eyes Were Watching God. Philadelphia: Lippincott, 1937. (novel)

Tell My Horse. Philadelphia: Lippincott, 1938. (folklore)

Moses, Man of the Mountain. Philadelphia: Lippincott, 1939. (novel)

Dust Tracks on a Road. Philadelphia: Lippincott, 1942. (autobiography)

Seraph on the Suwanee. New York: Scribner's, 1948. (novel)

I Love Myself When I Am Laughing . . . And Then Again When I Am Looking Mean and Impressive: A Zora Neale Hurston Reader. Ed. Alice Walker. Old Westbury, NY: Feminist Press, 1979.

The Sanctified Church: The Folklore Writings of Zora Neale Hurston. Intro. Toni Cade Bambara. Berkeley, CA: Turtle Island, 1981.

Spunk: The Selected Short Stories of Zora Neale Hurston. Berkeley, CA: Turtle Island, 1985.

(With Langston Hughes). *Mule Bone: A Comedy of Negro Life*. New York: HarperCollins, 1991. (play)

The Complete Stories of Zora Neale Hurston. Ed. Henry Louis Gates Jr., and Sieglinde Lemke. New York: Harper, 1995.

Zora Neale Hurston: Folklore, Memoirs and Other Writings. Ed. Cheryl A. Wall. New York: Library of America, 1995.

"Three by Zora Neale Hurston: Story, Essay, and Play." *Southern Quarterly* 36.3 (1998): 94–102.

Studies of Zora Neale Hurston

Awkward, Michael, ed. *New Essays on Their Eyes Were Watching God*. Cambridge: Cambridge University Press, 1990.

Beilke, Debra. " 'Yowin' and Jawin': Humor and the Performance of Identity in Zora Neale Hurston's *Jonah's Gourd Vine*." *Southern Quarterly* 36.3 (1998): 21–33.

Benesch, Klaus. "Oral Narrative and Literary Text: Afro-American Folklore in *Their Eyes Were Watching God*." *Callaloo* 11 (1988): 627–35.

Bethel, Lorraine. " 'This Infinity of Conscious Pain': Zora Neale Hurston and the Black Female Literary Tradition." In *All the Women Are White, All the Blacks Are Men, But Some of Us Are Brave: Black Women's Studies*. Ed. Gloria T. Hull, Patricia Bell Scott, and Barbara Scott. Old Westbury, NY: Feminist Press, 1982. 176–88.

Bloom, Harold, ed. *Zora Neale Hurston: Modern Critical Views*. New York: Chelsea House, 1986.

———. *Zora Neale Hurston's Their Eyes Were Watching God*. New York: Chelsea House, 1987.

Bordelon, Pam. "New Tacks on Dust Tracks: Toward a Reassessment of the Life of Zora Neale Hurston." *African American Review* 31 (1997): 5–21.

Boxwell, D. A. " 'Sis Cat' as Ethnographer: Self-Presentation and Self-Inscription in Zora Neale Hurston's *Mules and Men*." *African American Review* 26 (1992): 605–15.

Brigham, Cathy. "The Talking Frame of Zora Neale Hurston's Talking Book: Storytelling as Dialectic in *Their Eyes Were Watching God.*" *CLA Journal* 37 (1994): 402–18.

Byrd, James W. "Zora Neale Hurston: A Novel Folklorist." *Tennessee Folklore Bulletin* 21 (1955): 37–41.

Caron, Timothy P. " 'Tell Ole Pharaoh to Let My People Go': Communal Deliverance in Zora Neale Hurston's *Moses, Man of the Mountain.*" *Southern Quarterly* 36.3 (1998): 47–60.

Cobb-Moore, Geneva. "Zora Neale Hurston as Local Colorist." *The Southern Literary Journal* 26.2 (1994): 25–34.

Cooper, Jan. "Zora Neale Hurston Was Always a Southerner Too." In *The Female Tradition in Southern Literature.* Ed. Carol S. Manning. Urbana: University of Illinois Press, 1993. 57–69.

Crabtree, Claire. "The Confluence of Folklore, Feminism and Black Self-Determination in Zora Neale Hurston's *Their Eyes Were Watching God.*" *Southern Literary Journal* 17.2 (1985): 54–66.

Crosland, Andrew. "The Text of Zora Neale Hurston: A Caution." *CLA Journal* 37 (1994): 42–44.

Dance, Daryl C. "Zora Neale Hurston." In *American Women Writers: Bibliographical Essays.* Ed. Maurice Duke, Jackson R. Bryer, and M. Thomas Inge. Westport, CT: Greenwood, 1983. 321–51.

Daniel, Janice. " 'De Understandin' to Go 'Long Wid It': Realism and Romance in *Their Eyes Were Watching God.*" *Southern Literary Journal* 24.1 (1991): 66–76.

Davie, Sharon. "Free Mules, Talking Buzzards, and Cracked Plates: The Politics of Dislocation in *Their Eyes Were Watching God.*" *PMLA* 108 (1993): 446–59.

Davies, Kathleen. "Zora Neale Hurston's Poetics of Embalmment: Articulating the Rage of Black Women and Narrative Self-Defense." *African American Review* 26 (1992): 147–59.

Davis, Rose Parkman. *Zora Neale Hurston: An Annotated Bibliography and Reference Guide.* Westport, CT: Greenwood, 1997.

Dearborn, Mary V. "Black Women Authors and the Harlem Renaissance." *Pocahontas' Daughters: Gender and Ethnicity in American Culture.* New York: Oxford University Press, 1986. 61–70.

Dolby-Stahl, Sandra. "Literary Objectives: Hurston's Use of Personal Narrative in *Mules and Men.*" *Western Folklore* 51 (1992): 51–63.

Domina, Lynn. " 'Protection in My Mouf': Self, Voice, and Community in Zora Neale Hurston's *Dust Tracks on a Road* and *Mules and Men.*" *African American Review* 31 (1997): 197–209.

Donlon, Jocelyn Hazelwood. "Porches: Stories: Power: Spatial and Racial Intersections in Faulkner and Hurston." *Journal of American Culture* 19 (1996): 95–110.

Dubek, Laura. "The Social Geography of Race in Hurston's *Seraph on the Suwanee.*" *African American Review* 30 (1996): 341–51.

Faulkner, Howard J. "*Mules and Men*: Fiction as Folklore." *CLA Journal* 34 (1991): 331–39.

Fox-Genovese, Elizabeth. "My Statue, My Self: Autobiographical Writings of Afro-American Women." *Reading Black, Reading Feminist: A Critical Anthology.* Ed. Henry Louis Gates Jr. New York: Meridian, 1990. 176–203.

Gates, Henry Louis, Jr. "Zora Neale Hurston and the Speakerly Text." In *The Signifying*

Monkey: A Theory of Afro-American Literary Criticism. New York: Oxford University Press, 1988: 170–216.

Gates, Henry Louis, Jr., and K. A. Appiah, eds. *Zora Neale Hurston: Critical Perspectives Past and Present*. New York: Amistad, 1993.

Glassman, Steve, and Kathryn Lee Seidel, eds. *Zora in Florida*. Orlando: University of Central Florida Press, 1991.

Harris, Trudier. "Performing Personnel in Southern Hospitality: Zora Neale Hurston in *Mules and Men*." In *The Power of the Porch: The Storyteller's Craft in Zora Neale Hurston, Gloria Naylor, and Randall Kenan*. Athens: University of Georgia Press, 1996. 1–50.

Hemenway, Robert E. *Zora Neale Hurston: A Literary Biography*. Urbana: University of Illinois Press, 1978.

Hill, Lynda Marion. *Social Rituals and the Verbal Art of Zora Neale Hurston*. Washington, DC: Howard University Press, 1996.

Holloway, Karla F. C. *The Character of the Word: The Texts of Zora Neale Hurston*. New York: Greenwood, 1987.

Howard, Lillie P. *Alice Walker and Zora Neale Hurston: The Common Bond*. Westport, CT: Greenwood, 1993.

———. *Zora Neale Hurston*. Boston: Twayne, 1980.

Hubbard, Dolan. " ' . . . Ah said Ah'd Save De Text for You': Recontextualizing the Sermon to Tell (Her) story in Zora Neale Hurston's *Their Eyes Were Watching God*." *African American Review* 27 (1993): 167–78.

Jacobs, Karen. "From 'Spy-Glass' to 'Horizon': Tracking the Anthropological Gaze in Zora Neale Hurston." *Novel* 30 (1997): 329–60.

Johnson, Barbara. "Thresholds of Difference: Structures of Address in Zora Neale Hurston." *Critical Inquiry* 12 (1985): 278–89.

Jordan, Jennifer. "Feminist Fantasies: Zora Neale Hurston's *Their Eyes Were Watching God*." *Tulsa Studies in Women's Literature* 7 (1988): 105–17.

Kalb, John D. "The Anthropological Narrator of Hurston's *Their Eyes Were Watching God*." *Studies in American Fiction* 16 (1988): 169–80.

Knudsen, Janice L. "The Tapestry of Living: A Journey of Self-Discovery in Hurston's *Their Eyes Were Watching God*." *CLA Journal* 40 (1996): 214–29.

Krasner, James N. "The Life of Women: Zora Neale Hurston and Female Autobiography." *Black American Literature Forum* 23 (1989): 113–26.

Kubitschek, Missy Dehn. " 'Tuh De Horizon and Back': The Female Quest in *Their Eyes Were Watching God*." *Black American Literature Forum* 17 (1983): 109–115.

Lionnet, Francois. "Autoethnography: The An-Archic Style of Dust Tracks on a Road." *African American Autobiography*. Ed. William L. Andrews. Englewood Cliffs, NJ: Prentice Hall, 1993, 113–37.

Lowe, John. *Jump at the Sun: Zora Neale Hurston's Cosmic Comedy*. Champaign: University of Illinois Press, 1994.

———. "Hurston, Humor, and the Harlem Renaissance." In *Harlem Renaissance Re-Examined*. Ed. Victor A. Kramer. New York: AMS Press, 1987. 283–313.

McKay, Nellie. "Race, Gender, and Cultural Context in Zora Neale Hurston's *Dust Tracks on a Road*." *Life/Lines: Theorizing Women's Autobiography*. Ed. Bella Brodski and Celeste M. Schenck. Ithaca, NY: Cornell University Press, 1988. 175–88.

Meisenhelder, Susan. "Conflict and Resistance in Zora Neale Hurston's *Mules and Men*." *Journal of American Folklore* 109 (1996): 267–88.

Morris, Robert J. "Zora Neale Hurston's Ambitious Enigma: *Moses, Man of the Mountain.*" *CLA Journal* 40 (1997): 305–35.

Newsom, Adele S. *Zora Neale Hurston: A Reference Guide.* Boston: G. K. Hall, 1987.

O'Connor, Mary. "Zora Neale Hurston and Talking Between Cultures." *Canadian Review of American Studies* 8.2 (1992): 141–61.

Peters, Pearlie M. " 'Ah Got the Law in My Mouth': Black Women and Assertive Voice in Hurston's Fiction and Folklore." *CLA Journal* 37 (1994): 293–302.

Plant, Deborah G. *Every Tub Must Sit on Its Own Bottom: The Philosophy and Politics of Zora Neale Hurston.* Urbana: University of Illinois Press, 1995.

Rayson, Ann. "*Dust Tracks on a Road*: Zora Neale Hurston and the Form of Black Autobiography." *Negro American Literature Forum* 7 (1973): 39–45.

Robey, Judith. "Generic Strategies in Zora Neale Hurston's *Dust Tracks on a Road*." *Black American Literature Forum* 24 (1990): 667–82.

Sheffey, Ruthe T. "Zora Neale Hurston's *Moses, Man of the Mountain*: A Fictionalized Manifesto on the Imperatives of Black Leadership." *CLA Journal* 29 (1985): 206–20.

Sollors, Werner. "Of Mules and Mares in a Land of Difference; Or, Quadrupeds All?" *American Quarterly* 42 (1990): 167–90.

Southerland, Ellease. "The Influence of Voodoo on the Fiction of Zora Neale Hurston." In *Sturdy Black Bridge: Visions of Black Women in Literature.* Ed. Roseann P. Bell, Bettye J. Parker, and Beverly Guy-Sheftall. Garden City, NY: Anchor, 1979. 172–83.

Speisman, Barbara. "From 'Spears' to *The Great Day*: Zora Neale Hurston's Vision of a Real Negro Theater." *Southern Quarterly* 36.3 (1998): 34–46.

St. Clair, Janet. "The Courageous Undertow of Zora Neale Hurston's *Seraph on the Suwanee*." *Modern Language Quarterly* 50 (1989): 38–57.

Stein, Rachel. "Remembering the Sacred Tree: Black Women, Nature, and Voodoo in Zora Neale Hurston's *Tell My Horse* and *Their Eyes Were Watching God*." *Women's Studies* 25 (1996): 465–82.

Story, Ralph D. "Gender and Ambition: Zora Neale Hurston in the Harlem Renaissance." *Black Scholar* 20.3–4 (1989): 25–31.

Thompson, Gordon E. "Projecting Gender: Personification in the Works of Zora Neale Hurston." *American Literature* 66 (1994): 737–63.

Trefzer, Annette. " 'Let Us All Be Kissing-Friends?': Zora Neale Hurston and Race Politics in Dixie." *Journal of American Studies* 31 (1997): 69–78.

Turner, Darwin T. "Zora Neale Hurston: The Wandering Minstrel." In *In a Minor Chord: Three Afro-American Writers and Their Search for Identity.* Carbondale: Southern Illinois University Press, 1971. 89–120.

Vickers, Anita M. "The Reaffirmation of African-American Dignity through the Oral Tradition in Zora Neale Hurston's *Their Eyes Were Watching God*." *CLA Journal* 37 (1994): 303–15.

Wald, Patricia. "Becoming 'Colored': The Self-Authorized Language of Difference in Zora Neale Hurston." *American Literary History* 2.1 (1990): 79–100.

Walker, Alice. "In Search of Zora Neale Hurston." *Ms. Magazine* (March 1975): 74–79, 85–89.

Wall, Cheryl A. "*Mules and Men* and Women: Zora Neale Hurston's Strategies of Narration and Visions of Female Empowerment." *Black American Literature Forum* 23 (1989): 661–80.

————, ed. *"Sweat": Zora Neale Hurston*. New Brunswick, NJ: Rutgers University Press, 1997.

Wallace, Michele. "Who Owns Zora Neale Hurston: Critics Carve Up the Legend." In *Invisibility Blues: From Pop to Theory*. London: Verso, 1990. 172–86.

Washington, Mary Helen. "'I Love the Way Janie Crawford Left Her Husbands': Zora Neale Hurston's Emergent Female Hero." In *Invented Lives: Narratives of Black Women, 1886–1960*. New York: Doubleday, 1987. 237–54.

Werner, Craig. "Zora Neale Hurston." In *Modern American Women Writers*. Ed. Elaine Showalter, Lea Baechler, and A. Walton Litz. New York: Scribner's, 1990. 221–33.

Wilentz, Gay. "Defeating the False God: Janie's Self-Determination in Zora Neale Hurston's *Their Eyes Were Watching God*." In *Faith of a (Woman) Writer*. Eds. Alice Kessler-Harris and William McBrien. Westport, CT: Greenwood Press, 1988. 285–91.

Wright, Richard. "Between Laughter and Tears." *New Masses* (October 1937): 22–25.

REBECCA COX JACKSON
(1795–1871)

Joyce L. Cherry

BIOGRAPHY

Rebecca Cox was born in a small community near Philadelphia on February 15, 1795, to an apparently free African American couple. Many details of her formative years are not known, and she provides few clues about her early life in her autobiographical writing. Her father apparently died when she was yet in her infancy, and Rebecca's early nurturing was provided by her mother, with the support of her grandmother and, eventually, a stepfather. After her mother died, when Rebecca was about thirteen years old, she was apparently taken into the household of her older brother Joseph Cox, a prominent minister in the African Methodist Episcopal Church, who lived in a free black community in Philadelphia. Thus, her formative years were spent in an apparently stable environment where she experienced relative financial and emotional security and spiritual nurture.

She began her autobiographical writings in 1830, when she was about thirty-five years old. In this body of writing, she reveals some insight into the years covering the period of her early adulthood. She refers at points to her marriage to Samuel Jackson, also apparently a free black of the laboring class, and her own activities and responsibilities in her brother's household as housekeeper and caregiver for her brother's children. She also tells of her work as a seamstress, through which she was able to contribute to her own financial support and that of her extended family.

Against this backdrop of relative quiescence in her home life, Jackson reveals further insight into her life through her account of her spiritual conversion and her rise to Shaker eldress and founder of a black Shaker community in Philadelphia. Influenced by the evangelical movement of the 1820s and 1830s among Protestant churches in general and within the Methodist churches in particular, Jackson relates a traumatic and visionary experience during a thunderstorm in July 1830, which led to a personal spiritual awakening. Catapulted by the experience, she devotes the remainder of her life and activities toward a search for the guidance of God and her personal quest for the authenticity of her inner voice through which she could know, with assurance, God's purposes for her life. Early in this quest, she participates in, and leads, prayer meetings, seeks divine guidance in daily activities, responds to inspired commands to engage in healing and prophecy, and seeks to obtain for herself a state of holiness and, beyond that, personal sanctification.

The years between 1840 until her death marked the period of her most important spiritual activism. Her preaching ventures beyond the Philadelphia community eventually brought her into contact with a group of religious perfectionists known as the "Little Band," based in Albany, New York. Through these associates, it appears that she was introduced to the Shaker community at Watervliet, with which she developed an extensive association. She eventually went to live at Watervliet in 1847, along with a companion and disciple, Rebecca Perot. She lived in the Shaker community until 1851, at which time she returned to Philadelphia with Rebecca Perot, established her own residence, and began a ministry to spread the Shaker teachings to other black Philadelphians. Her mission, based on her journal entry for February 17, 1850, was divinely inspired: "I received an encouraging word in confirmation to the word of God which He gave to me concerning my people, which work He has called me to do. And when the time arrives, no man can hinder me from doing it through the help of God" (*Gifts of Power* 219). Rebecca Jackson and Rebecca Perot remained in Philadelphia until February 1858, when Jackson decided to return to Watervliet. Her motivation for the return seems to be twofold: by her own account, she received divine inspiration to further purge herself from all sin, which may be threefold—"the lust of the flesh, the lust of the eye, and the pride of life" (267)— and she was intent on seeking official support and status for her efforts to establish a black Shaker community in Philadelphia.

When Jackson began her second residence at Watervliet in early 1858, she experienced six months of debilitating illness. Upon recovery, her work became more politically directed toward gaining the sanctions she needed for her proposed Philadelphia project. She received this commission on Tuesday, October 5, 1858, and returned to Philadelphia to begin this work on Friday, October 8, 1858. Jackson's work to recruit black converts to the Shaker community and to officially establish a black Shaker community in Philadelphia apparently reached fruition in 1866 (see the letter by an anonymous Philadelphian in the *Shaker Manifesto*, 19.9, 110–11). Jackson died in 1871, but her journal entries ceased in 1864, apparently prior to the establishment of her Philadelphia Shaker community.

MAJOR WORK AND THEMES

Rebecca Jackson's major work is her spiritual autobiography, composed over a period of thirty-four years, apparently unfinished, and unpublished during her lifetime. Her writing has been carefully researched and edited in an authoritative text by Jean McMahon Humez, entitled *Gifts of Power*, which provides the best access to her ideas and themes. Humez' text in *Gifts of Power* is based on two extant manuscripts of Jackson's autobiography in Jackson's handwriting—one housed in the collection of the Berkshire Athenaeum in Pittsfield, Massachusetts; the other, a part of the archive of Shaker documents at Case Western Reserve University. Humez' careful methodology for the production of an authentic text is explained in the text's prefatory essay. Jackson's spiritual autobiography is important for its portrait of the early American female preacher, its insight into the evangelical movement in nineteenth-century America, and its presentation of issues relating to gender, race, and class.

Although the itinerant nature of Jackson's ministry is limited in scope, her activities provide a view of the personal impact of the movement known as the Second Great Awakening in nineteenth-century America. In her early religious exposure, through the African Methodist Episcopal Church, Jackson experienced the fervency of the evangelical movement of the period, with its emphasis on home-based prayer cells, fiery-styled preaching in worship services, and emotion-packed revival meetings featuring shouting and speaking in tongues. Jackson's writing is particularly inspired by her need to recount her personal quest for freedom from what she viewed as purposeless spirituality. Her impetus comes out of her fear of thunderstorms. Ironically, she reacts by identifying this personal phobia as the voice of God and commits herself to follow only God's divine imperatives. As she frees herself from her personal phobia, she also declares herself independent of an apparently domineering brother and from any further obligations, legal and conjugal, to her husband. With single-mindedness, she begins her spiritual quest, holding prayer meetings, traveling and preaching, prophesying and healing, and eventually holding seances.

Jackson's narrative also resonates with the theme of literacy and freedom. For Jackson, learning to read and write was the greatest gift, an "unspeakable gift of Almighty God" (*Gifts of Power* 108) and she vowed to use it in God's service all of her life. As she relates her experience of learning to read, she recalls the burden of dependence on her older brother Samuel to read her mail and write her responses. The siblings experience conflict when Samuel presumes to "word" her letters for her, to which she takes great exception. She recalls with fervency her decision to kneel in prayer and meditate on a chapter from the Old Testament book of James, asking God to help her to read. When she opens her eyes, she found, miraculously, that she could read the entire chapter. Literacy thus becomes central to her life, as her means of defining personal freedom and of focusing her life's work. She would, she declared, become an instrument of God in tribute to his beneficence.

Jackson's association with the Shaker movement provides unique insight into the Shaker community as she relates tensions within the Watervliet community with regard to race. During her residency at Watervliet, she becomes sensitive to differences in the quality of life for a group of African Americans who joined the society. Her perceptions and divinely inspired insights led her to the conclusion that the needs of this segment of the community were not being fully addressed. She decided that it was God's will that she should establish a ministry expressly designed for her own people. Her plan was to establish a Shaker community in Philadelphia, and she sought, and eventually gained, official approval and support, though not without some political intrigue. Her narrative ends as she is engaged in establishing this community. However, records attesting to the success of her efforts do exist in journal writings and other documents of the Shaker movement.

CRITICAL RECEPTION

Very little, if any, analysis of Jackson's work has been done. The major scholarship remains the definitive textual study done by Jean McMahon Humez, *Gifts of Power*. One earlier study by Richard E. Williams, *Called and Chosen*, tells the story of Mother Jackson's life, focusing particularly on race relations among the Shakers. Williams' study provides some details in his analysis that give insight into Jackson's motivation for starting the black Shaker community in Philadelphia. However, Humez' text remains, to date, the best general resource for further research on Jackson. In Humez' assessment, Jackson's autobiography makes "a remarkable contribution to visionary literature and to our understanding of the American past" (50).

A critical chapter on Jackson appears in J. H. Evans' work *Spiritual Empowerment in Afro-American Literature—Douglass, Frederick; Jackson, Rebecca; Washington, Booker T.; Wright, Richard, and Morrison, Toni*. Jackson is included in Kimberly Rae O'Connor's *Conversions and Visions in the Writings of African-American Women*.

BIBLIOGRAPHY

Primary Sources

Humez, J. M., ed. *Gifts of Power: The Writings of Rebecca Jackson, Black Visionary, Shaker Eldress*. Amherst: University of Massachusetts Press, 1981.
Williams, Richard E. *Called and Chosen*. Metuchen, NJ: Scarecrow Press, 1981.

Studies of Rebecca Cox Jackson

Andrews, Edward Deming. *The People Called Shakers: A Search for the Perfect Society*. New York: Dover, 1963.

Bassard, Katherine Clay. "Spiritual Interrogations: Conversion, Community and Author-ship in the Writings of Phillis Wheatley, Ann Plato, Jarena Lee, and Rebecca Cox Jackson." Diss., Rutgers University, New Brunswick, 1994. DAI 54.12: 4439A.

Brekus, Catherine A. *Strangers and Pilgrims: Female Preaching in America, 1740–1845.* Chapel Hill: University of North Carolina Press, 1998.

Bryant, Sylvia. "Speaking into Being: The Gifts of Rebecca Jackson, 'Black Visionary, Shaker Eldress.'" In *Women's Life-Writing: Finding Voice/Building Community.* Bowling Green, OH: Bowling Green State University Popular Press, 63–79.

Evans, J. H. *Spiritual Empowerment in Afro-American Literature—Douglass, Frederick; Jack-son, Rebecca; Washington, Booker T.; Wright, Richard, and Morrison, Toni.* Lewiston, NY: E. Mellen Press, 1987.

Hardesty, Nancy, Lucille Sider, and Donald W. Dayton. "Women in the Holiness Move-ment: Feminism in the Evangelical Tradition." In *Women of Spirit: Female Lead-ership in the Jewish and Christian Traditions.* New York: Simon and Schuster, 1979.

Hull, Gloria T. "Rebecca Cox and the Uses of Power." Tulsa Studies in Women's Liter-ature 1.2 (1982): 203–209.

Laprade, Candis Anita. "Pens in the Hand of God: The Spiritual Autobiographies of Jarena Lee, Zilpha Elaw, and Rebecca Cox Jackson." Diss., University of North Carolina, Chapel Hill, 1996. *DAI* 56.7 (1996): 2682A.

Madden, Etta. "Reading, Writing and the Race of Mother Figures: Shakers Rebecca Cox Jackson and Alonzo Giles Hollister." In *A Mighty Baptism: Race, Gender, and the Creation of American Protestantism.* Ed. Susan Juster and Lisa MacFarlane. Ithaca, NY: Cornell University Press, 1996. 210–34.

O'Connor, Kimberly Rae. "Womanist Parables in *Gifts of Power*: The Autobiography of Rebecca Cox Jackson." *Auto/Biography Studies* 10.2 (1995): 21–38.

——— *Conversions and Visions in the Writings of African-American Women.* Knoxville: University of Tennessee Press, 1995.

HARRIET ANN JACOBS
(c. 1813–1897)

Terry Novak

BIOGRAPHY

Harriet Ann Jacobs was born a slave in Edenton, North Carolina, around the year 1813. She was orphaned by age six. Until her mother's death, Jacobs was not consciously aware of her status as a slave. She lived a fairly idyllic early childhood under the roof of her free grandmother, Molly Horniblow. Upon the death of her mother, however, Jacobs was sent to the home of her mistress. Her mistress taught her reading and sewing. When her mistress died, the eleven-year-old Jacobs was sent to the Norcom household. She had been willed by her mistress to three-year-old Mary Matilda Norcom. Mary's father was the unscrupulous Dr. James Norcom. Before long, Jacobs became the victim of repeated sexual harassment by Dr. Norcom. In an effort to persuade Dr. Norcom to cease his harassment of her, Jacobs began an affair at age sixteen with a neighbor of the Norcoms', the white lawyer Samuel Tredwell Sawyer. It was Jacobs' desperate belief that Sawyer would protect her from Norcom's advances or that, at the very least, she would have some personal choice over which white man would possess her sexually.

Two children resulted from Jacobs' liaison with Sawyer: Joseph, born around 1829, and Louisa Matilda, born around 1833. The pregnancies only further enraged Dr. Norcom, who vowed never to sell Jacobs. Jacobs felt the further threat that Norcom would sell her children. Jacobs' fears prompted her to run away in 1835, in the hopes that in her absence her children would be sold to their father, which they were. For seven years Jacobs hid away in a crawl space in the attic of her grandmother's home. Not even her children, who lived with Jacobs' grandmother, knew her whereabouts. In 1842 Jacobs escaped north and went to work for the family of the editor Nathaniel Parker Willis. Although reunited with her children in the North, Jacobs was still pursued by Norcom. After Norcom's death, Mary Norcom and her husband traveled north under the guise of the Fugitive Slave Law to reclaim their "property." Facing a desperate situation, Jacobs allowed Mrs. Willis to purchase her freedom for her.

After being urged to do so by abolitionist friends, particularly Amy Post, Jacobs undertook the writing of her autobiography. Jacobs at first tried to interest Harriet Beecher Stowe in writing her story. Stowe, however, lost Jacobs' trust when she attempted to verify the facts of Jacobs' sexual abuse with Mrs. Willis, in whom Jacobs had not confided regarding the matter. The autobiography, finally titled *Incidents in the Life of a Slave Girl, Written by Herself*, did not see publication until 1861. The title page listed only the abolitionist and writer Lydia Maria Child as editor. Jacobs was fairly widely known as the author of the book, though, and she followed the book's publication with continued antislavery work, then ultimately Reconstruction work. Her daughter worked along with her in these efforts. Though Jacobs apparently had some health problems in the last years of her life, she continued her work until her death on March 7, 1897, in Washington, D.C.

MAJOR WORK AND THEMES

Harriet Ann Jacobs is known solely for her autobiographical account, *Incidents in the Life of a Slave Girl, Written by Herself*, which follows the history of her life as a slave. Certainly, the work is considered part of the slave narrative genre; what makes it a particularly significant slave narrative is the basis of the story it unfolds. This is not the type of slave narrative the reader is used to encountering with Frederick Douglass* or Olaudah Equiano.* Rather, this is very clearly the story of a slave woman, and it deals very openly with the issue of sexual abuse that was so accepted but so unspoken of in slavery days. Jacobs describes her plan to have a sexual relationship with her master's white neighbor as her only way out of a very desperate, very horrifying, very sad situation. It is not a decision she makes lightly. She has been raised to be a "good girl." She knows that throwing away her virtue will crush her grandmother, but she also knows that if she does not take this drastic measure, she will surely be forced to succumb to rape by her master. Aware of the sensibilities of her largely genteel nineteenth-century audience and indeed still feeling a sense of shame over her past, Jacobs attempts to gain the reader's understanding of her situation:

Pity me, and pardon me, O virtuous reader! You never knew what it is to be a slave; to be entirely unprotected by law or custom; to have the laws reduce you to the condition of a chattel, entirely subject to the will of another. You never exhausted your ingenuity in avoiding the snares, and eluding the power of a hated tyrant; you never shuddered at the sound of his footsteps, and trembled within hearing of his voice. I know I did wrong. No one can feel it more sensibly than I do. The painful and humiliating memory will haunt me to my dying day. Still, in looking back, calmly, on the events of my life, I feel that the slave woman ought not to be judged by the same standard as others. (55–56)

Jacobs changes the names of the principal characters, but not the facts, in her autobiography. She names herself Linda Brent. Her grandmother becomes Aunt Martha. Her children become Benny and Ellen. Dr. Norcom becomes Dr. Flint. Sawyer becomes Mr. Sands. As is typical with a slave narrative, there is a testimonial Introduction by a respected white abolitionist—in this case, Lydia Maria Child—followed by further testimony at the end of the volume by other respected citizens.

Also included in the work is a Preface by the author herself assuring her readers of the veracity of her story. This would have been a genuine concern. Jacobs must have been painfully aware that a number of her sheltered readers may have found the idea of such blatant sexual abuse taking place in their Christian country to be more unbelievable than appalling. Her periods of didacticism in the work may have served as a means of softening the blow of such knowledge.

Jacobs takes great pains to convince the reader of the perversity of her situation. She expresses sorrow at the birth of her daughter, realizing what the girl might one day have to face. When she describes the tiny space in which she imprisons herself for seven years in an attempt to be rid of her master's abuse, she goes to great lengths to explain to the reader how very unbearable her situation was. "I had always been kindly treated," she writes, "and tenderly cared for, until I came into the hands of Dr. Flint. I had never wished for freedom till then. But though my life in slavery was comparatively devoid of hardships, God pity the woman who is compelled to lead such a life!" (115).

In the context of the available canon of slave narratives, Jacob's *Incidents in the Life of a Slave Girl* takes a unique place. It supplies the reader with an important aspect of slavery, and it is written with sufficient style to keep the reader interested. It fills in many historical blanks, and its appeal remains, despite the passage of time.

CRITICAL RECEPTION

In her Introduction to the reprint of *Incidents in the Life of a Slave Girl*, which she edited, Jean Fagan Yellin tells of the publicity the work brought upon its initial publication, then of its twentieth-century reception. Yellin writes,

Despite this publicity, by the twentieth century both Jacobs and her book were forgotten. Those historians of the slave narrative who did recall *Incidents* associated it only vaguely, if at all, with Jacobs's name. Some thought it a narrative dictated by a fugitive slave, Jacobs, to Child; others thought it an antislavery novel that Child had written in the form of a slave narrative. In the 1960s the Civil Rights movement sparked republication of a number of slave narratives, including *Incidents*, and more recently the women's movement has created interest in the book. But Jacobs's achievement remained in obscurity until the accession of her letters in the Post Archive at the University of Rochester made it possible in 1981 to authenticate her authorship. (xxv)

Since that time, great critical interest has been shown in Jacobs' work. Many scholars have discussed it in terms of its comparative place in the canon of slave narratives. Others have focused on feminist issues. Almost all have given the work the serious attention and respect it is due. Both John Ernest and Maggie Sale discuss the importance of the motherhood theme in *Incidents*, especially as it relates to the time period in which it was written, when the idea of True Womanhood was more than a social slogan. Karen Sanchez-Eppler has written about Jacobs' use of sexual transgressions to draw parallels to the larger issues of slavery. She notes that Jacobs achieves such through her style of writing: "Jacobs's text juxtaposes the traditionally male adventures of the slave narrative with the white middle-class femininity of the domestic novel" (87).

Others have also seen Jacobs' textual dynamics as a distinct tool of the author. Both Carla Kaplan and Martha J. Cutter view the narrative as a form of freedom in and of itself. Cutter writes, "Jacobs . . . uses her critical literacy to create a reconfigured discursive community—a community in which language is true, communal, and sympathetic" (222). Anne Bradford Warner takes the narrative discussion further by focusing on the idea of a female trickster motif in *Incidents*, a motif that the reader finds in the doubling roles of the character Linda Brent.

SallyAnn H. Ferguson explores the contradictions of white American Christianity in the context of Jacobs' narrative and discusses the spiritual strength of slave women in general, Jacobs in particular. Frances Smith Foster, on the other hand, sees the role of spirituality in Jacobs' life and narrative somewhat differently:

Harriet Jacobs's text represents a development in women's literature that is parallel to those of the religious narrators who became empowered through spiritual transcendence. In Harriet Jacobs's text as in those of many writing at the time, spiritual transcendence is of less value than intellectual, moral, and personal empowerment. Her emphasis was upon the natural rights of women and others to personal autonomy and self-expression. (96)

A number of other scholars have also looked at Jacobs' work from the standpoint of feminist literary criticism. Carolyn Scorisio discusses the sense of self that Jacobs presents in *Incidents* and the power that Jacobs receives from that sense of self. Jean Fagan Yellin discusses Jacobs' presentation of herself in conjunction with the classic "madwoman in the attic" persona, being careful to note that Jacobs' woman in the attic is very far from mad. Furthering basic feminist arguments, Joanne M. Braxton and Sharon Zuber discuss the breaking of silences in *Incidents*. They write, "In her narrative, Jacobs also treats the implication of white women in the silence surrounding the sexual exploitation of slave women. White women participate in the silencing of black women when they are themselves silenced by the same patriarchal imperatives that oppress their black sisters" (148–49).

Critical attention continues to be given to Harriet Jacobs' *Incidents in the Life of a Slave Girl*, placing the work largely in the context of slave narrative and women's literature. Jacobs has earned a definite place in both American literature and American history with her autobiography. Her work has gained sufficient acceptance to garner discussions on literary merit, devices, and motifs as well as on the book's historical significance.

BIBLIOGRAPHY

Work by Harriet Ann Jacobs

Incidents in the Life of a Slave Girl, Written by Herself. 1861. Ed. Jean Fagan Yellin. Cambridge: Harvard University Press, 1987.

Studies of Harriet Ann Jacobs

Braxton, Joanne M., and Sharon Zuber. "Silences in Harriet 'Linda Brent' Jacobs's *Incidents in the Life of a Slave Girl*." In *Listening to Silences: New Essays in Feminist Criticism*, Ed. Elaine Hedges and Shelley Fisher Fishkin. New York: Oxford University Press, 1994. 146–55.

Cutter, Martha J. "Dismantling 'The Master's House': Critical Literacy in Harriet Jacobs's *Incidents in the Life of a Slave Girl*." *Callaloo* 19.1 (1996): 209–25.

Ernest, John. *Resistance and Reformation in Nineteenth-Century African-American Literature: Brown, Wilson, Jacobs, Delany, Douglass, and Harper.* Jackson: University Press of Mississippi, 1995.

Ferguson, SallyAnn H. "Christian Violence and the Slave Narrative." *American Literature* 68.2 (1996): 297–320.

Foster, Frances Smith. *Written by Herself: Literary Production by African-American Women, 1746–1892.* Bloomington: Indiana University Press, 1993.

Kaplan, Carla. "Narrative Contracts and Emancipatory Readers: *Incidents in the Life of a Slave Girl*." *The Yale Journal of Criticism* 6.1 (1993): 93–119.

Sale, Maggie. "Critiques from within: Antebellum Projects of Resistance." *American Literature* 64.4 (1992): 696–718.

Sanchez-Eppler, Karen. *Touching Liberty: Abolition, Feminism, and the Politics of the Body.* Berkeley: University of California Press, 1993.

Scorisio, Carolyn. " 'There Is Might in Each': Conceptions of Self in Harriet Jacobs's *Incidents in the Life of a Slave Girl, Written by Herself*." *Legacy* 13.1 (1996): 1–18.

Warner, Anne Bradford. "Santa Claus Ain't a Real Man." In *Haunted Bodies: Gender and Southern Texts*. Ed. Anne Goodwyn Jones and Susan V. Donaldson. Charlottesville: University Press of Virginia, 1997. 185–200.

Yellin, Jean Fagan. "Harriet Jacobs's Family History." *American Literature* 66.4 (1994): 765–767.

———. "Introduction." In *Incidents in the Life of a Slave Girl, Written by Herself*. Ed. Jean Fagan Yellin. Cambridge: Harvard University Press, 1987.

AMELIA E. JOHNSON
(1858–1922)

Elaine Saino

BIOGRAPHY

Amelia Etta Hall Johnson was born in Toronto, Canada, in 1858. After receiving her education in Montreal, she moved with her family in 1874 to Baltimore, Maryland the native state of her parents. Three years after moving to Baltimore, she met and married Rev. Harvey Johnson, the author, civil rights activist, and famed minister of Union Baptist Church. The Johnsons had three children, a daughter and two sons.

Amelia E. Johnson never achieved the fame that her remarkable accomplishments should have accorded her. Her novels were the first by an African American to be used as Sunday school literature. Her novel *Clarence and Corinne; or, God's Way* was only the second novel by an African American woman to be published in book form and was also the first novel by an African American to be published by the American Baptist Publication Society, one of the largest publishing companies in the United States. Yet, she has fallen into relative obscurity.

Johnson began her literary career after her marriage by contributing articles and poetry to various newspapers and periodicals. Her literary interests were always centered around the instruction and enlightenment of young people. In 1887, seeing the need for a literary periodical aimed at young African Americans, Johnson started *The Joy*. She filled the eight pages of this monthly paper with short stories and articles solicited from African American women. In 1888 she started a second periodical, *The Ivy*, also aimed at young children. In addition to Johnson's work as editor of these well-received periodicals, she wrote for newspapers and had her own regular column in the early 1890s in the *Baltimore Sower and Reaper* called the "Children's Corner."

Johnson is best remembered now not for these early endeavors in editing and newspaper work but for her novels for children and adolescents. She was the author of three novels, all of which were aimed at a young Sunday school audience. Her first novel, *Clarence and Corinne; or, God's Way*, appeared in 1890. Johnson followed her first success with two other novels: *The Hazeley Family* (1894) and *Martina Meriden; or, What Is My Motive?* (1901).

Johnson died after a two-day illness at the age of sixty-four on March 29, 1922, in Baltimore.

MAJOR WORKS AND THEMES

Each of Amelia Johnson's three novels has a strong didactic, religious purpose. Like the periodicals she started, these novels are meant to encourage children and young adults to aspire to a religious life. However, unlike these periodicals, the novels did not have a strictly African American audience. In fact, they were published by the American Baptist Publication Society, a large white publishing house. Probably because of Johnson's predominantly white audience, the characters in her novels are scrupulously racially ambiguous. Although Johnson does not address race, she confronts other contemporary issues such as temperance, family unity, and devotion to God.

In Johnson's first novel, young Clarence and Corinne are in their late childhood when their long-suffering, unchristian mother dies of a heart attack, and their drunkard father abandons them. Cast upon the mercy of society, Clarence and Corinne are separated from each other as different persons take over their care. Eventually, they both find spiritual guides who teach them the virtues of Christianity. When both have become thoroughly Christian on their own, they are reunited quite by accident in the little town of Brierton, where Corinne has been staying with the Stone family. Clarence comes to live with them as well, and by the end, they are married to another pair of siblings, the minister's children.

The themes of the focus on family, the terrors of alcohol, and the reliance on God that are so prominent in *Clarence and Corinne* are prominent in Johnson's other works as well. Johnson's second novel, *The Hazeley Family*, also begins by portraying a family in distress. The protagonist, Flora Hazeley, starts life in a home with a largely absent father and an unchristian mother. An aunt takes pity on Flora and offers to raise her in her home, where Flora learns the values of Christian living, housekeeping, and thrift. When this benevolent aunt dies, Flora returns to her family to find her brothers straying from home and her father dead. Through her positive example, Flora reunites her family and converts them all to Christianity. Although one brother almost ruins his life in a fit of drunken debauchery, he later reforms and becomes a minister.

Johnson's third novel, *Martina Meriden: or, What Is My Motive?*, is her least successful. Johnson proposes the same ideology as she does in her other novels, advising readers that the way to happiness is to devote oneself to God and the service of others. This novel, however, lacks the spark of the earlier two and is much more overtly didactic and ponderous.

CRITICAL RECEPTION

Until the recent Schomburg Library editions of *Clarence and Corinne* and *The Hazeley Family*, Amelia E. Johnson had fallen into obscurity. This fact is due in part to the fame of her husband, Dr. Rev. Harvey Johnson, who is remembered as one of the great civic and religious leaders of African Americans in Baltimore.

In spite of these explanations, her obscurity is especially shocking given Johnson's popularity in the 1890s and 1900s. *Clarence and Corinne* was commercially and critically successful. White and African American contemporary reviewers praised it for its didactic message and for its ability to capture and keep the reader's attention. The *Baltimore Baptist* wrote, "Mrs. Johnson is a fine writer," and "The interest of the reader is early excited, and held steadily to the close" (qtd. in Penn 425). *The Missionary Visitor* praised it as a novel whose "tale is healthy in tone, holds the attention, and is well adapted to the intermediate classes of Sunday-school readers" (qtd. in Penn 425). Finally, The *Home Protector* of Baltimore claimed that it "ought to be in every home; and parents should secure it for their children, and see that they read and re-read it, until they make the principles set forth by the writer the rule of their life" (qtd. in Penn 426).

Little is known about the reception of *The Hazeley Family* and *Martina Meriden*, but as they followed the same basic formula as *Clarence and Corinne*, one can assume they reached a similar audience.

Few recent scholars have explored Johnson's novels. The Schomburg Library's editions of *Clarence and Corinne* and *The Hazeley Family* contain valuable Introductions by Hortense J. Spillers and Barbara Christian, respectively. These Introductions impart biographical information and critical interpretations of the texts. In addition, M. Giulia Fabi treats *Clarence and Corinne* in light of two other novels by African American women of the late nineteenth century, Frances Harper's* *Iola Leroy* and Pauline Hopkins'* *Contending Forces*. She points out that, while the issue of passing plays a role in the other two novels, Johnson's characters never have to pass; their race is indeterminate. In essence, Johnson's novel "passes." For Hortense Spillers, the issue of race for Johnson is secondary to issues of morality, religion, and temperance. Spillers argues that while "Mrs. Johnson's readers—black and white—smuggle in race, the narrative's subtitle insinuates its own supplementary meanings. *God's Way* renders the *other* theme of the work" (xxxiii). As Barbara Christian points out, *The Hazeley Family*'s characters are also racially ambiguous. However, Johnson was by no means alone in presenting race-free novels. Other African American female novelists of her era also removed race from their works. One should not interpret Johnson's novels as ignoring the race issue but instead value them for their explorations of the issues of temperance, family, and Christian living.

BIBLIOGRAPHY

Works by Amelia E. Johnson

Novels

Clarence and Corinne; or, God's Way. Philadelphia: American Baptist Publication Society, 1890.
The Hazeley Family. Philadelphia: American Baptist Publication Society, 1894.
Martina Meriden; or, What Is My Motive?. Philadelphia: American Baptist Publication Society, 1901.

Studies of Amelia E. Johnson

Christian, Barbara. "Introduction." In *The Hazeley Family*. Oxford: Oxford University Press, 1988. xxvii–xxxvii.
Fabi, M. Giulia. "Taming the Amazon? The Price of Survival in Turn-of-the-Century African American Women's Fiction." In *The Insular Dream: Obsession and Resistance*. Ed. Kristiaan Versluys. Amsterdam: VU University Press, 1995.
"Johnson, Amelia E." In *The Oxford Companion to African American Literature*. Ed. William L. Andrews, Frances Smith Foster, and Trudier Harris. New York: Oxford University Press, 1997.
Majors, Monroe Alphus. *Noted Negro Women, Their Triumphs and Activities*. Chicago: Donohue and Henneberry, 1893.
Pegues, A. W. *Our Baptist Ministers and Schools*. Springfield, MA: Wiley, 1892.
Penn, I. Garland. *The Afro-American Press and Its Editors*. 1891. Reprint ed., New York: Arno Press and New York Times, 1969.
Shockley, Ann Allen. *Afro-American Women Writers 1746–1933: An Anthology and Critical Guide*. Boston: G. K. Hall, 1988.
Spillers, Hortense J. "Introduction." In *Clarence and Corinne; or, God's Way*. Oxford: Oxford University Press, 1988.
———. "Moving on Down the Line." *American Quarterly* 40.1 (1988): 84.
Tate, Claudia. *Domestic Allegories of Political Desire: The Black Heroine's Text at the Turn of the Century*. New York: Oxford University Press, 1992.

GEORGIA DOUGLAS JOHNSON
(1880?–1966)

Gwendolyn S. Jones

BIOGRAPHY

Biographers disagree on the birth date of Georgia Blanche Douglas Camp: the most frequently quoted date is September 10, 1886, but the best documented date is September 10, 1880. A discrepancy also exists in the reporting of her place of birth, with both Rome and Atlanta, Georgia, being listed. She received her early education in public and private schools in Rome and in Atlanta. Ann Shockley reports that Johnson completed the Normal School at Atlanta University in 1893; Gloria Hull reports 1896. She taught herself violin while at Atlanta University, then later studied violin, piano, and composition at Oberlin Conservatory of Music. In her later years, she also studied at Howard University.

Georgia Douglas Johnson and her husband, Henry Lincoln Johnson, and their two sons moved to Washington, D.C., in 1910 and enjoyed a prestigious social and political life. She was a leader or a participant in many organizations. In addition to writing stories and poems and composing songs, Johnson taught music and was church organist. Following her husband's death in 1925, she was free to write and travel, but it was also necessary for her to work to support her sons. Johnson held such jobs as substitute teacher, librarian, file clerk, then later in her life, immigrant inspector in the Department of Labor and labor inspector.

Although Harlem was its central location, Washington, D.C., was a mecca for the New Negro Renaissance. Beginning in 1920, Johnson was host to the Saturday Nighter's Club at her home, for the benefit of the younger and the established writers and other artists. Johnson's literary salon provided a place to rest, to share ideas, and to discuss projects. Young writers, including Countee Cullen,* Bruce Nugent,* Zora Neale Hurston,* and Langston Hughes,* mingled with the older generation of writers, which included W.E.B. Du Bois, Alain Locke,* and

James Weldon Johnson.* This activity lasted approximately forty years; she also called this literary salon the Halfway House. Gwendolyn Bennett* mentions the Saturday Nighter's Club in her column, "The Ebony Flute," in *Opportunity: A Journal of Negro Life*.

After the close of the Harlem Renaissance, Johnson maintained her participation in the literary arts. She continued to publish poetry in *Opportunity*, *Phylon*, *Journal of Negro History*, and anthologies; read poetry on radio broadcasts; contributed to two magazines based in Washington, D.C., *Negro Woman's World Magazine* and *The Women's Voice*; studied journalism at Howard University; and wrote short stories. She remained in her home on S Street and continued to write until her death in 1966.

MAJOR WORKS AND THEMES

Georgia Douglas Johnson's literary career began before the Harlem Renaissance and extended into the 1960s. She was published as early as 1905 in *Voice of the Negro* and in 1916 in *Crisis: A Record of the Darker Races*. Writing romantic, conventional verse, her lyrics were based on introspection and instinct. She was inspired by William Stanley Braithwaite,* who later became a promoter of her first collection of poetry.

Because she wished to be recognized as a poet who would appeal to all readers, she did not address racial issues in *The Heart of a Woman and Other Poems* and she was criticized for this. The prevailing notion was that black writers should address racial issues. Instead, she addressed several themes that white women poets treated, and she revealed the heart of any woman.

The title poem deals with the nature of a woman's heart and sets the tone for the volume. Other poems include "The Dreams of Dreamers," "Sympathy," and "Peace." The poems about love express the love of a woman for her mate or her beloved, whom she loves emotionally. She treats death, which is expressed in such poems as "Whither," "Gethsemane," "Posthumous," and "When I Am Dead," and the daily experience of time—as in day and night. In "Nightfall," for example, God sends nightfall so that the speaker can rest. In some of her poems, tears represent pain or relief or may be refreshing; in other words, tears are a natural response for a woman.

Her second volume of poetry, *Bronze*, was written in response to negative criticism Johnson received for not writing about racial issues in *The Heart of a Woman and Other Poems*. She addresses race riots, lynching, and random violence. The book is divided into nine sections with titles such as "Exhortation," "Supplication," and "Martial." The section on "Motherhood" contains "The Mother," "Maternity," "Black Woman, Guardianship" and treats such issues as the likelihood of no future for a child, the pride a mother has for her child, and the prejudice and racism a child must face. In spite of prejudice and racism, the speaker advises her son to strive for success. The poems in Appreciations praise people who had a positive influence on Johnson's life and on the black race, including Abraham Lincoln, William Stanley Braithwaite, W.E.B. Du Bois, Mary Church Terrell,* and her husband, Henry Lincoln Johnson.

An Autumn Love Cycle is a companion volume to The Heart of a Woman and Other Poems. It treats the same theme of love, but through a more mature speaker. The speaker ponders over lost love but is grateful to have been loved. In the first of five sections, "The Cycle," the persona is a mature woman who is aware of the positive and the negative aspects of love. In the second section, "Contemplation," the speaker speaks of the certainty of sorrow and the impermanence of happiness. In the poem "I Wonder" the speaker wonders how older women remember their past. One of the most popular of Johnson's poems, "I Want to Die While You Love Me," appears in the third section, "Intermezzi." In the section entitled "Penseroso," the poems express despair, a broken heart, and lost hope. "Break, Break My Heart" expresses that love is over. "Cadence" is the final section. She closes this section with the idea that the speaker would relive her life in spite of the pain and dejection she has suffered.

Share My World, published in 1962, is a collection of poems that had been sent to friends over the years. It also contains poems from earlier collections and selections from "Homely Philosophy," a series of newspaper articles providing inspiration for daily living. The speaker reflects, then concludes that she had a happy life.

Georgia Douglas Johnson was also a productive playwright. In contrast to black males, black women playwrights usually wrote about happenings in any geographic area, presented a broader perspective on black culture and problems, and portrayed the main characters as women who had to make major decisions. Only six of her more than thirty plays were published. Her two best-known plays are Blue Blood and Plumes; both won literary awards, and Plumes was published in Opportunity. The theme of Sunday Morning in the South and Blue Eyed Black Boy is lynching. In Sunday Morning in the South, Johnson uses dialect to depict illiterate southern blacks. Two historical plays, Frederick Douglass and William and Ellen Craft, are about slaves' attempts to escape and gain freedom. Johnson intended that these two dramas be used to educate young blacks about their heritage.

Johnson wrote several short stories that were not published. "Gesture" and "Tramp Love" were published under the pseudonym Paul Tremain. "The Skeleton" won first prize through the Washington Tribune. Some short stories were written in collaboration with Gypsy Drago.

Fiction writers and poets of the Harlem Renaissance were also journalists. They wrote newspaper or magazine columns directed to a growing black readership. Johnson's syndicated column, "Homely Philosophy," published from 1926 to 1932, appeared in approximately thirty weekly newspapers. The editorials were intended to cheer, encourage, and motivate readers during the depression era. They contained motivational sentiments, inspiration, and advice. She also wrote columns entitled "Wise Sayings" and "Beauty Hints by Nina Temple."

CRITICAL RECEPTION

Georgia Douglas Johnson, a prolific writer, was considered by some critics the most popular since Frances Ellen Watkins Harper.* However, she was considered a "minor" poet because she was overshadowed by the "masculine literature of the New Negro" (Fletcher 153). Some of her critics and editors make only brief remarks about her work. James Weldon Johnson, in *The Book of American Negro Poetry*, describes her as a lyricist. Sterling Brown,* in *Negro Poetry and Drama*, notes that Johnson's poetry is conventional in certain technical aspects but that she is also a skilled and fluent poet. Brown observed that many poets of the period insisted on being poets, not black poets, and that their poetry was escapist. Davis and Redding consider that Johnson treats subjects superficially.

Alain Locke considers that *The Heart of a Woman and Other Poems* is her finest book. He feels that she set out to document the feminine heart. She does succeed in documenting the experience of love. Cedric Dover, a Eurasian, referred to the fact that the subject is "the heart of a colored woman" (634); he noted further that Johnson, a person of "mixed blood" herself, "was the first to give to peoples of mixed origin the pride in themselves that they so badly needed" (635).

In "Notes on the New Books," Alain Locke and Jessie Fauset* applaud the fact that Johnson writes on experiences related to race in *Bronze*. In the Introduction, Du Bois writes that the volume, "as a revelation of the soul struggle of the women of a race . . . is invaluable" (7).

Few critical analyses are available for Johnson's literary productions other than the poetry. Claudia Tate reviews the plays and short stories in the Introduction to *Selected Works*.

BIBLIOGRAPHY

Works by Georgia Douglas Johnson

Poetry

The Heart of a Woman and Other Poems. 1918. Freeport: Books for Libraries, 1971.
Bronze: A Book of Verse. Boston: B. J. Brimmer, 1922.
An Autumn Love Cycle. New York: H. Vinal, 1928.
Share My World. Binghamton, NY: Vail-Ballou, 1962.

Drama

A Sunday Morning in the South. 1925. *Georgia Douglas Johnson: The Selected Works of Georgia Douglas Johnson*. Intro. Claudia Tate. New York: G. K. Hall, 1997. 385–93.
Blue Blood. 1926. *Georgia Douglas Johnson: The Selected Works of Georgia Douglas Johnson*. "Intro." Claudia Tate. New York: G. K. Hall, 1997. 307–17.

Plumes: A Folk Tragedy. 1927. *Opportunity: A Journal of Negro Life* (July 1927): 200–201,
217–18.
Blue Eyed Black Boy. 1935. Ed. Kathy A. Perkins. *Black Female Playwrights: An Anthology
of Plays before 1950.* Bloomington: Indiana University Press, 1989.
Frederick Douglass. 1935. *Georgia Douglas Johnson: The Selected Works of Georgia Douglas
Johnson.* "Intro." Claudia Tate. New York: G. K. Hall, 1997. 333–52.
William and Ellen Craft. 1935. *Georgia Douglas Johnson: The Selected Works of Georgia
Douglas Johnson.* "Intro." Claudia Tate. New York: G. K. Hall, 1997. 353–76.

Short Stories

(As Paul Tremaine). "Tramp Love." *Challenge: A Literary Quarterly* 2.1 (Spring 1937): 3–
11.
(As Paul Tremaine). "Gesture." *Challenge: A Literary Quarterly* 1.1 (June 1936): 13–17.
"Free." *The Sleeper Wakes: Harlem Renaissance Stories by Women.* Ed. Marcy Knopf. New
Brunswick, NJ: Rutgers University Press, 1993. 55–59.

Nonfiction Prose

Numerous editorials.
The weekly "Homely Philosophy" was published in more than thirty-two newspapers
1926–1932, including the *Pittsburgh Courier,* the *Chicago Defender,* and the *Baltimore Afro-American.*

Studies of Georgia Douglas Johnson

Bloom, Harold. *Black American Poets and Dramatists of the Harlem Renaissance.* New York:
Chelsea House, 1995.
Bontemps, Arna, ed. *Harlem Renaissance Remembered: Essays Edited with a Memoir.* New
York: Dodd, Mead, 1972.
Brown, Sterling. *Negro Poetry and Drama.* Washington, DC: Associates in Negro Folk
Education, 1937.
Cullen, Countee. *Caroling Dusk: An Anthology of Verse by Negro Poets.* New York: Harper
and Row, 1927.
Davis, Arthur P., and Saunders Redding, eds. *Cavalcade: Negro American Writing from
1760 to the Present.* Boston: Houghton, 1971.
Dover, Cedric. "The Importance of Georgia Douglas Johnson." *Crisis* 59 (December 1952),
633–36, 647.
Fletcher, Winona. "Georgia Douglas Johnson." In *Dictionary of Literary Biography.* Ed.
Thadious M. Davis and Trudier Harris. Detroit: Gale, 1984. 153–64.
Georgia Douglas Johnson: The Selected Works of Georgia Douglas Johnson. "Intro." Claudia
Tate. New York: G. K. Hall, 1997.
Henderson, Dorothy F. "Georgia Douglas Johnson: A Study of Her Life and Literature."
Diss., Florida State University, 1995.
Honey, Maureen. "Georgia Douglas Johnson." In *Oxford Companion to African American
Literature.* Ed. William L. Andrews, Frances Smith Foster, and Trudier Harris. New
York: Oxford University Press, 1997. 403–4.
Hull, Gloria, "Black Women Poets from Wheatley to Walker." In *Sturdy Black Bridges:*

Visions of Black Women in Literature. Garden City, NY: Anchor Books/Doubleday, 1979. 69–86.

————. *Color, Sex, and Poetry*. Bloomington: Indiana University Press, 1987.

Johnson, James Weldon. *The Book of American Negro Poetry*. New York: Harcourt, Brace, and World, 1922.

Lewis, David Levering. *When Harlem Was in Vogue*. New York: Knopf, 1981.

Locke, Alain, ed. *The New Negro: His Heritage and Literature*. 1925. New York: Arno Press, 1968.

Locke, Alain, and Jessie Fauset. "Notes on the New Books." *Crisis* 256 (February 1923): 161.

Redmond, Eugene B. *Drumvoices: The Mission of Afro-American Poetry. A Critical History*. Garden City, NY: Anchor Books, 1976.

Roses, Lorraine Elena, and Ruth Elizabeth Randolph. *Harlem's Glory: Black Women Writing 1900–1950*. Cambridge: Harvard University Press, 1997.

————. *The Harlem Renaissance and Beyond: Literary Biography of 100 Black Women Writers, 1900–1945*. Boston: G. K. Hall, 1990. 201–8.

Shockley, Ann Allen. *Afro-American Women Writers 1746–33: An Anthology and Critical Guide*. New York: New American Library, 1989.

Stetson, Erlene, ed. *Black Sister: Poetry by Black American Women, 1746–1980*. Bloomington: Indiana University Press, 1981.

Wall, Cheryl A. *Women of the Harlem Renaissance*. Bloomington and Indianapolis: Indiana University Press, 1995.

Watson, Steven. *The Harlem Renaissance; Hub of African-American Culture, 1920–1930*. New York: Pantheon Books, 1995.

HELENE JOHNSON
(1906–1995)

Barbara L. J. Griffin

BIOGRAPHY

Considered a "bright light" in the Harlem Renaissance whose radiant genius promised lasting fame, poet Helene Johnson today is recognized as only a "minor" poet. Born on July 7, 1906, in Boston to Ella Johnson and William Johnson (a father she was never to meet), Helene led a middle-class New England existence. The family possessed two residences: a Boston address at 478 Brookline Avenue and a house in Oak Bluff on Martha's Vineyard, Massachusetts, purchased by Helene's grandfather, Benjamin Benson, shortly after following his three daughters (including Helene's mother) from their southern home in South Carolina to the north (Bryan 587).

Although there are little biographical data available on Helene Johnson, who guarded her private life, scant information became available when poet and critic William Stanley Braithwaite* included a poem of hers in his *Anthology of Magazine Verse for 1926*. She wrote that she attended, in Boston, the Lafayette School, the Martin School, and the Girls' Latin High School. After graduation, she took courses at Boston University but had no desire to pursue a degree. Already a member of the Saturday Evening Quill Club of Boston, founded by a group of young black writers, the nineteen-year-old wrote that her favorite writers were Walt Whitman, Lord Tennyson, Percy Bysshe Shelley, and Carl Sandburg (Patterson 164). Evidence of their influence, as well as that of Claude Mckay* and Langston Hughes,* can be detected in many of her popular poems. A year earlier, she had won first prize in a short story contest sponsored by the *Boston Chronicle*.

Although Helene Johnson grew up secure within a stable, middle-class, supportive family, her childhood was anything but typical. The house at 478 Brookline Avenue was populated and managed primarily by females—her mother, Ella, along with her mother's two sisters, Minnie and Rachel. Each of the sisters gave birth to a daughter within a one-year span, between 1906 and 1907. Writer Dorothy West, Helene's cousin, was born to sister Rachel. The only male Helene remembered encountering regularly was the father of Dorothy West, Isaac Christopher West, known during the early twentieth century as the Banana King of Boston. In writing her 1948 novel *The Living Is Easy*, West draws upon her memory of living in a "society of females." This unique dynamic helped shape a feminine consciousness central to Johnson's works. Her Aunt Rachel, Dorothy West's mother, nurtured her love for the theater and suggested that Helene, born Helen, give her name a more glamorous twist by adding an "e" at the end.

Ella, Helene's mother, a bright, perceptive woman, was to her daughter the perfect model of a new, twentieth-century woman. Despite her modest salary as a domestic for Boston elites, she introduced her daughter to a world of adventure, like taking her to see the Wright brothers (Bryan 588). Exposure to new experiences and to men and women with backbone and imagination led Helene to avoid the staid and the predictable in her work.

In 1925 Helene's star began to rise. She won a short story contest sponsored by the *Boston Chronicle*, and her poem "Trees at Night" won honorable mention in the first literary contest sponsored by *Opportunity*, the official journal of the National Urban League and one of the top three black magazines committed to nurturing talented young black artists. The *Crisis*, official organ of the National Association for the Advancement of Colored People (NAACP), then edited by W.E.B. Du Bois,* and the *Messenger* were the other two. Langston Hughes won first prize for "The Weary Blues" in the same contest in which Helene won honorable mention. Subsequent to her first honorable mention, Helene was to win honorable recognition in at least three other *Opportunity* contests. In 1926 three of her poems won first honorable mention: "Fullfillment," "Magalu," and "The Road." Judges were William Rose Benét, Alain Locke,* Vachel Lindsay, and Robert Frost.

From 1925 to 1935 Helene Johnson was assured a place in all the important Renaissance periodicals and anthologies. In 1925 *Opportunity*, edited by Charles S. Johnson, published her "Trees at Night" and later that year published her poem "My Race." Alain Locke included in his 1925 groundbreaking anthology *The New Negro* Helene Johnson's "The Road," a clarion call for a resurgence of black pride. In 1926 *Opportunity* published six of her poems; and in 1927 *Vanity Fair* published "Bottled," a poem on the theme of the reclamation of African roots, often considered her finest work. Landing a place in such a prestigious journal secured Johnson's position among the Harlem literati. She was gaining fame as a young writer not afraid to experiment with injecting into her work a bold new black attitude that strutted to a new beat and spoke in new black language. The inhabitants of her poetic world longed *unambivalently* for Africa. "Black" themes were explored by other Harlem Renaissance female poets, but none engaged the vernacular and primitivism as effectively as Helene Johnson.

Throughout the period, she was published in the *Messenger, Palms,* and *The Saturday Evening Quill.* Poet Countee Cullen,* especially fond of traditional forms, published in his first and only anthology *Caroling Dusk* (1927) eight of her poems. James Weldon Johnson* included five in the revised edition of *The Book of American Negro Poetry,* lauding particularly her poems written in the colloquial style, making the vernacular style seem easy (279).

Unable to resist the lure of Harlem, Helene and cousin Dorothy West moved to New York in 1927 to take classes at the Extension Division of Columbia University. (One of her teachers was novelist John Erskine.) She stayed in that city for more than half a century. Harlem was a whirlwind of excitement for the two Boston girls: they networked with Harlem luminaries and made the round of social events. Helene counted among her closest friends Zora Neale Hurston* and the irascible novelist and critic Wallace Thurman,* who wrote her and cousin Dorothy into his 1932 satire of the Harlem Renaissance, *The Infants of the Spring.* Within the malaise of an overrated Harlem art world, Helene Johnson (fictionalized as Hazel Jamison), and her cousin Doris Westmore (Dorothy West) represented "a freshness and a naivete which [the protagonist—Raymond Taylor] and his cronies had lost" (231). The one and only issue of *Fire!!*—the legendary 1926 avant-garde journal founded by Wallace Thurman, Langston Hughes, Zora Neale Hurston, and others—included Helene Johnson's poem "A Southern Road."

After 1929 Helene Johnson's level of productivity lessened dramatically. The stock market crash of 1929 decimated the cadre of black writers dependent on the goodwill of publishing companies now driven out of the business of "black books" by economic realities. The Harlem cluster broke up with a number of writers scattering to different parts of the country. Some joined New Deal programs like the Federal Writers' Project, but Helene Johnson dropped out of public view. She began contributing poems to the first edition of Dorothy West's journal *Challenge: A Literary Quarterly,* launched in 1934, but stopped after the journal increased its socialistic emphasis in 1937 under the associate editorship of Richard Wright.* In the 1930s she married William Warner Hubbell, a motorman she met in New York City, and in 1940 gave birth to a daughter, Abigail Calachaly Hubbell. Helene worked a number of years as a correspondent at Consumers Union in Mount Vernon, New York. Although she maintained her love for poetry and continued to write "for herself," she could never re-create the lyrically precise pieces of her youth. In the 1980s, she returned to Massachusetts for a brief time, but ill health forced her to return to New York to live with her daughter. She died in 1995 (Bryan 590).

MAJOR WORKS AND THEMES

Helene Johnson wrote barely two dozen poems during her career as a creative artist, many on the sentimental themes of love and death popular during the period. Her literary reputation, however, rests primarily upon the eight poems that reflect popular Harlem Renaissance ideals: a new black aesthetic, the nos-talgic longing for an African past, and a reconfiguration of nature as erotic meta-phor of black femininity. In "The Road," for example, within a little "trodden" road, she discerns the majesty of her people, who must not bow down but "rise!" Johnson's message is reminiscent of Paul Laurence Dunbar's,* who in "Not They Who Soar" formulates an aesthetic based on toil and suffering. Eugene Redmond in *Drumvoices* suggests a comparison to James Weldon Johnson's "Lift Every Voice and Sing" (209). In "My Race," Helene Johnson celebrates the reputed emotional spontaneity of her people (a popular Harlem Renaissance theme). Through explosive, staccato rhythms, she draws a contrast between "blackness" and "whiteness." She ends by positing faith in the potential of the black race as they "fumble" toward rebirth. "Poem" plunges headlong into the new urbanized jazz-age themes as the speaker flirts with, and culturally identifies with, a banjo player who sports patent-leather shoes and "flashing" eyes and teeth, prompting James Weldon Johnson to remark that in "Poem," Helene Johnson extols the very qualities that blacks once felt "called for apology or defense" (279). Clearly, one of her best poems is "Bottled," published by *Vanity Fair* in 1927, where she exhibits remarkable skill in combining the black aesthetic theme with alien/exile hypothesis central to much of the writing during the Renaissance—that blacks are captives in a corrupt United States, "bottled" like the delicate sand from the Sahara Desert sitting upon a shelf of the 135th Street Library. Johnson is dazzling as she skillfully employs the vernacular to peer into the soul of a Harlem strutter who should be a prince in Africa. In "Magalu," Johnson undertakes the same concept but relocates her poem within precolonial Africa, a breathtakingly par-adisaical land where a Jeremiah-type speaker cautions Magalu, a glorious daughter of Eden, to fear the man in a "white collar," whose creed will not allow her to dance. In *Sturdy Black Bridges*, Gloria T. Hull argues that "Magalu" should be better known since it provides one of the most superior treatments available of the "pro-African primitivism theme" (80).

In "Sonnet to a Negro in Harlem," the speaker understands the "disdain" for his environment a Harlem black man feels when he experiences subconscious memories of a glorious African past. Bernard Bell suggests that, unlike many Harlem Renaissance poets who wrote on this theme, Johnson was not victim to the double-consciousness raised by W.E.B. Du Bois. She believed that "African tradition is the only true cultural heritage of the African American" (918).

Even in Johnson's best poems based on the romantic themes of love and the exuberance of blooming sensuality, she adeptly transmutes the negative stereo-types of night into effective expressions of a black female aesthetic. In "What Do I Care for Morning," the glaring, noisy images of the day are contrasted with the seductively rich images of night, and in "Trees at Night," she establishes the same paradigm by focusing on silhouetted trees whose impressionistic beauty is born of the intermingling of moonlight and shadow. Shifting images of delicate "lacy" branches that reach longingly for the moon are masterfully stenciled on nearby objects. In *Shadowed Dreams: Women's Poetry of the Harlem Renaissance*,

Maureen Honey writes that Johnson's preference for night in her poems was a characteristic theme in the poems of women during the Renaissance because "it [asserted] the primacy of Blackness in a world that favored white things." Night was considered a necessary time for "contemplation" in that it "brought serenity to a restless, discontented spirit" (15). Except for "Fulfillment," obviously influenced by Whitman, Shelley, and Sandburg, in which the speaker yearns for a full life punctuated by moments that satisfy the hunger for sensate experiences, many of Johnson's conventional romantic poems are pastorals, typical of the period, locating female sexuality within the fertile, sentient realm of nature, such as in "Summer Matures," "Metamorphism," and "Invocation," where death and romantic passion find common ground.

CRITICAL RECEPTION

Helene Johnson's poems based on popular Harlem Renaissance themes have received favorable critical reviews from 1925 to the present, but because the poet's output is so small, it is difficult to make conclusive statements regarding her reputation or her impact in the field. In *Sturdy Black Bridges*, Gloria T. Hull remarks upon the paucity of works not only from Helene Johnson but from the other women poets of the period. Regrettably, only one of the female Harlem Renaissance poets—Georgia Douglas Johnson*—produced a book. Consequently, "they end up being 'interesting,' 'minor'—a kind of secondary wave which helped to make up the Renaissance tide" (81–82). Hull blames the poor level of production on the difficulty of women's being "insiders" in a movement that was "a predominantly masculine affair" (81–82).

Clearly, however, Helene Johnson's contemporaries judged her to be an exceptionally gifted artist, and that opinion of her work seems to have continued. Since her debut as a writer, she consistently found a place in major collections and periodicals. After appearing in three Harlem Renaissance landmark anthologies: Locke's *The New Negro* (1925), Cullen's *Caroling Dusk* (1927), and James Weldon Johnson's revised *The Book of American Negro Poetry* (1931), she was included in *The Negro Caravan* (1941), edited by Sterling Brown,* Arthur P. Davis, and Ulysses Lee; and in Arna Bontemps'* *Golden Slippers: An Anthology of Negro Poetry for Young Readers* (1941). Although Langston Hughes does not mention her in his 1940 autobiography, *The Big Sea*, she is included in Bontemps and Langston Hughes' 1970 anthology *The Poetry of the Negro: 1746–1970*, and Bontemps includes her in his *American Negro Poetry* (1970). She appears in Arnold Adoff's *The Poetry of Black America* (1973); *The Norton Anthology of African American Literature* (1997), edited by Henry L. Gates and Nellie McKay; and *The Riverside Anthology of the African American Literary Tradition* (1998), edited by Patricia Liggins Hill.

A major critical study in African American literature, Jean Wagner's *The Black Poets of the United States* (1973) briefly notes her versatility and genius in using modern forms and themes, but thus far, there has been no book-length study of her works. The most comprehensive treatment of the writer is in *Shadowed Dreams: Women's Poetry of the Harlem Renaissance* (1989), edited by Maureen Honey; *Sturdy Black Bridges: Visions of Black Women in Literature* (1979), edited by Roseann P. Bell, Bettye J. Parker, and Beverly Guy-Sheftall; Eugene Redmond's *Drumvoices* (1976); T. J. Bryan's "Helene Johnson" in *Notable Black American Women* (1992), edited by Jessie Carney Smith; and Raymond Patterson's "Helene Johnson" in the *Dictionary of Literary Biography*, vol. 51 (1987), edited by Trudier Harris. The consensus regarding Helene Johnson is that as a craftsperson of the "racial" poems of the period, she had few peers. But lamentably, she failed to fulfill the promise indicated by her extraordinary gifts.

BIBLIOGRAPHY

Works by Helene Johnson

Poems in Collections

"A Southern Road." In *Fire!!* (November 1926): 17.

"What Do I Care for Morning," "Sonnet to a Negro in Harlem," Summer Matures," "Poem," "Fulfillment," "The Road," "Bottled," and "Magalu." In *Caroling Dusk: An Anthology of Verse by Negro Poets*. Ed. Countee Cullen. New York: Harper and Row, 1927. 223–24.

"Poem," "The Road," "Sonnet to a Negro in Harlem," "Remember Not," and "Invocation." In *The Book of American Negro Poetry*, rev. ed. Ed. James Weldon Johnson. New York: Harcourt, Brace, 1931. 279–82.

"Summer Matures," "Fulfillment," "Magalu," "Remember Not," "Invocation," and "The Road." In *The Poetry of the Negro 1746–1970*. Ed. Langston Hughes and Arna Bontemps. Garden City, NY: Anchor/Doubleday, 1970. 261–66.

"What Do I Care for Morning," "Invocation," and "Trees at Night." In *Shadowed Dreams: Women's Poetry of the Harlem Renaissance*. Ed. Maureen Honey. New Brunswick, NJ: Rutgers University Press, 1989. 97–102.

"My Race," "Metamorphism," and "Bottled." In *Harlem's Glory: Black Women Writing 1900–1950*. Ed. Lorraine Elena Roses and Ruth Elizabeth Randolph. Cambridge: Harvard University Press, 1996. 326–28.

Studies of Helene Johnson

Bryan, T. J. "Helene Johnson." In *Notable Black American Women*. Ed. Jessie Carney Smith. Detroit: Gale, 1992. 587–91.

Honey, Maureen, ed. *Shadowed Dreams: Women's Poetry of the Harlem Renaissance*. New Brunswick, NJ: Rutgers University Press, 1989.

Hull, Gloria T. "Black Women Poets from Wheatley to Walker." In *Sturdy Black Bridges: Visions of Black Women in Literature*. Ed. Roseanne Bell, Bettye Parker, and Beverly Guy-Sheftall. New York: Anchor Books/Doubleday, 1979. 69–86.

Patterson, Raymond. "Helene Johnson." In *Dictionary of Literary Biography: Afro-American*

Writers from the Harlem Renaissance to 1940. Vol. 51. Ed. Trudier Harris. Detroit: Gale, 1987.

Redmond, Eugene. *Drumvoices: The Mission of Afro-American Poetry.* New York: Anchor/Doubleday, 1976.

Roses, Lorraine, and Ruth E. Randolph, eds. *Harlem Renaissance and Beyond: Literary Biographies of 100 Black Women Writers 1900–1945.* Boston: G. K. Hall, 1990.

Wagner, Jean. *The Black Poets.* Urbana: University of Illinois Press, 1973.

JAMES WELDON JOHNSON
(1871–1938)

Louis Hill Pratt

BIOGRAPHY

James Weldon Johnson was born June 17, 1871, to Helen (Dillet) and James Johnson in Jacksonville, Florida. Early in his life, James became aware of the family legacy of black pride and public service, exemplified by his maternal grandfather, Stephen Dillet, who held the position of postmaster in Nassau and served in the Bahaman House of Assembly for thirty years. By precept, the elder Johnson taught his young son the value of hard work, while Mrs. Johnson taught the boy to read and play the piano. She inspired his classical education. Soon James was reading *David Copperfield, Pickwick Papers, Pilgrim's Progress*, and the works of Sir Walter Scott and the Brothers Grimm. Johnson's middle-class values were firmly rooted in the church, and he attended regularly with his parents.

Having graduated from the eighth grade at Stanton School in 1887, Johnson entered the Preparatory Division at Atlanta University, where he excelled in oratory and athletics. After his graduation in 1894, Johnson returned to Jacksonville as principal at Stanton. By 1901 he had expanded the Stanton curriculum to the high school level, thereby establishing the first high school for blacks in the state of Florida. During this seven-year period, Johnson founded *The Daily American* (1895), the first black daily newspaper in America. Two years later, he became the first black man to be admitted to the Florida bar.

Ironically, Johnson's crowning achievement also came during these early years. On an early February afternoon in 1900, he penned the lyrics for "*Lift Every Voice and Sing*" in recognition of the ninety-first anniversary of President Abraham Lincoln's birth. Set to music by his brother, J. Rosamond, the song was first performed by the Stanton chorus on February 12 during the local celebration. Over the years, the song gained a gradual popularity, and some twenty years later, the National Association for the Advancement of Colored People (NAACP) named it the Negro national anthem. In 1971 it won the Lewis Carroll Shelf Award, and today it has reached international acclaim as the national black anthem.

By 1901 Johnson had resigned as principal at Stanton and joined J. Rosamond and Bob Cole in New York to form a successful musical team. Together they wrote musical plays, light operas, and over 200 songs, including "Under the Bamboo Tree," "Congo Love Song," "Maiden with the Dreamy Eyes," "O Didn't He Ramble," and "Louisiana Lize."

In 1904 Johnson received the honorary A.M. degree from Atlanta University, and from 1906 to 1909 he served as U.S. consul to Puerto Cabello, Venezuela. He married Grace Elizabeth Nail of New York City on February 3, 1910, and he was appointed U.S. consul to Corinto, Nicaragua, where he served until 1913. The following year he was appointed chief of the Editorial Staff of the oldest black newspaper in New York, The New York Age. In 1915 his English version of the libretto to the grand opera Goyescas was performed at the Metropolitan Opera House.

Johnson was appointed field secretary for the National Association for the Advancement of Colored People in 1916, and from 1920 to 1930 he served as the executive secretary. Under his leadership, the NAACP expanded its chapters in the South and began the first statistical analysis of lynching in this country. Johnson initiated the fight to save the Houston Martyrs, black soldiers of the twenty-fourth U.S. Infantry at Fort Sam Houston, who were charged with creating a riot in 1917. Through his direct appeal, President Wilson commuted death sentences for five of these soldiers. Most significant, however, was his valiant, but unsuccessful, fight to have the U.S. Senate pass the Dyer Anti-Lynching Bill in 1922.

Honorary Litt.D. degrees from Talladega College (1917) and Howard University (1923) were conferred on Johnson, and he was awarded the Spingarn Medal in 1925. His folk poem "The Creation" was set to music and performed at a chamber concert in Town Hall, New York City, in 1926, and he received a Julius Rosenwald Fellowship in 1929. The next year Johnson was appointed Adam K. Spence Professor of Creative Literature at Fisk University, and in 1934, he accepted a concurrent appointment as professor of creative literature at New York University.

Johnson died in an automobile-train collision in Great Barrington, Massachusetts, on June 26, 1938, and he was memorialized by his colleagues as a freedom fighter and a man of letters. But Fiorello H. La Guardia, mayor of New York City, appropriately typified him "as a true symbol of man's fight against prejudice, and for the eternal values of truth, justice, and equity" (Baxter 291). Most appropriately, Johnson penned his own epitaph in "The Reward," some twenty years earlier, in two couplets of iambic pentameter verse: "No greater earthly boon than this I crave,/That those who some day gather 'round my grave,/

In place of tears, may whisper of me then,/'He sang a song that reached the hearts of men.' "

MAJOR WORKS AND THEMES

Perhaps James Weldon Johnson's heritage of strong racial pride and dedicated public service led him to the backwoods of rural Georgia for a teaching assignment. As a young college student, urbanized by his experiences in Jacksonville and Atlanta, Johnson was profoundly affected by the folk in the community, and he learned to appreciate John Donne's concept of the interrelationship of all humanity. Johnson developed an affinity for the black masses, and he described a feeling of kinship and oneness: "they were me, and I was they . . . a force stronger than blood made us one" (*Along This Way* 19).

Richard A. Carroll has identified four fundamental principles that influenced Johnson's writings: "(1) black people have made significant contributions to American culture; (2) black writers, to achieve their best results, should treat black material in their works; (3) black people possess a unique racial spirit which can best be represented in literature by black writers; and (4) black writers must develop new literary forms to express adequately this unique racial spirit" (345).

Johnson's reverence for history, his strong religious background, and his sensitivity to folk customs and traditions led him to edit *The Book of American Negro Spirituals* (1925) and *The Second Book of American Negro Spirituals* (1926). These collections reflect his awareness of the fragility and ephemerality of these cultural artifacts, as well as the need to give honor and praise to their creators. Four years later, *Black Manhattan* (1930) was published out of this same awareness; the need to document the unique presence and artistic achievements of blacks in New York City.

The need for experimentation led Johnson to edit *The Book of American Negro Poetry* (1922). In the Preface, he calls for a new form, "capable of voicing the deepest and highest emotions and aspirations, and allow the widest range of subjects and the widest scope of treatment" (*American Negro Poetry*, rev. 1931, 42). The chief value in this volume, however, is that it provided exposure not only for established poets like Paul Laurence Dunbar* and William Stanley Braithwaite* but also for unrecognized writers like Phillis Wheatley,* George Moses Horton,* and Frances E. W. Harper.* Finally, it featured rising stars like Fenton Johnson, Georgia Douglas Johnson,* and Claude Mckay.* The revised, expanded edition published in 1931 gave voice to younger poets like Langston Hughes,* Countee Cullen,* and Arna Bontemps.*

Critics who have examined Johnson's literary contributions seem to be unanimous in their judgment that his literary reputation rests firmly on his poetry. Although he began to write stories and poems while he studied at Stanton, Johnson did not become aware of the race issue until he entered Atlanta University. During these early adult years, he took part in the frequently intense campus discussions of race, which found their way into his poetry. However, although he wrote poetry in nondialect, he continued to experiment with dialect verse. Examples of his early poetry can be seen in "Sence You Went Away," published in *Century Magazine*, and in "Fifty Years" (written to celebrate the contributions of blacks fifty years after the Emancipation Proclamation), which was featured on the editorial page of the *New York Times* on January 1, 1913.

Johnson's first collection of poetry, *Fifty Years*, appeared in 1917. Typically, the poems are written in couplets, or quatrains, sestets, or octets, with alternating rhyme. Exceptions such as "Brothers" and "Vashti" are written in free verse, a form that Johnson used later in his most successful volume, *God's Trombones*. Common themes include love ("Morning, Noon, Night," "Nobody's Lookin' but De Owl and De Moon"); death ('De Little Pickaninny's Gone to Sleep," "The Glory of the Day Was in Her Face"); racial pride ("O Black and Unknown Bards"); sulf-sufficiency ("Answer to Prayer"); and brotherhood ("O Southland").

The division of this collection into an opening section of forty-nine nondialect poems, followed by "Jingles and Croons," an accumulation of sixteen poems written entirely in dialect, reflects a certain ambivalence, intended or not, between the two modes that Johnson had experienced for nearly twenty years. This dichotomy began to surface during the summer of 1900, Johnson later tells us, when he read Whitman's *Leaves of Grass*, which left him "engulfed and submerged" and led him to the conclusion "that nothing I had written, with the exception of the hymn for the Lincoln celebration, rose above puerility" (*Along This Way* 158). He began to recognize dialect poetry "as an instrument of expression to but two emotions, pathos and humor, thereby making every poem either only sad or only funny" (*Along This Way* 159). This problem intensified when Johnson joined the Johnson-Cole songwriting team and discovered that he was "bound largely by the white man's stereotypes and prejudices" and that he was compelled to "compromise" his art (Adelman 134).

Consequently, Johnson abandoned dialect in 1917, and by 1920 he had assumed leadership of the younger poets of the Harlem Renaissance—Georgia Douglas Johnson, Langston Hughes, Countee Cullen, Claude Mckay, and Fenton Johnson—in their search for a form that would adequately express the essential substance of the black experience. According to Eugenia Collier, Johnson's conviction "that folk experience was a rich source of poetic material, . . . virtually untouched by colored writers . . . [influenced] Johnson's shift to the use of folk idiom in Negro poetry" ("James" 354). Form and substance found their collective embodiment, however, when Johnson published his most critically acclaimed work, *God's Trombones*, in 1927.

In the Preface to this volume, Johnson embraces the folk sermon as an art form and declares his purpose of trying "sincerely to fix something of the old-time Negro preacher" (11). More importantly, however, he praises the *intrinsic* value of the dialect as "the exact instrument for voicing certain traditional phases of Negro life" (7). On the other hand, he justifies his objection to the form on the basis of those *extrinsic* values that have restricted this vehicle of expression to pathos and humor. Johnson makes it clear that this rejection is "not due to any defect of the dialect, but to the mould of convention in which Negro dialect in the United States has been set, to the fixing effects of its long association with the Negro only as a happy-go-lucky or a forlorn figure" (7).

Willingly, Johnson suspends his avowed agnosticism and reaches back to the sermons of his childhood and later life to create "Seven Negro Songs in Verse," as the subtitle of the volume announces. Using the metaphor of the preacher as God's instrument of expression, he exchanges the regular, rigid patterns of stanza and rhyme for the relaxed style of free verse, which allows the full range of religious fervor and praise. Johnson shifts from the omniscient first-person narrator to third person, as his poetic demands require. Instead of focusing on form, Johnson uses the sermons to capture the oldtime preacher's manipulation of repetition, pauses, and cadence to emphasize the Christian messages of love, deliverance, accountability, mercy, salvation, and resurrection.

St. Peter Relates an Incident presents eight dialect poems, as well as twenty-nine nondialect contributions reprinted from *Fifty Years*. The satirical title poem, printed earlier in 1917 in a separate edition, presents St. Peter as the narrator who recalls the consternation of the good white patriots on Resurrection morning when they open the tomb of the unknown soldier and discover that he is black. Unsure of what to do, they finally abandon the soldier entirely and free him to achieve heroic stature by singing and climbing his way into heaven alone. The most famous of the additions, "Lift Every Voice and Sing," appears near the end of the volume, and five other poems are also featured. Written in sonnet form with slight variations, "My City" is an ode to Johnson's beloved Manhattan. "Mother, Farewell," written by Placido on the eve of his execution and translated by Johnson, is similar in form. Johnson describes the "budding girl" and the "maiden in full bloom" in "If I Were Paris," and he rejects both for the mature woman, the "woman sweetly ripe." In "A Poet to His Baby Son," the narrator satirizes the new poets who have abandoned their roles as "dreamers of the essential dreams" and "interpreters of the eternal truth," who "talk abracadabra/in an unknown tongue." The antithesis of the previous poem, "Envoy," employs a poet-narrator who prays for words of "beauty, truth, strength" that "fall sweetly," "burn like beacon fires," or "speed like arrows, swift and sure to the mark."

Johnson's only novel, *The Autobiography of an Ex-Colored Man*, was published anonymously in 1912. Here the interracial narrator traces his boyhood from his being raised by a mulatto mother to a boardinghouse in Atlanta and a cigar factory in Jacksonville. His next adventure finds him wandering in New York, where he adopts a Bohemian lifestyle and winds up touring Europe with his white benefactor. The story comes full circle when the narrator returns to the rural South, where he is traumatized by the lynching of a black man, and feelings of shame cause him to abandon his plan for major contributions to the black race. Following in his father's footsteps, he marries a white woman, becomes independently wealthy, and takes refuge in the white world. By the narrator's own admission, he is a "moral coward," as Robert Bone calls him, because he chooses a life of comfort and convenience over one of satisfaction and fulfillment (47). Because Johnson wanted to avoid the possibility of controversy, he refused to associate himself with a story that might be rejected by the public as dishonest or unrealistic. But contrary to these misgivings, the book was widely praised. Johnson claimed authorship when the book was reissued in 1927, and the theme of the novel, racial pride, forged an important link with the writers of the Harlem Renaissance.

Johnson closes the first stanza of "O Southland" with a statement that reflects Johnson the humanist and the optimist: "Man shall be saved by man." This credo, though evident throughout Johnson's writings, is nowhere more apparent than in his extended essay, *Negro Americans, What Now?* (1934). He admonishes black Americans to resist the encroachment of racism and the erosion of their individual rights. In his detailed plan for progress, Johnson counsels that the fates of blacks and whites are inextricably bound, and, therefore, full integration, not cultivated isolation, is the logical course. He cautions against physical force and prejudice as weapons of retaliation; instead, he counsels strategy and struggle and interracial harmony. We must increase our knowledge and pride in our culture and history, and we must recognize that the black church has unlimited potential for advancing the cause of freedom.

CRITICAL RECEPTION

Criticism of Johnson's writings, in the main, has been favorable, and negative assessments, generally, have been muted. Nearly all of the current criticism, written during the 1960s and 1970s, focuses on his three volumes of poetry and his novel. Citing the meticulous scholarship of the 1970s, appropriately, Julian Mason has called for the intensive study of Johnson's autobiography as a complement to the earlier comprehensive studies of his writing. Sondra K. Wilson's two edited volumes of Johnson's selected writings (1995) are noteworthy because of her efforts to widen the context for viewing Johnson's writings and for the inclusion of heretofore uncollected pieces, especially those published when Johnson served as contributing editor of the *New York Age*.

The Autobiography of an Ex-Colored Man has received its share of generous praise and commendation. Robert Bone accords Johnson preeminent status among early black novelists (4), and he views the novel as a prototype for Renaissance writers because Johnson subordinates "racial protest to artistic consideration" (48). Roger Whitlow reaffirms this influence and argues that Johnson is the major bridge between Charles W. Chesnutt* and the major black writers of the 1920s (65). Arthur P. Davis credits Johnson with breaking from the tradition of the protest novel and presenting the race issue in forthright, unimpassioned prose (31). Moreover, Davis admires the comprehensive picture of black bohemia that the novel presents, as well as the fact that Johnson touches "ever so lightly" and briefly on a romantic relationship between a black man and a white woman. Roger Rosenblatt and Nicholas Canaday discuss Johnson's narrator as an atypical hero whose story lies outside the tradition of black autobiography. Joseph T. Skerrett Jr., Marvin P. Garrett, and Robert E. Fleming explore the use of irony and the development of themes of contemporary interest. Houston A. Baker Jr., and Lucinda Mackethan have conducted studies that compare *Autobiography* with Richard Wright's* *Black Boy* and Ralph Ellison's *Invisible Man*. Eugenia Collier and Roger Whitlow consider the psychological dimensions of the novel that impact the narrator's conflicting duality, resulting in his vacillations between the white and the black worlds.

Richard A. Long and Arthur P. Davis trace the techniques and the messages in Johnson's early poetry as it evolves into the verse of the mature poet. Eugenia W. Collier discusses Johnson's search for the "folk idiom" as a new medium of expression for his poetry.

Of particular significance are contributions published in *The Crisis*. The James Weldon Johnson Memorial (September 1938) and Centennial (June 1971) issues contain valuable assessments of his life and achievements. Sondra K. Wilson's tribute, "James Weldon Johnson Remembered on the Fiftieth Anniversary of His Death" (January 1989), also highlights Johnson's life and legacy.

There are only two full-length studies of Johnson's contributions: Eugene Levy's *James Weldon Johnson: Black Leader, Black Voice* (1973) and Robert E. Fleming's *James Weldon Johnson* (1987). However, recent anthologies supplementing this scholarship have appeared under the editorship of Deirdre Mullane (*Crossing the Danger Water: Three Hundred Years of African-American Writing*, 1993); Henry Louis Gates and Nellie Y. McKay (*The Norton Anthology of African American Literature*, 1997); William L. Andrews et al. (*The Oxford Companion to African American Literature*, 1997); and Bernard Bell, et al. (*Call and Response: The Riverside Anthology of the African American Literary Tradition*, 1998). Jane Tolbert-Rouchaleau's *James Weldon Johnson* is also a vital book in the Black Americans of Achievement series, which is available for young readers.

BIBLIOGRAPHY

Works by James Weldon Johnson

Novel

The Autobiography of an Ex-Colored Man. Boston: Sherman, French, 1912. Reprinted as *The Autobiography of an Ex-Coloured Man*. New York: Knopf, 1927. Reprinted, New York: Penguin Classics, 1990. Reprinted, with an Introduction by Henry Louis Gates Jr. New York: Alfred A. Knopf, 1990.

Essays/History

Black Manhattan. New York: Alfred A. Knopf, 1930. Reprinted, New York: Arno Press, 1968. Reprinted, New York: Atheneum, 1972. Reprinted, with an Introduction by Sondra K. Wilson. New York: Da Capo Press, 1991.

Negro Americans, What Now? New York: Viking Press, 1934. Reprinted, New York: AMS Press, 1938. Reprinted, New York: AMS Press, 1971.

Poetry/Spirituals

Fifty Years and Other Poems. Boston: Cornhill, 1917.

The Book of American Negro Poetry. Ed. and Intro. James Weldon Johnson. New York: Harcourt, Brace, and World, 1922. Rev. ed., 1931. Reprinted, New York: Harcourt, Brace, and World, 1958. Reprinted, New York: Harcourt Brace Jovanovich, 1969. Reprinted, San Diego: Harcourt Brace Jovanovich, 1983.

The Book of American Negro Spirituals. Ed. James Weldon Johnson, with J. Rosamond Johnson. New York: Viking Press, 1925. Reprinted, New York: Da Capo Press, 1989.

The Second Book of American Negro Spirituals. Ed. James Weldon Johnson, with J. Rosamond Johnson. New York: Viking Press, 1926.

God's Trombones: Seven Negro Sermons in Verse. New York: Viking Press, 1927. Reprinted, New York: Penguin Books, 1976. Reprinted, New York: Penguin Classics, 1990. Produced on audiotape by Sondra K. Wilson for Penguin-Highbridge, 1993.

St. Peter Relates an Incident. Private edition. New York: Viking Press, 1930.

St. Peter Relates an Incident: Selected Poems by James Weldon Johnson. New York: Viking Press, 1935. Reprinted, with a Preface by Sondra K. Wilson. New York: Penguin Classics, 1992.

Autobiography

Along This Way: The Autobiography of James Weldon Johnson. New York: Viking Press, 1933. Reprinted, New York: Da Capo Press, 1973. Reprinted, with an introduction by Sondra K. Wilson. New York: Penguin Classics, 1990.

Collected Works

The Selected Writings of James Weldon Johnson. Ed. Sondra K. Wilson. 2 vols. New York: Oxford University Press, 1995.

Studies of James Weldon Johnson

Adelman, Lynn. "A Study of James Weldon Johnson." *Journal of Negro History* 52 (April 1967): 128–45.

Andrews, William L., Frances Smith Foster, and Trudier Harris, eds. *The Oxford Companion to African American Literature.* New York: Oxford University Press, 1997.

Baker, Houston A., Jr. "A Forgotton Prototype: *The Autobiography of an Ex-Colored Man* and *Invisible Man*." *The Virginia Quarterly Review* 49.3 (1973): 433–49.

Baxter, J. Harvey L., ed. "James Weldon Johnson Memorial Issue." *The Crisis* 45.9 (September 1938): 290–310.

Bell, Bernard W., Trudier Harris, William J. Harris, R. Baxter Miller, and Sondra A. O'Neale, eds. *Call and Response: The Riverside Anthology of the African American Literary Tradition.* New York: Houghton-Mifflin, 1998.

Bone, Robert. *The Negro Novelist in America.* New Haven, CT: Yale University Press, 1965.

Canady, Nicholas. "*The Autobiography of an Ex-Coloured Man* and the Tradition of Black Autobiography." *Obsidian* 6.1–2 (Spring/Summer 1980): 76–81.

Carroll, Richard A. "Black Racial Spirit: An Analysis of James Weldon Johnson's Critical Perspective." *Phylon* 32.4 (1971): 344–64.

Collier, Eugenia. "The Endless Journey of an Ex-Coloured Man." *Phylon* 32.4 (1971): 365–73.

———. "James Weldon Johnson: Mirror of Change." *Phylon* 21.4 (1960): 351–59.

Davis, Arthur P. *From the Dark Tower*. Washington, DC: Howard University Press, 1974.

Fleming, Robert E. "Contemporary Themes in Johnson's *Autobiography of an Ex-Coloured Man*. *Negro American Literature Forum* 4.4 (Winter 1970): 120–24.

———. "Irony as a Key to Johnson's *The Autobiography of an Ex-Coloured Man*." *American Literature* 43.1 (March 1971): 83–96.

———. *James Weldon Johnson*. Boston: G. K. Hall, 1987.

Garrett, Marvin P. "Early Recollections and Structural Irony in *The Autobiography of an Ex-Colored Man*." *Critique* 13.2 (1971): 5–14.

Gates, Henry Louis, and Nellie Y. McKay, eds. *The Norton Anthology of African American Literature*. New York: W. W. Norton, 1997.

Harris, Trudier, ed. *Dictionary of Literary Biography*. Vol. 51: *Afro-American Writers from the Harlem Renaissance to 1940*. Detroit: Gale Research, 1987.

Levy, Eugene. *James Weldon Johnson: Black Leader, Black Voice*. Chicago: University of Chicago Press, 1973.

Long, Richard A. "A Weapon of My Song: The Poetry of James Weldon Johnson." *Phylon* 32.4 (1971): 374–82.

Mackethan, Lucinda H. "*Black Boy* and *Ex-Coloured Man*: Version and Inversion of the Slave Narrator's Quest for Voice." *College Language Association Journal* 32.2 (December 1988): 123–47.

Mason, Julian. "James Weldon Johnson." In *Fifty Southern Writers after 1900*. Ed. Joseph M. Flora and Robert Bain. New York: Greenwood Press, 1987. 280–89.

Moon, Henry Lee, ed. "James Weldon Johnson Centennial Issue." *The Crisis* 78.4 (June 1971): 112–41.

Mullane, Deirdre, ed. *Crossing the Danger Water: Three Hundred Years of African-American Writing*. New York: Doubleday, 1993.

Pratt, Louis H. "Lift Every Voice and Sing: The Life of James Weldon Johnson, Educator, Writer, Civil Rights Leader." *Forum: The Magazine of the Florida Humanities Council* 15.2 (Fall 1991): 6–11.

Rosenblatt, Roger. *Black Fiction*. Cambridge: Harvard University Press, 1975.

Skerrett, Jr., Joseph T. "Irony and Symbolic Action in James Weldon Johnson's *The Autobiography of an Ex-Coloured Man*." *American Quarterly* 32.5 (Winter 1980): 540–58.

Tolbert-Rouchaleau, Jane. *James Weldon Johnson*. Philadelphia: Chelsea House, 1998.

Whitlow, Roger. *Black American Literature*. Totowa, NJ: Littlefield, Adams, 1973.

Wilson, Sondra K. "James Weldon Johnson Remembered on the Fiftieth Anniversary of His Death." *The Crisis* (Winter January 1989): 48–51+.

ELIZABETH KECKLEY
(1818/1819–1907)

Lynn Domina

BIOGRAPHY

Elizabeth Keckley was born in either 1818 or 1819 in Dunwiddie Court House, Virginia. Although both of her parents were slaves, they did not reside on the same plantation, so Elizabeth initially saw her father, George Pleasant, only at holidays. While she was still a young girl, her father's owner moved west, and Elizabeth never saw her father again. She and her mother, Agnes Hobbs, belonged to a Colonel A. Burwell.

When Elizabeth was fourteen, she began living with the family of Colonel Burwell's son, Robert, and moved with them to North Carolina when she was eighteen. While living in North Carolina, she gave birth to one son, George, whose father was a white man.

Eventually, Elizabeth returned to Virginia to live with Colonel Burwell's daughter, Ann, and her husband, Mr. Garland. They subsequently moved to St. Louis. While living in St. Louis, Elizabeth obtained work as a seamstress and also made the acquaintance of James Keckley, who proposed marriage. Because she objected to being married as a slave and hence potentially giving birth to further slave children, Elizabeth petitioned Mr. Garland for her freedom. He agreed to sell her and her son for $1,200, a sum Elizabeth proposed to raise through her earnings and loans. Although she had not yet raised the money, she married James Keckley soon thereafter; the marriage was dissolved after eight years due to James' drinking. Eventually, Elizabeth did raise the $1,200, and her manumission papers are dated November 15, 1855.

In 1860 Keckley moved to Baltimore and then to Washington, D.C., intending to earn her living as a dressmaker. She acquired several prestigious clients, including Mrs. Jefferson Davis and Mary Todd Lincoln. When the Civil War began,

Keckley remained in Washington, working frequently in the White House. Her son died fighting in the war.

Because so many former slaves arrived in Washington during the war, especially after the Emancipation Proclamation took effect, Keckley proposed the establishment of the "Contraband Relief Association," an organization of African Americans dedicated to meeting the needs of these newly free persons. Keckley served as president of the association.

After the war, Keckley visited the Garlands in Virginia, claiming that she had suffered little as their slave. The reunion was apparently a happy one, and Keckley visited with the Garlands for several weeks.

When Lincoln was assassinated, Mary Todd Lincoln owed clothing debts of tens of thousands of dollars. To escape this embarrassment, which had received substantial attention in the press, she enlisted the aid of Keckley. They met in New York and attempted to sell several items of Mary Todd Lincoln's clothing and jewelry. This endeavor was unsuccessful, and Keckley received no remuneration for her time or efforts. As a result, she wrote *Behind the Scenes, Or, Thirty Years a Slave and Four Years in the White House*, hoping it would sell enough copies to support her. The publication of this book essentially ended the friendship between Keckley and Lincoln.

During the remaining decades of Keckley's life, she was less engaged in public acts. She died on May 26, 1907.

MAJOR WORK AND THEMES

Elizabeth Keckley's single work is her narrative *Behind the Scenes, or, Thirty Years a Slave and Four Years in the White House*. Keckley dictated this text to an amanuensis who has never been certainly identified but was probably a writer named James Redpath. This book is part slave narrative and autobiography but primarily memoir. Her "thirty years a slave" are covered in the opening three chapters, while the comparatively few years she spent working in Washington constitute the bulk of the book. Because this book was originally published after the Civil War, it is not a militant antislavery text—in fact, Keckley sometimes seems to be understating the degree of violence she witnessed and experienced:

One of my uncles . . . lost a pair of ploughlines, and when the loss was made known the master gave him a new pair, and told him that if he did not take care of them he would punish him severely. In a few weeks the second pair of lines was stolen, and my uncle hung himself rather than meet the displeasure of his master. . . . Rather than be punished the way Colonel Burwell punished his servants, he took his own life. Slavery had its dark side as well as its bright side. (30)

Most of the book is devoted to a discussion of the lives of Abraham and Mary Todd Lincoln rather than to revelations regarding Keckley's personal life. For example, the death of their son, William Lincoln, is the focus of an entire chapter, while Keckley refers to the death of her own son in a single paragraph within that chapter. While Keckley's comments regarding Abraham Lincoln are entirely positive, her responses to Mary Todd Lincoln are sometimes more ambivalent— as they might well be given the fact that Mary Todd Lincoln at least occasionally failed to pay Keckley for her services.

Within the text, Keckley claims that she does not reveal anything about Mary Todd Lincoln that is not already public knowledge, referring to the stories that had already appeared in the press. Much of this information concerns Mary Todd Lincoln's response to the assassination of Abraham, as well as her pecuniary embarrassments and attempts to extricate herself from debt. Perhaps subtly contrasting herself with Mary Todd Lincoln, who had been unpopular as a First Lady, Keckley concludes her narrative with the assertion, "Though poor in worldly goods, I am rich in friendships, and friends are a recompense for all the woes of the darkest pages of life" (330).

CRITICAL RECEPTION

Behind the Scenes was initially reviewed quite negatively, primarily because reviewers believed Keckley had betrayed the trust of those for whom she worked, and the publication of this material was considered at best distasteful. A review in the *New York Times* concludes with these assertions:

As mere gossip, the book is mainly a failure. Mrs. Keckley really knew very little about life in the White House, and she ekes out her scanty stock of story and anecdote with extracts from newspapers, moral reflections and other expedients of like character. The public will be disappointed when they come to read her book. They will find it less piquant, less scandalous, than was expected, considering its source, while as a literary work it can lay claim to very little merit indeed. (10)

Reviews such as this, coupled with Robert Lincoln's attempts to have the book suppressed, resulted in very low sales and no income to Keckley.

In subsequent decades, the book received attention primarily as a historical source regarding the Lincolns. Contemporary biographers of Mary Todd Lincoln particularly cite *Behind the Scenes* and regard it as reliable. Like many books written by African Americans during the nineteenth and early twentieth centuries, this text received little attention from literary critics until comparatively recently.

In the last decade, however, critics have turned their attention to *Behind the Scenes* in increasing numbers and tend to focus their attention on Keckley the narrator and protagonist rather than primarily on her insights into the Lincolns. These critics have taken various approaches to the book and situate it within various contexts, although most contemporary critics do classify it as a slave narrative. In her book, *Mastering Slavery: Memory, Family, and Identity in Women's*

Slave Narratives, Jennifer Fleischner takes a psychoanalytic approach to race and to slavery. Her discussion of Keckley is detailed, and she is one of the few contemporary critics relying on psychoanalytic theory for its insights into group rather than individual behavior.

William Andrews' article, "Reunion in the Postbellum Slave Narrative," was among the first to discuss *Behind the Scenes* as a literary text. He compares Keckley's narrative to Frederick Douglass'* autobiographies. Andrews focuses on the passage in Keckley's text when she returns to visit the Garlands in Virginia. Andrews argues that Keckley was likely sincerely optimistic at the conclusion of the Civil War and saw her reunion with her former owners as a portent of the happy reunion of the various regions of the United States.

In her article "I Was Re-Elected President," Lynn Domina argues that Keckley situates herself primarily as an American rather than as an ex-slave. Domina suggests that Keckley aligns herself with Abraham Lincoln in this endeavor, despite the book's later focus on Mary Todd Lincoln. In her desire to be American, Domina asserts, Keckley can emphasize neither her race nor her gender since, for her, both of those identities contradict American identity; rather, Keckley emphasizes the American virtues such as honesty and self-reliance that she demonstrates.

Although Keckley's book has not yet received the amount of critical attention that has been devoted to some other slave narratives, *Behind the Scenes* is likely to continue garnering interest for the next several years.

BIBLIOGRAPHY

Work by Elizabeth Keckley

Behind the Scenes, Or, Thirty Years a Slave and Four Years in the White House. 1868. New York: Oxford University Press, 1988.

Studies of Elizabeth Keckley

Andrews, William. "Reunion in the Postbellum Slave Narrative: Frederick Douglass and Elizabeth Keckley." *Black American Literature Forum* 23.1 (1989): 5–16.
Domina, Lynn. "I Was Re-Elected President: Elizabeth Keckley as Quintessential Patriot in *Behind the Scenes, Or, Thirty Years a Slave and Four Years in the White House.*" In *Finding Voice/Building Community: Women's Life-Writing.* Ed. Linda Coleman. Bowling Green, OH: Bowling Green State University Popular Press, 1997. 139–51.
Fleischner, Jennifer. *Mastering Slavery: Memory, Family, and Identity in Women's Slave Narratives.* New York: New York University Press, 1996.
Rev. of *Behind the Scenes: Thirty Years a Slave and Four Years in the White House*, by Elizabeth Keckley. *New York Times*, April 19, 1868, 10.

Ryan, Barbara. "Elizabeth Keckley." In *The Historical Encyclopedia of World Slavery*. Vol. 1. Santa Barbara, CA: ABC-CLIO, 1997. 389.

Turner, Justin G., and Linda Levitt Turner. *Mary Todd Lincoln: Her Life and Letters*. New York: Knopf, 1972.

Washington, John E. *They Knew Lincoln*. New York: Dutton, 1942.

EMMA DUNHAM KELLEY-HAWKINS

(?–?)

Julie L. Williams

BIOGRAPHY

While very little is known about Emma D. Kelley-Hawkins, some information can be presumed from the evidence provided by her two novels. The first, *Megda*, was published in 1891 under the pseudonym "Forget-Me-Not." This edition and its reprint in 1892 contain a photograph of the author in the frontispiece, with the inscription "Yours very truly Emma Dunham Kelley." The photograph depicts a young woman of ambiguous race, while scholars express no doubt that Kelley-Hawkins is an African American. Like many postbellum African American writers and professionals, Kelley-Hawkins appears to be mulatto, "whose parentage could be traced back to the master himself during slave times and who found it easier to escape to the North and, after the war, to work their way up the economic ladder than did their darker, more brutalized brothers and their descendants" (Elder 34). Kelley-Hawkins' exposure to higher education reveals itself through her writing, and her subject matter contributes to the assumption of her middle-class status: "Black middle-class writers most often produced for middle-class readers of both races and not for the majority of their people" (Elder 34). Neither *Megda* nor her second novel, *Four Girls at Cottage City*, contains an African American main character.

Like her first novel, *Four Girls at Cottage City* (copyright 1895; publication 1898) was published in Boston. The characters of both novels visit Cottage City, which was renamed Oak Bluffs in 1907, and is located at Cape Cod, Massachusetts. During this period, Cottage City was known as a black resort community. This information implies that Kelley-Hawkins was familiar with Cottage City and may have been a Boston native. Also, the alteration of her surname from Kelley in 1891 to Kelley-Hawkins in 1895 suggests marriage within this four-year gap. She dedicated *Megda* to "My Widowed Mother" and her second novel to "Dear Aunt Lottie Whom I Have Often and Truly Called My 'Second Mother.' "

MAJOR WORKS AND THEMES

Megda and *Four Girls at Cottage City* are linked by a number of thematic similarities. Within the greater picture, the two novels are considered "girl's fiction" (Baym 296)—a branch of the popular, domestic, sentimental novel of the mid-nineteenth century. While also didactic in nature, "girl's fiction" differs from its predecessor, labeled "woman's fiction" by Nina Baym, since it avoids the conflicts faced by women and focuses more on the development of young girls, using a nostalgic tone. By providing behavioral models, "much of this writing targets a youthful reading audience because adolescents, in search of entertaining leisure activities, were especially susceptible to the growing influence of reading for behavioral modification and because social change was effectively sustained by influencing the future generation of adults" (Tate, *Domestic Allegories* 172). During this period, many other African American novelists openly battled against racial injustice and prejudice through their works, while Kelley-Hawkins' novels focus on spiritual uplift without the presence of racial distinction in order to promote change.

Rather than advocating racial egalitarianism in her novels, Kelley-Hawkins confronts class discrimination. In *Megda*, the main character, most often called Meg, becomes enraged when the most pious character of the novel, who also happens to be the poorest, is accused of stealing Meg's essay. With Ruth, who is " 'so poor and so good' " (78), and Maude, who was " 'born rich and wicked' " (78), as the two suspects for the crime, the schoolmistress blatantly overlooks Maude as a possibility and unjustly suspends Ruth from school. When Meg forces Maude to confess her guilt to Ruth and beg for forgiveness, Ruth demonstrates her steadfast faith by immediately accepting her apology and leading a prayer of thanks to God. The young women of *Four Girls at Cottage City* encounter and befriend Charlotte Hood, who is also a poor woman of great faith. Unable to afford proper medical care for her invalid son, Robin Hood, Charlotte accepts her station as God's will and works diligently as a laundrywoman. Becoming a conversion model for her young friends, Charlotte is rewarded when they pool their money together to provide an operation for Robin, who will become a successful doctor.

The evangelical intention of the two novels is quite evident. Debate over the sinfulness of theater and dancing spills over pages and pages in *Four Girls*, and Meg's cherished literary club becomes boycotted by converters due to its public dramatization of *Macbeth*. Due to her love for both theater and dance, Meg struggles to reconcile her interests with the desire to convert. While lynching and other injustices may seem more relevant in a novel written by an African American woman during this period, like many, Kelley-Hawkins portrays the belief that "only the elevation of the spirit would obliterate racism and other 'earthly' injustices" (McDowell xxix). By depicting characters such as Ruth and Charlotte Hood as happy and peaceful, the other characters, as well as the audience, "learned that reward was a product of rational reflection, commitment, and meritorious performance and not a result of one's racial, class, and sexual identity" (Tate, *Domestic Allegories* 174). Within Christian society, all members are considered equal.

Indeed, these novels also aim to uplift the status of women through religious and literary example. Spiritually, "women, largely because they were excluded from male domains, were believed to be morally superior to men and thus better spiritual leaders" (McDowell xxxi). For this reason, Charlotte, not the church, encourages and greatly influences the conversion of the young girls. Charlotte shares her conversion story with them and reveals that reading a woman's novel initiated her own reform. In *Megda*, Meg feels compelled to convert as her friends and siblings gradually do so and positively change. Also, God represents a female figure in these novels, as "these contemporary black women writers see God as maternal, as a spiritual force within the female self, a force detached from the institutional, hierarchical, male-dominated church" (McDowell xxxvii). The God encountered within the novels is loving and merciful rather than wrathful and dominating.

Meanwhile, Kelley-Hawkins asserts her own motivation for writing by affirming "the corrective value of reading appropriate fiction" (Tate, *Domestic Allegories* 172–73) within her novels. Her young models illustrate independence and love for literature while they also strongly react to the portrayal of weak women in the works of their favorite authors. Meg scoffs at the idea of playing Shakespeare's Ophelia since neither she nor Dell, the other possible candidate for the role, could credibly play her: " 'I think I have my share of imagination, but I have not enough to imagine such an impossibility as that. She would more probably send him about his business in double-quick time. No, girls, I cannot imagine Dell speaking like that to any man any more than I can imagine myself doing it' " (44–45). Vera of *Four Girls* adores Tennyson's *Lady of Shalott* but criticizes the work because "['h]e makes his women too weak' " (60). While these works are still considered "appropriate," they are meant to be read critically. Since the Kelley-Hawkins' girls cannot see themselves within these female characters, they acknowledge the differences between themselves and the inferior characters and continue reading. Within her own novels, Kelley-Hawkins can provide female characters worthy of admiration and imitation, which many works lack.

While *Megda* and *Four Girls* provide female characters rich in talent and intelligence, they cannot possibly sustain their independence. As in "woman's fiction," the ultimate resolution in "girl's fiction" is marriage, "represented by harmonious family formations and productive domesticity" (Tate, *Domestic Allegories* 68). These novels are also structured by female Christian bildungsroman, which "defines the experience of achieving adulthood as an experience of renouncing the self and acknowledging total dependence on God" (Hite xxxiii). As married, Christian women, characters such as Meg and Vera must adapt to their roles as wives and mothers. While they can exert their will within the home, very few acceptable roles existed outside the domestic realm for women of this period. Realistically, Meg and Jessie from *Four Girls* could not grow to be great elocutionists despite their indisputable talent. Therefore, "growing up can seem oddly like growing *down*" (Hite xxxiii) for these young women. During this period, "the word 'slavery' was used to describe everything from the domestic condition of women to the practice of pirating works published by foreign authors" (Warren 11). While the characters in Kelley-Hawkins' novels seem to enjoy a sense of equality within their marriages, their lack of freedom is apparent. While Meg's mother, Mrs. Randal, runs her household since Mr. Randal is inexplicably absent and most likely dead, her source of income also remains unknown since she does not leave the home to seek employment. As a middle-class Christian mother of three, Mrs. Randal could not possibly maintain her status within society while working as a laundry woman, such as Charlotte Hood. Due to the restrictions accompanying womanhood, the moral development of the young girls remains central to the novels, and the marriages of Vera and Jessie are briefly touched upon in the last chapter of *Four Girls*.

Through spiritual fulfillment, the characters of *Megda* and *Four Girls at Cottage City* discover a sense of equality within a discriminating world. While Kelley-Hawkins overlooks racial issues in her novels by solely providing white characters (excluding the occasional black servant), she confronts prejudices regarding class and gender, which are also damaging to society. As Claudia Tate suggests, "By making racial difference unimportant, this novel (*Megda*) already presumes as gratified the political objectives of racial equality depicted in traditional black works" (*Psychoanalysis* 24). Despite the absence of racial themes in her novels, through her evangelical theme, Kelley-Hawkins invites her readers to view others through God's eyes—in which all are considered equal.

CRITICAL RECEPTION

Criticism regarding Kelley-Hawkins' novels remains limited. *Four Girls* has been described as "naive and frivolous in its depiction of four carefree girls 'in their pretty summer dresses' off for vacation at a Massachusetts resort" (McDowell xxix) and "a plotless Christian moralizing story stretched through 26 unexciting chapters" (Shockley 177). Meanwhile, it is understood that the expectations of today's audience greatly differ from those of the novels' original readers. Due to the volatile time period and the intended adolescent audience, writers like Kelley-Hawkins "produced less artistic subtlety and more direct moralizing than we late-twentieth-century readers have come to expect or admire" (Tate, *Domestic Allegories* 172). While *Megda* is equally guilty of "direct moralizing" as *Four Girls*—if not more so—its popularity remains evident due to its reprint in 1892. During the 1890s, "[t]hat first audience undoubtedly found pleasurable self-affirmation that reflected their racial and gender aspirations to live in a world where such stories were possible" (Tate, *Domestic Allegories* 6). Today such stories *are* possible, and the recovery of the novels also recovers the sense of hope in which they were once written.

BIBLIOGRAPHY

Works by Emma Dunham Kelley-Hawkins

Novels

(As Forget-Me-Not or Emma Dunham Kelley). *Megda*. Boston: James H. Earle, 1891.
Four Girls at Cottage City. Boston: James H. Earle, 1898.

Studies of Emma Dunham Kelley-Hawkins

Baym, Nina. *Woman's Fiction: A Guide to Novels by and about Women in America, 1820–1870*. 2d ed. Urbana: University of Illinois Press, 1993.
Elder, Arlene A. *The "Hindered Hand": Cultural Implications of Early African-American Fiction*. Contributions in Afro-American and African Studies, 39. Westport, CT: Greenwood Press, 1978.
Hite, Molly. "Introduction." In *Megda*. The Schomburg Library of Nineteenth-Century Black Women Writers. New York: Oxford University Press, 1988.
McDowell, Deborah E. "Introduction." In *Four Girls at Cottage City*. The Schomburg Library of Nineteenth-Century Black Women Writers. New York: Oxford University Press, 1988.
Shockley, Ann Allen. *Afro-American Women Writers 1746–1933: An Anthology and Critical Guide*. Boston: G. K. Hall, 1988.
Tate, Claudia. *Domestic Allegories of Political Desire: The Black Heroine's Text at the Turn of the Century*. New York: Oxford University Press, 1992.
———. *Psychoanalysis and Black Novels: Desire and the Protocols of Race*. New York: Oxford University Press, 1988.
Warren, Kenneth W. *Black and White Strangers: Race and American Literary Realism*. Chicago: University of Chicago Press, 1993.

NELLA LARSEN
(1891–1964)

Emmanuel S. Nelson

BIOGRAPHY

Thadious M. Davis, in her monumental biography of Nella Larsen, offers a compelling narrative of her subject's fascinating life. Davis' reconstruction of Larsen's life is thoughtful and meticulous; yet Larsen emerges as an enigmatic figure, the contours of life shrouded in mystery. Larsen herself is entirely responsible for rendering her life an intriguing puzzle to readers curious about biographical details. Her aloofness, coupled with her deliberate distortions and artful obfuscations, ensured that the story of her life would remain largely fragmentary.

It appears that Nella Larsen was born Nellie Marie Walker in Chicago on April 13, 1891—though she claimed 1893 as the year of her birth—to Marie Hanson, an impoverished Danish woman with no formal education, and Peter Walker, a working-class Afro-Caribbean immigrant. In 1910 she graduated from Fisk Normal School in Nashville and then briefly attended the University of Copenhagen in Denmark. In 1919 she married Dr. Elmer S. Imes, an African American physicist; this marriage to a distinguished scientist granted her considerable prominence within elite social circles. She began to write short stories, two of which were published in *Young's Realistic Stories Magazine* in 1926. *Quicksand*, published in 1928, was Larsen's first major work of fiction; in the following year she published *Passing*, her second and final novel. Both works helped establish her as one of the finest writers of the Harlem Renaissance and a major woman writer of her generation. However, a short story titled "Sanctuary," which she published in 1930, probably ended her writing career. She was accused of plagiarism, and, though she defended herself vigorously, she never attempted to publish anything after the embarrassing scandal.

In the meantime, Larsen's marriage began to falter. In 1933 she attempted suicide twice, first by cutting her wrists and then by jumping out of a first-floor window. Later that year she divorced her husband.

In 1937 in a bizarre quest for anonymity, Larsen pretended to emigrate to South America. This feigned act of emigration was a calculated attempt on her part to disconnect herself from her many friends and to begin a quiet life away from the spotlight. Subsequently, she began to work as a nurse in a New York City hospital. Though her colleagues there considered her reliable and competent, she concealed from them her earlier status as a celebrity. Larsen died alone at age seventy-three: on March 30, 1964—several days after her death from an apparent heart attack—her body was found in her studio apartment by her landlady.

MAJOR WORKS AND THEMES

The two short stories Nella Larsen published in 1926—titled "The Wrong Man" and "Freedom"—contain in embryonic forms some of the major themes she would later explore in her novels. She published both stories under the pseudonym Allen Semi (Nella Imes spelled backwards). Perhaps she intended the white-sounding male name to conceal her gender and racial identities, to "pass" as a white male author in order to enhance the chances of her work being accepted for publication in a white periodical. "The Wrong Man" examines the dilemma of Julia Hammond, once a poor young woman and a mistress of the wealthy Ralph Taylor but now married to a prosperous and influential man. At a glamorous dance party that she attends with her husband, she is terrified to see Ralph Taylor, whom she suspects might expose her secret past. She sends him a message asking him to meet her in a dimly lit area, where she pleads with him not to reveal her secret to her husband. The man agrees. When he lights a cigarette, however, a startled Julia realizes that she had been confessing to a complete stranger, the wrong man. This theme of mistaken identity, in all its complexity and drama, would surface later in her novel *Passing*. "Freedom," Larsen's other short story, anticipates *Quicksand*. The male protagonist of the story decides to leave his pregnant mistress in order to be free. After two years of self-imposed exile in exotic places, he returns to reunite with his mistress. He is devastated when he learns that she had died during childbirth on the same day he had abandoned her. He gradually sinks into depression and ultimately commits suicide by jumping out the window of a high-rise building. Larsen examines this theme of exilic wandering in search of an inadequately defined personal freedom on a much grander scale in her first major work of fiction, *Quicksand*.

Quicksand maps the tragic journey of Helga Crane, who frantically travels from place to place in search of a sense of personal wholeness that eludes her. At the novel's beginning Helga, the daughter of a Danish mother and an Afro-Caribbean father, is an elegant and sophisticated young woman who teaches at Naxos, a black school in the South. The school's pretentious and provincial environment makes her uneasy; her recent engagement to one of her colleagues,

James Vayle, makes her deeply ambivalent about her future status as a staid, middle-class, married woman. Rejecting her job and terminating her engagement, Helga goes to Chicago to see Peter Nilssen, her maternal uncle. Uncle Peter's new wife, when she realizes Helga's mixed racial background, rejects her. Humiliated and distraught, Helga moves to New York, where she manages to become part of Harlem's high society. But the nagging restlessness she felt at Naxos returns, and she begins to feel estranged and uneasy in Harlem as well. Seeking new possibilities, she moves to Denmark to visit some of her mother's relatives in Copenhagen. Her exotic appearance makes her a minor celebrity in the nearly all-white Scandinavian city, but soon she begins to sense that she is seen by the people as a mere curiosity, an exotic and often eroticized object. The crude sexual advances of Axel Olsen, a Danish painter, merely confirm Helga's indignant realization of her racially and sexually fetishized position in a white environment. She longs for the color and vitality of middle-class Harlem. Soon after her return to New York, in a move that is nearly irrational, she marries the Reverend Pleasant Green, an illiterate preacher from the black South. With him she moves to Alabama and proceeds to have a series of children. The novel ends on the unmistakable note that Helga, as she awaits the birth of her fifth child in as many years, is on her deathbed. Her frenetic journey is over, and her quest remains sadly thwarted. As if trapped in quicksand, Helga sinks into oblivion.

Quicksand is a study in alienation, but the roots of Helga's profound sense of estrangement remain unclear. The passage from a Langston Hughes'* poem that Nella Larsen uses as the epigraph for her novel seems to suggest that the protagonist's feelings of disconnection stem from her biraciality: that she feels unsettled, uprooted, and dislocated because of her divided sense of racial self that renders her culturally schizophrenic. At home in neither the black nor the white cultural environment, Helga feels a disabling sense of nonbelonging. But perhaps it is unwise to attribute Helga's alienation entirely to her biracial background because in a variety of contexts—in both black and white social settings—her exquisite, mixed-race body makes her especially desirable and alluring. Therefore, one has to wonder if her disengagement from others as well as her simultaneous and conflicting desire for, and rejection of, intimacy might stem from her dysfunctional family background. She was abandoned by her father and rejected by several members of her mother's family. Therefore, it is indeed quite possible that her fear of intimacy and commitment is linked to her deep-seated fear of abandonment by those whom she begins to care for.

But Quicksand is more than a study in alienation. It is a sensitive portrayal of a woman's attempt to navigate the complex terrain of sexuality marked by racial stereotypes and shaped by historical circumstances. Helga's longing for sexual freedom and autonomy is compromised by her early twentieth-century, conservative, black, middle-class sense of sexual morality forged in response to racist and sexist constructions of the black female body. While Quicksand may not be a full-fledged feminist text in the postmodern sense, it does indeed address with remarkable insightfulness the complex and conflicting positionality of the middle-class black woman situated in the sharp intersections of race, gender, and class. Gently but relentlessly, Larsen exposes the maiming impact of conventional marriage as well as middle-class values and expectations on women's lives and possibilities.

Larsen published her second novel, *Passing*, in 1829. Divided into three sections—"Encounter," "Re-Encounter," and "Finale"—the novel's plot pivots on the relationship between two main characters: Irene Redfield and Clare Kendry. Both women are light-skinned enough to pass for white. Irene, who is married to a Harlem-based physician, passes for white whenever she can use her pseudo-whiteness to gain social privileges that she would be denied otherwise. Clare, however, is married to a pathologically racist white businessman who believes his wife is white. Therefore, Clare carefully conceals her cultural identity and passes for white on a full-time basis. Irene and Clare were childhood friends but had lost touch with each other. The novel begins with their accidental encounter in a sleek Chicago restaurant. They reestablish their friendship. Irene feels vaguely tantalized by Clare, her toughness as well as daring and her haughty disregard for conventional beliefs and values. Yet she is also faintly uncomfortable with the emotional intensity that begins to characterize their friendship. In the second section of the book, Clare visits Irene in New York. The visit, ostensibly, is prompted by Clare's desire to reconnect with her cultural roots, but her motives remain ambiguous. Her friendly overtures to Irene increasingly reveal a subtle, but unmistakable, erotic component. Irene seems to recognize that dimension of their friendship, and that recognition simultaneously excites as well as intimidates her. In the final section of the novel, Larsen stages a dramatic confrontation: Clare's racist husband, in search of Clare, walks into a glamorous party in Harlem and finds her there. Clare's elaborate masquerade collapses; her "real" identity is revealed. Moments later Clare falls out a window and dies. Larsen deliberately leaves unclear the exact cause of Clare's fatal fall. Whether her death was an accident, suicide, or murder—a murder committed either by her irate husband or by a confused Irene—is left to the reader's speculation.

In *Passing*, as in *Quicksand*, Larsen critiques the pretensions and foibles of the black middle class and reveals the many limits that conventional marriage imposes on women's lives. Her primary focus, however, is on exploring the phenomenon of passing from multiple perspectives. That Clare could pass for white undetected even by her bigoted husband raises intriguing questions about the very concept of "race" itself. More so than any other American writer, Larsen uses the not uncommon practice of passing by some light-skinned African Americans to deconstruct the thoroughly unscientific notion of race. The ability of individuals like Irene and Clare to pass for whites successfully subverts the presumed rigidity and impenetrability of racial categories. By destabilizing the idea of race, Larsen exposes it for what it really is: that race is not a biological reality but an elaborate cultural fiction grounded in the politicized pseudoscientific theories of nineteenth-century Europe.

What is even more revolutionary in this seemingly conventional novel is its author's use of the practice of passing—a process that involves establishing and sustaining concocted identities to mislead potentially hostile others and to gain otherwise inaccessible privileges—to examine sexual categories as well. The surface narrative in *Passing* appears innocuous: it deals with the evolving friendship between two middle-class, married women. The subtextual narrative, however, suggests a potential lesbian relationship between the two friends. By embedding two parallel narratives in a single text—a phenomenon that can be termed "bitextuality"—Larsen disrupts the simplistic classifications of complex human sexual responses and behaviors. Larsen unsettles the traditional binary construction of human sexual identity as "homosexual" and "heterosexual" and insists on viewing human sexuality as a continuum: sexuality identity, like racial identity, is not fixed but fluid.

Larsen's final work, which perhaps ended her writing career, was published in a periodical called *Forum* in 1930. Titled "Sanctuary," this short story is set in the rural South; a middle-aged black woman hides a young black man in her house to help him avoid arrest only to discover later that the young man was being sought by the police for the murder of her only son. Soon after its publication several readers found it to be remarkably similar to a short story by Sheila Kaye-Smith, a British author. Larsen, at the request of the editor of *Forum*, wrote an explanatory essay to defend herself against charges of plagiarism. While the editor claimed to be convinced of Larsen's innocence, many questions remained unanswered. The similarities between Larsen's story and that of Kaye-Smith are simply too numerous to be mere coincidences (Davis *Nella Larsen: Novelist of the Harlem Renaissance* 350–53). Perhaps because of the public humiliation caused by this incident, Larsen never attempted to publish anything after 1930.

CRITICAL RECEPTION

Both *Quicksand* and *Passing* received generally favorable reviews when they were published but were soon largely forgotten. However, both works were rescued from their relative obscurity when they were reissued in 1986 by the Rutgers University Press as part of its American Women Writers Series. The republication also coincided with the dramatic new academic as well as popular interest in black American women's writing in general. The considerable critical attention that Larsen's works have received since the mid-1980s has helped reestablish her reputation as one of the most gifted artists of the Harlem Renaissance.

Many of the initial reviews and early criticism of Larsen's novels tended to view both books as elaborations on the theme of the painful predicament of mixed-race women—a frequent theme in nineteenth- and early twentieth-century African American literature. More recent criticism, however, has begun to acknowledge and examine the considerable thematic and narrative complexities of Larsen's art. Ann E. Hostetler, in her 1990 *PMLA* article on *Quicksand*, points out that the novel "deserves serious critical consideration not only as a bold and innovative novel about race and gender but also a searching metaphor for the experiences of many Americans trapped by narrow definitions of race, caught in cultural transition, and alienated from the traditional anchors of family and ethnic tradition" (45). Ann DuCille offers an intriguing reading of *Quicksand*: she argues that a highly developed blues sensibility undergirds Larsen's representation of female sexuality in the novel. Claudia Tate, in her *Psychoanalysis and Black Novels*, proposes a pioneering interpretation of *Quicksand*. She argues that Helga's sexual repression is not merely a result of prevailing ethos but stems from her "incestuous impulse that the text paradoxically conceals and reveals" (147). Tate identifies the object of Helga's psychological quest as the father who abandoned her when she was an infant. Cheryl Wall praises "Larsen's depiction of a memorable protagonist, her adept narration, and her skillful development of the cultural metaphor expressed by the novel's title" and concludes that *Quicksand* "is one of the best novels of the Harlem Renaissance" (105).

Passing, especially in the last few years, has received wider critical attention and acclaim than *Quicksand*. Mary Mabel Youman's superb study of Larsen's clever use of irony remains one of the best articles yet published on *Passing*. Here Youman arrives at the provocative conclusion that Clare, though she passes for white, remains far more connected to her cultural roots than Irene, who thinks and acts like a dull, upper-class, white matron (though, ironically, she does not seem aware of the extent to which she has internalized white values). Peter J. Rabinowitz's essay offers particularly useful ideas on how to teach *Passing* in a way that would challenge what he characterizes as the students' "self-congratulatory liberalism, a liberalism more alert, at least on the surface, to racism than to homophobia" (201). He calls *Passing* "a novel about lesbians passing as heterosexuals that passes as a novel about racial passing" (201). The focus of Jennifer DeVere Brody's article is on Larsen's treatment of social class and its ideological underpinnings, while the subject of Deborah R. Grayson's lively essay is Larsen's shrewd deconstructions of the "raced and gendered bodies in American culture" (37).

Thadious M. Davis, in her critical biography of Nella Larsen, offers useful interpretations of both *Quicksand* and *Passing*. But especially valuable are Davis' close readings of Larsen's short stories, which have received very little scholarly attention.

Larsen and her novels, as the following bibliography indicates, continue to be the subject of numerous sophisticated critical readings. There is more than some irony in the fact that a writer who deliberately sought obscurity during the last three decades of her life should now emerge as a major canonical figure in African American women's tradition in fiction.

BIBLIOGRAPHY

Works by Nella Larsen

(As Allen Semi). "The Wrong Man." *Young's Realistic Stories Magazine* 50 (January 1926): 243–46.
(As Allen Semi). "Freedom." *Young's Realistic Stories Magazine* 51 (April 1926): 241–43.

Quicksand. New York: Alfred A. Knopf, 1928.
Passing. New York: Alfred A. Knopf, 1929.
"Sanctuary." *Forum* 83 (January 1930): 15–18.
"The Author's Explanation." *Forum* Supplement 4, 83 (April 1930): 41–42.

Studies of Nella Larsen

Barnett, Pamela. "My Picture of You Is, After All, the True Helga Crane: Portraiture and Identity in Nella Larsen's Quicksand." *Signs: Journal of Women in Culture and Society* 20.3 (Spring 1995): 575–600.

Blackmer, Corrine E. "African Masks and the Arts of Passing in Gertrude Stein's 'Melanetha' and Nella Larsen's *Passing.*" *Journal of the History of Sexuality* 4.2 (1993): 230–63.

Brody, Jennifer DeVere. "Clare Kendry's 'True Colors': Race and Class Conflict in Nella Larsen's *Passing.*" *Callaloo* 15.4 (1992): 1053–65.

Caughie, Pamela L. " 'Not Entirely Strange, . . . Not Entirely Friendly': *Passing* and Pedagogy." *College English* 54.7 (November 1992): 775–93.

Conde, Mary. "Passing in the Fiction of Jessie Redmon Fauset and Nella Larsen." *Yearbook of English Studies* 24 (1994): 94–104.

Davis, Thadious M. "Nella Larsen's Harlem Aesthetic." In *The Harlem Renaissance: Revaluations.* Ed. Amritjit Singh. New York: Garland, 1989. 245–56.

———. *Nella Larsen: Novelist of the Harlem Renaissance.* Baton Rouge: Louisiana State University Press, 1994.

Dittmar, Linda. "When Privilege Is No Protection: The Woman Artist in *Quicksand* and *The House of Mirth.*" In *Writing the Woman Artist: Essays on Poetics, Politics, and Portraiture.* Ed. Joseph Smith. Philadelphia: University of Pennsylvania Press, 1991. 133–54.

duCille, Ann. "Blue Notes on Black Sexuality: Sex and the Texts of Jessie Fauset and Nella Larsen." *Journal of the History of Sexuality* 3.3 (1993): 418–44.

Fleming, Robert. "The Influence of *Main Street* on Nella Larsen's *Quicksand.*" *Modern Fiction Studies* 31.3 (Autumn 1985): 547–53.

Goldsmith, Meredith. "Edith Wharton's Gift to Nella Larsen: *The House of Mirth* and *Quicksand.*" *Edith Wharton Review* 11.2 (Fall 1994): 3–5, 15.

Gray, Jennifer. "Essence and the Mulatto Traveler: Europe as Embodiment in Nella Larsen's *Quicksand.*" *Novel: A Forum on Fiction* 27.3 (Spring 1994): 257–70.

Grayson, Deborah R. "Fooling White Folks, or, How I Stole the Show: The Body Politics of Nella Larsen's *Passing.*" *Bucknell Review* 39.1 (1995): 27–37.

Horton, Merrill. "Blackness, Betrayal, and Childhood: Race and Identity in Nella Larsen's *Passing.*" *CLA Journal* 28.1 (September 1994): 31–45.

Hostetler, Ann E. "Aesthetics of Race and Gender in Nella Larsen's *Quicksand.*" *PMLA* 105.1 (January 1990): 35–46.

Howard, Lillie. " 'A Lack Somewhere': Nella Larsen's *Quicksand* and the Harlem Renaissance." *Harlem Renaissance Re-Examined.* Ed. Victor E. Kramer. New York: AMS, 1987. 223–33.

Johnson, Barbara. "Lesbian Spectacles: Reading *Sula, Passing, Thelma and Louise,* and *The Accused.*" In *Media Spectacles.* Ed. Marjorie Garber et al. New York: Routledge, 1993. 160–66.

———. "The Quicksands of Self: Nella Larsen and Heinz Kohut." *Telling Facts: History and Narration in Psychoanalysis*. Ed. Joseph Smith and Humphrey Morris. Baltimore: Johns Hopkins University Press, 1992. 184–99.

Larson, Charles. *Invisible Darkness: Jean Toomer and Nella Larsen*. Iowa City: University of Iowa Press, 1993.

Madigan, Mark. "Miscegenation and 'the Dicta of Race and Class': The Rhinelander Case and Nella Larsen's *Passing*." *Modern Fiction Studies* 35.4 (Winter 1990): 523–29.

———. " 'Then Everything Was Dark'?: The Two Endings of Nella Larsen's *Passing*." *Papers of the Bibliographical Society of America* 83.4 (December 1989): 521–23.

McDowell, Deborah E. " 'That Nameless . . . Shameful Impulse': Sexuality in Nella Larsen's *Quicksand* and *Passing*." In *Black Feminist Criticism and Critical Theory*. Ed. Joe Weixlmann and Houston A. Baker Jr. Greenwood, FL: Penkevill, 1988. 139–67.

McLendon, Jacquelyn. "Self-Representation and Art in the Novels of Nella Larsen." *Redefining Autobiography in Twentieth-Century Women's Writing*. Ed. Janice Morgan et al. New York: Garland, 1991. 149–68.

Newman, Richard. "Two Letters from Nella Larsen." *Biblion: The Bulletin of the New York Public Library* 2.2 (Spring 1994): 124–29.

Rabinowitz, Peter J. " 'Betraying the Sender': The Rhetoric and Ethics of Fragile Texts." *Narrative* 2.3 (October 1996): 201–13.

Silverman, Debra. "Nella Larsen's *Quicksand*: Untangling the Web of Exoticism." *African American Review* 27.4 (Winter 1993): 599–614.

Tate, Claudia. "Nella Larsen's *Passing*: A Problem of Interpretation." *Black American Literature Forum* 14.4 (Winter 1980): 142–46.

———. *Psychoanalysis and Black Novels*. New York: Oxford University Press, 1998.

Wall, Cheryl. "Passing for What?: Aspects of Identity in Nella Larsen's Novels." *Black American Literature Forum* 20.2 (1986): 97–111.

Williams, Bettye. "Nella Larsen: Early Twentieth-Century Novelist of Afrocentric Feminist Thought." *CLA Journal* 39.2 (December 1995): 155–78.

Youman, Mary Mabel. "Nella Larsen's *Passing*: A Study in Irony." *CLA Journal* 18 (December 74): 235–44.

JARENA LEE
(1783–?)

Riché Richardson

BIOGRAPHY

Jarena Lee, who became "the first female preacher of the First African Methodist Episcopal Church" (Gates 97), was born February 11, 1783, in Cape May, New Jersey, to free parents. That when she was seven she was sent not far away from her birthplace to be a servant in the Sharp family is among the few known details about her childhood. Hearing a sermon by Richard Allen, who was to become bishop of the African Methodist Episcopal Church in 1816, was the most significant capstone of a sequence of experiences that eventually led to Lee's conversion to Christianity in 1804 at age twenty-one. Months later, after a conversation with a man named William Scott, Lee prayerfully sought and received sanctification of her soul to God as the third and final step in spiritual development beyond conviction and justification from sin.

Lee received the call to preach a few years after her sanctification and went to see Richard Allen "to tell him that I felt it was my duty to preach the gospel" (11). Methodism, as Allen told her, permitted women to exhort and hold prayer meetings but "did not call for women preachers" (11). A marriage in 1811 to Joseph Lee, a pastor, took her six miles away from her familiar surroundings in Philadelphia to Snow Hill. She was unhappy in the Snow Hill church community until she had a dream revealing the importance of Joseph Lee's ministry there. Within six years, death had claimed five members of her family, including her husband. Thus, Lee was "left alone in the world" with an infant and a two-year-old child (14).

Eight years after her initial call, she claimed a space at Mother Bethel Church in Philadelphia to stand and exhort the congregation on the basis of the presiding minister's text; it confirmed for Richard Allen that she was meant to preach, and he gave her his blessing. Subsequently, Lee, who had been a servant into her young adulthood, began her life as a preacher, traveling to places such as New Jersey, New York, Canada, and Ohio. Over the years, she traveled thousands of miles and preached hundreds of sermons. For instance, in 1833 she traveled almost 2,800 miles. In 1835 she preached 692 sermons. Often, Lee traveled on foot with little money and was frequently ill. Most typically, she preached at houses in the communities that she visited to sometimes integrated congregations of blacks and whites, and on several occasions, Indians. Her authority to preach was challenged frequently, and, as in the case of Sojourner Truth,* Lee even suffered the indignity of having her gender questioned. She supported the cause of abolitionism and joined the American Anti-Slavery Society in 1840.

In 1836 Lee paid for the publication of 1,000 copies of her autobiographical narrative, *The Life and Religious Experience of Jarena Lee, a Coloured Lady*, and for its reprinting in 1839. She later expanded this narrative into *The Religious Experience and Journal of Mrs. Jarena Lee*, which was published in 1849. The exact date of Jarena Lee's death is unknown.

MAJOR WORKS AND THEMES

Jarena Lee's two autobiographical narratives provide the most detailed records of her life. Like writings by Zilpha Elaw, Julia Foote, and Rebecca Cox Jackson,* Lee's narratives thematically highlight Christian conversion experience and, as scholars have pointed out, fall within the tradition of spiritual autobiography in the United States. *The Life and Religious Experience of Jarena Lee* consists of twenty pages or so. An introductory chapter provides sketchy details about Lee's personal background and, in keeping with the spiritual autobiography genre, focuses on her conversion to Christianity and subsequent sanctification. Three chapters follow, entitled "My Call to Preach the Gospel," "My Marriage," and "The Subject of My Call to Preach Renewed." Embedded in this text is a subtle argument for sanctification of the soul as a final step in spiritual maturation in the sense outlined by Methodist John Wesley. In the text's epigraph, Lee's modification of Joel 2:28 through a highlighting of the word "daughters" immediately sets forth one of the most important thematic concerns of her spiritual narrative discourse: the assertion of her authority to preach the gospel. Furthermore, Lee stages a general critique of church injunctions against women preachers: "O how careful ought we be, lest through our by-laws of church government and discipline, we bring into disrepute even the word of life. For as unseemly as it may appear now-a-days for a woman to preach, it should be remembered that nothing is impossible with God. And why should it be thought impossible, heterodox, or improper, for a woman to preach? seeing the Savior died for the woman as well as the man" (Andrews 36). Crucial to Lee's narrative methodology is the incorporation of biblical Scriptures from books such as Psalms, Isaiah, and Romans. At times, she likens herself to biblical figures such as Paul, Belshazzar, the disciple Mary, and Jonah. This work is frequently read as an intertext or conflated with *Religious*

Experience and Journal of Mrs. Jarena Lee. However, that it was published just a year after the first set of Maria Stewart's* writings appeared and that it is a sample of spiritual writing from the period in the United States when the abolitionist movement was gaining ground are just two factors that make *The Life and Religious Experiences of Jarena Lee* worthy of engagement on its own terms.

Religious Experience and Journal of Mrs. Jarena Lee embeds within this prior text an extended narrative that is more thematically attentive to Lee's public life as an "incessantly travelling" preacher (Gates 96). As scholars have noted, this volume underscores repetition and nonlinearity as important aspects of Lee's narrative discourse. Black narratives produced within the spiritual autobiography genre manifest what Wilson Jeremiah Moses calls the black Jeremiad by not prioritizing a narrativization of blacks as essentially moral or messianic. Even if there is an articulation of racism and slavery as evils, these narratives generally extend the sin problematic to blacks and whites alike. Frequently, Lee implies that divine retribution has befallen "enemies of the cross" (46), or more specifically, those who have attempted to hinder her preaching. For example, she notes that James Ward, a black preacher in Reading, Pennsylvania, who had adamantly refused to let her speak in his pulpit, "was in a few weeks after I left there, turned out of the church" (44). Numerous passages lay bare the evangelical purposes of this text. For instance, Lee entreats her readers to repent: "Though I may never see you in the flesh, I leave on this page my solemn entreaty that you delay not to obtain the pardoning favor of God; that you leave not the momentous subject of religion to a sick bed or dying hour, but NOW, even now, seek the Lord with full purpose of heart, and he will be found of thee" (31). Interestingly, Lee's rhetorical tropings of concepts set forth in the Declaration of Independence such as "life" and "liberty" have been virtually ignored in critical discussions. Lee chronicles moments when "the word had its more perfect effect" (63) on people to whom she ministered, as well as a few disappointing times when "I shook the dust off my feet and left them in peace" (59). This narrative reveals her as a person who stimulated the growth of schools and churches in the communities that she encountered, as a spiritual mentor for other women, and as one for whom family was at times a touchstone.

Scholars such as Henry Louis Gates Jr., William Andrews, Ann Allen Shockley, Dorothy Porter, Bert James Loewenberg, and Ruth Bogin have made Lee's works readily available. She was a "measurably self-taught person" who had no more than three months of schooling (96). This makes her narrative discourse all the more compelling and remarkable.

CRITICAL RECEPTION

Perhaps Lee has not received much critical attention because so little is known about her life. Frances Smith Foster's important study of black women in the nineteenth century, *Written by Herself*, contextualizes Lee's narrative discourse within African American and women's literary history and highlights "the influences of her multicultural literary heritage" upon her writing (59). In *To Tell a Free Story*, William Andrews suggests that in her 1836 narrative, Lee uses the topos of gender, specifically, an assertion of "her right to the name of preacher, regardless of sexual identity," to further the practice of "rehabilitating alien names" in the African American context (69–70). In his Introduction to *Sisters of the Spirit*, he asserts that this work "offers us the earliest and most detailed firsthand information we have about the traditional roles of women in organized black religious life in the United States and about the ways in which resistance to those roles began to manifest itself" (2). Interestingly, in pointing out the hermeneutic challenges posed by Lee's 1849 narrative, which, as he notes, "reads very much like a log of distances traveled" (23), Andrews seems to invoke iron-ically the AME Book Concern's claim in 1845 that her writing was "impossible to decipher" (Payne 190). On the other hand, Susan E. Houchins has argued that "the travelbook quality of the autobiography emphasizes the theme of the woman preacher's literal search for a locus from which to speak" (Houchins xli). Furthermore, in "*Doers of the Word*," Carla L. Peterson suggests the importance of considering Lee's longer work in light of its rhetorical qualities like orality. However, Peterson is mainly concerned in her discussion with issues relating to the body, space, and writing production. She argues that "the act of composition itself allowed Lee both to deflect a curious public's gaze from her bodily self and to discourage invidious speculations about her gender, as well as to assert her possession of a narrative authority and power of interpretation sanctioned by God" (76). In her essay entitled "Nineteenth-Century Black Women's Spiritual Autobiographies: Religious Faith and Self-Empowerment," Nellie McKay notes that "her text is impressive for its overt feminist qualities: her rejection of the traditional woman's place as wife and mother, her determination to defy gender biases against women's spiritual leadership, and her physical ability to carry out the ministry she did" (149).

BIBLIOGRAPHY

Works by Jarena Lee

The Life and Religious Experience of Jarena Lee, a Coloured Lady, Giving an Account of Her Call to Preach the Gospel: Revised and Corrected from the Original Manuscript by Herself. Philadelphia: Printed and published for the author, 1836.
Religious Experience and Journal of Mrs. Jarena Lee, Giving an Account of Her Call to Preach the Gospel. Philadelphia: Printed and published for the author, 1849.

Studies of Jarena Lee

Andrews, William. *Sisters of the Spirit: Three Black Women's Autobiographies of the Nine-teenth Century.* Bloomington: Indiana University Press, 1986.

————. *To Tell a Free Story: The First Century of Afro-American Autobiography, 1760–1865*. Urbana: University of Illinois Press, 1986.

Bassard, Katherine Clay. "Spiritual Interrogations: Conversion, Community, and Authorship in the Writings of Phillis Wheatley, Ann Plato, Jarena Lee, and Rebecca Cox Jackson." Diss., Rutgers University 1992. *DAI* 54 (1994): 4439A.

Braxton, Joanne M. *Black Women Writing Autobiography: A Tradition within a Tradition*. Philadelphia: Temple University Press, 1989.

Davidson, Phebe. "Jarena Lee (1783–18??)." *Legacy: A Journal of American Women Writers* 10 (1993): 135–41.

Dickerson, Dennis. "The History of Women in Ministry of the African Methodist Episcopal Church." Foreword to *Religious Experiences and Journal of Mrs. Jarena Lee: A Preachin' Woman*. Nashville: AMEC Sunday School Union/Legacy, 1991.

Dodson, Jualynne. "Nineteenth-Century A.M.E. Preaching Women: Cutting Edge of Women's Inclusion in Church Polity." In *Women in New Worlds: Historical Perspectives on the Wesleyan Tradition*. Ed. Hilah F. Thomas and Rosemary S. Keller. Nashville: Abington, 1981. 276–89.

Foster, Frances Smith. "Adding Color and Contour to Early American Self-Portraitures: Autobiographical Writings of Afro-American Women." In *Conjuring: Black Women, Fiction, and Literary Tradition*. Ed. Marjorie Pryse and Hortense J. Spillers. Bloomington: Indiana University Press, 1985. 25–38.

————. "Neither Auction Block nor Pedestal: The Life and Religious Experience of Jarena Lee, a Coloured Lady." *New York Literary Forum* 12 (1984): 143–169.

————. *Written by Herself: Literary Production by African American Women, 1746–1842*. Bloomington: Indiana University Press, 1993.

Gates Jr., Henry Louis. Ed. *Spiritual Narratives*. New York: Oxford University Press, 1988.

Houchins, Susan E. "Introduction." In *Spiritual Narratives*. Ed. Henry Louis Gates Jr. New York: Oxford University Press, 1988. xxix–xliv.

Laprade, Candis Anita. "Pens in the Hands of God: The Spiritual Autobiographies of Jarena Lee, Zilpha Elaw, and Rebecca Cox Jackson." Diss., University of North Carolina, Chapel Hill, 1995. *DAI* (1996): 2682A.

McKay, Nellie Y. "Nineteenth-Century Black Women's Spiritual Autobiographies: Religious Faith and Self-Empowerment." In *Interpreting Women's Lives: Feminist Theory and Personal Narratives*. Ed. Personal Narratives Group. Bloomington: Indiana University Press, 1989. 139–54.

Payne, Daniel. *History of the African Methodist Episcopal Church*. Nashville: AME Sunday School Union, 1891.

Peterson, Carla. *"Doers of the Word": African American Women Speakers and Writers in the North (1830–1880)*. New York: Oxford University Press, 1995.

————. " 'Doers of the Word': Theorizing African-American Writers in the Antebellum North." In *The (Other) American Traditions: Nineteenth-Century Women Writers*. Ed. Joyce Warren. New Brunswick, NJ: Rutgers University Press, 1993. 183–202.

————. "Secular and Sacred Space in the Spiritual Autobiography of Jarena Lee." In *Reconfigured Spheres: Feminist Explorations of Literary Space*. Ed. Margaret R. Higonnet and Joan Templeton. Amherst: University of Massachusetts Press, 1994. 37–59.

Williams, Delores S. "Visions, Inner Voices, Apparitions, and Defiance in Nineteenth-Century Black Women's Narratives." *Women's Studies Quarterly* 21(1993): 81–90.

ALAIN LOCKE
(1886–1954)

Emmanuel S. Nelson

BIOGRAPHY

Alain Locke, one of the formidable intellectuals of his generation, was born on September 13, 1886, to solidly middle-class parents in Philadelphia. After graduating from the Philadelphia School of Pedagogy, Locke enrolled at Harvard University in 1904 and graduated with distinction three years later with a degree in philosophy. In 1907 he became the first African American to win the prestigious Rhodes Scholarship to study at Oxford University. After three years at Oxford, where he earned a degree in literature, Locke pursued graduate studies in philosophy at the University of Berlin for a year before returning to the United States. In 1912 he became an assistant professor of English and philosophy at Howard University in Washington, D.C. However, he returned to Harvard in 1916 for doctoral work. Two years later he received his Ph.D. in philosophy and resumed teaching at Howard University. Although he lectured and taught at a number of American universities during his brilliant academic career, Howard remained his "home" until his retirement in 1952.

Among the many noteworthy aspects of Locke's life is his management of his nontraditional sexuality: Locke was a gay man who, despite the strident homophobia of his times, did little to conceal his homosexuality.

Even after his retirement, Locke continued to be a prolific writer. At the time of his death in June 1954, he left behind not only an impressive body of published work but also a large number of unpublished manuscripts. Several of those manuscripts were published posthumously.

MAJOR WORK AND THEMES

Locke was not a creative writer in the conventional sense of the term. He was a philosopher and literary critic by training, though his intellectual interests

included a variety of disciplines—such as art, music, anthropology, political theory, and African studies, among others. Truly a Renaissance man, Locke published over 200 articles on an astonishing range of topics and edited as well as
authored several significant books.

Among Locke's publications, the work that most interests scholars of African
American literature is his groundbreaking anthology *The New Negro*. This volume, published in 1925, not only signaled the advent of the Harlem Renaissance
but ensured its continuity well into the 1930s. Initially conceived as a special
issue of the journal *Survey Graphic*, Locke's *The New Negro* consists of two parts.
The first section is devoted largely to creative works—short fiction and poetry—
but also has a few formal articles on African art, African American theater, and
related topics. The second section of the volume is devoted exclusively to nonfiction prose pieces that analyze various aspects of African American history,
politics, and culture. The book was, by any standards, a pioneering achievement:
it brought together the works of many important and influential African American thinkers of the early twentieth century. Some of the writers whose works
appear in the volume are Jean Toomer,* Richard Bruce Nugent,* Langston
Hughes,* Countee Cullen,* Claude Mckay,* Jessie Fauset,* James Weldon Johnson,* Zora Neale Hurston,* Walter White,* and W.E.B. Du Bois.*

Regarded as one of the architects of the Harlem Renaissance, Locke nurtured
the talents of several young artists of the era. Many aspiring writers viewed him
as their mentor. As an educator for over four decades, he helped legitimate and
institutionalize the study of African American literature. As an articulate political theorist, he was one of the early multiculturalists who, rejecting the racist
notion of an American melting pot, advocated instead the principles of cultural
pluralism. He was an integrationist, but his integrationist ideology was founded
on his uncompromising belief in cultural relativism, that is, "the assertion of the
parity of different cultures and rejection of the social Darwinian hierarchy that
supported the nineteenth-century racial and political theories inimical to African
Americans and other groups" (Long 461). A thoroughly cosmopolitan intellectual, Locke was intimately familiar with the European classics but was equally at
home in the traditions of African American expressive folk culture. In *The Negro
and His Music*, for example, Locke not only reveals his deep interest in an appreciation of African American music—particularly the blues and jazz—but
boldly asserts his belief that black music is central to the formation of twentieth-
century American culture.

That Locke, like W.E.B. Du Bois, subscribed to the idea of a Talented Tenth—
the notion that the gifted among African Americans can undermine white racist
theories of black inferiority and provide uplifting leadership to the black masses—
has rendered him vulnerable to charges of elitism. Such allegations, however,
largely lack substance; they tend to simplify the complex vision of Locke. There
is no doubt that his ideological stances were shaped in part by his middle-class
background and his international education. He did, indeed, reject the false
certainties of cultural nationalism and the parochial restrictiveness of monocul-

tural identities. Yet he was fully conscious of the ultimately self-defeating lure of rootless cosmopolitanism. He was too much of a pragmatist to be merely a cosmopolitan; he was too much of a humanist to view himself as inherently superior to the masses of less privileged people. In fact, much of his writing reveals his quest for a synthesis of cosmopolitan sophistication and folk sensibility: his desire to arrive at a definition of racial self that is grounded in a multicultural, global vision.

CRITICAL RECEPTION

Alain Locke's philosophical ideas have received considerable scholarly attention and analysis. Johnny Washington, who has authored two book-length assessments of Locke's philosophy, views him as a canonical figure in the American philosophical tradition and confidently asserts that "Locke's views will remain timely and continue to have a worldwide appeal into the twenty-first century" (A Journey 14). Many critics also acknowledge Locke's considerable contribution to cultural theory and criticism. Patricia Liggins Hill, for example, insists that Locke remains "one of the earliest and most significant black cultural critics in America" who has "provided us with a scholarly, technical analysis of black music" (122).

Locke's politics, however, has evoked widely divergent responses. Critics such as Henry Louis Gates Jr.—who are sometimes identified with the neoconservative wing of the African American political spectrum—view Locke as a central and indispensable figure in African American cultural history (160–67). Others, however, view him with some suspicion. Even George E. Kent, a critic noted for his judicious moderation and impeccable civility, adopts a slightly dismissive tone when he alludes to Locke's politics. Kent characterizes Locke's sensibility as "essentially middle-class" and "somewhat simplistically integrationist" (33). Much more hostile are Patricia Liggins Hill et al., the editors of Call and Response: The Riverside Anthology of the African American Literary Tradition. They accuse him of "conservative cowardice" and "aristocratic inclinations"; they see him as a mere formalist who "believed passionately in the universality of literary texts that were independent of history or social circumstance" (856). While they acknowledge that "he believed in and promoted the black folk tradition in theory," they insist that he "separated himself from real folk in fact" (856).

Nevertheless, there is consensus that Alain Locke is a pivotal figure in the Harlem Renaissance of the 1920s and 1930s. His nurturing presence helped energize that extraordinary cultural phenomenon; once the renaissance was under way, he helped expand its boundaries and enhance its visibility. George E. Kent, though skeptical of Locke's politics, concedes that Locke demonstrates "a critical and cultural sensitivity that has not been surpassed." Indeed, few informed critics of African American literature would contest Kent's unequivocal assertion that "it is difficult to imagine the Renaissance without [Locke's] services, critical and otherwise" (33).

BIBLIOGRAPHY

Works by Alain Locke

Decade of Negro Self-Expression. Ann Arbor, MI: University Microfilms, 1928.

The Negro in America. Chicago: American Library Association, 1933.

Negro Art: Past and Present. Washington, DC: Associates in Negro Folk Education, 1936.

The Negro and His Music. Washington, DC: Associates in Negro Folk Education, 1936.

The Negro in American Culture: Based on Material Left by Alain Locke. Ed. Margaret Just Butcher. New York: Alfred A. Knopf, 1956.

The Critical Temper of Alain Locke: A Selection of His Essays on Art and Culture. Ed. Jeffrey C. Stewart. New York: Garland, 1983.

Race Contacts and Interracial Relations: Lectures on the Theory and Practice of Race. Washington, DC: Howard University Press, 1992.

Edited Works

The New Negro. New York: A and C Boni, 1925.

Four Negro Poets. New York: Simon and Schuster, 1927.

Plays of Negro Life. New York: Harper, 1927.

The Negro in Art: A Pictorial Record of the Negro Artist and of the Negro Theme in Art. Washington, DC: Associates in Negro Folk Education, 1940.

When People Meet: A Study in Race and Culture Contacts. New York: Progressive Education Association, 1942.

Studies of Alain Locke

Akam, Everett H. "Community and Culture Crisis: The 'Transfiguring Imagination' of Alain Locke." *American Literary History* 3.2 (Summer 1991): 225–76.

Gates, Henry Louis, Jr. "Harlem on Our Minds," *Rhapsodies in Black: Art of the Harlem Renaissance* Ed. David A. Bailey. Berkeley: University of California Press, 1997. 160–67.

Harris, Leonard. *The Philosophy of Alain Locke*. Philadelphia: Temple University Press, 1989.

Hill, Patricia Liggins. "Alain Locke on Black Folk Music." In Linnemann, 122–31.

Hill, Patricia Liggins, et al., eds. *Call and Response: The Riverside Anthology of the African American Literary Tradition*. Boston: Houghton Mifflin, 1998.

Kent, George E. *Blackness and the Adventure of Western Culture*. Chicago: Third World Press, 1972.

Linnemann, Russell J., ed. *Alain Locke: Reflections on a Modern Renaissance Man*. Baton Rouge: Louisiana State University Press, 1982.

Long, Richard. "Locke, Alain." *Oxford Companion to African American Literature*. Ed. William L. Andrews et al. New York: Oxford University Press, 1997. 460–61.

Mason, Ernest Douglass. "Alain Locke." In *Dictionary of Literary Biography*. Vol. 51. Ed. Trudier Harris. Detroit: Gale Research, 1981. 313–21.

———. "Alain Locke and Social Realism." *Obsidian* 5.3 (1979): 22–32.

Scruggs, Charles W. "Alain Locke and Walter White: Their Struggle for Control of the Harlem Renaissance." *Black American Literature Forum* 14 (1980): 91–99.

Singh, Amritjit, et al., eds. *The Harlem Renaissance: Revaluations*. New York: Garland, 1989.

Tidwell, John Edgar, and John Wright. "Alain Locke: A Comprehensive Bibliography of His Published Writings." *Callaloo* 4.1–3 (1981): 175–92.

Washington, Johnny. *Alain Locke and Philosophy. A Quest for Cultural Pluralism*. Westport, CT: Greenwood Press, 1986.

———. *A Journey into the Philosophy of Alain Locke*. Westport, CT: Greenwood Press, 1994.

Wintz, Cary D., ed. *Remembering the Harlem Renaissance*. New York: Garland, 1996.

JOHN MARRANT
(1755–1791)

Roland L. Williams Jr.

BIOGRAPHY

An African American born free in New York during the spring of 1755, Marrant produced a memoir and a journal that convey the bulk of what is known about him. Remembering his youth in the given narrative, he pictures himself as a lost boy who began to stray in the wake of a move to the South with his mother, prompted by the death of his father. Since the road that he travels down cuts through territories thick with black slavery, one might expect racial injustice to take the blame for his going wrong. Instead, he cites an ignorance of modesty and morality. Following stopovers in Florida and Georgia, his parent settled him in the port of Charleston, a town busier with the slave trade than any other metropolis. Nevertheless, he says, the city "opened to me a large door of vanity and vice." By thirteen, he recalls, he was "a slave" to the pursuit of every possible evil pleasure that tended to elate him, especially music and dance as well as "fishing and hunting on the Sabbath." According to Marrant, "unstable as water" (430), he was lucky to see the light in time and save himself from doom.

He underwent a change of course that calls to mind the fate of the biblical Saul struck on the road to Damascus by a religious revelation that converts him from a scoundrel to a paragon named Paul. The transformation happened one night when, on his way to play the French horn for a casual crowd, Marrant passed a big assembly hall where the popular evangelist George Whitefield was set to preach. Curious to hear the sermon, he stepped inside the building. More or less immediately, rocked by Whitefield's words, hitting him as profound wisdom, Marrant fell unconscious, collapsed on the floor, and thereafter awoke to find himself a new person. Annoying his former friends and family, he turned into a strict Christian who read the Bible often. Ridicule from them chased him into the wilderness; there the Cherokees took him into captivity and assailed him with awful threats and terrible affronts. Luckily, he talked his way into a secure place among the natives and felt redeemed by his newfound religion. Once let go, following futile efforts to proselytize his captors, he felt called to spend the rest of his days spreading the gospel dear to him, and, except for a brief period of pressed service on a British ship in the midst of the American Revolution, he concentrated on little else.

In his journal, published the year before his death in 1791, he tells of going to London for training to become an ordained minister. Upon accomplishing his goal, he sailed to Nova Scotia and whirled throughout the region for four years on a mission to introduce the tenets of his faith to untold fugitives from American slavery, besides other inhabitants. He participated in the building of a church before he headed to Boston. The New England district rendered racism an unequivocal issue for him as a hateful mob tried to run him out of town to keep him from talking in any meetinghouses. A good friendship with Prince Hall, founder of the first black Masons lodge in the land, helped Marrant stay true to his elected business. In the spring of 1789, he delivered a homily to Hall's association, railing against racial prejudice and spotting in it a shallow sense of humanity on top of history. A year later, burdened with a heavy heart, he returned to England in search of a more agreeable climate. The prospect eluded him at his death and burial in the borough of Islington. Yet and still, dying, he had reason to be proud, for, to his contemporaries, his life signaled the possibility of individual salvation and sanctioned the exercise of human freedom in a spiritual manner that lent him a heroic cast.

MAJOR WORK AND THEMES

Marrant's discourse suggests that he grew disposed to applaud seeing people born to captain their fates in the fashion of swimmers at sea, unable to turn the tide but ready to rise above it, following sound study. This outlook surfaces in his memoir, A Narrative of the Lord's Wonderful Dealings with John Marrant, a Black (1785). The manuscript dismisses an Old World belief in fixed destinies mandating obedience to the orders of a Council or Crown, in effect, the fiats of a pyramidal form of institution placing the average individual on a low rank. In the sixteenth century, Martin Luther posted an early sign of the break from the preceding line of reasoning when he nailed his ninety-five theses against papal rule on the door of a church and stirred up the Reformation. By the time that Marrant came of age, mavericks like George Whitefield, eulogized by the poet Phillis Wheatley,* were flooding the country with cries for "men" to abide by their own consciences in lieu of custom. In private Bible study, true believers of the nonconformist persuasion witnessed just conduct, for they trusted that it permitted people to lift themselves to plateaus of reason from where they could pursue their salvation without dependence on a sovereign ministry. Swayed by the passing tides of thought, Marrant filled his narrative with echoes of scriptural learning that give his personal history the look of a climb to a lofty perch realized through intelligent effort.

Cardinally, revolving around a religious conversion, A *Narrative of the Lord's Wonderful Dealings* bears a striking resemblance to the Numidian autobiography from the fifth century titled the *Confessions of St. Augustine*, sparingly copied by Jonathan Edwards in the composition of his *Personal Narrative*. Additionally, since the text covers a deliverance from captivity attributed to a worship of Providence, it contains a property peculiar to American letters and classically manifested in A *True History of the Captivity and Restoration of Mrs. Mary Rowlandson*. While Marrant's story drew inspiration from a foreign source, its primary thrust was forged by the social currents that ushered in the American Revolution. On the whole, it stands as an embryonic form of art indigenous to the national culture and later raised to the level of a novel epic by the appearance of the *Autobiography of Benjamin Franklin*, along with that of numerous slave narratives, like *The Interesting Narrative of the Life of Olaudah Equiano** or *Gustavus Vassa, the African*, portraying learning as a passage to success. Overall, in substance, Marrant's work symbolizes a strand of an artery in the literary mainstream.

CRITICAL RECEPTION

Other than the first known review of Marrant's writing, criticism of the author has fathomed his memoir as an instance of a formative development in American literature. The oldest extant critique of the work was written by a British writer and published in a 1785 edition of the *Monthly Review*; snide remarks pour from it; the judgment implies that the narrative amounts to little more than a tall tale, like an Irish legend about St. Patrick swimming a river after being beheaded, told to comfort the blind followers of a creed. Still, as Angelo Costanzo notes, the black's story at home and abroad found a very receptive audience that warranted several printings and a few translations. It struck a responsive chord in its time by appealing to a taste for a rising convention, in sum, a spiritual autobiography, remembering a conscientious rebirth and celestial rescue from a grim captivity in the hands of strangers. Recognizing its ties to its milieu, William Andrews labels A *Narrative of the Lord's Wonderful Dealings* "a kind of slave narrative in spiritual terms" (45). Rafia Zafar sees it as a seed of an African American "branch" (57) in a rudimentary field of American literature.

Until the final years of the 1980s, critics suspected that Marrant's narrative betrays an indifference to racism. The majority concurred with Andrews' finding that the black man simply deemed himself a "Christian pilgrim" (45). But, inquiries of his *Journal* (1790) and *Sermon* (1789) overturned the verdict. The diary shows that Marrant faced and fought racial discrimination. His speech expresses an aversion to color prejudice because it licensed inequity for blacks through a denial of their God-given dignity exemplified by the momentous achievements of famous Christians with African roots like Augustine, Chrysostom, Cyprian, Origen, and Tertullian. These discoveries make it likely that, writing his memoir,

Marrant hoped to assure his readers, contrary to conventional wisdom, that black people have the power to set a fine example for everyone to follow by obtaining and employing useful knowledge.

BIBLIOGRAPHY

Works by John Marrant

A Narrative of the Lord's Wonderful Dealings with John Marrant, a Black. London: Gilbert and Plummer, 1785. Included Early Negro Writing, ed. Dorothy Porter. Boston: Beacon Press, 1971.
A Sermon Preached on the 24th Day of June 1789. Boston: Bible and Heat, 1789.
A Journal of the Rev. John Marrant, from August the 18th, 1785, to the 16th of March, 1790. London: J. Taylor, 1790.

Studies of John Marrant

Andrews, William. To Tell a Free Story. Chicago: University of Illinois Press, 1986.
Costanzo, Angelo. Surprizing Narrative. New York: Greenwood Press, 1987.
Kaplan, Sidney. The Black Presence in the Era of the American Revolution. Amherst: University of Massachusetts Press, 1989.
Rev. of Narrative of the Lord's Wonderful Dealings with John Marrant, a Black. Monthly Review 52 (November 1785): 399.
Zafar, Rafia. We Wear the Mask. New York: Columbia University Press, 1997.

CLAUDE MCKAY
(1889 – 1948)

Sarala Krishnamurthy

BIOGRAPHY

One of the most prominent writers of the Harlem Renaissance, Claude Mckay was born in Jamaica, the son of a poor peasant farmer, on September 15, 1889. In his childhood, his education was handled initially by his older brother and later by an Englishman, Walter Jekyll. Jekyll taught Mckay the literary uses of native dialect, which he used effectively later in his poetry and in his novels to create culturally authentic texts. He published two collections of poetry, *Songs of Jamaica* and *Constab Ballads* in England in 1912 and a volume of poetry in 1920 entitled *Spring in New Hampshire and Other Poems*. Subsequently, he moved to the United States to study agriculture. He attended Tuskegee Institute and Kansas City College for two years before giving up his course altogether and moving to New York. He aspired to become a writer. His encounters with the rabid racism of New York engendered in him a violent hatred of the racists. He published another collection of poetry, the first in America, entitled *Harlem Shadows*. Soon he left for Russia and traveled for twelve years in Germany, France, Spain, and Morocco. During his absence from America he wrote and published his fictional works: *Home to Harlem, Banjo, Banana Bottom,* and *Gingertown*. Apart from a compilation of essays, *Harlem: A Negro Metropolis*, and his autobiography, *A Long Way from Home*, he did not publish anything of significance after his three novels. He was married for a brief while, and he had a daughter from this relationship. He formally converted to Roman Catholicism shortly before his death on May 22, 1948.

Mckay combined the rigors of traditional poetry and its conventional metered form with contemporary themes that sprang from his experiences as a black man in a white-dominated society. Often in his poetry and fiction he celebrates the vitality and the spontaneity of the black race by contrasting it with the crass, materialistic society of white people and Western civilization.

MAJOR WORKS AND THEMES

The Harlem Renaissance marked the emergence of a new class of writers in the literary history of the United States. Not only has it been hailed as the point of spiritual, cultural, and artistic reawakening for the African American, but the radical poetics of the movement created a set of politically conscious people sensitive to race issues. Along with Langston Hughes,* Countee Cullen,* Zora Neale Hurston,* and others, Claude Mckay is considered one of the major writers of the Harlem Renaissance. But, whereas the former were American Negroes in search of their racial heritage through an exploration of jazz, the spiritual, and the folk forms, Mckay drew upon his native Jamaican African roots for his literary sustenance. He took immense pride in being black and celebrated what made many middle-class African Americans uncomfortable: the idea of black primitivism. His writings have also been appropriated by the negritude movement. Yet his works embody the deep schism in his personal philosophy and his ambivalent attitude toward everything in life.

All his fictional works and a majority of his poems deal with the concept of cultural dualism—the belief that there is a polarity between the instinctual African self, on one hand, and the intellectualized Western self, on the other. For Mckay, the black embodies disorder, which is associated with vagabondage and animalism, seen as positive forces in his writings, and he contrasted these forces with order, civilization, and rationalism, which he associated with the West. The hedonistic lifestyle of his protagonists in *Home to Harlem* and *Banjo* invokes the deep desire of the Negro searching for his or her identity in an increasingly crass and materialistic white society and the need to forge a new sense of identity through a relationship with other black people to form a community that shares the same joys and sorrows. While Mckay asserts his individuality as a writer, he recognizes the need for an artist to have a sense of a self that is rooted in a nation or a race. He repeatedly affirms his pride in the black race and his belief in the black people.

While Mckay is more famous for his poetry, he has also written five works of fiction, a collection of essays, and an autobiography. His fictional works include three novels—*Home to Harlem*, *Banjo*, and *Banana Bottom*—and his short story collections are entitled *Gingertown* and *Trial by Lynching*, retranslated from Russian to English. The collection of essays is called *Harlem: A Negro Metropolis*, and *A Long Way from Home* is his autobiography.

Home to Harlem has been described as one of the first successful early novels by a black writer and was hugely acclaimed during the year of its publication, selling thousands of copies. The novel delineates in detail the life of Jake, who returns home to Harlem after abandoning his military assignment. The novel traces Jake's spatial and temporal movement in his search for selfhood and ends

with his attainment of happiness with a former prostitute, whom he had immediately picked upon his return to Harlem. The night after his tryst with the
prostitute, Felice, to whom he hands over his last fifty-dollar bill, he awakens to
find himself alone with the money in his hand. Felice, in her generosity, leaves
him the money that she has earned from him. From then on, the mainspring of
Jake's actions is to lead a life of the vagabond, working on a railroad and indulging
himself with good food, good liquor, and beautiful women. In presenting Jake's
style of living, Mckay gets an opportunity to create for his readers Harlem with
the various nightclubs and to describe the pimps and the prostitutes who make
up a part of the world of Harlem. The black women are enticingly beautiful, and
Mckay deals with the problem of prostitution with great sensitivity. He acknowledges that many women of his race have had to resort to this profession because
of their economic situation. However, he suggests that even though black women
turn to prostitution, it does not necessarily rob them of their spontaneity,
warmth, and humanity. Often because black women find acceptance and employment in a white society, unlike their male counterparts, not infrequently the
woman is the breadwinner. Yet it does not mean that she does not long for male
companionship. In *Home to Harlem* Congo Rose, the cabaret dancer, is willing
to share her earnings, meager as they are, with any man who is willing to stay
with her. But she does not find permanent happiness, because she is always
deserted by the men, who exploit her generosity. Therefore, she turns as hard as
a stone and sadomasochistic. As far as she is concerned, men are only the means
for her sexual gratification, and cruelly she demands this from her men.

At the core of the novel is Jake's relationship with another character, Ray,
who is the son of a Haitian government official. Ray's initial education has been
based on the great European classics: the works of Joyce, Shaw, Lawrence, Ibsen,
and others. Subsequently, he goes to the United States of America to study.
When he is a student at Howard University, American troops invade Haiti, and
his father is jailed. Cast adrift, anchorless, in a turbulent Harlem, Ray is unable
to articulate the tensions that crisscross and ravage his consciousness. Though
he has the desire to become a writer, coming from a colonized country and
educated in the colonizer's language and culture, he feels alienated from himself
and is unable to forge an identity through his connection with Negroes in Harlem. For example, though he falls in love with Agatha, he feels intellectually
disconnected from her. His reluctance to establish contact with the Harlem men
and women and his rejection of Agatha's offer of marriage result from the ambivalence created in him by his education. His predicament is partly resolved in
his friendship with Jake. Through Jake's grasp of blackness, life's problems, and
the ease with which he is able to submerge his identity in the Harlem spirit, Ray
gets a glimmer of understanding of the cause of his alienation. But he is not able
to act upon his newfound knowledge and construct a selfhood for himself.
Therefore, at the end of the novel he leaves Harlem and takes up a menial
job as a worker on an Australian freighter, leaving behind his aspirations and
his friendships.

The Negro's quest for identity is the theme that is addressed again in *Banjo*, Mckay's second novel. While the scene has shifted from Harlem to Marseilles, the cultural dualism as configured in the personae of Jake and Ray finds its echoes in a new pair in *Banjo*, Banjo himself, the protagonist of the novel, and Ray, his doppelgänger. The choice of Marseilles as the setting is significant because it is the chief port of Mediterranean commerce and connects Europe to Africa. Mckay indicts Western society for its dehumanizing attitude toward people of a different race, for its hypocrisy, its Christianity, and its sexual purity. In his desire to impose "civilizing" norms on the colonized peoples, Western man has distorted the naturalness of human sexuality. Marseilles is symbolic of the zenith of European civilization and progress; but within its underbelly it hides the ugly, sordid, exploitative, and avaricious nature of the so-called civilized society.

By writing about Banjo, Mckay has succeeded in creating a character who not only convinces because of his authenticity but becomes a symbol in the novel. Banjo is a folk artist and a jazz musician. Playing the instrument for the sheer love of music and not for any monetary benefit, he embodies the true spirit of vagabondage. He is a wandering minstrel, impudent and carefree in his attitude toward life, innovative in his music, and completely shorn of the hypocrisy and restraint exercised by the white jazz musicians of Marseilles. The novel portrays the lower-class Negro's struggle to retain his racial identity and his refusal to get assimilated into the bourgeois mainstream.

As in the previous novel, Ray is the intellectual spokesman for the black people in *Banjo*. Sophisticated, educated, and articulate, Ray is interested in African folktales, African sculpture, and primitivism. In Marseilles, he comes into contact with blacks from the different regions of Africa and derives from them a sense of belonging. Mckay states: "They made him feel that he definitely belonged to a race, weighed, tested and poised in the universal scheme. They inspired him with confidence in them. Short of extermination by the Europeans, they were a safe people, protected by their own indigenous culture" (320). Through Ray, Mckay points out that the African Americans are a deracinated and emasculated lot because of the enfeeblement brought about by miscegenation. Therefore, in order to gain a thorough understanding of themselves and to affirm their racial identity, it is necessary for African Americans to go back to their African roots. Ray is able to derive his vigor from Banjo and feels "buttressed by the boys with a rough strength and sureness that gave him spiritual passion and pride to be his human self in an inhumanly alien world" (322).

As a writer from the Third World, Mckay was cognizant of the devitalizing effect of colonization. The white imperialists not only robbed the land that they had colonized of its riches but also stole from the people their consciousness and a sense of identity. In *Banjo*, Ray mentions the massacre of innocent Indians at Jallianwallah Bagh in Amritsar and urges his compatriots to draw inspiration from the freedom movement in India as led by Gandhi. Mckay emphasized the need for the blacks in America to get organized as a political group so that they can as a community and in one voice fight for their rights. In his autobiography,

A *Long Way from Home*, he says, "When you have your own voting strength, you can make demands on whites, they will have respect for your potential strength. Every other racial group in America is organized as a group, except Negroes" (178). In this, Mckay anticipated the Civil Rights movement and paved the way for black nationalism in America.

In *Banana Bottom*, Mckay reaches the culmination of his artistic endeavors. It is his final novel in terms of both his vision and his art. Described as "the first West-Indian prose classic," and its heroine described as "the first West-Indian heroine" (Ramchand 273), *Banana Bottom* is situated in Mckay's native Jamaica. The Caribbean islands in Mckay's hands take on a paradisial quality, and he evokes the sensuous warmth of the tropics in poetic detail. Jamaica represents all that is pure and natural as contrasted with the sordid artificiality of the metropolitan centers of the Western civilization in his earlier novels. He describes the peace and tranquility of the islands with the rare sensitivity and lyricism that are possible only for an insider. Even in his poetry collection, *Songs of Jamaica*, he recaptures with nostalgia the essence of Jamaica, which is its folk culture. In *Banana Bottom*, he invokes the local culture and the native rhythms by his depiction of the harvest festivals, pimiento picking, house parties, composing of ballads, and other acts of community togetherness.

Against this background, the heroine of the novel, Bita Plant, forges her self-identity. Unlike Jake, Banjo, and Ray of the previous novels, who eke out their existence in the lap of Western civilization, struggling to reconcile their differences in order to acquire an identity, in *Banana Bottom*, Bita Plant is able to integrate herself with her community and her land. The cultural dualism and the violent debates between the polarized pair of heroes of *Home to Harlem* and *Banjo* do not appear in the third novel. The antithetical notions of emotion and intellect, vagabondage and civilization, order and disorder, instinct and rationality do not form the thesis of this novel. Bita Plant combines within herself the dual aspects that caused a conflict in the earlier novels. The success of the novel rests on her ability to relate to her environment and to discover herself.

Banana Bottom traces the progress of Bita Plant from the debilitating influence of an imposed, superficial culture to a discovery of the self through an identification with her inherent nature and culture. She is adopted by Mr. and Mrs. Craig, the white missionaries who rescue her from a troubled past. They send her to England to get educated and take pride in the fact she is completely Westernized. However, the education that she has acquired does not cut her off from her roots. She returns to her homeland and draws tremendous contentment and satisfaction from the simple things in life: "But the pure joy that Bita felt in the simple life of her girlhood was child-like and almost unconscious. The noises of the market were sweeter in her ears than a symphony. Accents and rhythms, movements and colors, nuances that might have passed unnoticed if she had never gone away, were now revealed to her in all their striking detail" (41).

Bita's relationship with Hopping Dick marks the triumph of the instinctual over the rational. The Craigs, in their desire to curb Bita's rebellion against their wishes, arrange a match with the young divinity student Herald Newton Day. However, his act of defilement with a goat releases her from the burden of obeying her adoptive parents, and she is free to be herself. She says: "I thank God that although I was brought up and educated among white people, I have never wanted to be anything but myself. I take pride in being colored and different, just as an intelligent white person does in being white. I cannot imagine anything more tragic than people torturing themselves to be different from their natural unchangeable selves" (169).

Bita's confrontational attitude toward Mrs. Craig is emblematic of the clash between two cultures and two ways of life. She is hostile toward the Craigs' act of charity of taking her in because she believes herself to be a part of an experiment that the imperial race conducts in order to assert its own superiority. She reacts violently to the experiment and to Western education. Her belief in her self and her black identity engenders a sense of pride in being black. She says, "It was murder of the spirit to cultivate a black child to hanker after the physical characteristics of the white," and proclaimed passionately, "rather teach it to delight in its own created self upon the earth, in heaven and in hell" (268). Thus, at the end of the novel Bita marries Jubban, a Jamaican peasant and an uneducated man. For Mckay, Bita is the ideal black girl, mature and proud. She comprehends her racial identity, and her marriage to Jubban is the bedrock of their happiness. This does not mean that she is contemptuous of Western education. Jubban satisfies the physical aspect of her nature, being himself of the earth and in total harmony with his environment, but education gives her gratification of being in touch with the collective wisdom of the white people. Bita represents the best aspect of the black woman, for she has a perfect understanding of the intellectual and physical needs of her self. Even as she is married to Jubban, she continues her education by going to the library. More than anything else, she is supportive of Jubban when he is lost and lonely. Their child is the symbol of the synthesis of African vigor and spontaneity, on one hand, with Western education and civilization, on the other.

An analysis of the three novels of Claude Mckay clearly reveals an emphasis on racial pride and a celebration of blackness and black identity. According to Mckay, the Negroes are capable of unstructured emotional behavior. This strength enables them to resist dehumanization by the white power structure. From Mckay's novels, a theory of black aesthetics developed that anticipated an interest in black culture, music, art and dancing, and developing Third World sensitivity.

In the ultimate analysis it must be noted that Mckay's intellectual proclivities were unrestricted by notions of race or any other consideration. He did not advocate cultural separatism, and he himself was nourished by the great philosophical traditions of Europe and America. He believed that great ideas transcended the barriers of race, class, and creed.

CRITICAL RECEPTION

Critical opinion on Claude Mckay was most favorable subsequent to the publications of his poetry collections. In the 1920s he was regarded as the main driving force behind the Harlem Renaissance. His writings provided an impetus to other black writers who learned to take pride in their racial heritage and their color. But later, he was attacked by many black writers for his depiction of the "lowlife" of the black people. They felt that he was perpetuating the stereotypical notions of the black as immoral, unscrupulous, shiftless, and poor. He used the sonnet form in some of his poetry. His poetry was rejected by many for being too conventional and too limited to sustain the urgency and intensity of his ideas. His prose was condemned for being formless, and he was accused of pandering to the tastes of white society for incorporating exoticism in his writings. However, in recent years, there has been a revival of interest in Mckay, and there is a remarkable change in the critical reception of his works for his ability to transform protest poetry into great art. The primacy of place has been given to him in the canon of African American literature.

Mckay's first volume of poetry, *Songs of Jamaica*, was published when he was still in Jamaica, and it is a compilation of folk verse in native dialect. It has been praised both for its lyrical quality and for the "substantial portrait" (Thurman 555) that it gives of the Jamaican soul. His later poetry was militant in nature because he came under the influence of communism. He did not believe in passive resistance and urged his compatriots to take up cudgels against their oppressors and fight for their rights. He became famous when he published the poem "If We Must Die," protesting against lynching of black people in the Deep South. Wagner calls him a poet of resistance and believes that with this poem he became "the incarnation of the new spirit and the spokesman for a whole people at last resolved to witness no longer, in resignation and submissiveness, the massacre of its own brothers at the hands of the enraged white mob, but to return blow for blow, and if necessary, to die" (229).

While for Wagner, Mckay is, in essence, a black poet, Drayton opines that his poetry is universal. The vitality of his verse, he says, is based on something more than bitterness; it depends on a stubborn resistance to articulating the Negro suffering as a mere racial suffering. Mckay is moved by the resilience of the Negro race and believes that it devolves upon the Negro race to restore the dignity of the human race through its suffering. Drayton states, "Sometimes, too, there is a certain poignancy as he [Mckay] attempts to reconcile his reaction as a Negro with his larger reaction as a human being. To see his verse in terms of mere racialism is to miss this quality" (78). Fully conscious of the Negro plight and sensitive to the pain and misery of the black, he nevertheless strives to maintain his equilibrium. He loses neither his sense of balance nor breadth of vision; he is at once protesting as a Negro and at the same time uttering a cry for humankind as a member of that race.

When *Home to Harlem* was first published, it received mixed reviews. While

it was praised by several reviewers for its depiction of the working-class Negroes—
the longshoremen and roustabouts, housemaids and Pullman porters, waiters and
washroom attendants, cooks and scullery maids—others, like W.E.B. Du Bois,
rejected it vehemently. Du Bois believed that though Mckay had all the materials
of a great piece of fiction, he deliberately set out "to cater for the prurient demand
on the part of the white folk for a portrayal in Negroes of the utter licentiousness
which conventional civilization holds white folk back from enjoying—if enjoyment it can be called" (202). The novel, he said, nauseated him. Robert Bone
states that the plot of *Home to Harlem* is simply a device used by Mckay to help
Jake, the protagonist of the novel, to find the prostitute, Felice. The narrative
structure is "loose and vagrant," and the novel, "unable to develop its primary
conflict bogs down in the secondary contrast between Jake and Ray" (67). Traditionally, there have been two disparaging views of *Home to Harlem*: one, that
it is full of repugnant realism and two, that the plot lacks unity and that the
episodicity of the novel is detrimental to its success because of the lack of coherence and unity in its structure. However, Richard Barksdale explicates that
the episodic nature of the plot is a recapitulation of the picaresque novel in
which the picaro, Jake, is "a carefree hedonist" (339) and that the novel is
actually a study of a symbolic conflict that occurs on two levels. On the first
level, the conflict is between order and disorder, and Jake is "the wise primitive
who has been blessed with an intuitive sense of order" (339). This conflict is
reinforced by another conflict at the second level between "the rational and
animalistic" (343). Thus, the novel is not just an exposé of the joy belt of Harlem
but a symbolic journey undertaken by Jake. Barksdale suggests that the title *Home
to Harlem* is ironic because "in a world in which men are everywhere disorderly
and animalistic, a man like Jake can never find a home" (344).

The theme of cultural dualism that forms the core of *Home to Harlem* is played
out again in Mckay's second novel, *Banjo*. Ray, Jake's alter ego in the first novel,
is retained in Banjo and is more articulate. Bone describes the central conflict
in the novel as black vagabondage versus white civilization being represented by
Banjo, the protagonist, and Ray, Mckay's spokesman. Bone states that Mckay is
unable to sustain the conflict to its very end, and Ray, the intellectual, joins
Banjo's bandwagon. He opines that "the novel slips out of a clear-cut dualism
into a fuzzy dialectical *structure*—thesis, white civilization; antithesis, Banjo; synthesis, Ray" (72).

Banana Bottom, Mckay's last novel, has been proclaimed as his best and most
mature. Ramchand says that the novel is about the "return of the native" (239).
The writer is in full control of his medium. The violent debates of the two earlier
novels are resolved, and the polarized pair of heroes is replaced by a single heroine, Bita Plant. Bone calls *Banana Bottom* "the culmination of Mckay's search
for form" (71). Even though Bita is caught between two cultures, she is free to
return to her folks. Unlike *Home to Harlem* and *Banjo*, *Banana Bottom* has a lyrical
quality and a tranquil tone. Much of the novel is given to the creation of the
idyllic environment of Jamaica. The pastoral element has been described as "ex-

oticism" by some critics, but all critics agree that in *Banana Bottom* Mckay has found artistic fulfillment and that his spiritual journey carried him all over the world but came to rest in his native land. Chellappan states that the success of the novel is due to the fact that it "relates an individual's self-discovery as a discovery of a way of life," and the novelist posits a "psychic integration of setting the work in Jamaica and making his heroine merge with it" (33).

In recent years there has been a revival of interest in Claude Mckay, his poetry, novels, and other writings. While his contribution to the Harlem Renaissance is acknowledged, his status as a writer belonging to the Commonwealth has been given a tremendous boost. His writings have been appropriated by postcolonial critics, like Emmanuel S. Nelson, who sees Ray's dilemma as the predicament of "the colonial and the post-colonial peoples, who, victimized by the flow of imperial history, find themselves as denigrated outsiders in the metropolitan centers of the West" (107). While Nelson argues that *Banana Bottom* is a flawed novel mainly because of the ease with which Bita Plant is able to handle her caste and class identity, he says that the novel, nevertheless, reveals that Mckay's vision of the interconnectedness of self, the other, and the community has essential validity.

P. S. Chauhan states that Mckay's works have seemed paradoxical because they have been read in an "inappropriate frame of reference" (25). To read Mckay as belonging to the Harlem Renaissance and in the context of African American studies is to "dislocate his emotional geography" (23). To treat Mckay as a writer who belongs to the African American tradition is simply to state Jamaica's contribution to the African diaspora since there is no urgent political need as well as contingent expedience for this inclusion. However, if Claude Mckay were to be analyzed as a writer of the colonial world, it would be possible to gain a richer insight into his works, which would lead to a better and a more realistic understanding of his creative energy and his black consciousness. Chauhan states that in order to accommodate all of his works we must take Mckay for what he is: "a colonial writer who happened to stop over in Harlem on his life-long quest for a spiritual home; on a quest, incidentally, that no writer has effectively escaped" (23).

BIBLIOGRAPHY

Works by Claude Mckay

Novels

Home to Harlem. New York: Harper, 1928; reprinted, Chatham, NJ: Harper, 1973.
Banjo, a Story without a Plot. New York: Harper, 1929; reprinted, New York: Harcourt, 1970.
Banana Bottom. New York: Harper, 1933; reprinted, Chatham, NJ: Harper, 1970.

Short Stories

Gingertown. Chatham, NJ: Harper, 1932.
Trial by Lynching: Stories about Negro Life in America. (Retranslated into English from
     Russian language version by Robert Winter). Ed. Alan L. Mcleod. Port Washing-
     ton, NY: Kennikat Press, 1979.

Poetry

Constab Ballads. London: Watts, 1912.
Songs of Jamaica. London: Gardner, 1912; reprinted, London: Mnemosyne, 1969.
Spring in New Hampshire and Other Poems. London: Grant Richards, 1920.
Harlem Shadows: The Poems of Claude Mckay. New York: Harcourt, 1922.

Autobiography

A Long Way from Home. New York: Furman, 1937; reprinted, New York: Harcourt, 1970.

Nonfiction

Harlem: A Negro Metropolis. New York: Dutton, 1940; reprinted, New York: Harcourt,
     1970.

Studies of Claude Mckay

Barksdale, Richard K. "Symbolism and Irony in Mckay's *Home to Harlem.*" *CLA Journal*
     25.3 (March 1972): 84–134.
Beier, Ulli, ed. *Introduction to African Literature: An Anthology of Critical Writing from "Black
     Orpheus."* London: Longmans, 1967.
Bone, Robert. *The Negro Novel in America.* New Haven, CT: Yale University Press, 1958.
Brawley, Benjamin. *The Negro Genius: A New Appraisal of the Achievement of the American
     Negro in Literature and Fine Arts.* New York: Dodd, 1937.
Chamberlain, John. "The Negro as a Writer." *The Bookman* 70.6 (February 1930): 603–
     11.
Chauhan, P. S. "Polarities of the Colonial Imaginations." In *Claude Mckay: Centennial
     Studies.* Ed. A. L. Mcleod. 22–31.
Chellappan, K. "Cultural Dualism in *Banana Bottom*: An Indian Perspective." In *Claude
     Mckay: Centennial Studies.* Ed. A. L. Mcleod. 32–40.
Collier, Eugenia W. "The Four-Way Dilemma of Claude Mckay." *CLA Journal* 15 (1972):
     345–54.
Cooper, Wayne F. *Claude Mckay: Rebel Sojourner in the Harlem Renaissance. A Biography.*
     Baton Rouge: Louisiana State University Press, 1930.
Drayton, Arthur D. "Claude Mckay's Human Pity: A Note on His Protest Poetry." In
     Beier, Ed. London: Longmans, 1967. 76–88.
Du Bois, W.E.B. "The Browsing Reader: 'Home to Harlem.' "*The Crisis* 35.6 (June 1928):
     208.
Giles, James R. *Claude Mckay.* Boston: Twayne, 1976.
Kent, George E. *Blackness and the Adventure of Western Culture.* Chicago: Third World
     Press, 1972.

Mcleod, A. L., ed. *Claude Mckay: Centennial Studies*. New Delhi: Sterling, 1992.

Nelson, Emmanuel S. "Community and Individual Identity in the Novels of Claude Mckay." In *Claude Mckay: Centennial Studies*. Ed. A. L. Mcleod, 106–13.

Ramchand, Kenneth. *The West-Indian Novel and Its Background*. London: Faber and Faber, 1970; 2nd ed., London: Heinemann, 1983.

Thurman, Wallace. "Negro Poets and Their Poetry." *The Bookman* 67.5 (July 1928): 555–61.

Wagner, Jean. "Claude Mckay." *Black Poets of the United States: From Paul Laurence Dunbar to Langston Hughes*. Trans. Kenneth Douglas. Urbana: University of Illinois Press, 1973. 197–257.

RICHARD BRUCE NUGENT
(1906–1987)

Maxine J. Sample

BIOGRAPHY

Writer and artist Richard Bruce Nugent is one of the lesser-known figures of the Harlem Renaissance. Sometimes known as Bruce Nugent and sometimes as Richard Bruce, he was born on July 2, 1906, into a socially prominent African American family and spent much of his early childhood in Washington, D.C. Through poet Georgia Douglas Johnson,* Nugent met Langston Hughes,* and he would later return to New York and develop close friendships with other notable Harlem Renaissance writers. In an autobiographical sketch in Countee Cullen's* anthology of poetry, *Caroling Dusk,* Nugent describes New York as "a glorious something torn from a novel" (205). Nugent, who worked an assortment of menial jobs and traveled extensively, often described himself as penniless but nonetheless happy. Reportedly, many of his poems and drawings were created on pieces of scrap paper.

Nugent published the short story "Sahdji" in *The New Negro* in 1925. This work is considered the earliest known gay text written by an African American. An adaptation of the story, *Sahdji, an African Ballet,* was anthologized in Alain Locke's* *Plays of Negro Life* (1927) and performed at the Eastman School of Music in 1932. Nugent coedited the short-lived *Fire!!* (1926), a literary journal that was to voice the unrestrained expression of the younger Harlem Renaissance artists. Nugent contributed drawings and the story "Smoke, Lilies, and Jade," a semiautobiographical work that has been called the most explicit homoerotic text of the Harlem Renaissance. After the failure of *Fire!!* Nugent found work in the cast of DuBose Hayward's *Porgy.* He again contributed drawings as well as an essay in *Harlem: A Forum of Negro Life,* another short-lived periodical edited by Wallace Thurman* in 1928. In 1927 *Ebony* published his series of artwork *Drawings for Mulattos.*

After the Harlem Renaissance Nugent, like many of his contemporaries, found work with the Federal Arts Project and the Federal Theatre, contributing the "Negroes of New York" manuscript. He later published poetry in *Trend* magazine. Along with artist Romare Bearden, Nugent helped found the Harlem Cultural Council in 1960. In 1970 *Crisis* published the story "Beyond Where the Star Stood Still."

MAJOR WORKS AND THEMES

Nugent published two poems under the name Richard Bruce. "Shadows" voices the racial consciousness characteristic of Harlem Renaissance poetry. "Cavalier" expresses in its solitary, six-lined stanza the speaker's undaunted acceptance of his "new mistress . . . Lady Death" (line 6), calling for the food, drink, and merriment that are to accompany the occasion. Three short stories reflect homosexual themes. "Sahdji," an African morality tale, condemns murder, not homosexual love. Sahdji, the youthful, favored wife of African chief Konombju, is also loved by the chief's son, Mrabo, who patiently waits for the proper moment to express his feelings. However, in his love for Mrabo, Numbo, "a young buck . . . [who] would do anything to make Mrabo happy" (113), kills the chief during a hunting expedition. Ironically, a grieving Sahdji throws herself upon the burning funeral pyre. Similar in style to "Smoke, Lilies, and Jade," this story uses the ellipsis to render a self-conscious modernist text with its fluid stream of consciousness.

Published in *Fire!!*, "Smoke, Lilies, and Jade" features an artist protagonist "content to lay and smoke and meet friends at night . . . to argue and read Wilde . . . Freud . . . Boccaccio and Schnitzler" (34). Alex lies in bed, shrouded with memories of his father's death and his mother's condemnation of his bohemian lifestyle. Nugent uses ellipses to blend memory, dialogue, and sensory impressions as the reader navigates the stream of Alex's thoughts through this prose poem with its self-conscious reflection and dream sequence. Images of blue smoke are woven throughout the story, creating a tapestry of sensuality in Nugent's erotic depiction of the male body as he describes Alex's sexual encounter with Adrian, a male lover. Alex's bisexuality is revealed in his affirmation that he loves both Adrian (Beauty) and Melva, his sweetheart. The story closes with Alex's statement that "one can love two at the same time" (39). The calla lily, with its funnel-shaped flower, and jade, a hard, precious stone that the Portuguese called "stone of the loins," function as sexually suggestive symbols in Nugent's multilayered, lyrical prose.

"Beyond Where the Star Stood Still" recounts the biblical journey of the three Magi to Bethlehem. When they visit an ailing King Herod, he entreats the trio to reveal the Messiah's whereabouts once they find him. As they resume their journey, Casper, the young king of Ethiopia, is approached by Carus, a fourteen-year-old boy described as "the favorite of Herod" (408). Carus warns Casper of King Herod's sinister plan to kill Jesus, professes his attraction to Casper, and begs to accompany the Magi. The story ends with Casper's embracing and consoling a weeping Carus, whose betrayal will bring certain death. Nugent's interjection of homosexuality into a biblical context is apparent in the unmistakably homoerotic portrait of Carus' attraction to Casper.

CRITICAL RECEPTION

Though proponents of "moral uplift" in black artistic expression, such as W.E.B. Du Bois, were troubled by such themes as blatant homosexuality, Nugent's talents were recognized by his contemporaries. Wallace Thurman's *Infants of the Spring*, a satiric portrait of the Harlem Renaissance literary scene, includes a thinly disguised portrait of Nugent. Outliving many major Harlem Renaissance writers, Nugent served as a valuable resource to scholars studying the period. In addition to a few published interviews, critical material on Nugent can be found in *Dictionary of Literary Biography*'s (Garber) volume on writers from the Harlem Renaissance. In his profile Eric Garber writes that Nugent "enjoyed shocking the prudish with his overtly erotic drawings and poetry and his tales of amorous adventure, many of which were unabashedly homosexual" (216). Much more attention has been given to Nugent's work as an artist. Thomas Wirth notes that Nugent "has been legendary for his erotic, art-deco drawings," all of which contain elements of eroticism (16). Ellen McBreen has examined the politics of sexual identity in Nugent's art, examining in particular the homoeroticized bodies of Nugent's Salome series. In general, the exploration of New York's gay community and gay and lesbian studies have brought Nugent and his work additional attention.

BIBLIOGRAPHY

Works by Richard Bruce Nugent

(As Bruce Nugent). "Sahdji." *The New Negro*. Ed. Alain Locke. New York: Boni, 1925. 113–114.
"Shadows." *Opportunity* 3 (October 1925): 296.
(As Richard Bruce). "Smoke, Lilies, and Jade." *Fire!!* 1 (November 1926): 405–8.
(As Richard Bruce). "Cavalier." *Caroling Dusk*. Ed. Countee Cullen. New York: Harper, 1927. 207.
Sahdji, an African Ballet. Plays of Negro Life: A Sourcebook of Native American Drama. Ed. Alain Locke and Montgomery Gregory. New York: Harper, 1927. 388–400.
Sahdji, an African Ballet. Rochester, NY, Eastman School of Music, 1932. (play)
"Narcissus." *Trend* 1 (January/March 1933):127.
"Beyond Where the Star Stood Still." *Crisis* 77 (December 1970):405–8.
Lighting Fire!! Metuchen, NJ: *Fire!!* Press, 1982.

Studies of Richard Bruce Nugent

Garber, Eric. "Richard Bruce Nugent." In *Dictionary of Literary Biography*. Vol. 51: *Afro-American Writers from the Harlem Renaissance*. Ed. Trudier Harris and Thadious Davis. Detroit: Gale, 1987.

Hatch, James. "An Interview with Bruce Nugent: Actor, Artist, Writer, Dancer." New York: Hatch-Billops Collection, 1982. 99.

Hudson, Jean. Interview with Richard Bruce Nugent. April 14, 1982. Special Collections, Schomburg Center for Research in Black Culture, New York.

McBreen, Ellen. "Biblical Gender Bending in Harlem: The Queer Performance of Nugent's *Salome*." *Art Journal* 57.3 (Fall 1998):22–28.

Nelson, Emmanuel S. "African American Literature, Gay Male." In *Gay and Lesbian Literary Heritage*. Ed. Claude J. Summers. New York: Henry Holt, 1995. 8–12.

Wirth, Thomas H. "Richard Bruce Nugent." *Black American Literature Forum* 9 (Spring 1985): 16–17.

ELIZA C. POTTER
(1820–?)

Nikolas Huot

BIOGRAPHY

Although born in Cincinnati, Eliza Potter, née Johnson, was raised in New York City, where, at a young age, she started to work as a domestic for "people of *ton*" (*Hairdresser's* 11). Soon weary of this sedentary life and "being at liberty to choose [her] own course," the free Eliza Potter left New York and traveled west to Buffalo, where she "committed a weakness" and married (12). After a brief stay with her husband, she resumed her travels by journeying north to Canada and then south to Cincinnati, where she briefly settled and spent most of her later life (11). After spending three months in jail for giving information on, and directions to, Canada to a slave, Eliza Potter sailed to Europe as maid and governess, where she witnessed with great pleasure the baptisms of the Prince of Wales and count of Paris, the funeral of the duke of Orleans, and other such events featuring European aristocrats; this fascination with the higher social spheres would be a lifetime attraction that would shape her entire life. Upon returning to the United States, she refused employment as governess and concentrated instead on hairdressing, a skill learned in France that became her principal occupation and wage earner. In 1844 she traveled across the country following the wealthy families to the trendy retreats (Saratoga, Newport, New Orleans), combing and styling ladies' hair for the numerous balls, receptions, and parties. Privy to the gossip and sordid affairs of the upper classes, Eliza Potter decided to share anonymously with the public the wretchedness found "among the rich and fashionable of every land and nation" and, in 1859, published her only work, *A Hairdresser's Experience in High Life* (iv). Written the same year as Harriet Wilson's *Our Nig*, this behind-the-scenes autobiography focuses more, however, on the lives of wealthy white women than on her own; seemingly more preoccupied with white society in the mid-nineteenth century, the author, who is called Iangy by her customers and friends, tells very little about her life. Moreover, although some brief passages reveal Potter's views on slavery, abolition, and colorism, the greater part of the narrative is spent criticizing white standards of beauty and those who long to climb the social ladder.

MAJOR WORK AND THEMES

Written at a time when fugitive slave laws and the unrestricted traveling of free blacks were significant issues, slavery and the plight of the race are rarely mentioned in the autobiography. Seemingly more interested in the predicaments of her white customers, Potter rarely comments on slavery and on the treatment of slaves unless compelled to impart her opinion by one of her customers. One of her recurring observations about slavery, however, is that blacks themselves make the worst and cruelest masters; when visiting New Orleans, she even started a petition "to prevent the colored people from owning slaves" (191). Criticizing mostly the thoughtlessness of some slaveholders rather than the slavery system as a whole, she contends that not all slaves are mistreated and that a good number of them are very well taken care of. Potter, as a free and economically independent mulatto and as one who does not associate with slaves, seems unable to condemn slavery and the system that supports it. Indeed, when a customer reveals herself as an abolitionist, Potter replies:

I am very sorry indeed to hear that . . . I don't like abolitionists, nor any that bear the name, as I have seen so much injustice and wrong, and actually speculation done in that name, that I hate to hear it; but I like every person—slave-holders, free-holders, or any other kind of holders who treat all people right, regardless of nation, station or color; and all men and women who love their Redeemer, will do this without confining themselves to any one name to make themselves conspicuous. (249)

In her autobiography, rather than denouncing slaveholders and slave traders and their poor treatment of slaves, Potter prefers to condemn and stigmatize the nouveau riche and their attempts at climbing the social ladder.

Offering her services exclusively to the high upper classes, Potter treats with contempt all who try to enter high society without good social credentials. Strongly believing in what should be an unchanging and steadfast hierarchy among classes, she contends that all people should stay in their proper social spheres and not attempt to rise through them. By the time Potter was writing, the closed higher social classes of Cincinnati were composed of four distinct circles: the genuine aristocracy, the "moneyed" aristocracy, the church aristocracy, and the school aristocracy composed of "girls whose parents send them to such or such a school because Miss So-and-So goes there; so that, by these means, they may have an *entree* into the higher circles" (196). Interspersed throughout her narrative are examples of belles who tried to make an entry into those higher social circles and miserably failed. Explaining how every class in "every city has its own mode of putting down those they think are getting along too fast," Potter describes how when "passing along the street [she] saw hanging on the knob of a lady's door, an old dress, with needles, thimble, spools of cotton, scissors and everything belonging to a dress-maker. . . . it was done by a neighbor, who thought the lady had forgotten her mother's occupation, so that she might be reminded from what she had sprung" (292–93). Potter, however, not only observes passively but actively plays many roles in the lives of her rich clients. Due to her special status as confidante to ladies who give large parties, Potter is able to obtain invitations for some of her customers who would not otherwise get invited to these soirees. Moreover, in many instances, Potter willingly gives helpful advice to her younger customers just starting out in high life. At the same time, however, those customers have to suffer through what some defined as Iangy's crossness and pride (277). Not satisfied by vehemently criticizing and denouncing the social climbers, the sharp-tongued hairdresser also reproves her established customers and scolds their unladylike attitudes. Indeed, Potter's temperament was so well known in Cincinnati, and her personality was "so opinionated and extroverted that, when her autobiography was published, the public instantly recognized her as the author" (Dean, Introduction xlvii).

CRITICAL RECEPTION

Very little attention has been given to Potter's autobiography so far. Alvin Harlow gathers that, at first, Cincinnati "society was startled" by the publication of *A Hairdresser's Experience in High Life*. "Generally known to have been, in the words of a reviewer, the work of 'the bold, if not very polished pen of Mrs. Potter,' " Harlow comments, "Naturally it was a best seller" (171). Sharon Dean, who is responsible for bringing Potter's book out of anonymity and the first one to analyze the text, sees this work as an inside-outsider look at white society. Moreover, this "protofeminist autobiography," Dean argues, not only offers the reader a "high-spirited account of one very free black woman's refusal to become a stereotype, a refusal to be anything but self-defined" (Introduction lviii-lix) but also "provides a crucial context for Harriet E. Wilson's *Our Nig* . . . and for Toni Morrison's *Beloved*" (Dean, "Eliza" 598). Despite its flaws, this important book, "the first of the genre of behind-the-scenes, tell-all autobiographies," (Dean, "Eliza" 598), contributes largely in bringing black women "from the margin to the center" of history. One would hope that its recent republication by the Schomburg Library of Nineteenth-Century Black Women Writers will help generate more interest in this significant work in African American literature and history.

BIBLIOGRAPHY

Work by Eliza C. Potter

A Hairdresser's Experience in High Life. 1859. The Schomburg Library of Nineteenth-Century Black Women Writers. New York: Oxford University Press, 1991.

Studies of Eliza C. Potter

Blassingame, John W. *Black New Orleans, 1860–1880.* Chicago: University of Chicago Press, 1973.

Dean, Sharon G. "Eliza Potter." In *The Oxford Companion to African American Literature.* New York: Oxford University Press, 1997. 598.

———. "Introduction." In *A Hairdresser's Experience in High Life,* by Eliza Potter. New York: Oxford University Press, 1991. xxxiii–lix.

Graber, Susan P. "*A Hairdresser's Experience in High Life* by Mrs. Eliza Potter: Cincinnati in the Mid-Nineteenth Century." *Bulletin of the Historical and Philosophical Society of Ohio* 25.3 (1967): 215–24.

Harlow, Alvin Fay. *The Serene Cincinnatians.* New York: E. P. Dutton, 1950.

MARY PRINCE
(c. 1788–?)

Nanette Morton

BIOGRAPHY

Born into slavery in Brakish Pond, Bermuda, about 1788, Mary Prince was the first woman to publish a slave narrative. In the fractured tradition of slave families, her mother, a domestic slave, and her father, a sawyer named Prince, had different owners. Mother and child were soon sold to Captain Darrel, who presented them to his granddaughter, Betsey Williams. The white child's "pet" and "little nigger," Mary Prince recalled that she "was too young to understand rightly my condition as a slave" (57). She was hired out as a nurse at the age of twelve and was taught how to spell by a child in that household. When Betsey Williams' mother died, however, her father ignored his daughter's property rights and sold Mary and two of her five siblings. Mary's weeping mother "shrouded" her children for sale and saw each of her daughters bought by a different owner (61).

Mary was bought by Captain I—, who took her to Spanish Point. Upon her arrival she learned what was expected of her by watching her new master and mistress abuse Hetty, the slave who cared for the master's house, children, and livestock. When Hetty, who was repeatedly beaten, miscarried and eventually died, the overtaxed Mary took her place as the family's scapegoat and general factotum. "I was licked, and flogged, and pinched by [the mistress'] pitiless fingers" she later recalled (66). Seeking succor, Mary ran away to her mother, only to be returned by her father, who begged her owner to "be a kind master to her in future" (70).

Captain I—later sold Mary to Mr. D—, the equally abusive owner of a salt-works on Turks Island. Living on a diet of boiled cornmeal, the slaves on Turks Island worked long hours in a deadly combination of salt water and burning sun. Here Mary saw her ailing mother for what proved to be the last time. Her master took her back to Bermuda, where she performed the agricultural and household tasks she had performed for Captain L__. Mr. D__ also forced her to wash his naked body, a task that suggests further sexual abuse. Unable to endure this, she asked to be sold to John Wood, who took her to Antigua. Although she managed to accumulate some savings by taking in extra washing and selling provisions to ships, Mary later developed rheumatism and was unable to do the vast amounts of washing her mistress required. Neglected and abused, she depended on the ministrations of neighbors. Wood and his wife were angered by her inability to work and her decision, made after her religious conversion, to marry. Refusing to let Mary buy herself, they took her to England and threatened to abandon her when she again suffered from rheumatism. Knowing she could obtain freedom in England, Mary Prince left her owners and sought out the Anti-Slavery Society. Eventually, she became the housemaid of abolitionist Thomas Pringle, who wrote both a Preface and an Afterword for her dictated narrative. Since she could not return to Antigua without being reenslaved, the society made several attempts to buy her, all of which seem to have failed.

MAJOR WORK AND THEMES

Most of what we know of Prince comes from her own narrative, published in 1831. Pringle's Preface states that the "idea of writing Mary Prince's history was first suggested by herself": she wanted "the good people of England" to "hear from a slave what a slave had felt and suffered" (55). In the third edition, printed the same year, he reported that Mary was almost blind; any profits from her book would be used for her maintenance.

Though Mary Prince spoke through both an editor and an amanuensis, and although her transcribed words are surrounded by a plethora of material designed to establish her veracity (including the short narrative of a man who has also escaped slavery), her narrative is notable for its authoritative, confident tone. That she maintained this confidence during slavery is evident, for the conversion and marriage that so angered the Woods were a declaration of selfhood: the Moravian Church, to which Mary belonged, emphasized spiritual equality and recognized slave marriages. Although semiliterate, she claimed the right to tell her experience: "I have been a slave myself—I know what slaves feel—I can tell by myself what other slaves feel, and by what they have told me. The man that says slaves be quite happy in slavery . . . that man is either ignorant or a lying person" (94). That she maintained control over her narrative is evident in the editor's added notes, which indicate that "strong expressions . . . are given verbatim as uttered by Mary Prince" (64). Indeed, while emphasizing her trustworthiness, Pringle felt obliged to acknowledge that one of the former slave's "faults" was "a considerable share of natural pride and self-importance" (115). In spite of this, the narrative is bound by the constraints imposed by the Anti-Slavery Society: only the assurances of a white editor of standing could guarantee credibility.

The publication caused controversy, and Mary Prince was called upon to repeat her story orally, in public, on two occasions. She testified in a suit Pringle won against a pro-slavery journalist who had attacked the narrative's veracity and Pringle's reputation. When her former owner tried to defend his own reputation by suing Pringle, however, Pringle lost: in the absence of a white witness, the former slave woman's forthright testimony was not enough. Save for a brief mention in the correspondence of Susanna Strickland, who served as her amanuensis, Mary Prince then disappeared from written records.

CRITICAL RECEPTION

Although several modern editions of Mary Prince's narrative have been produced—most notably, in Henry Louis Gates' *The Classic Slave Narratives* (1987) and William L. Andrews' *Six Women's Slave Narratives* (1988)—the one with the most supplementary information was edited by Moira Ferguson (1987; rev. 1997). In her Introduction and in a more detailed examination of the narrative in *Subject to Others*, Ferguson writes that Mary Prince was forced to encode her abusive sexual experiences because she was subject to the moral constraints of an English public that demanded sexual purity. Unlike the later narratives of American slaves, which tended to portray the slave woman as "a double victim of the two-headed monster of the slavocracy, the lecherous master and the jealous mistress,' " British slave women appeared in Antislavery Society publications "as pure, Christlike victims and martyrs" ("Introduction" 4). Knowing this, Mary's former owner attempted to undermine her authority and restore his reputation as a slave owner by publicly revealing her premarital sexual history. Although the English church's nonrecognition of slave marriage, coupled with the prevalence of sexual coercion, made Prince's history commonplace in the colonies, revelations of premarital liaisons could render her story suspect in England. In spite of this, Lean'tin Bracks notes that this distance between the British public and colonial customs enabled Mary Prince to attack her owners on moral grounds by revealing their cruelty. Bracks links the strength of Mary Prince's resistance to the ongoing rebellions of Caribbean slaves, about which Mary must have heard. Noting that Mary Prince's mother aided her in her first escape attempt, Brenda Berrian writes that her mother, in spite of her enforced absence, showed support for Mary's attempts to resist. Of Prince's relationship to her fellow slaves, Sandra Pouchet Paquet writes that "Mary Prince is as much the subject of her narrative as slavery is," for "the tortured body of [the] female slave speaks through and on behalf of the tortured bodies of men and women and children alike" (131–132). Although exiled to England, Mary, unlike Olaudah Equiano,* still sees the Caribbean as her " 'native place' ": indeed, "telling her life story is a civic and political act that links Prince's individual quest for freedom as a black West Indian woman to the revolutionary restructuring of West Indian society" (132).

BIBLIOGRAPHY

Work by Mary Prince

The History of Mary Prince, a West Indian Slave, Related by Herself. 1831. Rev. ed., Moira Ferguson. Ann Arbor: University of Michigan Press, 1997.

Studies of Mary Prince

Berrian, Brenda F. "Claiming an Identity: Caribbean Writers in English." *Journal of Black Studies* 25.2 (1994): 200–216.

Bracks, Lean'tin L. "*The History of Mary Prince, a West Indian Slave, Related by Herself*: History, Ancestry, and Identity." In *Writings on Black Women of the Diaspora: History, Language, and Identity.* Crosscurrents in African American History. Vol. 1. New York: Garland, 1998. 29–52.

Ferguson, Moira. Introduction to the Revised Edition. "The Voice of Freedom: Mary Prince." *The History of Mary Prince, a West Indian Slave, Related by Herself.* Rev. ed., Moira Ferguson. Ann Arbor: University of Michigan Press, 1997. 1–51.

———. *Subject to Others: British Women Writers and Colonial Slavery, 1670–1834.* New York: Routledge, 1992.

Grant, Joan. "Call Loud: The History of Mary Prince." *Trouble and Strife* 14 (Autumn 1988): 9–12.

Paquet, Sandra Pouchet. "The Heartbeat of a West Indian Slave: *The History of Mary Prince*." *African American Review* 26 (1992): 131–46.

NANCY PRINCE
(1799–c.1856)

Loretta G. Woodard

BIOGRAPHY

Nancy Gardner Prince was born on September 15, 1799, in Newburyport, Massachusetts. She was the second oldest of eight children and had little formal education. After her stepfather died, Prince was forced to become a domestic worker to support her mother and six younger siblings. At age fourteen, Prince went to Essex, then to Salem, where she worked for a family of seven for three months. Due to harsh labor, her health failed, and Prince was returned to her mother in Gloucester to recover. Prince tried, often unsuccessfully, to keep watch over her family. During the winter of 1815–1816, Prince rescued her older sister Silvia from a house of ill repute in Boston. In 1817, while working in Boston, Prince's idea to combine the wages of herself and eldest siblings, to better provide for her family, was short-lived when her mother married a man who expected the older children to support him. To sustain her, while she labored to assist her mother and find homes and employment for her siblings, Prince was baptized on May 9, 1817, by Rev. Thomas Paul. She became a devoutly religious woman and dedicated her life and work to religious teachings.

At the age of twenty-three, Prince left her position in Boston to learn a trade (possibly sewing) and made up her mind to leave her country in 1822. On September 1, 1823, a Mr. Prince, a seaman who had been a visitor in the home of Prince's mother when she was around twelve or thirteen years old, arrived from an earlier voyage to Russia. A year later she married Mr. Prince, on February 15, 1824, and departed with him for St. Petersburg in April.

The Princes arrived in St. Petersburg on June 21, 1824 and were later presented to Emperor Alexander I and Empress Elizabeth. Prince learned the language of the nobility in six months and boarded children, which led to her making baby linen and children's garments. The success of her business warranted employing a journeywoman and apprentices.

In 1833 Prince left St. Petersburg for reasons of health. Mr. Prince stayed two years longer and accumulated some property. However, he died in Russia before he could follow her, leaving his thirty-four-year-old wife on her own in Boston, where she devoted herself to humanitarian service. She organized an institution for homeless children who were shut out of the asylums because of their color, but the orphan asylum closed due to a lack of sufficient funds. Prince also attended meetings of the antislavery societies and was encouraged by friends in the ministry to assist the emancipated slaves in Jamaica.

Prince sailed to Jamaica in 1840, where she helped with the mission in St. Ann. Prince became ill and gave up her position with the St. Ann school. In April 1841 she traveled to Kingston and established a Free Labor School for poor little girls. She returned to America in July 1841 and successfully raised funds for her school throughout Boston, New York, and Philadelphia.

Prince's second voyage to Jamaica was in May 1842 in the aftermath of a bloody insurrection. For three months she managed her Free Labor School but soon realized the devious motives of her colleagues and departed from Jamaica. The voyage was dangerous for Prince, a free woman of color traveling without a companion. Her life was threatened, and her personal belongings were stolen. Though Prince recovered some of her possessions, with the assistance of Lewis Tappan and others in New York City, before heading to Boston in August 1843, her failing health and business setbacks left her financially dependent on her friends from 1848 to 1849.

The following year, in hope of supporting herself, Prince published the first edition of her work *A Narrative of the Life and Travels of Mrs. Nancy Prince*. Between the second and third editions of her narrative, 1853–1856, Prince's health seriously declined. In the Preface to the third and last edition, she added that she had lost the power of her arms. Little is known of Prince's life after the 1856 edition of her narrative, and how Nancy Prince died is not known.

MAJOR WORKS AND THEMES

As a blend of travel literature, essay, and "spiritual" autobiography, Prince's *Narrative* (1850) focuses on her experiences in Russia in the 1820s and 1830s and her missionary work in Jamaica in the 1840s. By also incorporating into her *Narrative* her fifteen-page pamphlet *The West Indies: Being a Description of the Islands, Progress of Christianity, Education, and Liberty among the Colored Population Generally* (1841), she documents, with keen observation, pivotal moments in history and presents detailed accounts of the geography, manners, and customs of the people she encountered.

Most dominant throughout her work, however, are her quest for a self-defining identity, her drive for self-sufficiency and public respect, and her desire to make a contribution to her race (Braxton 51). From the beginning of the narrative, Prince is separated from her family and friends in a quest for a better life. Eventually, deeply affected by her personal experience of racial, sexual, and economic oppression while working as a "free" servant in Massachusetts, Prince decides to leave America for Russia with her husband, Mr. Prince. After he dies, she establishes herself as an independent black woman who works not only to support herself but specifically because it is the right thing for her to do. In her Preface, fifty-four-year-old Prince states, "There are many benevolent societies for the support of Widows, but I am desirous not to avail myself of them, as long as I can support myself by my endeavors." Prince's self-definition comes through her understandings of God's intentions for her as an individual. Consequently, her quest is fulfilled as seen in her attempts to establish schools, asylums, and programs of spiritual instruction, mostly to benefit the children.

Prince's writing reveals her remarkable courage, intelligence, and dedication to helping people. Moreover, it reveals her tireless efforts as a reformer to bridge cultural and geographical gaps in her fight against slavery and her advocacy for woman's rights. Though she is not always open about her own personal life, her narrative broadens our understanding of antebellum life for "free" blacks.

CRITICAL RECEPTION

To date, the critical studies of Prince's major work have been limited to articles in books, which have tried to locate the work within a genre and historical frame. While Vernon Loggins argues that Prince's *Narrative* is "a naive description of the impressions received by an American Negro woman during a sojourn of several years in Russia . . . and . . . Jamaica" (229), Kari J. Winter claims the work "records an extraordinary nineteenth-century life and mind" (600). Putting the narrative into more of a historical perspective, Ronald Walters sees it as "an adventure story, an enigma, and a treasure" [which] stands as one of the few surviving autobiographical accounts by a free black woman in the pre–Civil War North" (ix).

Other critics point to Prince's narrative form and style. Hazel Carby notes how Prince uses "the structure of spiritual autobiography, not to conform to a conventional representation of experience, but to begin to question the limits of those conventions as they contradicted aspects of her own experience" (43). Another critic asserts that the work is "a secularized autobiography that incorporated elements of several genres" (Smith 85). Joanne Braxton notes that Prince's "autobiography is marked by shifts in the patterns of movements that contribute to the overall impression that the story lacks order" (51), but then she further observes that "these changes in narration reflect Prince's discontinuous experience" (51). In examining Prince's writing style, Allison Blakely points out how "her vivid, firsthand account is stirkingly reminiscent of the product of Pushkin's artistic imagination" (18).

One critic claims that the element of mystery "at the center of Nancy Prince's *Narrative* is the author herself" (Walters xxii). Perhaps it is just enough to keep readers and critics "fascinated" with such a historical document.

BIBLIOGRAPHY

Works by Nancy Prince

The West Indies: Being a Description of the Islands, Progress of Christianity, Education, and Liberty among the Colored Population Generally. Boston: Dow and Jackson, 1841.
A Narrative of the Life and Travels of Mrs. Nancy Prince . . . Written by Herself. Boston: Published by the author, 1850.

Studies of Nancy Prince

Andrews, William L., ed. *Sisters of the Spirit: Three Black Women's Autobiographies of the Nineteenth Century.* Bloomington: Indiana University Press, 1986.
Barthelemy, Anthony G., ed. *Collected Black Women's Narratives.* New York: Oxford University Press, 1988.
Blakely, Allison. "Negro Servants in Imperial Russia." In *Russia and the Negro: Blacks in Russian History and Thought.* Washington, DC: Howard University Press, 1986. 15–19.
Braxton, Joanne M. "Fugitive Slaves and Sanctified Ladies: Narratives of Vision and Power." In *Black Women Writing Autobiography: A Tradition within a Tradition.* Philadelphia: Temple University Press, 1989. 50–52.
Carby, Hazel. " 'Hear My Voice, Ye Careless Daughters' ": Narratives of Slave and Free Women before Emancipation." In *Reconstructing Womanhood: The Emergence of the Afro-American Woman Novelist.* New York: Oxford University Press, 1987. 40–43.
Curtin, Philip D. *Two Jamaicas: The Role of Ideas in a Tropical Colony, 1830–1865.* Cambridge, MA: Harvard University Press, 1955.
Foster, Frances Smith. "Adding Color and Contour to Early American Self-Portraitures: Autobiographical Writings of Afro-American Women." In *Conjuring: Black Women, Fiction, and Literary Tradition.* Ed. Marjorie Pryse and Hortense J. Spillers. Bloomington: Indiana University Press, 1985. 27–29.
———. "Gendered Writing for Promiscuous Audiences." *Written by Herself: Literary Production by African American Women, 1746–1892.* Indianapolis: Indiana University Press, 1993. 85–86.
Logan, Rayford W., and Michael R. Winston. *Dictionary of American Negro Biography.* New York: Norton, 1982.
Loggins, Vernon. *The Negro Author: His Development in America.* New York: Columbia University Press, 1931.
Hine, Clark D., ed. "Prince, Nancy Gardner." *Black Women in America: An Historical Encyclopedia.* Vol. 2. New York: Carlson, 1993. 946–47.
Loewenberg, Bert James, and Ruth Bogin, eds. *Black Women in Nineteenth-Century American Life.* University Park: Pennsylvania State University Press, 1976.

McEwan, Jo Dawn. *Notable Black American Women 1607–1950*. Vol. 3. Ed. Jessie Carney Smith. Cambridge: Harvard University Press, 1992. 882–84.

Shockley, Ann Allen, ed. "Nancy Gardner Prince." *Afro-American Women Writers, 1746–1933: An Anthology and Critical Guide*. Boston: G. K. Hall, 1988. 48–51.

Smith, Sidonie. *Where I'm Bound*. Westport, CT: Greenwood Press, 1974.

Spradling, Mary M., ed. *In Black and White*. 3d ed. Detroit: Gale, 1980.

Sterling, Dorothy, ed. *We Are Your Sisters: Black Women in the Nineteenth Century*. New York: W. W. Norton, 1984.

Walters, Ronald G. *A Black Woman's Odyssey through Russia and Jamaica: The Narrative of Nancy Prince*. New York: M. Wiener, 1990.

Winter, Kari J. "Nancy Prince." In *The Oxford Companion to African American Literature*. Ed. William L. Andrews, Frances Smith Foster, and Trudier Harris. New York: Oxford University Press, 1997. 600.

HENRIETTA CORDELIA RAY
(c.1849–1916)

Marva Osborne Banks

BIOGRAPHY

Henrietta Cordelia Ray was born in 1849 in New York City. She was the second daughter and the youngest of the five surviving children of Charlotte Augusta (Burrough) Ray and Charles Bennett Ray. Early biographer Maritcha R. Lyons, writing in *Homespun Heroines*, notes that Ray's family roots extended to "early Negroes of New England, and included aboriginal Indian, and English stock of Massachusetts" (171). Her father, a blacksmith, journalist, and minister, was editor of *The Colored American*, the third black-owned newspaper in the United States. Cordelia (the name she preferred) grew up in a privileged environment where she no doubt enjoyed the advantages of being a member of a prominent black family. Lyons further notes that Charles Ray and his wife, Charlotte, created a home where "birth, breeding and culture were regarded as important assets" (172). He encouraged his children to excel and ensured that all of them earned a college degree.

Details of Ray's formative education are somewhat sketchy; however, records indicate that she earned a master of pedagogy degree from the University of the City of New York (New York University) in 1891. She also studied at the Sauveneur School of Languages, where she became proficient in Greek, Latin, French, and German. Influenced, no doubt, by her sister Florence, who was a teacher, Ray began teaching. She taught for thirty years in the New York City Schools, in the girls' department of Colored American Grammar School No. 1 and at School No. 80, where the noted educator, essayist, and poet Charles Reason was the principal. After an illustrious teaching career, Ray moved with her sister Florence to Woodside, Long Island, where she gave private lessons in music, mathematics, and languages. She also offered a course in English literature for teachers, served as corresponding secretary to *New Era*, a publication of the National Colored Democratic League, and devoted more time to her literary interests.

After her retirement from public school teaching she pursued her literary career more consistently. Ray wrote several poems, and upon her father's death she coauthored with her sister Florence a biography of their father entitled *Sketches of the Life of Rev. Charles B. Ray* (1887). The seventy-nine-page biography, which detailed their father's work as an editor and as an abolitionist, contained a sonnet, "To Our Father," written by Ray.

Six years later in April 1876, Ray's poetry received considerable attention when William E. Matthews read her eighty-line ode "Lincoln: Written for the Occasion of the Unveiling of the Freedmen's Monument in Memory of Abraham Lincoln, April 14, 1876," the eleventh anniversary of Lincoln's death. Ray's poem and Frederick Douglass'* oration were the highlights of the event. In "Lincoln" Ray extols the fallen president for his humane qualities and for his role in alleviating the suffering of the slaves. Though widely circulated, the poem was not published until 1893.

Ray published two volumes of poetry, *Sonnets* in 1893, the same year her tribute to Lincoln was printed, and *Poems* in 1910. *Poems* signaled the end of Ray's literary career. Records indicate that nothing else was published. She died in New York City on January 5, 1916.

MAJOR WORKS AND THEMES

Ray's writing consistently explores the intricacies of such familiar themes as nature, love, moral responsibility, the complexities of life, and literature. Ray's writing mirrors many of her life experiences. She writes of events and individuals close to her. Her tribute to Abraham Lincoln in 1876 garnered tremendous public attention; her eight-stanza poem praises the fallen president, "whose destiny was not worlds to conquer, but men's hearts ("Lincoln" 1)." Ray celebrates Lincoln's role in ending the suffering of slaves. She predicts that Lincoln will not be forgotten, that the world will forever remember him and his noble deeds. The poem was published in 1893. After the death of her father Ray coauthored with her sister Florence a tribute entitled *Sketches of the Life of Rev. Charles B. Ray* (1887). This volume highlighted her father's contributions to the causes of education, abolition, and journalism. Ray's sonnet entitled "To Our Father" introduced the sketch. Ray continued to write poetry, contributing to various periodicals. Her poem "Charles Lamb" appeared in the AME Church *Review* in July 1891. Her poetry is considered her greatest literary strength.

Her volume *Poems* (1910) contains 145 poems on various themes. The table of contents shows a range of topics: "Rosary of Fancies," "The Perfect Orchestra," "Meditations," "Sonnets Reprinted," "Champions of Freedom," "Ballads and Other Poems," "Chansons D'Amour," "Quatrains," "The Procession of the Season," "The Sea," "The Singer and the Sage," and "Heroic Echoes."

Though her poetry covers a variety of themes, it falls into three discrete categories. The first class, the philosophical poems, are serious, idealistic, and deeply pious. "In Broken Heart" Ray expresses deep pain, which she finally surrenders to Jesus. In "Failure" she expresses the disappointment she feels because of the sometimes unfavorable response her poetry receives: "What is failure?," she queries (*Poems* 59). Ray wonders why success or failure should be determined by her audience.

"Chansons D'Amour" introduces the second section. Here she ponders the complexities and dynamics of love. In "Reunited," a once lonely and mournful maiden is suddenly joyous when she learns that her valiant prince has long loved her. In "Recompensed?" a maiden is seeking love; "she roams the meadows with hope. . . . she'd meet her youth with golden hair" (*Poems* 140). In "Oh Restless Heart, Be Still!," Ray chides the restless heart to be calm. In these poems, Ray expresses deep and profound emotion.

The third category of Ray's poems is dedicated to the champions of freedom's cause and includes eulogies to William Lloyd Garrison, Frederick Douglass, Abraham Lincoln, and Toussaint L'Ouverture. This section entitled, "Heroic Echoes," also contains tributes to writers Paul Laurence Dunbar* and Harriet Beecher Stowe. In "In Memoriam Paul Laurence Dunbar," Ray passionately laments the poet's death. She begs that others would mourn him and remember his fame with "the fondest pride" (*Poems* 167).

Both collections, *Sonnets* and *Poems*, represent her best and most prolific work. The collections also mark the end of her literary career, for after the publication of *Poems* (1910), no other work by Ray appeared.

CRITICAL RECEPTION

Although Ray wrote her first poem at age ten, her early efforts seemed an avocation. She was not a full-time writer but did write occasionally, contributing several poems to *The AME Church Review*, the official publication of the African Methodist Episcopal Church. However, not until 1876 did her poetry attract public attention. She was among the few black American women whose writing received even moderate acclaim. Leela Kapai notes, in an entry on Ray published in the *Dictionary of Literary Biography*, "that Henrietta Cordelia Ray . . . was one of the few black women in the genteel tradition who achieved a certain amount of local recognition in the nineteenth century" (233).

Regarding *Poems*, Jessie Redmon Fauset,* the reviewer in the *Crisis*, praised "the themes of images and the versatility of the author" (183). Maritcha R. Lyons also commented on Ray's versatility but also recognized other attributes such as "her love of nature, classical knowledge, delicate fancy, and unaffected piety" (175). An entry in *Black Writers: A Selection of Sketches from Contemporary Authors* maintains that "Ray is best remembered for her skill in poetic form and technique and for the genteel quality, versatility, and idealism characteristic of her verse" ("Ray" 473).

It seems somewhat paradoxical that some of the qualities for which Ray is praised are some of the same ones for which she is condemned. Her critics generally object to the genteel character of her writing. Many accuse her of imitating traditional Western models. William Robinson, writing in his *Early Black Poets*, notes that "Ray's work shows too much of her intellectual learning in both subject matter and in routine conventionally academic rendition" (138). Blyden Jackson in his study *A History of Afro-American Literature* notes "Ray's predilection in her poetry for subjects and themes, as well as modes of utterance, which identify her with . . . white culture of Western civilization" (261). Jackson, however, defends Ray against the general charges that she paid little attention to the issues that concerned the masses of blacks during her day; he argues that "it can hardly be said . . . she never remembers her color. She wrote safely. She did not write poorly" (263). Jackson also recognizes Ray's ingenuity and creativity: "She seems to have invented a new stanza here and there" (263).

Ray's biographical tribute to her father, which she coauthored with her sister, was generally held to be mediocre and lacking distinction. Yet despite its lackluster reputation, comments published in *The AME Review* praised it roundly: "In the twenty years of editorial work, we do not remember having received so unique a volume, high judgment, good taste, literary tact and excellence all combine to put it absolutely beyond the criticism. As a work of the kind, it is as near perfect as can be conceived" (qtd. in Lyons 172). Ray's poetic tribute to her father which introduced the sketch was favorably received. Blyden Jackson declares that Ray wrote "no better sonnet than that to her father: A leaf from Freedom's golden Chaplet fair we bring you dear father" (263).

Ray's writing has qualities identifiable in the works of white authors in the Victorian tradition. Critic Jessie Carney Smith compares Ray's "Verses to My Heart's Sister," a tribute she writes on the occasion of her sister Florence's death, to the sentimental poetry of white women writers in Rufus Griswold's *Female Poets of America* (925).

BIBLIOGRAPHY

Works by Henrietta Cordelia Ray

Book

Ray, Henrietta Cordelia, and Florence Ray. *Sketches of the Life of Rev. Charles B. Ray.* New York: J. J. Little, 1887.

Poetry

"Lincoln: Written for the Occasion of the Unveiling of the Freedmen's Monument in Memory of Abraham Lincoln, April 14, 1876." New York: J. J. Little, 1893.
Sonnets. New York: J. J. Little, 1893.
Poems. New York: Grafton Press, 1910.

Periodical Publication

"Charles Lamb." *The AME Review* 8 (July 1891): 1–9.

Studies of Henrietta Cordelia Ray

Fauset, Jessie Redmon. Rev. of *Poems. Crisis* 3–4 (August 1912): 183.
Frazier, S. Elizabeth. "Some Afro-American Women of Mark." *AME Review* 8 (April 1892): 373–86.
Jackson, Blyden. *A History of Afro-American Literature.* Vol. 1: *The Long Beginning, 1746–1895.* Baton Rouge: Louisiana State University Press, 1989.
Kapai, Leela. "Henrietta Cordelia Ray." In *The Dictionary of Literary Biography.* Vol. 50: *Afro American Writers before the Harlem Renaissance.* New York: Gale, 1986. 233–36.
Kerlin, Robert T. *Negro Poets and Their Poems.* Washington, DC: Associated, 1947.
Lyons, Maritcha R. "Henrietta Cordelia Ray." In *Homespun Heroines and Other Women of Distinction.* Ed. Hallie Quinn Brown. Xenia, OH: Aldine, 1926. 169–75.
"Ray, H(enrietta) Cordelia." In *Black Writers: A Selection of Sketches from Contemporary Authors.* Ed. Linda Metzer et al. Detroit: Gale Research, Inc., 1989.
Robinson, William Henry, Jr. *Early Black American Poets.* Dubuque, IA: William C. Brown, 1996.
Sampson, Henry T. *Blacks in Black and White.* Metuchen, NJ: Scarecrow Press, 1977.
Sanders, Kimberly Wallace. "Henrietta Cordelia Ray." In *The Oxford Companion to African American Literature.* Ed. William L. Andrews et al. New York: Oxford University Press, 1997. 261–62.
Sherman, Joan R. *Invisible Poets: Afro-Americans of the Nineteenth Century.* Urbana: University of Illinois Press, 1974.
———, ed. *Collected Black Women's Poetry.* New York: Oxford University Press, 1988.
Shockley, Ann Allen. *Afro-American Women Writers (1746–1933).* New York: Dutton, 1988.
Smith, Jessie Carney, ed. *Notable Black Women.* New York: Gale Research, 1992.
Ward, Jerry W., Jr., ed. "Henrietta Cordelia Ray." In *Trouble the Water: 250 Years of African-American Poetry.* New York: Penguin, 1997. 55.

MARY SEACOLE
(1805-1881)

Laura L. Moakler

BIOGRAPHY

As the title of her autobiography implies, *Wonderful Adventures of Mrs. Seacole in Many Lands*, Mary Seacole, indeed, led a life filled with adventure. In 1805 in Kingston, Jamaica, she was born Mary Jane Grant to a Scottish father, an officer in the British army, and a free black woman, the proprietor of a boardinghouse and, as Seacole describes, "an admirable doctress" (2). She attributes her medical talent to her mother but her "energy and activity" to her father because these qualities, she states, "are not always found in the Creole race" (1). Seacole did not grow up in her mother's house but instead lived with an old woman, referred to as her "patroness," "among her own grandchildren" (2). However, Seacole often visited her mother, feeding her passion for medicine. She first honed her medical skills on her doll, working her way up to unwitting cats and dogs. Finally, at the age of twelve, she began to assist her mother, "learning a great deal of Creole medicinal art" (5).

As Seacole matured, she "began to indulge that longing to travel" (4). While still a young woman, she had two lengthy stays in London and visited other Caribbean islands, including Haiti and Cuba. After her travels and a medical apprenticeship of sorts with her mother, she married Mr. Seacole, whom she observes was "very delicate" (5). The couple owned and ran a store in Black River, but as Mr. Seacole suffered from ill health, they were forced to return to Kingston. He died soon after their arrival despite Seacole's efforts to nurse him back to health. After her mother's death and turning away "the pressing candidates for the late Mr. Seacole's shoes" (8), she embarked upon a life of independence.

In 1850, after Seacole's "reputation as a skilful [sic] nurse and doctress" was firmly established (7), and she had learned "many hints as to [cholera's] treatment" from a doctor during a cholera epidemic in Jamaica (9), she left Kingston to join her brother's entrepreneurial pursuits on the Isthmus of Panama. She helped her brother manage his Independent Hotel in Cruces until she opened one of her own, the British Hotel. She later relocated the hotel, which offered meals and sold provisions to travelers, to Gorgona. Not only did she sharpen her business skills, but also she was able to practice and expand her medical skills, treating infectious and tropical diseases, tending knife and gunshot wounds, and even, with the plentiful supply of dead bodies, performing secret autopsies. She returned only briefly to Jamaica, "just in time to find my services . . . needful," combating an outbreak of yellow fever (59), before she was back to the isthmus, running a store first in Navy Bay and then in Escribanos. Finally in 1854, tired of a land "as capital a nursery for ague and fever as Death could hit upon" (11), and where "the refuse of every nation . . . meet together" (10), she left, sailing from Navy Bay directly to Britain in hopes of finding an opportunity to serve the British troops fighting in the Crimea.

Seacole's offer of help, however, was not welcomed by the British officials. Likely because of her race and age, she was denied a position in Florence Nightingale's nursing corps. Unwilling to bow to defeat, though, she arranged for her own passage to the Crimea and, once there, set up a hotel, much like the ones that she had managed in Central America. "Mother Seacole," as she was known to the British soldiers, achieved fame for her hospitality and her nursing skills. In her time she was as well known as Nightingale.

At the war's conclusion, Seacole returned to England, where she opened a store in Aldershot. Unfortunately, the venture was not a success, and, combined with the financial losses she suffered from overstocking provisions in her Crimean hotel, she went bankrupt. Publications such as the *London Times* and *Punch* advertised appeals for donations on her behalf. For four nights at the Royal Surrey Gardens, the Seacole Festive, featuring musical entertainments, was held as a benefit for her. These efforts were less than successful, forcing Seacole to look elsewhere for financial solvency. Capitalizing on her fame as a "Crimean *heroine*" (76), she wrote her autobiography in 1857.

Regaining some fiscal security after the publication of *Wonderful Adventures*, she worked with war widows and orphans. She also received decorations from the French, the Turkish, and (most probably) the British governments for her service during the war effort. In her later life, she developed a relationship with the Princess of Wales, working as the princess' masseuse. At the time of her death on May 14, 1881, with her substantial assets, she was hardly still in need of a benefit. She was buried in London in St. Mary's Catholic Cemetery.

MAJOR WORK AND THEMES

Mary Seacole did not hold literary aspirations. She wrote only one book, her autobiography, and she wrote it to rescue herself from bankruptcy. However, her narrative is not merely a self-serving attempt to raise funds. She uses the public forum of print to relate some of her deeply held beliefs. While much of the book seems to praise British imperialism, privilege white culture, and, at times, indulge in some unfortunate ethnic stereotyping, she is also very critical of slavery and racism. She mainly confines her critique to the Americans she encounters in Central America, but she does not hesitate to raise doubts about British racial attitudes as well. She also makes the point that an unmarried woman—a member of a minority, no less—can be independent and successful while maintaining her femininity. Her personal story assaults the Victorian notions of race and womanhood.

CRITICAL RECEPTION

Wonderful Adventures was not reprinted this century until the 1980s. Only in the 1990s are scholars beginning an in-depth examination of Seacole's narrative. Sandra Pouchet Paquet, among the first critics to investigate the work, observes that Seacole reveals "the conflicts and contradictions of identity, authority, and freedom" (651). Paquet's study goes on to explore the ways in which "Seacole crafts her self-image in a journey from the perceived margins of civilization to its center" (652). According to Paquet, Seacole "self-consciously redefines 'true womanhood' around her individual accomplishments as a Jamaican woman of color" (652) and simultaneously marginalizes issues of race, gender, and colonialism. That is, Seacole claims British values as her own and celebrates the British empire, while challenging those values and that empire with a life story that contradicts Victorian assumptions of race and gender and, through relating various observations, unwittingly exposing negative consequences of colonialism.

Other critics, including Amy Robinson, Bernard McKenna, Cheryl Fish, and Catherine Judd, also note this conflict with *Wonderful Adventures.* Robinson sees Seacole "reattach[ing] herself to a tradition of colonial subjectivity which her narrative overtly rejects" (538). McKenna observes that as a result of this conflict Seacole "subverts the British colonial discourse both implicitly and explicitly" (221). According to Fish, although Seacole may espouse views that "might be considered the colonizing paradigm with its assumption of Western superiority and endorsement" (479), there are moments in the text when "she ironically undercut[s] that flattery" (480). Finally, Judd "explore[s] the ways Seacole creates oblique resistance to her otherwise evident acceptance of 'English values at the margins of Empire' " (101) and contends that "through her rewriting of both the Homeric epic and the popular hagiography of Florence Nightingale . . . , Seacole creates a heroic self that cannot be contained by the exigencies of her English audience" (101). Almost every scholar studying Seacole today explores the dynamics of a radical subtext present in *Wonderful Adventures.*

BIBLIOGRAPHY

Work by Mary Seacole

Wonderful Adventures of Mrs. Seacole in Many Lands. 1857. Schomburg Library of Nineteenth-Century Black Women Writers Series. Ed. Henry Louis Gates, Jr. New York: Oxford University Press, 1988.

Studies of Mary Seacole

Alexander, Ziggi, and Audrey Dewjee. "Editor's Introduction." *Wonderful Adventures of Mrs. Seacole in Many Lands.* 1857. Ed. Ziggi Alexander and Audrey Dewjee. Bristol: Falling Wall, 1984. 9–45.

Andrews, William L. "Introduction". *Wonderful Adventures of Mrs. Seacole in Many Lands.* 1857. Schomburg Library of Nineteenth-Century Black Women Writers Series. Ed. Henry Louis Gates Jr. New York: Oxford University Press, 1988.

Fish, Cheryl. "Voices of Restless (Dis)continuity: The Significance of Travel for Free Black Women in the Antebellum Americas." *Women's Studies* 26.2 (1997): 475–95.

Judd, Catherine. *Bedside Seductions: Nursing and the Victorian Imagination.* New York: St. Martin's, 1998. 101–21.

McKenna, Bernard. " 'Fancies of Exclusive Possession': Validation and Dissociation in Mary Seacole's England and Caribbean." *Philological Quarterly* 76.2 (Spring 1997): 219–39.

Mercer, Lorraine Susan Gallicchio. "Skirting Traditions: Travel Texts of Three Nineteenth-Century Women Writers (Anna Leonowens, Margaret Fuller, Mary Seacole, Narrative)." Diss. University of Oregon, 1996.

Paquet, Sandra Pouchet. "The Enigma of Arrival: *The Wonderful Adventures of Mrs. Seacole in Many Lands.*" *African American Review* 26.4 (Winter 1992): 651–663.

Robinson, Amy. "Authority and Public Display of Identity: *Wonderful Adventures of Mrs. Seacole in Many Lands.*" *Feminist Studies* 20.3 (Fall 1994): 537–57.

MARIA W. STEWART
(1803–1879)

Barbara Ryan

BIOGRAPHY

Born free in 1803 in Hartford, Connecticut, Maria Miller was orphaned at the age of five and "bound out" in a minister's family. As an adult, she deplored the way this man neglected her formal education since she was a dependent in his household. Luckily, her appetite for learning was awakened by his books. When the term of "binding" was complete, and the fifteen-year-old Miller supported herself as a domestic servant, she sought education in Sunday school classes. In 1826 she married James W. Stewart, a veteran of the War of 1812 who had become a shipping agent in Boston. For three years, the couple engaged in a life rich with religious observations and political activity based on attempts to uplift Americans of African descent. After James Stewart's death in December 1829, the childless widow was defrauded by a group of white businessmen and forced to start again financially. In tribute to her husband, Stewart took his middle initial, "W.," for her own.

Undeterred by her scrappy education and devoted to social reform, Stewart was inspired by the incendiary manifesto that David Walker* published in 1829. She also steeped herself in the women's history compiled by a Briton named John Adams. Finally, she underwent a religious recommitment that fueled her sense of mission. In 1831 she published a pamphlet, *Religion and the Pure Principles of Morality*. It was followed by a collection of religious writings, including prayers, called *Meditations from the Pen of Mrs. Maria W. Stewart*. Religious conviction played a large part in Stewart's political critiques of race-based exploitation, for she believed that God had called on her to represent the oppressed.

In 1833 and 1834 Stewart addressed the Afric-American Female Intelligence Society of America, delivered a lecture at Boston's Franklin Hall, and spoke in the African Masonic Hall. A remarkable aspect of her early career was that she lectured to what were called "promiscuous" audiences, meaning a group comprising women and men. Though Stewart addressed all of her lectures to black Americans, an essay called "Cause for Encouragement" and a poem entitled "The Negro's Complaint" were published in the *Liberator*, an abolitionist organ published and controlled by whites. Years later, the editor of that paper, William Lloyd Garrison, recalled Stewart's "intelligence and excellence of character" (Richardson 89). It is not known why Stewart left "Cause for Encouragement" out of the two book-length collections of her work. It has been suggested, though, that she was disillusioned by comments about the impropriety of what she was trying to do. "I find," she told a Boston audience in a reproachful "Farewell Address" that she elected to publish in her book, "it is no use for me as an individual to try to make myself useful among my color in this city" (Richardson 70). Historians surmise that many of Stewart's ideas about gender alarmed those who led Boston's African American community. Stewart's last lecture suggests as much but also mentions dislike for the evangelical aspects of her campaign.

After publishing a book of her lectures, Stewart moved to New York, became a teacher, attended the Women's Anti-Slavery Convention in 1837, and participated in a literary society for black women. She almost certainly lectured on a small scale in New York; more definitely, though, she was made assistant principal of a public school in Williamsburg, New York, in 1847. Three years later, she gave public support to Frederick Douglass'* newspaper, the *North Star*. The next thing known of her is a move to Baltimore before the Civil War. After emancipation, Stewart was named head housekeeper of the Freedmen's Hospital in Washington, D.C. In Washington, she befriended Elizabeth Keckley,* the slave who earned her own purchase price with the dressmaking skills that made her a sought-after modiste in Washington during the Civil War.

In 1878 Stewart applied for a government pension as the relict of a veteran of the War of 1812. Granted this small stipend, she used it to bring out a new edition of her collected works in 1879. For this book, which reused the title *Meditations from the Pen of Mrs. Stewart*, she wrote a brief memoir called "Sufferings during the War" and collected several "Letters and Commendations," which rounded out the story of her life and career. Stewart died on December 17, 1879. She is buried in Graceland Cemetery in Washington, D.C.

MAJOR WORKS AND THEMES

Though Stewart published relatively little, in comparison to a professional writer like Frederick Douglass, it is fair to call all of her early works "major" because each promoted radical new ideas with a gender slant. The evangelical texts are the least oppositional, in political terms, but do broach the idea that black women have a role to play in advancing African Americans' status in U.S. society. Lectures about uplift articulate more confrontational ideas about black leadership and suggest that Stewart would advocate black self-defense when necessary. Suggestions of this sort were risky in the wake of Nat Turner's slave revolt. Equally disturbing, from a different angle, was Stewart's call for black women to take on leadership roles in business, education, religion, and politics. If, as scholars avow, Stewart's work in the 1830s was an early call for black cultural nationalism, then it is significant that she delegated this agenda to black women in preacherlike tones. "O woman, woman!" she told the Afric-American Female Society. "Upon you I call; for your exertions almost entirely depend whether the rising generation shall be any thing more than we have been or not" (Richardson 55). Though the idea of changing the world through right-minded child nurture fitted within the "true woman" philosophy that meant so much in antebellum America, Stewart's decision to lecture clashed with the idea that good women exerted their influence within the confines of their homes. Rejecting the dictate that women circumscribe their proselytizing efforts, Stewart pointed to biblical heroines like Deborah and Esther. In so doing, she paved the way for activists like Sojourner Truth,* Harriet Jacobs,* and Frances E. W. Harper.*

Stewart was adamant about the need for black parents to push their children to aspire. She told audiences that "such is the horrible idea that I entertain respecting a life of servitude, that if I conceived of there being no possibility of my rising above the condition of a servant, I would gladly hail death as a welcome messenger" (Richardson 46). These were strong words, considering the barriers to employment that free black Americans faced. But Stewart scorned accommodation to injustice in any form and called on more open defiance from the victimized. "Had the free people of color in these United States nobly and boldly contended for their rights," she charged, "had they held up, encouraged and patronized each other, nothing could have hindered us from being a thriving and flourishing people" (Richardson 62).

In works written after the Civil War, Stewart focused on her commitment to the Episcopalian Church during troubled times. The burden of her "Sufferings during the War" is a lament about sectarian Christians' intolerance for each other. This autobiographical fragment seems the work of a writer unacquainted with the fiery polemic that Stewart disseminated when the U.S. abolitionist movement was new.

CRITICAL RECEPTION

The best overview of Stewart's life and thought is Marilyn Richardson's *Maria W. Stewart, America's First Black Woman Political Writer: Essays and Speeches*. For Richardson, Stewart's "original synthesis of religious, abolitionist, and feminist concerns places her squarely in the forefront of a black female activist and literary tradition only now beginning to be acknowledged as of integral significance to the understanding of the history of black thought and culture in America" (xiii). From a different angle, Lora Romero recently contended that Stewart's writings signify in terms of "their . . . erasure from the black nationalist consciousness" because they expose the extent to which "the deployment of gender as a sign of oppositionality limits the egalitarian politics expressed in domestic ideology" (54). Paula Giddings views Stewart as a thinker far ahead of her times: many of "Stewart's assumptions," according to Giddings, "would later become known as modernist thinking" (52).

BIBLIOGRAPHY

Works by Maria W. Stewart

Religion and the Pure Principles of Morality. Boston: Garrison and Knapp, 1831.
"Cause for Encouragement." *The Liberator* (July 14, 1832):110.
Meditations from the Pen of Mrs. Maria W. Stewart. Boston: Garrison and Knapp, 1832.
Productions of Mrs. Maria W. Stewart. Boston: Friends of Freedom and Virtue, 1835.
Meditations from the Pen of Mrs. Maria W. Stewart. Washington, DC: For the author, 1879.

Studies of Maria W. Stewart

Giddings, Paula. *When and Where I Enter: The Impact of Black Women in Race and Sex in America.* New York: William Morrow, 1984.
Richardson, Marilyn. *Maria W. Stewart, America's First Black Woman Political Writer: Essays and Speeches.* Bloomington: Indiana University Press, 1987.
Romero, Lora. *Home Fronts: Domesticity and Its Critics in the Antebellum United States.* Durham, NC: Duke University Press, 1997.

MARY CHURCH TERRELL
(1863–1954)

Shara McCallum

BIOGRAPHY

Mary "Mollie" Church Terrell was born September 23, 1863, in Memphis, Tennessee. Her parents, Louisa (Ayres) and Robert Church, were newly emancipated slaves and part of the growing black middle class that firmly established itself after slavery. Throughout her early life, Terrell's parents endeavored to shield her from racial prejudice and provide her with every educational and financial opportunity possible. At the age of six, she was sent to Ohio to attend the Model School on the campus of Antioch College. Later, she attended public school in Oberlin, Ohio, and completed her B.A. from Oberlin College in 1884. At the time, it was customary for women to complete a two-year course instead of the four-year "gentleman's course," which included the study of Latin and Greek. Despite recommendations from many against pursuing the latter program of study, Terrell did.

After college, Terrell again asserted her independence. Going against the wishes of her father, who believed that "ladies" should not engage in a profession, Terrell worked as a faculty member at Wilberforce University from 1885 to 1887. Moving to Washington, D.C., the following year, she became assistant to her future husband, Robert Terrell, teaching Latin at the famous M Street High School. From 1888 to 1890 Terrell traveled throughout Europe, where she studied French and German and witnessed the different treatment of blacks in Europe versus that in the United States. Turning down proposals of marriage, educational opportunities, and the chance for a life less fraught by the constant struggle of overt racism, Terrell made the decision to return to the United States. In her autobiography, *A Colored Woman in a White World*, Terrell describes this decision as stemming from her felt "duty" and "responsibility" to "promote the welfare of [her] race in [her] native land" (99).

After her return to the United States, Terrell began her life as a public speaker, activist, writer, and leader in several movements and organizations for black "uplift" and civil rights and for woman's rights. In 1895 Terrell was appointed to the District of Columbia Board of Education and served for five years. She was the first black woman to sit on any school board in the United States. One of the founders of the National Association of Colored Women (NACW), formed in 1896, she was also the first president. Serving three terms, she played a vital role not only in the direction of the NACW but also in the black women's club movement of the late nineteenth and early twentieth centuries. On February 18, 1898, she delivered one of her most famous speeches, "The Progress of Colored Women," at the National American Women's Suffrage Association's biennial meeting. In 1904 she spoke at the International Congress of Women in Berlin. The only black woman present, Terrell was also the only American woman to deliver her speech in French and German as well as English.

Throughout her life, Terrell wrote and spoke in protest of the many injustices heaped against blacks and women in the United States. Her autobiography, *A Colored Woman in a White World*, published in 1940, stands as a testimony to her life, her struggles, and her achievements. Toward the end of her life, Terrell's political views and activities became more militant. Preceding the formal Civil Rights movement in the early 1950s, Terrell, then in her late eighties, organized a campaign of protests, picketing, and sit-ins that successfully desegregated Washington, D.C., restaurants. Terrell's personal life consistently reflected her public philosophies. Vocally committed to the "home," she successfully combined marriage and motherhood (raising two daughters, Phillis and Mary) with a vibrant career in public speaking and activism.

MAJOR WORKS AND THEMES

While Terrell wrote several short stories and poems and even plotted a novel that was never completed, her published writings consist of her autobiography, *A Colored Woman in a White World*, and her many speeches and essays. The themes of her nonfiction are consistent and fall into one of two main categories. Her essays and speeches, delivered primarily to white audiences, reflect the need to educate white women and men about various injustices facing blacks and women and to press for the eradication of these injustices. Her essays in praise of historical figures such as Phillis Wheatley,* Frederick Douglass,* and Samuel Coleridge Taylor seek to educate blacks and whites about the great achievements of blacks. Her autobiography and several essays, such as "The Progress of Colored Women," represent a combination of these two approaches.

Her writing reflects her ardent belief in the necessity of racial "uplift" and of a "moral" womanhood. Subscribing to W.E.B. Du Bois'* idea of the "Talented Tenth," as well as to a conservative vision of women, Terrell's writing seeks to replace the prevailing stereotypical and degrading notions of both blacks and women with positive images. For example, in "The Progress of Colored Women" Terrell argues against accusations of black women's impropriety:

The immorality of colored women is a theme upon which those who know little about them or those who maliciously misrepresent them love to descant. . . . And yet, in spite of the fateful heritage of slavery, even though the safe guards usually thrown around maidenly youth and innocence are in some sections entirely withheld from colored girls, statistics compiled by men not inclined to falsify in favor of my race show that immorality among the colored women of the United States is not so great as among women with similar environment and temptations in Italy, Germany, Sweden, and France. (Jones 184)

Recognizing the authority vested in male (presumably white) findings and evidence by her audience, Terrell shows her astuteness as a rhetorician here and supports her claim that environment, not some inherited inferiority in blacks and women, accounts for differences in moral behavior where they exist.

Her autobiographical writings uphold this position time and time again. In a conversation with a white woman related in her autobiography, Terrell uses the woman's own racist argument to debunk itself and simultaneously assert her own agenda: "Then I suggested that, since colored women and girls were so bad as she depicted them, they were a constant menace to the men and boys of all races, and for that reason if no other, some effort should be made to uplift them" (327).

Another strategy Terrell uses to undermine racist and sexist notions of black women is to provide descriptions of her achievements to belie these false and destructive ideas. In the close of her autobiography, she explains that she chose to present the incidents she did precisely because they highlight what she has accomplished "in spite of the prejudice encountered because of both [her] race and [her] sex" (417). If in doing so she seems a "conceited prig," as she shows some concern of appearing, her motives are clearly guided by her need to "lift as she climbs," to present herself as a positive example of black womanhood (417).

Stylistically and aesthetically, Terrell's writing is sympathetic to her goals and themes. Her work is journalistic and propagandistic. The language she uses is direct while revealing a sophisticated understanding of rhetoric. Terrell situates herself within the black middle class and within established notions of "true womanhood" to validate her ethos. Through retelling various incidents of racial prejudice and human degradation as well as survival, she makes frequent appeals to the reader's and listener's sense of pathos. Her writing reflects Terrell's balance in her own life between racial indignation and middle-class values and conservatism.

CRITICAL RECEPTION

While Terrell's life has received revived attention in the last thirty years, providing several articles and a handful of books, her writing has received almost none. Often, Terrell's writing is mentioned only in passing within the former context. Two examples, notable for their insights into her writing despite their lack of sustained focus, are Dorothy Sterling's *Black Foremothers* and Beverly Jones' *Quest for Equality*. In Peterson's biography on Terrell, she discusses the difficulties of time that restricted Terrell from becoming the writer she had wanted to be, a fact acknowledged by Terrell herself in her autobiography. She also critiques Terrell's autobiography, her writing opus, for its reticence:

Throughout her life she had suppressed her anger, schooling herself to meet rebuffs, she said, "with a kind of rebellious resignation and a more or less genuine smile." The smile made white people feel comfortable in her presence, but it kept the book from having the fire and bite that she often revealed in her diaries. (152)

Jones' book on Terrell is important not only for its insights into her life and work but also because it contains reprints of many of Terrell's most significant essays and speeches, uncollected anywhere else. Her discussion of Terrell's writing centers on summaries of theme and plot and connects her unpublished fiction to her published nonfiction: "Ever mindful of her goal, Terrell's short stories were often imbued with the same objectivity and thoroughness that had characterized her articles. Each story depicted true incidents of racial discrimination" (40).

Similarly, Karlyn Kohrs Campbell's essay "Style and Content in the Rhetoric of Early Afro-American Feminists" provides a summary of the major themes in Terrell's nonfiction, focusing entirely on her speeches. She goes beyond this summary, though, and also advances a rhetorical analysis of the speeches, describing Terrell's style as "feminine":

She spoke from her personal experience, which she extended to the personal experiences of other individuals she knew about. The speech developed inductively; it relied on arousing empathy and through it, appealing to the feelings of the audience. . . . It was a speech by a woman who conformed to traditional notions about women, and it used forms of appeal and support that were highly appropriate for a white, middle-class, largely female audience. (442–43)

One of the only sustained "literary" analyses of Terrell's writing is Nellie McKay's article comparing the autobiographies of Harriet Jacobs,* Mary Church Terrell, and Anne Moody. McKay uses "a paradigm of development from Carol Pearson's study of archetypes of the hero in Western culture" to discuss how Terrell's childhood prefigures her later life. She views Terrell's autobiography, thus, as a way for her to "explain vital connections between childhood and adulthood, and to show us why [she] became who [she] was" (320).

BIBLIOGRAPHY

Works by Mary Church Terrell

"The Progress of Colored Women: An Address Delivered before the National American Women's Suffrage Association, at the Columbia Theatre, Washington D.C., February

18, 1898, on the Occasion of Its Fiftieth Anniversary." Washington, DC: Smith Brothers, Printers, 1898.

Harriet Beecher Stowe: An Appreciation. Washington, DC: Murray Brothers Press, 1911.

A Colored Woman in a White World. Washington, DC: Ransdell, 1940; reprinted, Salem, NH: Ayer, 1986.

The Papers of Mary Church Terrell, 1863–1954 (microform; contains all unpublished and published writings). Washington, DC: Library of Congress, 1955.

Studies of Mary Church Terrell

Campbell, Karlyn Kohrs. "Style and Content in the Rhetoric of Early Afro-American Feminists." Quarterly Journal of Speech 72 (1986): 434–45.

Giddings, Paula. When and Where I Enter. New York: William Morrow, 1984.

Harley, Sharon, and Rosalyn Terborg-Penn. Afro-American Woman: Struggles and Images. New York: Kennikat Press, 1978.

Jones, Beverly W. Quest for Equality: The Life and Writings of Mary Eliza Church Terrell, 1863–1954. New York: Carlson, 1990.

McKay, Nellie. "The Girls Who Became the Women: Childhood Memories in the Autobiographies of Harriet Jacobs, Mary Church Terrell, and Anne Moody." Traditions and the Talents of Women. Ed. Florence Howe. Urbana: University of Illinois Press, 1991. 105–24.

Sterling, Dorothy. Black Foremothers: Three Lives. New York: Feminist Press, 1988.

LUCY TERRY
(c. 1730–1821)

Paula C. Barnes

BIOGRAPHY

Little is known of the early life of the woman who is the author of the "earliest extant poem written by a black person in North America" (Foster 28). It is generally agreed that Lucy Terry was born in Africa and kidnapped into slavery. At age five, she was brought to Rhode Island and sold to Ebenezer Wells of Deerfield, Massachusetts. In 1746 Terry composed the poem "Bars Fight."

In 1756 Terry married Abijah (or Obijah) Prince, a free black twice her age who purchased her freedom. They moved to Guilford, Vermont, and had six children. Terry made history three more times when she appealed to various governing bodies on behalf of her family. In 1785, when neighbors threatened them, Terry appealed in person to the governor and his Council, and the Princes were ordered protection. Some years later, Terry appealed to the trustees of Williams College to admit one of her sons. He was still denied admission, but not before Terry had presented a three-hour speech. Terry's last recorded political act—to contend a land dispute—went to the Supreme Court, which ruled in Terry's favor.

In 1803, nine years after her husband's death, Terry moved to Sunderland but would travel the eighteen miles by horseback annually to visit his grave. In 1821, at age ninety-one, she died.

MAJOR WORK AND THEMES

Lucy Terry's fame as a poet rests solely on "Bars Fight," which was first published in 1855 in Josiah Holland's *History of Western Massachusetts*. The poem, which tells of the 1746 Indian raid on colonial settlers, is considered an accurate account of the historical event. The poem consists of twenty-eight lines of rhymed tetrameter couplets. While some critics and historians suggest that there may be other versions of the poem, only William Katz in *Eyewitness: the Negro in American History* records a variant, which has thirty lines (24).

CRITICAL RECEPTION

Having survived in the oral tradition for almost 100 years suggests that "Bars Fight" was well received during its time. Twentieth-century critics before the present decade, however, have described the poem as a doggerel, a "semi-literate effort" (qtd. in Hughes and Bontemps xxii) or a "rough hewn ballad" (Kaplan 209). Most conclude that "Bars Fight" hardly rates Terry's being called a poet; what makes the poem noteworthy is its being the earliest work by an African American.

Critics have also varied in their assessment of the poem's tone. Greene recognizes its tragic theme but asserts that the humor in the poem was "not always intentional" (242). Stetson states the work has "color, tragedy, and adventure" (3). Mason claims that the poem's form, while owing "a clear debt to the oral heroic tradition," is "more of a lament" than a celebration (1433). Andrews states that the poem "conveys great sympathy" (719), while Shields identifies its tone as "hardbitten remorse" (872).

Terry's poem has received much critical attention during the 1990s, with exceptions being taken to the earlier assessments. Warren asserts that "Bars Fight" is possibly equal to any early American verse, including that of Anne Bradstreet (882). Harris, noting the poem's "satirical humor," places it in the captivity narrative tradition (11); Hill et al. place it within the African American oral tradition (90). Frances Smith Foster, however, offers the fullest explication of the poem to date.

Reminding readers that few Americans in the eighteenth century could read or write, Foster argues that "Bars Fight" is "an exceptional occasion in eighteenth century American literature" (28). In her extended analysis of the poem, Foster asserts that although the poem begins with "apparent objectivity," it later defines "the relationship between the audience and narrator," a narrator who not only relates history but also manipulates historical events and thereby "creates a more melodramatic situation" (29). Foster also points to the various pronouns in the poem as indicators of the poet's persona. These suggest, for Foster, that Terry "is taking artistic control" (30). Foster's close reading indeed suggests "new possibilities for interpreting the text" (24).

BIBLIOGRAPHY

Work by Lucy Terry

"Bars Fight." *Black Poets*. Ed. Dudley Randall. New York: Bantam Books, 1971.

Studies of Lucy Terry

Andrews, William L. "Lucy Terry." In *Oxford Companion to African American Literature*. Ed. William L. Andrews, Frances Smith Foster, and Trudier Harris. New York: Oxford University Press, 1997. 19–20.

Foster, Frances Smith. " 'Sometimes by Simile, a Victory's Won': Lucy Terry Prince and Phillis Wheatley." In *Written by Herself: Literary Production by African American Women, 1746–1892*. Bloomington: Indiana University Press, 1993. 23–43.

Greene, Lorenzo. *The Negro in Colonial New England*. New York: Columbia University Press, 1942. 242–43, 314–15.

Harris, Sharon, ed. *American Women Writers to 1800*. New York: Oxford University Press, 1996. 11, 317–18.

Hill, Patricia, et al., eds. "Lucy Terry." In *Call and Response: The Riverside Anthology of the African American Literary Tradition*. Boston: Houghton Mifflin. 90–92.

Holland, Josiah. *History of Western Massachusetts*. Vol. 2. Springfield, MA: Willey, 1855.

Hughes, Langston, and Arna Bontemps, eds. "Lucy Terry." In *The Poetry of the Negro, 1746–1970*. New York: Anchor, 1970. xxi, 3, 622.

Jackson, Blyden. *A History of Afro American Literature: The Long Beginning 1746–1895*. Baton Rouge: Louisiana University Press, 1989. 29–33.

Kaplan, Sidney. "Lucy Terry Prince." In *The Black Presence in the Era of the American Revolution, 1770–1800*. Washington, DC: Smithsonian, 1973. 209–11.

Katz, William. *Eyewitness: The Negro in American History*. New York: Pitman, 1967. 24, 37.

Mason, Julian. "Lucy Terry." In *American Writers before 1800: A Biographical and Critical Dictionary*. Vol. 3. Ed. James Levernier and Douglas Wilmes. Westport, CT: Greenwood, 1983. 1433–34.

Robinson, William, ed. "Lucy Terry." In *Early Black American Poets*. Dubuque, IA: William C. Brown, 1969. 3–4.

Shields, David. "Lucy Terry." In *Oxford Companion to Women's Writing*. New York: Oxford University Press, 1995. 872–73.

Stetson, Erlene, ed. *Black Sister. Poetry by Black American Women, 1746–1980*. Bloomington: Indiana University Press, 1981. 3, 12.

Warren, Nagueyalti. "Lucy Terry Prince." In *Notable Black American Women*. Vol. 4. Ed. Jessie Carney Smith. Detroit: Gale, 1992. 881–82.

WALLACE THURMAN
(1902–1934)

Linda M. Carter

BIOGRAPHY

Wallace Henry Thurman, son of Oscar and Beulah Thurman, was born on August 16, 1902, in Salt Lake City, Utah. Thurman was raised by his maternal grandmother, Emma Jackson, and attended public schools in Salt Lake City. Reading, writing, and attending movies were major childhood interests for Thurman. In his unpublished manuscript, "Notes of a Stepchild," Thurman commented that he wrote his first "novel" at the age of ten and rewrote movie serials two years later. After graduating from high school in 1919, he enrolled in premed courses at the University of Utah and transferred to the University of Southern California. During his years in Los Angeles, Thurman wrote "Inklings," a column for a local African American newspaper, and worked at a post office, where he met Arna Bontemps,* who like Thurman, would later participate in the Harlem Renaissance. Inspired by the cultural activity in Harlem, New York, Thurman published *The Outlet*, a literary magazine he financed. When *The Outlet* folded six months later, Thurman moved to Harlem.

Thurman arrived in New York at the zenith of the Harlem Renaissance. Langston Hughes* remembered his friend Thurman as

a strangely brilliant black boy, who had read everything, and whose critical mind could find something wrong with everything he read . . . [Thurman] had read so many books because he could read eleven lines at a time. He would get from the library a great pile of volumes that would have taken me a year to read. But he would go through them in less than a week, and be able to discuss each one at great length with anybody. (234)

Dorothy West recalled that Thurman, who was called Wally by his friends, had a "ballast of self-assurance and talent . . . [as well as] the most agreeable smile in

Harlem and a rich, infectious laugh. His voice was . . . the most memorable thing about him, welling up out of his too frail body and wasting its richness in un-printable recountings" (215). Literary critic Arthur P. Davis, who was an English major at New York's Columbia University during the Harlem Renaissance, cited Thurman's "intelligence, his cynical wit, and his flair for satire" (Dark Tower 113). Although he was not the Renaissance's most creative or eloquent writer, he was one of its most prolific and influential authors. Thurman's first writing job in New York was as an editorial writer and reporter for the Looking Glass. The newspaper ceased publishing when financial difficulties arose. In 1926 Thur-man became the managing editor of The Messenger, a magazine founded in 1917 by A. Philip Randolph and Chandler Owen devoted to African American eco-nomic and political issues. During his brief tenure at The Messenger, Thurman published his own work as well as short stories, sketches, and poems and/or essays by other young Harlem Renaissance writers such as Hughes, Bontemps, Zora Neale Hurston,* and Dorothy West. Later in 1926 Thurman became the circu-lation manager for The World Tomorrow, a religious magazine. Thurman was the first African American hired at the magazine in an editorial position.

Thurman was the "enfant terrible of the New Negro Movement" (Warren 1118), the Harlem Renaissance writer most dedicated to art and excellence (Hug-gins 240), and a "scathing critic of the bourgeois attitude that motivated the Harlem Renaissance old guards like [Alain] Locke* and [W.E.B.] Du Bois* charg-ing that they professed their intellectual and artistic freedom while seeking white approval with slanted portrayals of African Americans" (Ferguson 729). Thus, younger Harlem Renaissance members (Hughes, Hurston, Gwendolyn Bennett,* Aaron Douglas, Richard Bruce, and John Davis) selected Thurman to edit Fire!! A Quarterly Devoted to the Younger Negro Artists (1926). Fire!!, published one year after Locke's The New Negro, the Harlem Renaissance's landmark anthology, was "an alternative manifesto to The New Negro" (Watson 91). As editor, Thurman, who "had almost single-handedly produced Fire!!" (Huggins 191), led his fellow younger artists' quest for literary independence from organizational publications such as the Crisis of the National Association for the Advancement of Colored People (NAACP) and the Urban League's Opportunity and inspired them to focus on art rather than propaganda as well as not to restrict their subject matter to the black middle class. By this time, Thurman was considered a spokesman for the younger Harlem Renaissance writers, who recognized him as "a symbolic alternative to the repressed dictydom of the Talented Tenth" (Watson 88). In 1928 Thurman edited another magazine, Harlem: A Forum of Negro Life; among those who contributed were Walter White*, Hughes, Aaron Douglas, Helene Johnson,* Locke, George S. Schuyler, Alice Dunbar Nelson,* Georgia Douglas Johnson,* Theophilus Lewis, and Richard Bruce. Thus, unlike Fire!!, Harlem included the works of older, established members of the Harlem Renaissance as well as its younger members. Both magazines failed after their premier issues "not because they lacked literary merit but because they lacked funds" (Fergu-son 730).

A personal milestone was marked in 1928; Thurman married Louise Thompson, a stenographer for Hughes' *Not without Laughter*, a typist for Hughes and Hurston's *Mulebone*, and a former college instructor. However, the marriage lasted six months. Also in 1928 Thurman joined the editorial staff of McFadden Publications; thus, he was the first black American to hold such a position with a white publishing company. The following year marked the publication of Thurman's first novel, *The Blacker the Berry: A Novel of Negro Life*, as well as the debut of *Harlem: A Melodrama of Negro Life in Harlem*, a play he cowrote with William Jourdan Rapp, a white writer. The play, based on Thurman's short story "Cordelia the Crude," which appeared in *Fire!!* (1926), was the first black play successfully produced on Broadway that appealed to white theatergoers. Although there were ninety-three performances of the play in New York as well as elsewhere in the United States and Canada, *Harlem* received "mixed reviews and complaints from old guard African Americans that it focused too much on the lowlife in Harlem" (Warren 1120). Prior to *Harlem*, Thurman, Richard Bruce Nugent,* and a number of their contemporaries were extras in the Theatre Guild's *Porgy*. Thurman accepted a walk-on part that paid $16.50 weekly in an effort to learn more about stagecraft. His battle for a pay increase for extras was won one week before he left *Porgy* to sit in at rehearsals for *Harlem*. Later members of the *Harlem* cast waged a similar fight for more money (West 222).

As a result of Thurman's articles that began appearing in 1927 in major publications such as the *New Republic, Independent, The World Tomorrow*, the *Bookman*, and *Dance Magazine*, along with the success of *The Blacker the Berry* and *Harlem* (the play), Thurman was "Harlem's best-known inhabitant" (Lewis 238). Henderson offers a similar assessment of Thurman: "But for a brief period, no personality among the 'New Negroes' shone so brilliantly as that of Wallace Thurman who found himself on a floodtide of success" (148). Thurman remained supportive of other writers who sought his attention (Singh xvii).

Although Thurman frequently experienced melancholy, he continued to write. There were times when he served as a ghostwriter for books and magazines, including *True Story*, using pen names such as Ethel Belle Mandrake and Patrick Casey. His second and third novels, *Infants of the Spring* and *The Interne* (cowritten with the white author Abraham Furman), were published in 1932 by the Macaulay Company, the same year that Thurman was appointed editor in chief at Macaulay. Again Thurman achieved another first; he was the first African American in such a position with a major white publishing company. Two years later, Thurman returned to California, where he wrote two screenplays: *Tomorrow's Children* and *High School Girl*.

In 1934 Thurman, losing a battle with tuberculosis, returned to New York. Ironically, he spent the final six months of his life at the same Welfare Island hospital that he exposed in *The Interne*. Thirty-two-year-old Wallace Thurman, novelist, playwright, short story writer, poet, literary critic, editor, and journalist, died on December 21, the same week that fellow Harlem Renaissance writer Rudolph Fisher* died. Arna Bontemps commented that "Thurman was like a flame which burned so intensely, it could not last for long, but quickly consumed itself" (qtd. in Henderson 147), while Thurman's other contemporary Dorothy West acknowledged that his death "caused the first break in the ranks of the 'New Negro' " (227).

MAJOR WORKS AND THEMES

Thurman was a prolific author who wrote in various genres, yet his most memorable contributions are his novels *The Blacker the Berry* and *Infants of the Spring*. Armed with honesty, a propensity to criticize, and an ability to write satire, Thurman was the Harlem Renaissance's gadfly who advocated self-acceptance and self-examination. Since the publication of the first slave narratives, African American novels, and short stories, most black writers created protagonists who were victims of racial discrimination and/or models to be emulated in efforts to uplift the race. However, Thurman was one of the first black writers to present African American characters who are victims of their own foibles.

The Blacker the Berry's dark-skinned heroine, Emma Lou Morgan, "had always been the alien member of the family and of the family's social circle" (15) because her family believes "[w]hiter and whiter, every generation. The nearer white you are the more white people will respect you" (21). Thus, Thurman audaciously reveals a forbidden subject in black literature—intraracial discrimination. Emma Lou suffers because lighter-skinned African Americans in Boise, Los Angeles, and Harlem reject her. This victim of a color caste system is worthy of readers' scorn because she dislikes other dark-skinned people and values bleaching cream more than her high school diploma. It is not until the end of the novel that Emma Lou accepts herself, and Thurman offers a didactic message to African Americans with hatred or shame for black skin:

For the first time in her life she felt that she must definitely come to some conclusion about her life and govern herself accordingly. After all she wasn't the only black girl alive. There were thousands on thousands, who, like her, were plain, untalented, ordinary, and who, unlike herself, seemed to live in some degree of comfort. Was she alone to blame for her unhappiness? Although this had been suggested to her by others, she had been too obtuse to accept it. She had ever been eager to shift the entire blame on others when no doubt she herself was the major criminal.

But having arrived at this—what did it solve or promise for the future? . . . What she needed to do now was to accept her black skin as being real and unchangeable, to realize that certain things were, had been, and would be, and with this in mind begin life anew, always fighting, not so much for acceptance by other people, but for acceptance of herself by herself. (226–27)

Just as Thurman mocks Emma Lou for her foibles, in *Infants of the Spring*, the only novel of the Harlem Renaissance written by a member of the Harlem Renaissance, he ridicules Harlem Renaissance writers for their failures. The protagonist, Raymond Taylor (Thurman), tries to awaken his contemporaries Sweetie Mae Carr (Hurston), Tony Crews (Hughes), DeWitt Clinton (Countee Cullen*), Cedric Williams (Eric Walrond*), Manfred Trout (Fisher), Doris Westmore (West), Hazel Jamison (Helene Johnson), and others. Thurman's criticism of his own works, his peers' writings, and the Harlem Renaissance in general is evident in his protagonist. Raymond realizes that African American writers are caught up in the glamour of the era: "[They] had climbed aboard the bandwagon [and unless they] began to do something worth while, there would be little chance of their being permanently established" (62). Raymond disapproves of black writers who are creating fads rather than art and/or attempting to uplift the race: "He was tired of Negro writers who had nothing to say, and who only wrote because they were literate and felt they should apprise white humanity of the better classes of Negro humanity" (91). Thurman's protagonist also has little tolerance for black artists who feel inferior: "He had no sympathy whatsoever with Negroes who contended that should their art be Negroid, they, the artist, must be considered inferior. As if a poem or a song or a novel by and about Negroes could not reach the same heights as a poem or a song or a novel by or about any other race" (108). Thus, Thurman argues for self-examination. Once the artists realize their limitations, they can strive to produce worthier works.

CRITICAL RECEPTION

Thurman acknowledged that his creative writing was not as strong as his journalistic abilities. Critics from the 1920s to the present day agree that Thurman's talents as a novelist are lacking. However his stature has grown over the decades.

Earlier critics such as Carter misinterpreted Thurman's novels by failing to recognize his use of satire; she classifies *The Blacker the Berry*'s Emma Lou as "an incredibly stupid character" (162). Indeed, Emma Lou is stupid, but Carter misses the purpose of Thurman's portrayal; he wants readers to see Emma Lou as an object of ridicule. Other scholars from earlier years such as Bone have psychoanalyzed Thurman. Bone goes as far as to label *Infants of the Spring* "a neurotic novel" (93) and calls Thurman "the undertaker" (93) of the Harlem Renaissance who "was simply working out his self-destructive impulses on the level of a literary movement" (94). More accurate assessments of Thurman's novels are provided by Brown, who identifies Thurman as "devil's advocate in his two novels" (146), and Davis, who recognizes Thurman's messages about insincerity and writing freedom in *Infants of the Spring* (*From the Dark* 118). There appears to be a consensus among the critics, past or present, that *Infants of the Spring* provides valuable insight into the Harlem Renaissance. Singh accurately assesses the novel as "a coming-of-age of the Harlem Renaissance literati" (36) and as "the only document from the period that attempted self-evaluation" (33).

Singh, Klotman, Gaither, and Ferguson are among the recent scholars who tend to regard Thurman as a central figure of the Harlem Renaissance; they are primarily influenced by Thurman's critical abilities as displayed in his novels and articles. Klotman rates Thurman "the most trenchant . . . [and] most incisive critic" (261) of the era. Thus, these scholars view Thurman's critical talents as his legacy.

Huggins, when describing the protagonist of *Infants of the Spring*, elaborates upon Thurman's legacy and reveals Thurman's role in defining an African American aesthetic:

Raymond Taylor attempts to find solid ground, in terms of the Harlem Renaissance, for his own artistic integrity. He wonders through the maze: the Negro as artist or advocate, the writer as individual or race man, art as self-expression or expression of ethnic culture. Explicit or not, these were the problems of Afro-American artists then and now. Wallace Thurman, more than any other writer of the period, tried to address himself to these issues. (183)

The literary career of Wallace Thurman, a brilliant, yet enigmatic, Harlem Renaissance figure, merits more study.

BIBLIOGRAPHY

Works by Wallace Thurman

Novels

The Blacker the Berry: A Novel of Negro Life. 1929. New York: Collier, 1972. *Infants of the Spring.* 1932. Boston: Northeastern University Press, 1992.
(And Abraham Furman). *The Interne.* New York: Macaulay, 1932.

Drama

(And William Jourdan Rapp). *Harlem: A Melodrama of Negro Life in Harlem.* Unpublished, 1929.
Jeremiah the Magnificent. Unpublished.

Poetry

"The Last Citadel." *Opportunity* (April 1926): 128.
"Confession." *Messenger* (June 1926): 167.
"God's Edict." *Opportunity* (July 1926): 216.

Booklet

The Negro Life in New York's Harlem. Girard, KS: Haldeman-Julius, 1928.

Magazines

Fire!! A Quarterly Devoted to the Younger Negro Artists (November 1926).
Harlem: A Forum of Negro Life (November 1928).

Essays/Reviews

"Eugene O'Neill's *All God's Chilluns Got Wings.*" *Outlet* (October 1924): 19–20.
"Whither Are We Drifting?" *Outlet* (November 1924): 9–11.

"Christmas: Its Origin and Significance." *Outlet* (December 1924): 11–12.

"In the Name of Purity." *Messenger* (April 1926): 125.

"Quoth Brigham John:—This Is the Place." *Messenger* (August 1926): 235–36.

"Fire Burns, Editorial Comment." *Fire!! A Quarterly Devoted to the Younger Negro Artists* (November 1926): 47–48.

"Singers at the Crossroads." *Greenwich Village Quill* (March 1927): 14–16.

"Harlem: A Vivid Picture of the World's Greatest Negro City." *American Monthly* (May 1927): 19–20.

"Negro Artists and the Negro." *New Republic* (August 31, 1927): 37–39.

"Nephews of Uncle Remus." *Independent* (September 24, 1927): 296–98.

"Harlem Facets." *World Tomorrow* (November 1927): 465–67.

"Harlem's Place in the Sun." *Dance Magazine* (May 10, 1928): 23+.

"Negro Poetry and Their Poetry." *Bookman* (July 1928): 555–61.

"Editorial." *Harlem: A Forum of Negro Life* (November 1928): 21–22.

"High, Low, Past and Present." Rev. of *The Walls of Jericho*, by Rudolph Fisher, *Quicksand*, by Nella Larsen, *and Adventures of an African Slaver*, by Captain Canot. *Harlem: A Forum of Negro Life* (November 1928): 31–32.

(And William Jourdan Rapp). "Harlem-as Others See It." *Negro World* (April 13, 1929): 3.

"Notes of a Stepchild." (Ms. excerpt in Mae Gwendolyn Henderson, "Portrait of Wallace Thurman.") *The Harlem Renaissance Remembered: Essays with a Memoir*. Ed. Arna Bontemps. New York: Dodd, Mead, 1972. 147–89.

Rev. of *Infants of the Spring*. Ms., n.d. Reprinted in *The Harlem Renaissance 1920–1940: The Critics and the Harlem Renaissance*. Ed. Gary D. Wintz. New York: Garland, 1996. 236–37.

Rev. of *Not without Laughter*, by Langston Hughes. Reprinted in *The Harlem Renaissance 1920–1940: The Critics and the Harlem Renaissance*. Ed. Gary D. Wintz. New York: Garland, 1996. 225.

Short Stories

"You Never Can Tell." *Outlet* (September 1924): 6–8.

"You Never Can Tell, Part 2." *Outlet* (October 1924): 14–15.

"Cordelia the Crude, a Harlem Sketch." *Fire!! A Quarterly Devoted to the Younger Negro Artists* (November 1926): 5–6.

"Grist in the Mill." *Black Writers of America: A Comprehensive Anthology*. Ed. Richard Barksdale and Keneth Kinnamon. New York: Macmillan, 1972. 606–11.

Screenplays

Tomorrow's Children. Bryan Foy Productions, 1934.
High School Girl. Bryan Foy Productions, 1935.

Studies of Wallace Thurman

Abramson, Doris. *Negro Playwrights in the American Theatre, 1925–1929*. New York: Columbia University Press, 1969.

Anderson, Jarvis. *This Was Harlem: A Cultural Portrait, 1900–1950*. New York: Farrar, Straus, Giroux, 1981.

Bone, Robert A. *The Negro Novel in America*. 1958. New Haven, CT: Yale University Press, 1970.

Brown, Sterling. *The Negro in American Fiction*. 1937. New York: Atheneum, 1969.

Carter, Eunice Hunton. Rev. of *The Blacker the Berry*. *Opportunity* (May 1929): 162–63.

Davis, Arthur P. *From the Dark Tower: Afro-American Writers 1900–1960*. 1974. Washington, DC: Howard University Press, 1982.

———. "Growing Up in the New Negro Renaissance." *Negro American Literature Forum* 2 (1968): 53–55.

Du Bois, W.E.B. "The Browsing Reader." Rev. of *The Blacker the Berry*. *Crisis* (July 1929): 248.

Ferguson, SallyAnn H. "Wallace Thurman." In *The Oxford Companion to African American Literature*. Ed. William L. Andrews, Frances Smith Foster, and Trudier Harris. New York: Oxford University Press, 1997. 729–30.

Gaither, Renoir W. "The Moment of Revision: A Reappraisal of Wallace Thurman's Aesthetics in *The Blacker the Berry* and *Infants of the Spring*." *CLA Journal* 37 (1993): 81–93.

Gloster, Hugh M. "The Van Vechten Vogue." In *Negro Voices in American Fiction*. 1948. Chapel Hill: University of North Carolina Press, 1975. 157–73.

Haslam, Gerald. "Wallace Thurman: A Western Renaissance Man." *Western American Literature* (Spring 1971): 53–59.

Hemenway, Robert E. *Zora Neale Hurston: A Literary Biography*. 1977. Urbana: University of Illinois Press, 1980.

Henderson, Mae Gwendolyn. "Portrait of Wallace Thurman." In *The Harlem Renaissance Remembered: Essays with a Memoir*. Ed. Arna Bontemps. New York: Dodd, Mead, 1972. 147–89.

Hicks, Granville. "The New Negro: An Interview with Wallace Thurman." *Churchman* (April 30, 1927): 10–11.

Holt, Elvin. "*The Blacker the Berry: A Novel of Negro Life*." In *Masterpieces of African-American Literature*. Ed. Frank N. Magill. New York: HarperCollins, 1992. 61–64.

Huggins, Nathan Irvin. *Harlem Renaissance*. 1971. New York: Oxford University Press, 1973.

Hughes, Langston. *The Big Sea: An Autobiography*. 1940. New York: Thunder's Mouth, 1986.

Klotman, Phyllis R. "Wallace Henry Thurman." In *Dictionary of Literary Biography*. *Afro-American Writers from the Harlem Renaissance to 1940*. Ed. Trudier Harris. Vol. 51. Detroit: Gale, 1987. 260–73.

Lewis, David Levering. *When Harlem Was in Vogue*. 1981. New York: Oxford University Press, 1989.

Perkins, Huel D. "Renaissance 'Renegade'?: Wallace Thurman." *Black World* (February 1976): 29–35.

Perry, Margaret. *Silence to the Drums: A Survey of the Literature of the Harlem Renaissance*. Westport, CT: Greenwood, 1976.

Singh, Amritjit. *The Novels of the Harlem Renaissance: Twelve Black Writers 1923–1933*. University Park: Pennsylvania State University Press, 1976. 1–40.

Taylor, Lois. Rev. of *Infants of the Spring*. *Journal of Negro Life* (March 1932): 89.

Walden, Daniel. "The Canker Galls . . . ," or the Short Promising Life of Wallace Thurman." In *Harlem Renaissance Re-Examined*. Rev. ed. Ed. Victor A. Kramer and Robert A. Russ. Troy, NY: Whitston, 1997. 229–37.

"Wallace Thurman." *Twentieth-Century Literary Criticism*. Ed. Sharon K. Hall. Vol. 6. Detroit: Gale, 1982. 444–51.

Warren, Nagueyalti. "Wallace Thurman." In *Notable Black American Men*. Ed. Jessie Carney Smith. Detroit: Gale, 1999. 1118–21.

Watson, Steven. *The Harlem Renaissance: Hub of African-American Culture, 1920–1930*. New York: Pantheon, 1996.

West, Dorothy. "Elephant's Dance." 1970. In *The Richer, the Poorer: Stories, Sketches, and Reminiscences*. New York: Doubleday, 1995. 215–27.

Young, James O. "Black Reality and Beyond." In *Black Writers of the Thirties*. Baton Rouge: Louisiana State University Press, 1973. 203–36.

KATHERINE DAVIS CHAPMAN TILLMAN
(1870–?)

Kirsten Saunders

BIOGRAPHY

Katherine Davis Chapman Tillman was born February 19, 1870, in Mound City, Illinois. She would later relocate with her parents, Charles and Laura, to Yankton, South Dakota, where she completed high school. Her first published work, a poem titled "Memory," appeared in the *Christian Recorder* when she was eighteen. Although little else is known about Tillman's formative years, what is acknowledged is that her educational pursuits took her to State University of Louisville in Kentucky and to Wilberforce University in Ohio. Presumably, in Yankton, South Dakota, she first met and married George Tillman, a young African Methodist Episcopal (AME) minister who was on his first ministerial assignment. George Tillman, who also studied at Wilberforce University, would later go on to become a diligent and successful minister in the AME Church. Katherine Tillman's active involvement and association with the AME Church, in particular her prolific publications in the *AME Church Review* and the *Christian Recorder* and her work with the *AME Book Concern*, most likely came as a direct result of her marriage to George Tillman. Indeed, wherever her husband established a ministry, Tillman's involvement with church and civic associations flourished.

Presently, any further biographical information regarding Katherine Tillman remains scant. Her last known publications appear in 1922, while the exact year and date of her death remain unknown.

MAJOR WORKS AND THEMES

Tillman's writing, like that of most African American female authors in the post-Reconstruction period of 1877–1915, was thematically centered around issues or pursuits of a profession, marriage, mothering/motherhood, and domesticity. While some of these prescribed roles for European Americans would serve as attainable goals, for the majority of African American women who were a generation removed from slavery, the highly idealized images and themes of Tillman's works would be problematized by race and class. In the novella *Beryl Weston's Ambition: The Story of an Afro-American Girl's Life* (1893), published as a serial in the *AME Church Review*, the protagonist or heroine, Beryl Weston, is a young black woman "regarded as a great prodigy among her untutored acquaintances" (213) and the firstborn of a wealthy planter and a "dainty and refined" (213) schoolteacher. Upon the death of her mother, Beryl must leave college to oversee the physically taxing task of running the family household, thus deferring her own intellectual ambition of becoming an "instructress in the modern languages and higher mathematics" (217).

The other Tillman novella (again serialized by the *AME Church Review*), *Clancy Street* (1898–1899), was a departure thematically from *Beryl Weston's Ambition*. Its setting, a street in Louisville, Kentucky, that was "the home of a large settlement of Negroes" (251), offers the reader a panoramic view of poverty-stricken urban postemancipation black life. Its heroine, Caroline Waters, although virtuous, is a stark contrast to the idealized Beryl Weston. Whereas Beryl was born a child of means, Caroline was raised on a street "filled with rickety tenements and mouldy cottages" (254). The contrast is further underscored by Tillman's acknowledgment of the licentious behavior of the inhabitants of *Clancy Street*, behavior that Tillman identifies not as innate pathologies but rather as retainers from slavery. Thus, for Caroline Waters, the negotiation of life is imbued not only with the despair of poverty but also with the sin and moral decay of theft, drinking, prostitution, and gambling. In keeping with the novella's didactic stance against these ills, Tillman, through Caroline's mother, Anne, proffers this sentiment: "You're only a colored girl . . . but I'd rather see you going barefooted in your little sunbonnet and calico slip, and know you're alright, than to see you in silks and satins and know you didn't come by them honest" (273).

The body of Katherine Tillman's essays varies widely. In her essay "Paying Professions for Colored Girls" (1907), Tillman, as in *Beryl Weston's Ambition*, thematically pairs the intellect with the physical responsibility of domestic life as a necessary framework for good Christian African American women. Conversely, in other essays published in the *AME Book Review*, Tillman predominately charts the literary accomplishments of notable African American authors. In "Afro-American Poets and Their Verse" (1898) and "The Negro among Anglo-Saxon Poets" (1898), as well as in her biographical essays, "Alexander Dumas, Père" (1907) and "Alexander Sergeivich Pushkin" (1909), Katherine Tillman chronicles these achievements with a decidedly vindicationist thrust. In "Afro-American Poets and Their Verse," she contends that "no man who loves the Negro race [can] decry poetry, for it is by this and other proofs of genius that our race will be enabled to take its place among the nations of the earth" (95). The level of sophistication and didactic discourse Tillman achieves in her novellas and essays is not as intrinsic in her five dramas but is, however, infused into some of her poems published between 1888 and 1902, as well as in her book of verse, *Recitations* (1902). In *Recitations*, poems ranging from the religiously charged "Faith's Vision" to the aesthetically relevant and humorous "When Mandy Combs Her Head" serve as cultural and literary milestones, in part because Katherine Tillman's utilization of African American dialect and social, historical, and religious experiences aids in painting a realistic picture of black culture of the day. Tillman's writing substantiates definitively that nineteenth-century African American women-authored work was not confined to the prescribed notions of the time.

CRITICAL RECEPTION

The proliferation of publications by Tillman in the *Christian Recorder* and the *AME Church Review* not only suggests a correlation to her active involvement in the AME Church but also is a testament to her popularity as an author within the church.

In 1991 Claudia Tate edited: *The Works of Katherine Davis Chapman Tillman*, a seminal collection of Tillman's publications. In the Introduction, Tate assesses the relevance and importance of Tillman's literary contributions as a black woman writer in the nineteenth century: "Her work approximates that of many early, minor, black authors, heretofore obscure, who similarly asserted their authority to interpret black culture, question its values, and preserve its integrity through the dissemination of the written word" (9). Indeed, Tillman's tireless dissemination of the written word into the heart of the black community will undoubtedly attract the critical study it demands.

BIBLIOGRAPHY

Works by Katherine Davis Chapman Tillman

Novellas

Beryl Weston's Ambition: The Story of an Afro-American Girl's Life. AME Church Review 10 (July 1893): 173–91; 10 (October 1893): 308–22.
Clancy Street. AME Church Review 15 (October 1898):643–50; 15 (July 1899):152–59; 15 (October 1899):241–51.

Short Stories

"Miles the Conqueror." *American Citizen* (April 20, 1894): n.p.
"The Preacher at Hill Station." AME Church Review 19 (January 1903):634–43.

Essays

"Some Girls That I Know." AME Church Review 9 (January 1893):288–92.
"Afro-American Women and Their Work." AME Church Review 11 (April 1895):477–99.

"Afro-American Poets and Their Verse." AME Church Review 14 (April 1898):421–28.
"The Negro among Anglo-Saxon Poets." AME Church Review 14 (1898):106–12.
"Alexander Dumas, Père." AME Church Review 24 (January 1907):257–63.
"Paying Professions for Colored Girls." Voice of the Negro (January–February 1907):54–55.
"Alexander Sergeivich Pushkin." AME Church Review 25 (July 1909):27–32.

Poetry

"Memory." Christian Recorder (July 12, 1888):1.
"Only a Letter." Christian Recorder (August 9, 1888):1.
"My Queen." Christian Recorder (September 10, 1891):5.
"The Glad New Year." Christian Recorder (January 10, 1893):1.
"Lift Me Higher Master." Christian Recorder (April 26, 1894):1.
"Lines to Ida B. Wells." Christian Recorder (July 5, 1894):1.
"The Pastor." Christian Recorder (October 18, 1894):1.
"A Rest Beyond." The Work of the Afro-American Woman. Ed. N. F. Mossell. Philadelphia: George S. Ferguson, 1894; reprinted, New York: Oxford University Press, 1988.
"Allen's Army." Christian Recorder (February 7, 1895):6.
"A Psalm of the Soul." Christian Recorder (January 9, 1896):1.
"Heart-Keeping." Christian Recorder (March 12, 1896):1.
"Afro-American Boy." Christian Recorder (June 24, 1897):1.
"Faith's Vision." Christian Recorder (July 29, 1897):1.
"A Tribute to Negro Regiments." Christian Recorder (June 9, 1898):1.
"The Superannuate." Christian Recorder (March 16, 1899):1.
"Which?" Christian Recorder (July 6, 1899):1.
"The Highest Life." Christian Recorder (November 8, 1900):1.
"Soul Visions." Christian Recorder (August 21, 1902):1.
"The Warrior's Lay." Christian Recorder (October 22, 1902):1.
Recitations. Philadelphia: AME Book Concern, 1902.

Drama

Aunt Betsy's Thanksgiving. Philadelphia: AME Book Concern, n.d.
Thirty Years of Freedom: A Drama in Four Acts. Philadelphia: AME Book Concern, 1902.
Heirs of Slavery. Philadelphia: AME Publishing House, 1909.
Fifty Years of Freedom, or From Cabin to Congress: A Drama in Four Acts. Philadelphia: AME Book Concern, 1910.
The Spirit of Allen: A Pageant of African Methodism. N.p., 1922.

Anthologies

Quotations from Negro Authors. Fort Scott, KS: N.p., 1921.
The Works of Katherine Davis Chapman Tillman. Ed. Claudia Tate. New York: Oxford University Press, 1991.

Studies of Katherine Davis Chapman Tillman

"Book List." AME Church Review (April 1904):418.
Dunnigan, Alice. "Early History of Negro Women in Journalism." Negro History Bulletin 28 (Summer 1965):178.
Majors, Monroe A. Noted Negro Women. Chicago: Donohue and Henneberry, 1893.

MELVIN BEAUNORUS TOLSON
(1898–1966)

Pierre-Damien Mvuyekure

BIOGRAPHY

Of African, Irish, French, and Native American heritage, an ethnic mixture that has influenced some of his work, Melvin Beaunorus Tolson was born February 6, 1898, in Moberly, Missouri, though his family constantly moved from town to town in Missouri and Iowa due to his father's being a minister in the Methodist Episcopal Church. Before his family moved to Iowa, Melvin B. Tolson had discovered the arts, especially painting, and one day he was given a book about the French Revolution, in which he saw the picture of Toussaint L'Ouverture. The picture of Toussaint L'Ouverture would instill racial pride in the young Tolson's mind, one of the major themes that underlie his work. Equally important is how the move to Iowa would shape Tolson's future literary career. In 1912 he lived in Oskaloosa, Iowa, where he published his first poem in an Oskaloosa newspaper. A year later, his family moved from Oskaloosa to Mason City, Iowa, where a white teacher not only helped him become a good public speaker but taught him to be "a perfectionist by hearing him say one poem over and over and by snapping her fingers to indicate when a word should be accented" (*Melvin B. Tolson* Flasch 23). Also while living in Iowa, Tolson discovered Paul Laurence Dunbar,* whose dialect poems he would try to imitate.

After graduating from Lincoln University in Oxford, Pennsylvania, Tolson became an instructor of English and speech at Wiley College in Marshall, Texas, where he not only led team debates but also wrote poems, short stories, novels, and plays. But the biggest influence on Melvin Tolson's poetry would come in 1930, when he worked on a master's degree at Columbia University, where he wrote a thesis on the Harlem Renaissance writers, "The Harlem Group of Negro Writers." Although in one way or another all the Harlem Renaissance writers on whom Tolson worked may have influenced his own work, greater influence came from George S. Schuyler and Langston Hughes,* the former for speaking for the underprivileged, the latter for his experimentation with blues in poetry. From his discovery of, and experiences in, Harlem, Tolson wrote two great collections of poems, *A Gallery of Harlem Portraits* (completed in 1932) and *Harlem Gallery, Book I: The Curator* (1953). After the critics and publishers rejected *A Gallery of Harlem Portraits*, Tolson waited until 1940 to mark his impact on the literary scene, when his poem "Dark Symphony" won the National Poetry Contest organized by Chicago's American Negro Exposition. "Dark Symphony" was later published in the *Atlantic Monthly* and collected in *Rendezvous with America* in 1944. When, in 1947, Tolson was appointed the poet laureate of Liberia by the Liberian president Tubman, he began working on *Libretto for the Republic of Liberia*, an ode poem for Liberia, utterly anticolonial in tone, that forever marked Tolson as a modern poet.

MAJOR WORKS AND THEMES

Rendezvous with America, Tolson's first published collection of poems, exemplifies the influences that Tolson received from reading and imitating the techniques of Whitman, Shakespeare, Pound, Eliot, Baudelaire, and other poets whom he admired. The controlled form ranges from the Shakespearean sonnet, through quatrains and couplets, to the Whitmanesque free verse. In "Rendezvous with America," the title poem, Tolson defines America and its history and through the process claims it as not only his country as a black man but also the country of the yellows, the reds, the browns, and the whites. Through Plymouth Rock, Jamestown, and Ellis Island, the opening stanza of section 1 conjures up images of how the Pilgrims/Puritans, the Africans, and the immigrants bridged the ocean between the Old World and the New World. In the next section, the speaker makes it clear how diverse breeds and mixed bloods these men became, some of them becoming martyrs whose bones served as America's "foundation stones." The next section demonstrates how the making of the republic was made possible by waves of people from Europe, Africa, and Asia; through images of river, color, and orchestra, the poet defines America as a rainbow of diverse, multicolored ethnicities playing thousands of instruments as a tribute to America. In the next sections, America is defined through some of its popular sports and folk heroes and philosophers, including Daniel Boone, Jesse James, John Henry, Casey Jones, Johnny Appleseed, Joe Dimaggio, Joe Louis, Thomas Paine, Abe Lincoln, Marian Anderson, and Fred Douglass.* But in section 7, America, personified through Uncle Sam, is debunked for being sometimes somnolent and complacent, which anti-Semites and the Ku Klux Klan see as an opportunity to undermine democracy and the Constitution. The last two sections of "Rendezvous with America" not only speak of Whitman's influence as far as free verse and anaphora are concerned but also point to Tolson's interest in music.

Though not as unified as "Rendezvous with America," poems in "Woodcuts for Americana" continue the definition of America in terms of race, law, and patriotism. In "An Ex-Judge at the Bar," an eight-stanza interior monologue poem with two rhyming couplets for each stanza (*aabb*), the speaker begins by asking the bartenders to make a drink for two, one for the bartender in the speaker and another for the bartender in the ex-judge. Then the speaker tells the story about how he became an ex-judge after returning from France (probably as a fighter in World War I). When he was singing *Dixie* in a bar named Tony's Lady of Romance, the Goddess Justice challenged the way he became a judge, by participating in the lynching of a "Negro." In the concluding stanza, the ex-judge orders three straight shots, one for the lynched black man and two for the bartender and him. The same ironies of race are expressed in "The Town Fathers," in which a mayor, a judge, and a sheriff celebrate the Fourth of July by both lamenting the death of the Confederacy and pondering ways to express the blackness of the land and the whiteness of people living in town. But Tolson's treatment of race is probably best expressed in "The Man Inside," a poem dedicated to V. F. Calverton, editor of the *Modern Quarterly*, who had introduced Tolson to several writers in New York. The main point of the poem is that black and white colors are not determining factors insofar as the man inside is neither. In "Esperanto," however, race matters to the extent that Arab, Jew, Chinese, Saxon, Eskimo, Slav, Tartar, Kru, Latin, Danakil, and Crow speak Esperanto as their "catholic tongue" of grief. Yet, the speaker notes that their race is the human race.

With "Dark Symphony," Tolson returns to the theme of music, both in form and in content, to celebrate the accomplishments of his race, past and present, including the New Negro. First, each of the six sections is named after a musical tempo (in Italian) at which it should be played: "Allegro Moderato," "Lento Grave," "Andante Sostenuto," "Tempo Primo," "Larghetto," and "Tempo di Marcia." Second, the poem celebrates how black slaves challenged the white world through Negro spirituals such as "One More River to Cross," "Steal Away to Jesus," "The Crucifixion," "Swing Low, Sweet Chariot," and "Go Down Moses." Then the poem defines the New Negro, a breed sprung from the strong "loins" of Nat Turner, Joseph Cinquez, Frederick Douglass,* Sojourner Truth,* and Harriet Tubman.

While "Song of Myself" echoes Whitman and demonstrates the influence of Emily Dickinson on Tolson, the poems in the "Sonnets" section are all Shakespearean sonnets, the subject matter of which ranges from a schoolteacher, to Iago, to Hamlet, to language of the wolf, to a meeting in Versailles between Woodrow Wilson (America), Clemenceau (France), and Lloyd George (England). Through poems like "Vesuvius," "The Bard of Addis Ababa," "Damascus Blade," "Babylon," "The Idols of the Tribe," and "Tapestries of Time," the last three sections of *Rendezvous with America* challenge the reader's knowledge of world history, cultures, and politics.

Critics have pointed out how Tolson is a "multicultured citizen of the world," and no work of his proves this more than the *Libretto for the Republic of Liberia*, an ode poem structured after the notes of the musical scale: "do," "re," "mi," "fa,"

"sol," "la," "ti," "do." Although Liberia and its thriving history are the underpinnings of the libretto, the poem mixes references and allusions from European and
American canons—Virgil, Shakespeare, Blake, Aeschylus, Hawthorne, Boccaccio, Camus, Nietzsche, Apollinaire, Ronsard, Ovid, Lamartine, Boileau, Dante,
Xenophanes—and celebratory references to African-rich traditions such as griots,
poetry, proverbs, and Benin art. This modernist aspect of the poem led Allen
Tate to argue, in his Preface to the poem, that "there is a great gift for language,
a profound historical scene, and a first-rate intelligence at work in this poem
from the first to last" (10). The same aspect, however, has led to the difficult
reading of the poem by readers who do not possess Tolson's stupendous knowledge of world history and culture. Karl Shapiro, in his Introduction to *The Harlem
Gallery*, has rightly pointed out that *Libretto for the Republic of Liberia* "pulls the
rug out from under the poetry of the Academy; on the stylistic level, outpounding
Pound, it shocks the learned into a recognition of their own ignorance" (12).
Furthermore, that Tolson provided 737 notes, many of them long paragraphs,
suggests that he, too, realized how complex and quasi-esoteric (to some readers)
Libretto for the Republic of Liberia was likely to be.

The "do" section opens with a question about Liberia, which is repeated
throughout the section; Liberia is defined not only as the epitome of "survival
dawn" that has escaped America but also as both the future of Africa and the
shining star of Europe and Asia. What is more, the poet sees Liberia not as a
shame to Africa but as a "Black Lazarus" who arose from the grave of the white
man. In the sixth stanza, the poem discusses the shape of the map of Africa from
two African schools of thought: one sees the shape of Africa as a question mark
to the white world, while the other sees it as a "ham bone" destined to carve
European imperialism. From this perspective, the rest of the first section negates
Bismarck's argument that blacks are the distorted imitations of white men. Also,
the last part of the section insists that Liberia has not yet surrendered its soul of
the nation as the Gold Coast was forced by Sir Frederich Hodgson or been
conquered as Songhai was by Ed-dehebi. Anticolonial and postcolonial moments
abound in *Libretto for the Republic of Liberia*.

Through three chants by the good old Bard of Timbuktu, the "re" section
points out that before Liberia and before Americans and Europeans went to
Africa to plunder ivory and gold, there were Songhai with Sankoré University
and a powerful ruler like Askia. With the second one-line chant in Kiswahili,
the Bard of Timbuktu laments that women are having babies at an alarming rate
and that it is the work of the white man. In the third chant, the Bard of Timbuktu
calls Europe an "empty python" hiding in the grass, a metaphor that is further
explained in the next two stanzas, whose main subject is the destruction of Timbuktu by the Portuguese and the Spanish renegades. Because the rivers Wagadu
and Bagana cry, cobras and mambas hiss in the golden caves of Falémé and
Bambuk, and adders and scorpions inhabit the now weedy halls of Sankoré, the
Bard of Timbuktu no longer sings.

In "mi," the third section, the origins of Liberia are traced back to the American "Pilgrim Fathers' " ill-fated first voyage to found what is now Liberia. This small beginning is contrasted to the momentous role that Liberia was to later play during World War I by both providing rubber to Allied countries and serving as an air base for Allied forces. In a note, Tolson informs us that the "airplanes from Liberia dropped 17,000 bombs a month against Rommel's *Africa Korps*" (61). Through the images of a boa, an assassin eagle, and a tiger holding a human skull between its paws, however, the poet warns in the "fa" section that the threats for war still loom large. The "sol" section evokes the history of slavery through the images of the Middle Passage, where sharks fatten on "pounds of flesh" whose stench incites God to hold his nose. Additionally, the poem travels back to ancient Africa through the voyage of Elijah Johnson, who recrosses the Middle Passage and from the belly of a whale hears the griots, whom Tolson defines as "living encyclopedias," present Africa's wisdom and philosophy through proverbs. The importance of the forty-one proverb-verses is underlined in a long note provided by Tolson: "Giryama, Bantu, Amharic, Swahili, Yoruba, Vai, Thonga, Zulu, Jaba, Sudanese these tribal scholars speak, with no basic change in idea and image, from line 173 to 214. The Africans have their *avant garde* in oral literature" (63). It is worth noting that the proverbs in this section are intended to disprove Guernier's words in French, mockingly repeated by the parrots, that of all continents Africa is the only one that does not possess any history.

That Africa possesses a rich and vast history is accounted for in "la," the sixth section, which tells the story of how glaciers caused antelopes, lions, leopards, giraffes, elephants, rhinoceroses, and apes to migrate south of the Sahara. The section ends with Jehudi Ashmun, who is believed to have founded Liberia, telling his black "kingsmen" that while America is his mother and Liberia his wife, Africa is his brother. A note informs the reader that Lincoln University was created as "Ashmun Institute" and that the "memory of the white pilgrim survives in old Ashmun Hall" (64).

In "ti," the second largest section, the poet reminds us that he is celebrating the centennial birthday of Liberia and prays that no venom destroys the African earth. Through the remaining part of the section, the poet displays a great sense of universalism through countless references to European masterpieces, classical and modern, as signposts of European epistemology and philosophy. The last lines of the section show, however, that the universal man was probably not meant to be African, as Greek and Latin scholars transformed Gorii into gorilla. A note tells us that Gorii originally referred to the aborigines of Liberia as seen by Hanno, a Carthaginian general, and that Gorii in Wolof language today means " 'These too are men' " (71).

In "do," the final and longest section of *Libretto for the Republic of Liberia*, Liberia becomes the lenses through which Africa, Asia, and Europe are viewed. Not only is Liberia the "Futureafrique" of the whole world, but it is also the "United Nations Limited" of Chaka, Seretse Khama in Bechuanaland. Liberia is also hailed as the "Bula Matadi," a reference to the Congolese port city of the western Democratic Republic of Congo (formerly Zaire) on the Congo River, which connects the Niger to Picayune, San Salvador, Hiroshima, Tel Aviv, Monrovia, and Peiping. Furthermore, Liberia is called "*Le Premier des Noirs*," a reference to Toussaint L'Ouverture, who addressed Napoleon, when the latter became first consul, as follows: "*Du Premier des Noirs au Premier des Blancs*" (From the First of the Blacks to the First of the Whites). The last part of the "do" section describes Liberia through the "Parliament of African Peoples," whose decrees become the decrees of Everyman and are eternalized in "*Africa Sikelel Africa*" (Africa save Africa), a pun on "Nkosi Sikeleli Africa" (God Bless/Save Africa)—the national anthem of at least two African countries, including South Africa. Noteworthy is that, thanks to the "Parliament of African Peoples," the hyenas no longer lament over the "barren bones" of Songhai's sultans, as in the "re" section, after Timbuktu's destruction.

Thus, in *Libretto for the Republic of Liberia* Tolson envisions a Liberia that is more than a nation, as demonstrated by countless and complex references to world history, culture, literature, and philosophy. A note to "Shikata pai nai" in the last section, a Japanese phrase that refers to "the stoicism with which Japanese villagers meet the earth convulsions of Fujiyama," could summarize Tolson's vision in the poem: "the flux of men and things is set forth in symbols whose motions are vertical-circular, horizontal-circular, and rectilinear. In spite of the diversity of phenomena, the unity of the past is represented by the ferris wheel; the present by the merry-go-round; and the future by the automobile, the train, the ship, and the aeroplane" (79).

As noted earlier, Harlem played a momentous role in Tolson's public life and literary career and was therefore crowned with two important collections of poetry, *The Harlem Gallery, Book I: The Curator* and *A Gallery of Harlem Portraits* (more than 160 poems completed in 1935 but posthumously published in 1979). The poems of *The Harlem Gallery* are organized according to the Greek alphabet and resemble a Platonic dialogue between the Curator, the Bantu expatriate Dr. Nkomo, Hideho Heights, the beatnik poet, and several other Harlemite characters. Throughout the twenty-four sections, Harlem is celebrated through the Curator's views on artists, art, and their importance to society as they clearly and meaningfully express human experiences, views that are supplemented by the Socratic questions of Dr. Nkomo. It is worth noting that before he died, Tolson had planned several books of *The Harlem Gallery*.

CRITICAL RECEPTION

In his Afterword to *A Gallery of Harlem Portraits*, Robert M. Farnsworth states, "Critics and readers have been ducking the challenge of [Tolson's] work for years except for a few who have been willing to let loose some critical haymakers" (256). Karl Shapiro echoes the same sentiment when he points out, in his Introduction to *The Harlem Gallery, Book I: The Curator*, that a "great poet has been living in our midst for decades and is almost totally unknown, even by the literati, even by poets" (11). Farnsworth and Shapiro summarize the state of the critical reception of Tolson's work since 1965. They suggest that because of its complexity and modernist poetic style, Tolson's work has not received the critical attention it deserves. According to David Shevin, Tolson's poetry, "as a published legacy, is a difficult one" insofar as it "bridges styles and schools, functioning as a record of an intellectual fabric rather than the product of any given school. The evaluation remains incomplete, and Tolson's unique contribution continues to unfold" (446).

But since 1965 things have improved, as some critics started paying attention to Tolson's poetic contribution to American and world literature. Noteworthy critical studies of Tolson's work include Joy Flasch's *Melvin B. Tolson* (1972), Robert M. Farnsworth's *Melvin B. Tolson, 1898–1966: Plain Talk and Poetic Prophecy* (1984), Mariann Russell's *Melvin B. Tolson's Harlem Gallery: A Literary Analysis* (1980), Michael Berube's *Marginal Forces/Cultural Centers: Tolson, Pynchon, and the Politics of the Canon* (1992), and some critical essays in literary journals. Nevertheless, there is no doubt that much more needs to be done, because works such as the *Libretto for the Republic of Liberia* have scarcely received any critical attention. With the inclusion of the *Libretto for the Republic of Liberia* in the first *The Norton Anthology of African American Literature*, there is hope that many readers and critics will have access to this out-of-print important work. Also, a forthcoming collection of Tolson's poetry from the University Press of Virginia, with an Introduction by Rita Dove, will further give ample exposure to Tolson's work. Furthermore, there is a need for critics to study Tolson's columns collected in *Caviar and Cabbage*, for therein Tolson has expressed his views on Christ and radicalism, race and class, World War II, black slavery and white slavery, and the racist overtones of *Gone with the Wind* and *Birth of a Nation*, themes that are likely to shed more light on Tolson's poetic work.

BIBLIOGRAPHY

Works by Melvin Beaunorus Tolson

Poems

Rendezvous with America. New York: Dodd, Mead, 1944.
The Harlem Gallery, Book I: The Curator. New York: Twayne, 1953; New York: Collier Books, 1970.
Libretto for the Republic of Liberia. London: Collier Books, 1970.
A Gallery of Harlem Portraits. Ed. Robert M. Farnsworth. Columbia: University of Missouri Press, 1979.
"Harlem Gallery" and Other Poems of Melvin B. Tolson. Ed. Raymond Nelson. Charlottesville: University Press of Virginia, 1999.

Essays

Caviar and Cabbage: Selected Columns by Melvin B. Tolson from the Washington Tribune, 1937–1944. Ed. Robert M. Farnsworth. Columbia: University of Missouri Press, 1982.

Studies of Melvin Beaunorus Tolson

Basler, Roy P. "The Heart of Blackness: M. B. Tolson's Poetry." *News Letter* 39.3 (1973): 63–76.

Berube, Michael. "Avant-Gardes and De-Authorizations: *Harlem Gallery* and the Cultural Contradiction of Modernism." *Callaloo* 12.1 (1989): 192–215.

———. *Marginal Masks/Cultural Forces: Tolson, Pynchon, and the Politics of the Canon.* Ithaca, NY: Cornell University Press, 1992.

———. "Masks, Margins and African American Modernism: Melvin Tolson's *Harlem Gallery*." *PMLA* 105.1 (1990): 57–69.

Cansler, Ronald L. "The White and Non-White Dichotomy of Melvin B. Tolson's Poetry." *Negro-American Literature-Forum* 7 (1993): 115–118.

Dove, Rita. "Telling It Like It I-S Is: Narrative Techniques in Melvin Tolson's *Harlem Gallery*." *New England Review and Bread Loaf Quarterly* 8.1 (1985): 109–117.

Farnsworth, Richard M. *Melvin B. Tolson, 1898–1966: Plain Talk and Poetic Prophecy.* Columbia: University of Missouri Press, 1984.

Flasch, Joy. *Melvin B. Tolson.* New York: Twayne, 1972.

———. "Preface to Melvin B. Tolson's *Caviar and Cabbage* Columns." *News Letter* 47.4 (1981): 101–2.

Hansell, William H. "Three Artists in Melvin B. Tolson's *Harlem Gallery*." *Black American Literature Forum* 18.3 (1984): 122–27.

McCall, Dan. "The Quicksilver Sparrow of M. B. Tolson." *American Quarterly* 18 (1966): 538–42.

Mootry, Maria K. " 'The Step of Iron Feet': Creative Practice in the War of Sonnets of Melvin B. Tolson and Gwendolyn Brooks." *Obsidian II: Black Literature in Review* 2.3 (1987): 69–87.

Nelson, Raymond. Ed. *Harlem Gallery, and Other Poems by Melvin B. Tolson.* Charlottesville: University of Virginia Press, 1999.

Nielsen, Aldon L. "Melvin B. Tolson and the Deterritorialization of Modernism." *African American Review* 26.2 (1992): 241–55.

Russell, Mariann. *Melvin B. Tolson's Harlem Gallery: A Literary Analysis.* Columbia: University of Missouri Press, 1980.

Shapiro, Karl. "Introduction." In *The Harlem Gallery, Book I: The Curator,* by Melvin B. Tolson. New York: Twayne, 1965. 11–15.

Shevin, David. "The Poetry of Melvin Tolson." In *Masterpieces of African-American Literature.* Ed. Frank N. Magill. New York: HarperCollins, 1992. 443–46.

Shroeder, Patricia R. "Point and Counterpoint in *Harlem Gallery*." *CLA* 27.2 (1983): 152–68.

Smith, Gary. "A Hamlet Rives Us: The Sonnets of Melvin B. Tolson." *CLA* 29.3 (1986): 261–75.

Tompson, Gordon E. "Ambiguity in Tolson's *Harlem Gallery*." *Callaloo* 9.1 (1986): 159–70.

Woodson, Jon. "Melvin Tolson and the Art of Being Difficult." In *Black American Poets between Worlds, 1940–1960.* Ed. Miller R. Baxter. Knoxville: University of Tennessee Press, 1986. 19–42.

EUGENE (JEAN) PINCHBACK TOOMER
(1894–1967)

Emma Waters Dawson

BIOGRAPHY

Jean Toomer was a novelist, poet, and essayist whose publication of the collection *Cane* (1923) heralded the beginning of the Harlem Renaissance. Born December 26, 1894, in Washington, D.C., he was the only child of Nathan, a southern planter, and Nina Pinchback Toomer, the daughter of Pinckney Benton Stewart Pinchback (P.B.S.), former lieutenant governor of Louisiana during Reconstruction and former U.S. senator. Nina Pinchback had married—over her father's objections—the illegitimate mulatto son of a wealthy white North Carolina landowner. Nathan Toomer passed as white and owned, at one time, a large farm in Georgia. A year after the marriage and shortly after Toomer's birth, he left wife, debts, and son to the Pinchbacks after discovering that the family patriarch kept firm control of the family's finances.

David Levering Lewis notes that the early childhood of Jean Toomer was "ambiguously white, temporarily affluent, and politically well connected . . . passed in a silver spoon" (60). Indeed, the indolent luxury on Bacon Street, where the Pinchbacks resided, recalled the Old South, and, according to Toomer, the family belonged to "an aristocracy—such as never existed before and perhaps never will exist again in America—midway between the white and black world" (60). This midway intersection of life in a wealthy white neighborhood included fine wines at dinner and African American domestics serving and anticipating the needs of the family, which lasted until the senator's gambling excesses at Saratoga and other eastern racetracks forced an incessant liquidation of vast real estate holdings. In 1904, when the Pinchbacks had moved to New Rochelle, where the elder Pinchback had received a patronage slot in a New York Customs House, his annual salary of $10,000 had been reduced to barely enough for family sustenance due to his gambling intemperance.

In 1905 Nina remarried, again over her father's objections, though after she and her new husband moved to Brooklyn, the Pinchback family joined her. Toomer's stepfather, according to Lewis, was "poor white . . . known to posterity only as Coombs" (61). Four years after remarrying, Nina Pinchback Toomer Coombs died due to complications following an appendectomy. Significant to his growing sense of insecurity, stemming from an unhappy childhood, particularly the death of his mother, Toomer ended his life as a white youth.

After Nina's death, the family moved back to Washington to an African American neighborhood in the 1300 block of U Street, not far from Howard University. For the first time in his life, Toomer lived in an African American world, where there is no question that his ancestry was in some part African, despite its being mixed and complicated racially. By physical appearance he was white; by race, Toomer was mixed. At this time in his life, Toomer fell under the tutelage of his uncle Bismarck, who had dropped out of Yale Medical School and who taught Toomer how to read books critically. Toomer attended Dunbar High School for an elite, though publicly financed, education, where he completed his education in three and a half years, despite sexual indulgences affecting his health and resulting in his withdrawal from friends and hours spent brooding at home. Turner writes of this adolescent period in Toomer's life:

Believing himself in love, newly aware of sexual desires but unwilling to gratify them with girls of his group, superstitiously fearful that his body would weaken unless he experienced intercourse, envious of other youths who boasted of their conquests, unable to discuss his dilemma, Toomer behaved in a manner already characterizing his response to any situation he could not dominate. He contemptuously withdrew from his friends. In isolation, he dedicated himself to developing his body through diet and exercise. (6)

Here in adolescence, Toomer established a pattern of searching for new interests, excitement at the possibility of accomplishment, frantic pursuit of the new interest, abrupt withdrawal, and a despondent attitude caused by fear of failure. These adolescent behaviors subsequently appeared in almost all of Toomer's future endeavors.

Had finances permitted, Toomer, like his Uncle Bismarck, would have chosen Yale. Instead, he went to the University of Wisconsin, majoring in agriculture. He finished the semester and then withdrew. Returning to Washington, Toomer became a "bon vivant" in the disrespectable circle of Washington artists and theater people, where he assisted his uncle Bismarck in managing a theater. This experience in theater he undoubtedly creatively adapted to his later sketch of Dorris in "Theatre" in the second section of Cane. After his fleeting enrollment at the University of Wisconsin in 1914 and brief sojourn home to Washington, Toomer spent a hasty stint at Massachusetts College of Agriculture the next fall. In February 1916 he attended American College of Physical Training in Chicago. Boredom with this project soon led him to enroll in a premedical program at the University of Chicago. There he lectured on philosophy and economics in addition to studying his major course work. He left there also to return to his grandfather's house as an unwelcome guest. Dismissing agriculture and body-building, he attended lectures at New York University in the summer of 1917, enrolling in City College in the fall and majoring in history, where Toomer received his first and last A. He tried and failed to enlist in the army (he had bad eyesight and a hernia) and to join the Red Cross, and the Young Men's Christian Association (YMCA). Despite his enrollment at the University of Wisconsin, the Massachusetts College of Agriculture, the American College of Physical Training in Chicago, the University of Chicago, New York University, and the City College of New York, Toomer never became a serious degree candidate. Unsettled, he read psychology and Shaw, whom he later credited with having made him "aware of literary style and having introduced him to the intellectual life" (9). In a relatively brief time period, Toomer sold Ford cars, taught physical education near Milwaukee, rode rails to Washington, and hitch-hiked to New York. He learned to play piano, hoboed, was a bodybuilder, and welded in New Jersey shipyards "in order to gain among the working classes the practical experience which he considered necessary to his work as a socialistic reformer" (9). He also started to write, although the wandering continued. According to Turner, "While chasing many gleams, he had read extensively in atheism, naturalism, socialism, sociology, psychology, and the dramas of Shaw. To these scientific, philosophical, and social writings, he had added *Wilhelm Meister* of Goethe, the romances of Victor Hugo, and the verse of Walt Whitman (10). In his middle twenties and at the end of World War I, Toomer returned to his grandfather's home in Washington, although he never doubted that the most important thing about life was the way he lived it.

Lewis comments that "being *colored* in Washington turned out to be a social carnival and an intellectual calamity for Toomer" (62). Experiencing alienation, prompted by an ambivalence about his racial identity, he could have had no trouble passing for white. With this state of mind, Toomer formed a close friend-ship with a group of New York intellectuals that included Paul Rosenfeld, Hart Crane, Kenneth Burke, Gorham Munson, Alfred Stieglitz, and Waldo Frank, the latter of whom he met in 1920 at a party given by Lola Ridge, editor of the American edition of *Broom*. The literary party in New York affected him profoundly, prompting self-identification. Around 1920 he denied his African American racial heritage, claiming that his grandfather pretended to be of African ancestry in order to gain personal profit in Louisiana during Reconstruction. No doubt, Toomer felt bridled by the burden of America's rigid and simplistic racial and ethnic categories. He discussed such feelings with Waldo Frank, a novelist and essayist well established by 1920 who influenced Toomer. They critiqued each other's work and sharpened ideas about what modern American literature should be.

Of particular note is the reception of Toomer at his initial contact with *The Liberator*, edited by Claude Mckay.* Rejecting Toomer's submission to the magazine, Mckay wrote that the staff found "Miss Toomer's point of view" interesting, but "her" short story was, unfortunately, "a little too long, not clear enough, and lacking unity." Such reception was ironic, considering Toomer had placed poems and stories in avant-garde little magazines such as *The Double Dealer, Broom, The Crisis, The Little Review, S4N, Secession, The Modern Review, Nomad, Prairie,* and *Opportunity.* Nevertheless, the two met briefly prior to Mckay's departure for Russia—after a warm correspondence. Interestingly enough, both Toomer and Mckay had similarities in their work and lives. Deeply troubled escapists who held contempt for propagandist literature and disdain for literary politics, they struggled simply to be themselves, testing "the outermost limits of what was possible for persons of African ancestry dedicated to the creative life" (Lewis 50). Both were deeply immersed in the universe of the Lost Generation. For Toomer, especially, his relationship to the Lost Generation contributed to his literary success and subsequent lack thereof.

MAJOR WORKS AND THEMES

In 1921 Toomer accepted a temporary position in rural Sparta, Georgia, as superintendent of a small black school. Spending four months there, he saturated himself in the essence of the region and its people and derived the first and third parts of *Cane.* Specifically, the setting is rural Georgia and its presentation of the life of black folk in physical and psychic dimensions. Structured as a series of short stories, sketches, poems, and a "novella-play," *Cane* involves the idea of transformation and quest for a meaningful identity, which underlie a number of pieces. The unity of the text is achieved through structure, style, and theme. Structured through a series of vignettes, sketches, poems, and a few short stories, the work contains recurrent imagery of dusk and cane. In this Georgia setting, Toomer sought for meaning in the vanishing of black peasant life in the South, yet the integrity and beauty present in the first section of *Cane* are relatively absent in the Washington and Chicago settings of the second part of the text. Instead, corruption and sterility dominate, prompted by materialism of an urban society.

The relationships of both the rural and urban settings reflect the nature of the restrictions between the sexes. On a larger scale, the male–female associations in the novel make a statement about human alliances in modern society. Although Toomer gives vivid descriptions of his women characters, he paints a picture of despair and futility as a result of the community's failure to recognize female individuals within that setting. In Part I, the character sketch of "Karintha" addresses fornication, motherhood, death, and promiscuity to converge on a theme of a submerged population, women.

The next sketch of "Becky," "the white woman who had two Negro sons" (5), reveals the South's conspiracy to ignore miscegenation. "Common, God-forsaken, insane white shameless wench, said the white folks' mouths. . . . Poor Catholic poor-white crazy woman, said the black folks' mouths" (5). The stage for the "crudest melodrama" is set when the narrator relates of Carma, "Her husband's in the gang. And it's her fault he got there" (11). The reader recognizes a story based on a romantic plot and developed sensationally. Upon Bane's confronting her with the gossip about her infidelity, Carma becomes hysterical, grabs a gun, rushes off into a canebrake, and fires it. Bane believes she has killed herself and forms a search with neighboring men. They soon find Carma and return home. However, Carma fakes her injury, and Bane takes it as evidence of her infidelity in marriage. "Twice deceived, and one deception proved the other. . . . His head went off. Slashed one of the men who'd helped. . . . Now he's in the gang" (11). It is, indeed, "the crudest melodrama" that Carma's infidelity leads to her husband's tragicomic fate, although in a real sense she cannot be blamed; Bane had alternatives. Toomer's character sketches of "Fern" and "Esther" further illustrate a strong sense of alienation, isolation, and estrangement from the community.

The particularly horrendous sketch of "Blood-Burning Moon," however, gives a much more vivid example of the detrimental effects racial and sexual restrictions have on a black woman's life that help destroy her sanity and cause violent death. The sketch may be seen as the most fully developed story of the first section in *Cane*. Focusing on the life of Louisa, a black woman in Georgia, it also strongly reflects a southern setting and the ways of southern men, both black and white. When Tom Burwell, a black man, and Bob Stone, a white man, discover the presence of the other in Louisa's life, each reacts negatively and reveals the vanity of male pride. Tom Burwell fought the men who had talked and laughed about the silk stockings Louisa had received from Bob Stone, and Stone denied that Louisa saw Tom: "No sir. No nigger had ever been with his girl. He'd like to see one try. Some position for him to be in. Him Bob Stone, of the old Stone family, in a scrap with a nigger over a nigger girl" (32). In self-defense, Tom kills Bob when the latter attacks him with a knife. In punishment, a white mob, out of fear and hatred, burns Tom to death beneath the "blood-burning moon." In the aftermath of the lynching, Louisa, paying the price of vain male pride, loses her mind because she has caused two men to lose their lives: "The full moon, an evil thing, an omen, soft showering the homes of folks she knew. Where were they, these people? She'd sing, and perhaps they'd come out and join her. Perhaps Tom Burwell would come" (35). Seductress-goddess, mother, wife, lady, educated woman, old maid, and mistress are all characterizations of Jean Toomer's women in the first section of *Cane*. The spectator-narrator perceives them as the embodiment of fulfilled female sexuality in harmony with natural rhythms of existence. In actuality, they are stock characters who represent stifled or thwarted creativity. Not one woman is allowed to fully develop or express her own identity. In their relations with men, they fail to conquer male egotism, self-assertion, abuse, or adoration and devotion, qualities that act as barriers to complete human relationships because such concepts bear no necessary relation to the women's actual being. According to Alice Walker, the women in *Cane* were:

driven to a numb and bleeding madness by the springs of creativity in them for which there was no release. They were Creators, who lived lives of spiritual waste, because they were so rich in spirituality—which is the basis of Art—that the strain of enduring their unused and unwanted talent drove them insane. ("In Search of Our Mothers' Gardens" 89)

Cane was published in 1923. Shortly after the publication of this critically reviewed work, Toomer and Waldo Frank had a rift that resulted in the end of their friendship. Toomer had fallen in love with Margaret Naumburg, Frank's wife. By 1924, he had abandoned black writing in favor of more didactic and philosophical work. Toomer felt that "complete identification with black culture was not possible . . . he regretted that literary critics and editors wanted him to write another *Cane*" (Rusch xii). The truth of the matter is that Toomer did not feel sustained by black life beyond the publication of this monumental work. He even stated, "I do not know whether colored blood flows through my veins. . . . I am of no particular race. . . . I am of the human race, a man at large in the human world preparing a new race" (Barksdale and Kinnamon 501). For him, black life could not be his only subject.

Toomer succumbed to a state of psychological disarray: in quest of elusive principles of unity, he, along with several other intellectuals, turned to philosophies of F. Matthias Alexander, P. D. Ouspensky, and George I. Gurdjieff, a Russian who combined elements of yoga, religious mysticism, and Freud into a system called unitism. The Gurdjieffian philosophy emphasized two aspects of human beings: personality and essence. According to the philosophy, personality shaped by people's social environment is superficial; strong personality hides essence, which is the true nature and core of being. Gurdjieff, therefore, proposed to help people find the essence. Gurdjieffian philosophy held attraction to Toomer after completion of *Cane*, for he felt burned out, and the philosophy held out the possibility of being and personal unity. Consequently, Toomer spent the summer of 1924 and several summers thereafter at the Gurdjieff Institute in France. He also taught the Gurdjieffian message in Chicago and New York, where some of his pupils included major figures of the Harlem Renaissance: Wallace Thurman,* Aaron Douglass, and Nella Larsen.* He also taught Margery Latimer, a white writer whom he married in 1931 but who died in childbirth the following year. In 1934 Toomer married his second wife, Margery Content, who was also white.

After *Cane*, Toomer continued to write, but he had difficulty getting published. His life was motivated by "a quest for meaning, for certainty, for a sense of psychological stability in a world of chaos and flux" (Turner, *The Wayward* 500). The fact is that Toomer had a sparse publishing record after 1923, and what was printed did not deal with African American subjects. His scanty published output, however, obscures that he produced a tremendous amount of writing after the publication of *Cane*. Though Toomer moved away from portrayal of African Americans, he was still concerned with the meaning of being black in America in a long 1929 essay, "Race Problems and Modern Society" (*The Wayward* 108–140). Eventually, readers and critics forgot about him. The rediscovery and republication of *Cane* in the 1960s, thanks to scholars and critics such as Robert

Bone, Darwin T. Turner, and S. P. Fullinwider, led to Toomer's great role in the canon of African American literature. Turner reported that Toomer's body of work includes "two novels, two books of poems, a collection of stories, books of non-fiction, two books of aphorisms, a half-dozen plays, three of which were written in the early 1920's. Despite such a prolific output, Toomer's published and unpublished work after *Cane* became more abstract and disconnected from physical reality" (18).

In essence, Toomer produced a body of work reflective of the vast dilemmas he experienced as a young man largely shaped by his environment; however, his perceptions were altered by his quest for meaning, attempted in various sources: the vanishing black peasant life in the South and in the Freudian mysticism of George Ivanovitch Gurdjieff. Finally, in the 1940s, he sought meaning in the Society of Friends when he turned to the Quaker faith for spiritual sustenance. He died on March 30, 1967. Toomer had much earlier summed up his life: "Perhaps . . . , our lot on this earth is to seek and to search. Now and again we find just enough to enable us to carry on. I now doubt that any of us will completely find and be found in this life" (Turner, *The Wayward* 500).

During his life and following the publication of *Cane*, Toomer published "Balo" in *Plays of Negro Life* (1927), edited by Alain Locke* and Montgomery Gregory; "Winter on Earth" in *The Second American Caravan* (1928), edited by Alfred Kreymbourg and others; "York Beach," a novella in *The New American Caravan* (1929), edited by Alfred Kreymbourg and others; "Race Problems and Modern Society" in *Problems of Civilization* (1929), edited by Baker Brownell; *Essentials: Definitions and Aphorisms* (1931), privately printed; "As the Eagle Soars," *The Crisis* 41 (1932): 116; "The Hill," an essay in *America and Alfred Stieglitz* (1934), edited by Waldo Frank and others; *Work-Ideas I* and *Living Is Developing* (1937), privately printed pamphlets; and two Quaker pamphlets, *An Interpretation of Friends Worship* (1947) and *The Flavor of Man* (1949). Excerpts from an unpublished autobiography, "Earth Being," appeared in *Black Scholar* 2 (January 1971): 3–13. Toomer's vision of the new race in the new America is expressed in a long poem, "Blue Meridian" (1936). All of these works are included in Darwin T. Turner's *A Wayward and the Seeking: A Collection of Writings by Jean Toomer.*

CRITICAL RECEPTION

Jean Toomer's legacy to African American literature has received steady critical acclaim since the republication and rediscovery of *Cane* in 1975. Since that time, book articles, journal articles, dissertations, and full-length books have been written. Most notable among them is the text *Jean Toomer: A Critical Evaluation* (1988), edited by Therman B. O' Daniel. A collection of critical essays, the work explores aspects of Jean Toomer's life and art; his relationships with Waldo Frank, Sherwood Anderson, and Hart Crane; the Toomer-Ouspensky-Gurdjieff connection; selected interpretations of *Cane*; Jean Toomer as the *Cane* short story writer; Jean Toomer as poet of the *Cane* poems and of "Blue Meridian"; Jean

Toomer as playwright; women and male–female relationships in *Cane*; and such subjects as celebration, biblical myth, surrealism, and the blues in *Cane*. O'Daniel also includes a classified bibliography, using categories of books, poems, and stories before, during, and after *Cane*. He also lists autobiographies, plays, essays, literary criticism and book reviews, pamphlets, and Toomer's contributions to *The Friends Intelligencer*. Works about Toomer extend to the listing of some anthologies, dissertations, and books, articles, and reviews. What this venture reveals is that—with little exception—much of the valuable work to have appeared thus far devotes itself to *Cane*. A more recent edited collection, by Robert B. Jones, is *Jean Toomer: Selected Essays and Literary Criticism* (1996). As of the submission of this chapter, the MLA Bibliography lists eighty-three records from 1981 to 1998 assessing the work of Jean Toomer. Twelve of these analyses are book articles; forty-eight journal articles; fifteen dissertations; and eight books. Of this number, more than half treat some aspect of *Cane*. However, some works do offer as well treatments of Toomer's other writings. A *Jean Toomer Reader: Selected Unpublished Writings* (1993), edited by Frederik L. Rusch, includes correspondence from Toomer to his colleagues of the Lost Generation, Lola Ridge, Gorham Munson, and Waldo Frank as well as his publisher, Horace Liveright. Since 1981, another text, *Invisible Darkness: Jean Toomer and Nella Larsen* (1993), written by Charles R. Larson, examines the fiction of Jean Toomer and compares his treatment of race to that by Nella Larsen. Rudolph P. Byrd explores Toomer's relationship with Gurdjieff in *Jean Toomer's Years with Gurdjieff: Portrait of an Artist, 1923–1936* (1990). Important biographical studies include *The Lives of Jean Toomer: A Hunger for Wholeness* (1988), written by Cynthia Earl Kerman and Richard Eldridge, and *Jean Toomer, Artist: A Study of His Literary Life and Work, 1894–1936*, authored by Nellie Y. McKay.

BIBLIOGRAPHY

Works by Eugene (Jean) Pinchback Toomer

Novel

Cane. New York: Boni and Liveright, 1923; Reprinted, New York: Liveright, 1975. *Cane: An Authoritative Text, Backgrounds, Criticism*. Ed. Darwin T. Turner. New York: Norton, 1988.

Poetry

The Collected Poems of Jean Toomer. Ed. Robert B. Jones and Margery Toomer Latimer; intro. Jones. Chapel Hill: University of North Carolina Press, 1988.

Other Collections

Essentials: Definitions and Aphorisms. Chicago: Lakeside, 1931; (reprinted, ed. Rudolph P. Byrd. Athens: University of Georgia Press, 1980.

The Wayward and the Seeking: A Collection of Writings by Jean Toomer. Ed. with intro. Darwin T. Turner. Washington, DC: Howard University Press, 1980.

A Jean Toomer Reader: Selected Unpublished Writings. Ed. Frederik L. Rusch. New York and Oxford: Oxford University Press, 1993.

Studies of Eugene (Jean) Pinchback Toomer

Barksdale, Richard and Keneth Kinnamon. *Black Writers of America: A Comprehensive Anthology.* New York: Macmillan, 1972.

Benson, Brian Joseph, and Mabel Mayle Dillard. *Jean Toomer.* Boston: Twayne, 1980.

Byrd, Rudolph P. *Jean Toomer's Years with Gurdjieff: Portrait of an Artist, 1923–1936.* Athens: University of Georgia Press, 1990.

Clarys, Francoise. " 'The Waters of My Heart': Mythe et identite dans Cane de Jean Toomer." *Etudes-Anglaise* 50.4 (October–December 1997): 422–33.

Dawson, Emma Waters. "Images of the Afro-American Female Character in Jean Toomer's *Cane,* Zora Neale Hurston's *Their Eyes Were Watching God,* and Alice Walker's *The Color Purple.*" Diss., University of South Florida, 1987.

Dorris, Ronald. "Early Criticism of Jean Toomer's *Cane*: 1923–1932." In *Perspectives of Black Popular Culture.* Ed. Harry B. Shaw. Bowling Green, OH: Popular, 1990.

Durham, Frank, ed. *The Merrill Studies in Cane.* Columbus, OH: Merrill, 1971.

Foley, Barbara. "Jean Toomer's Washington and the Politics of Class: From 'Blue Veins' to Seventh-Street Rebels." *Modern Fiction Studies* 42.2 (Summer 1996): 289–321.

Fullinwider, S. P. "The Renaissance in Literature." In *The Mind and Mood of Black America.* Homewood, IL: Dorsey, 1969. 123–71.

Hamalian, Leo. "D. H. Lawrence and Black Writers." *Journal of Modern Literature* 16.4 (Spring 1990): 579–96.

Hutchinson, George. "Jean Toomer and American Racial Discourse." *Texas Studies in Literature and Language* 35.2 (Summer 1993): 226–50.

Jones, Robert B. *Jean Toomer and Selected Essays and Literary Criticism.* Knoxville: University of Tennessee Press, 1996.

Kerman, Cynthia Earl, and Richard Eldridge. *The Lives of Jean Toomer: A Hunger for Wholeness.* Baton Rouge: Louisiana University Press, 1988.

Larson, Charles R. *Invisible Darkness: Jean Toomer & Nella Larsen.* Iowa City: University of Iowa Press, 1993.

Lewis, David Levering. *When Harlem Was in Vogue.* New York: Oxford University Press, 1981.

Lindberg, Kathryne V. "Raising Cane on the Theoretical Plane: Jean Toomer's Personae." In *Cultural Difference and the Literary Text: Pluralism and the Limits of Authenticity in North American Literatures.* Ed. Winfried Siemerling. Iowa City: University of Iowa Press, 1996.

McKay, Nellie Y. *Jean Toomer, Artist: A Study of His Literary Life and Work, 1894–1936.* Chapel Hill: University of North Carolina Press, 1984.

Mitchell, Carolyn A. "Henry Dumas and Jean Toomer: One Voice." *Black American Literature Forum* 22.2 (Summer 1988): 297–309.

O'Daniel, Therman B., ed. *Jean Toomer: A Critical Evaluation.* Washington, DC: Howard University Press, 1988.

Scruggs, Charles. " 'My Chosen World': Jean Toomer's Articles in *The New York Call*." *Arizona Quarterly* 51.2 (Summer 1995): 103–26.

Turner, Darwin T. *In a Minor Chord: Three Afro-American Writers and Their Search for Identity*. Carbondale and Edwardsville: Southern Illinois University Press, 1971.

SOJOURNER TRUTH
(1797, 1800?–1883)

Suzanne Hotte Massa

BIOGRAPHY

Isabella, who later named herself Sojourner Truth, was born to James "Bomefree" and Betsey "Mau-Mau Bett," who were slaves owned by Colonel Ardenburgh in Ulster County, New York. She was their second-to-last child. Because she was the child of slaves, her biographical data are imprecise. However, historians agree that she was born sometime between 1797 and 1800. Isabella lived with her parents and her younger brother, Peter, until she was around nine years old. Then, like most of her eleven or twelve siblings, she was sold into slavery.

As the chattel in a series of slave trades, she was prevented from settling in one place until she was sold to John J. Dumont of New Paltz, where she spent her adolescence and young womanhood: 1810–1828. While working on Mr. Dumont's farm, she married another slave, Thomas, with whom she had four or five children; the exact number is uncertain. But census records show evidence of only four children, which has led some historians to conclude that one son, James, died shortly after birth. What became of her husband is unclear, and there is no evidence that she remarried.

In 1826 Isabella left the Dumonts' house and walked to freedom under the cover of darkness. She was subsequently directed to the home of Isaac S. and Maria VanWagenen, who treated her with kindness and respect. In fact, she had so much respect for them that she adopted their last name as her own.

Isabella began her religious studies as a young child, along with her younger brother, Peter, under the tutelage of her mother, Mau-Mau Bett. Once her religious awakening began, it became a lifelong endeavor and ultimately her life's work. Isabella moved to New York City where she continued her religious education. She was easily deceived by one of her teachers: the exploitative, misogynist, fanatic Matthias. But even this encounter provided a valuable contribution to her spiritual quest. Finally, in 1843 she left New York City—on foot—to travel as a spokesperson for peace and the antislavery movement in New England. She changed her name to Sojourner Truth to represent her journey toward the truth. For some time she settled in a utopian commune, Fruitlands, at Northampton, Massachusetts, and continued to preach as a servant of God.

When that community dissolved, Truth went back on the road to continue her travels and began speaking as an advocate for woman's rights. By the time *The Narrative of Sojourner Truth* was published in 1850, she had become so popular that she needed an office. She set up her headquarters at the *Anti-Slavery Bugle*, a newspaper in Salem, Ohio. At a woman's rights convention in Akron, Ohio, in 1851 she delivered her celebrated speech: "Ain't I a Woman?" In each place that she stopped to speak, her *Narrative* was always available for purchase. Her motto in defense of what appeared to be a mercenary tactic was, "I sell the shadow to support the substance" (Washington, *Narrative Sojourner Truth* xiii). In time, her travels took her farther west. She settled permanently in Battle Creek, Michigan, in 1857. She continued to travel and give her passionate and powerful speeches until her death in 1883.

MAJOR WORKS AND THEMES

As an illiterate ex-slave, Truth was unable to pen her own story. So the *Narrative of Sojourner Truth* is her story as it was related to Olive Gilbert. Truth was a spiritual orator. Therefore, her religious education is critical to both her history and her narrative. The *Narrative* tells the story of Isabella's spiritual journey from her birth until she began her career as a traveling preacher. Truth is depicted as soundly spiritual, someone who, in spite of a horrific life, was able to find solace in spirituality. As a young child, Isabella was greatly influenced by her Mau-Mau Bett's religious teachings. "She taught them to kneel and say the Lord's prayer. She entreated them to refrain from lying and stealing, and to strive to obey their masters" (7). Even though the concept of the Lord was alien to Isabella, she spent her life searching for the meaning of that concept, carrying the memory of her mother's lessons with her throughout her life.

The *Narrative* focuses on how Truth maintained her constant dignity in the face of unyielding oppression. To affirm Truth's steadfast faith, Gilbert paints several vivid pictures of the horrors of slavery. She describes living conditions unfit for a rat; she underscores the crime against humanity when people—women, children, and the aged—are treated as chattel and discarded when deemed worthless; she reiterates the frivolity with which marriages among slaves were treated; she relates vivid tales of brutal beatings and the scars they leave; and she admonishes the masters for nonchalantly breaking promises. All of these abominations provide a stark contrast to Truth's unflagging piety and innate integrity.

Isabella spent her adolescent and young adult years as a slave for the Dumont family, where she earned a reputation for being an efficient, hard worker. Not only did she do everything well, but she did the work of several people. Isabella found that Mr. Dumont had agreeable, or at least tolerable, qualities, even though he beat her. He often praised Isabella in front of Mrs. Dumont and her white maid, Kate, increasing their resentment of Isabella. Together, they conspired to ruin Isabella's reputation in the eyes of Mr. Dumont. One day, Kate began to make a fuss about Isabella's ruining the potatoes, and Mr. Dumont had no choice but to agree that the potatoes were indeed "dingy" and "dirty" (19). Isabella, naturally, felt terrible that she had ruined her master's meal. So the next morning, Isabella vowed to make the potatoes right. Dumont's young daughter, Gertrude, offered to stay and help Isabella prepare breakfast. When she saw Kate flipping ashes from the fire into the pot of potatoes, Gertrude told her father the truth, thus exonerating Isabella. Sojourner Truth insisted that this incident be included in the *Narrative* to illustrate "how God shields the innocent" (18). This incident not only shows the rewards of being faithful to God but is also a testament to the concept that the truth will always prevail.

At one point, Mr. Dumont felt the need to reward the faithful Isabella with her " 'free papers,' one year before she was legally free by statute" (26). The emancipation law of 1817 stipulated that blacks born before July 4, 1799, would be freed: women at the age of twenty-five and men at the age of twenty-eight. (This law might have some bearing on why one of Isabella's birth dates is 1797.) That meant that legally, Isabella should have been freed in 1827. However, when the time arrived, Mr. Dumont refused to fulfill his promise. Devastated by his sudden change of mind, Isabella sought a solution to her problem by praying to God for advice. Shortly thereafter, it occurred to her that she could just walk out before sunrise. Nobody else would be awake yet, so she could leave undetected. The plan worked; Isabella escaped and moved in with the VanWagenens. Naturally, she credited God with providing her with such a clever idea.

At the VanWagenens, she met her spiritual equal. Because Isabella was still legally Mr. Dumont's chattel, Isaac VanWagenen had to buy Isabella from Mr. Dumont so that she could retain her freedom. Therefore, Isabella expected VanWagenen to assume the role of her master. He told her that she was not to call him master because "there is but *one* master; and he who is *your* master is *my* master" (30). To show her gratitude for their consistent compassion, Isabella borrowed their surname for herself and her children.

Shortly before Isabella left the Dumonts' house, they had sold her son, Peter, into slavery in Alabama. At that time a law prohibited the sale of slaves across state lines. So Isabella confronted Mrs. Dumont, who assured her that she would never be reunited with her son. But she was not daunted, because she was confident that God would aid her in effecting a reunion with her son. During her emotionally charged conversation with Mrs. Dumont—in which she declared: "*I'll have my child again*" (31)—Isabella displayed the passionate rhetorical style and quaint dignity that were to become her trademark:

The impressions made by Isabella on her auditors, when moved by lofty or deep feeling, can never be transmitted to paper, (to use the words of another,) till by some Daguerrian act, we are enabled to transfer the look, the gesture, the tones of voice, in connection with the quaint, yet fit expressions used, and the spirit-stirring animation that, at such a time, pervades all she says. (31)

Once again, Isabella's persistent faith helped her to find a solution to her problem: her son was returned to her.

Isabella continued to follow her spiritual path, even though she stumbled along the way. Her hardest fall came in New York City when she became involved in a religious hoax perpetrated by the impostor Matthias. She blindly became a disciple of this misogynist fraud and foolishly invested her life's savings in his trust. She lost her investments, but the spiritual education that she obtained from that experience was profound. Her experiences helped her to realize that the lessons she learned from her mother as a young girl were still the truth: "Through her life, and all its chequered changes, she has ever clung fast to her first permanent impression on religious subjects" (80). It was then, June 1, 1843, that she changed her name to Sojourner Truth and left New York City to begin her journey as a traveling preacher.

On the road, Sojourner Truth began to hone her oratorical skills, for which she already had a natural gift. At one meeting in New England, a large group of young white male hecklers threatened to turn the meeting into a riot. But Sojourner summoned the strength from God to confront and transform the group into enthusiastic supporters. A large part of her success in that endeavor is a result of her dynamic and inspirational speaking style. "Her speech had operated on the roused passions of the mob like oil on agitated waters; they were, as a whole, entirely subdued, and only clamored when she ceased to speak or sing" (95).

By the time Truth delivered her famous "Ain't I a Woman?" speech in 1851 at a woman's rights convention in Akron, Ohio, she had become a supporter of rights for women as well as the antislavery movement. But still, audiences were struck by her speeches. The "Ain't I a Woman?" speech was delivered numerous times, but the actual text does not exist. The version that Frances Gage has published repeatedly is full of colloquialisms that are not necessarily part of Truth's typical way of speaking. In Margaret Washington's 1993 edition of the *Narrative*, she includes a version of the speech entitled: "Ar'n't I a Woman?" that is almost entirely free of colloquialisms and dramatically different from the more often published version. This version is written as it was recorded by the staff of the *Anti-Slavery Bugle* but delivers a very similar sentiment: although both blacks and women are oppressed, black women suffer from dual oppression. Today, her speech continues to be an anthem for advocates of freedom from oppression.

CRITICAL RECEPTION

When the *Narrative* was first published, it received little critical attention. However, a fair amount of historical commentary about Sojourner Truth is available. Jean M. Humez's lengthy and useful article on Margaret Washington's edition of the *Narrative* remains the only substantial critical study of Sojourner Truth's autobiography. Included in Washington's edition are her Introduction, extensive notes on the text, a version of "Ar'n't I a Woman?," William Lloyd Garrison's Preface to the 1850 edition, and an extensive bibliography.

At times the narrative is poorly organized, making it difficult to follow. In spite of the confusion, though, the narrative is generally reliable and informative. Another question that arises concerning a nineteenth-century collaboration is the authenticity of the text. However, Humez believes that the text is largely accurate:

Although this text contains only the skeletal structure of the full spiritual autobiography that we might have had if Truth had had direct access to the pen, there is still plenty of rich material, particularly in the core stories, that illuminates Truth's midlife understanding of her religious experience and of such religious issues as the origin and nature of evil. (36)

Nonetheless, the reader should read with caution and read between the lines. In the Preface to the 1993 edition, Margaret Washington recommends that "anyone who studies the *Narrative* and is familiar with the plight of female slaves can easily read between the lines—and should do so whenever reading narratives of black women unable to write for themselves" (xxxi). Clearly, there are topics and issues that are avoided or distorted. Without too much difficulty, Gilbert's voice can easily be distinguished from Truth's. "We should reconceptualize the mediated text as a truly collaborative project undertaken by two fully engaged personalities situated in different social locations and attempt to identify the distinct voices and agendas of the two parties" (Humez 37).

Overall, the Gilbert–Truth collaboration produced a fine and largely reliable account of Truth's experiences. Humez applauds Gilbert's lack of condescension toward Truth and obvious commitment to their collaboration:

Unlike other writers who attempted to record Truth's speech, including Harriet Beecher Stowe and Frances Gage, Gilbert did not use dialect to convey her sense of Truth's otherness in her language. This decision makes a tremendous difference in the dignity of the portrait she drew—perhaps especially for the modern reader. Gilbert's decision may reflect a genuine respect for Truth's eloquence in speaking. (30)

Together, these women created a rare and valuable document that remains a compelling commentary on an important chapter in American history.

BIBLIOGRAPHY

Works by Sojourner Truth

(And Olive Gilbert). *Narrative of Sojourner Truth*. New York: Penguin, 1998.
Narrative of Sojourner Truth. Ed. Margaret Washington. New York: Vintage Classics, 1993.

Studies of Sojourner Truth

Humez, Jean. "Reading the *Narrative of Sojourner Truth* as a Collaborative Text." *Frontiers: A Journal of Women Studies* 16.1 (1996): 29–52.

Joseph, Gloria I. "Sojourner Truth: Archetypal Black Feminist." In *Wild Women in the Whirlwind*. Ed. Joanne Braxton and Andrée McLaughlin. New Brunswick, NJ: Rutgers University Press, 1990. 35–47.

DAVID WALKER
(1785–1830)

Montye P. Fuse

BIOGRAPHY

David Walker was born on September 28, 1785, in Wilmington, North Carolina, to a slave father and a free black mother (thus, under the laws of slavery he was born into freedom). The known facts of Walker's life are sparse, but as a young man he became literate and left Wilmington to travel around the United States so that he could study the peculiarities of slavery, having first become acquainted with it through his father's experience. He lived for a period in Charleston, South Carolina, before making Boston his home in 1825, where he would spend the rest of his abbreviated life. In 1827 Walker entered the used clothing business near Boston's wharves, and a year later he married a fugitive slave.

Whatever time was available Walker spent studying history, the Bible, and slavery in its historic and present manifestations. He had become familiar with the evils of slavery through his travels to the slave states, and Walker recognized that even for a "free" black man life was extremely limited. Walker had left behind in Wilmington, North Carolina, a city in which blacks greatly outnumbered whites, but only a small percentage of the city's black population was free. Further, most jobs in the labor market, either skilled or unskilled, were held by slaves. Free men like Walker probably felt as though their options were few. Upon his arrival in Boston, however, Walker quickly realized the extent of racial inequality faced by free blacks in the North. Under Massachusetts law, blacks were prohibited from holding public office and faced racial discrimination at nearly every level in Boston society.

Walker and his family took up residence in a traditionally black section of Boston, where Walker became an outspoken community leader recognized for his antislavery activism and speech making. Upon his arrival in Boston, Walker had established contacts with a number of black Bostonians engaged in abolitionist work. He was also a supporter of two black abolitionists in New York who published the first African American newspaper, *Freedom's Journal*, in March 1827. Walker contributed several articles to *Freedom's Journal* before it suspended publication in 1829, most notably, his speech "Address, Delivered before the General Colored Association at Boston," published on December 19, 1828. Walker remained outspoken on issues of racial discrimination and slavery, publishing the first edition of the *Appeal* in 1829. Between 1829 and 1830 he would publish two subsequent editions, each more strident and outspoken in its attack on slavery than its predecessor. By 1830 white hysteria over the *Appeal* escalated as the pamphlet circulated throughout the South, and purportedly a $3,000 bounty was placed on Walker's life. On August 3, 1830, Walker died suddenly in his home under mysterious circumstances.

MAJOR WORKS AND THEMES

In addition to his contributions to *Freedom's Journal*, David Walker's only published work were three editions of his small pamphlet, *David Walker's Appeal, in Four Articles; Together with a Preamble, to the Coloured Citizens of the World.* Published by Walker himself in 1829, the *Appeal* was the most strident and militant voice of early black protest writing. Walker's was an outspoken indictment of the institution of chattel slavery and its ideological cousins, racial injustice and race prejudice. Walker's rhetorical goal was clear: to produce an inspirational document for the masses of enslaved and free black people in America, with the intention of inciting them to seize their own freedom. Familiar with both the indignities of slavery and abolitionist efforts in the North, Walker realized that if African Americans were to be free, they had to muster the will and determination to claim their own freedom and not rely on the benevolence of whites.

Walker's challenge to whites who were sympathetic to the abolitionist cause was not only to accept African Americans as equals but to take the extraordinary step of extending to African Americans the full rights and privileges of American citizenship. Walker challenged white Americans by reminding them of the very principles upon which the union was founded—those words so carefully crafted by Thomas Jefferson and others in the Declaration of Independence of the United States. Walker asked white Americans:

Do you understand your own language? Hear your language, proclaimed to the world, July 4th, 1776 [.] "We hold these truths to be self evident that ALL men are created EQUAL!! that *they are endowed by their Creator with certain unalienable rights. . . .*" Compare your own language . . . with your cruelties and murders inflicted . . . on our fathers and on us.

By posing the dilemma of continued slavery and racial injustice as he did, Walker relentlessly challenged whites to live up to those principles that they recognized as foundational to American democracy. Walker's goal was to demonstrate the hypocrisy of democracy as practiced by those who remained unwilling to accept African Americans as equal to themselves.

Further, Walker understood the importance of Christianity and the Bible to America's grand imagination of itself in the making. As such, Walker's *Appeal* was also relentless in its insistence that the Bible had been misinterpreted as sanctioning the subjugation and enslavement of blacks. In other words, Walker challenged the notion promulgated by many southern whites that as a consequence of ancestral sin, the Bible dictates that the "natural" condition of blacks is subservient to that of whites. Walker denounced the hypocrisy of prevailing religious doctrine, while he underscored for blacks the necessity of maintaining faith that God would eventually send a messenger to lead them out of bondage. By suggesting that this prophet would emerge from the ranks of enslaved black people, Walker also maintained that blacks must act on their own accord if freedom is to be won. As William L. Andrews suggests in *The Norton Anthology of African American Literature*, "by demonstrating that biblical as well as American history amply justified forcible resistance against tyranny, Walker tried to galvanize into purpose both the religious and worldly communities of black America" (178).

While Walker's *Appeal* was steadfastly antislavery, much of its poignancy was due to its being grounded in this history of slavery and the surprising formality and rhetorical sophistication with which it was written. These qualities amazed some, for Walker was largely self-educated. Also interesting about Walker's pamphlet is its discussion of other social issues concerning free and enslaved blacks. Like W.E.B. Du Bois* some seventy-five years later, Walker was interested in wholesale social change for African Americans, articulating an agenda for black political, spiritual, and social empowerment. In this sense, Walker was much less interested in instigating retributive violence against white Americans than he was in putting forth a plan for complete black liberation.

CRITICAL RECEPTION

When it was first published in 1829, Walker faced the challenge of circulating what was surely seen as a seditious document. That his clothing business was located close to Boston's wharves gave Walker access to sailors on the many local and oceangoing vessels that docked in Boston. Walker formed friendships with some of these sailors, who carried the *Appeal* both north and south. As whites read the pamphlet, particularly those in the South, state governors from Louisiana, Mississippi, and Virginia were forced to convene meetings to discuss ways to limit the *Appeal*'s influence. Eventually, whites caught disseminating the pamphlet were subject to fines and jail time, and blacks were threatened under penalty of death. Further, Walker found himself a marked man by southern slaveholders, who, concerned about the possibility of slave insurrection, conspired to delay slavery's demise. Southern whites were correct in anticipating that Walker's *Ap-*

peal would be a source of inspiration and pride for blacks fortunate enough to secure a copy.

More recently, Walker's *Appeal* has been recognized as an important statement of antebellum black protest writing. Walker's sense that African Americans might benefit greatly from a perspective of the larger world as gained through liberal education witnessed a rearticulation in the writings of W.E.B. Du Bois, as did the idea that black progress comes only through the determined efforts of black people themselves. As many contemporary scholars point out, this message was also embraced to varying degrees by Marcus Garvey* and Booker T. Washington.* In the 1960s the militancy of Walker's message and his radical call to action based on fundamental principles of justice were a welcomed legacy to civil rights and black nationalist activists. Walker's *Appeal* should be thought of as seminal text, preceding in tone and intention such diverse twentieth-century texts as Du Bois' *The Souls of Black Folk* (1903), Richard Wright's* "Blueprint for Negro Writing" (1937), and Eldridge Cleaver's *Soul on Ice* (1967). Although it has been recognized as an early voice of black militancy and nationalism, Walker's *Appeal* has yet to receive the extensive critical attention it so richly deserves.

BIBLIOGRAPHY

Works by David Walker

David Walker's Appeal, in Four Articles; Together with a Preamble, to the Coloured Citizens of the World, but in Particular, and Very Expressly, to Those of the United States of America. Boston, 1829.

David Walker's Appeal, in Four Articles; Together with a Preamble, to the Coloured Citizens of the World. Intro. William Loren Katz. New York: Arno Press, 1969.

David Walker's Appeal, in Four Articles; Together with a Preamble, to the Coloured Citizens of the World. Intro. James Turner. Baltimore: Black Classic Press, 1993.

David Walker's Appeal, in Four Articles; Together with a Preamble, to the Coloured Citizens of the World. Intro. Sean Wilentz. New York: Hill and Wang, 1995.

Studies of David Walker

Andrews, William L. "David Walker." In *The Norton Anthology of African American Literature.* Ed. Henry Louis Gates and Nellie McKay et al. New York: W. W. Norton, 1997. 178–79.

Aptheker, Herbert. *One Continual Cry: David Walker's Appeal to the Coloured Citizens of the World (1829–1830): Its Setting and Its Meaning.* New York: Humanities Press, 1965.

Eaton, Clement. "A Dangerous Pamphlet in the Old South." *Journal of Southern History* 2 (1936): 323–34.

Garnet, Henry Highland. *David Walker's Appeal with a Brief Sketch of His Life.* New York: J. H. Tobitt, 1848.

Hinks, Peter P. *To Awaken My Afflicted Brethren: David Walker and the Problem of Ante-bellum Slave Resistance.* University Park: Pennsylvania State University Press, 1997.
———. " 'We Must and Shall be Free': David Walker, Evangelicalism, and the Problem of Antebellum Black Resistance." Diss., Yale University, 1993.
Hubbard, Dolan. *"David Walker's Appeal* and the Puritan Jeremiadic Tradition." *The Centennial Review* 30.3 (Summer 1986): 331–46.
Mitchell, Verner. "To Steal Away Home: Tracing Race, Slavery and Difference in Selected Writings of Thomas Jefferson, David Walker, William Wells Brown, Ralph Waldo Emerson and Pauline Elizabeth Hopkins." Diss., Rutgers University, 1995.
Pease, William H., and Jane H. Pease. *"Walker's Appeal* Comes to Charleston: A Note and Documents." *Journal of Negro History* 59 (1974): 287–92.

ERIC WALROND
(1898–1966)

Cora Agatucci

BIOGRAPHY

Eric Derwent Walrond was born December 18, 1898, in Georgetown, British Guiana (now Guyana). By 1906 his Guyanese father had left the family, as thousands had, to seek work on the Panama Canal. Deserted by her husband, Ruth Walrond took the children to her native Barbados. Young Walrond attended St. Stephen's Boys School in Black Rock. In "White Man, What Now?" (1935), he would deride his "English education" "at the expense of everything African" ("Winds" 279).

By 1911 Mrs. Walrond uprooted the family again to search out her husband in the Canal Zone. The marital reconciliation failed, and Walrond resumed public school and private tutoring and acquired fluent Spanish. Colon Latinos gave the boy his "first taste of prejudice" against Anglophone blacks ("White Man, What Now?", "Winds" 280). The Health Department of the Canal Commission gave Walrond his first job as a clerk. In 1916 he began reporting for the *Panama Star and Herald*, an important Latin American newspaper. "I used to write up brawls, murders, political scandals, voodoo rituals, labor confabs, campaigns, concerns, dramatic affairs, shipping intelligence," Walrond reports in a 1924 biographical sketch ("Winds" 333, n. 161).

Beckoned by "a bigger world of endeavor," Walrond resumed his migrations ("Winds" 333, n. 161). He arrived in New York City on June 30, 1918. Denied employment equal to his journalistic qualifications by white-run Harlem newspapers, he worked as porter, secretary, stenographer, and janitor between 1918 and 1921. While secretary at the British Recruiting Mission and the Broad Street Hospital, Walrond resumed writing. His utopian sketch of a united Africa, "A Senator's Memoirs" (1921), won a prize sponsored by Marcus Garvey's* Universal Negro Improvement Association. Walrond became assistant, then associate editor of *Negro World* (1921–1923) at the height of its circulation.

Walrond studied at the City University of New York (1922–1924) and briefly co-owned and edited the *Brooklyn and Long Island Reformer* until 1923. In an increasing variety of venues, Walrond published fictional vignettes, political articles, and cultural reviews. He translated early U.S. experiences with racial discrimination into "On Being Black" (1922), "On Being a Domestic" (1923), and "Vignettes of the Dusk" (1924). These vivid, impressionistic collages use irony, metaphor, and a range of voices to probe the dehumanizing effects of prejudice, bald and subtle. "It is low, mean, degrading—this domestic serving. . . . By its internal spirit wounds, it is responsible for the Negro's enigmatic character. It dams up his fountains of feeling and expression" ("On Being a Domestic," "*Winds*" 86). The narrator of "Vignettes of the Dusk" identifies himself as a "listening post . . . anchored in the middle of life's gurgling stream," up in the "anthropologically exotic. . . . Negro belt" ("*Winds*" 92). This narrative persona afforded the black insider-Caribbean outsider some "armor" (93) in a seductive, hostile land.

Walrond began to articulate an independent aesthetics in the forums of New Negro cultural politics. In "Developed and Undeveloped Negro Literature" (1922), he identifies the debilitating race consciousness that America imposes on its black writers as a primary obstacle to their creating great literature about themselves. Too many, including W.E.B. Du Bois,* had deserted the "Great Field of Folk-Life" for "reform and propaganda" ("*Winds*" 62, 63). In "The New Negro Faces America" (1923), Walrond criticizes the leadership of Du Bois, Booker T. Washington,* and Marcus Garvey, marking a growing split with Garveyism and *Negro World*. Wanting neither "to be like the white man" or "to go back to Africa," the New Negro finds himself "at the crossroads" looking for means to transcend race consciousness and "realize great possibilities within himself" ("*Winds*" 111, 112).

Walrond's first sustained short story, "Miss Kenny's Marriage" (1923), dramatizes internalized prejudices of color and caste stratifying black New York society. Miss Kenny, a West Indian émigré, is caught in the self-defeating trap of aspiring to be white. The story attracted the notice of Charles S. Johnson and the National Urban League, and Walrond began writing for *Opportunity*. While studying creative writing at Columbia University (1924–1926), Walrond continued his experiments in fiction. "The Stone Rebounds" (1923), monologue of a bigoted white writer who exoticizes "dark Harlem" ("Winds" 88), is "one of [Walrond's] few examinations of the white psyche" (Parascandola 21).

In 1924 Walrond was among the young black writers Charles Johnson invited to a Civic Club literary symposium—"dress rehearsal" for the Harlem Renaissance (David Lewis 90). Walrond turned to Caribbean subjects for his short stories "The Godless City" (1924), "The Voodoo's Revenge" (1925), and "The Palm Porch" (1925). A rare optimism infuses the biographical sketch accompanying "Godless City": "*I love America!* I am spiritually a native of Panama," owing "the sincerest kind of allegiance to it" because "I grew up," worked, loved, struggled, "rambled and roamed and adventured" there (*"Winds"* 332, n. 161). The *"dreaming"* young man proclaims, "I must find my place in the sun!" (333, n. 161). However, Walrond confesses to anxiety and depression inhibiting his creativity in letters to Alain Locke* dating from 1924 (cited in Parascandola 35).

In 1925 *Opportunity* awarded "Voodoo's Revenge" third prize in a literary contest, and Locke included "The Palm Porch" in *The New Negro*, cultural manifesto of the Harlem Renaissance. By the mid-1920s Walrond had moved from Brooklyn to Harlem, divorced his Jamaican-born wife, Edith, with whom he had three daughters, and become a social celebrity among New Negro literati (Arthur P. Davis, cited in Bogle 475). Walrond worked as business manager of *Opportunity* from 1925 to 1927, promoting young black writers and artists and expanding the journal's international scope (Parascandola 24).

Walrond continued to examine multiple facets of the U.S. color problem in articles and reviews of this period. Abiding concern with its damaging effects on black literature is expressed in "The New Negro Literati" (*Winds* 1925). From the distanced perspective of "a foreigner," Walrond implores black artists to break free of their "inferiority complex" and reject propagandistic "Uplift work" proscribing subject matter "which may put the black race in a disparaging light" (*"Winds"* 130, 131). Like Jean Toomer,* the black writer should paint true "pictures of people—tantalizing black people—he knows" (130). Such pictures would distinguish *Tropic Death* (1926), a collection of short stories drawing deeply upon Walrond's Caribbean past.

Hailed as a major achievement of the Harlem Renaissance, *Tropic Death* earned Walrond an advance for a new book on the building of the Panama Canal—to be called *The Big Ditch*—and three major awards in 1927–1928: a Harmon Fellowship in literature, a Zona Gale Scholarship at the University of Wisconsin, and a Guggenheim award to "[t]ravel and study in the West Indies for the purpose of obtaining material for a series of novels and short stories depicting native life there" (Letter to Henry Allen Moe, March 13, 1928, qtd. in Parascandola 31). Walrond meant to weave into these works "legends, folktales, pleasant songs and voodoo myths" of the region (qtd. in Ramchand 74). High expectations followed Walrond out of New York in September 1928.

Over the next two years, Walrond traveled Panama, Haiti, the Dominican Republic, St. Kitts, Barbados, and the Virgin Islands, before requesting permission from Henry Allan Moe of the Guggenheim Foundation to continue research in France for *The Big Ditch* (Parascandola 31). Arriving in Paris in the summer of 1929, Walrond pursued an extravagant lifestyle that exhausted his finances and produced little writing. His time in France in the early 1930s is not well documented (Parascandola 31–32). Evidence suggests that Walrond continued research for *The Big Ditch* (Parascandola 32), yet he produced no second book-length work in his lifetime.

On a 1929 Caribbean visit, Walrond proclaimed himself more American than West Indian; two years later a brief return to the United States brought him "no thrill" (qtd. in Parascandola 32–33, 36). In a 1933 interview, Walrond explained that, while conditions for blacks were easier in France than in the United States, he could remain in neither country (cited in Parascandola 33). His migrations brought him to rest not in his native Caribbean but in London. There Walrond settled in 1932, with a second wife (Bogle 476). English racism stirred the embittered émigré. Reestablishing his relationship with Marcus Garvey, Walrond began writing for *The Black Man* in the mid-1930s.

In 1939 Walrond moved to Wiltshire, and his wartime journalism for the *People's Voice* attacked the racist treatment of black soldiers (Parascandola 34). Walrond fictionalized this theme in "By the River Avon" (1947); an accompanying biographical note announced plans for a short story collection (cited in Parascandola 34). A troubled 1940 letter to Henry Allan Moe suggests that unfulfilled literary promise weighed heavily on Walrond (cited in Ramchand 74). He voluntarily admitted himself to the Roundway Psychiatric Hospital from 1952 to September 1957 (Parascandola 39, n. 15). Walrond's last two stories, memories of his Caribbean youth, were published in the *Roundway Review* in 1954.

Later returning to London, Walrond and Rosey E. Pool edited *Black and Unknown Bards* (1958), based on a program of African American poetry at the Royal Court Theatre. Although he vowed to pursue original work in a 1960 letter to Moe, Walrond failed to find publishers for a book on the Panama Canal or a revision of *Tropic Death* (Parascandola 35). He died of a heart attack in 1966.

MAJOR WORKS AND THEMES

Eric Walrond capped his best writing years with *Tropic Death*, a collection of ten short stories. The stimulating debates of New Negro cultural politics spawned an aesthetics that carried Walrond back to his Caribbean roots. In a 1923 review of "El Africano," Afro-Hispanic Nestor Martin Fernandez de la Torre, Walrond acknowledges: "In every artist's life it is inexorable that environment—early environment—play a determining part" (*"Winds"* 67). *Tropic Death* (1926) centers on the black life Walrond knew best: Caribbean folk shaped by pride, adversity, dislocation, and migration. With an ear attuned to the rhythms of that life, Walrond code-switches among the rich languages of the Americas to enunciate complex Caribbean identities. Challenging American stereotypes of "a monolithic Caribbean" (Parascandola 26), *Tropic Death* re-creates the region's linguistic and cultural diversity in bold sensory strokes.

Impressionistically rendered as seductive and vengeful or harshly indifferent, the tropics impend upon human struggles in both rural and urban settings. Painful U.S. experiences sharpened Walrond's focus on the destructive effects of racism. The best stories of *Tropic Death* cast penetrating light into Caribbean hearts twisted by color and caste prejudice. Volatile mixtures of indigenous and colonizing forces impel these dramas of self-destruction and self-assertion, accommodation and resistance, violent death and resilient survival.

In "Drought," "grim, sun-crazed blacks" (19) carve a marginal existence from the "white burning" hills of Barbados at the height of the dry season. Against an ominous landscape and an unhearing God, black peasants struggle for survival in "the gap" (21). Ubiquitous, life-choking marl dust—agent of unforgiving nature and colonial exploitation—exacts a family tragedy. The light-skinned young daughter of Coggins Rum, "yellow" Beryl of " 'too hard ears,' " must satisfy her strange, self-destructive hunger for white marl. The irony-charged scene unfolds at dusk, under a "sensuous tropic sky," as the poverty-stricken Rums sit for the "absurdly regal" rite of English "tea" (29). In a swirling haze, pounded by images of the desecration of black bodies, epiphany slowly comes to Coggins: " 'Marl . . . dust,' " the old white doctor concludes after autopsy, is indeed death's agent (32).

"The Yellow One," on a ship full of migrants, offers a microcosm of the Caribbean world. Under the relentless sun, the human mixture seethes with desire, hostility, and desperation. Code-switching narrative and dialogue expose identities and relationships misshapen by color prejudice. Migrations of "work and daring" lead Alfred St. Xavier Mendez to a prized and envied wife, the lovely mestiza *la madurita*, won over the objections of her Honduran "*chumbo*-hating folk" (54–55). Restless to return home to Jamaica, Alfred uproots wife and child, but his laziness and her prayers will not secure even hot water for their starving baby. Desperate, the "yellow one" dodges lecherous white hands and plunges into the hell below deck to seek help from another mestizo, Jota, of the crew. The ensuing tragedy indicts a color system that privileges and scapegoats such "yellow" ones—"the nearest thing to a white" (61)—in the underclass world. The black cook's mate Hubigon hates "yellow" Jota's success with women. *La madurita*'s innocent interaction with the Cuban inflames Hubigon, and he attacks Jota in a murderous rage. *La madurita*, a hapless victim, is trampled to death in the melee. Above, her husband wonders at her absence, while "hosannas to Jesus" rise to greet Jamaica's "dead blue hills" (66).

Layered conflicts converge in the plot of "The Wharf Rats" (in *Tropic*). Color and caste prejudices, perpetrated by American imperialism, assign "shadowy, obdurate" (69) Maffi to the bottom of Canal Zone society. She resents her immediate employers, an upwardly aspiring black family whose migrations lead only to Coco Te, impoverished black tenements outside Cristobal. The patriarch Jean Baptiste apes the mannerisms of the white Yankee foreman across the tracks and piously espouses the "harsh" English Plymouth Brethren faith (69). His "petulant patois" bespeaks a St. Lucian transplant thrice-colonized, and the male family members dismiss obeah, powerful in Black Coco Te (68). Moon-dreaming Maffi, wielder of obeah, concentrates her hostility on Jean Baptiste's son Philip. "Wharf rats," Philip and his brother dive recklessly into the shark-infested waters for coins thrown by affluent whites. Maffi begrudges Philip's attempts to protect the romantic dreams of color-favored Maura. Ironically, Maura's love object, Chinese half-breed San Tie, wants nothing to do with the Bantu girl. Maffi vows, " 'Ah go stop it, yes' " (78). Her chosen instrument, a "bloaty, stone-colored mankiller" shark, catches Philip lured again into the fatal sea by white gold (84).

Prostitution and murder lurk beneath exotic illusions in "The Palm Porch," a lavish bordello situated high above the "squalid world of Colon" (89). An "armor of leafy laces" and tropical greenery screens out Western imperialism's ravages in the Canal Zone (88–89). Miss Buckner, the madam, is a paradox of native pride and colonial prejudice. Even as she regrets the loss of Panama's "virgin past" (86), she prostitutes her many daughters of mysterious parentage to the agents of the land's destruction. She speaks "blazing meteors" of rich mulatto patois and harbors a secret wish that she were white (90). But Miss Buckner is a shrewd survivor in a hostile land, tough and predatory as the dehumanizing system that made her. She nurtures her clients' illusions and courts Canal Zone elite. Two defiant daughters have run off with too-black, too-poor clients, and Miss Buckner will stop at nothing to prevent a third from repeating this disaster. The recesses of her genteel Victorian dress conceal a dagger, and an unsuitable British suitor falls victim to her ambition.

"Tropic Death" (in *Tropic*) is the initiation story of eight-year-old Gerald Bright, migrating from Barbados to Panama, from innocence to experience, in search of his father. The title story is the most autobiographical of the collection. Close bonds unite mother and son in the absence of Lucian Bright, another Caribbean drawn to the Canal Zone in search of "work and daring." Aboard the British packet, young Gerald is introduced to a teeming new world, from which his proper mother, Sarah, and her devout Plymouth Brethren prayers cannot protect him. They find Lucian in Colon's Bottle Alley, its "lecherous huts" and rum-soaked byways haunted by disease, poverty, racism, and violence (181). But here Gerald comes "to take on the color of life" (177). The child learns through his senses, flooded with rich images of the dangerous, fascinating streets, matured by violent, tearful scenes between his parents. Visual postures of poor, urbanized Caribbean peasants seeking atonement and salvation, dull in their transformation, impress Gerald, but he sleeps through the long, hot prayer meetings at the Sixth Street Mission. Leprosy, rather than Sarah's earnest prayers, finally subdues her wild, dissipated husband. In the final scene of parting, her faith in the Lord's "mysterious" ways dries Sarah's eyes. Winds take her sustaining "mirage," while father and son weep on (192). Briefly, indelibly, Gerald comes to know his father.

Walrond's 1933 self-assessment best summarizes the forces that drove four decades of writing and converge magnificently in *Tropic Death*: "My duty and my *raison d'etre* are to give an accurate portrayal of my race, its history, its sufferings, its hopes and its rebellions. Therein lies a rich source of emotion and pain. It is there that I draw the essence of my work, and I will dedicate my energy as a writer to serving the Black race" (qtd. in Parascandola 37, 40, n. 19).

CRITICAL RECEPTION

Walrond's contemporaries acclaimed *Tropic Death* as a brilliant, if flawed, achievement of New Negro writing. Robert Herrick judged *Tropic Death* "careless of composition, as the younger writers of the day often are, disdaining unity and coherence in their effort to seize a deep reality" (332). Herrick distinguished the collection for working the "rich new field" of black West Indian experience and capturing the "African temperament, modes of thought": Walrond's "dramatic presentation of character in dialogue, in a vernacular so literal as not always to be readily intelligible, is masterly convincing" (332).

Tropic Death's impressionistic style and Caribbean vernacular drew mixed reviews. Thomas Oxley was entranced by the stories' "immaculate beauty and West Indian weirdness" and Walrond's use of "the dialect of the peasants" to voice "the poetry of their soul" (1). Theophilus Lewis quarreled with the sometimes "unintelligible jargon, disconnected sentences," and "exotic and pagan character," which conformed to white stereotypes of blacks (27, 28). W.E.B. Du Bois was discomfited by the folk languages and experimental style but nevertheless concluded that "on the whole, [*Tropic Death*] is a human document of deep significance and great promise" (152).

Treatment of "prostitution, colorism, poverty, crime, and vengeance" also stirred controversy (Parascandola 29). Pre-*Tropic Death* articles like Walrond's "The New Negro Literati" (*Winds* 1925) and Langston Hughes'* "The Negro Artist and the Racial Mountain" (1926) asserted black artistic freedom from the constraints of propaganda, and *Tropic Death* provided a rich example of what such freedom would yield. Hughes admired "[t]he throbbing life and sun-bright hardness of these pages," "untainted by racial propaganda" ("Marl-Dust" 9). In 1927 Benjamin Brawley pronounced *Tropic Death* "the most important contribution made by a Negro to American letters since the appearance of Dunbar's* *Lyrics of Lowly Life*" (179).

Walrond's luster faded steadily after 1928. In 1937 Sterling Brown distinguished Walrond from most Harlem writers for depicting the "tragedy and pain in his milieu rather than the joy of living" (155). Brown judged *Tropic Death* "unapologetically naturalistic," admired its imagery and command of "diverse West Indian dialects," but faulted the prose style (154, 155). A decade later, Hugh M. Gloster also called *Tropic Death* naturalistic, depicting "helpless animal[s] impelled primarily by instinct and controlled mainly by capricious forces" (181).

Interest in black arts stimulated the reprinting of *Tropic Death* in 1972. Robert Bone gave it serious attention in *Down Home* (1975), examining the "interface of Walrond's life and art" derived from "the known facts and the known fictions" (176). Bone rejects *Tropic Death*'s classification as naturalistic: instead, Walrond uses "primitive and atavistic" metaphors to "explor[e] the complexities of his black identity" (171). His "images of horrifying death, his fascination with the supernatural, and . . . the dark underside of human consciousness betray the workings of a Gothic imagination" (171). Bone attributes Walrond's Gothicism to "the anguish of a fragmented self," tragic outcome of racial trauma, crisis, and rebellion for this "black Englishman," with a "secret longing" for "whiteness" (173). Its quality "uneven," *Tropic Death* nevertheless features some of the best fiction "of the Harlem Renaissance" (195).

In *When Harlem Was in Vogue* (1979), David Lewis describes *Tropic Death* as "one of the truly avant-garde experiments of the Harlem Renaissance" (189). Lewis joins Bone in ranking some of the stories "among the fine Gothic tales of early twentieth-century American literature" (190). Walrond seemed confident "that what he had to say about his own past was . . . universally meaningful to the condition of Exiled America" (190).

In 1970 Kenneth Ramchand pointed a different direction for Walrond studies. He declares *Tropic Death* "one of the startling treasures in the lost literature of the West Indies" (67). Enid E. Bogle picks up this overlooked trail in 1986: *Tropic Death*'s focus on "Black people outside of the United States" and the "venomous experiences . . . inescapable to those who migrate" adds "a new dimension to the writings of the Harlem Renaissance" (481). Walrond's depictions of "the disillusions and aspirations and human interactions of the Caribbean people" in migration speak to "the plight of [all] Black people" (480, 481). Even so, *Tropic Death* is now out of print.

"Recent critics have had relatively little to say about his writing, and even less about his life . . ." ("Eric Walrond" 1195). Louis J. Parascandola substantially redresses these problems in *"Winds Can Wake Up the Dead"* (1998), making accessible a selection of Walrond's best work in several genres spanning four decades, including seven stories from *Tropic Death*. For Parascandola, *Tropic Death* holds a "unique place in Black literature" for representing the "Pan-African element of the Harlem Renaissance" (25). Walrond's dominant themes—"migration, discrimination, and racial pride—are still relevant to today's readers" (11). A core problem obstructing Walrond's reclamation is "the difficulty of categorizing him" (Parascandola 37). His multinational, "multifaceted literary output over several decades" confounds "nationalist criteria used to construct African American and Caribbean literary canons" (37). Walrond's work should be examined as Caribbean literature and as world literature enunciating the global condition of "homelessness" (Parascandola 37). May Parascandola's reader indeed blow "winds" strong enough to "wake up the dead."

BIBLIOGRAPHY

Works by Eric Walrond

Books

Tropic Death. New York: Boni and Liveright, 1926; reprinted, New York: Collier-Macmillan, 1972.
(Ed. with Rosey E. Pool). *Black and Unknown Bards: A Collection of Negro Poetry*. Aldington, England: Hand and Flower Press, 1958.
"Winds Can Wake Up the Dead": An Eric Walrond Reader. Ed. Louis J. Parascandola. Detroit: Wayne State University Press, 1998.

Short Fiction

"A Senator's Memoirs." *Negro World* 17 (December 1921): 6.
"On Being Black." *New Republic* 1 (November 1922): 244–46.

"On Being a Domestic." *Opportunity* (August 1923): 234.

"Miss Kenny's Marriage." *Smart Set* 72 (September 1923): 73–80.

"The Stone Rebounds." *Opportunity* 1 (September 1923): 277–78.

"The Godless City." *Success* (January 1924): 32+.

"Vignettes of the Dusk." *Opportunity* 2 (January 1924): 19–20.

"The Voodoo's Revenge." *Opportunity* 3 (July 1925): 209–13.

"The Palm Porch." In *The New Negro*. Ed. Alain Locke. New York: Albert and Charles Boni, 1925; reprinted, 1992. *The New Negro: Voices of the Harlem Renaissance*. New York: Touchstone-Simon and Schuster, 1997. 115–26.

"City Love." *The American Caravan*. Ed. Van Wyck Brooks et al. New York: Macaulay, 1927. 485–93.

"By the River Avon." *Crisis* (January 1947): 16–17.

Articles and Reviews

"Art and Propaganda." *Negro World* 31 (December 1921): 4

"Marcus Garvey—A Defense." *Negro World* 11 (February 1922): 4.

"The Dice of Destiny." *Negro World* 11 (March 1922): 4.

"The Negro Poet." Rev. of *The Book of American Negro Poetry*, by James Weldon Johnson. *Negro World* 1 (April 1922): 4.

"Visit to Arthur Schomburg's Library Brings out Wealth of Historical Information." *Negro World* 22 (April 1922): 6.

"Book Notes." Rev. of *Harlem Shadows*, by Claude Mckay. *Negro World* 6 (May 1922): 4.

"Developed and Undeveloped Negro Literature: Writers Desert Great Field of Folk-Life for Propagandism." *Dearborn Independent* 13 (May 1922): 12.

"Florida Girl [Augusta Savage] Shows Amazing Gift for Sculpture." *Negro World* 16 (December 1922): 3.

"The New Negro Faces America." *Current History* 17 (February 1923): 786–88.

"West Indian Labor." *International Interpreter* 26 (May 1923): 240–42.

"The Negro Comes North." *New Republic* 18 (July 1923): 200–201.

"El Africano." *Crisis* 23 (August 1923): 168–69.

"The Negro Exodus from the South." *Current History* 18 (September 1923): 942–44.

"The Black City." *Messenger* 6 (January 1924): 13–14.

Rev. of *There Is Confusion*, by Jessie Fauset. *The New Republic* 9 (July 1924): 192.

"Imperator Africanus, Marcus Garvey: Menace or Promise?" *Independent* 114, January 3, 1925, 8–11.

"The Negro Literati." *Brentano's Book Chat* (March/April 1925): 31–33.

"Negro Folk-Song." Rev. of *The Negro and His Songs*, by Howard W. Odum and Guy B. Johnson. *The Saturday Review of Literature* 11 (July 1925): 891.

"A Poet for the Negro Race." Rev. of *Color*, by Countee Cullen. *New Republic* 31 (March 1926): 179.

"From Cotton, Cane, and Rice Fields." *The Independent* (September 4, 1926: 260–62; reprinted, *"Winds Can Wake Up the Dead"* 138–41.

"The Epic of a Mood." Rev. of *Nigger Heaven*, by Carl Van Vechten. *The Saturday Review of Literature* 2 (October 1926): 153.

"The Color of the Caribbean." *World Tomorrow* (May 1927): 225–27.

"A Rich Field." Rev. of *Plays of Negro Life*, ed. Alain Locke and Montgomery Gregory. *New York Herald Tribune*, November 27, 1927, sec. 7: 3–4.

"Harlem, la Perle Noire de New York." Trans. Mathilde Camhi. *Voila* [Paris] 27 (May 1933): n.p.

"Como el Hizo el Canal de Panama." *Ahora* [Madrid] 19 (August 1934): n.p.

"Book Reviews." Rev. of *Jonah's Gourd Vine*, by Zora Neale Hurston, and *The Ways of White Folks*, by Langston Hughes. *Keys* [London] (January/March 1935): 61.

"White Man, What Now?" *Spectator* [London] 5 (April 1935): 562–63.

"The Negro in London." *The Black Man* [London] (late March 1936): 9–10.

"The Negro in the Armies of Europe." *The Black Man* [London] (September-October 1936): 8–9.

"The Negro before the World." *The Black Man* [London] (March 1938): 4–5.

"On England." *The Black Man* [London] (July 1938): 18.

"White Airmen in England Protest Treatment of Negro Comrades." *People's Voice* 9 (December 1944): 16.

"Indian Troops Employed for British Dirty Work." *People's Voice* 15 (December 1945): 13.

"Reviews of Books." Rev. of *Twelve Million Black Voices*, by Richard Wright. *Life and Letters* (November 1948): 176+.

Studies of Eric Walrond

Bassett, John E. "Reviews of *Tropic Death* by Eric Walrond." In *Harlem in Review: Critical Reactions to Black American Writers, 1917–1939*. Selinsgrove, PA: Susquehanna University Press, 1992. 65–67.

Berry, Jay. "Eric Walrond (1898–1966)." In *Afro-American Writers from the Harlem Renaissance to 1940*. Vol. 51 of *Dictionary of Literary Biography*. Ed. Trudier Harris. Detroit: Gale Research-Bruccoli Clark Layman, 1987. 296–300.

Bogle, Enid E. "Eric Walrond (1898–1966)." In *Fifty Caribbean Writers: A Bio-Bibliographical Critical Sourcebook*. Ed. Daryl Cumber Dance. New York: Greenwood Press, 1986. 474–482.

Bone, Robert. "Eric Walrond." In *Down Home: A History of Afro-American Short Fiction from Its Beginnings to the End of the Harlem Renaissance*. New York: Putnam: 1975. 171–203; reprinted, *Down Home: Origins of the Afro-American Short Story*. Morningside ed. Preface Robert Bone. New York: Columbia University Press, 1988. 171–203.

Brawley, Benjamin. "The Negro Literary Renaissance." *The Southern Workman* 56.4 (April 1927): 177–84.

Brown, Sterling. *The Negro in American Fiction*. Washington, DC: Associates in Negro Folk Education, 1937. 154–55.

Du Bois, W.E.B. "Five Books." Rev. of *Tropic Death*. *Crisis* 33 (January 1927): 152.

"Eric Walrond, 1898–1966." In *The Norton Anthology of African American Literature*. Ed. Henry Louis Gates Jr. and Nellie Y. McKay. New York: Norton, 1997. 1195.

Gloster, Hugh M. "Eric Walrond." In *Negro Voices in American Fiction*. Chapel Hill: University of North Carolina Press, 1948. 181–83.

Herrick, Robert. "Tropic Death." *New Republic* 48 (November 10, 1926): 332.

Hughes, Langston. "Marl-Dust and West Indian Sun." *New York Herald Tribune Books* (December 5, 1926): 9.

Lewis, David Levering. *When Harlem Was in Vogue*. 1979. New York: Oxford University Press, 1989.

Lewis, Theophilus. "New Year's Message to Big Shroud-and-Coffin Man." Rev. of *Tropic Death. The Messenger* 9.1 (January 1927): 27–28.

Locke, Alain, ed. *The New Negro: An Introduction.* New York: Boni, 1925. Reprinted, 1992.

———. *The New Negro: Voices of the Harlem Renaissance.* Intro. Arnold Rampersad. New York: Touchstone-Simon and Schuster, 1997.

Martin, Tony. "The Defectors—Eric Walrond and Claude McKay." In *Literary Garveyism.* Dover: Majority Press, 1983. 124–38.

Oxley, Thomas L. G. "Tropic Death." *Chicago Defender*, November 13, 1926, part 2, p. 1.

Parascandola, Louis J. Intro. *"Winds Can Wake Up the Dead": An Eric Walrond Reader.* Ed. Louis J. Parascandola. African American Life Series. Detroit: Wayne State University Press, 1998. 11–42. (Gives complete bibliography of Walrond's known work, 341–48.)

Ramchand, Kenneth. "The Writer Who Ran Away: Eric Walrond and *Tropic Death.*" *Savacou* 2 (September 1970): 67–75.

BOOKER T. WASHINGTON
(1856–1915)

Ted Olson

BIOGRAPHY

Likely born in the spring of 1856 (there was no official record of the birth, as he was born into slavery), Booker T. Washington spent his first nine years living in a tiny cabin on James Burroughs' 207-acre Franklin County, Virginia, tobacco farm. Washington's mother, Jane, was one of Burroughs' slaves, while his biological father was a never-disclosed white man living in the neighborhood. Jane bestowed upon her son both his first name—derived from the first name of her former slave owner, Bowker Preston—and his middle name, Taliaferro, probably co-opted from the last name of prominent white families living nearby. Washington acquired his last name after the Civil War. His family, having been emancipated, left Virginia to join Jane's husband, Washington Ferguson, in Malden, West Virginia, where Ferguson was employed by the local salt industry. Booker, attending school for the first time at the age of nine, needed to declare a last name; he chose his stepfather's first name.

During his first years in Malden, Booker T. Washington attended school intermittently while working as a salt-packer to help support his family; in his spare time, he taught himself to read using a copy of Webster's spelling book given him by his mother. By 1867 he was a servant in the home of the Ruffners, Malden's most prominent white family. The matriarch, Viola Ruffner, a New Englander, fostered in Washington an appreciation for order and cleanliness.

A few years later, while working at a nearby coal mine, Washington heard about Hampton Normal and Agricultural Institute, an experimental school in the Virginia tidewater that allowed African American students to pay tuition and boarding fees through on-campus work. Enrolling at Hampton Institute in 1872, Washington met Samuel Chapman Armstrong, the institute's founder and director and the Reconstruction era's chief proponent of industrial education as a means for empowering African Americans. Formerly a general in the Union army, Armstrong not only advocated self-reliance, self-discipline, work, and morality but also demonstrated paternalistic generosity toward the dispossessed. Washington subsequently modeled himself and his activities on Armstrong's example.

Graduating with honors from Hampton in 1875, Washington returned to Malden to rejoin his family and teach at the same neighborhood school he had once attended. Overseeing the education of nearly 200 African American students (100 children during the day and an equal number of adults at night), Washington prepared his most capable students to attend Hampton Institute; one of these was his future wife, Fannie N. Smith. As testament to Washington's effectiveness as a teacher, several of his Malden students went on to notable professional careers.

In 1878, wanting to explore new career possibilities, Washington attended Wayland Seminary, a Baptist theological school in Washington, D.C. The next year, dissatisfied with urban life and disillusioned with the urbane attitudes of his fellow seminary students, Washington accepted Armstrong's invitation to return to Hampton Institute as a teacher. Washington's duties during his two-year teaching stint at Hampton included serving as dormitory supervisor of some Native American students sent there for acclimatization into white society.

In 1881 Armstrong recommended Washington, now twenty-five years old, to Alabama educators seeking someone to direct a new school for African American students to be established in Tuskegee, Alabama. Initially resisting the idea of hiring a young African American man for the position, these educators eventually heeded Armstrong's recommendation. Washington immediately proved an effective leader of Tuskegee Normal and Industrial Institute. To ensure that Tuskegee Institute would remain immune from the vagaries of Alabama state politics, he purchased school property without public funds. This approach, of course, necessitated the procuring of financial support. Washington realized that Tuskegee Institute's program of industrial education (modeled on that of Hampton Institute) would need to win the respect and financial support of whites (locally, regionally, and nationally). Local whites were won over after Tuskegee students began to make high-quality material products (such as bricks). Other southern whites grew sympathetic when Washington assured them the school would help the region economically through keeping the African American labor force from leaving the Black Belt of Alabama for opportunities elsewhere. White northerners, respecting Washington's dedication to education and finding his views on race nonthreatening, donated much of the funding on which Tuskegee Institute depended. Under Washington's leadership, Tuskegee Institute by the early years of the twentieth century was serving over 1,000 students, employing nearly 200 faculty and staff, and offering a competitive academic program as well as its signature program in industrial training.

Washington's primary position on race was his belief that his generation of

African Americans, instead of insisting upon immediate social and political equality with whites, should first endeavor to improve themselves economically and morally. He believed that, once blacks achieved self-respect, they would inevitably garner respect from whites and thus gain civil rights. Whites, praising Washington for his position on race relations, nicknamed him "the Great Accommodator."

While gaining public acclaim at Tuskegee Institute, Washington was experiencing personal setbacks. His wife, Fannie, whom he married in 1882, died suddenly in 1884. The next year he married Olivia A. Davidson, who had served Tuskegee Institute since its beginnings; she died in 1889. With three children to support and a rapidly expanding educational institution to supervise, Washington welcomed his 1892 marriage to Margaret J. Murray, as it was to bring him lasting stability.

Washington's power in state and national politics increased dramatically during the 1890s. In 1892 he was recruited to secure the African American vote in Alabama for white politician Thomas G. Jones' gubernatorial campaign. The event that, more than any other, boosted Washington's national reputation was his address at the 1895 Cotton States and International Exposition in Atlanta. Washington's speech, eloquently conveying his accommodationist position on the race issue, drew wildly enthusiastic reactions. Not only was the text of the speech published in major newspapers across the country, but Washington received compliments from President Grover Cleveland and many other white politicians.

In 1896, the same year the U.S. Supreme Court upheld the legality of state laws advocating racial segregation (in the *Plessy v. Ferguson* decision), Harvard University awarded Washington an honorary degree, the first such degree given to an African American by a New England university. In 1898 President William McKinley, while visiting Tuskegee Institute, publicly confessed admiration for that school's founder. During their 1899 trip to Europe, Washington and his wife were invited to join Queen Victoria for tea at Windsor Castle. In 1901 President Theodore Roosevelt, seeking advice regarding political appointments in southern states, invited Washington to dine in the White House. Throughout this period, philanthropists like Andrew Carnegie and John D. Rockefeller, in recognition of Washington's efforts to help African Americans in the South, made significant monetary donations to Tuskegee.

The African American response to Washington was less positive. Numerous black ministers and journalists thought the 1895 Atlanta speech too sympathetic toward southern whites and not enough concerned with the rights of their own race. Washington, of course, had to coexist with southern whites on an everyday basis; his reaction to racial discrimination in the South had to be checked by his need to mollify potentially angry whites. Nevertheless, though Washington claimed in his 1901 autobiography *Up from Slavery* to have won over his critics, several African American intellectuals were, in fact, growing increasingly suspicious of him, believing that, given Washington's personal clout in national politics, he was not doing enough to oppose racially motivated lynching and other hate crimes rampant in the southern states at the turn of the century. Some African Americans criticized Washington's passivity toward the race riots then occurring in both southern and northern cities. Washington maintained that once the economic disparity between blacks and whites had been reduced, such conflict would inevitably end. Thus, he concentrated his attention on expanding the possibilities for African American advancement through entrepreneurship. In 1900 Washington, co-opting an idea from W.E.B. Du Bois, founded the National Negro Business League, an influential organization that encouraged the development of African American–run businesses nationally. This endeavor, though, spawned additional controversy, as Washington excluded Du Bois from the league's governing committee. Disgruntled at this slight and not respecting Washington's conservative accommodationist position, Du Bois persuasively ensured the exclusion of his former mentor from African American circles by condemning Washington in his influential book *The Souls of Black Folk* (1903):

The black men of America have a duty to perform, a duty stern and delicate,—a forward movement to oppose a part of the work of their greatest leader. So far as Mr. Washington preaches Thrift, Patience, and Industrial Training for the masses, we must hold up his hands and strive with him, rejoicing in his honors and glorying in the strength of this Joshua called of God and of man to lead the headless host. But so far as Mr. Washington apologizes for injustice, North or South, does not rightly value the privilege and duty of voting, belittles the emasculating effects of caste distinctions, and opposes the higher training and ambition of our brighter minds,—so far as he, the South, or the Nation, does this,—we must unceasingly and firmly oppose them. (185)

In the *Encyclopedia of Southern Culture*, Louis R. Harlan, Washington's principal biographer, succinctly summarized Washington's final decade, a time marked by divided intentions and mixed results:

Washington kept his white following by conservative policies and moderate utterances, but he faced growing black and white liberal opposition in the Niagara Movement (1905–9) and the NAACP [National Association for the Advancement of Colored People] (1909–), groups demanding civil rights and encouraging protest in response to white aggressions such as lynchings, disenfranchisement, and segregation laws. Washington successfully fended off these critics, often by underhanded means. At the same time, however, he tried to translate his own personal success into black advancement through secret sponsorship of civil rights suits, serving on the boards of Fisk and Howard universities, and directing philanthropic aid to these and other black colleges. His speaking tours and private persuasion tried to equalize public educational opportunities and to reduce racial violence. These efforts were generally unsuccessful, and the year of Washington's death [1915] marked the beginning of the Great Migration from the rural South to the urban North. Washington's racial philosophy, pragmatically adjusted to the limiting conditions of his own era, did not survive the change. (229)

Despite such controversy, Washington after his death (on November 14, 1915) was widely commemorated by both blacks and whites as the most significant African American of his generation. Even today, historians refer to the period between 1895 and 1915 as "the Era of Booker T. Washington."

MAJOR WORKS AND THEMES

Booker T. Washington's life story is legendary, a consequence of the popularity of his one literary classic, *Up from Slavery* (1901). That book, an autobiography, traces its author's transformation from slave to internationally recognized educator and social reformer. Washington's underlying motivation for writing *Up from Slavery* was to provide a personal illustration of his conviction that he and other former slaves were responsible for their own social advancement.

As it chronicles Washington's achievements, conveys the widening scope of his influence, and imparts to others his social agenda, *Up from Slavery* is highly didactic. To Washington, writing and oratory (he was renowned for his speeches) were equally important modes of communication; he utilized both in his effort to persuade Americans to solve that era's racial problems constructively through his preferred course of action: accommodation.

Otherwise markedly inspirational in tone, *Up from Slavery* begins sardonically, with Washington confessing, "I was born a slave on a plantation in Franklin County, Virginia. I am not quite sure of the exact place or exact date of my birth, but at any rate I suspect I must have been born somewhere and at some time" (7). This statement suggests that, despite his acceptance by whites and his accommodationist position on race relations, Washington as an adult had not forgotten his subjugated position in American society during his formative years. Clearly, Washington's rise within postemancipation white society necessitated that he sublimate feelings of anger.

Washington wrote two additional autobiographical books, both stylistically inferior to *Up from Slavery*. *The Story of My Life and Work* (1900) was a subscription title written exclusively for African American readers, while *My Larger Education* (1911) was Washington's late attempt to reevaluate his life's work and recover some of the power he had lost within the African American community (his authority was then being questioned by African American intellectuals).

Two books by Washington dealt directly with U.S. race relations. *The Future of the American Negro* (1899) compiled some of Washington's most compelling articles and speeches about race, while *The Man Farthest Down: A Record of Observation and Study in Europe* (1912) contained Washington's controversial opinion, formed during his time in Europe, that his fellow African Americans fared better in the United States than did many dispossessed Europeans in Europe. Some of Washington's more provocative speeches were published in 1932 as *Selected Speeches of Booker T. Washington*, edited by his son Ernest Davidson Washington.

Virtually all of Washington's works were composed with the assistance of ghostwriters. For example, a white man, Max Bennett Thrasher, helped Washington write *Up from Slavery*. Ironically, that book's didactic power—its combination of direct statement, restrained testimony, and stylistic simplicity—owes much to the presence of Thrasher, who ensured that Washington's story would appeal to the largest possible readership.

CRITICAL RECEPTION

Up from Slavery most closely resembles, of all the texts in the American literary canon, Benjamin Franklin's *Autobiography*. Both these autobiographical works are generally deemed to be definitive literary treatments of the prototypically American concept of upward mobility; both works suggest that social success is inevitable for individuals who heed traditional American virtues of responsibility, tenacity, thrift, and practicality. A primary difference between Franklin's *Autobiography* and Washington's *Up from Slavery* is the fact that, whereas Franklin achieved success in colonial society by remaining true to himself, Washington, a marginalized minority, gained acceptance in post–Civil War society through hiding his real identity.

Washington's self-characterization in *Up from Slavery* is thus highly idealized; it is also at times untrustworthy. While Washington extensively discusses his successes (quoting liberally from letters and speeches), he is far less forthcoming about his failures. *Up from Slavery*, for example, provides few details on Washington's unsuccessful attempt to become a minister at Wayland Seminary in Washington, D.C. Washington might have been more disclosing concerning this personal setback, as his year in the nation's capital bred in him a deep distrust of organized religion, urban life, and conventional approaches to higher education (attitudes that strongly influenced his later work at Tuskegee Institute). Yet, according to scholar William L. Andrews, Washington's selectivity regarding self-revelation is part of his rhetorical strategy: "Washington, a former slave who became the most powerful African American of his era, rhetorically converted his liabilities into assets that, when organized into an autobiographical narrative, became one of the most compelling personal myths in the history of American literature" ("Preface" viii).

Full appreciation of *Up from Slavery* today hinges upon an awareness of how the book reflected and capitalized upon its author's unique experience of being the first African American wholeheartedly embraced by white Americans. When portions of the manuscript were serialized in the popular magazine *Outlook* in late 1900 and early 1901, Washington was a national celebrity. After the 1901 publication of the entire manuscript, white readers tended to be in agreement over *Up from Slavery*, finding its spin on the Horatio Alger success myth inspiring. African American readers, however, were divided over the book. While most accepted Washington's characterization of himself as the self-made leader of the race, some African American intellectuals distrusted *Up from Slavery*, believing that the book portrayed not a noble racial visionary but rather a political tactician who alternated between ruthless self-aggrandizement and shameless compromise.

Paradoxically, despite its importance as a historic document, *Up from Slavery* is unreliable as a record of history. Not only does it feature a rather sketchy account of Washington's life, but the book contains factual inaccuracies; for instance, whereas Washington speculated that his birth year was either 1858 or 1859, Louis H. Harlan determined the correct year to have been 1856. Furthermore, given its date of publication, *Up from Slavery* provides no information on the last fifteen years of Washington's life. Harlan's two-volume biography provides a fuller, more reliable, more objective account of Washington's remarkable career than does *Up from Slavery*.

Scholarly interest in Washington has generally focused on his historical roles rather than on his literary work. For the 1996 "Norton Critical Edition" of *Up from Slavery*, William L. Andrews compiled compelling analyses of Washington's writing by a variety of scholars, including August Meier (who wrote the first systematic interpretation of Washington), Sidonie Smith (who studied the "masks" that Washington, as African American autobiographer, wore), Houston A. Baker Jr. (who traced Washington's appropriation of the "minstrel form"), Robert B. Stepto, and James Olney (the latter two, in separate articles, illuminated the subtleties in Washington's seemingly artless "style"). In his Preface to this edition of *Up from Slavery*, Andrews acknowledged that many facets of Washington's writing remain critically unexplored.

BIBLIOGRAPHY

Works by Booker T. Washington

Autobiographical Writings

The Story of My Life and Work. Naperville, IL: J. L. Nichols, 1900.
Up from Slavery. New York: Doubleday, Page, 1901.
My Larger Education. New York: Doubleday, Page, 1911.

Compilations of Articles and Speeches

The Future of the American Negro. Boston: Small, Maynard, 1899.
The Man Farthest Down: A Record of Observation and Study in Europe. Garden City, NY: Doubleday, 1912.
Selected Speeches of Booker T. Washington. Ed. E. Davidson Washington. Garden City, NY: Doubleday, 1932.

Collected Works

Harlan, Louis R., et al., eds. *The Booker T. Washington Papers*. 14 vols. Urbana: University of Illinois Press, 1972–1989.

Studies of Booker T. Washington

Biographical Studies

Harlan, Louis R. "Booker T. Washington." In *Encyclopedia of Southern Culture*. Ed. Charles Reagan Wilson and William Ferris. Chapel Hill: University of North Carolina Press, 1989. 228–29.

———. "Booker T. Washington in Biographical Perspective." *American Historical Review* 75.4 (October 1970): 1581–99.

———. *Booker T. Washington: The Making of a Black Leader, 1856–1901*. New York: Oxford University Press, 1972.

———. *Booker T. Washington: The Wizard of Tuskegee, 1901–1915*. New York: Oxford University Press, 1983.

Criticism of Up from Slavery

Andrews, William L. "Preface." In *Up from Slavery*. Norton Critical Edition. Ed. William L. Andrews. New York: W. W. Norton, 1996. vii–xi.

———. *To Tell a Free Story: The First Century of Afro-American Autobiography, 1760–1865*. Urbana: University of Illinois Press, 1986.

Baker, Houston A., Jr. *Modernism and the Harlem Renaissance*. Chicago: University of Chicago Press, 1987.

Du Bois, W.E.B. *The Souls of Black Folk*. Chicago: A. C. McClung, 1903.

Gibson, Donald B. "Strategies and Revisions of Self-Representation in Booker T. Washington's Autobiographies." *American Quarterly* 45.3 (September 1993): 370–93.

Hedin, Raymond. "Paternal at Last: Booker T. Washington and the Slave Narrative Tradition." *Callaloo* 2 (October 1979): 95–102.

McElroy, Frederick L. "Booker T. Washington as Literary Trickster." *Southern Folklore* 49.2 (1992): 89–107.

Meier, August. *Negro Thought in America, 1880–1915: Racial Ideologies in the Age of Booker T. Washington*. Ann Arbor: University of Michigan Press, 1963.

Miller, Kelly. *Race Adjustment*. New York: Neale, 1908.

Olney, James. "The Founding Fathers—Frederick Douglass and Booker T. Washington." In *Slavery and the Literary Imagination*. Ed. Deborah McDowell and Arnold Rampersad. Baltimore: Johns Hopkins University Press, 1989. 1–24.

Rev. of *Up from Slavery*. *The Nation* 72 (April 4, 1901): 281–82.

Rev. of *Up from Slavery*. *Colored American Magazine* 8 (March 1905): 161–62.

Smith, Sidonie. *Where I'm Bound: Patterns of Slavery and Freedom in Black American Autobiography*. Westport, CT: Greenwood, 1974.

Stepto, Robert B. "Lost in a Cause: Booker T. Washington's *Up from Slavery*." In *From behind the Veil: A Study of Afro-American Narrative*. Urbana: University of Illinois Press, 1979. 32–51.

FRANK WEBB
(?–?)

Rennie Simson

BIOGRAPHY

Very little is known about Frank Webb, and what little we do know comes mainly from Harriet Beecher Stowe's Preface to Webb's only major work, *The Garies and Their Friends* (1857). Mrs. Stowe describes Webb as a "colored young man, born and reared in the city of Philadelphia" (xv). She notes that Philadelphia in the 1850s was a city that included a large population of mixed-race people and that this group constituted a "peculiar society of their own" (xv).

A well-known family in that society was the Fortens, one of whose members, Charlotte Forten,* wrote a journal that was not published until 1953. In that journal she makes reference to Frank Webb and his wife, Ann. On Monday, March 1, 1858, Forten included the following observation in her journal: "Lucy tells me that Mr. Frank Webb has received an appointment as postmaster in Jamaica. Probably Annie Webb will accompany him" (116). The editor of Forten's *Journal*, Ray Allen Billington, elaborates this observation in a corroborating entry he found in *The Liberator* on March 5, 1858:

Mr. and Mrs. Frank J. Webb of Philadelphia had just returned to the United States after a long visit in southern France occassioned [sic] by Mrs. Webb's poor health. Mrs. Webb had been forced to abandon giving the "readings" that had won her fame. While in England Mr. Webb had, through the intervention of friends, received the appointment of poastmaster at Kingston, Jamaica. (257)

From this quote we see that Frank Webb traveled and lived outside the United States. We can conjecture that *The Garies and Their Friends*, published in London and dedicated by Webb to Lady Noel Byron by her "grateful friend the author," indicates the likelihood that he spent some time in England. The two stories that he published in 1870 in *The New Era*, "Two Wolves and a Lamb" and "Marvin Hayle," deal with high society in London and Paris.

While most of what we know about Webb remains in the realm of hypothesis, we have sufficient clues to place him in the upper crust of African American society of Philadelphia in the mid-nineteenth century. He was probably well educated, well traveled, and well connected.

MAJOR WORKS AND THEMES

Although Webb published two novelettes, "Two Wolves and a Lamb" and "Marvin Hayle," his literary reputation rests entirely on his 1857 novel *The Garies and Their Friends*.

The story revolves around three families: the Garies, the Ellises, and the Stevenses. The Garies hail from the South. Garie is a white southerner who desires to legalize his relationship with his mulatto mistress, Emily, thus making her his wife and their two children his legal heirs. To accomplish this he moves to Philadelphia, where he and Emily do marry but where they are subjected to all the racial prejudices of the North and meet their end as the victims of a mob. Their two children are separated. The girl, Emily, is raised by a black family, the Ellises, and the boy, Clarence, is sent off to school to pass for white. When they attain adulthood, Emily marries the Ellis son and leads an emotionally and financially secure existence. Clarence "dies of grief" when his racial identity is revealed to the family of his white fiancée, and the family completely rejects him. The Ellis family consists of a black carpenter (who earns a comfortable living in Philadelphia), his wife, and their three children, a son and two daughters. The family is close-knit, yet the individual members possess much personal strength and independence of spirit. The children all succeed in making their way in the world, but the family's life is not without tragedy. The same mob that kills the Garies leaves Mr. Ellis disabled and shattered in mind and body. He never works again, nor is he able to actively partake in family life. He remains a physical and emotional invalid. The Stevens family, with the exception of the young daughter, is a collection of villains in the true Dickensian tradition. Stevens, a white lawyer, is a bigoted and totally corrupt individual whose sole interest in life lies in lining his own pocket. When he learns that he and the Garies are related, he decides to gain for himself the inheritance a distant relative has left to Garie. To achieve this goal he manages to arouse an antiblack mob of which he becomes a part, and he slays Garie himself. He then bribes a poor client of his, McCloskey, to steal Garie's will. Without Garies' children specifically designated as his heirs, Stevens acquires the fortune for himself. Unfortunately for him, he is not able to enjoy his newly acquired wealth. McCloskey constantly threatens to expose Stevens if he does not keep McCloskey supplied with money. Stevens spends his last years as a frightened alcoholic attended only by his daughter. Stevens Jr. comes across Clarence Garie accidentally and reveals his racial background. At the conclusion of the novel McCloskey, on his deathbed, produces Garie's will, and the lone Garie survivor, Emily, inherits a fortune.

Webb intended to show that the conflict in mid-nineteenth-century America was not primarily North versus South, but black versus white. He wanted to show that white prejudice against black Americans was just as intense in the North as in the South. Webb demonstrated that black people survived in nineteenth-century America not by assimilating with whites or by passing as white but by establishing their own way of life and adhering to it. To emphasize this point Webb created the strong, independent Ellis family and the wealthy black businessman, Walters. All of these people are too dark-skinned to pass as whites, and they show no desire to be assimilated into white society. Accommodating to positions that whites have assigned to blacks is unacceptable to the strong-willed black characters in *The Garies and Their Friends*. When Mrs. Ellis desires her son, Charlie, "go into service" for a white lady, Mr. Ellis, Mr. Walters, and even Charlie himself are indignant: "I won't live at service—I'd rather be a sweep or sell apples on the dock. . . . I'll cut my own head first" (27).

Mr. Ellis finally consents to let Charlie take the job on the condition that he will definitely return to school after the holiday. After the maiming of his father by the mob, Charlie feels obligated to support his mother and sisters, but he desires a profession, not a menial job. He has a hard time securing the type of position he wants, and in a conversation held between two clerks who work for a company that is considering Charlie for employment, the hypocrisy of northerners is demonstrated in the words of a clerk from New Orleans: "I must say you Northern people are perfectly incomprehensible. You pay to have niggers educated, and made fit for such places—and then won't let them fill them when they are prepared to do so" (292).

Survival in the white man's world includes fighting if necessary. When Walters learns that his home is about to be attacked by a mob, he seeks assistance from the mayor, who offers a couple of policemen. Walters rejects this offer: "If that is the extent of the aid you can afford me I must do what I can to protect myself" (202).

Before the mob strikes, Walters gives the following instructions to his friends:

We are not the aggressors, Thank God! And the results, be they what they may, are not of our seeking. I have asked protection of the law, and it is too weak or indifferent to give it; so I have no alternative but to protect myself. . . . if they resort to firearms, then we will do the same; I want to be strictly on the defensive—but at the same time we must defend ourselves fully and energetically. (208, 211)

The Ellises show their courage during the attack. Mr. Ellis risks life and limb to warn the Garies of the mob, Esther (the elder Ellis daughter) assists by loading rifles, and Caddy (the younger Ellis daughter) and a friend dispel the mob by pouring boiling water filled with several pounds of cayenne pepper on the heads of the crowd below. Her encounter with the mob leaves Caddy very bitter.

What these white devils will have to answer for! When I think of how much injury they have done us, I *hate* them! I know it's wrong to hate anybody—but I can't help it; and I believe God hates them as much as I do. (267)

Walters and the Ellises survive and prosper in the white-dominated northern states. They do so in spite of, not because of, the white northerners.

The racially mixed Garie family does not fare as well. Their entire lifestyle is an attempt to escape the harsh realities of the society in which they live. In the South they live on a luxurious plantation in a scenic setting. They associate with few people, but Garie's retirement from society was "entirely voluntary, therefore by no means disagreeable" (97). When they arrive in the North, they hope for a more social existence, but this does not come to pass, and since Garie's retirement from society in his northern home is not voluntary, he finds it very disagreeable. The Garie children are placed in a private school intended only for whites but are asked to leave when their racial identity becomes known. Unlike Walters and the Ellises, the Garies don't stand their ground when the mob attacks. Garie attempts to calm the mob and is shot. Emily and the children escape to a woodshed, where she dies in childbirth. Significantly, the new baby, her first to be born on "free" soil, is born dead. Little Emily is raised by the Ellises; she accepts herself as a black woman, is proud of her heritage, and prospers. Charlie is sent off to school to pass for white; he is never able to accept or reveal his black heritage, and this proves his undoing.

The white man's Christianity is also given "the once-over" by Webb. The white minister who is to perform the marriage ceremony between Garie and Emily refuses to go through with the proceedings.

After Mrs. Garie's death she is refused burial in the white cemetery, a fact that astonishes and outrages the Garies' white attorney, whom Mr. Walters considers quite naive.

They refuse us permission to kneel by the side of the white communicants at the Lord's Supper, and give us separate pews in obscure corners of their churches. All this you know—why, then be surprised that they carry their prejudices into their graveyards? (234)

Webb is at his best in describing childhood, which he handles with a superb blend of realism and nostalgia. When one considers that *Tom Sawyer* was published in 1876 and *Huck Finn* in 1884, Webb's marvelous depictions of childhood appear all the more remarkable, and the academic neglect of the Ellis children, the Garie children, and Kinch, Charlie's close friend, is shameful. Charlie and Kinch are forerunners of Tom Sawyer and Huck Finn, respectively. The reader identifies with the mischievous spirit of Charlie's youth and sees in Charlie a revival of his own childhood. Kinch, like Huck, has no adult who is particularly concerned about him. His mother is dead, and his father, an old clothes dealer, doesn't bother much about the boy. Like Huck, Kinch is a free spirit, and the reader feels somewhat envious of this freedom.

When Kinch learns that Charlie is to "go into service," he gives him some advice. "If it was me I should act so bad that the people would be glad to get rid of me" (30). This advice Charlie decides to follow. He manages to irritate his employer in a number of ways, but the climax comes at a big banquet Mrs. Thomas is holding. Unfortunately, the sparsity of Mrs. Thomas' hair compels her to wear a wig, and Charlie decides to take advantage of this situation.

Now to Charlie was assigned the important duty of removing the cover from the soup tureen which was placed before his mistress and the little rogue had settled upon that moment as the most favorable for the execution of his purpose. He therefore secretly affixed a nicely crooked pin to the elbow of his sleeve, and, as he lifted the cover, adroitly hooked it into her cap, to which he knew the wig was fastened and in a twinkling had it off her head. . . . The guests stared and tittered at the grotesque figure she presented. . . . In her haste to put it on, she turned it wrong side foremost; the laughter of the guests could now no longer be restrained. (76)

Webb does not confine his descriptions of childhood to humorous interludes. He showed much compassion for the bleaker moments of childhood. Charlie's sister Caddy, in a fit of rage, accidentally pushes her brother down a flight of stairs. He not only breaks a leg but is dangerously ill for some time. Caddy is in a state of despair, which Webb described as even affecting her compulsion for cleanliness.

The saddest moment for the Ellis children is the injury done to their father by a mob. Webb captures their unhappiness very well; Charlie even gives up marbles, but they do not despair about the future. On the whole, Webb describes the Ellis children as mischievous, independent, and fun-loving. The Garie children, by contrast, are rather sober, dependent, and unrealistic. When the racial identity of the Garie children is revealed, they are reluctantly dismissed by the young teacher who has become very fond of them. Clarence doesn't comprehend why he is being rushed out of school. When little Emily leaves, she says to her teacher, "Don't cry, teacher, I love you . . . don't cry. I'll come back again tomorrow" (160). When Clarence learns of his mother's death, his grief is understandably overwhelming. "The cry of grief [that] sprung up from the heart of that orphan boy, rang in those women's ears for long years after" (225).

Webb does a superb job of utilizing children, the most vulnerable and least self-sufficient members of society, to show how unjust and downright foolish the race caste systems of North and South were. His children are people any reader can identify with. They like to laugh and play and have fun, but they also possess compassion and are easily hurt. Caddy and Kinch are not cruel children but in self-defense feel compelled to pour boiling water on their attackers. Clarence is a sensitive, loving child, but a cruel world crushes his spirit. Webb expertly guides his characters from childhood to adulthood by giving the reader ample insight into why and how they develop as they do.

As Jean Toomer* is known almost exclusively for *Cane* and Ralph Ellison for

The Invisible Man, so Webb is known for one work, and this work is a nineteenth-century masterpiece deserving far more recognition than it has had to date.

CRITICAL RECEPTION

Critical reception of Webb's book has been as mixed as it has been infrequent. After *The Garies* was reissued by the Arno Press in 1969, the novel attracted a modest amount of scholarly attention between 1969 and 1974, when the attention petered out along with the publication of *The Garies*, which is no longer in print.

A major point of discussion has been the novel as an early piece of realism. Gregory Candela observes that "the novel is structurally sound and realistically details many of the issues confronting Afro Americans in the 1850s" (245). R. F. Bogardus also focuses on *The Garies* as an early black novelist's venture into realism. Bogardus feels that Webb defines and delineates the major obstacles standing in the way of success for African Americans: the genteel, white middle class, the white clergy, the political authorities, and even the abolitionists (17). Considering the harsh reality of the black man's existence in America, Bogardus particularly praises Webb's realistic depiction of the wealthy black businessman Walters, who understands the importance of a "comfortable" survival in a hostile world. Walters "knows that money is power, one of the few powers available to the Black man in America" (18). Walters takes no abuse from whites without attempting retaliation, and Bogardus sees him as a realistic forerunner of the militant participants in the Civil Rights movement.

Another aspect of Webb's writing that has drawn praise is his use of humor (presented in the prior discussion of *The Garies*). Robert Fleming acknowledges Webb's use of that familiar humorous figure in African American literature, the trickster, who perpetuates a joke on the white dupe, thus affording the black reader "the dual pleasure of identifying with the player of the joke as well as laughing at the victim" (257). The superb blend of realism and humor is particularly evident in Webb's portrayal of childhood. As James DeVries points out, Webb's children "participate in childhood fantasies such as marking a certain board fence with a skull and crossbones to tell the other he has already gone to school" (248). DeVries also notes that "Kinch, like the later Huck, aids Charles in his mischievous rebellion against his parents" (248). Indeed, the similarities between Webb's and Twain's two young boys are so great that one is forced to wonder if Twain had not, indeed, read *The Garies* before creating Tom and Huck.

The novel's lack of popularity in its own day (and subsequently) probably rests to a large extent, as DeVries points out, to the fact that its major subject matter is northern racism (242). Arthur Davis called the novel "a goodwill book" and criticized Webb for not being "a strong protest writer" (33). For his day, Webb's strong black characters, who fought with violence against a lynch mob and who referred to white people as "white devils," were probably too strong and thus intimidating to a white audience. Indeed, they may still be intimidating to some, and this is very unfortunate because, as Simson pointed out, *The Garies* deserves recognition "as the first outstanding 19th Century novel to be written by a Black author" (21).

BIBLIOGRAPHY

Works by Frank Webb

The Garies and Their Friends. London: Routledge, 1857; reprinted, New York: Arno Press, 1969.
"Two Wolves and a Lamb." *New Era* 1 (January/February 1870): N.p.
"Marvin Hayle." *New Era* 1 (March/April 1870): N.p.

Studies of Frank Webb

Barbour, James, and Robert Fleming. "Nineteenth Century Black Novelists: A Checklist." *Minority Voices* 2 (Fall 1969): 27–30.
Billington, Ray. *The Journal of Charlotte L. Forten*. New York: W. W. Norton, 1981.
Bogardus, R. F. "Frank J. Webb's The Garies and Their Friends: An Early Black Novelist's Venture into Realism." *Studies in Black Literature* 5.2 (Spring 1974): 15.
Bone, Robert. *The Negro Novel in America*. New Haven, CT: Yale University Press, 1965.
Candela, Gregory. "Frank Webb." *Dictionary of Literary Biography*. Vol. 50: *African American Writers before the Harlem Renaissance*. Detroit: Gale, 1986. 242.
Davis, Arthur. "*The Garies and Their Friends*: A Neglected Pioneer Novel." *CLA Journal* 13.1 (1969): 27–32.
DeVries, James. "The Tradition of the Sentimental Novel in The Garies and Their Friends." *CLA Journal* 17.2 (1973): 250–55.
Fleming, Robert. "Humor in the Early Black Novel." *CLA Journal* 17.2 (1973): 250–54.
Gloster, Hugh. *Negro Voices in American Fiction*. Chapel Hill: University of North Carolina Press, 1948.
Simson, Rennie. "*The Garies and Their Friends*: The Black American Novel Comes of Age." *Educational Dimensions* 2 (1981): 21–22.

IDA B. WELLS-BARNETT
(1862–1931)

Loretta G. Woodard

BIOGRAPHY

Ida B. Wells was born in Holly Springs, Mississippi, on July 16, 1862, to James Wells and Elizabeth " 'Lizzie" (Bell) Wells. The eldest of eight children, Wells attended Shaw University, later renamed Rust College, a freedmen's high school and industrial school, where she was an excellent student. When the 1878 yellow fever epidemic swept through Holly Springs, claiming her parents and her nine-month-old brother, Stanley, sixteen-year-old Wells assumed responsibility of caring for her younger siblings. After passing the teacher's examination, she taught for a short time in the rural school district of Holly Springs, earning a monthly salary of twenty-five dollars. To be closer to her family and to obtain a better-paying teaching position, Wells moved to Memphis, Tennessee, in 1884.

That same year, Wells sued the Chesapeake, Ohio, and Southwestern Railroad Company after she was forcibly removed from the first-class ladies' coach designated for "whites only." In December 1884, the circuit court ruled in her favor, but the Tennessee Supreme Court reversed the decision three years later. The loss of her suit was the beginning of her lifelong public campaign against the inequities and injustices faced by blacks throughout the South. Subsequently, journalism was to serve as an important avenue for her to eradicate ignorance and to create a new level of humanity.

Wells became editor of a small church paper, the *Evening Star*, and she became the editor of the newspaper *Living Way*, a religious weekly, writing her editorials under the pen name "Iola." For the next few decades, Wells would write for several African American newspapers and periodicals such as the *Detroit Plaindealer*, *Gate City Press*, *New York Freeman*, and *AME Review*. In 1889 she became editor and co-owner of a local black newspaper, the *Memphis Free Speech and*

Headlight. Writing about the poor conditions of the local black schools and the inadequacies of the teachers, Wells lost her teaching position in 1891. To financially support herself, Wells devoted full-time to traveling for the *Free Speech* and expanding its circulation throughout the Delta region in Mississippi, Arkansas, and Tennessee.

On March 9, 1892, events in Memphis changed the course of Wells' life. Three young black managers of grocery stores, Thomas Moss, Calvin McDowell, and Henry Steward, Wells' friends, were lynched. During her investigation of the rationale for lynching, Wells concluded that it was a racist device for eliminating financially independent black Americans. Wells used her pen to attack the evils of lynching and encouraged the black citizens of Memphis to go west. Hundreds of blacks began to move away, including entire church congregations. She also encouraged blacks to boycott white businesses and introduced the first black boycott.

While Wells attended the African Methodist Episcopal Church conference in Philadelphia, a mob of whites, responding to an editorial Wells left behind to be printed, demolished the *Free Speech* printing press and office on May 27, 1892. Threats of personal violence forced Wells not to return to Memphis. Instead, she went to New York, joined the staff of the *New York Age,* and launched into an antilynching campaign. On June 7, 1892, Wells' thorough investigative research culminated in a feature story, a full seven-column page, published by the *New York Age.* Later, in October 1892, this report became the foundation for two booklets, *Southern Horrors: Lynch Law in All Its Phases,* published in 1892, and *A Red Record: Tabulated Statistics and Alleged Causes of Lynching in the United States, 1892–1893–1894,* published in 1895. Following her publications, she lectured on lynching throughout England, Wales, and Scotland, where she sparked an international awareness on lynching. Wells' speeches during her return trip to England in 1894 led to the formation of the Anti-Lynching Committee.

Wells was also a strong voice at the Chicago World's Fair in 1893. That same year, along with Frederick Douglass,* black journalist Ferdinand Barnett, and I. Garland Penn, she wrote *The Reason Why the Colored American Is Not in the Columbian Exposition,* a protest pamphlet about the exclusion of blacks from the Chicago World's Fair.

Remaining in Chicago, she continued to use her investigations as proof of the atrocities toward black Americans. Her efforts spawned the growth of the black women's club movement. Earning the title "Mother of Clubs," Wells formed women's groups throughout New England and Chicago. Two such associations in Chicago were the Ida B. Wells Club and the Negro Fellowship League, where she served as president of the former for five years and led the club in the establishment of the first black orchestra in Chicago and in the opening of the first kindergarten for black children.

Wells joined the staff of the *Chicago Conservator,* and married the editor and founder, Ferdinand L. Barnett, a black attorney. Barnett shared his wife's interests, and together they championed the black cause for equal rights. Following the birth of her children, Charles Aked, Herman Kohlsaat, Ida B. Wells Jr., and Alfreda M., Wells-Barnett continued to write and to broaden her reformist activities.

Wells-Barnett led a delegation to President William McKinley to protest lynchings in 1898. Two years later she published the pamphlet *Mob Rule in New Orleans: Robert Charles and His Fight to the Death* and that same year became the secretary to the national Afro-American Council until 1902. In 1909 she was one of the original group who with W.E.B. Du Bois conceived the National Association for the Advancement of Colored People (NAACP). In 1913 Wells-Barnett was appointed adult probation officer in Chicago. That same year, she also founded the Alpha Suffrage Club, the first suffrage group composed of black women, and marched in suffrage parades. Two years later she was elected vice president of Chicago's Equal Rights League.

For the next decade Wells-Barnett continued her crusade against violence. She covered the race riot in East Saint Louis, Illinois, in 1918 and wrote a series of articles on the riot for the *Chicago Defender*. She returned south four years later to investigate the indictment for murder of twelve innocent Arkansas farmers. Her report was published in 1922 as *The Arkansas Race Riot*. Toward the end of her life, in 1928, Wells-Barnett began an autobiography, which was edited and published posthumously by her daughter, Alfreda Duster, as *Crusade for Justice: The Autobiography of Ida B. Wells* (1970). She also kept a diary in 1930, the year she entered the political arena and ran unsuccessfully as an independent candidate for state senator. Wells-Barnett died in Chicago of uremia, a kidney disease, on March 25, 1931.

Wells-Barnett was widely known as a "fearless" journalist and ardent activist who made an indelible mark on the history of the United States and offered a critique of racial, sexual, and economic exploitation that still rings true today.

MAJOR WORKS AND THEMES

Wells-Barnett is best known for her courageous exposé of lynching in the American South in both the black and white press and in her two most popular works, *Southern Horrors: Lynch Laws in All Its Phases* (1892) and *A Red Record: Tabulated Statistics and Alleged Causes of Lynching in the United States, 1892–1893–1894* (1895). Together, with strong, concrete language, these thorough analyses of lynching in America make a scathing indictment against the injustices brought about by Jim Crow. In *Southern Horrors* she argues, quiet convincingly, the falseness of the rape charge as a means for lynching the black man and exposes the deep-seated reason for these rapes as ways to conceal interracial love affairs between black men and white women. At the center of America's race war, however, Wells-Barnett uses the miscegenation laws and points to the deeper irony of the sexual double standard. She reveals that white men exploit black women without penalty, under the pretense of white womanhood, while black men "succumb" to white women and are murdered. Asserting that white women in the

South would be willing to marry black men if laws or society did not forbid it, Wells-Barnett supports her assertions by using evidence from "respected" white newspapers.

Wells-Barnett ultimately exposes the underlying political intentions of the cry of "rape" by noting its extreme effectiveness to instill panic and fear of the black man. Once lynching is established as an institutionalized practice, endorsed and encouraged by prominent southern leaders and the press they influenced, Wells-Barnett names those accomplices responsible for the perpetuation of such barbarism. In an effort for blacks to "secure their rights" and to become a strong economic force within the community, she seems convinced that it would take "a Winchester rifle . . . in every black home" (*Southern Horrors* 23) in order for potential lynchers to have more regard for the lives of black people.

Written for mass appeal, *A Red Record* presents both lynching statistics and the history of blacks and others since the Emancipation Proclamation. Again, as in *Southern Horrors*, Wells relies upon many of the incidents verified in the reputable *Chicago Tribune*. Her detailed analysis reveals that a number of men, including women and children, were lynched for petty crimes such as hog stealing, quarreling, "sassiness," and for no offense at all. She gives three main excuses used by whites to justify the lynching or killing of blacks. The often-cited reason was to repress "race riots," which lacks evidence or proof of injuries or fatalities due to any massacres or insurrections. To keep blacks from exercising their right to vote and become citizens, an actual dominant political force, was the second reason that organized mobs, the Ku Klux Klan, and Regulators killed blacks. A third argument, already used in *Southern Horrors*, was the cry of "rape," a strategy effectively designed to mobilize the black race.

Throughout her work, Wells-Barnett demonstrates that many of the men, women, and children who were lynched were not guilty of any crime. The symbolic significance of such an act and Wells-Barnett's conscious recognition of this fact led her on her "crusade" to rid the United States of its "atrocities."

CRITICAL RECEPTION

Critical assessments of Wells-Barnett's works have been limited mostly to scholarly articles in books. Speaking of *Southern Horrors* as a political and social commentary, Frances Smith Foster notes her "boldness" for writing about "impolite topics" not generally expected of female journalists and her use of "many literary strategies . . . to establish her authority and veracity" (180). She further observes that "Well's structure was factual and her testimony was certainly naked." Noting that she does not use the usual "sentimental diction" with which others had masked their critique of society, Foster as well examines how Wells-Barnett "presented . . . a strong and compelling series of quotations and examples taken from the public media" (181).

Scholars highly praise the importance of *A Red Record*. Joanne M. Braxton claims it is the "most substantial and best-known antilynching book" (120).

Another critic applauds it as "a "sophisticated analysis of lynching" (Carby 112) but claims Wells-Barnett's analysis "led her into direct confrontation with individuals which considered themselves progressive" (113). Even one of her contemporaries, Frederick Douglass, also affirms the significance of her work and states in a letter, "You have dealt with the fact, and cool, painstaking fidelity and left those naked and uncontradicted facts to speak for themselves." Overall, as "a notable work" (Shockley 215), critics, especially Frances Foster Smith, believe that Wells-Barnett's works have "literary and social significance" (182).

BIBLIOGRAPHY

Works by Ida B. Wells-Barnett

Southern Horrors: Lynch Law in All Its Phases. New York: New York Age Print, 1892.
The Reason Why The Colored American Is Not in the World's Columbian Exposition—the Afro-American's Contribution to Columbia Literature. Chicago: Author, 1893.
A Red Record: Tabulated Statistics and Alleged Causes of Lynchings in the United States, 1892–1893–1894. Chicago: Donohue and Henneberry, 1895.
Mob Rule in New Orleans: Robert Charles and His Fight to the Death. Chicago: Author, 1900.
The Arkansas Race Riot. Chicago: Author, 1922.
On Lynchings: Southern Horrors; A Red Record; Mob Rule in New Orleans. New York: Arno Press, 1969.

Essays

"Afro-Americans and Africa." *AME Zion Church Review* (July 1892): 40–45.
"Lynch Law in All Its Phases." *Our Day* (May 1893): 333–47.
"Lynch Law in America." *Arena* 23 (January 1900): 15–24.
"The White Man's Problem." *Arena* 23 (January 1900): 1–30.
"The Negro's Case in Equity." *Independent* (April 26, 1900): 1010–11.
"Lynching and the Excuse for It." *Independent* 53 (May 1901): 1133–36.
"Booker T. Washington and His Critics." *World Today* (April 1904): 518–21.
"Lynching: Our National Crime." *National Negro Conference Proceedings* (1909): 174–79.
"How Enfranchisement Stops Lynchings." *Original Rights Magazine* (June 1910): 42–53.
"Our Country's Lynching Record." *Survey* (February 1, 1913): 573–74.

Short Story

"Two Christmas Days: A Holiday Story." *AME Zion Quarterly* (January 1894): 129–40.

Studies of Ida B. Wells-Barnett

Adams, Russell L. "Ida B. Wells: Anti-Lynch Crusader." In *Great Negroes Past and Present*. 3d ed. Chicago: Afro-Am, 1991. 109.
Aptheker, Bettina, ed. *Lynching and Rape: An Exchange of Views*. Occasional Paper no. 25. San Jose, CA: American Institute for Marxist Studies, 1977.

Barker-Benfield, G. J., and Catherine Clinton, eds. *Portraits of American Women: From Settlement to the Present*. New York: St. Martin's Press, 1991.

Bontemps, Arna, and Jack Conroy. *Anyplace but Here*. New York: Hill and Wang, 1966.

Braxton, Joanne M. "Crusader for Justice: Ida B. Wells." In *Black Women Writing Autobiography: A Tradition within a Tradition*. Philadelphia: Temple University Press, 1989. 102–38.

Carby, Hazel V. "Black Feminist Thought after Emancipation." In *Reconstructing Womanhood: The Emergence of the Afro-American Woman Novelist*. New York: Oxford University Press, 1987. 108–16.

Church, Roberta, and Ronald Walter. *Nineteenth Century Memphis Families of Color, 1850–1900*. Memphis: Murdock, 1987.

Cutler, James E. *Lynch-Law: An Investigation into the History of Lynching in the United States*. New York: Longmans, Green, 1905.

Daniels, Sadie Iola. *Women Builders*. Rev. ed. Ed. Charles H. Wesley and Thelma D. Perry. Washington, DC: Associated, 1970.

Dannett, Sylvia G. L. *Profiles of Negro Womanhood*. Vol. 2: *20th Century*. Yonkers, NY: Educational Heritage, 1966.

Davis, Elizabeth Lindsay. *Lifting as They Climb*. Washington, DC: National Association of Colored Women, 1933.

————. *The Story of the Illinois Federation of Colored Women's Clubs, 1900–1922*. N.p., n.d.

Decosta-Willis, Miriam. "Ida B. Wells-Barnett." In *The Oxford Companion to African American Literature*. Ed. William L. Andrews, Frances Smith Foster, and Trudier Harris. New York: Oxford University Press 1997. 763–64.

————, ed. *The Memphis Diary of Ida B. Wells*. Boston: Beacon Press, 1995.

Detweiler, Frederick G. *The Negro Press in the United States*. Chicago: University of Chicago Press, 1922.

Douglass, Frederick. Letter to Ida B. Wells. October 25, 1892. Frederick Douglass Collection, Library of Congress, Washington, DC.

Duster, Alfreda M. Letter to Joanne M. Braxton. January 30, 1983.

————, ed. *Crusade for Justice: The Autobiography of Ida B. Wells*. Chicago: University of Chicago Press, 1970.

Flexner, Eleanor. "Ida B. Wells-Barnett." In *Notable Black American Women 1607–1950*. Vol. 3. Ed. Jessie Carney Smith. Cambridge: Harvard University Press, 1971. 1232–37.

Fortune, T. Thomas. "Ida B. Wells, A.M." In *Women of Distinction: Remarkable in the Works and Invincible in Character*. Ed. Lawson A. Scruggs. Raleigh, NC: Author, 1893.

Foster, Frances Smith. " 'A Woman Question and a Race Problem': The Black Woman's Era." In *Written by Herself: Literary Production by African American Women, 1746–1892*. Indianapolis: Indiana University Press, 1993. 180–83.

Franklin, V. P. "Ida B. Wells-Barnett: To Tell the Truth Freely." In *Living Our Stories, Telling Our Truths*. New York: Oxford University Press, 1995. 59–93.

Gibson, John W., and W. H. Crogman, eds. *Progress of a Race, or, The Remarkable Advancement of the Colored American*. Rev. ed. Miami, FL: Mnemosyne, 1969.

Giddings, Paula. *When and Where I Enter: The Impact of Black Women on Race and Sex in America*. New York: Morrow, 1984.

Harris, Trudier, ed. *Selected Works of Ida B. Wells-Barnett.* New York: Oxford University Press, 1991.

Hendricks, Wanda. "Wells-Barnett, Ida Bell." In *Black Women in America: An Historical Encyclopedia.* Vol. 2. Ed. Darlene Clark Hine. New York: Carlson, 1993. 1242–46.

Holt, Thomas C. "The Lonely Warrior: Ida B. Wells and the Struggle for Black Leadership." In *Black Leaders of the Twentieth Century.* Ed. John Hope Franklin and August Meier. Urbana: University of Illinois Press, 1982. 39–61.

Hughes, Langston. *Famous Negro Heroes of America.* New York: Dodd, Mead, 1958.

Hutchins, Fred L. *What Happened in Memphis.* Kingsport and Memphis, TN: Kingsport, 1965.

Lerner, Gerda. "Early Community Work of Black Club Women." *Journal of Negro History* 59 (April 1954): 158–67.

———, ed. *Black Women in White America: A Documentary History.* New York: Pantheon Books, 1972.

Loewenberg, Bert James, and Ruth Bogin. *Black Women in Nineteenth-Century American Life: Their Words, Their Thoughts, Their Feelings.* University Park: Pennsylvania State University Press, 1976.

Low, Augustus, and Virgil A. Clift. "Ida B. Wells." In *Encyclopedia of Black Americans.* New York: McGraw-Hill, 1981. 849–50.

Majors, Gerri, and Doris Saunders. *Black Society.* Chicago: Johnson, 1976.

Majors, Monroe Alphus. *Noted Negro Women, Their Triumphs and Activities.* Chicago: Donohue and Henneberry, 1893.

McMurry, Linda O. *To Keep the Waters Troubled: The Life of Ida B. Wells.* New York: Oxford University Press, 1998.

Meier, August. "Introduction." In *On Lynchings,* by Ida B. Wells Barnett. New York: Arno Press, 1969.

Mossell, N. F. *The Work of the Afro-American Woman.* New York: Oxford University Press, 1988.

Neverdon-Morton, Cynthia. *Afro-American Women of the South and the Advancement of Race, 1895–1925.* Knoxville: University of Tennessee Press, 1989.

Noble, Jeanne. *Beautiful, Also, Are the Souls of My Black Sisters: A History of the Black Woman in America.* Englewood Cliffs, NJ: Prentice-Hall, 1978.

Ottley, Roi. *The Lonely Warrior.* Chicago: Henry Regnery, 1955.

Pacyga, Dominic A., and Ellen Skerrett. *Chicago: City of Neighborhood Histories and Tours.* Chicago: Loyola University Press, 1986.

Penn, I. Garland. *The Afro-American Press and Its Editors.* 1891. Reprinted, New York: Arno Press, 1969.

Ploski, Harry A., and Roscoe C. Brown Jr., eds. *The Negro Almanac.* New York: Bellwether, 1967.

Salem, Dorothy. "Black Women and the NAACP, 1909–1922: An Encounter with Race, Class, and Gender." In *Black Women in America.* Ed. Kim M. Vaz. Thousand Oaks, CA: Sage, 1995. 55–57.

Scott, Anne Firor. *The Southern Lady: From Pedestal to Politics, 1830–1930.* Chicago: University of Chicago Press, 1970.

Shockley, Ann Allen. "Ida Bell Wells-Barnett." In *Afro-American Women Writers, 1746–1933: An Anthology and Critical Guide.* New York: New American Library, 1988. 248–53.

Spear, Allan H. *Black Chicago: The Making of a Negro Ghetto: 1890–1920.* Chicago: University of Chicago Press, 1967.

Sterling, Dorothy. *Black Foremothers: Three Lives.* Old Westbury, NY: Feminist Press, 1979.

Suggs, Henry L., ed. *The Black Press in the South, 1865–1929.* Westport, CT: Greenwood, 1983.

Thompson, Mildred. *Ida B. Wells-Barnett. An Exploratory Story of an American Black Woman, 1893–1930.* Vol. 15. In *Black Women in American History.* Ed. Darlene Clark-Hine. Brooklyn, NY: Carlson, 1990.

Truman, Margaret. *Women of Courage.* New York: William Morrow, 1976.

Tucker, David M. *Black Pastors and Leaders: The Memphis Clergy, 1819–1972.* Memphis: Memphis State University Press, 1975.

———. "Miss Ida B. Wells and Memphis Lynching." *Phylon* 32.2 (Summer 1971): 112–22.

Wilson, Charles R., and William Ferris. *Encyclopedia of Southern Culture.* Chapel Hill: University of North Carolina Press, 1989.

Wood, Norman B. *The White Side of a Black Subject.* Chicago: American, 1897.

PHILLIS WHEATLEY
(1754–1784)

Mona M. Choucair

BIOGRAPHY

Born in Africa in 1754 to parents whose names have never been revealed, Phillis Wheatley was captured and sold into slavery around the age of seven. John Wheatley, a well-known and respected Boston tailor, bought Phillis as a servant for his wife, Susannah, in 1761. Although her journey to America utimately proved philanthropic and noteworthy, Wheatley must have undergone extreme conditions before her arrival in America. However, despite such odds, she emerged as a self-taught reader and poet of the English language. One biographer notes that

it is probable that but few of the white children of Boston were brought up under circumstances better calculated for the full development of their natural abilities. Her ambition was stimulated; she became acquainted with grammar, history, ancient and modern geography, and astronomy, and studied Latin so as to read Horace with such ease and enjoyment. . . . A general interest was felt in the . . . prodigy; the best libraries were open to her: and she had opportunities for conversation with the most accomplished and distinguished persons in the city. (Mason xii)

Such opportunities allowed Phillis to succeed. She became an avid reader of the Bible and classical texts, especially the works of Virgil and Ovid. While many readers and critics alike may question the likelihood of a young slave girl mastering such classical works, it must be noted that Phillis was exposed to a very refined group of friends by her mistress, Mrs. Susannah Wheatley. Likewise, Mary, the Wheatleys' daughter, also helped Phillis emerge into an intelligent, self-confident child. The latter's private time included prayer, meditation, and reading. Although she was allowed special privileges and luxuries due to her respected position in the Wheatley household, Phillis maintained friendships with other slaves as well. Numerous letters prove such lifelong kinship. Drawing on the knowledge of her own readings and subsequent discussions of literature and politics with prominent citizens, Phillis Wheatley, at thirteen years of age, began to write her own poetry. Her first poem, "On Being Brought from Africa to America," written in 1770, exhibited great ability. As the young girl's talents were fully realized, her duties in the Wheatley household were lessened, and despite problems with her health and memory, Phillis Wheatley's writing career began to flourish.

Several incidents were significant in Phillis Wheatley's life after 1770. Specifically, in 1771 Mary Wheatley, by that time a very close friend and confidant to Phillis, married Rev. John Lathrop. Soon thereafter, Phillis' health began to fail considerably, and upon doctors' recommendations, she made plans to go to England. Meanwhile, she also became a "baptized communicant" of the Old South Meeting House in Boston, a notable exception to rules that had previously excluded slaves (Mason xiv). Yet perhaps the most important day for Phillis Wheatley was October 18, 1773—the day she received her freedom from slavery (Robinson, *Critical Essays* 5). As planned previously, in 1773 (by most sources—some date the trip several years later—see Robinson's *Critical Essays*), Phillis visited London and met many influential members of English society through the courtesy of the countess of Huntingdon. However, Phillis' excitement in London was cut short in 1773 as she received word that Mrs. Wheatley, her devoted mistress, was growing very ill. Phillis quickly returned to Boston to be with her—just as she was gaining recognition as an author in London. Susannah Wheatley died in March 1774, and most sources have noted that after this loss, Phillis was no longer a permanent resident at the Wheatley home; indeed, after John Wheatley's death in 1778, Phillis permanently left the residence. Biographers have thus marked Phillis' return from England as a downward trend in her life. Her marriage to John Peters brought no respite. The couple had three children; two died within a year's span, 1783–1784. When her husband was imprisoned (around 1784 and probably for his social and political ideas), Phillis and her remaining child lived in squalor. She took odd jobs in order to support herself and her child. On December 5, 1784, Phillis Wheatley Peters died. Sadly, her child died soon enough thereafter, to be buried in the same grave.

MAJOR WORKS AND THEMES

As mentioned earlier, Phillis Wheatley published her first poem in 1770, at a time when "only two other American Negroes had published anything" (Mason xviii). However, her real debut came in 1773, when it was said by biographer Julian Mason and others that "she was the first American Negro writer of any significance, and that her book of poems in 1773, entitled *Poems on Various Subjects, Religious and Moral*, was probably the first book—and was certainly the first book of poetry—published by an American Negro author (xviii–xix).

Although the works of Phillis Wheatley cover a wide variety of themes, the one for which she is most criticized and praised is subversion. Through her eloquent and witty word choice, Wheatley manages to protest against slavery. Perhaps literary critic John Shields in his essay entitled, "Phillis Wheatley's Subversive Pastoral" reveals one of the most intriguing approaches to her use of masking. He notes that foremost in her works, the persona "emerges as the subtle product of an author who wishes to, or who must, adopt a mask to make her or his critique of societal ills known in print, motivated by an intense desire to alter unacceptable or inappropriate behavior" (632). Speaking mainly of her poem "To Maecenas," Shields explains that the published volume of Wheatley's poetry was accompanied by a most unusual statement of Preface, written by the publisher, signaling the creation of a mask for the author: "The following Poems were written originally for the Amusement of the Author, as they were the Products of her leisure Moments. She had no Intention ever to have published them." Shields thus contends that although the London printer, Archibald Bell, makes such aforementioned claims concerning Wheatley's intentions in the Preface to her works, American readers surely would have remembered that the young black author indeed had sought publication at various intervals in Boston previously (634–35). Shields also mentions that the very frontispiece included in the volume portrays a rebelliousness in the young author: "Wheatley sits non-humbly and aggressively before a writing desk, on which one sees paper with writing on it, holding a pen and striking a contemplative pose, obviously promising still more writing to come" (634). Such a portrait stands in contrast to the apologetic tone of the poem "To Maecenas."

Later in the same poem, Wheatley ponders the question of African authorship. Realizing that no African authors other than Terence exist, Wheatley decries the status quo and exhorts her own abilities simultaneously with one ingenious stroke of the pen. Likewise, when she continues the poem's lines with "I'll snatch a laurel from thine honour'd head," she also exalts freedom. She implies that she will snatch her place in the world of art and that she will take it quickly and surreptitiously perhaps. Shields adds, "[S]he, the good black poet and a slave, finds herself so impoverished and dependent that she is forced either to be silent—which will not do for this aggressive voice . . . or to 'snatch' her place as a poetic voice" (637). Wheatley did not choose silence.

James Levernier, in his article on the same poem, reiterates the theme of subversion through the use of punning and masking in Wheatley's works: "Wheatley used her considerable linguistic talent to embed in the poem, at a very sophisticated level, a far different message than that which the poem superficially conveys" (25). The use of irony in the young poet's works proves noteworthy, especially in the last line: "Remember *Christians, Negroes, and Cain.*" Wheatley creatively "links the three terms rhetorically, thereby creating a level of ambiguity in line with the deeper message of the poem" (26).

Moreover, Phillis Wheatley explores religious themes in many of her poems. As Henri Gregoire notes, "Almost all her poetical productions have a religious or moral cast—all breathe a soft and sentimental melancholy" (qtd. in Robinson *Phillis Wheatley and Her Writings* 48). William J. Snelling agrees: "Her mind seems to have been peculiarly susceptible of religious impressions, as indeed, we have observed most of her race are, when anyone takes the pains to teach them" (qtd. in Robinson *Phillis Wheatley and Her Writings* 63). In his essay entitled, "Subjection and Prophecy in Phillis Wheatley's Verse," William J. Scheick advocates that in her poems on religion, Wheatley achieves a sense of freedom for herself and other slaves as well. Scheick proves this point by carefully investigating the young poet's use of ambiguities. He proposes that "from the pulpit, as well as from her reading and her discussions with others, Wheatley became familiar with select standard eighteenth-century Protestant commentaries on Scripture and, as well, with approved secular applications of biblical passages" (123). Such ambiguity can be found in her paraphrases of Scripture, such as the highly criticized poem "Goliath and Garth." Many literary critics surmise that Wheatley identifies with the character of David on many levels. Scheick, for example, notes that skin color and humble beginnings initially link the author and David (124). He concludes, "Wheatley manages her biblically-influenced art as a verbal double-edged sword. She prophetically reminds her readers that the tongue of God's enemies . . . will fatally 'fall upon themselves' " (129).

CRITICAL RECEPTION

Foremost in the scholarship of Phillis Wheatley, William H. Robinson presents the most reliable, thorough source of information on the author's personal history and scholarship. Also contributing to the scholarship on Wheatley are many literary critics, divided into two camps—those who find her work imitative and simple and those who find her work innovative and quite remarkable for a young African American woman in the 1800s.

Helen Burke, in an insightful essay entitled "The Rhetoric and Politics of Marginality: The Subject of Phillis Wheatley," reminds readers that although Wheatley was able to make her voice heard, she still remained a "culturally displaced person," someone who had to "reconstruct her symbolic identity" (33). Burke reiterates the deprivation of the slave girl who had "no other covering than a quantity of dirty carpet about her like a fillibeg," a marginal character who must earn acceptance and privilege (33). Wheatley achieved an identity and adopted a successful Muse, Burke notes, but "[w]hat Phillis Wheatley could not address was the difference that her ethnic background, sex, and class made in her ability to express herself freely, a difference that, if elaborated, would have exposed the inequity of the power relations in which she operated" (38). In her conclusion, Burke claims that such a "gap between the ideology . . . and historical reality" exists even today (41).

Similarly, Sondra O'Neale in her essay "A Slave's Subtle War: Phillis Wheatley's Use of Biblical Myth and Symbol" advocates that "any evaluation of Phillis

Wheatley must consider her status as a slave" (144). Employing a technique that retrospectively applauds the works of slaves who desired to express the truth to the outside world, O'Neale explains that slaves would first have "to acquire the requisite language skills, usually surreptitiously" (144). She convincingly shows that "[b]ecause critics have failed to consider her status as a slave . . . Wheatley has been undervalued as a poet and as an abolitionist" (145). "On Being Brought from Africa to America" provides the focal poem of the analysis. Wheatley's word choice as well as masking combine to "wage a subtle war against slavery" (157).

In perhaps one of the most ingenious essays written on Wheatley, entitled "The Difficult Miracle of Black Poetry in America or Something like a Sonnet for Phillis Wheatley," June Jordan poignantly portrays the realities of Wheatley's life from the slave auction onward. Rhythmically repeating phrases, almost in a chantlike manner, Jordan creates a vivid account of Wheatley's difficult life: "It was not natural. And she was the first. Come from a country of many tongues tortured by rupture, theft, by travel like mismatched clothing packed down into the cargo hold of evil ships sailing, irreversibly, into slavery; . . . to be docile and dumb" (252). The narrative as mantra illustrates the "Phillis Miracle. Phillis Miracle Wheatley: The first Black human being to be published in America. She was the second female to be published in America. And the miracle begins in Africa" (254). Jordan attests to Wheatley's "intrinsic ardor," considering what it must have taken for the "young African to undertake such a persona, such values, and mythologies a million million miles remote from her own ancestry, and her own darkly formulating race!" (257).

BIBLIOGRAPHY

Works by Phillis Wheatley

Poems on Various Subjects, Religious and Moral. London: A. Bell, 1773.
The Collected Works of Phillis Wheatley. Ed. John C. Shields. New York: Oxford University Press, 1988.

Studies of Phillis Wheatley

Burke, Helen M. "The Rhetoric and Politics of Marginality: The Subject of Phillis Wheatley." Tulsa Studies in Women's Literature 9–10 (1990–1991): 31–42.
Daly, Robert. "Powers of Humility and the Presence of Readers in Anne Bradstreet and Phillis Wheatley." Studies in Puritan-American Spirituality (1993): 1–24.
Erkkila, Betsy. "Revolutionary Women." Tulsa Studies in Women's Literature 6 (1987): 189–223.
Flanzbam, Hilene. "Unprecedented Liberties: Re-Reading Phillis Wheatley." The Journal for the Society for the Study of the Multi-Ethnic Literature of the United States 18 (1993): 71–81.

Gates, Henry Louis, Jr. *Figures in Black: Words, Signs, and the Racial Self.* New York: Oxford University Press, 1987.

———. *Reading Black, Reading Feminist.* New York: Penguin, 1990.

Hayden, Lucy K. "Classical Tidings from the Afric Muse: Phillis Wheatley's Use of Greek and Roman Mythology." *College Language Association Journal* 35 (1992): 432–47.

Isani, Mukhtar Ali. "The Methodist Connection: New Variants of Some Phillis Wheatley Poems." *Early American Literature* 21–22 (Spring 1986–1987): 108–13.

Jordan, June. "The Difficult Miracle of Black Poetry in America or Something like a Sonnet for Phillis Wheatley." *Massachusetts Review* 27 (1986): 252–63.

Kendrick, Robert. "Remembering America: Phillis Wheatley's Intertextual Epic." *African-American Review* 30 (1996): 71–88.

Levernier, James A. "Wheatley's On Being Brought from Africa to America." *Explicator* 40 (1982): 25–27.

Mason, Julian D. ed. *Poems.* Chapel Hill: University of North Carolina Press, 1966.

McKay, Michele, and William Scheick. "The Other Song in Phillis Wheatley's 'On Imagination.' " *Studies in the Literary Imagination* 27 (1994): 71–84.

Nott, Walt. "From 'Uncultivated Barbarian' to 'Poetical Genius': The Public Presence of Phillis Wheatley." *MELUS* 18 (1993): 21–32.

O'Neale, Sondra. "A Slave's Subtle War: Phillis Wheatley's Use of Biblical Myth and Symbol." *Early American Literature* 21–22 (Spring 1986–1987): 144–57.

Richards, Phillip M. "Phillis Wheatley, Americanization, the Sublime, and the Romance of America." *Style* (1993): 194–221.

Robinson, William H. *Critical Essays on Phillis Wheatley.* Boston: G. K. Hall, 1982.

———. *Phillis Wheatley and Her Writings.* New York: Garland, 1984.

———. *Phillis Wheatley in the Black American Beginnings.* Detroit: Broadside Press, 1975.

Rogal, Samuel J. "Phillis Wheatley's Methodist Connection." *Black American Literature Forum* 21 (1987): 1–2.

Scheick, William J. "Subjection and Prophecy in Phillis Wheatley's Verse Paraphrases of Scripture." *College Literature* 22 (1995): 122–30.

Scruggs, Charles. "Phillis Wheatley and the Poetical Legacy of Eighteenth-Century England." *Studies in Eighteenth Century Culture* 10 (1981): 279–95.

Shields, John C. "Phillis Wheatley's Subversive Pastoral." *Eighteenth Century Studies* 27 (Fall 1993–Summer 1994): 631–47.

Silvers, Anita. "Pure Historicism and the Heritage of Hero(in)es: Who Grows in Phillis Wheatley's Garden?" *Journal of Aesthetics and Art Criticism* 51 (1993): 475–82.

Steele, Thomas J. "The Figure of Columbia: Phillis Wheatley Plus George Washington." *The New England Quarterly* 54 (1981): 264–66.

Watson, Marsha. "A Classic Case: Phillis Wheatley and Her Poetry." *Early American Literature* 31 (1996): 103–32.

Willard, Carla. "Wheatley's Turns of Praise: Heroic Entrapment and the Paradox of Revolution." *American Literature: A Journal of Literary History, Criticism, and Bibliography* 67 (1995): 233–56.

WALTER WHITE
(1893–1955)

Emmanuel S. Nelson

BIOGRAPHY

Walter White is one of the minor literary figures of the Harlem Renaissance. Better known for his civil rights activism than for his literary achievement, White was born on July 1, 1893, in Atlanta, Georgia. His father, George White, was a mail carrier; his mother, Madeline White, was a schoolteacher. His childhood seems to have been generally pleasant and largely uneventful. However, he does recall with bitter clarity in his autobiography, *A Man Called White*, an incident that took place in 1906. During a race riot, the White family's house, which was adjacent to a white neighborhood, was nearly torched by a mob of white thugs. He recalls how he and his father were ready to shoot at the mob in self-defense. The mob retreated when shots were fired by one of the black neighbors. This nearly fatal encounter with racially motivated violence left a lasting impression on Walter White.

Ironically, however, White had blue eyes, blond hair, and pale complexion; often he was mistaken for a white person. When he was among whites who were unaware of his background, his physical appearance earned him easy acceptance. Later on during his years as a tireless civil rights activist, he often passed as a white man in the South to investigate lynchings of blacks.

After graduating from Atlanta University in 1916, White worked briefly for an insurance company before moving to New York City, where he became an assistant secretary at the headquarters of the National Association for the Advancement of Colored People (NAACP). He became its executive secretary in 1931 and guided that major civil rights organization for almost a quarter century.

White married Leah Gladys Powell, a coworker, in 1922. Twenty-six years later he divorced her and married Poppy Cannon, a white woman. Walter White died on March 21, 1955.

MAJOR WORKS AND THEMES

Considerably more significant than White's two novels are his nonfiction works. In *The American Negro and His Problems*, published in 1927, White offers a remarkably perceptive assessment of American race relations. A widely read man, he draws insights from a variety of disciplines—history, anthropology, sociology, and psychology—to present an engaging analysis of the black American predicament. Of particular interest to White throughout his life was the subject of racial violence. In 1943 he coauthored with Thurgood Marshall *What Caused the Detroit Riot?*—a work that examines the roots of racial violence in general. In *A Man Called White: The Autobiography of Walter White*, published in 1948, White offers not only a narrative of his personal life but also an insider's view of the NAACP during its formative years and its gradual consolidation of substantial political power. But perhaps the work that remains his most valuable contribution to American cultural studies is *Rope and Faggot: A Biography of Judge Lynch*. Published in 1929, it was the first major attempt to study a most hideous aspect of the culture of the white South: lynching. White was in a unique position to comment on this cultural practice. As an investigator for the NAACP, he was a black man who could pose as a white, gain the confidence of the white lynch mobs as well as their supporters, and thus observe firsthand their minds and their motives. But what White offers in his book is more than the grim details of individual lynchings; he locates the practice of lynching in its wider cultural contexts and examines its causes. Deeply implicated in lynching, according to White, is a cluster of factors: sexual mythologies, economic anxieties, religious beliefs, and psychological compulsions.

Lynching is also the subject of White's first novel, *The Fire in the Flint*. The protagonist, Kenneth Harper, is a young African American physician. Originally from the South but educated up north, he returns to his hometown in rural Georgia to practice medicine. His presence provokes white hostility. Undaunted, Harper begins to call for social change; with the help of a local black minister, he encourages blacks to organize and assert themselves. When he is away in Atlanta on a short visit, his house is ransacked by a mob of white men, and his sister is gang-raped. Harper's brother kills two of the men and, to avoid capture and lynching, commits suicide. When Harper returns home, he receives a call from a white woman who asks him to treat her ailing daughter. While on his way to her house, he is shot and killed by some Klansmen. The next day the local newspaper reports that D. Harper, "a Negro, was lynched here tonight, charged with attempted criminal assault on a white woman. . . . He is said to have confessed before being put to death by a mob which numbered five thousand. He was burned at the stake" (300).

Though the basic plot is compelling, White does not fully exploit its novelistic possibilities. He appears more interested in establishing his thesis rather than in exploring the complexities of the issues he has introduced into the narrative. At times the novel reads more like an overt piece of propaganda than like a polished work of art. Yet the sensational plot was sufficiently provocative to generate interest; the novel sold several thousand copies and was translated into a number of languages.

White's second novel, *Flight*, was less successful than the first—both critically and commercially. Here he deals with a theme that was especially popular during the 1920s and 1930s in African American fiction: the theme of racial passing. It is the story of Mimi Daquin, a young, fair-complexioned, black southerner who moves to New York City after a failed romance. In New York she passes for white in order to enhance her social and economic opportunities. She even marries a white banker, who assumes she is white. Incrementally, however, Mimi realizes the emptiness of her duplicitous life. She begins to long for freedom and spontaneity. She secretly visits Harlem cabarets for the music, dance, and a sense of community. Her transformation occurs when she listens to an African American blues singer at Carnegie Hall: the music awakens her repressed racial memories and frees her from her assumed white identity.

Flight, like *The Fire in the Flint*, has a sufficiently interesting plot. But what White continues to lack is the artistic ability to turn that plot into a compelling narrative. The characters lack psychological depth; the didactic tone is too apparent; and White's prose style is at times awkward. It appears that White had some powerful ideas that he wanted to articulate through his fiction; however, he was not adept at the craft of fiction to achieve his objective fully. White himself might have agreed with such a conclusion because, as Walter Daniel points out, White "never considered himself a professional writer" (305–6).

CRITICAL RECEPTION

White's prominent affiliation with the NAACP granted considerable publicity to his two novels. In fact, White himself was actively involved in promoting his works and sought blurbs for the book covers from his well-established contemporaries, such as H. L. Mencken, Sinclair Lewis, Carl Van Vechten, and Eugene O'Neill. He even used NAACP's extensive administrative network across the nation to encourage black Americans to buy his novels.

The Fire in the Flint, given its sensational plot, elicited several formal reviews and informal responses. Sinclair Lewis, while pointing out some flaws, declared that "he rejoice[d] immensely in the book" (qtd. in Waldron 63). Carl Van Vechten, in a generous blurb for the novel, noted that its "plot is most ingeniously articulated, its characters well-drawn" (qtd. in Waldron 64). H. L. Mencken, the iconoclastic American commentator, liked the novel for its antiracist politics. When some reviewers complained that all the white characters in the novel are presented as irredeemably evil, Mencken wrote an encouraging note to the author. Mencken, with exquisite accuracy, told White: "The Southern crackers, if anything, are worse than you make them" (qtd. in Waldron 58). Others did not respond so sympathetically. Some reviewers emphasized the novel's formal weaknesses; some even questioned White's command of the English language. Predictably, the reviews in the South were mostly hostile.

White attempted to promote his second novel just as vigorously as he had tried to push the sales of his first work. One of his tactics ended in an amusing controversy. When Frank Horne gave *Flight* a negative review in *Opportunity*—the official publication of the Urban League—White, using his clout as a top official of the NAACP, convinced the editor of the journal to solicit a rebuttal to Horne's review from Nella Larsen. Larsen, one of White's close friends at the time, agreed; she published in *Opportunity* a strident response to Horne. She attacked Horne and not very convincingly defended the merits of White's novel. Shortly thereafter Horne responded to Larsen with a letter to the editor. He accused Larsen of being an "illogical" woman and concluded that *Flight* was not a "jolly good book," as she insisted (qtd. in Waldron 105–6). In response to Horne, White himself wrote a letter to *Opportunity*. It appeared in the December 1926 issue of the journal. Here he defended his novel, praised Larsen's good taste, and launched a scathing personal attack on Horne (Waldron 100–107).

Even the entertainment provided by this epistolary exchange failed to interest many potential book buyers: *Flight* sold considerably fewer copies than *The Fire in the Flint*. The reviews were mixed. Even those who recognized the value of some of the ideas that White attempted to thematize felt compelled to point out the obvious flaws in structure, characterization, and style.

Edward E. Waldron's book-length study of White's life and work remains the most valuable scholarly work published on White so far. In recent years, Walter White's novels have received little attention. According to the Modern Language Association (MLA) bibliography, not a single scholarly article has been published on White's fiction since 1983.

BIBLIOGRAPHY

Works by Walter White

The Fire in the Flint. New York: Knopf, 1924.
Flight. New York: Knopf, 1926.
The American Negro and His Problems. Girard, KS: Haldeman-Julius, 1927.
Rope and Faggot: A Biography of Judge Lynch. New York: Knopf, 1929.
(With Thurgood Marshall). *What Caused the Detroit Riot?* New York: NAACP, 1943.
A Rising Wind: A Report on the Negro Soldier in the European Theater of War. Garden City, NY: Doubleday, 1945.
A Man Called White: The Autobiography of Walter White. New York: Viking, 1948.
How Far the Promised Land? New York: Viking, 1955.

Studies of Walter White

Bercovici, Konrad. "Almost Black and White." Rev. of *The Fire in the Flint*. *Nation* 119 (October 8, 1924): 384, 386.

Cooney, Charles. "Walter White and the Harlem Renaissance." *Journal of Negro History* 57 (July 1972): 231–40.

Daniel, Walter. "Walter Francis White." *Dictionary of Literary Biography*. Vol. 51. Ed. Trudier Harris and Thadious Davis. Detroit: Gale Research, 1987. 301–7.

Gruening, Ernest. "Going White." Rev. of *Flight*. *Saturday Review of Books* 2 (July 10, 1926): 918.

Horne, Frank. Rev. of *Flight*. *Opportunity* (July 1926): 227.

Larsen, Nella. "Correspondence." Opportunity (Sept. 1926): 295.

Rev. of *Flight*. *The Times Literary Supplement* (December 9, 1926): 908.

Scruggs, Charles W. "Alain Locke and Walter White: Their Struggle for Control of the Harlem Renaissance." *Black American Literature Forum* 14 (Fall 1980): 91–99.

Waldron, Edward E. *Walter White and the Harlem Renaissance*. Port Washington, NY: Kennikat Press, 1978.

JAMES MONROE WHITFIELD
(1822–1871)

James L. Hill

BIOGRAPHY

Never able to realize his potential as the leading African American abolitionist poet, James Monroe Whitfield remained a practicing barber most of his life. Whitfield, born April 10, 1822, in Exeter, New Hampshire, to free blacks, attended the neighborhood schools of Exeter, but little else is known about his youth. While still a young man, after a short stay in Boston, he eventually settled in Buffalo, New York, and married a local black woman with whom he had two sons and a daughter. A skilled barber, Whitfield opened a barbershop at 30 East Seneca Street in 1858, and his customers included many of Buffalo's prominent African American citizens and visitors, including Frederick Douglass.* The first black barber-poet in America, Whitfield began writing abolitionist poems before the 1850s; and Buffalo, one of the main centers of the abolitionist movement, provided a convenient platform for his abolitionist fervor. From 1849 to 1852, frequently voicing his racial pride and abhorrence of slavery, Whitfield contributed poems and letters to such publications as the *Liberator*, *North Star* and *Frederick Douglass' Paper*.

In 1853 Whitfield published *America and Other Poems*, his best-known work, and dedicated it to his friend Martin R. Delany, a leading advocate of colonization who for a time was coeditor of *Frederick Douglass' Paper*. Subsequently, he affiliated with the American Colonization Society and in 1854 joined Delany and Rev. James T. Holley as advocates and organizers for the black emigration movement. That same year, he supported the call for a National Emigration Convention for Colored Men, organized by Delany, and attended the convention in Cleveland, Ohio. An appeal to African Americans to support plans for colonizing free blacks in Central and South America and the West Indies, the convention sparked staunch opposition from many black leaders; and following the convention, which produced no tangible results, Whitfield and Frederick Douglass engaged in a lively newspaper debate about the merits of colonization. To further advance his position, Whitfield founded a short-lived quarterly periodical, the *African American Repository*. Although the first issue of the magazine was scheduled for publication in 1858, there is no evidence that the periodical was ever launched.

While all of Whitfield's activities between 1859 and 1861 are not known, there is evidence that he traveled abroad on a fact-finding tour of Central America, searching for emigration sites for free blacks. In 1861 he migrated to California, where he spent most of the remainder of his life. Since the Civil War was already in full force, colonization became an increasingly moot issue, and after 1862 there is no record of Whitfield's speaking publicly about it. Whitfield, however, did not withdraw from public affairs, for he continued his antislavery crusade, publishing letters and poems in the *San Francisco Elevator* and *Pacific Appeal*. Additionally, from 1864 to 1869, he served as the grand master of the California Prince Hall Masonic Lodge. Whitfield lived and worked as a barber variously in Portland, Oregon, and several cities in Idaho from 1863 to 1865; but in 1865 he returned to San Francisco and opened a barbershop at 916 Kearny Street. Later, in 1867, he moved to Elko, Nevada, where he became active in the literary and political activities of the Republican Club and was among the first group of blacks seated on a jury in Nevada. In 1870 he returned to San Francisco, where, at age forty-nine on April 23, 1871, he died and was buried in the Masonic Cemetery.

MAJOR WORKS AND THEMES

Though Whitfield has always been credited with the publication of his first volume of poetry, *Poems*, in 1846, the volume is not extant, and Joan R. Sherman indicates in *Invisible Poets: Afro-Americans of the Nineteenth Century* that the original attribution of this volume to Whitfield in George W. Williams' *History of the Negro Race* (1885) may even have been in error. Nonetheless, no record of the volume was found. Whitfield's reputation and legacy as a poet rest, however, on *America and Other Poems* and his later writings. A collection of twenty-three poems, *America* places Whitfield squarely in the protest tradition of African American poetry and establishes him as the leading nineteenth-century abolitionist poet. Two of the longest and most controversial poems in the volume, "America" and "How Long?," typify the militant abolitionist protest and invective tone Whitfield sustains throughout the volume. The title poem, "America," opens with a parody of the nationalistic hymn by the same name, which was familiar to all of Whitfield's contemporaries. Written in strong iambic tetrameter but strikingly similar to David Walker's* *Appeal* in its incendiary tone, import, and literary strategy, "America" demonstrates Whitfield's poetic skill and intellectual abilities, for the poem is a penetrating analysis of American hypocrisy and skillful dissection of the flaws of American democracy. With sardonic irony,

Whitfield recounts the democratic ideals that led to the Revolutionary War and juxtaposes these ideals to the nation's enslavement of blacks, who also participated in the war. "America" is also a frontal assault on slavery, illustrating the incongruities between slavery and American ideals; and like the *Narrative of the Life of Frederick Douglass*, it denounces the hypocrisy of American religion as practiced. The poem ends with a twenty-seven-line prayer that appeals to God to avenge enslaved blacks and to America to resolve the glaring discrepancies between slavery and its ideals. Whitfield's "How Long?" poses the cosmic question most common to antislavery prose and poetry. The poem asks why, despite their cries for deliverance, blacks still remain enslaved, while the so-called Christians of America sanction anything that brings them "wealth and rank and power." These two long, poetic jeremiads decry American hypocrisy and slavery and conclude with militant calls for justice and freedom, not unlike the works of other abolitionists of the 1850s. Other notable antislavery poems in the volume include "Lines on the Death of John Quincy Adams," "Ode for the Fourth of July," "To Cinque," "Prayer of the Oppressed," and "Stanzas for the First of August."

America also includes conventional hymns for Christmas, New Year's, and church dedications, several love poems, and a series of Romantic poems, the latter of which have influenced some critics to characterize Whitfield as a cynical and pessimistic poet imitative of Romantic poets, Byron in particular. In *Early Black American Poets*, however, William H. Robinson warns against over-emphasizing the poet's Romantic tendencies, pointing out correctly that Whitfield's anger and racial pride are genuine; but Whitfield, like his contemporaries, was not unaffected by the burgeoning Romanticism of mid-nineteenth-century America. Though a self-educated man, he was apparently familiar with some Romantic writers, for other than the obvious antislavery poems, the most compelling poems in *America* are the ones similar to Romantic poetry in form, themes, and philosophy, including "Self-Reliance," "Delusive Hope," "Ode for Music," "Yes, Strike Again That Sounding String," and "The Misanthropist." "Self-Reliance," for example, calls for reliance on God and the laws of nature, while "Delusive Hope" describes how life's miseries and hypocrisies conspire to diminish one's faith. The best of this group, "The Misanthropist" prefigures the double-consciousness W.E.B. Du Bois* describes in *The Souls of Black Folk*, and, like Countee Cullen's* "Yet Do I Marvel," the poem is a unique portrait of the estrangement and intellectual and cultural dissonance the African American poet experiences in America.

America clearly demonstrates Whitfield's talent as a poet and secures his place as perhaps the most technically skilled of the black abolitionist poets. As an orator-poet, imbued with genuine anger and antislavery fervency, he wrote his poems to be read aloud, and his poetry reflects his ability to control meter and rhyme, his broad use of classical imagery and allusions, and his sense of history. After 1854 Whitfield never published another collection and actually wrote fewer poems, although the majority of his writings have never been collected. He remained, however, a strong advocate for the antislavery cause and racial justice, sentiments that he was still expressing in his last two poems. In 1867, fourteen years after *America*, he read "Poem" at Platt's Hall in San Francisco to commemorate the celebration of the fourth anniversary of the Emancipation Proclamation, and in 1867 he read "Poem by J. M. Whitfield" in Virginia City, Nevada. The former is a 200-year survey of American history, including slavery, while the latter is a paean to law, order, racial justice, and liberty.

CRITICAL RECEPTION

Harbinger of a new poetic voice and talent, the publication of *America* brought accolades from the likes of M. R. Delaney,* William Wells Brown,* and Douglass who, in 1850 in the *Anti-Slavery Bugle*, wrote that the barber-poet "was intended by nature for a higher position in life" (1). So well received was the volume that Whitfield virtually ceased barbering, intending to devote himself to speaking and writing for the abolitionist cause. *America* did not, however, provide enough financial return to allow Whitfield to devote himself full-time to writing, obviously disappointing his contemporaries who had expected much more from him. Unfortunately for Whitfield, "the malignant arrangements of society" chained him to the barbershop (Douglass 1). Subsequently, his interests shifted increasingly from poetry to emigration. Like many of the early African American writers, Whitfield was not a prolific writer and has received scant critical attention until recently. Other than brief biographical accounts published in reference books, the two most valuable analyses of Whitfield's writings have been completed by Doris Lucas Laryea and Joan R. Sherman.

In an entry in the *Dictionary of Literary Biography* in 1986, Laryea provides a positive analysis of Whitfield's life and writings, concluding that he was "one of the most talented and forceful black poets of the nineteenth century" (260). Additionally, she delineates the antislavery and racial themes of the major poems in *America*. Sherman attempts the most extensive analysis of Whitfield's poetry to date in her *Invisible Poets*, demonstrating the interrelations between his antislavery and emigration activities and his writings. Contrary to some critics of Whitfield's poems, however, Sherman does not appear to believe that his anger is genuine, suggesting that the bitter tone of his poetry is attributable more to his failure to become a man of letters than his commitment to the antislavery cause and racial justice. Though she acknowledges his forceful combining of anger, pathos, and artistry, she concludes that his "poetry of protest and despair, like his own unfulfilled aspirations, remains a vivid testament to the alienation of the Afro-American in the nineteenth century" (52). While limited, most studies of Whitfield have typically concluded that he is a significant, though minor, antislavery poet. There has been, however, little or no commentary on several aspects of Whitfield's writings, including the diversity of themes and metrical patterns in his poetry, the Romantic tenets of major poems, the propaganda of his poems and uncollected prose, or his legacy as the nineteenth-century African American poet as culture hero. These alone indicate that his work needs more critical attention.

BIBLIOGRAPHY

Works by James Monroe Whitfield

America and Other Poems. Buffalo, NY: James S. Leavitt, 1853.
Emancipation Oration, by Dr. Ezra R. Johnson and Poems, by James M. Whitfield. San Francisco: Elevator Office, 1867.

Studies of James Monroe Whitfield

Brawley, Benjamin. *Negro Genius.* New York: Dodd, Mead, 1937.
Jackson, Blyden. *A History of Afro-American Literature.* Vol. 1. Baton Rouge: Louisiana State University, 1989.
Laryea, Doris Lucas. "James Monroe Whitfield." In *Dictionary of Literary Biography.* Vol. 50. Ed. Trudier Harris. Detroit: Gale Research, 1986. 260–63.
Loggins, Vernon. *The Negro Author: His Development in America to 1900.* New York: Kennikat Press, 1959.
Redmond, Eugene. *Drumvoices: The Mission of Afro-American Poetry, a Critical History.* Garden City, NY: Doubleday/Anchor Press, 1976.
Robinson, William H. *Black American Poets.* Dubuque, IA: W. C. Brown, 1996.
Sherman, Joan R. *Invisible Poets: Afro-Americans of the Nineteenth Century.* 2d ed. Urbana: University of Illinois Press, 1974.
———. "James Monroe Whitfield." In *Dictionary of American Negro Biography.* Ed. Rayford Logan. New York: W. W Norton, 1982. 650.
———. "James Monroe Whitfield." In *The Oxford Companion to African American Literature.* Ed. William L. Andrews, et al. New York: Oxford University Press, 1997. 773–74.
———. "James Monroe Whitfield, Poet and Emigrationist: A Voice of Protest and Despair." *Journal of Negro History* 57 (1972): 169–76.
Wagner, Jean. *Negro Poets in the United States.* Trans. Kenneth Douglas. Urbana: University of Illinois Press, 1973.

ALBERY ALLSON WHITMAN
(1851–1901)

Bettye J. Williams

BIOGRAPHY

Albery Allson Whitman was born a slave on a Green River plantation near Munfordville, Kentucky, on May 30, 1851. Photographs reveal a face where Caucasian features dominate over African. He was orphaned after the deaths of both parents, his mother in 1862 and his father in 1863. He wrote of his early life: "I was bred to the plow. Amid the rugged hills, along the banks of Green River in Kentucky, I enjoyed the inestimable blessings of cabin life and hard work during the whole of my early days. I was in bondage,—*I was never a slave* . . ." (Loggins 336). With seven months of formal education, he took to the road as a teenager, teaching in Carysville, Ohio, and then in Kentucky, near his first home. Then, after living in Louisville and Cincinnati, he went to Troy, Ohio, where he worked first in a shop where plows were made and then as a laborer in a railroad construction gang.

No later than 1870, Whitman resumed study at Wilberforce University, where he met Daniel A. Payne, a bishop of the African Methodist Episcopal (AME) Church and president of Wilberforce University. He was inspired by the zeal of Payne and considered himself for all of his life Bishop Payne's protégé and almost son. By the time he was twenty-six years old, he was the general financial agent of Wilberforce University and pastor of an AME Church in Springfield, Ohio. Afterward, his life was one of ceaseless activity as a pastor, evangelist, and writer. During this time, Whitman married a woman named Caddie, with whom he had two daughters. Small of stature and fair enough to pass for white, Whitman probably married into the white race and "responded to the America of his era in ways reflective of the values of middle-class whites" (Jackson 266). Known as a fine pulpiteer, he served as the pastor of churches in Ohio, Kansas, Texas, and

Georgia, until in 1899 he went to St. Philip's AME Church in Savannah, Georgia, which a storm destroyed. His last ministerial charge was Allen Temple in Atlanta. As a clergyman and writer, he did not have the training that comes from the best university education, but he had the taste and talent commensurate with such background.

His years as an itinerant preacher were plagued by ill health, poverty, and alcoholism. His excessive drinking may well have shortened his life, but alcoholism never occasioned his abandonment by his denomination or his wife, even though it destroyed any hopes he may have had for a bishopric in the AME Church. While he was on a visit to Anniston, Alabama, in 1901, he contracted pneumonia. Borne home to Atlanta, he survived only a week and was buried in Atlanta.

MAJOR WORKS AND THEMES

In 1877 Whitman published his first long poem, *Not a Man and Yet a Man*. It was written in the hope that the book might speak more effectively for Wilberforce University. In some 5,000 verses of easy couplets, *Not a Man* is infused with adventures and romantic episodes. It was commonly reputed to be the longest poem ever written by an African American and held that distinction until the 1903 publication of Robert E. Ford's 8,600-word poem, *Brown Chapel, a Story in Verse*. Opening in an Illinois pioneering town called Saville, *Not a Man* relates the heroic exploits of a mulatto slave named Rodney. The property of Sir Maxey, Rodney saves his wealthy master's daughter, Dora, from being massacred by Indians, and then he falls in love with her. But breaking his promise to give his daughter in marriage to any man who would save her, Sir Maxey sells Rodney to a slave trader from the Deep South. Rodney is seen next on a plantation in Florida, where he forgets his infatuation for Dora and falls in love with a beautiful Creole slave named Leeona. After a stirring sequence of events, the lovers are separated from each other for a while and then are permanently united. They win their way to Canada and freedom. Although the plot is well unified, and the characterization consistent, *Not a Man* reproduces musical stanzas and metrical configurations of many well-known, unrelated poems of the eighteenth and nineteenth centuries, such as Timothy Dwight's *Greenfield Hill*, Oliver Goldsmith's *The Deserted Village*, Sir Walter Scott's *Lady of the Lake*, John Greenleaf Whittier's *Snow-Bound*, and Henry Wadsworth Longfellow's *Hiawatha, Paul Revere's Ride*, and *Evangeline*. Yet, Whitman's genius lies in his extravagant, brisk narration. This may be seen in the following descriptive verse: "Where in her queenly pride the rose blooms fair," taken from "The Flight of Leeona."

The Rape of Florida is the best known of Whitman's works. It was published in 1884 and reprinted the next year with slight alterations as *Twasinta's Seminoles; or, Rape of Florida*. A third edition of *Twasinta's Seminoles* appeared in 1890, which included a second edition, carefully revised, of *Not a Man*, with a collection of unpublished short poems grouped into a special section called "Drifted

Leaves." Written in 257 Spenserian stanzas, *The Rape* is the story of the expulsion from Florida of a group of Seminole Indians who had always extended a brotherly welcome to fugitive slaves. Dense with love, romance, and adventure, *The Rape* imitates Lord Byron's *Childe Harold*. Vernon Loggins exclaims on the narrative portions, "The poem relates only indirectly to the Negro. . . . Byron's sound is felt all the more strongly" (339).

In 1901 Whitman published *An Idyl of the South*, an epic poem in two parts and written entirely in ottava rima. With tributes to Ulysses S. Grant and Robert E. Lee, "The Southland's Charms and Freedom's Magnitude" moralizes, not too coherently, on Whitman's varied impressions and beliefs of the South. Making up the major part of *An Idyl of the South*, "The Octoroon" uses the tragic theme of the honest love of Sheldon Maury, the son of a slaveholder, for Lena, a beautiful octoroon slave. Influenced by other poems of the era, *An Idyl of the South* is a reproduction of "The Charge of the Light Brigade" and other Tennyson poems.

CRITICAL RECEPTION

An impressive number of African American critics, including Loggins, Benjamin Brawley, Sterling A. Brown,* Blyden Jackson, and D. W. Culp, exclaim that Whitman was the ablest of all the African American poets between Phillis Wheatley* and Paul Laurence Dunbar.* Loggins says, "He had the soul of a poet" (337). Notwithstanding, many of the preceding critics regard Whitman as a "mockingbird" poet. He imitated British and American poets but was especially fond of Whittier, Longfellow, and William Cullen Bryant. Yet, his poems "repeatedly display excellencies of his own . . . [and] original genius" (Jackson 266).

Although Whitman was a narrative poet, he did write some lyrics. Appended to *Not a Man* is "Ye Bards of England," a poem that eulogizes Chaucer, Shakespeare, Byron, and other British poets. In the "Drifted Leaves" section, Whitman offers tributes to Stonewall Jackson, General George Armstrong Custer, and General Ulysses S. Grant. "The Great Strike" remarks on organized labor. From *An Idyl of the South*, "Tobe's Dream" is Whitman's effort at dialect verse. "Sally Ann's er cookin' ob de hoe cake bread" is the poet's attempt at vernacular verse, which would become popular with Dunbar. Whitman was a contemporary of both Dunbar and Frances Ellen Watkins Harper,* but he was not a spontaneous versifier (a primitive) of nineteenth-century Negro life, nor did he voice the striving of his people in the poetry.

BIBLIOGRAPHY

Works By Albery Allson Whitman

Poetry

Essays on the Ten Plagues and Miscellaneous Poems. 1871?
Leelah Misled. Elizabethtown, KY: Richard LaRue, 1873.

Not a Man and Yet a Man, with Miscellaneous Poems. Springfield, OH: Republican, 1877.
The Rape of Florida. St. Louis: Nixon, Jones, 1884; rev. as *Twasinta's Seminoles; or, Rape of Florida.* St. Louis: Nixon, Jones, 1885; 1890.
Twasinta's Seminoles/Not a Man and Yet a Man/Drifted Leaves: A Collection of Poems. St. Louis: Nixon, Jones, 1890.
The World's Fair Poem. Atlanta: Holsey Job, 1893.
An Idyl of the South, an Epic Poem in Two Parts. New York: Metaphysical, 1901.

Studies of Albery Allson Whitman

Brawley, Benjamin. *The Negro Genius: A New Appraisal of the Achievement of the American Negro in Literature and the Fine Arts.* New York: Dodd, Mead, 1937.
Brown, Sterling A. *Negro Poetry and Drama.* Washington, DC: Associates in Negro Folk Education, 1937.
Culp, D. W., ed. *Twentieth Century Negro Literature.* Naperville, IL, and Toronto: J. L. Nichols, 1902.
Jackson, Blyden. "Albery Allson Whitman." *Dictionary of Literary Biography: Afro-American Writers before the Harlem Renaissance.* Vol. 50. Ed. Trudier Harris. Detroit: Gale, 1987. 263–67.
Jackson, Blyden, and Louis D. Rubin Jr. *Black Poetry in America: Two Essays in Historical Interpretation.* Baton Rouge: Louisiana State University Press, 1974.
Loggins, Vernon. *The Negro Author, His Development in America.* New York: Columbia University Press, 1931.
Redmond, Eugene B. *Drumvoices: The Mission of Afro-American Poetry, a Critical History.* Garden City, NY: Anchor/Doubleday, 1976.
Sherman, Joan R. "Albery Allson Whitman: Poet of Beauty and Manliness." *CLA Journal* 15 (1971): 126–43.
———. *Invisible Poets: Afro-Americans of the Nineteenth Century.* Urbana, Chicago, and London: University of Illinois Press, 1974.
Wagner, Jean. *Black Poets of the United States: From Paul Laurence Dunbar to Langston Hughes.* Urbana: University of Illinois Press, 1973.
Williams, Kenny J. *They Also Spoke: An Essay on Negro Literature in America, 1787–1930.* Nashville, TN: Townsend, 1970.

HARRIET E. WILSON
(1827?–1863?)

Emmanuel S. Nelson

BIOGRAPHY

The publication of *Our Nig; or, Sketches in the Life of a Free Black* by Harriet E. Wilson was a remarkable event in American literary history. The first novel by a black person to be published in the United States, *Our Nig* inaugurated the African American women's tradition in fiction. Yet the novel received little attention and had little impact on the reading public. Only after its discovery and republication by Henry Louis Gates Jr. in 1983—the year when Alice Walker was awarded the Pulitzer Prize for *The Color Purple* and Gloria Naylor won the National Book Award for *The Women of Brewster Place*—did Harriet Wilson's novel regain its status as a pioneering text by an extraordinary woman. However, so far only scant information about Wilson's life exists. We know, for example, nothing at all about her parents; nor can we be sure of her dates of birth and death.

The little that we do know about Harriet Wilson is largely the result of Henry Louis Gates Jr.'s painstaking research; in his introductory essay to the novel he offers some biographical information that he has gleaned from a few extant documents. The details that he provides have been substantially augmented more recently by the first-rate investigative work of Barbara A. White. Both Gates and White conclude that Harriet Wilson was born Harriet Adams in New Hampshire in 1827 or 1828. She married Thomas Wilson, who was from Virginia, on October 6, 1851, in Milford, New Hampshire. For several years prior to her marriage she worked as a servant in the home of Nehemiah and Rebecca Hayward, a prosperous couple in Milford. The abuse that she suffered at the hands of Mrs. Hayward is the focus of her autobiographical novel. At the time of the publication of the book, however, it appears that Harriet Wilson was a widow and a resident of Boston. Her son, whose ill health she alludes to in the Preface to *Our Nig*, was probably her only child. Wilson wrote the book in order to earn some money to pay for her son's medical care, but the son—George Mason Wilson—died in 1860, a few months after the publication of his mother's work. Soon after the loss of her child Mrs. Wilson seems to have returned to New Hampshire. No record of her exists after 1860.

MAJOR WORK AND THEMES

The cumbersome subtitle of Wilson's novel boldly states one of the major themes of the book: *Our Nig, or, Sketches from the Life of a Free Black, in a Two-Story White House, North. Showing That Slavery's Shadows Fall Even There.* In the page-long prefatory statement with which the book begins, Wilson reiterates the theme she highlights in the subtitle: the North is just as brutally racist as the slaveholding South. In a daring move that could potentially alienate abolitionists and ensure the commercial failure of her writing venture, Wilson insinuates in her Preface that even northern abolitionists are not above racist beliefs and practices. The twelve chapters that follow narrate the story of Frado, the child of a white mother and black father. After the death of her father, Frado is abandoned at age six by her mother at the home of the Bellmonts. For the next several years Frado is forced to work as a servant in the Bellmont household. During those years she is subjected to appalling physical and emotional torture by Mrs. Bellmont and by her equally fiendish daughter, Mary. Though Mr. Bellmont and his two sons are largely sympathetic to Frado's plight, they do little to protect her from Mrs. Bellmont's pathological behavior. The final chapter briefly chronicles the departure of Frado, now a young woman, from the Bellmont household; her short marriage to Samuel, a man who falsely claims to be an escaped slave and dupes the abolitionists into making him a lecturer at their meetings; her subsequent abandonment by Samuel and the birth of their son; and her destitute condition and her various attempts to become self-employed to take care of herself and her child. The narrative is followed by an Appendix, which consists of three letters of endorsement. Apparently written by women who knew Harriet Wilson personally, the letters vouch for the veracity of Wilson's claims in the book and urge the readers to offer their support.

Our Nig resists generic classification because its author blends a variety of narrative forms to create a unique text that would articulate her vision. Clearly, the text is grounded in autobiographical facts; the letters of endorsement appended to the book confirm that *Our Nig* is largely a self-representational narrative. However, there is considerable conflation of fact and fiction: evident in the text are several stock characteristics of sentimental fiction. The book, after all, is about an abandoned and abused child—a staple of nineteenth-century sentimental novels. The melodramatic prose that Wilson often employs, too, is consistent with the norms of that type of fiction. At least one critic sees *Our Nig* as an elaborate allegorical narrative: Hazel Carby reads the book as an allegorical statement on the practice of slavery (44–45). *Our Nig* also has some of the attributes of a typical slave narrative. The letters of endorsement, for example, are devices of authentication that accompany most slave narratives. As do many slave narratives, *Our Nig* contains an elaborately described moment of confrontation with a white adversary: Frado rebels against Mrs. Bellmont and at least momentarily gains the upper hand and catches a glimpse of her own possibilities. This scene bears some resemblance to one of the most famous scenes in African American literature—Frederick Douglass'* epiphanic confrontation with Covey in Douglass' *Narrative of the Life of Frederick Douglass, an American Slave* (1845). *Our Nig* is similar to yet another form of narration that was popular during the eighteenth and nineteenth centuries: captivity narratives. Often written by white women, captivity narratives are records of their authors' alleged experiences as captives among Native Americans. *Our Nig* offers a subversive perspective on the theme of captivity: here a young African American woman is held captive in a brutally violent, middle-class, white American home.

This synthesis of several narrative forms is one of the most significant aspects of Wilson's *Our Nig*. Rather than simply align herself with a particular narrative tradition, Wilson innovatively blends many literary forms to create a hybrid text that could embody her complex vision. This hybridity positions her text in an indeterminate space where a variety of literary forms intersect. It also reveals Harriet Wilson's inventive struggle to find a new narrative form and to begin the African American women's tradition in fiction.

Just as intriguing as the form of *Our Nig* is a haunting silence that marks its pages. In her Preface to the book Wilson states, "I do not pretend to divulge every transaction in my own life, which the unprejudiced would declare unfavorable in comparison with the treatment of legal bondsmen; I have purposely omitted what would most provoke shame in our good anti-slavery friends at home" (n.p.). Precisely what information is being withheld from the reader is unclear. Since Wilson describes in great detail various forms of physical and emotional abuse that she suffered at the Bellmont home, it would be logical to conclude that she is withholding details of sexual abuse by Mrs. Bellmont or by one or more men in the household. But such a conclusion is problematic: since Wilson very specifically states that she has opted to be silent because her revelations would "provoke shame in our good anti-slavery friends," one has to wonder why disclosure of sexual abuse in the Bellmont household would so specifically shame the abolitionists. Barbara A. White offers a fascinating suggestion that perhaps the Bellmonts were members of the abolitionist movement. Revelation of that inconvenient fact would indeed shame the abolitionists (White 38). While White's speculation is compelling, it is not entirely convincing. Wilson pointedly announces in her Preface that she is not revealing "every transaction" in her life—transactions that would make her life seem even worse than that of an enslaved person in the South. Here she appears to be alluding to her personal *experience* rather than to any objective facts about the Bellmonts' politics. So Wilson's silence, like much of her life, remains enigmatic.

CRITICAL RECEPTION

After its republication in 1983, *Our Nig* generated considerable critical attention. Eric Gardner's article, for example, offers a superb overview of the book's publishing history. Bernard W. Bell considers *Our Nig* as a defining text in the African American as well as feminist traditions in fiction. More importantly, Bell uses Wilson's text to illustrate the hybrid nature of the early African American novel, which was influenced by "the Euro-American literary tradition" as well as "the Afro-American oral tradition" (50). The trope of silence in *Our Nig* has attracted a good deal of lively scholarly interest. Cynthia Davis, P. Gabrielle Foreman, and Barbara A. White offer various readings of Wilson's self-imposed silence. Julia Stern's "Excavating Genre in *Our Nig*" remains one of the best commentaries on the narrative and textual complexities of the work. Perhaps the most provocative article that has been published so far on Wilson's text is Elizabeth Breau's "Identifying Satire: *Our Nig*." Rejecting the views of some critics who characterize Wilson's struggle to create a new narrative form as "desperate" and "awkward," Breau insists on reading *Our Nig* as a brilliant piece of satire. Breau's essay is a lively piece of scholarship, and her arguments are as convincing as her conclusion that Harriet Wilson was a "woman . . . capable of both conceiving and executing a groundbreaking work of literature" (464).

BIBLIOGRAPHY

Work By Harriet E. Wilson

Our Nig; or, Sketches in the Life of a Free Black. Boston: G. C. Rand and Avery, 1859; New York: Random House, 1983.

Studies of Harriet E. Wilson

Bell, Bernard W. *The Afro-American Novel and Its Tradition*. Amherst: University of Massachusetts Press, 1987.

Breau, Elizabeth. "Identifying Satire: *Our Nig*." *Callaloo* 16.2 (Spring 1993): 455–65.

Carby, Hazel. *Reconstructing Womanhood: The Emergence of the Afro-American Novelist*. New York: Oxford University Press, 1987.

Cole, Phyllis. "Stowe, Jacobs, Wilson: White Plots and Black Counterplots." In *New Perspectives on Gender, Race, and Class in Society*. Ed. Audrey T. McCluskey. Bloomington: Indiana University Press, 1990. 23–45.

Davis, Cynthia. "Speaking the Body's Pain: Harriet Wilson's *Our Nig*." *African American Review* 27.3 (Fall 1993): 391–404.

Doriani, Beth Maclay. "Black Womanhood in Nineteenth-Century America: Subversion and Self-Construction in Two Women's Autobiographies." *American Quarterly* 43.2 (June 1991): 99–222.

Ernest, John. "Economics of Identity: Harriet E. Wilson's *Our Nig*." *PMLA* 199.3 (May 1994): 424–38.

Foreman, P. Gabrielle. "The Spoken and the Silenced in *Incidents in the Life of a Slave Girl* and *Our Nig*." *Callaloo* 13.2 (Spring 1990): 313–24.

Gardner, Eric. " 'This Attempt of Their Sister': Harriet Wilson's *Our Nig* from Printer to Readers." *New England Quarterly* 66.2 (June 1993): 226–46.

Gates, Henry Louis, Jr. "Harriet E. Adams Wilson." In *Dictionary of Literary Biography*. Vol. 50. Ed. Thadious M. Davis and Trudier Harris. Detroit: Gale, 1986. 268–71.

Herndl, Diane Price. "The Invisible (Invalid) Woman: African-American Women, Illness, and Nineteenth-Century Narrative." *Women's Studies: An Interdisciplinary Journal* 24.6 (September 1995): 553–72.

Jefferson, Margo. "Down and Out and Black in Boston." *Nation* 28 (May 1983): 675.

Jones, Jill. "The Disappearing 'I' in *Our Nig*." *Legacy: A Journal of American Women Writers* 13.1 (1996): 38–53.

Richardson, Marilyn. "The Shadow of Slavery." *Women's Review of Books* (October 1983): 14.

Stern, Julia. "Excavating Genre in *Our Nig*." *American Literature* 67.3 (September 1995): 439–66.

Tate, Claudia. "Allegories of Black Female Desire." In *Changing Our Own Words: Essays on Criticism, Theory, and Writing by Black Women*. Ed. Cheryl A. Wall. New Brunswick, NJ: Rutgers University Press, 1989. 98–126.

White, Barbara A. "*Our Nig* and the She-Devil: New Information about Harriet Wilson and the 'Bellmont' Family." *American Literature* 65.1 (March 1993): 19–52.

RICHARD WRIGHT
(1908–1960)

Eberhard Alsen

BIOGRAPHY

Richard Wright was born on a plantation near Natchez, Mississippi, on September 4, 1908. He was the older of two sons of the sharecropper Nathaniel Wright and the schoolteacher Ella Wilson Wright. In 1911 the family moved to Memphis, Tennessee, where the father abandoned the family, and the mother took on a series of menial jobs to support herself and her two sons. When Ella Wright fell ill in 1914, she was forced to put the six-year-old Richard and his four-year-old brother into an orphanage for six months. Sometime in 1916, she moved to Elaine, Arkansas, where she and her children stayed with her sister Maggie Hoskins, whose husband, Silas, owned a saloon. When Silas was murdered by whites so they could take over his business, Ella and Maggie and the two children fled and settled briefly in West Helena, Arkansas. In 1919 Ella Wright suffered a stroke, and the children went to live with an aunt and uncle in Greenwood, Mississippi. The eleven-year-old Richard constantly fought with his Aunt Jody and Uncle Clark until, in 1920, they shipped him off to Jackson, Mississippi, to live with his grandmother Wilson.

During the five years he stayed in Jackson, Richard began to attend school regularly for the first time in his life. Initially, he went to a Seventh-Day Adventist School where his aunt Addie was the only teacher, but in the fall of 1921 he enrolled in the fifth grade of the Jim Hill Public School but was advanced to the sixth grade within two weeks. Two years later he transferred to the Smith Robinson School. In 1925 he graduated from Smith as the class valedictorian. While at Smith, Wright published his first story, "The Voodoo of Hell's Half-Acre," in a black newspaper, the *Southern Register* of Jackson, Mississippi. Unfortunately, no copy of that story exists.

From 1925 to 1927 Richard Wright lived in Memphis, Tennessee, taking on various jobs in order to make enough money to go north to Chicago. During those two years in Memphis, Wright began to read literary magazines such as *Harper's*, the *Atlantic Monthly*, and H. L. Mencken's *American Mercury*. He became fascinated with Mencken because Mencken attacked American bigotry and used words as weapons. More importantly, Wright discovered the novels of Sinclair Lewis and Theodore Dreiser and could not read enough of them. Reading those novels evoked in him glimpses of life's possibilities and confirmed his plans to go north and become a writer himself.

In 1927 Wright finally made his escape from the South and went to Chicago. In Chicago Wright at first moved from one menial job to another while continuing to read voraciously and write stories. After the Depression hit, Wright was unemployed for a while until he found work with the Federal Writers' Project. In 1931 Wright published a short story, "Superstition," in *Abbott's Monthly Magazine* and made contacts with the communist-sponsored John Reed Club. The following year he was made secretary of that literary organization, and a year later, in 1933, he joined the Communist Party. Full of the zeal of the new convert, Wright cranked out dozens of political poems for the newspaper the *New Masses* and other communist publications. The best of these poems can be found in Michel Fabre's book *The World of Richard Wright*. During his Chicago years, Wright also finished his first attempt at a novel, *Cesspool*, but he could not find a publisher for it.

Wright's communist phase lasted until 1937, when he had a falling out with the communist leadership in Chicago and left for New York. In an essay entitled "I Tried to Be a Communist" (1944), Wright describes the quarrel. The party bosses told Wright that they weren't interested in his writing because all he was doing was to "dramatize Negro nationalism." Instead they wanted to make him into a "mass leader." When Wright refused to obey the party's orders, he was branded a "bourgeois degenerate" and an "incipient Trotskyite," and he was bodily thrown out of the communist ranks at the 1937 May Day parade. Even after he left Chicago, Wright still believed in the ideals of the Communist Party, but he could not abide their "tactics of terror, threat, invective, intimidation, suspicion" (*American Hunger* 111).

In New York, where the local communists had a low opinion of their Chicago comrades, Wright was hired as an editor by the Harlem office of the *Daily Worker*. Although he produced over 200 articles for the *Daily Worker* between 1937 and 1938, his first priority during that time was the writing of fiction.

Wright's literary efforts paid off in 1938, when he received an award of $500 as first prize from *Story* magazine for the best book-length manuscript by one of the 1,200 authors working for the Federal Writer's Project. Later that same year Harper published this collection of four stories under the title *Uncle Tom's Children*. The book received rave reviews and helped Wright to win a Guggenheim Fellowship. The financial ease provided by that fellowship and the royalties from

Uncle Tom's Children allowed Wright to concentrate all his efforts on a new novel he had begun. The new novel was *Native Son.*

Native Son was published on March 1, 1940. It turned out to be a phenomenal success, selling better than anything Harper had published in twenty years: over 200,000 copies in less than three weeks. It also outsold John Steinbeck's *The Grapes of Wrath*, which had been published a year earlier. Praised extravagantly by most reviewers, *Native Son* became an instant classic of American literature and made Richard Wright internationally famous. It also made him a wealthy man.

Having suddenly become a man of substance, Richard Wright decided to marry one of two white women he had been seeing, the dancer Dimah Rose Meadman. However, during their honeymoon in Mexico, Richard and Dimah found that they were incompatible, and they returned to New York separately. Wright divorced Dimah and married Ellen Poplar, who, like Wright himself, was a member of the Communist Party. The marriage turned out to be a happy one, and the couple had two daughters, Julia and Rachel, born in 1942 and 1949.

Following the fiasco of his first marriage, Wright traveled to Chicago to do research for a book on African American history. The book came out in 1941 and was entitled *Twelve Million Black Voices: A Folk History of the Negro in America*. Meanwhile, Harper decided to cash in on the popularity of *Native Son* by publishing an enlarged edition of *Uncle Tom's Children* (1940). Wright seized the opportunity to popularize his social and political ideas by adding two pieces that had previously appeared in communist publications, the essay "The Ethics of Living Jim Crow" and a story that deals with racial conflict in Marxist terms, "Bright and Morning Star." The same year Wright collaborated with the playwright Paul Green in turning *Native Son* into a stage play. Directed by Orson Welles, the play had a reasonably successful run at the St. James Theater in New York.

In 1943 Wright completed the manuscript of an autobiography. It was entitled "American Hunger" and dealt with his life up to 1937, when he left Chicago and went to New York. For reasons that are probably political, Harper published only the first half and gave it the title *Black Boy: A Record of Childhood and Youth* (1945). Wright's account of his ten years in Chicago eventually came out as *American Hunger*, seventeen years after Wright's death. *Black Boy* sold even better than *Native Son* but received reviews that were, on the whole, not quite as positive.

In 1946 the French government invited Richard Wright and his family to visit France as guests of the French state. Wright was overwhelmed by the cordial reception he received from the French intellectuals, including Jean-Paul Sartre and Simone de Beauvoir, and a year later, he moved his family to Paris for good and became a French citizen. Paris remained his base of operations until his death in 1960.

During his thirteen years of exile, Richard Wright wrote chiefly nonfiction. In addition to scores of book reviews and journal and newspaper articles, he wrote four books on race relations in countries other than the United States: *Black Power* (1954), which came out of his trip to Ghana; *The Color Curtain* (1956), which records his participation in the Bandung Conference of Third World Nations; *Pagan Spain* (1956), for which he traveled to Spain and studied its Muslim heritage; and *White Man, Listen!* (1957), which is a collection of lectures on the general topic of worldwide race relations.

In 1949 Wright turned *Native Son* into a screenplay, and the shooting of the film started later that year in Buenos Aires, Argentina. When the film was finished in 1950, American censors forced Wright and his French director to make extensive cuts. These may be partly to blame for the negative reviews the film received. It also didn't help the film that Richard Wright himself played the part of Bigger Thomas, the novel's protagonist. Wright was 41 at the time, and Bigger was supposed to be 20.

When Wright turned to fiction during his years in France the stories and the novels he produced were decidedly inferior to *Native Son* and *Uncle Tom's Children*. Three of the stories were later collected in *Eight Men* ("Man of All Work," "Man, God Ain't like That," and "Big Good Black Man"), and they are considered to be among Wright's weakest work. The three novels he wrote in Paris are also disappointing. *The Outsider* (1953) is the upshot of Wright's studying French and German existentialist philosophy, and *Savage Holiday* (1954) reflects his studying Freudian psychology. *Savage Holiday* was rejected by Wright's regular publisher, Harper, and was eventually published by Avon books as a paperback. It is a spectacularly bad novel, the only one of Wright's books in which all the major characters are whites. Wright's last novel, *The Long Dream* (1958), is the best of the three that he wrote in France because it draws on Wright's childhood and adolescence in the Deep South.

During the 1950s, Richard Wright became increasingly irritable and hard to get along with. This was partly due to the negative reviews that his fiction had been receiving, partly to his unhappiness about the growing Americanization of France, and partly to his declining health (he had recurring bouts with amebic dysentery, which he contracted during a trip to Ghana in 1953). He had a falling out with James Baldwin, who had been his protégé, and with several other expatriate African American writers in Paris, and he eventually suspected everyone of plotting against him, even a physician, Dr. Victor Schwartzmann, who admired his work and had been treating him for free. Eventually, Wright came to feel so alienated in Paris that he made plans to move to London.

In 1959 Wright put together a collection of short fiction from three different periods of his life. It is entitled *Eight Men*, and it contains three inferior stories that Wright wrote during his years in Paris and five much better stories that he wrote in New York and Chicago. Wright did not live to see the book published.

During the last year of his life, Wright finished the second book of the trilogy he had begun with *The Long Dream*. That novel was to be entitled *Island of Hallucinations*. It remains unpublished to this day. Another book that Wright did not live to see published is *Cesspool*, his first novel. Wright had put it aside after it was rejected by a number of publishers, first in Chicago and then in New York. But this book did appear posthumously as *Lawd Today* (1963).

Richard Wright died of a heart attack on November 28, 1960. He was only fifty-two years old.

MAJOR WORKS AND THEMES

When Wright was working as a publicity agent for the Federal Negro Theater in Chicago, he ran afoul of a group of black actors because he wanted the theater to produce plays of "dramatic realism" and assumed that the average African American would "pine for adult expression in the American theater; that he was ashamed of the stereotypes of clowns, mammies, razors, dice, watermelon, and cotton fields." He was aghast when the actors refused to put on a new play by Paul Green, entitled *Hymn to the Rising Sun*, because they considered it "indecent" and because they didn't think it was a play that "will make the public love us" (*American Hunger* 114–15). Wright's account of this incident reveals not only his view of what African American theater should be like but also what he considered to be his own mission as a literary artist.

Wright did not care if his work was "indecent" or if the public liked it. One of his chief concerns was to achieve a "dramatic realism" that would destroy the stereotypical image the public had of African Americans. As Michel Fabre points out, Wright deliberately wanted to shock "an audience not yet prepared to look beyond the mask of the smiling Negro to discover his hatred and his desire for revenge against white racism" ("Afterword" 136).

Wright's first book, *Uncle Tom's Children: Four Novellas* (1938), contains some of his best work. The four long stories are connected by a theme that is hinted at in an epigraph that states that "Uncle Tom is Dead": all four stories deal with African Americans who refuse to be subservient Uncle Toms but insist on asserting the dignity of black people even if it kills them.

The first story, "Big Boy Leaves Home," illustrates what happens to black males in the Deep South when white women feel threatened by them. In that story, Big Boy and his three friends Bobo, Buck, and Lester sneak a swim in a swimming hole located on the property of a white landowner, "old man Harvey." The fiancée of Jim Harvey, the landowner's son, stumbles upon the scene and screams in fear as the four naked adolescents come out of the water to retrieve their clothes. Alerted by her screams, Jim Harvey comes running with a rifle and shoots Buck and Lester. As Harvey aims at Bobo, Big Boy wrestles the gun away from him and tells him to back off. Ignoring the warning, Harvey attacks, and Big Boy shoots him dead. Knowing full well that the white people will be organizing a lynching party, Big Boy's father calls together the leaders of the black community and asks them to help Big Boy escape. Brother Sanders tells the group that his son Will is scheduled to leave for Chicago with a truckload of goods early the next morning. Big Boy is to hide out in a kiln near the edge of town until Will comes by with his truck. Then he is to make his escape by stowing away on the truck. The escape comes off as planned, but while Big Boy is waiting in the kiln that night, Bobo is captured by the lynch mob, and Big Boy watches helplessly as his friend is tortured, tarred and feathered, and then burned alive.

The second story, "Down by the Riverside," is less concerned with racism—although racism does play a role in the story—than with the role that chance plays in our lives, because three coincidences bring about the death of the protagonist, a small farmer by the name of Brother Mann. The story takes place during a major flood of the Mississippi Valley. Mann needs to get his pregnant wife, Lulu, to a hospital because she has been in labor for four days, and the baby needs to be delivered by cesarean section. In desperation, Mann uses a boat that his son has stolen from a white man. The first coincidence occurs when the current drives the boat against the house of the boat's owner, the postmaster Henry Heartfield. Heartfield recognizes his boat and orders Mann to give the boat back to him. Because Mann doesn't comply immediately, Heartfield fires several shots at him. In self-defense, Mann shoots back and accidentally kills Heartfield. All this is for naught, because by the time Mann gets to the hospital, his wife has died. In a second coincidence, the military authorities assigned Mann to a motorboat that is sent to rescue Mrs. Heartfield and her two children from the second floor of their house. When Heartfield's son recognizes him, Mann decides to kill the family. But as he lifts an ax to do so, yet another coincidence occurs: the flood suddenly makes the house lurch from its foundations, and Mann is knocked down and drops his ax. Before he can retrieve the ax, the driver of the motorboat comes to help him get the family out of the badly tilting house, and so Mann is unable to dispose of the witnesses of his murder. Once the family is safe, they report Mann to the general who is in charge of the rescue operations. Under martial law, Mann is sentenced to be shot for looting and murder. He tries to escape and dies in a hail of gunfire.

In the third story, "Long Black Song," the protagonist also kills a white man and is killed in return, but in this story there are no coincidences, and the conflict is both a racial and a sexual one. The story is told from the point of view of Sarah, a lonely black woman who allows a white phonograph salesman to seduce her while her husband, Silas, is away. Because Sarah has no money, the salesman leaves a gramophone with her and plans to return the next day to collect from her husband. But Silas finds out about Sarah's infidelity soon after he returns home, and when the salesman shows up the next morning, Silas kills him. Just like Big Boy in the first story, Silas knows that it is only a matter of time until a lynch mob will be after him. Instead of trying to escape, he sends his wife and child away and prepares to fight the white people. Before Sarah leaves, Silas makes a speech that contains the message of the story. Silas says: "The white folks ain never give me a chance. They ain never give no black man a chance. There ain nothin in yo life you kin keep from em! They take yo lan! They take yo freedom! They take yo women! N then they take yo life!" (125). As Sarah watches from a nearby hillside, the lynch mob arrives. Silas holds them off by shooting down several white men, but he can't prevent some others from setting fire to the house. Rather than surrendering and getting lynched, Silas chooses to die in the flames.

The fourth story in *Uncle Tom's Children* is entitled "Fire and Cloud," and it stands out because nobody gets killed. Also, it is the only one of the four stories that does not emphasize individual rebellion and instead emphasizes community action. Moreover, it advocates solidarity of all poor people, black and white. But most importantly, it is the only one of the four stories in which the protagonist comes to a positive realization. In "Fire and Cloud," the man who refuses to be an Uncle Tom is the Reverend Dan Taylor. For years, Taylor had cooperated with the white mayor in keeping racial peace in his town. Now unrest is brewing because there is large-scale unemployment, and the local relief agency claims it has no food to distribute, but people suspect that the food is being held back because the mayor and his cronies are selling it to line their own pockets. To exploit the unrest, the Communist Party has sent two organizers to town, one black and one white, and the two have called for a mass demonstration. As the story opens, the two communists are waiting in a back room at Taylor's church to ask him to support the demonstration, while the mayor and the chief of police are waiting in his parlor to pressure him into stopping the march. Taylor does not want to do either. When the deacons of his church ask him what they shall tell the black community, Taylor is evasive and says only that if the people decide to march, he will march with them. Then a group of white thugs show up, kidnap Taylor, take him to the woods, and beat him until he loses consciousness. This incident makes Taylor change his mind about his relationship to God and mankind, and he delivers a speech in favor of the demonstration. As a result, 5,000 blacks and 3,000 poor whites march downtown, too many protesters to be stopped by the town's police force. Afraid of a large-scale riot, the mayor promises to distribute relief if the marchers return to their homes peacefully. The story's upbeat ending illustrates the Reverend Martin's newfound belief: "We cant do nothin erlone. . . . All the will, all the strength, all the power, all the numbahs is in the people" (172).

A second, expanded edition of *Uncle Tom's Children* appeared in 1940. It is subtitled *Five Long Stories*, and it opens with an "autobiographical sketch" that is entitled "The Ethics of Living Jim Crow." This sketch consists of material gleaned from a work in progress that later became *Black Boy*. The other addition is the story "Bright and Morning Star." It is an even more political story than "Fire and Cloud" because it is about an old black woman, Aunty Sue, who chooses to die for the cause of communism. The story takes place in a rural area outside Memphis, Tennessee, where the protagonist's two sons work as communist organizers. One of them, Sug, is in jail, and the other one, Johnny Boy, has just called a meeting of all newly recruited members of the party. Although Johnny Boy says, "Ah cant see white n Ah cant see black. . . . Ah sees rich men n Ah sees po men" (192), his mother warns him not to trust some of the new white members of the party. The sheriff comes to arrest Johnny Boy and beats up Aunty Sue because she won't reveal the whereabouts of her son. After the sheriff leaves, a newly recruited white member of the party by the name of Booker (!) wheedles the names of Johnny Boy's associates out of his mother. When Aunty Sue finds out that Booker has betrayed Johnny Boy, she takes Johnny Boy's pistol and decides to kill Booker before he can betray the rest of his comrades. She finds the sheriff and his henchmen in a clearing in the forest, where they are torturing Johnny Boy because he refuses to talk. When Booker shows up, Aunty Sue shoots him dead before he can pass along to the sheriff the information she had given him. In retaliation, the sheriff and his men kill both her and her son. While the story is clearly sympathetic to the communist cause, it still shows that Johnny Boy's color-blind idealism is naive.

Richard Wright's masterpiece, *Native Son*, was published in 1940. In his essay "How Bigger Was Born," first published in the *Saturday Review* and later included as Preface to the novel, Wright explains that the overarching theme of *Native Son* is "the moral—or what *I* felt was the moral—horror of Negro life in the United States" (xxxiii). Related themes are familiar ones from *Uncle Tom's Children*: black aspirations thwarted by racism and the desire of oppressed blacks to strike back at whites. In addition, the novel develops several new themes. One of them is the role the ghetto environment plays in stunting the emotional growth of black people, another is the Marxist idea that religion is the opiate of the people, and a third is the notion that the only meaning that our lives can have is the meaning that we give them ourselves by our own actions.

The protagonist of *Native Son* is the twenty-year-old Bigger Thomas, who lives with his mother and two siblings in a run-down, rat-infested tenement building in the South Side of Chicago. In the opening scene of the novel, Bigger has to kill a rat before his mother can prepare the family's breakfast. After squashing the rat with a skillet, Bigger dangles its body in front of his sister Vera's face until the girl faints. Rats show up again and again in crucial scenes of the novel so that we can't help but identify them with the protagonist. But it isn't until late in the novel that we understand the symbolism: white people consider Bigger and other impoverished and undereducated blacks to be pests that need to be exterminated.

As Richard Wright explains in "How Bigger Was Born," he made Bigger into "a meaningful and prophetic symbol" (xiv) representing the average young black male whose coming-of-age involves the realization that the American Dream is only for whites and that racism will prevent him from achieving a life of dignity and self-fulfillment. This symbolism becomes apparent during one of the early scenes of the novel, when Bigger notices an airplane in the sky and expresses his desire to become an aviator. When one of his friends reminds Bigger that blacks are not allowed to become pilots, Bigger says that the whites are probably right in denying pilot licenses to blacks: "Cause if I took a plane up I'd take a couple of bombs along and drop them sure as hell" (20). Bigger's comment foreshadows the central conflict of the novel between Bigger and white society.

That conflict takes shape when Bigger becomes the chauffeur for the wealthy Dalton family. On the evening of his first day of work, Bigger is supposed to drive young Mary Dalton to a lecture at the university, but Mary instead orders him to pick up her boyfriend, Jan Erlone, and to take them to a black restaurant on the South Side of Chicago. Mary and Jan get very drunk, and after Bigger drives Jan home, he finds that Mary has passed out in the car. Unable to wake her and unwilling to compromise her by waking up her parents, Bigger carries Mary to her room and puts her on her bed. Before he can leave, Mary's mother, who is blind, comes into the room. Bigger is afraid that Mary may give away his presence, and so he presses a pillow over her mouth. When Mrs. Dalton leaves, he discovers that Mary has suffocated.

Bigger knows that no one will accept Mary's death as an accident, and he therefore decides to dispose of her body by decapitating it and burning it in the furnace of the Dalton mansion. The next day, he claims that Mary had sent him home by himself and suggests that her boyfriend Jan, a self-declared communist, might be able to explain her disappearance.

Sure that he has fooled everyone, Bigger feels "like a man reborn." By killing Mary Dalton, so Bigger believes, he has created something for himself that no one can take away from him. Although the killing was accidental, Bigger accepts it as a murder because in his mind he has murdered white people many times before. Now that what Bigger has so often imagined has become a reality, "the hidden meaning of his life—a meaning which others did not see and which he had always tried to hide—had spilled out" (101).

In this analysis of Bigger's thoughts on the day after the killing, the narrator develops the metaphor of blindness which recurs throughout the novel. When Bigger sits down to dinner with his family as if nothing out of the ordinary had happened, he realizes that they don't consider him capable of murdering a white person. Bigger realizes that people only see what they want to see and that they are blind to anything that doesn't fit into their preconceptions. He decides that everyone around him is blind in this way, his mother, his sister Vera, his brother Buddy, his friends Gus, Jack and G.H., and even Mary Dalton's boyfriend, Jan Erlone, despite all his college education. Most significantly, toward the end of the novel the narrator suggests that Bigger's sympathetic defense lawyer, Boris Max, is blind too, the cause of his blindess being his communist vision of life.

While the police are still holding Jan Erlone as the primary suspect, Bigger decides to pass Mary's disappearance off as a kidnapping and to collect ransom money from her parents. Bigger writes a ransom note that calls for Mr. Dalton to drive down Michigan Avenue at midnight and drop a shoe box with $10,000 in the snow when he sees a light in a window flash three times. Bigger does not want to risk picking up the money himself, and so he talks his girlfriend Bessie into doing it for him. But before that plan can be carried out, Mary's bones are discovered in the ashes of the Dalton's furnace, and Bigger goes into hiding. Because Bessie knows that he killed Mary, Bigger decides to take Bessie with him and kill her when it becomes necessary.

Bigger's murder of Bessie demonstrates the dehumanizing effect that the ghetto environment has had on his personality even more drastically than his panic-stricken dismemberment of Mary Dalton's body. By having Bigger plan the killing of Bessie in cold blood, Wright makes us give up whatever sympathy we may have felt for him up to this point. As Bigger and Bessie bed down for the night on the fourth floor of an abandoned building, Bigger looks around for a brick with which to kill Bessie. But before killing her, he forces Bessie to have sex with him against her will. After Bessie is asleep, Bigger grabs the brick and smashes it down into Bessie's face again and again until "he seemed to be striking a wet wad of cotton, of some damp substance whose only life was the jarring of the brick's impact" (222). Then he tosses the body down an airshaft, but we eventually learn that "the girl was not dead when she hit the bottom of that shaft; she froze to death later, trying to climb out" (378).

Richard Wright manages to make us feel sympathy for Bigger again after Bigger is caught and put on trial, because both the newspapers and the white prosecutor go out of their way to describe Bigger as a "jungle beast" and a "maddened ape." One Chicago newspaper says about Bigger: "All in all, he seems a beast utterly untouched by the softening influences of modern civilization" (260). This is bitter irony because the first part of the novel amply illustrates that white society has denied Bigger such "softening influences of modern civilization" as a good education and decent living conditions.

This idea—that African Americans are systematically denied the benefits of modern civilization—is the explanation that the communist defense lawyer Boris Max offers for Bigger's behavior. Max explains to the court that "men can starve from a lack of self-realization as much as they can from a lack of bread. And they can *murder* for it, too" (367). By denying blacks self-realization, so Max says, whites have instilled in them a profound hate and a desire to subvert white society:

"Excluded from, and unassimilated in our society, yet longing to gratify impulses akin to our own, but denied the objects and channels evolved through long centuries for their socialized expression, every sunrise and sunset makes him guilty of subversive actions. Every movement of his body is an unconscious protest. Every desire, every dream, no matter how intimate or personal, is a plot or a conspiracy." (367)

Toward the end of his speech, Max adds a political dimension to his argument when he blames not only racism but also capitalism for creating the environment that produces violent individuals such as Bigger. Turning to the judge, Max says that Bigger is a symbol representing all Americans who are denied self-fulfillment. When Max later talks to Bigger, he repeats the notion that the prejudice Bigger has been experiencing all his life is essentially not of a racial but of a socioeconomic nature. He tells him: "Your being black, as I told you before, makes it easy to single you out. . . . Bigger, they say that all people who work are inferior" (391). However, Bigger does not react to this Marxist analysis of his situation. Instead, he is preoccupied with the meaning of his life.

Knowing that he has only a few hours to live before he will be executed, Bigger expresses a view of his situation that is more philosophical than sociological or political. Just before he is taken to the electric chair, Bigger says to Boris Max: "I didn't want to kill . . . But what I killed for I *am!*" This statement of Bigger's has an existentialist ring to it, and so does his view of death. Bigger does not believe that he will be judged in an afterlife, because, as he says, "when they strap me into that chair and turn on the heat, I'm through, for always" (330). This life is all we have, so Bigger believes, and all that matters is that we give meaning to it by our actions. Bigger's outlook anticipates the existentialist ideas of Jean-Paul Sartre, for in his most famous essay, "Existentialism Is a Humanism" (1942), Sartre makes the same assumptions as Bigger, namely, that "God does not exist" and that "[m]an is nothing else but what he makes of himself" (18).

Next to *Native Son*, the autobiographical *Black Boy* (1945) is considered to be Richard Wright's greatest achievement. The importance of the book is that it shows where some of the major themes in Wright's fiction come from and that it sheds light on Wright's personality. Although Wright's biographer Michel Fabre has pointed out a number of instances in *Black Boy* where Wright fictionalizes events, the book still draws a brutally honest picture of Wright's character and spells out opinions that Wright must have known would offend many readers, both black and white.

The major themes in *Black Boy* echo those in Wright's fiction, especially white racism, the meaninglessness of human suffering, the pointlessness of religious belief, and, above all, the ways in which racial, economic, and cultural oppression stunts black people emotionally. Themes unique to *Black Boy* are that an exceptional black person can overcome the obstacles of racism and educational deprivation and that such a person is inevitably alienated from his or her own culture.

Like most of his fiction, Wright's autobiography illustrates the hundreds of indignities that black people have to suffer at the hands of whites who consider them subhuman. It also records several instances of Wright's having been threatened with physical violence by whites unless he acted subservient. Above all, it tells the story of the older brother of a school friend being killed by whites because he had been seeing a white prostitute and of Wright's own uncle Silas being killed by a white man who wanted to take over his saloon.

The theme of the meaninglessness of human suffering crops up for the first time when Wright's mother has her second stroke, which leaves her partially paralyzed. Wright says that his mother's suffering grew into a symbol in his mind and set the emotional tone of his life. At the age of twelve, so Wright says, "I had a conception of life that no experience would ever erase . . . a conviction that the meaning of living came only when one was struggling to wring a meaning out of meaningless suffering" (112).

Related to this theme is Wright's conviction that religion is a pernicious force in people's lives. One reason Wright turned away from religion is that his grandmother and his aunt Addie, who was also his teacher in school, were fanatic Seventh-Day Adventists and tried to force-feed him their beliefs. He came to hate his aunt Addie so much that he once pulled a knife on her and threatened to cut her if she did not leave him alone. Observing the behavior of supposedly religious people like his aunt, Wright concluded: "Whenever I found religion in my life, I found strife, the attempt of one individual or group to rule another in the name of God. The naked will to power seemed always to walk in the wake of a hymn" (150).

The most controversial theme in *Black Boy* is spelled out in the following passage, which several black critics have read as an attack on black culture. Commenting on the emotional life of black people, Wright says:

I used to mull over the strange absence of real kindness among Negroes, how unstable was our tenderness, how lacking in genuine passion we were, how void of great hope, how bare our traditions, how hollow our memories, how lacking we were in those sentiments that bind man to man, and how shallow was even our despair. (45)

Two things can be said in Wright's defense. For one thing, the statement is not an attack on black culture because in his *Twelve Million Black Voices* (1941), Wright demonstrates his deep pride in black culture, and he predicts correctly that it would one day transform the dominant white culture. For another thing, the statement about black people's lack of kindness and tenderness should be seen in the light of how Wright himself was brought up. After all, one of the first incidents he reports in *Black Boy* is that of his mother's beating him until he lost consciousness. This happened when he was four years old and had accidentally set fire to his grandmother's house. Moreover, Wright developed a searing hate for his father, who abandoned the family and caused them to live on the brink of starvation for many years. After his mother was too sick to take care of Richard, he was forced to live with his Fundamentalist grandmother and aunt, who never showed him any love or kindness. In short, Wright based the statement about black people's lack of kindness on the way he himself was treated by his own family.

A theme that is unique to *Black Boy* has to do with Wright's unusual sense of values. Throughout the nineteen years that *Black Boy* covers, Wright shows his own values to be radically different from those of everyone else around him. Not only did he value his personal dignity and often get into trouble because he didn't act subservient toward whites, but he also valued education more than anyone else he knew. Wright's thirst for education made him read voraciously, and his reading made him decide that he wanted to be a writer. He wrote his first story at the age of fifteen, a melodramatic tale about an unhappy Indian maiden who commits suicide. When he was sixteen, he had his first story published in a local black newspaper. Its suggestive title was "The Voodoo of Hell's Half-Acre." The publication of this story strengthened Wright's resolve to become a writer, even though he knew that for an African American such a career was impossible in the South. He therefore began to dream of "going north" (86).

While the theme of the alienation of the artist from his culture may be a cliché, it has a special poignancy in *Black Boy* because Wright felt alienated from the very people whose champion he had decided to be. His schoolmates "could not understand why anyone would want to write a story" (184), and they felt that he was doing something "that was vaguely wrong" (187). Later, when he was working in a hotel in Jackson, he decided not to tell his black fellow workers about his ambition. He explains: "Had a black boy announced that he aspired to be a writer, he would have been unhesitatingly called crazy by his pals," and what's more, his black pals "would have reported his odd ambition to the white boss" (216). Thus, Wright was determined to go north not only because of white racism but also because his own people did not understand his love for literature and his ambition to become a writer. Moreover, he felt that the South, both white and black, had never allowed him "to be natural, to be real, to be myself, except in rejection, rebellion, and aggression" (284). However, after he did escape to the North, Wright says: "I realized that I could never really leave the South, for my feelings had already been formed by the South, for there had been slowly instilled into my personality and consciousness, black though I was, the culture of the South" (284).

The Outsider (1953), Wright's first novel after Native Son (1940), shows a great thematic shift. Although the protagonist is black and does experience racial prejudice, matters of race take a back seat to philosophical concerns. The protagonist Cross Damon is a student of Nietzschean nihilism. To prove to himself that he is an Übermensch who is beyond good and evil, Cross commits two murders. When he is hunted down and shot, he realizes the wrongness of his Nietzschean outlook. As he lies dying, he makes a speech advocating a form of humanistic existentialism that echoes the ideas of Jean-Paul Sartre.

Savage Holiday (1954) is thematically even further removed from Wright's earlier fiction than The Outsider. For one thing, all the major characters in the novel are whites. For another, the plot revolves around the protagonist's feelings of hate for his father and his feelings of lust for his mother. This cheap Freudianism makes the novel an embarrassing failure.

The themes in Eight Men (1960), the collection that Wright put together shortly before his death, are once again the familiar ones of race relations. Two of the most recent stories take place in Europe. One of them deals with the racist attitude of the Danish protagonist toward a black American and the other with the racist attitude of a white American toward a native African. The remaining six stories, most of which were published before, take place in the United States. Two of these stand out because racism isn't the central theme. One is a coming-of-age story entitled "The Man Who Was Almost a Man." In that story there is no racial oppression at all, and the story would work just as well if the young protagonist were white, Native American, or Asian. The other outstanding piece is the novella The Man Who Lived Underground, about which Wright said that he deliberately wanted to go beyond race. A major theme in the novella is that of the artist's alienation from his society. The man who lives underground is Fred Daniels, who has been wrongly accused of a murder and has escaped from the police. He is hiding in a sewer and manages to gain access to the basements of various businesses and organizations whose secrets he ferrets out and exploits. He eventually gives himself up because he feels guilty about all the secrets he knows. In the meantime, he has been cleared of the murder, but the police shoot him to death anyway because he mentions that he has observed the police officers torturing a suspect.

The themes in *Lawd Today* (1963), the other book published after Wright's death, are similar to those in *Native Son*. Originally entitled *Cesspool*, the book dates back to 1937–1938. It is essentially a naturalist novel, explaining the sub-human personality of the protagonist in terms of the effects of the dehumanizing physical and social environment created by white racism. The novel details the activities of Jake Jackson, a black post office worker in Chicago, for one whole day. It begins with Jake's getting up in the morning and beating his sick wife, and it ends at night after a visit to a brothel when Jake passes out in a drunken stupor.

CRITICAL RECEPTION

The story of the critical reception of Richard Wright's fiction is a sad one. For one thing, his work was, on the whole, better received by white than by black reviewers. For another thing, while his first book received extravagant praise, the reviews became steadily more critical from his second book on, especially after Wright left the United States and settled in France. It is therefore easy to see why, during his last years, Wright became even more bitter toward America and Americans than he had been from the start.

Richard Wright's first book, *Uncle Tom's Children: Four Novellas* (1938), received lavish praise from most reviewers, with one of the few critical voices being that of black fellow novelist Zora Neale Hurston.* Many of the reviews mention that *Uncle Tom's Children* was the winner of a $500 award for the best book-length manuscript by a writer working for the Works Progress Administration (WPA) Federal Writers' Project. One of the three judges of the contest, Lewis Gannett, reviewed *Uncle Tom's Children* for his newspaper, the *New York Herald Tribune*, and reported that "Richard Wright's work stood head and shoulders above the rest." Gannett's prophetic judgment of the four stories in *Uncle Tom's Children* is this: "These stories are more than American literature. Their spirit is a part of a new American history." The anonymous review in *Time* magazine agreed in its estimation of Wright's talent. That review begins with the following: "The U.S. has never had a first-rate Negro novelist. Last week the promise of one appeared" ("Bad Nigger"). Novelist James T. Farrell, writing for the *Partisan Review*, also was profoundly impressed by Wright's first book. Farrell said about *Uncle Tom's Children*: "It is a book of bitter truths and bitter tragedies written by an able and sensitive talent. It is not merely a book of promise. It is a genuine literary achievement" (58).

Aside from the predictably negative reactions of reviewers writing for southern newspapers and magazines, one of the most negative reviews came from Zora

Neale Hurston. In her essay in the *Saturday Review of Literature*, she calls *Uncle Tom's Children* "a book about hatreds" and complains that "not one act of understanding and sympathy comes to pass in the entire work." Hurston sees "the wish-fulfillment theme" as central to the book: "In each story the hero suffers but he gets his man." Moreover, she resents that "all the characters in the book are elemental and brutish" and that "there is lavish killing here, perhaps enough to satisfy all male black readers." Finally, Hurston also attacks Wright's craftsmanship, claiming that he does a poor job with black dialogue: "Certainly he does not write by ear unless he is tone-deaf." Hurston's attack on Wright has to be seen in light of the fact that a year earlier Wright had written a narrow-minded and devastating review of Hurston's excellent novel *Their Eyes Were Watching God* (1937).

When *Native Son* was published in 1940, some of the reviews were as enthusiastic as those of *Uncle Tom's Children*. A number of them compared *Native Son* favorably to John Steinbeck's recent *The Grapes of Wrath* (1939) and to Theodore Dreiser's *An American Tragedy* (1923). Other reviews ranked Wright with Dickens and even Dostoyevsky. However, a number of reviews also suggested that the characterization of Bigger Thomas is overdrawn and that some of the violence in the novel is gratuitous. In short, critics questioned the implied premise of the book that Bigger Thomas is a representative of all young African Americans.

One of the first reviews of *Native Son* was that of Clifton Fadiman in the *New Yorker*. It came out one day after the publication of the novel. Fadiman begins his review by saying that "Richard Wright's 'Native Son' is the most powerful American novel to appear since 'The Grapes of Wrath' " (52). Yet Fadiman also notes that *Native Son* "has numerous defects as a work of art" (52). However, he admits that Wright is such a good storyteller that these defects become apparent only in retrospect. For one thing, Fadiman says that "Mr. Wright is too explicit. He says many things over and over again" (53). For another, he believes that Wright "overdoes his melodrama" (53). But ultimately, Fadiman finds *Native Son* an impressive achievement because Wright "does not base the argument of his horrifying story upon any facile thesis of economic determinism" (53). Instead, Wright "goes deeper than that, often into layers of consciousness where only Dostoyevsky and a few others have penetrated" (53).

The reviewer for the *Nation*, Margaret Marshall, also balanced her praise of *Native Son* with a discussion of its flaws. On one hand, Marshall says that Wright "displays a maturity of thought and feeling beside which the eloquence of 'The Grapes of Wrath' grows pale" (368). On the other hand, she points out three defects "which cannot be described as minor" (367). One defect is that "the author often ascribes to Bigger thoughts of which he is plainly incapable" (367). Another flaw is Wright's "flair for the melodramatic," which "could bear curbing" (367). A third defect that Marshall sees in the novel is the inconsistency of Wright's style, which changes from an almost biblical rhetoric to a style that has "a bookish quality often encountered in self-educated writers" (367). However,

Marshall is sure that these defects "can be overcome by a writer whose talent and seriousness are apparent on each page" (368).

The most insightful review of *Native Son* is the one that the distinguished literary critic Malcolm Cowley wrote for the *New Republic*. Cowley begins his essay by saying that " 'Native Son' is the most impressive American novel I've read since 'The Grapes of Wrath' " (382). He is particularly impressed with the political and philosophical dimensions of the message as it takes shape toward the end of the novel. Cowley says about *Native Son* that the long courtroom speech of Bigger's defense lawyer, Boris Max, "is at once its strongest and its weakest point" (383). Its weakness is that Max does not manage to convince the judge and therefore loses his fight to save Bigger from the electric chair. Its strength is that it "sums up the argument of the novel" (383). According to Cowley, that argument runs as follows: "Listen, you white folks . . . I want to tell you about all the Negroes in America. I want to tell you how they live and how they feel. I want you to change your minds about them before it is too late to prevent a worse disaster than any we have known" (382–83). Because Wright "speaks for and to the nation without ceasing to be a Negro," so Cowley says, "his book has more force than any other American novel by a member of his race" (383).

The reviews of *Black Boy* (1945) were, on the whole, positive as far as its display of Wright's talent is concerned. However, critics were divided about the book's content. A curious fact is that white reviewers, especially the liberals among them, liked the book better than did black reviewers.

The literary critic Lionel Trilling reviewed *Black Boy* for *Nation*. His review is one of the most uncritical ones. Trilling begins by calling *Black Boy* "a remarkably fine book" and by labeling it a sociological "document" (390). Trilling reads *Black Boy* as "a precise and no doubt largely typical account of Negro life in Mississippi" (390). He gives Wright credit for creating this account with "moral and intellectual power" (390). While Trilling lauds the "objectivity" with which Wright describes conditions in the Deep South, he also notes that " 'Black Boy' is an angry book, as it ought to be—we would be surprised and unhappy if it were not" (390). The anger is justified, so Trilling says, because it "is in proportion only to the social situation he is dealing with; it is also in proportion to the author's desire to live a reasonable and effective life" (390). Trilling notes that some of the anger is directed at black people because Wright has understood that white racism not only visits the moral flaws of the dominant culture on African Americans but also is likely to give them "other flaws of feeling and action" (390). Trilling winds up his review by saying that *Black Boy* teaches us that oppression "does not merely affect the body but also the soul" and that "it is only a grim and ironic justice that the deterioration is as great in the oppressor as in the oppressed" (392).

Another white reviewer who is silent about any flaws that *Black Boy* might have is the novelist Sinclair Lewis, writing for *Esquire* magazine. Lewis starts out by acknowledging Richard Wright as being "enormously talented." Then he takes issue with all the reviews that claim that *Black Boy* is "betraying too much 'emotion,' too much 'bitterness.' " Lewis believes that "not bitterness but fear charges this book," and he says it is beyond him how Richard Wright can look back on his early life "with anything except hatred." Then Lewis draws a poignant analogy between Jews in Nazi concentration camps and blacks in the Deep South. He suggests that Richard Wright might "mellow and speak amiably of the teachers who flattered him, his colored neighbors and relatives who denounced him, the merchants who cheated him, the white fellow-mechanics who threatened him" as soon as we get the first "successful comedy by an ex-prisoner about the kindness and humor of the warders in a German concentration camp." Like Lionel Trilling, Sinclair Lewis demonstrates his deep empathy for the persona of Richard Wright in *Black Boy* and does not question the accuracy of the account.

However, some reviewers of *Black Boy*, both black and white, noted that the book is not an objective account of conditions in the Deep South and that in some instances it might not even be a truthful account. In his review of *Black Boy* for the *New York Herald Tribune* the great black scholar W.E.B. Du Bois* begins by asking what the book's "relation to truth is," and he answers his own question by asserting that *Black Boy* "is probably intended to be fiction or fictionalized biography." Seeing the book this way allows Du Bois to interpret Wright's motives in writing the book. Du Bois notes, for example, that "the Negroes whom [Wright] paints have almost no redeeming qualities." Du Bois concludes that Wright depicts other blacks so negatively in order to make them contrast with the positive depiction of his own persona. Du Bois says that "the hero is only interested in himself, is self centered to the exclusion of everybody and everything else. . . . The world is himself and his suffering." Then Du Bois quotes part of the long passage in *Black Boy* where Wright talks about "the absence of real kindness in Negroes" and "how lacking we were in those intangible sentiments that bind man to man." Du Bois takes exception to this generalization and calls it a "misjudgment." He concludes his review with these words: "Nothing that Richard Wright says is in itself unbelievable or impossible; it is the total picture that is not convincing."

The reviews of Wright's other nonfiction were even more critical than those of *Black Boy*, but they were still better than the negative reviews that all his later fiction received. In 1953 reviewers were eagerly awaiting the appearance of the novel *The Outsider* because Wright had not published any fiction in thirteen years. They were disappointed. One of the most devastating reviews is that of black playwright Lorraine Hansberry in the Harlem newspaper *Freedom*. She calls *The Outsider* "a story of sheer violence, death and disgusting spectacle, written by a man who has seemingly come to despise humanity."

Wright's next novel, *Savage Holiday* (1954), wasn't even reviewed in the American press because it was published only as a paperback. Most later critics agree with Robert Felgar, who calls *Savage Holiday* Wright's "most disappointing" novel, the kind of "fiction that belongs in a sleazy drugstore book-rack" (121).

The Long Dream (1958) is probably the best of Wright's later novels, but reviewers still were unanimous in ranking it far below *Native Son*. The response of Granville Hicks in the *Saturday Review* is a typical one. Hicks notes that in its subject matter, *The Long Dream* is closer to *Native Son* than to *The Outsider* because its focus is on race relations rather than on philosophy but that it shares two flaws with those novels, "a preoccupation with scenes of violence" (13) and a plot "which turns into melodrama" (13). Additional flaws are unconvincing characterization, especially of the protagonist, and a style that is often overblown.

The two works of fiction that were published after Wright's death, the collection of stories entitled *Eight Men* (1960) and *Lawd Today* (1963), also received mostly negative reviews. As far as *Lawd Today* is concerned, Lewis Gannett's review in the *New York Herald Tribune* provides the fairest estimate. Gannett points out that *Lawd Today* was begun in 1936 and should be seen as an "apprentice work." Gannett concludes that "the book's chief interest is a stage in the development of a writer who, later, made his mark." The reviewers of *Eight Men* were divided in their estimate of the book's merits. One of the most negative reviews is that of Richard Gilman in *Commonweal*. Gilman calls the collection "a dismayingly stale and dated book" which is marred by "mechanical ineptitude" and "lapses in taste" (130). One of the most favorable reviews is a piece in the *New Republic* entitled "Richard Wright: A Word of Farewell." The reviewer, Irving Howe, not only evaluates *Eight Men* but also considers Richard Wright's place in American literature. Like other reviewers, Howe recognizes that the eight stories are very uneven, and he wonders how Wright can be "at once so brilliant and so inept" (17). However, Howe does give Wright credit for his "wish to keep learning and experimenting" (17). He believes that Wright's experimentation paid off in the novella *The Man Who Lived Underground* because it "shows a sense of narrative rhythm, a gift for shaping the links between sentences so as to create a chain of expectations, which is superior to anything in his full-length novels and evidence of the seriousness with which he kept working" (17). Looking back over Wright's creative career, Howe says that Wright will probably never be regarded as "a writer of the first rank, for his faults are grave and obvious" (17). But Howe concludes that literary history will have to give Richard Wright "an honored place," and he believes that "any estimate of his role in our cultural life will have to stress his importance as the pioneer Negro writer who in the fullness of his anger made it less possible for American society to continue deceiving itself" (18).

BIBLIOGRAPHY

Works by Richard Wright

Fiction

Uncle Tom's Children: Four Novellas. New York: Harper, 1938.
Native Son. New York: Harper, 1940, 1987.

Uncle Tom's Children: Five Long Stories. New York: Harper, 1940, 1976.
The Outsider. New York: Harper, 1953.
Savage Holiday. New York: Avon, 1954.
The Long Dream. Garden City, NY: Doubleday, 1958.
Eight Men. New York: World, 1960.
Lawd Today. New York: Walker, 1963.

Nonfiction

Twelve Million Black Voices: A Folk History of the Negro in the United States. New York: Viking, 1941.
Black Boy: A Record of Childhood and Youth. New York: Harper, 1945, 1984.
Black Power: A Record of Reactions in a Land of Pathos. New York: Harper, 1954.
The Color Curtain: A Report on the Bandung Conference. New York: World, 1956.
Pagan Spain: A Report of a Journey into the Past. New York: Harper, 1956.
White Man, Listen! Garden City, NY: Doubleday, 1957.
American Hunger. New York: Harper, 1977.

Studies of Richard Wright

"Bad Nigger." Rev. of *Native Son. Time* (March 4, 1940): 72.
Cowley, Malcolm. "The Case of Bigger Thomas." Rev. of *Native Son. New Republic* (March 18, 1940): 382–83.
Du Bois, W.E.B. "Richard Wright Looks Back." Rev. of *Black Boy. New York Herald Tribune [Books]* (March 4, 1945): 2.
Fabre, Michel. "Afterword." In *American Hunger.* New York: Harper, 1977. 136–46.
———. *The Unfinished Quest of Richard Wright.* Trans. Isabel Barzun. New York: Morrow, 1973.
———. *The World of Richard Wright.* Jackson: University Press of Mississippi, 1985.
Fadiman, Clifton. "A Black 'American Tragedy.' " Rev. of *Native Son. New Yorker* 16 (March 2, 1940): 52–53.
Farrell, James T. "Lynch Patterns." Rev. of *Uncle Tom's Children. Partisan Review* 4 (May 1938): 57–58.
Felgar, Robert. *Richard Wright.* Boston: Twayne, 1980.
Gannett, Lewis. "At Last, a Good Prize Book." Rev. of *Uncle Tom's Children. New York Herald Tribune,* March 25, 1938, 17.
———. "*Lawd Today.* By Richard Wright." *New York Herald Tribune [Books]* (May 5, 1963): 10.
Gayle, Addison. *Richard Wright: Ordeal of a Native Son.* New York: Doubleday, 1980.
Gilman, Richard. "The Immediate Misfortunes of Widespread Literacy." Rev. of *Eight Men. Commonweal* 28 (April 1961): 130–31.
Hansberry, Lorraine. "*The Outsider,* by Richard Wright." *Freedom* 14 (April 1953): 7.
Hicks, Granville. "The Power of Richard Wright." Rev. of *The Long Dream. Saturday Review* 41 (October 18, 1958): 13, 65.
Howe, Irving. "Richard Wright: A Word of Farewell." Rev. of *Eight Men. New Republic* 144 (February 13, 1961): 17–18.
Hurston, Zora Neale. "Stories of Conflict." Rev. of *Uncle Tom's Children. Saturday Review* 17 (April 2, 1938): 32.

Lewis, Sinclair. "Gentlemen, This Is Revolution." Rev. of *Black Boy*. *Esquire* 23 (June 1945): 76.

Marshall, Margaret. "Black Native Son." *Nation* 150 (March 16, 1940): 367–68.

Reilly, John. *Richard Wright: The Critical Reception*. New York: Franklin, 1978.

Sartre, Jean-Paul. "Existentialism." In *Existentialism and Human Emotion*. Trans. Bernard Frechtman. New York: Philosophical Library, 1957.

Trilling, Lionel. "A Tragic Situation." Rev. of *Black Boy*. *Nation* 160 (April 7, 1945): 391–92.

Walker, Margaret. *Richard Wright, Demonic Genius*. New York: Amistad, 1988.

ZARA WRIGHT
(?–?)

Loretta G. Woodard

BIOGRAPHY

Very little is known about the novelist Zara Wright. From what she reveals through her preface, introduction, and the front matter of her novels, Wright lived and published in Chicago in the 1920s. Included in John Taitt's *Souvenir of Negro Progress* (1925), with nine other prominent members of the black community, he mentions her as the "Author [of] *Tangled Threads*." This tends to suggest her novels were known among the community and testifies as well to both her stature in the community and the reputation of her work.

Wright was "inspired" to write *Black and White Tangled Threads* by her deceased husband, J. Edward Wright, to whom the book is dedicated. In her Introduction, Wright comments that she hopes her books are "food for sane and serious thought . . ." (7). Unfortunately, these works were "pushed" into obscurity. Although *Black and White Tangled Threads* and *Kenneth* were originally published privately and together in Chicago in 1920, Wright's novels immediately went out of print until they were reissued by AMS Press in 1975. Further details of Wright's life are currently unavailable.

MAJOR WORKS AND THEMES

Wright's melodramatic, romantic novel *Black and White Tangled Threads* and its sequel, *Kenneth*, explore the complex themes of race consciousness, passing, and interracial marriage, as do the books of her contemporaries of the Harlem Renaissance, with whom she shared a number of characteristics. Set in the upper-class social worlds of the United States, mostly in Louisville, Kentucky, England, and Italy, the novels follow two families from the generation after emancipation.

Zoleeta Andrews, the heroine of the first novel, is the daughter of Harold Andrews and Mildred Yates, son of a slaveholder and daughter of a slave. Zoleeta's
parents, who secretly left the plantation on which they were both raised and fell
in love for a life in India, both die when she is quite young. Adopted by Harold's
older brother, Paul, she is brought back to the plantation of her parents' youth,
where she is raised as a member of the formerly slaveholding family. Claretta,
the sister of Paul and Harold, hates Zoleeta's beauty and resents being forced to
live with someone whom she considers "tainted" with the blood of the slaves.
Consequently, she teaches Catherine, her daughter, to feel the same way. Much
of the plot of the first novel centers on Claretta's vindictiveness to ruin Zoleeta's
marriage prospects. Zoleeta is eventually united with Lord Blankleigh, the man
of her dreams, who knows and accepts her racial heritage, and she spends three
years in England as Lady Blankleigh. In order to speak and work on behalf of
the newly freed women and men of the South, she returns to the United States,
without her husband and son but pregnant with her daughter.

In a subplot of the novel, Catherine, Zoleeta's cousin, marries a young painter,
Guy Randolf, who discovers after his marriage and the birth of their son, Kenneth, that he is the illegitimate son of a wealthy, but deceased, slaveholder named
Guy Slayton and his slave Hebe, a woman who had escaped slavery and, disguised
as a nurse, raised Randolf. Though he inherits a large fortune, he loses his wife,
who accuses him of being deceptive regarding his identity, and she finds both
him and their son repulsive to her. *Kenneth*, the second novel, traces the life of
Guy and Catherine's son as a rising young lawyer in Louisville and also examines
the troubled life of Dr. Philip Grayson, Kenneth's dark-skinned friend.

Interestingly, Wright challenges a number of cultural assumptions in her novels. In *Threads* she addresses the notion that African Americans want to inter-
marry with whites in order to elevate their status and that they see this as positive
and unproblematic. Ralph, Mildred's dark-skinned brother, who had returned to
the plantation in order to stop Claretta's plot to ruin Zoleeta, decides instead to
leave town to prevent her from being excluded by her friends. After closer examination, Zoleeta's Uncle Paul comes to realize Ralph's "intellectual ability"
and becomes convinced that "he was a man to be trusted," but from the puzzle-
ment on Paul Andrews' face he seems uncomfortable with his niece's kinship to
the ex-slave. In fact, Paul wishes "that his brother had chosen one from his own
race to be the mother of his child" (*Threads* 142–43). Actually, both men suffer
from the same thought, for Zoleeta's ex-slave uncle also wishes "his sister had
chosen one of her race for her life's companion" (*Threads* 143). Ralph considers
Harold's and Mildred's marriage to be problematic for their daughter, despite the
fact that it has brought her wealth and a secure status in upper-class society.
Because of his own racial superiority, Paul takes for granted that Ralph and even
other ex-slaves like him desire whiteness and the status it brings. Ralph's decision
to leave the area to protect Zoleeta and her prospect of a secure future with a
white family was indeed painful, yet he put her welfare first, which is quite
difficult for him.

With a different set of characters in *Kenneth* and with different implications, Wright focuses on some of the same concerns of the black man as other writers did. The sequel opens with the handsome, dark-skinned Dr. Philip Grayson treating the victims of a railroad accident. Among the victims is Alice Blair, the white daughter of a wealthy banker, whom Dr. Grayson saves, and then she falls hopelessly in love with him. She pursues him and eventually becomes seriously ill after he rejects her. In love with a younger black woman with whom he grew up, he politely tells Alice the dangers of returning her "unlooked-for attentions." He could be run out of Louisville, if not killed, if she continues her unsolicited visits to his office. Here, Wright, like Ida B. Wells-Barnett* in *Southern Horrors*, points to the common southern practice of lynching black men for any attention or insults to white women. Here, however, Alice is the aggressor, concerned only with her own gratification, and is careless of the danger she brings to Dr. Grayson. By using a white woman in this manner, Wright challenges the stereotypical notions that black men always desire white women, that relationships are always initiated or created by black men, and that black men are generally the aggressors and white women always the passive victims. Though Dr. Grayson is not lynched, the predicament he finds himself in implies that black men are often lynched not for their own aggressions but for those of white women, as documented in the works of Ida B. Wells-Barnett and others.

CRITICAL RECEPTION

Published in Chicago in 1920, Wright's novels have not received the scholarly attention they deserve. In the only existing review of the novels in the *Chicago Defender*, the city's leading black newspaper, the reviewer called *Black and White Tangled Threads* and its sequel, *Kenneth*, "remarkable," noting "the realistic portrayal of individuals and events" [as well as how] "the facts are given in a clear and concise manner." The reviewer further asserted that "to read this story will be convincing proof that as a writer, Mrs. Wright is unexcelled" (8).

Critic Ann Allen Shockley points out that "the uniqueness of [*Black and White Tangled Threads* was] its mulatto story with a different twist; it showed the effects of miscegenation upon a white antebellum southern family who acknowledges a mulatto as a legitimate family member" (280). She concludes that Wright's books, . . . are fairy tales created by a fanciful imagination building on nineteenth-century models and adding a few twists of her own" (382). Maggie Sale discovered that "Wright's novels challenge us to interrogate the critical standards and assumptions that privilege what we imagine to be new, different, and original, and to thereby discover the significance and originality in the older and familiar" (xxx–xxxi).

Scholars seem to believe that the republication of *Black and White Tangled Threads* and *Kenneth* (1969) by AMS Press and by G. K. Hall in the new thirty-volume series, *African-American Women Writers, 1910–1940* (Gates 1995), is certainly a crucial first step in expanding and broadening our critical attention to African American culture.

BIBLIOGRAPHY

Works by Zara Wright

Black and White Tangled Threads. Chicago: Barnard and Miller, 1920; New York: AMS Press, 1975.
Kenneth. 1920. New York: AMS Press, 1975.

Studies of Zara Wright

Gates, Henry Louis, Jr., ed. *African-American Women Writers: 1910–1940.* New York: G. K. Hall, 1995.
Rev. of *Black and White Tangled Threads* and *Kenneth. Chicago Defender,* December 25, 1920, 8.
Sale, Maggie. "Introduction." In *African-American Women Writers: 1910–1940.* Ed. Henry Louis Gates Jr. New York: G. K. Hall, 1995. xv–xxxiv.
Shockley, Ann Allen. Introduction to "The Little Orphan." In *Afro-American Women Writers, 1746–1933: An Anthology and Critical Guide.* New York: New American Library, 1988. 380–82.
Taitt, John. *Souvenir of Negro Progress.* Chicago: De Saible Association, 1925.

SELECTED BIBLIOGRAPHY

Andrews, William. *The Oxford Companion to African American Literature*. New York: Oxford University Press, 1997.

Baker, Houston, Jr. *Modernism and the Harlem Renaissance*. Chicago: University of Chicago Press, 1987.

Bassett, John Earl. *Harlem in Review*. Selinsgrove: Susquehanna University Press, 1992.

Bell, Bernard. *The Afro-American Novel and Its Tradition*. Amherst: University of Massachusetts Press, 1987.

Bone, Robert. *Down Home: A History of Afro-American Short Fiction from Its Beginnings to the End of the Harlem Renaissance*. New York: G. P. Putnam's Sons, 1976.

———. *The Negro Novel in America*. New Haven, CT: Yale University Press, 1965.

Bontemps, Arnold, ed. *Harlem Renaissance Remembered*. New York: Dodd, Mead, 1972.

Braxton, Joanne. *Black Women Writing Autobiography: A Tradition within a Tradition*. Philadelphia: Temple University Press, 1989.

Bruce, Dickson D., Jr. *Black American Writing from the Nadir: The Evolution of a Literary Tradition, 1877–1915*. Baton Rouge: Louisiana State University Press, 1989.

Carly, Hazel V. *Reconstructing Womanhood: The Emergence of the Afro-American Woman Novelist*. New York: Oxford University Press, 1989.

De Jongh, James. *Vicious Modernism: Black Harlem and the Literary Imagination*. New York: Cambridge University Press, 1990.

Elder, Arlene. *The "Hindered Hand": Cultural Implications of Early African-American Fiction*. Westport, CT: Greenwood Press, 1978.

Ernest, John. *Resistance and Reformation in Nineteenth-Century African American Literature: Brown, Wilson, Jacobs, Delany, Douglass, Harper*. Jackson: University Press of Mississippi, 1995.

Foster, Frances Smith. *Witnessing Slavery: The Development of Ante-Bellum Slave Narratives*. Westport, CT: Greenwood Press, 1979.

———. *Written by Herself: Literary Production by African American Women, 1746–1892*. Bloomington: Indiana University Press, 1993.

Fox, Robert Elliott. *Masters of the Drum: Black Lit/Oratures across the Continuum.* Westport, CT: Greenwood Press, 1995.

Gates, Henry Louis, Jr. *Figures in Black: Words, Signs, and the "Racial" Self.* New York: Oxford University Press, 1987.

———. *The Signifying Monkey: A Theory of Afro-American Literary Criticism.* New York: Oxford University Press, 1988.

Greene, J. Lee. *Blacks in Eden. The African American Novel's First Century.* Charlottesville: University Press of Virginia, 1996.

Harris, Trudier, and Thadious M. Davis. *Dictionary of Literary Biography: Afro-American Writers before the Harlem Renaissance.* Vol. 50. Detroit: Gale Research, 1984.

———. *Dictionary of Literary Biography: Afro-American Writers from the Harlem Renaissance to 1940.* Vol. 5. Detroit: Gale Research, 1987.

Hull, Gloria T. *Color, Sex and Poetry.* Bloomington: Indiana University Press, 1987.

Jackson, Blyden. *A History of Afro-American Literature.* Vol. 1. Baton Rouge: Louisiana State University Press, 1989.

Kawash, Samira. *Dislocating the Color Line: Identity, Hybridity, and Singularity in African-American Narrative.* Stanford, CA: Stanford University Press, 1997.

McLendon, Jacquelyn Y. *The Politics of Color in the Fiction of Jessie Fauset and Nella Larsen.* Charlottesville: University of Virginia Press, 1995.

Nelson, Emmanuel. *Gay and Lesbian Writers of Color: Critical Essays.* New York: Haworth Press, 1994.

O'Neale, Sandra A. *Jupiter Hammon and the Beginnings of African-American Literature.* Metuchen, NJ: Scarecrow, 1993.

Posnick, Ross. *Color and Culture: Black Writers and the Making of the Modern Intellectual.* Cambridge: Harvard University Press, 1998.

Pryse, Marjorie, and Hortense J. Spillers, ed. *Conjuring: Black Women, Fiction, and Literary Tradition.* Bloomington: Indiana University Press, 1985.

Rosenblatt, Roger. *Black Fiction.* Cambridge: Harvard University Press, 1974.

Singh, Amritjit. *The Harlem Renaissance: Revaluations.* New York: Garland, 1989.

Stepto, Robert B. *From behind the Veil: A Study of Afro-American Narrative.* Urbana: University of Illinois Press, 1979.

Wagner, Jean. *Black Poets of the United States.* Trans. Kenneth Douglas. Urbana: University of Illinois Press, 1973.

Wall, Cheryl A. *Women of the Harlem Renaissance.* Bloomington: Indiana University Press, 1995.

Yellin, Jean Fagan, and Cynthia D. Bond. *The Pen Is Ours: A Listing of Writings by and about African American Women before 1910 with Secondary Bibliography to the Present.* New York: Oxford University Press, 1991.

INDEX

ABOUT THE EDITOR AND CONTRIBUTORS

CORA AGATUCCI teaches African and Asian cultures and literatures, writing, and women's studies at Central Oregon Community College.

EBERHARD ALSEN a widely published scholar, is Professor of English at SUNY-Cortland. His most recent major publication is *Romantic Postmodernism in American Fiction* (1997).

MARVA OSBORNE BANKS is Professor of English at Albany State University, Georgia.

PAULA C. BARNES teaches in the English Department of Hampton University.

LINDA M. CARTER is Assistant Professor of English at Morgan State University.

LAURIE CHAMPION is Assistant Professor of English at San Diego State University.

HARISH CHANDER is Professor of English at Shaw University, North Carolina.

JOYCE L. CHERRY is Professor of English at Albany State University, Georgia.

MONA M. CHOUCAIR is a doctoral candidate in English at Baylor University; she is completing a dissertation on the works of Toni Morrison.

PETER G. CHRISTENSEN teaches in the School of Library and Information Science at the University of Wisconsin, Milwaukee.

ADENIKE MARIE DAVIDSON is Assistant Professor of English at the University of Central Florida, Orlando.

KAREN M. DAVIS is a graduate student at the Women's Studies Institute of Georgia State University, Atlanta.

EMMA WATERS DAWSON is Professor of English at Florida A&M University.

LYNN DOMINA teaches in the Humanities Division at SUNY-Delhi. She has published a collection of poetry, *Corporal Works* (1995), and edited *Understanding A Raisin in the Sun: A Student Casebook to Issues, Sources, and Historical Documents* (Greenwood, 1998).

DAVID L. DUDLEY is Associate Professor of Literature and Philosophy at Georgia Southern University. He is the author of *My Father's Shadow: Intergenerational Conflict in African American Men's Autobiography*.

MONTYE P. FUSE is Assistant Professor of English at Arizona State University.

BRUCE A. GLASRUD is Dean of the School of Arts and Sciences at Sul Ross State University at Alpine, Texas.

BARBARA L. J. GRIFFIN is Associate Professor of English at Howard University. A specialist in African American literature, her articles have appeared in a variety of journals, such as *Melus*, *CLA Journal*, *Callaloo*, and *The Black Scholar*.

TRACIE CHURCH GUZZIO is an instructor in the English Department at the University of Nevada, Las Vegas.

JAMES L. HILL is Professor of English and Dean of the College of Arts and Sciences at Albany State University, Georgia. His scholarly articles have appeared in numerous journals.

NIKOLAS HUOT is a Ph.D. candidate at Georgia State University, Atlanta.

YMITRI JAYASUNDERA is a doctoral candidate at the University of Massachusetts, Amherst.

LONNELL E. JOHNSON is a Professor of English at Otterbein College, Ohio.

GWENDOLYN S. JONES is Professor of English at Tuskegee University.

JACQUELINE C. JONES is Assistant Professor of English and American Studies at Washington College, Maryland.

LEELA KAPAI is Professor of English at Prince George's Community College, Maryland. She has published several articles on multicultural literature.

ROY KAY is Assistant Professor of English at Macalester College. He is currently writing a book titled *Rewriting the Self in Emergent Literature*.

SARALA KRISHNAMURTHY is Reader in the Postgraduate Department of English at Bangalore, India.

ROBIN LUCY is completing her doctoral dissertation on the African American literary response to World War II at McMaster University, Ontario.

SUZANNE HOTTE MASSA teaches multicultural literature at a private high school in Ithaca, New York.

VIVIAN M. MAY is Assistant Professor of Women's Studies at Texas Woman's University.

SHARA McCALLUM is the author of a collection of poems, *The Water between Us* (1999).

JACQUELYN Y. McLENDON is Associate Professor of English and Director of Black Studies at the College of William and Mary. She is the author of *The Politics of Color in the Fiction of Jessie Fauset and Nella Larsen* (1999).

ROBERT L. MILDE is completing his doctoral dissertation on rhetorical depictions of Haiti in American literature at the University of North Carolina, Greensboro.

VERNER D. MITCHELL is Associate Professor of English at the U.S. Air Force Academy in Colorado. He is currently editing a book on the poetry of Helen Johnson.

LAURA L. MOAKLER is a graduate student in English at Georgia State University, Atlanta.

GILBERT N.M.O. MORRIS directs the African American Studies Program at George Madison University.

NANETTE MORTON is completing her doctoral dissertation on the autobiographies of Frederick Douglass at McMaster University, Ontario.

PIERRE-DAMIEN MVUYEKURE is Assistant Professor of English at the University of Northern Iowa.

EMMANUEL S. NELSON is Professor of English at SUNY-Cortland. Author of over thirty articles on various international literatures in English, he has edited several books, including *Connections: Essays on Black Literatures* (1988), *Contemporary Gay American Novelists* (Greenwood, 1993), and *Contemporary African American Novelists* (Greenwood, 1999).

TERRY NOVAK teaches in the Department of English at the University of Nevada, Las Vegas.

RUSSELL JAY NURICK is a graduate student in English at the University of South Carolina, Columbia.

KIRK NUSS is a doctoral candidate in English at Georgia State University, Atlanta.

TED OLSON teaches in the Department of English at Union College, Kentucky. He is the author of *Blueridge Folk Life* (1997).

LOUIS HILL PRATT is Professor of English at Florida A&M University. Author of *James Baldwin* (1978), he has edited *Alice Malsenior Walker: An Annotated Bibliography* (1988) and *Conversations with James Baldwin* (1989).

PEGGY STEVENSON RATLIFF is Chairperson of the Division of Humanities and Social Sciences at Claflin College, South Carolina.

ROOSEVELT RATLIFF Jr., is Vice President for Leadership Development at Claflin College, South Carolina.

GEETHA RAVI is Reader in the Department of English at Fatima College, India.

RICHÉ RICHARDSON is Assistant Professor of English at the University of California, Davis.

DEBRA J. ROSENTHAL is Assistant Professor of English at John Carroll University, Ohio.

JOYCE RUSSELL-ROBINSON teaches in the English Department at Fayetteville State University, North Carolina.

BARBARA RYAN is Assistant Professor of English at the University of Missouri, Kansas City.

ELAINE SAINO is a Ph.D. candidate at Georgia State University, Atlanta.

MAXINE J. SAMPLE is Associate Professor of English at the State University of West Georgia, Carrollton.

KIRSTEN SAUNDERS teaches in the English Department at Hampton University.

RENNIE SIMSON is Lecturer in the African-American Studies Department at Syracuse University.

LORI LEATHERS SINGLE is a doctoral candidate in English at Georgia State University, Atlanta.

HEATHER E. SPAHR is a graduate student in English at Georgia State University, Atlanta.

JESSE G. SWAN is Assistant Professor of English at the University of Northern Iowa.

RONALD A. TYSON is a doctoral candidate in English at Rutgers University.

BETTYE J. WILLIAMS is Associate Professor of English at the University of Arkansas, Pine Bluff.

JULIE L. WILLIAMS is a graduate student in English at Georgia State University, Atlanta.

ROLAND L. WILLIAMS JR., the great grandson of an American slave, is Assistant Professor of English at Temple University. He is the author of *African American Autobiography and the Quest for Freedom through Learning* (Greenwood, 2000).

LORETTA G. WOODARD is Associate Professor of English at Marygrove College, Detroit.

ISBN 0-313-30910-8

90000>

EAN

9 780313 309106

HARDCOVER BAR CODE